"If you are looking for a job ... before you go to the newspapers and the help-wanted ads, listen to Bob Adams, publisher of *The Metropolitan New York JobBank*."
> **-Tom Brokaw,** *NBC*

"Help on the job hunt ... Anyone who is job-hunting in the New York area can find a lot of useful ideas in a new paperback called *The Metropolitan New York JobBank* ..."
> **-Angela Taylor,** *New York Times*

"For those graduates whose parents are pacing the floor, conspicuously placing circled want ads around the house and typing up resumes, [*The Carolina JobBank*] answers job-search questions."
> *-Greensboro News and Record*

"Because our listing is seen by people across the nation, it generates lots of resumes for us. We encourage unsolicited resumes. We'll always be listed [in *The Chicago JobBank*] as long as I'm in this career."
> **-Tom Fitzpatrick, Director of Human Resources**
> **Merchandise Mart Properties, Inc.**

"Job-hunting is never fun, but this book can ease the ordeal ... [*The Los Angeles JobBank*] will help allay fears, build confidence, and avoid wheel-spinning."
> **-Robert W. Ross,** *Los Angeles Times*

"*The Florida JobBank* is an invaluable job-search reference tool. It provides the most up-to-date information and contact names available for companies in Florida. I should know -- it worked for me!"
> **-Rhonda Cody, Human Resources Consultant**
> **Aetna Life and Casualty**

"*The Boston JobBank* provides a handy map of employment possibilities in greater Boston. This book can help in the initial steps of a job search by locating major employers, describing their business activities, and for most firms, by naming the contact person and listing typical professional positions. For recent college graduates, as well as experienced professionals, *The Boston JobBank* is an excellent place to begin a job search."
> **-Juliet F. Brudney, Career Columnist**
> *Boston Globe*

"*The Phoenix JobBank* is a first-class publication. The information provided is useful and current."
-Lyndon Denton
Director of Human Resources and Materials Management
Apache Nitrogen Products, Inc.

"*The Seattle JobBank* is an essential resource for job hunters."
-Gil Lopez, Staffing Team Manager
Battelle Pacific Northwest Laboratories

"I read through the 'Basics of Job Winning' and 'Resumes' sections [in *The Dallas-Fort Worth JobBank*] and found them to be very informative, with some positive tips for the job searcher. I believe the strategies outlined will bring success to any determined candidate."
-Camilla Norder, Professional Recruiter
Presbyterian Hospital of Dallas

"*The San Francisco Bay Area JobBank* ... is a highly useful guide, with plenty of how-to's ranging from resume tips to interview dress codes and research shortcuts."
-A.S. Ross, *San Francisco Examiner*

"[*The Atlanta JobBank* is] one of the best sources for finding a job in Atlanta!"
-Luann Miller, Human Resources Manager
Prudential Preferred Financial Services

"This well-researched, well-edited, job hunter's aid includes most major businesses and institutional entities in the New York metropolitan area ... [*The Metropolitan New York JobBank* is] highly recommended."
-Cheryl Gregory-Pindell, *Library Journal*

"*The Florida JobBank* is the key to networking successfully in today's competitive job market."
-Anthony LaMorte, Placement Specialist
City of Hialeah Adult and Youth Service

"If you are looking for a job, you need to know which industries are hiring. Then you need to know which employers fall within those industries. *The Houston JobBank* tells you this and much more."
-Joel C. Wagher, Labor Market Analyst
Texas Workforce Commission

What makes the
JobBank series
the nation's premier
line of employment guides?

With vital employment information on thousands of employers across the nation, the JobBank series is the most comprehensive and authoritative set of career directories available today.

Each book in the series provides information on **dozens of different industries** in a given city or area, with the primary employer listings providing contact information, telephone and fax numbers, addresses, Websites, a summary of the firm's business, and in many cases descriptions of the firm's typical professional job categories, the principal educational backgrounds sought, internships, and the fringe benefits offered.

In addition to the **detailed primary employer listings,** JobBank books give telephone numbers and addresses for **thousands of additional employers,** as well as information about executive search firms, placement agencies, and professional associations.

All of the reference information in the JobBank series is as up-to-date and accurate as possible. Every year, the entire database is thoroughly researched and verified by mail and by telephone. Adams Media Corporation publishes **more local employment guides more often** than any other publisher of career directories.

In addition, the JobBank series features current information about the local job scene -- **forecasts on which industries are the hottest** and **lists of regional professional associations,** so you can get your job hunt started off right.

The JobBank series offers **33 regional titles**, from Minneapolis to Houston, and from Boston to San Francisco. All of the information is organized geographically, because most people look for jobs in specific areas of the country.

A condensed, but thorough, review of the entire job search process is presented in the chapter **The Basics of Job Winning**, a feature which has received many compliments from career counselors. In addition, each JobBank directory includes a section on **resumes and cover letters** the *New York Times* has acclaimed as "excellent."

The JobBank series gives job hunters the most comprehensive, timely, and accurate career information, organized and indexed to facilitate the job search. An entire career reference library, JobBank books are the consummate employment guides.

Top career publications from Adams Media Corporation

The JobBank Series:
each JobBank book is $16.95

The Atlanta JobBank, 1999
The Austin/San Antonio JobBank, 2nd Ed.
The Boston JobBank, 1999
The Carolina JobBank, 5th Ed.
The Chicago JobBank, 1999
The Connecticut JobBank, 1st Ed.
The Dallas-Fort Worth JobBank, 1999
The Denver JobBank, 11th Ed.
The Detroit JobBank, 9th Ed.
The Florida JobBank, 1999
The Houston JobBank, 10th Ed.
The Indiana JobBank, 2nd Ed.
The Las Vegas JobBank, 2nd Ed.
The Los Angeles JobBank, 1999
The Minneapolis-St. Paul JobBank, 11th Ed.
The Missouri JobBank, 2nd Ed.
The Northern New England JobBank, 1st Ed.
The New Jersey JobBank, 1st Ed.
The New Mexico JobBank, 1st Ed.
The Metropolitan New York JobBank, 1999
The Upstate New York JobBank, 1st Ed.
The Ohio JobBank, 1999
The Greater Philadelphia JobBank, 1999
The Phoenix JobBank, 7th Ed.
The Pittsburgh JobBank, 2nd Ed.
The Portland JobBank, 2nd Ed.
The Salt Lake City JobBank, 1st Ed.
The San Francisco Bay Area JobBank, 1999
The Seattle JobBank, 1999
The Tennessee JobBank, 4th Ed.
The Virginia JobBank, 2nd Ed.
The Metropolitan Washington DC JobBank, 1999
The Wisconsin JobBank, 1st Ed.

The JobBank Guide to Computer & High-Tech
    Companies, 2nd Ed. ($17.95)

The JobBank Guide to Health Care Companies,
    1st Ed. ($16.95)

The National JobBank, 1999
    (Covers the entire U.S.: $350.00 hc)

The JobBank Guide to Employment Services,
    1998 -1999
    (Covers the entire U.S.: $199.00 hc)

Other Career Titles:

The Adams Cover Letter Almanac ($10.95)
The Adams Electronic Job Search Almanac, 1999
    ($10.95)
The Adams Executive Recruiters Almanac
    ($16.95)
The Adams Job Interview Almanac ($12.95)
The Adams Jobs Almanac, 1999 ($16.95)
The Adams Resume Almanac ($10.95)
America's Fastest Growing Employers, 2nd Ed.
    ($16.00)
Career Shifting ($9.95)
Cold Calling Techniques, 3rd Ed. ($7.95)
College Grad Job Hunter, 4th Ed. ($14.95)
The Complete Resume & Job Search Book for
    College Students ($10.95)
Cover Letters That Knock 'em Dead, 3rd Ed.
    ($10.95)
Every Woman's Essential Job Hunting & Resume
    Book ($10.95)
The Harvard Guide to Careers in the Mass Media
    ($7.95)
High Impact Telephone Networking for Job
    Hunters ($6.95)
How to Become Successfully Self-Employed, 2nd
    Ed. ($9.95)
How to Get a Job in Education, 2nd Ed. ($15.95)
The Job Hunter's Checklist ($5.95)
The Job Search Handbook ($6.95)
Knock 'em Dead, 1999 ($12.95)
The Lifetime Career Manager ($20.00 hc)
The MBA Advantage ($12.95)
The Minority Career Book ($9.95)
The National Jobline Directory ($7.95)
The New Rules of the Job Search Game ($10.95)
Outplace Yourself ($15.95)
Over 40 and Looking for Work? ($7.95)
Reengineering Yourself ($12.95)
The Resume Handbook, 3rd Ed. ($7.95)
Resumes That Knock 'em Dead, 3rd Ed. ($10.95)
Richard Beatty's Job Search Networking ($9.95)
300 New Ways to Get a Better Job ($7.95)
The 250 Job Interview Questions You'll Most
    Likely Be Asked ($9.95)

Adams JobBank FastResume Suite (CD-ROM)
(Please call for details.)

If you are interested in variations of JobBank company profiles in electronic format for job search or sales
mailings, please call 800/872-5627x5304 or e-mail us at jobbank@adamsonline.com.

To order books, please send check or money order (including $4.95 for postage) to:
Adams Media Corporation, 260 Center Street, Holbrook MA 02343.
(Foreign orders please call for shipping rates.) Discounts available for standing orders.

Ordering by credit card? Just call 800/USA-JOBS (In Massachusetts, call 781/767-8100). Fax: 800/872-5687.
Please check your favorite retail outlet first.

—VISIT OUR WEBSITE—
http://www.careercity.com

11th Edition
THE Minneapolis–St. Paul
JobBank

Managing Editor:	Steven Graber
Assistant Managing Editor:	Marcie DiPietro
Senior Editor:	Michelle Roy Kelly
Senior Associate Editor:	Heidi E. Sampson
Associate Editor:	Jayna S. Stafford
Editorial Assistants:	Thom Blackett
	Heather L. Vinhateiro
	Jennifer M. Wood

Adams Media Corporation
HOLBROOK, MASSACHUSETTS

Published by Adams Media Corporation
260 Center Street, Holbrook, MA 02343

Manufactured in the United States of America.

Copyright © 1999 by Adams Media Corporation. All rights reserved. No part of the material printed may be reproduced or used in any form or by any means, electronic or mechanical, including photocopying, recording, or by any information storage retrieval system without permission from the publisher.

The Minneapolis-St. Paul JobBank, 11th Edition and its cover design are trademarks of Adams Media Corporation.

Brand name products in the employer listings are proprietary property of the applicable firm, subject to trademark protection, and registered with government offices.

Because addresses and telephone numbers of smaller companies change rapidly, we recommend you call each company and verify the information before mailing to the employers listed in this book. Mass mailings are not recommended.

While the publisher has made every reasonable effort to obtain and verify accurate information, occasional errors are inevitable due to the magnitude of the database. Should you discover an error, or if a company is missing, please write the editors at the above address so that we may update future editions.

"This publication is designed to provide accurate and authoritative information with regard to the subject matter covered. It is sold with the understanding that the publisher is not engaged in rendering legal, accounting, or other professional advice. If legal advice or other expert assistance is required, the services of a competent professional person should be sought."
--From a Declaration of Principles jointly adopted by a Committee of the American Bar Association and a Committee of Publishers and Associations

The appearance of a listing in the book does not constitute an endorsement from the publisher.

ISBN: 1-58062-151-1
ISSN: 1072-5768

This book is available at quantity discounts for bulk purchases.
For information, call 800/872-5627.

Visit our exciting job and career site at http://www.careercity.com

TABLE OF CONTENTS

SECTION FOUR: EMPLOYMENT SERVICES

Temporary Employment Agencies/266

Includes addresses, phone numbers, and descriptions of companies specializing in temporary placement of clients. Also includes contact names, specializations, and a list of positions commonly filled.

Permanent Employment Agencies/269

Includes addresses, phone numbers, and descriptions of companies specializing in permanent placement of clients. Also includes contact names, specializations, and a list of positions commonly filled.

Executive Search Firms/272

Includes addresses, phone numbers, and descriptions of companies specializing in permanent placement of executive-level clients. Also includes contact names, specializations, and a list of positions commonly filled.

Contract Services Firms/281

Includes addresses, phone numbers, and descriptions of companies specializing in contract services.

Resume/Career Counseling Services/283

Includes addresses, phone numbers, and descriptions of companies providing resume writing services and/or career counseling services.

SECTION FIVE: INDEX

Alphabetical Index of Primary Employers/286

Includes larger employer listings only. Does not include employers that fall under the headings "Additional Employers."

INTRODUCTION

HOW TO USE THIS BOOK

Right now, you hold in your hands one of the most effective job-hunting tools available anywhere. In *The Minneapolis-St. Paul JobBank*, you will find a wide array of valuable information to help you launch or continue a rewarding career. But before you open to the book's employer listings and start calling about current job openings, take a few minutes to learn how best to use the resources presented in *The Minneapolis-St. Paul JobBank*.

The Minneapolis-St. Paul JobBank will help you to stand out from other jobseekers. While many people looking for a new job rely solely on newspaper help-wanted ads, this book offers you a much more effective job-search method -- direct contact. The direct contact method has been proven twice as effective as scanning the help-wanted ads. Instead of waiting for employers to come looking for you, you'll be far more effective going to them. While many of your competitors will use trial and error methods in trying to set up interviews, you'll learn not only how to get interviews, but what to expect once you've got them.

In the next few pages, we'll take you through each section of the book so you'll be prepared to get a jump-start on your competition.

Basics of Job Winning

Preparation. Strategy. Time-management. These are three of the most important elements of a successful job search. *Basics of Job Winning* helps you address these and all the other elements needed to find the right job.

One of your first priorities should be to define your personal career objectives. What qualities make a job desirable to you? Creativity? High pay? Prestige? Use *Basics of Job Winning* to weigh these questions. Then use the rest of the chapter to design a strategy to find a job that matches your criteria.

In *Basics of Job Winning,* you'll learn which job-hunting techniques work, and which don't. We've reviewed the pros and cons of mass mailings, help-wanted ads, and direct contact. We'll show you how to develop and approach contacts in your field; how to research a prospective employer; and how to use that information to get an interview and the job.

Also included in *Basics of Job Winning*: interview dress code and etiquette, the "do's and don'ts" of interviewing, sample interview questions, and more. We also deal with some of the unique problems faced by those jobseekers who are currently employed, those who have lost a job, and college students conducting their first job search.

Resumes and Cover Letters

The approach you take to writing your resume and cover letter can often mean the difference between getting an interview and never being noticed. In this section, we discuss different formats, as well as what to put on (and what to leave off) your resume. We review the benefits and drawbacks of professional resume writers, and the importance of a follow-up letter. Also included in this section are sample resumes and cover letters which you can use as models.

CD-ROM Job Search

Jobseekers who are looking for an edge against the competition may want to check out these CD-ROM products.

The Employer Listings

Employers are listed alphabetically by industry, and within each industry, by company names. When a company does business under a person's name, like "John Smith & Co.," the company is usually listed by the surname's spelling (in this case "S"). Exceptions occur when a company's name is widely recognized, like "JCPenney" or "Howard Johnson Motor Lodge." In those cases, the company's first name is the key ("J" and "H" respectively).

The Minneapolis-St. Paul JobBank covers a very wide range of industries. Each company profile is assigned to one of the industry chapters listed below.

Accounting and Management Consulting
Advertising, Marketing, and Public Relations
Aerospace
Apparel, Fashion, and Textiles
Architecture, Construction, and Engineering
Arts and Entertainment/Recreation
Automotive
Banking/Savings and Loans
Biotechnology, Pharmaceuticals, and Scientific R&D
Business Services and Non-Scientific Research
Charities and Social Services
Chemicals/Rubber and Plastics
Communications: Telecommunications and Broadcasting
Computer Hardware, Software, and Services
Educational Services
Electronic/Industrial Electrical Equipment

Environmental and Waste Management Services
Fabricated/Primary Metals and Products
Financial Services
Food and Beverages/Agriculture
Government
Health Care: Services, Equipment, and Products
Hotels and Restaurants
Insurance
Legal Services
Manufacturing: Miscellaneous Consumer
Manufacturing: Miscellaneous Industrial
Mining/Gas/Petroleum/Energy Related
Paper and Wood Products
Printing and Publishing
Real Estate
Retail
Stone, Clay, Glass, and Concrete Products
Transportation/Travel
Utilities: Electric/Gas/Water
Miscellaneous Wholesaling

Many of the company listings offer detailed company profiles. In addition to company names, addresses, and phone numbers, these listings also include contact names or hiring departments, and descriptions of each company's products and/or services. Many of these listings also feature a variety of additional information including:

Common positions - A list of job titles that the company commonly fills when it is hiring, organized in alphabetical order from Accountant to X-ray Technician. Note: Keep in mind that *The Minneapolis-St. Paul JobBank* is a directory of major employers in the area, not a directory of openings currently available. Many of the companies listed will be hiring, others will not.

However, since most professional job openings are filled without the placement of help-wanted ads, contacting the employers in this book directly is still a more effective method than browsing the Sunday papers.

Educational backgrounds sought - A list of educational backgrounds that companies seek when hiring.

Benefits - What kind of benefits packages are available from these employers? Here you'll find a broad range of benefits, from the relatively common (medical insurance) to those that are much more rare (health club membership; child daycare assistance).

Special programs - Does the company offer training programs, internships, or apprenticeships? These programs can be important to first time jobseekers and college students looking for practical work experience. Many employer profiles will include information on these programs.

Parent company - If an employer is a subsidiary of a larger company, the name of that parent company will often be listed here. Use this information to supplement your company research before contacting the employer.

Number of employees - The number of workers a company employs.

Company listings may also include information on other U.S. locations and any stock exchanges the firm may be listed on.

Because so many job openings are with small and mid-sized employers, we've also included the addresses and phone numbers of such employers. While none of these listings include any additional hiring information, many of them do offer rewarding career opportunities. These companies are found under each industry heading. Within each industry, they are organized by the type of product or service offered.

A note on all employer listings that appear in *The Minneapolis-St. Paul JobBank*: This book is intended as a starting point. It is not intended to replace any effort that you, the jobseeker, should devote to your job hunt. Keep in mind that while a great deal of effort has been put into collecting and verifying the company profiles provided in this book, addresses and contact names change regularly. Inevitably, some contact names listed herein have changed even before you read this. We recommend you contact a company before mailing your resume to ensure nothing has changed.

At the end of each industry section, we have included a directory of other industry-specific resources to help you in your job search. These include: professional and industrial associations, many of which can provide employment advice and job-search help; magazines that cover the industry; and additional directories that may supplement the employer listings in this book.

Employment Services

Immediately following the employer listings section of this book are listings of local employment services firms. Many jobseekers supplement their own efforts by contracting "temp" services, headhunters, and other employment search firms to generate potential job opportunities.

This section is a comprehensive listing of such firms, arranged alphabetically under the headings Temporary Employment Agencies, Permanent Employment Agencies, and Executive Search Firms. Each listing includes the firm's name, address, telephone number, and contact person. Most listings also include the industries the firm specializes in, the type of positions commonly filled, and the number of jobs filled annually.

Index

The Minneapolis-St. Paul JobBank index is a straight alphabetical listing.

THE JOB SEARCH

THE BASICS OF JOB WINNING: A CONDENSED REVIEW

This chapter is divided into four sections. The first section explains the fundamentals that every jobseeker should know, especially first-time jobseekers. The following three sections deal with special situations faced by specific types of jobseekers: those who are currently employed, those who have lost a job, and college students.

THE BASICS:
Things Everyone Needs to Know

Career Planning   The first step to finding your ideal job is to clearly define your objectives. This is better known as career planning (or life planning if you wish to emphasize the importance of combining the two). Career planning has become a field of study in and of itself.

If you are thinking of choosing or switching careers, we particularly emphasize two things. First, choose a career where you will enjoy most of the day-to-day tasks. This sounds obvious, but most of us have at one point or another been attracted by a glamour industry or a prestigious job title without thinking of the most important consideration: Would we enjoy performing the everyday tasks the position entails?

The second key consideration is that you are not merely choosing a career, but also a lifestyle. Career counselors indicate that one of the most common problems people encounter in job-seeking is that they fail to consider how well-suited they are for a particular position or career. For example, some people, attracted to management consulting by good salaries, early responsibility, and high-level corporate exposure, do not adapt well to the long hours, heavy travel demands, and constant pressure to produce. Be sure to ask yourself how you might adapt to not only the day-to-day duties and working environment that a specific position entails, but also how you might adapt to the demands of that career or industry choice as a whole.

Choosing Your Strategy   Assuming that you've established your career objectives, the next step of the job search is to develop a strategy. If you don't take the time to develop a strategy and lay out a plan, you may find yourself going in circles after several weeks of randomly searching for opportunities that always seem just beyond your reach.

The most common job-seeking techniques are:

- following up on help-wanted advertisements
- using employment services
- relying on personal contacts
- contacting employers directly (the Direct Contact method)

Many professionals have been successful in finding better jobs using each one of these approaches. However, the Direct Contact method boasts twice the success rate of the others. So unless you have specific reasons to believe that other strategies would work best for you, Direct Contact should form the foundation of your job search.

If you prefer to use other methods as well, try to expend at least half your effort on Direct Contact, spending the rest on all of the other methods combined. Millions of other jobseekers have already proven that Direct Contact has been twice as effective in obtaining employment, so why not benefit from their experience?

With your strategy in mind, the next step is to work out the details of your search. The most important detail is setting up a schedule. Of course, since job searches aren't something most people do regularly, it may be hard to estimate how long each step will take. Nonetheless, it is important to have a plan so that you can monitor your progress. **Setting Your Schedule**

When outlining your job search schedule, have a realistic time frame in mind. If you will be job-searching full-time, your search could take at least two months or more. If you can only devote part-time effort, it will probably take at least four months.

You probably know a few currently employed people who seem to spend their whole lives searching for a better job in their spare time. Don't be one of them. If you are presently working and don't feel like devoting a lot of energy to job-seeking right now, then wait. Focus on enjoying your present position,

> **The first step in beginning your job search is to clearly define your objectives.**

performing your best on the job, and storing up energy for when you are really ready to begin your job search.

Those of you who are currently unemployed should remember that job-hunting is tough work physically and emotionally. It is also intellectually demanding work that requires you to be at your best. So don't tire yourself out by working on your job campaign around the clock. At the same time, be sure to discipline yourself. The most logical way to manage your time while looking for a job is to keep your regular working hours.

If you are searching full-time and have decided to choose several different contact methods, we recommend that you divide up each week, designating some time for each method. By trying several approaches at once, you can evaluate how promising each seems and alter your schedule accordingly. But be careful -- don't judge the success of a particular technique just by the sheer number of interviews you obtain. Positions advertised in the newspaper, for instance, are likely to generate many more interviews per opening than positions that are filled without being advertised.

If you are searching part-time and decide to try several different contact methods, we recommend that you try them sequentially. You simply won't have enough time to put a meaningful amount of effort into more than one method at once. Estimate the length of your job search, and then allocate so many weeks or months for each contact method, beginning with Direct Contact.

And remember that all schedules are meant to be broken. The purpose of setting a schedule is not to rush you to your goal but to help you periodically evaluate how you're progressing.

The Direct Contact Method

Once you have scheduled your time, you are ready to begin your search in earnest. If you decide to begin with the Direct Contact method, the first step is to develop a checklist for categorizing the types of firms for which you'd like to work. You might categorize firms by product line, size, customer type (such as industrial or consumer), growth prospects, or geographical location. Your list of important criteria might be very short. If it is, good! The shorter it is, the easier it will be to locate a company that is right for you.

Now you will want to use this *JobBank* book to assemble your list of potential employers. Choose firms where *you* are most likely to be able to find a job. Try matching your skills with those that a specific job demands. Consider where your skills might be in demand, the degree of competition for employment, and the employment outlook at each company.

Separate your prospect list into three groups. The first 25 percent will be your primary target group, the next 25 percent will be your secondary group, and the remaining names you can keep in reserve.

After you form your prospect list, begin work on your resume. Refer to the Resumes and Cover Letters section following this chapter to get ideas.

Once your resume is complete, begin researching your first batch of prospective employers. You will want to determine whether you would be happy working at the firms you are researching and to get a better idea of what their employment needs might be. You also need to obtain enough information to sound highly informed about the company during phone conversations and in mail correspondence. But don't go all out on your research yet! You probably won't be able to arrange interviews with some of these firms, so save your big research effort until you start to arrange interviews. Nevertheless, you should plan to spend several hours researching each firm. Do your research in batches to save time and energy. Start with this book, and find out what you can about each of the firms in your primary target group. Contact any pertinent professional associations that may be able to help you learn more about an employer. Read industry

> The more you know about a company, the more likely you are to catch an interviewer's eye. (You'll also face fewer surprises once you get the job!)

publications looking for articles on the firm. (Addresses of associations and names of important publications are listed after each industrial section of employer listings in this book.) Then try additional resources at your local library. Keep organized, and maintain a folder on each firm.

If you discover something that really disturbs you about the firm (they are about to close their only local office), or if you discover that your chances of getting a job there are practically nil (they have just instituted a hiring freeze), then cross them off your prospect list. If possible,

---

DEVELOPING YOUR CONTACTS:
NETWORKING

Some career counselors feel that the best route to a better job is through somebody you already know or through somebody to whom you can be introduced. These counselors recommend that you build your contact base beyond your current acquaintances by asking each one to introduce you, or refer you, to additional people in your field of interest.

The theory goes like this: You might start with 15 personal contacts, each of whom introduces you to three additional people, for a total of 45 additional contacts. Then each of these people introduces you to three additional people, which adds 135 additional contacts. Theoretically, you will soon know every person in the industry.

Of course, developing your personal contacts does not work quite as smoothly as the theory suggests because some people will not be able to introduce you to anyone. The further you stray from your initial contact base, the weaker your references may be. So, if you do try developing your own contacts, try to begin with as many people that you know personally as you can. Dig into your personal phone book and your holiday greeting card list and locate old classmates from school. Be particularly sure to approach people who perform your personal business such as your lawyer, accountant, banker, doctor, stockbroker, and insurance agent. These people develop a very broad contact base due to the nature of their professions.

---

supplement your research efforts by contacting individuals who know the firm well. Ideally you should make an informal contact with someone at that particular firm, but often a direct competitor, or a major supplier or customer, will be able to supply you with just as much information. At the very least, try to obtain whatever printed information the company has available -- not just annual reports, but product brochures and any other printed materials that the firm may have to offer, either about its operations or about career opportunities.

Getting the Interview

Now it is time to arrange an interview, time to make the Direct Contact. If you have read many books on job-searching, you may have noticed that most of these books tell you to avoid the personnel office like the plague. It is said that the personnel office never hires people; they screen candidates. Unfortunately, this is often the case. If you can identify the appropriate manager with the authority to hire you, you should try to contact that person directly. However, this will take a lot of time in each case, and often you'll be bounced back to personnel despite your efforts. So we suggest that initially you begin your Direct Contact campaign through personnel offices. If it seems that the firms on your prospect list do little hiring through personnel, you might consider some alternative courses of action.

The three obvious means of initiating Direct Contact are:

- Showing up unannounced
- Mail (postal or electronic)
- Phone calls

Cross out the first one right away. You should never show up to seek a professional position without an appointment. Even if you are somehow lucky enough to obtain an interview, you will appear so unprofessional that you will not be seriously considered.

Mail contact seems to be a good choice if you have not been in the job market for a while. You can take your time to prepare a letter, say exactly what you want, and of course include your resume. Remember that employers receive many resumes every day. Don't be surprised if you do not get a response to your inquiry, and don't spend weeks waiting for responses that may never come. If you do send a letter, follow it up (or precede it) with a phone call. This will increase your impact, and because of the initial research you did, will underscore both your familiarity with and your interest in the firm.

Another alternative is to make a "cover call." Your cover call should be just like your cover letter: concise. Your first statement should interest the employer in you. Then try to subtly mention your familiarity with the firm. Don't be overbearing; keep your introduction to three sentences or

> **Always include a cover letter if you are asked to send a resume.**

less. Be pleasant, self-confident, and relaxed. This will greatly increase the chances of the person at the other end of the line developing the conversation. But don't press. If you are asked to follow up with "something in the mail," this signals the conversation's natural end. Don't try to prolong the conversation once it has ended, and don't ask what they want to receive in the mail. Always send your resume and a highly personalized follow-up letter, reminding the addressee of the phone conversation. *Always* include a cover letter if you are asked to send a resume.

Unless you are in telephone sales, making smooth and relaxed cover calls will probably not come easily. Practice them on your own, and then with your friends or relatives.

If you obtain an interview as a result of a telephone conversation, be sure to send a thank-you note reiterating the points you made during the

DON'T BOTHER WITH MASS MAILINGS OR BARRAGES OF PHONE CALLS

Direct Contact does not mean burying every firm within a hundred miles with mail and phone calls. Mass mailings rarely work in the job hunt. This also applies to those letters that are personalized -- but dehumanized -- on an automatic typewriter or computer. Don't waste your time or money on such a project; you will fool no one but yourself.

The worst part of sending out mass mailings, or making unplanned phone calls to companies you have not researched, is that you are likely to be remembered as someone with little genuine interest in the firm, who lacks sincerity -- somebody that nobody wants to hire.

HELP WANTED ADVERTISEMENTS

Only a small fraction of professional job openings are advertised. Yet the majority of jobseekers -- and quite a few people not in the job market -- spend a lot of time studying the help wanted ads. As a result, the competition for advertised openings is often very severe.

A moderate-sized employer told us about their experience advertising in the help wanted section of a major Sunday newspaper:

It was a disaster. We had over 500 responses from this relatively small ad in just one week. We have only two phone lines in this office and one was totally knocked out. We'll never advertise for professional help again.

If you insist on following up on help wanted ads, then research a firm before you reply to an ad. Preliminary research might help to separate you from all of the other professionals responding to that ad, many of whom will have only a passing interest in the opportunity. It will also give you insight about a particular firm, to help you determine if it is potentially a good match. That said, your chances of obtaining a job through the want ads are still much smaller than they are with the Direct Contact method.

conversation. You will appear more professional and increase your impact. However, unless specifically requested, don't mail your resume once an interview has been arranged. Take it with you to the interview instead.

Preparing for the Interview

Once the interview has been arranged, begin your in-depth research. You should arrive at an interview knowing the company upside-down and inside-out. You need to know the company's products, types of customers, subsidiaries, parent company, principal locations, rank in the industry, sales and profit trends, type of ownership, size, current plans, and much more. By this time you have probably narrowed your job search to one industry. Even if you haven't, you should still be familiar with the trends in the firm's industry, the firm's principal competitors and their relative performance, and the direction in which the industry leaders are headed.

Dig into every resource you can! Read the company literature, the trade press, the business press, and if the company is public, call your stockbroker (if you have one) and ask for additional information. If possible, speak to someone at the firm before the interview, or if not, speak to someone at a competing firm. The more time you spend, the better. Even if you feel extremely pressed for time, you should set aside several hours for pre-interview research.

> You should arrive at an interview knowing the company upside-down and inside-out.

If you have been out of the job market for some time, don't be surprised if you find yourself tense during your first few interviews. It will probably happen every time you re-enter the market, not just when you seek your first job after getting out of school.

Tension is natural during an interview, but knowing you have done a thorough research job should put you more at ease. Make a list of questions that you think might be asked in each interview. Think out your answers carefully and practice them with a friend. Tape record your responses to the problem questions. If you feel particularly unsure of your interviewing skills, arrange your first interviews at firms you are not as interested in. (But remember it is common courtesy to seem enthusiastic about the possibility of working for any firm at which you interview.) Practice again on your own after these first few interviews. Go over the difficult questions that you were asked.

Interview Attire

How important is the proper dress for a job interview? Buying a complete wardrobe of Brooks Brothers pinstripes or Donna Karan suits, donning new wing tips or pumps, and having your hair styled every morning are not enough to guarantee you a career position as an investment banker. But on the other hand, if you can't find a clean, conservative suit or won't take the time to wash your hair, then you are just wasting your time by interviewing at all.

Top personal grooming is as important as finding appropriate clothes for a job interview. Careful grooming indicates both a sense of thoroughness and self-confidence. This is not the time to make a statement -- take out the extra earrings and avoid any garish hair colors not found in nature. Women should not wear excessive makeup, and both men and women should refrain from wearing any perfume or cologne (it only takes a small spritz to leave an allergic interviewer with a fit of sneezing and a bad impression of your meeting). Men should be freshly shaven, even if the interview is late in the day, and men with long hair should have it pulled back and neat.

Men applying for any professional position should wear a suit, preferably in a conservative color such as navy or charcoal gray. It is easy to get away with wearing the same dark suit to consecutive interviews at the same company; just be sure to wear a different shirt and tie for each interview.

Women should also wear a businesslike suit. Professionalism still dictates a suit with a skirt, rather than slacks, as proper interview garb for women. This is usually true even at companies where pants are acceptable attire for female employees. As much as you may disagree with this guideline, the more prudent time to fight this standard is after you land the job.

SKIRT VS. PANTS:
An Interview Dilemma

For those women who are still convinced that pants are acceptable interview attire, listen to the words of one career counselor from a prestigious New England college:

I had a student who told me that since she knew women in her industry often wore pants to work, she was going to wear pants to her interviews. Almost every recruiter commented that her pants were "too casual," and even referred to her as "the one with the pants." The funny thing was that one of the recruiters who commented on her pants had been wearing jeans!

The final selection of candidates for a job opening won't be determined by dress, of course. However, inappropriate dress can quickly eliminate a first-round candidate. So while you shouldn't spend a fortune on a new wardrobe, you should be sure that your clothes are adequate. The key is to dress at least as formally or slightly more formally and more conservatively than the position would suggest.

What to Bring   Be complete. Everyone needs a watch, a pen, and a notepad. Finally, a briefcase or a leather-bound folder (containing extra, *unfolded*, copies of your resume) will help complete the look of professionalism.

Sometimes the interviewer will be running behind schedule. Don't be upset, be sympathetic. There is often pressure to interview a lot of candidates and to quickly fill a demanding position. So be sure to come to your interview with good reading material to keep yourself occupied and relaxed.

The Interview   The very beginning of the interview is the most important part because it determines the tone for the rest of it. Those first few moments are especially crucial. Do you smile when you meet? Do you establish enough eye contact, but not too much? Do you walk into the office with a self-assured and confident stride? Do you shake hands firmly? Do you

---

BE PREPARED:
Some Common Interview Questions

Tell me about yourself...

Why did you leave your last job?

What excites you in your current job?

Where would you like to be in five years?

How much overtime are you willing to work?

What would your previous/present employer tell me about you?

Tell me about a difficult situation that you
faced at your previous/present job.

What are your greatest strengths?

What are your greatest weaknesses?

Describe a work situation where you took initiative
and went beyond your normal responsibilities.

Why do you wish to work for this firm?

Why should we hire you?

---

make small talk easily without being garrulous? It is human nature to judge people by that first impression, so make sure it is a good one. But most of all, try to be yourself.

Often the interviewer will begin, after the small talk, by telling you about the company, the division, the department, or perhaps, the position. Because of your detailed research, the information about the company should be repetitive for you, and the interviewer would probably like nothing better than to avoid this regurgitation of the company biography. So if you can do so tactfully, indicate to the interviewer that you are very familiar with the firm. If he or she seems intent on providing you with background information, despite your hints, then acquiesce.

But be sure to remain attentive. If you can manage to generate a brief discussion of the company or the industry at this point, without being forceful, great. It will help to further build rapport, underscore your interest, and increase your impact.

Soon (if it didn't begin that way) the interviewer will begin the questions, many of which you will have already practiced. This period of the interview usually falls into one of two categories (or somewhere in between): either a structured interview, where the interviewer has a prescribed set of questions to ask; or an unstructured interview, where the interviewer will ask only leading questions to get you to talk about

> **The interviewer's job is to find a reason to turn you down; your job is to not provide that reason.**
>
> -John L. LaFevre, author,
> *How You Really Get Hired*
>
> Reprinted from the 1989/90 *CPC Annual,* with permission of the National Association of Colleges and Employers (formerly College Placement Council, Inc.), copyright holder.

yourself, your experiences, and your goals. Try to sense as quickly as possible in which direction the interviewer wishes to proceed. This will make the interviewer feel more relaxed and in control of the situation.

Remember to keep attuned to the interviewer and make the length of your answers appropriate to the situation. If you are really unsure as to how detailed a response the interviewer is seeking, then ask.

As the interview progresses, the interviewer will probably mention some of the most important responsibilities of the position. If applicable, draw parallels between your experience and the demands of the position as detailed by the interviewer. Describe your past experience in the same manner that you do on your resume: emphasizing results and achievements and not merely describing activities. But don't exaggerate. Be on the level about your abilities.

The first interview is often the toughest, where many candidates are screened out. If you are interviewing for a very competitive position, you will have to make an impression that will last. Focus on a few of your greatest strengths that are relevant to the position. Develop these points carefully, state them again in different words, and then try to summarize them briefly at the end of the interview.

Often the interviewer will pause toward the end and ask if you have any questions. Particularly in a structured interview, this might be the one chance to really show your knowledge of and interest in the firm. Have a list prepared of specific questions that are of real interest to you. Let your questions subtly show your research and your knowledge of the firm's activities. It is wise to have an extensive list of questions, as several of them may be answered during the interview.

> **Getting a job offer is a lot like getting a marriage proposal. Someone is not going to offer it unless they're pretty sure you're going to accept it.**
>
> -Marilyn Hill,
> Associate Director,
> Career Center,
> Carleton College

Do not turn your opportunity to ask questions into an interrogation. Avoid reading directly from your list of questions, and ask questions that you are fairly certain the interviewer can answer (remember how you feel when you cannot answer a question during an interview).

Even if you are unable to determine the salary range beforehand, do not ask about it during the first interview. You can always ask about it later. Above all, don't ask about fringe benefits until you have been offered a position. (Then be sure to get all the details.)

Try not to be negative about anything during the interview (particularly any past employer or any previous job). Be cheerful. Everyone likes to work with someone who seems to be happy.

Don't let a tough question throw you off base. If you don't know the answer to a question, simply say so -- do not apologize. Just smile. Nobody can answer every question -- particularly some of the questions that are asked in job interviews.

Before your first interview, you may be able to determine how many rounds of interviews there usually are for positions at your level. (Of course it may differ quite a bit even within the different levels of one firm.) Usually you can count on attending at least two or three interviews, although some firms are known to give a minimum of six interviews for all professional positions. While you should be more relaxed as you return for subsequent interviews, the pressure will be on. The more prepared you are, the better.

Depending on what information you are able to obtain, you might want to vary your strategy quite a bit from interview to interview. For instance, if the first interview is a screening interview, then be sure a few of your strengths really stand out. On the other hand, if later interviews are primarily with people who are in a position to veto your hiring, but not to push it forward, then you should primarily focus on building rapport as opposed to reiterating and developing your key strengths.

If it looks as though your skills and background do not match the position the interviewer was hoping to fill, ask him or her if there is another division or subsidiary that perhaps could profit from your talents.

Write a follow-up letter immediately after the interview, while it is still fresh in the interviewer's mind (see the sample follow-up letter format found in the Resumes and Cover Letters chapter). Then, if you haven't heard from the interviewer within a week, call to stress your continued interest in the firm, and the position, and request a second interview. **After the Interview**

THE BALANCING ACT:
Looking for a New Job While Currently Employed

For those of you who are still employed, job-searching will be particularly tiring because it must be done in addition to your normal work responsibilities. So don't overwork yourself to the point where you show up to interviews looking exhausted and start to slip behind at your current job. On the other hand, don't be tempted to quit your present job! The long hours are worth it. Searching for a job while you have one puts you in a position of strength.

If you're expected to be in your office during the business day, then you have additional problems to deal with. How can you work interviews into the business day? And if you work in an open office, how can you even call to set up interviews? As much as possible you should keep up the effort and the appearances on your present job. So maximize your use of the lunch hour, early mornings, and late afternoons for calling. If you keep trying, you'll be surprised how often you will be able to reach the executive you are trying to contact during your out-of-office hours. You can catch people as early as 8 a.m. and as late as 6 p.m. on frequent occasions. **Making Contact**

Your inability to interview at any time other than lunch just might work to your advantage. If you can, try to set up as many interviews as possible for your lunch hour. This will go a long way to creating a relaxed atmosphere. But be sure the interviews don't stray too far from the agenda on hand. **Scheduling Interviews**

Lunchtime interviews are much easier to obtain if you have substantial career experience. People with less experience will often find no alternative to taking time off for interviews. If you have to take time off, you have to take time off. But try to do this as little as possible. Try to take the whole day off in order to avoid being blatantly obvious about your job search, and try to schedule two to three interviews for the same day. (It is

> **Try calling as early as 8 a.m. and as late as 6 p.m. You'll be surprised how often you will be able to reach the executive you want during these times of the day.**

very difficult to maintain an optimum level of energy at more than three interviews in one day.) Explain to the interviewer why you might have to juggle your interview schedule -- he/she should honor the respect you're showing your current employer by minimizing your days off and will probably appreciate the fact that another prospective employer is interested in you.

References   What do you tell an interviewer who asks for references? Just say that while you are happy to have your former employers contacted, you are trying to keep your job search confidential and would rather that your current employer not be contacted until you have been given a firm offer.

IF YOU'RE FIRED OR LAID OFF:
Picking Yourself Up and Dusting Yourself Off

If you've been fired or laid off, you are not the first and will not be the last to go through this traumatic experience. In today's changing economy, thousands of professionals lose their jobs every year. Even if you were terminated with just cause, do not lose heart. Remember, being fired is not a reflection on you as a person. It is usually a reflection of your company's staffing needs and its perception of your recent job performance and attitude. And if you were not performing up to par or enjoying your work, then you will probably be better off at another company anyway.

> **Be prepared for the question "Why were you fired?" during job interviews.**

A thorough job search could take months, so be sure to negotiate a reasonable severance package, if possible, and determine what benefits, such as health insurance, you are still legally entitled to. Also, register for unemployment compensation immediately. Don't be surprised to find other professionals collecting unemployment compensation -- it is for everyone who has lost their job.

Don't start your job search with a flurry of unplanned activity. Start by choosing a strategy and working out a plan. Now is not the time for major changes in your life. If possible, remain in the same career and in the same geographical location, at least until you have been working again for a while. On the other hand, if the only industry for which you are trained is leaving, or is severely depressed in your area, then you should give prompt consideration to moving or switching careers.

Avoid mentioning you were fired when arranging interviews, but be prepared for the question "Why were you fired?" during an interview. If you were laid off as a result of downsizing, briefly explain, being sure to reinforce that your job loss was not due to performance. If you were in fact fired, be honest, but try to detail the reason as favorably as possible and portray what you have learned from your mistakes. If you are confident one of your past managers will give you a good reference, tell the interviewer to contact that person. Do not to speak negatively of your past employer and try not to sound particularly worried about your status of being temporarily unemployed.

Finally, don't spend too much time reflecting on why you were let go or how you might have avoided it. Think positively, look to the future, and be sure to follow a careful plan during your job search.

THE COLLEGE STUDENT:
How to Conduct Your First Job Search

While you will be able to apply many of the basics covered earlier in this chapter to your job search, there are some situations unique to the college student's job search.

Perhaps the biggest problem college students face is lack of **Gaining** experience. Many schools have internship programs designed to give **Experience** students exposure to the field of their choice, as well as the opportunity to make valuable contacts. Check out your school's career services department to see what internships are available. If your school does not have a formal internship program, or if there are no available internships that appeal to you, try contacting local businesses and offering your services -- often, businesses will be more than willing to have any extra pair of hands (especially if those hands are unpaid!) for a day or two each week. Or try contacting school alumni to see if you can "shadow" them for a few days, and see what their day-to-day duties are like. Either way, try to begin building experience as early as possible in your college career.

THE GPA QUESTION

You are interviewing for the job of your dreams. Everything is going well: You've established a good rapport, the interviewer seems impressed with your qualifications, and you're almost positive the job is yours. Then you're asked about your GPA, which is pitifully low. Do you tell the truth and watch your dream job fly out the window?

Never lie about your GPA (they may request your transcript, and no company will hire a liar). You can, however, explain if there is a reason you don't feel your grades reflect your abilities, and mention any other impressive statistics. For example, if you have a high GPA in your major, or in the last few semesters (as opposed to your cumulative college career), you can use that fact to your advantage.

What do you do if, for whatever reason, you weren't able to get experience directly related to your desired career? First, look at your previous jobs and see if there's anything you can highlight. Did you supervise or train other employees? Did you reorganize the accounting system, or boost productivity in some way? Accomplishments like these demonstrate leadership, responsibility, and innovation -- qualities that most companies look for in employees. And don't forget volunteer activities and school clubs, which can also showcase these traits.

On-Campus Recruiting

Companies will often send recruiters to interview on-site at various colleges. This gives students a chance to get interviews at companies that may not have interviewed them otherwise, particularly if the company schedules "open" interviews, in which the only screening process is who is first in line at the sign-ups. Of course, since many more applicants gain interviews in this format, this also means that many more people are rejected. The on-campus interview is generally a screening interview, to see if it is worth the company's time to invite you in for a second interview. So do everything possible to make yourself stand out from the crowd.

The first step, of course, is to check out any and all information your school's career center has on the company. If the information seems out of date, call the company's headquarters and ask to be sent the latest annual report, or any other printed information.

Many companies will host an informational meeting for interviewees, often the evening before interviews are scheduled to take place. DO NOT MISS THIS MEETING. The recruiter will almost certainly ask if you attended. Make an effort to stay after the meeting and talk with the company's representatives. Not only does this give you an opportunity to find out more information about both the company and the position, it also makes you stand out in the recruiter's mind. If there's a particular company that you had your heart set on, but you weren't able to get an interview with them, attend the information session anyway. You may be able to convince the recruiter to squeeze you into the schedule. (Or you may discover that the company really isn't suited for you after all.)

Try to check out the interview site beforehand. Some colleges may conduct "mock" interviews that take place in one of the standard interview rooms. Or you may be able to convince a career counselor (or even a custodian) to let you sneak a peek during off-hours. Either way, having an idea of the room's setup will help you to mentally prepare.

Be sure to be at least 15 minutes early to the interview. The recruiter may be running ahead of schedule, and might like to take you early. But don't be surprised if previous interviews have run over, resulting in your 30-minute slot being reduced to 20 minutes (or less). Don't complain; just use whatever time you do have as efficiently as possible to showcase the reasons *you* are the ideal candidate.

LAST WORDS

A parting word of advice. Again and again during your job search you will be rejected. You will be rejected when you apply for interviews. You will be rejected after interviews. For every job offer you finally receive, you probably will have been rejected a multitude of times. Don't let rejections slow you down. Keep reminding yourself that the sooner you go out and get started on your job search, and get those rejections flowing in, the closer you will be to obtaining the job you want.

RESUMES AND COVER LETTERS

When filling a position, a recruiter will often have 100-plus applicants, but time to interview only a handful of the most promising ones. As a result, he or she will reject most applicants after only briefly skimming their resumes.

Unless you have phoned and talked to the recruiter -- which you should do whenever you can -- you will be chosen or rejected for an interview entirely on the basis of your resume and cover letter. Your cover letter must catch the recruiter's attention, and your resume must hold it. (But remember -- a resume is no substitute for a job search campaign. *You* must seek a job. Your resume is only one tool.)

RESUME FORMAT:
Mechanics of a First Impression

The Basics Recruiters dislike long resumes, so unless you have an unusually strong background with many years of experience and a diversity of outstanding achievements, keep your resume length to one page. If you must squeeze in more information than would otherwise fit, try using a smaller typeface or changing the margins.

Keep your resume on standard 8-1/2" x 11" paper. Since recruiters often get resumes in batches of hundreds, a smaller-sized resume may get lost in the pile. Oversized resumes are likely to get crumpled at the edges, and won't fit easily in their files.

First impressions matter, so make sure the recruiter's first impression of your resume is a good one. Print your resume on quality paper that has weight and texture, in a conservative color such as white, ivory, or pale gray. Use matching paper and envelopes for both your resume and cover letter.

Getting it on Paper Modern photocomposition typesetting gives you the clearest, sharpest image, a wide variety of type styles, and effects such as italics, bold-facing, and book-like justified margins. It is also much too expensive for many jobseekers. And improvements in laser printers mean that a computer-generated resume can look just as impressive as one that has been professionally typeset.

A computer or word processor is the most flexible way to type your resume. This will allow you to make changes almost instantly and to store different drafts on disk. Word processing and desktop publishing systems also offer many different fonts to choose from, each taking up different amounts of space. (It is generally best to stay between 9-point and 12-point font size.) Many other options are also available, such as bold-facing for emphasis, justified margins, and the ability to change and manipulate spacing.

The end result, however, will be largely determined by the quality of the printer you use. You need at least "letter quality" type for your resume. Do not use a "near letter quality" or dot matrix printer. Laser printers will generally provide the best quality.

Household typewriters and office typewriters with nylon or other cloth ribbons are *not* good enough for typing your resume. If you don't have access to a quality word processor, hire a professional who can prepare your resume with a word processor or typesetting machine.

Don't make your copies on an office photocopier. Only the personnel office may see the resume you mail. Everyone else may see only a copy of it, and copies of copies quickly become unreadable. Either print out each copy individually, or take your resume to a professional copy shop, which will generally offer professionally-maintained, extra-high-quality photocopiers and charge fairly reasonable prices.

Proof with Care Whether you typed it yourself or paid to have it produced professionally, mistakes on resumes are not only embarrassing, but will usually remove you from further consideration (particularly if something obvious such as your name is misspelled). No matter how much you paid someone else to type, write, or typeset your resume, *you* lose if there is a mistake. So proofread it as carefully as possible. Get a friend to help you. Read your draft aloud as your friend checks the proof copy. Then have your friend read aloud while you check. Next, read it letter by letter to check spelling and punctuation.

> The one piece of advice I give to everyone about their resume is: Show it to people, show it to people, show it to people. Before you ever send out a resume, show it to at least a dozen people.
>
> -Cate Talbot Ashton,
> Associate Director,
> Career Services,
> Colby College

If you are having it typed or typeset by a resume service or a printer, and you can't bring a friend or take the time during the day to proof it, pay for it and take it home. Proof it there and bring it back later to get it corrected and printed.

If you wrote your resume on a word processing program, also use that program's built-in spell checker to double-check for spelling errors. But keep in mind that a spell checker will not find errors such as "to" for "two" or "wok" for "work." It's important that you still proofread your resume, even after it has been spell-checked.

Types of Resumes The two most common resume formats are the functional resume and the chronological resume (examples of both types can be found at the end of this chapter). A functional resume focuses on skills and de-emphasizes job titles, employers, etc. A functional resume is best if you have been out of the work force for a long time and/or if you want to highlight specific skills and strengths that your most recent jobs don't necessarily reflect.

Choose a chronological format if you are currently working or were working recently, and if your most recent experiences relate to your desired field. Use reverse chronological order. To a recruiter your last job and your latest schooling are the most important, so put the last first and list the rest going back in time.

Organization

Your name, phone number, and a complete address should be at the top of your resume. Try to make your name stand out by using a slightly larger font size or all capital letters. Be sure to spell out everything -- never abbreviate St. for Street or Rd. for Road. If you are a college student, you should also put your home address and phone number at the top.

Next, list your experience, then your education. If you are a recent graduate, list your education first, unless your experience is more important than your education. (For example, if you have just graduated from a teaching school, have some business experience, and are applying for a job in business, you would list your business experience first.)

Keep everything easy to find. Put the dates of your employment and education on the left of the page. Put the names of the companies you worked for and the schools you attended a few spaces to the right of the dates. Put the city and state, or the city and country, where you studied or worked to the right of the page.

This is just one suggestion that may work for you. The important thing is simply to break up the text in some way that makes your resume visually attractive and easy to scan, so experiment to see which layout works best for your resume. However you set it up, stay consistent. Inconsistencies in fonts, spacing, or tenses will make your resume look sloppy. Also, be sure to use tabs to keep your information vertically lined up, rather than the less precise space bar.

RESUME CONTENT:
Say it with Style

Sell Yourself

You are selling your skills and accomplishments in your resume, so it is important to inventory yourself and know yourself. If you have achieved something, say so. Put it in the best possible light. But avoid subjective statements, such as "I am a hard worker" or "I get along well with my coworkers." Just stick to the facts.

While you shouldn't hold back or be modest, don't exaggerate your achievements to the point of misrepresentation. Be honest. Many companies will immediately drop an applicant from consideration (or fire a current employee) if inaccurate information is discovered on a resume or other application material.

Keep it Brief   Write down the important (and pertinent) things you have done, but do it in as few words as possible. Your resume will be scanned, not read, and short, concise phrases are much more effective than long-winded sentences. Avoid the use of "I" when emphasizing your accomplishments. Instead, use brief phrases beginning with action verbs.

While some technical terms will be unavoidable, you should try to avoid excessive "technicalese." Keep in mind that the first person to see your resume may be a human resources person who won't necessarily know all the jargon -- and how can they be impressed by something they don't understand?

Also, try to keep your paragraphs at six lines or shorter. If you have more than six lines of information about one job or school, put it in two or more paragraphs. The shorter your resume is, the more carefully it will be examined. Remember: Your resume usually has between eight and 45 seconds to catch an employer's eye. So make every second count.

Job Objective   A functional resume may require a job objective to give it focus. One or two sentences describing the job you are seeking can clarify in what capacity your skills will be best put to use.

Examples: An entry-level position in the publishing industry.
A challenging position requiring analytical thought and excellent writing skills.

Don't include a job objective in a chronological resume. Even if you are certain of exactly what type of job you desire, the presence of a job objective might eliminate you from consideration for other positions that a recruiter feels are a better match for your qualifications. But even though you may not put an objective on paper, having a career goal in mind as you write can help give your resume a sense of direction.

Work Experience   Some jobseekers may choose to include both "Relevant Experience" and "Additional Experience" sections. This can be useful, as it allows the jobseeker to place more emphasis on certain experiences and to de-emphasize others.

Emphasize continued experience in a particular job area or continued interest in a particular industry. De-emphasize irrelevant positions. Delete positions that you held for less than four months (unless you are a very recent college grad or still in school). Stress your results, elaborating on how you contributed in your previous jobs. Did you increase sales, reduce costs, improve a product, implement a new program? Were you promoted? Use specific numbers (i.e., quantities, percentages, dollar amounts) whenever possible.

Mention all relevant responsibilities. Be specific, and slant your past accomplishments toward the position that you hope to obtain. For example, do you hope to supervise people? If so, then state how many people, performing what function, you have supervised.

Keep it brief if you have more than two years of career experience. **Education** Elaborate more if you have less experience. If you are a recent grad with two or more years of college, you may choose to include any high school activities that are directly relevant to your career. If you've been out of school for awhile, list post-secondary education only.

Mention degrees received and any honors or special awards. Note individual courses or research projects you participated in that might be relevant for employers. For example, if you are an English major applying for a position as a business writer, be sure to mention any business or economics courses.

USE ACTION VERBS

How you write your resume is just as important as *what* you write. The strongest resumes use short phrases beginning with action verbs. Below are a few action verbs you may want to use. (This list is not all-inclusive.)

achieved	developed	integrated	purchased
administered	devised	interpreted	reduced
advised	directed	interviewed	regulated
analyzed	discovered	invented	reorganized
arranged	distributed	launched	represented
assembled	eliminated	maintained	researched
assisted	established	managed	resolved
attained	evaluated	marketed	restored
budgeted	examined	mediated	restructured
built	executed	monitored	revised
calculated	expanded	negotiated	scheduled
collaborated	expedited	obtained	selected
collected	facilitated	operated	served
compiled	formulated	ordered	sold
completed	founded	organized	solved
computed	generated	participated	streamlined
conducted	headed	performed	studied
consolidated	identified	planned	supervised
constructed	implemented	prepared	supplied
consulted	improved	presented	supported
controlled	increased	processed	tested
coordinated	initiated	produced	trained
created	installed	proposed	updated
designed	instituted	provided	upgraded
determined	instructed	published	wrote

Highlight Impressive Skills   Be sure to mention any computer skills you may have. You may wish to include a section entitled "Additional Skills" or "Computer Skills," in which you list any software programs you know. An additional skills section is also an ideal place to mention fluency in a foreign language.

Personal Data   This section is optional, but if you choose to include it, keep it very brief (two lines maximum). A one-word mention of hobbies such as fishing, chess, baseball, cooking, etc., can give the person who will interview you a good way to open up the conversation. It doesn't hurt to include activities that are unusual (fencing, bungee jumping, snake-charming) or that somehow relate to the position or the company you're applying to (for instance, if you are a member of a professional organization in your industry). Never include information about your age, health, physical characteristics, marital status, or religious affiliation.

References   The most that is needed is the sentence, "References available upon request," at the bottom of your resume. If you choose to leave it out, that's fine.

HIRING A RESUME WRITER:
Is it the Right Choice for You?

If you write reasonably well, it is to your advantage to write your own resume. Writing your resume forces you to review your experience and figure out how to explain your accomplishments in clear, brief phrases. This will help you when you explain your work to interviewers.

If you write your resume, everything will be in your own words -- it will sound like you. It will say what you want it to say. If you are a good writer, know yourself well, and have a good idea of which parts of your background employers are looking for, you should be able to write your own resume better than

> Those things [marital status, church affiliations, etc.] have no place on a resume. Those are illegal questions, so why even put that information on your resume?
>
> -Becky Hayes, Career Counselor Career Services, Rice University

anyone else can. If you decide to write your resume yourself, have as many people review and proofread it as possible. Welcome objective opinions and other perspectives.

When to Get Help   If you have difficulty writing in "resume style" (which is quite unlike normal written language), if you are unsure of which parts of your background you should emphasize, or if you think your resume would make your case better if it did not follow one of the standard forms outlined either here or in a book on resumes, then you should consider having it professionally written.

There are two reasons even some professional resume writers we know have had their resumes written with the help of fellow professionals. First, they may need the help of someone who can be objective about their background, and second, they may want an experienced sounding board to help focus their thoughts.

The best way to choose a writer is by reputation -- the **If You Hire** recommendation of a friend, a personnel director, your school placement **a Pro** officer, or someone else knowledgeable in the field.

Important questions:
- "How long have you been writing resumes?"
- "If I'm not satisfied with what you write, will you go over it with me and change it?"
- "Do you charge by the hour or a flat rate?"

There is no sure relation between price and quality, except that you are unlikely to get a good writer for less than $50 for an uncomplicated resume and you shouldn't have to pay more than $300 unless your experience is very extensive or complicated. There will be additional charges for printing.

Few resume services will give you a firm price over the phone, simply because some resumes are too complicated and take too long to do for a predetermined price. Some services will quote you a price that applies to almost all of their customers. Once you decide to use a specific writer, you should insist on a firm price quote before engaging their services. Also, find out how expensive minor changes will be.

COVER LETTERS:
Quick, Clear, and Concise

Always mail a cover letter with your resume. In a cover letter you can show an interest in the company that you can't show in a resume. You can also point out one or two skills or accomplishments the company can put to good use.

The more personal you can get, the better. If someone known to the **Make it** person you are writing has recommended that you contact the company, **Personal** get permission to include his/her name in the letter. If you have the name of a person to send the letter to, address it directly to that person (after first calling the company to verify the spelling of the person's name, correct title, and mailing address). Be sure to put the person's name and title on both the letter and the envelope. This will ensure that your letter will get through to the proper person, even if a new person now occupies this position. But even if you don't have a contact name and are simply addressing it to the "Personnel Director" or the "Hiring Partner," definitely send a letter.

Type cover letters in full. Don't try the cheap and easy ways, like using a computer mail merge program, or photocopying the body of your letter and typing in the inside address and salutation. You will give the impression that you are mailing to a host of companies and have no particular interest in any one.

Cover letter do's and don'ts

- *Do* keep your cover letter brief and to the point.
- *Do* be sure it is error-free.
- *Don't* just repeat information verbatim from your resume.
- *Don't* overuse the personal pronoun "I."
- *Don't* send a generic cover letter -- show your personal knowledge of and interest in that particular company.
- *Do* accentuate what you can offer the company, not what you hope to gain from them.

FUNCTIONAL RESUME
(Prepared on a word processor
and laser printed.)

ELIZABETH HELEN LaFRANCE
129 Shoreline Drive
Harbor Point OH 45822
419/555-6652

Objective
A position as a graphic designer commensurate with my acquired skills and expertise.

Summary
Extensive experience in plate making, separations, color matching, background definition, printing, mechanicals, color corrections, and personnel supervision. A highly motivated manager and effective communicator. Proven ability to:

- **Create Commercial Graphics**
- **Produce Embossed Drawings**
- **Color Separate**
- **Control Quality**
- **Resolve Printing Problems**
- **Analyze Customer Satisfaction**

Qualifications

Printing:
Knowledgeable in black and white as well as color printing. Excellent judgment in determining acceptability of color reproduction through comparison with original. Proficient at producing four- or five-color corrections on all media, as well as restyling previously reproduced four-color artwork.

Customer Relations:
Routinely work closely with customers to ensure specifications are met. Capable of striking a balance between technical printing capabilities and need for customer satisfaction through entire production process.

Specialties:
Practiced at creating silk screen overlays for a multitude of processes including velo bind, GBC bind, and perfect bind. Creative design and timely preparation of posters, flyers, and personalized stationery.

Personnel Supervision:
Skillful at fostering atmosphere that encourages highly talented artists to balance high-level creativity with maximum production. Consistently meet or beat production deadlines. Instruct new employees, apprentices, and students in both artistry and technical operations.

Experience
Graphic Arts Professor, Ohio State University, Columbus OH (1987-1993).
Manager, Design Graphics, Lima OH (1993-present).

Education
Massachusetts Conservatory of Art, Ph.D. 1987
University of Massachusetts, B.A. 1984

CHRONOLOGICAL RESUME
(Prepared on a word processor
and laser printed.)

RANDALL ELLIS
557 Pine Street
Seattle, WA 98404
(206) 555-6584

EXPERIENCE

THE CENTER COMPANY   Seattle, WA
Systems Programmer   1993-present
- Develop and maintain over 100 assembler modules.
- Create screen manager programs, using Assembler and Natural languages, to trace input and output to the VTAM buffer.
- Install and customize Omegamon 695 and 700 on IBM mainframes.
- Develop programs to monitor complete security control blocks, using Assembler and Natural.
- Produce stand-alone IPLs and create backrests on IBM 3380 DASD.

INFO TECH, INC.   Seattle, WA
Technical Manager   1991-1993
- Designed and managed the implementation of a network providing the legal community with a direct line to Supreme Court cases, using Clipper on IBM 386s.
- Developed a system which catalogued entire library inventory, using Turbo Pascal on IBM AT.
- Used C to create a registration system for university registrar on IBM AT.

EDUCATION

SALEM STATE UNIVERSITY   Salem, OR
    B.S. in Computer Science.   1989
    M.S. in Computer Science.   1991

COMPUTER SKILLS

- Programming Languages: C, C++, Assembler, COBOL, Natural, Turbo Pascal, dBASE III+, and Clipper.
- Software: VTAM, Complete, TSO, JES 2, ACF 2, Omegamon 695 and 700, and Adabas.
- Operating Systems: MVS/XA, MVS/SP, MS-DOS, and VMS.

FUNCTIONAL RESUME
(Prepared on an office-quality typewriter.)

MEAGHAN O'LEARY
703 Mulberry Avenue
Chicago, IL 60601
(312) 555-8841

OBJECTIVE:
To contribute over eight years of experience in promotion, communications, and administration to an entry-level position in advertising.

SUMMARY OF QUALIFICATIONS:
* Performed advertising duties for small business.
* Experience in business writing and communications skills.
* General knowledge of office management.
* Demonstrated ability to work well with others, in both supervisory and support staff roles.
* Type 75 words per minute.

SELECTED ACHIEVEMENTS AND RESULTS:
Promotion:
Composing, editing, and proofreading correspondence and PR materials for own catering service. Large-scale mailings.

Communication:
Instruction; curriculum and lesson planning; student evaluation; parent-teacher conferences; development of educational materials. Training and supervising clerks.

Computer Skills:
Proficient in MS Word, Lotus 1-2-3, Excel, and Filemaker Pro.

Administration:
Record-keeping and file maintenance. Data processing and computer operations, accounts receivable, accounts payable, inventory control, and customer relations. Scheduling, office management, and telephone reception.

WORK HISTORY:
Teacher; Self-Employed (owner of catering service); Floor Manager; Administrative Assistant; Accounting Clerk.

EDUCATION:
Beloit College, Beloit, WI, BA in Education, 1987

CHRONOLOGICAL RESUME
**(Prepared on a word processor
and laser printed.)**

PAUL K. NORTON
16 Charles Street
Marlborough CT 06447
203/555-9641

EDUCATION

Keene State College, Keene NH
Bachelor of Arts in Elementary Education, 1995
- Graduated *magna cum laude*
- English minor
- Kappa Delta Pi member, inducted 1993

EXPERIENCE
September 1995-
Present

Elmer T. Thienes Elementary School, Marlborough CT
Part-time Kindergarten Teacher
- Instruct kindergartners in reading, spelling, language arts, and music.
- Participate in the selection of textbooks and learning aids.
- Organize and supervise class field trips and coordinate in-class presentations.

Summers
1993-1995

Keene YMCA, Youth Division, Keene NH
Child-care Counselor
- Oversaw summer program for low-income youth.
- Budgeted and coordinated special events and field trips, working with Program Director to initiate variations in the program.
- Served as Youth Advocate in cooperation with social worker to address the social needs and problems of participants.

Spring 1995

Wheelock Elementary School, Keene NH
Student Teacher
- Taught third-grade class in all elementary subjects.
- Designed and implemented a two-week unit on Native Americans.
- Assisted in revision of third-grade curriculum.

Fall 1994

Child Development Center, Keene NH
Daycare Worker
- Supervised preschool children on the playground and during art activities.
- Created a "Wishbone Corner," where children could quietly look at books or take a voluntary "time-out."

ADDITIONAL INTERESTS
Martial arts, skiing, politics, reading, writing.

GENERAL MODEL
FOR A COVER LETTER

Your mailing address
Date

Contact's name
Contact's title
Company
Company's mailing address

Dear Mr./Ms. _____:

Immediately explain why your background makes you the best candidate for the position that you are applying for. Describe what prompted you to write (want ad, article you read about the company, networking contact, etc.). Keep the first paragraph short and hard-hitting.

Detail what you could contribute to this company. Show how your qualifications will benefit this firm. Describe your interest in the corporation. Subtly emphasizing your knowledge about this firm and your familiarity with the industry will set you apart from other candidates. Remember to keep this letter short; few recruiters will read a cover letter longer than half a page.

If possible, your closing paragraph should request specific action on the part of the reader. Include your phone number and the hours when you can be reached. Mention that if you do not hear from the reader by a specific date, you will follow up with a phone call. Lastly, thank the reader for their time, consideration, etc.

Sincerely,

(signature)

Your full name (typed)

Enclosure (use this if there are other materials, such as your resume, that are included in the same envelope)

SAMPLE COVER LETTER

16 Charles Street
Marlborough CT 06447
March 16, 1999

Ms. Lia Marcusson
Assistant Principal
Jonathon Daniels Elementary School
43 Mayflower Drive
Keene NH 03431

Dear Ms. Marcusson:

Janet Newell recently informed me of a possible opening for a third grade teacher at Jonathon Daniels Elementary School. With my experience instructing third-graders, both in schools and in summer programs, I feel I would be an ideal candidate for the position. Please accept this letter and the enclosed resume as my application.

Jonathon Daniels' educational philosophy that every child can learn and succeed interests me, since it mirrors my own. My current position at Elmer T. Thienes Elementary has reinforced this philosophy, heightening my awareness of the different styles and paces of learning and increasing my sensitivity toward special needs children. Furthermore, as a direct result of my student teaching experience at Wheelock Elementary School, I am comfortable, confident, and knowledgeable working with third-graders.

I look forward to discussing the position and my qualifications for it in more detail. I can be reached at 203/555-9641 evenings or 203/555-0248 weekdays. If I do not hear from you before Tuesday of next week, I will call to see if we can schedule a time to meet. Thank you for your time and consideration.

Sincerely,

Paul K. Norton

Paul K. Norton

Enclosure

GENERAL MODEL FOR A
FOLLOW-UP LETTER

Your mailing address
Date

Contact's name
Contact's title
Company
Company's mailing address

Dear Mr./Ms._____:

Remind the interviewer of the reason (i.e., a specific opening, an informational interview, etc.) you were interviewed, as well as the date. Thank him/her for the interview, and try to personalize your thanks by mentioning some specific aspect of the interview.

Confirm your interest in the organization (and in the opening, if you were interviewing for a particular position). Use specifics to re-emphasize that you have researched the firm in detail and have considered how you would fit into the company and the position. This is a good time to say anything you wish you had said in the initial meeting. Be sure to keep this letter brief; a half-page is plenty.

If appropriate, close with a suggestion for further action, such as a desire to have an additional interview, if possible. Mention your phone number and the hours that you can be reached. Alternatively, you may prefer to mention that you will follow up with a phone call in several days. Once again, thank the person for meeting with you, and state that you would be happy to provide any additional information about your qualifications.

Sincerely,

(signature)

Your full name (typed)

CD-ROM JOB SEARCH

Jobseekers who are looking for any edge they can find may want to check out the following selected CD-ROM products. Since most of these databases cost upwards of $500, and are designed for use by other businesses or libraries, don't expect to find these at your local software store. Of course, not all libraries will have all of these resources. Depending on how technologically advanced your library is, you may find only one or two of these electronic databases. Call your library to find out what electronic resources it has available. Many of these databases can also be found in the offices of career counselors or outplacement specialists, and are used as part of your service.

ADAMS JOBBANK FASTRESUME SUITE
260 Center Street
Holbrook MA 02343
800/872-5627
The CD-ROM version of the best-selling *JobBank* series contains 22,000 detailed profiles of companies in all industries, 1,800 executive search firms, and 1,100 employment agencies. For most companies, you will find the name, address, company description, and key contact name. The database also lists common professional positions and information on benefits for most companies. You can search the database by company name, state, industry, and job title. Calling itself a "total job search package," the CD-ROM also creates personalized resumes and cover letters and offers advice on job interviews, including over 100 sample interview questions and answers. *Adams JobBank FastResume Suite* CD-ROM is for Windows®98, Windows®95, and Windows®3.1.

AMERICAN BIG BUSINESS DIRECTORY
5711 South 86th Circle
P.O. Box 27347
Omaha NE 68127
800/555-5211
Provides profiles of 160,000 privately and publicly held companies employing over 100 people. The CD-ROM contains company descriptions which include company type, industry, products, and sales information. Also included are contact names for each company, with a total of over 340,000. You can search the database by industry, SIC code, sales volume, employee size, or zip code.

AMERICAN MANUFACTURER'S DIRECTORY
5711 South 86th Circle
P.O. Box 27347
Omaha NE 68127
800/555-5211
Made by the same company that created *American Big Business Directory*, *American Manufacturer's Directory* lists over 531,000 manufacturing

companies of all sizes and industries. The directory contains product and sales information, company size, and a key contact name for each company. The user can search by region, SIC code, sales volume, employee size, or zip code.

BUSINESS U.S.A.
5711 South 86th Circle
P.O. Box 27347
Omaha NE 68127
800/555-5211
Also from the makers of *American Big Business Directory* and *American Manufacturer's Directory*, this CD-ROM contains information on 10 million U.S. companies. The profiles provide contact information, industry type, number of employees, and sales volume. Each listing also indicates whether the company is public or private, as well as providing information about the company's products. There are a number of different search methods available, including key words, SIC code, geographic location, and number of employees.

CAREER SEARCH - INTEGRATED RESOURCE SYSTEM
21 Highland Circle
Needham MA 02194-3075
617/449-0312
Career Search is a database which contains listings for over 490,000 privately and publicly held companies. It has contact information, including names of human resources professionals or other executives, for companies of virtually all sizes, types, and industries. The database can be searched by industry, company size, or region. This product is updated monthly.

COMPANIES INTERNATIONAL
835 Penobscot Building
645 Griswald Street
Detroit MI 48226
800/877-GALE
Produced by Gale Research Inc., this CD-ROM is compiled from *Ward's Business Directory* and the *World's Business Directory*, and contains information on more than 300,000 companies worldwide. You can find industry information, contact names, and number of employees. Also included is information on the company's products and revenues. The database can be searched by industry, company products, or geographic location.

CORPTECH DIRECTORY
12 Alfred Street, Suite 200
Woburn MA 01801-1915
800/333-8036
The *CorpTech Directory* on CD-ROM contains detailed descriptions of over 45,000 technology companies. It also lists the names and titles of nearly 155,000 executives -- CEOs, sales managers, R&D managers, and human resource professionals. World Wide Web and e-mail addresses are also available. In

addition to contact information, you can find detailed information about each company's products or services and annual revenues. The *CorpTech Directory* also lists both the number of current employees, and the number of employees one year ago. Some companies also list the number of employees they project having in one year. You can search the database by type of company, geographic location, or sales revenue. This product is updated quarterly.

DISCOVERING CAREERS & JOBS
835 Penobscot Building
645 Griswald Street
Detroit MI 48226
800/877-GALE
Provides overviews on 1,200 careers, 1,000 articles from trade publications, and contact information for professional associations. This CD-ROM also contains self-assessment tests, college profiles, and financial aid data.

DISCOVERING CAREERS & JOBS PLUS
835 Penobscot Building
645 Griswald Street
Detroit MI 48226
800/877-GALE
This CD-ROM gives users contact information on more than 45,000 companies, with 15,000 in-depth profiles and 1,000 company history essays. In addition, the product also provides profiles and application procedures for all major two- and four-year U.S. colleges and universities.

DUN & BRADSTREET MILLION DOLLAR DISC PLUS
3 Sylvan Way
Parsippany NJ 07054
800/526-0651
This CD-ROM provides information on over 400,000 companies in virtually every industry. About 90 percent of the companies listed are privately held, and all have at least $3 million in annual sales or at least 50 employees. Each company's listing includes the number of employees, sales volume, name of the parent company, and corporate headquarters or branch locations. The *Million Dollar Disc Plus* also provides the names and titles of top executives, as well as biographical information on those executives, including education and career background. Searches can be done by location, industry, SIC code, executive names, or key words in the executive biographies. This directory is updated quarterly.

ENCYCLOPEDIA OF ASSOCIATIONS:
NATIONAL ORGANIZATIONS OF THE U.S.
835 Penobscot Building
645 Griswald Street
Detroit MI 48226
800/877-GALE

Contains descriptions and contact information for nearly 23,000 national organizations. You can search by association name, geographic location, and key words. This CD-ROM is available in both single- and multi-user formats.

GALE BUSINESS RESOURCES CD-ROM
835 Penobscot Building
645 Griswald Street
Detroit MI 48226
800/877-GALE
This two CD-ROM set contains detailed profiles on certain industries and covers the major companies in each industry, with statistics on over 200,000 businesses nationwide. You can search by company name, industry type, products, and more. This product is available in both single- and multi-user formats.

HARRIS INFOSOURCE NATIONAL
2057 East Aurora Road
Twinsburg OH 44087
800/888-5900
This directory of manufacturers profiles thousands of companies. Although the majority of the companies listed are located in the United States, there are also listings for some Canadian businesses. The listings include the number of employees, plant size, and sales revenue, as well as the names and titles of top executives. This CD-ROM is updated annually and can be purchased in smaller regional or state editions.

MOODY'S COMPANY DATA
99 Church Street
New York NY 10007
800/342-5647
Moody's Company Data is a CD-ROM which has detailed listings for over 10,000 publicly traded companies. In addition to information such as industry, company address, and phone and fax numbers, each listing includes the names and titles of its top officers, including the CEO, president, and vice president; company size; number of shareholders; corporate history; subsidiaries; and financial statements. Users can conduct searches by region, SIC codes, industry, or earnings. This CD-ROM is updated monthly.

STANDARD & POOR'S REGISTER
65 Broadway
8th Floor
New York NY 10004
800/221-5277
The CD-ROM version of this three-volume desk reference provides the same information as its printed companion. The database lists over 55,000 companies, including more than 12,000 public companies. In addition to contact information, which includes the names and titles of over 500,000 executives, you can find out about each company's primary and secondary sources of

business, annual revenues, number of employees, parent company, and subsidiaries. When available, the *Standard & Poor's Register* also lists the names of banks, accounting firms, and law firms used by each company. Also, the directory provides biographies of more than 70,000 top executives, which include information such as directorships held and schools attended. There are 55 different search modes available on the database. You can search geographically, by zip code, industry, SIC code, or stock symbol. You can also limit your search to only private or only public companies. This directory is updated quarterly.

ACCOUNTING AND MANAGEMENT CONSULTING

 *Accounting and management consulting firms are facing more competitive pressures than ever, coupled with declining profits. Competition is forcing accounting firms to redesign the services they offer, cut costs significantly, and upgrade their recruiting efforts to attract more highly-skilled accountants. Fortunately, innovations in tax software and other technologies have made accounting practices more efficient, though resulting in fewer overall opportunities. The U.S. Department of Labor expects the number of opportunities in this industry to increase 10 to 20 percent by 2006, most notably in the areas of management consulting and other advisory positions.*

The nation's largest and most dominant accounting firms are focusing more on management consulting. As a result, revenues in the consulting arena have grown significantly. The split of Arthur Andersen into a separate division, Andersen Consulting, reflects a trend that will continue to transform the larger accounting firms and push some business customers toward smaller divisions or private firms.

The largest firms are continuing to create partnerships worldwide, and some of the smaller firms are following suit. In July 1998, Price Waterhouse and Coopers & Lybrand merged to form PricewaterhouseCoopers, a global professional services firm. The majority of the mid-sized accounting firms, however, concentrate on maintaining strong regional client relationships. According to Inc. magazine, while some accounting firms will be forced out of business due to competition, many have responded by specializing in a particular area.

ARTHUR ANDERSEN LLP
45 South Seventh Street, Minneapolis MN 55402-1607. 612/332-1111. **Contact:** Human Resources. **Description:** A global provider of professional services. Business is conducted through two business units: Arthur Andersen for audit, tax, and other consulting services; and Andersen Consulting for systems integration, change management services, and advanced systems. The company operates in 74 countries with 358 member offices. **Number of employees worldwide:** 72,000.

EMA SERVICES, INC.
1970 Oakcrest Avenue, St. Paul MN 55113. 651/639-5600. **Toll-free phone:** 800/800-2110. **Fax:** 651/639-5635. **Contact:** Human Resources. **E-mail address:** hrinfo@ema-inc.com. **World Wide Web address:** http://www.ema-inc.com. **Description:** A specialized consulting firm that works with utilities and selected manufacturers to help clients develop and implement operational strategies for improving work practices, addressing organizational development, and leveraging technology. Services focus on helping clients improve productivity and long-term performance in competitive business environments. Founded in 1975. **NOTE:** The company offers entry-level positions. **Company slogan:** Linking people and technology for business results. **Common positions include:** Computer Programmer; Consultant; Database Manager; Design Engineer; Draftsperson; Electrical/Electronics Engineer; Industrial Engineer; Management Analyst/ Consultant; Manufacturing Engineer; Mechanical Engineer; MIS Specialist; Project Manager; Systems Analyst. **Educational backgrounds include:** Business Administration; Communications; Computer Science; Engineering; Software Development; Software Tech. Support. **Benefits:** 401(k); Dental Insurance; Disability Coverage; Flexible Schedule; Life Insurance; Medical Insurance; Profit Sharing; Telecommuting; Tuition Assistance. **Office hours:** Monday - Friday, 8:00 a.m. - 5:00 p.m. **Corporate headquarters location:** This Location. **Other U.S. locations:** Phoenix AZ; Tucson AZ; Los Angeles CA; Sacramento CA; San Francisco CA; Orlando FL;

Boston MA; Philadelphia PA. **International locations:** Canada. **Listed on:** Privately held. **CEO:** Alan Manning. **Facilities Manager:** Peggy McCarthy. **Annual sales/revenues:** $21 - $50 million. **Number of employees at this location:** 80. **Number of employees nationwide:** 180. **Number of employees worldwide:** 185.

ERNST & YOUNG
1400 Pillsbury Center, 200 South Sixth Street, Minneapolis MN 55402. 612/343-1000. **Contact:** Recruiter. **World Wide Web address:** http://www.ey.com. **Description:** A certified public accounting firm that also provides its clients with management consulting services. Ernst & Young operates more than 300 offices in 70 countries worldwide. The consulting staff is comprised of more than 1,000 consultants and support staff worldwide, involved in such fields as data processing, financial modeling, financial feasibility studies, production planning and inventory management, management sciences, health care planning, human resources, and cost accounting and budgeting systems. The company provides services to numerous industries, including health care, finance, insurance, manufacturing, retail, government, utilities, and transportation. **Number of employees at this location:** 8,500. **Number of employees nationwide:** 16,000.

GRANT THORNTON
500 Pillsbury Center North, 200 South Sixth Street, Minneapolis MN 55402. 612/332-0001. **Contact:** Roger Richters, Personnel Director. **World Wide Web address:** http://www.gt.com. **Description:** An international, certified public accounting organization offering a comprehensive scope of consulting and accounting services as well as strategic and tactical planning assistance to a diverse clientele. **Other U.S. locations:** Nationwide.

THE HAY GROUP
121 South Eighth Street, Suite 1350, Minneapolis MN 55402. 612/339-0555. **Contact:** Human Resources. **World Wide Web address:** http://www.haygroup.com. **Description:** An international human resources and management consulting firm that provides services ranging from total compensation planning to strategic management, business culture, employee surveys, and outplacement. **NOTE:** All hiring is conducted through the Chicago office. Jobseekers should address resumes to Rod Fralick, Resource Operations Manager, The Hay Group, 205 North Michigan Avenue, Suite 4000, Chicago IL 60601. **Common positions include:** Management Analyst/Consultant. **Benefits:** Dental Insurance; Disability Coverage; Life Insurance; Medical Insurance; Pension Plan; Tuition Assistance. **Corporate headquarters location:** Philadelphia PA. **Other U.S. locations:** Nationwide. **Operations at this facility include:** Field Office.

HEWITT ASSOCIATES
45 South Seventh Street, Suite 2100, Minneapolis MN 55402. 612/339-7501. **Contact:** Jane Kelley, Personnel. **World Wide Web address:** http://www.hewitt.com. **Description:** Hewitt Associates is an international firm of consultants and actuaries specializing in the design, financing, communication, and administration of employee benefit and compensation programs. **Corporate headquarters location:** Lincolnshire IL.

KPMG PEAT MARWICK LLP
90 South Seventh Street, 4200 Norwest Center, Minneapolis MN 55402. 612/305-5000. **Contact:** Nancy Joanis, Recruiting Coordinator. **World Wide Web address:** http://www.kpmg.com. **Description:** KPMG Peat Marwick LLP delivers a wide range of value-added assurance, tax, and consulting services, and is the U.S. member firm of KPMG International, the worldwide professional services firm. **NOTE:** For immediate consideration, jobseekers need to mail, fax, or e-mail a resume to the following location: KPMG Human Resources Service Center, P.O. Box 560787, Dallas TX 75356-0787. 888/ONE-KPMG. Fax: 214/200-7710. Please specify Department #NETCCY in all correspondence. **Common positions include:** Accountant/Auditor; Management Analyst/Consultant; Tax Specialist. **Educational backgrounds include:** Accounting; Finance; Health Care; Tax. **Benefits:** 401(k); Dental Insurance; Disability Coverage; Life Insurance; Medical Insurance; Pension Plan; Tuition Assistance. **Special programs:** Internships. **Corporate headquarters location:** Montvale NJ. **Parent company:** KPMG International has more than 85,000 employees worldwide, including 6,500 partners and 60,000 professional staff members, serving clients in 844 cities in 155 countries. **Operations at this facility include:** Service.

McGLADREY & PULLEN
801 Nicollet Avenue, Suite 1300, Minneapolis MN 55402. 612/332-4300. **Contact:** Kathy Pedersen, Human Resources Director. **World Wide Web address:** http://www.mcgladrey.com. **Description:** Provides accounting and auditing services, business planning, taxation, and consulting services. **Corporate headquarters location:** Davenport IA. **Other U.S. locations:** Nationwide.

McGLADREY & PULLEN
227 West First Street, Suite 700, Duluth MN 55802-1913. 218/727-5025. **Fax:** 218/727-1438. **Contact:** Karen S. Andresen, Recruiter. **World Wide Web address:** http://www.mcgladrey.com. **Description:** Provides accounting and auditing services, business planning, taxation, and consulting services. **Common positions include:** Accountant/Auditor; Bank Officer/Manager; Branch Manager; Chemist; Civil Engineer; Clerical Supervisor; Computer Programmer; Credit Manager; Customer Service Representative; Financial Analyst; General Manager; Health Services Manager; Hotel Manager; Human Resources Specialist; Management Analyst/Consultant; Manufacturer's/Wholesaler's Sales Rep.; MIS Specialist; Operations/Production Manager; Paralegal; Property and Real Estate Manager; Purchasing Agent/Manager; Quality Control Supervisor; Systems Analyst; Telecommunications Manager; Typist/Word Processor. **Educational backgrounds include:** Accounting; Economics; Management/Planning; Personnel Relations. **Corporate headquarters location:** Davenport IA. **Other U.S. locations:** Nationwide.

PERSONNEL DECISIONS INTERNATIONAL (PDI)
900 Peavey Building, 730 Second Avenue South, Minneapolis MN 55402. 612/339-0927. **Fax:** 612/573-7800. **Contact:** Cathy Nelson, Human Resources Director. **Description:** A worldwide consulting firm of organizational psychologists and consultants who specialize in assessment-based development and who have created and implemented innovative programs, services, and products that are tailored to client needs. PDI's services and products cover the selection and promotion of employees at all levels, the development of managers and executives, the fostering of a positive group dynamic for the organization as a whole, and outplacement and career transition. **Corporate headquarters location:** This Location. **Other U.S. locations:** San Francisco CA; Denver CO; Washington DC; Atlanta GA; Chicago IL; Boston MA; Detroit MI; New York NY; Dallas TX; Houston TX.

PRICEWATERHOUSECOOPERS
650 Third Avenue South, Suite 1300, Minneapolis MN 55402. 612/370-9300. **Fax:** 612/373-7163. **Contact:** Anne M. Johnson, Recruiting Manager. **World Wide Web address:** http://www.pwcglobal.com. **Description:** One of the largest certified public accounting firms in the world. PricewaterhouseCoopers is the result of the July 1998 merger between Price Waterhouse and Coopers & Lybrand. **Special programs:** Internships. **Corporate headquarters location:** New York NY. **Other U.S. locations:** Nationwide. **Number of employees at this location:** 450.

SCHECHTER DOKKEN KANTER
100 Washington Avenue South, Suite 1600, Minneapolis MN 55401. 612/332-5500. **Contact:** Joanne Scherber, Human Resources. **Description:** A regional accounting and management consulting firm performing audits, accounting, tax, employee benefits plan consulting, litigation support, and management consulting services. **Common positions include:** Accountant/Auditor. **Educational backgrounds include:** Accounting; Business Administration. **Benefits:** Disability Coverage; Medical Insurance; Profit Sharing; Savings Plan. **Corporate headquarters location:** This Location. **Operations at this facility include:** Service. **Number of employees at this location:** 50.

TOWERS PERRIN
8300 Norman Center Drive, Suite 600, Minneapolis MN 55437. 612/897-3300. **Contact:** Kathy Halverson, Office Administrator. **World Wide Web address:** http://www.towers.com. **Description:** A management consulting firm. **Corporate headquarters location:** New York NY. **Other U.S. locations:** Washington DC; Atlanta GA; Chicago IL; Boston MA; Charlotte NC; Philadelphia PA; Pittsburgh PA.

Note: Because addresses and telephone numbers of smaller companies can change rapidly, we recommend you call each company to verify the information below before inquiring about job opportunities. Mass mailings are not recommended.

Additional small employers:

ACCOUNTING, AUDITING, AND BOOKKEEPING SERVICES

Boulay Heutmaker Zibell
5151 Edina Industrial Blvd, Minneapolis MN 55439-3013. 612/893-9320.

Deloitte & Touche
400 1st Ave NE, Minneapolis MN 55413-2208. 612/397-4000.

Larson Allen Weishair
220 S 6th St, Ste 1000, Minneapolis MN 55402-4500. 612/376-4500.

Lurie Besikof Lapidus & Co.
2501 Wayzata Blvd, Minneapolis MN 55405-2139. 612/377-4404.

McGladrey & Pullen LLP
3600 W 80th St, Ste 500, Bloomington MN 55431-4510. 612/835-9930.

Olsen Thielen & Co. Ltd.
223 Little Canada Road E, St. Paul MN 55117-1367. 651/483-4521.

Olsen Thielen & Co. Ltd.
6640 Shady Oak Rd, Ste 250, Eden Prairie MN 55344-7709. 612/941-9242.

BUSINESS CONSULTING SERVICES

BI Performance Services
PO Box 1610, Minneapolis MN 55440-1610. 612/835-4800.

BI Performance Services
479 Meeker Ave E, Eden Valley MN 55329-1629. 320/453-2600.

Brady & Company Inc.
2001 Killebrew Dr, Ste 311, Minneapolis MN 55425-1886. 612/851-9922.

Johnson Enterprises
PO Box 979, Brainerd MN 56401-0979. 218/829-4781.

MHC Consulting LLC
820 Promontory Pl, St. Paul MN 55123-2297. 651/228-3890.

NQI
340 Pierce Ave, Mankato MN 56003-2249. 507/387-7237.

Preferred One Management
200 S 6th St, Ste 300, Minneapolis MN 55402-1428. 612/623-8282.

Tena Companies Inc.
251 Lafayette Rd S, St. Paul MN 55107. 651/293-1234.

Watson Wyatt Worldwide
8400 Normandale Lake Blvd, Minneapolis MN 55437-1085. 612/921-8700.

For more information on career opportunities in accounting and management consulting:

<u>Associations</u>

AMERICAN ACCOUNTING ASSOCIATION
5717 Bessie Drive, Sarasota FL 34233. 941/921-7747. World Wide Web address: http://www.aaa-edu.org. American Accounting Association is an academically-oriented accounting association that offers two quarterly journals, a semi-annual journal, a newsletter, as well as a wide variety of continuing education programs.

AMERICAN INSTITUTE OF CERTIFIED PUBLIC ACCOUNTANTS
1211 Avenue of the Americas, New York NY 10036. 212/596-6200. World Wide Web address: http://www. aicpa.org. American Institute of Certified Public Accountants is a national professional organization for all CPAs. AICPA offers a comprehensive career package to students.

AMERICAN MANAGEMENT ASSOCIATION
1601 Broadway, New York NY 10019. 212/586-8100. World Wide Web address: http://www.amanet.org. American Management Association provides a variety of publications, training videos, and courses, as well as an Information Resource Center, which provides management information, and a library service.

ASSOCIATION OF GOVERNMENT ACCOUNTANTS
2208 Mount Vernon Avenue, Alexandria VA 22301. 703/684-6931. World Wide Web address: http://www. rutgers.edu/accounting/raw/aga. Association of Government Accountants serves financial management professionals and offers continuing education workshops.

ASSOCIATION OF MANAGEMENT CONSULTING FIRMS
521 Fifth Avenue, 35th Floor, New York NY 10175. 212/697-9693. World Wide Web address: http://www. amcf.org.

THE INSTITUTE OF INTERNAL AUDITORS
249 Maitland Avenue, Altamonte Springs FL 32701. 407/830-7600. World Wide Web address: http://www. theiia.org. The Institute of Internal Auditors publishes magazines and newsletters. Provides information on current issues, a network of more than 50,000 members in 100 countries, and professional development and research services. Also offers continuing education seminars.

INSTITUTE OF MANAGEMENT ACCOUNTANTS
10 Paragon Drive, Montvale NJ 07645. 201/573-9000. World Wide Web address: http://www.imanet.org. Offers a Certified Management Accountant Program, periodicals, seminars, educational programs, a research program, a financial management network, and networking services. The association has about 80,000 members and 300 local chapters.

INSTITUTE OF MANAGEMENT CONSULTANTS
521 Fifth Avenue, 35th Floor, New York NY 10175. 212/697-8262. World Wide Web address: http://www. imc.org. Offers certification programs, professional development, and a directory of members.

NATIONAL ASSOCIATION OF TAX PRACTITIONERS
720 Association Drive, Appleton WI 54914-1483. 414/749-1040. World Wide Web address: http://www. natptax.com. Offers seminars, research, newsletters, preparer worksheets, state chapters, insurance, and other tax-related services.

NATIONAL SOCIETY OF ACCOUNTANTS
1010 North Fairfax Street, Alexandria VA 22314. 703/549-6400. World Wide Web address: http://www. nsacct.org. Offers professional development services, government representation, a variety of publications, practice aids, low-cost group insurance, annual seminars, and updates for members on new tax laws.

<u>Magazines</u>

CPA JOURNAL
The New York State Society, 530 Fifth Avenue, 5th Floor, New York NY 10036. 212/719-8300. Monthly.

CPA LETTER
American Institute of Certified Public Accountants, 1211 Avenue of the Americas, New York NY 10036. 212/596-6200. World Wide Web address: http://www. aicpa.org/pubs/cpaltr.

THE FINANCE AND ACCOUNTING JOBS REPORT
Career Advancement Publications, Jamestown NY. World Wide Web address: http://www.jobreports.net. This publication is dedicated to finance and accounting professionals who are looking for a job. Each issue includes several hundred job openings in the United States and abroad. This report also offers

subscribers networking opportunities through its contact and referral program.

JOURNAL OF ACCOUNTANCY
American Institute of Certified Public Accountants, 1211 Avenue of the Americas, New York NY 10036. 212/596-6200.

<u>Online Services</u>

ACCOUNTANTS FORUM
Go: Aicpa. A CompuServe forum sponsored by the American Institute of Certified Public Accountants.

FINANCIAL/ACCOUNTING/INSURANCE JOBS PAGE
http://www.nationjob.com/financial. This Website provides a list of financial, accounting, and insurance job openings.

JOBS IN ACCOUNTING
http://www.cob.ohio-state.edu/dept/fin/jobs/account. htm#Link7. Provides information on the accounting profession, including salaries, trends, and resources.

MANAGEMENT CONSULTING JOBS ONLINE
http://www.cob.ohio-state.edu/~opler/cons. Provides information and resources for jobseekers looking to work in the field of management consulting.

ADVERTISING, MARKETING, AND PUBLIC RELATIONS

Professionals in advertising, marketing, and public relations face an industry that is constantly changing and extremely competitive due to the high salaries it commands. Growth is forecast for all areas of advertising, and the public relations sector is projected to be one of the fastest-growing through 2006.

Advertising executives are reporting that certain trends are dictating the industry's direction. Perhaps the most prominent are a renewed emphasis on corporate branding and the strategy of advertising products to individual consumers rather than larger groups or corporations.

Internet advertising is the fastest-growing area of the industry. Jobseekers with new media and interactive marketing skills will have an advantage over the competition. Companies are investing in "pop-up ads" that are linked to Websites related to the types of products and services they offer. This allows Internet advertisers to target specific audiences. New companies, such as AdKnowledge and Personify, contract with Internet advertisers to monitor the success of specific ads, detailing who bought products or services, how much they bought, and the overall profit from the sale. Online advertisers are also using well known search engines as springboards to their sites, but at great expense. It costs millions of dollars for companies to have their logos displayed on these high-traffic areas of the Web.

Direct mail is another advertising sector which has seen a great deal of recent success. The growth in this sector is fueled by newer, more precise data-collection databases, and the volume of "junk mail" is expected to triple in the next decade.

ADVO SYSTEM INC.
4216 Park Glen Road, St. Louis Park MN 55416. 612/929-1441. **Contact:** Human Resources. **World Wide Web address:** http://www.advo.com. **Description:** A direct mail company. Advo distributes Mailbox Values advertising coupon booklets and missing children alert cards through the mail.

BOZELL KAMSTRA
100 North Sixth Street, Suite 800-A, Minneapolis MN 55403. 612/371-7500. **Contact:** President. **World Wide Web address:** http://www.bozell.com. **Description:** An advertising agency.

CAMPBELL-MITHUN-ESTY, INC.
222 South Ninth Street, Minneapolis MN 55402. 612/347-1000. **Contact:** Robert Seper, Human Resources Director. **Description:** An advertising agency.

CARLSON COMPANIES, INC.
CARLSON MARKETING GROUP
P.O. Box 59159, Minneapolis MN 55459-8246. 612/540-5000. **Contact:** Vern Lovstad, Human Resources. **World Wide Web address:** http://www.carlson.com. **Description:** A highly diversified corporation doing business through a variety of subsidiaries. Business areas include hotels, restaurant operations, and retail and wholesale travel. Carlson Marketing Group (also at this location) provides a variety of marketing services for sporting events and airlines; incentive programs for employees of other companies; and strategic consulting to help client companies create customer/brand loyalty. **Corporate headquarters location:** This Location. **Number of employees nationwide:** 50,000.

CARMICHAEL-LYNCH ADVERTISING
800 Hennepin Avenue, Minneapolis MN 55403. 612/334-6000. **Fax:** 612/334-6171. **Contact:** Christina Schulte, Director of Human Resources. **Description:** A full-service advertising agency. Carmichael-Lynch Advertising offers a variety of services including direct marketing, public relations, new media design, and market research. Founded in 1962. **NOTE:** This company offers entry-level positions. **Common positions include:** Account Manager; Account Representative; Accountant/Auditor; Administrative Assistant; Art Director; Graphic Designer; Market Research Analyst; Production Manager; Public Relations Specialist; Secretary. **Educational backgrounds include:** Accounting; Advertising; Art/Design; Communications; Journalism; Marketing; Public Relations. **Benefits:** 401(k); Dental Insurance; Disability Coverage; Employee Discounts; Flexible Dependent Care; Life Insurance; Medical Insurance; Pension Plan; Profit Sharing; Savings Plan; Tuition Assistance. **Special programs:** Internships; Training. **Corporate headquarters location:** This Location. **Operations at this facility include:** Administration; Divisional Headquarters; Regional Headquarters; Research and Development; Service. **Listed on:** Privately held. **Annual sales/revenues:** More than $100 million. **Number of employees at this location:** 200.

COLLE & McVOY ADVERTISING AGENCY, INC.
8500 Normandale Lake Boulevard, Suite 2400, Bloomington MN 55437. 612/897-7500. **Contact:** Bob Hettlinger, Human Resources Director. **World Wide Web address:** http://www.collemcvoy. com. **Description:** An advertising agency.

THE DUFFY DESIGN GROUP
901 Marquette Avenue South, Suite 3000, Minneapolis MN 55402. 612/321-2333. **Contact:** Joe Duffy, President. **World Wide Web address:** http://www.duffy.com. **Description:** An advertising agency.

FABER SHERVEY ADVERTISING
160 West 79th Street, Minneapolis MN 55420. 612/881-5111. **Contact:** Paul Shervey, President. **Description:** An advertising firm that specializes in print advertising for agricultural and industrial clients. **Common positions include:** Art Director; Copywriter; Services Sales Representative; Technical Writer/Editor. **Educational backgrounds include:** Art/Design; Communications; Marketing. **Benefits:** Medical Insurance; Pension Plan; Profit Sharing. **Corporate headquarters location:** This Location. **Operations at this facility include:** Sales; Service.

FALLON McELLIGOTT
901 Marquette Avenue, Suite 3200, Minneapolis MN 55402. 612/321-2345. **Contact:** Human Resources Department. **World Wide Web address:** http://www.fallon.com. **Description:** An advertising firm.

FUNARI ADVERTISING
3948 West 50th Street, Suite 210, Edina MN 55424. 612/944-5050. **Contact:** Personnel. **Description:** An advertising firm.

HMS
204 North First Street, Minneapolis MN 55401. 612/332-4565. **Contact:** Tim Pearson, Executive Vice President. **Description:** An advertising agency focusing on corporate advertising. **Common positions include:** Account Representative; Art Director; Buyer; Copywriter; Media Specialist; Planner. **Educational backgrounds include:** Art/Design; Business Administration; Liberal Arts; Marketing. **Benefits:** 401(k); Dental Insurance; Disability Coverage; Life Insurance; Medical Insurance; Profit Sharing; Tuition Assistance. **Special programs:** Internships. **Corporate headquarters location:** This Location. **Number of employees at this location:** 45.

MARTIN WILLIAMS ADVERTISING INC.
60 South Sixth Street, Suite 2800, Minneapolis MN 55402. 612/340-0800. **Contact:** Tena Murphy, Director of Human Resources. **World Wide Web address:** http://www.martinwilliams.com. **Description:** An advertising agency. **Common positions include:** Marketing Specialist. **Educational backgrounds include:** Communications; Marketing. **Benefits:** Daycare Assistance; Dental Insurance; Disability Coverage; Life Insurance; Medical Insurance; Profit Sharing; Tuition Assistance. **Special programs:** Internships. **Corporate headquarters location:** This Location. **Operations at this facility include:** Regional Headquarters.

PEDERSON, HERZOG, AND NEE INC.
219 Logan Parkway, Minneapolis MN 55432. 612/333-1234. **Contact:** Creative Director. **Description:** An advertising agency.

RADA RECRUITMENT COMMUNICATIONS
7808 Creekridge Circle, Suite 300, Bloomington MN 55439. 612/941-3199. **Fax:** 612/941-6911. **Contact:** Marianne Kulka, Vice President. **Description:** Rada Recruitment Communications is a national recruitment advertising agency. **Common positions include:** Customer Service Representative; Sales Executive. **Benefits:** Dental Insurance; Life Insurance; Medical Insurance; Profit Sharing; Tuition Assistance. **Corporate headquarters location:** Chicago IL. **Parent company:** Grey Advertising (New York NY) has expertise in marketing, consultation, direct response, research, product publicity, public relations, sales promotion, and cooperative advertising. **Operations at this facility include:** Sales; Service.

RISDALL LINNIHAN ADVERTISING
2475 15th Street NW, New Brighton MN 55112. 651/631-1098. **Contact:** John Risdall, Chairman. **World Wide Web address:** http://www.rla.net. **Description:** Risdall Linnihan Advertising is an advertising firm specializing in environmental, high-tech, industrial, and business-to-business advertising.

SAXTON-FERRIS
11900 Wayzata Boulevard, Suite 114, Minnetonka MN 55305. 612/544-9300. **Contact:** June Ferris, General Manager. **World Wide Web address:** http://www.saxton-ferris.com. **Description:** Saxton-Ferris is a national Yellow Pages advertising agency. **Common positions include:** Advertising Clerk. **Corporate headquarters location:** This Location. **Parent company:** Ferris Marketing, Inc. **Operations at this facility include:** Service. **Number of employees at this location:** 15.

TMP WORLDWIDE
7825 Washington Avenue South, Suite 800, Minneapolis MN 55439. 612/903-4600. **Contact:** Carrie Young, Agency Manager. **World Wide Web address:** http://www.tmpw.com. **Description:** TMP Worldwide is a Yellow Pages advertising agency. **Other U.S. locations:** Chicago IL. **Operations at this facility include:** Administration; Regional Headquarters; Research and Development; Service.

TRADEMARK COMMUNICATIONS, INC.
14500 Martin Drive, Suite 1000, Eden Prairie MN 55344-2015. 612/934-5555. **Contact:** Manager. **Description:** An advertising agency.

W.B.K. MARKETING AND DESIGN
10 South Fifth Street, Suite 950, Minneapolis MN 55402. 612/341-2500. **Contact:** Personnel. **World Wide Web address:** http://www.wbk.com. **Description:** A direct response advertising agency.

Note: Because addresses and telephone numbers of smaller companies can change rapidly, we recommend you call each company to verify the information below before inquiring about job opportunities. Mass mailings are not recommended.

Additional small employers:

DIRECT MAIL ADVERTISING SERVICES

Arrowhead Promotional Fulfillment Inc.
PO Box 808, Grand Rapids MN 55744-0808. 218/327-1165.

Electrolink
277 12th Avenue North, Minneapolis MN 55401-1026. 612/341-2633.

Fulfillment Systems Inc. (FSI)
PO Box 636, Monticello MN 55362-0636. 612/295-3400.

Fulfillment Systems Inc. (FSI)
4001 Clearwater Road, St. Cloud MN 56301-9636. 320/255-0800.

SBI
7389 Bush Lake Road, Minneapolis MN 55439-2027. 612/844-0166.

United Mailing Inc.
PO Box 86, Little Falls MN 56345-0086. 320/632-2901.

MISC. ADVERTISING SERVICES

3M Promotional Marketing
PO Box 1997, North Mankato MN 56003. 507/625-4796.

John Ryan Company
3033 Excelsior Blvd, Minneapolis MN 55416-4688. 612/924-7700.

Rapp Collins Communications
901 Marquette Avenue,

Minneapolis MN 55402-3205. 612/373-3000.

PUBLIC RELATIONS SERVICES

Gage Marketing Group
10000 State Hwy 55, Plymouth MN 55441. 612/595-3800.

Gage Marketing Group
5130 Industrial Street, Maple Plain MN 55359-8001. 612/479-4100.

Shandwick
8400 Normadale Lake #500, Minneapolis MN 55437. 612/832-5000.

For more information on career opportunities in advertising, marketing, and public relations:

Associations

ADVERTISING RESEARCH FOUNDATION
641 Lexington Avenue, 11th Floor, New York NY 10022. 212/751-5656. Fax: 212/319-5265. E-mail address: email@arfsite.org. World Wide Web address: http://www.arfsite.org. A nonprofit organization comprised of advertising, marketing, and media research companies. For institutions only.

AMERICAN ASSOCIATION OF ADVERTISING AGENCIES
405 Lexington Avenue, 18th Floor, New York NY 10174. 212/682-2500. World Wide Web address: http://www.commercepark.com/aaaa. Offers educational and enrichment benefits such as publications, videos, and conferences.

AMERICAN MARKETING ASSOCIATION
250 South Wacker Drive, Suite 200, Chicago IL 60606. 312/648-0536. World Wide Web address: http://www.ama.org. An association with nearly 45,000 members worldwide. Offers a reference center, 25 annual conferences, and eight publications for marketing professionals and students.

INTERNATIONAL ADVERTISING ASSOCIATION
521 Fifth Avenue, Suite 1807, New York NY 10175. 212/557-1133. Fax: 212/983-0455. E-mail address: iaa@ibnet.com. World Wide Web address: http://www.iaaglobal.org. Over 3,600 members in 89 countries. Membership includes publications; professional development; congresses, symposia, and conferences; annual report and membership directory; and worldwide involvement with governments and other associations. Overall, the organization looks to promote free speech and the self-regulation of advertising.

MARKETING RESEARCH ASSOCIATION
1344 Silas Deane Highway, Suite 306, Rocky Hill CT 06067. 860/257-4008. World Wide Web address: http://www.mra-net.org. Publishes several magazines and newsletters.

PUBLIC RELATIONS SOCIETY OF AMERICA
33 Irving Place, New York NY 10003-2376. 212/995-2230. World Wide Web address: http://www.prsa.org. Publishes three magazines for public relations professionals.

Directories

AAAA ROSTER AND ORGANIZATION
American Association of Advertising Agencies, 405 Lexington Avenue, 18th Floor, New York NY 10147. 212/682-2500.

DIRECTORY OF MINORITY PUBLIC RELATIONS PROFESSIONALS
Public Relations Society of America, 33 Irving Place, New York NY 10003-2376. 212/995-2230.

O'DWYER'S DIRECTORY OF PUBLIC RELATIONS FIRMS
J. R. O'Dwyer Company, 271 Madison Avenue, Room 600, New York NY 10016. 212/679-2471.

PUBLIC RELATIONS CONSULTANTS DIRECTORY
American Business Directories, Division of American

Business Lists, 5711 South 86th Circle, Omaha NE 68137. 402/593-4500.

STANDARD DIRECTORY OF ADVERTISING AGENCIES
Reed Elsevier, 121 Chanlon Road, New Providence NJ 07974. Toll-free phone: 800/521-8110.

Magazines

ADVERTISING AGE
Crain Communications Inc., 220 East 42nd Street, New York NY 10017-5846. 212/210-0100. World Wide Web address: http://www.adage.com.

ADWEEK
BPI Communications, 1515 Broadway, 12th Floor, New York NY 10036-8986. 212/764-7300. World Wide Web address: http://www.adweek.com.

BUSINESS MARKETING
Crain Communications Inc.,. 220 East 42nd Street, New York NY 10017-5846. 212/210-0100. World Wide Web address: http://www.netb2b.com.

JOURNAL OF MARKETING
American Marketing Association, 250 South Wacker Drive, Suite 200, Chicago IL 60606. 312/648-0536.

THE MARKETING NEWS
American Marketing Association, 250 South Wacker Drive, Suite 200, Chicago IL 60606. 312/648-0536. A biweekly magazine offering new ideas and developments in marketing.

PR REPORTER
PR Publishing Company, P.O. Box 600, Exeter NH 03833. 603/778-0514. World Wide Web address: http://www.prpublishing.com.

PUBLIC RELATIONS NEWS
Phillips Business Information, Inc., 1201 Seven Locks Road, Suite 300, Potomac MD 20854. 301/424-3338. Fax: 301/309-3847. World Wide Web address: http://www.phillips.com.

Newsletters

PUBLIC RELATIONS CAREER OPPORTUNITIES
1575 I Street NW, Suite 1190, Washington DC 20005. 202/408-7900. Fax: 202/408-7907. Wide Web address: http://www.careeropps.com/prcareer1. Newsletter listing public relations, public affairs, special events, and investor positions nationwide compensating above $35,000 annually. Available on a subscription basis, published 24 times a year. Published on behalf of the Public Relations Society of America. Company also publishes other newsletters, including *CEO Job Opportunities Update* and *ASAE Career Opportunities* (for the American Society of Association Executives).

Online Services

ADVERTISING & MEDIA JOBS PAGE
http://www.nationjob.com/media. This Website offers advertising and media job openings that can be searched by a variety of criteria including location, type of position, and salary. This site also offers a service that will perform the search for you.

DIRECT MARKETING WORLD'S JOB CENTER
http://www.dmworld.com. Posts professional job openings for the direct marketing industry. This site also provides a career reference library, a list of direct marketing professionals, and a list of events within the industry.

MARKETING CLASSIFIEDS ON THE INTERNET
http://www.marketingjobs.com. Offers job listings by state, resume posting, discussions with other marketing professionals, links to other career sites, and company home pages.

Visit our exciting job and career site at http://www.careercity.com

AEROSPACE

 *Slow growth is predicted for the aerospace industry through 2006. Recent U.S. Defense Department spending cuts have increased competition for aerospace jobs, yet that is being offset by the high demand for commercial aircraft. According to* Standard & Poor, *aerospace industry profits for the first two quarters of 1998 were down 24 percent from profits for the same period of 1997. This is causing major companies, such as Boeing, to make significant changes. At the end of 1998, Boeing announced it would cut 48,000 jobs by 2001. The layoffs demonstrate the company's new focus on efficiency, increasing worker productivity, and ultimately profit margins. Boeing planned on building and selling 550 aircraft during 1998; however, the Asian economic crisis forced Boeing to find new buyers for some aircraft ordered by Asian companies.*

AERO SYSTEMS ENGINEERING
358 East Fillmore Avenue, St. Paul MN 55107. 651/227-7515. **Contact:** Tom Sletten, Human Resources Director. **Description:** An aerospace engineering firm serving both defense and commercial clients.

CIRRUS DESIGN
4515 Taylor Circle, Duluth MN 55811. 218/727-2737. **Contact:** Human Resources Department. **World Wide Web address:** http://www.cirrusdesign.com. **Description:** Cirrus Design manufactures aircraft.

R.M.S. COMPANY
8600 Evergreen Boulevard NW, Coon Rapids MN 55433. 612/786-1520. **Contact:** Human Resources. **Description:** Manufactures connectors for aircraft.

SIGNATURE FLIGHT SUPPORT
Hubert H. Humphrey Terminal, 7100 34th Avenue South, Minneapolis MN 55450. 612/726-5700. **Contact:** Laura Johnson, Human Resources. **Description:** A fixed-base aviation operator at the Minneapolis-St. Paul International Airport. Signature Flight Support provides fuel, hangar, avionics, maintenance, and parts services to the corporate aircraft market.

WATKINS AIRCRAFT SUPPORT PRODUCTS (WASP)
P.O. Box 100, Glenwood MN 56334. 320/634-5126. **Contact:** Human Resources. **Description:** Manufactures ground support equipment for airlines.

For more information on career opportunities in aerospace:

Associations

AHS INTERNATIONAL -- THE VERTICAL FLIGHT SOCIETY
217 North Washington Street, Alexandria VA 22314. 703/684-6777. Fax: 703/739-9279. E-mail address: ahs703@aol.com. World Wide Web address: http://www.vtol.org. Promotes the advancement of vertical flight technology.

AMERICAN ASTRONAUTICAL SOCIETY
6352 Rolling Mill Place, Suite 102, Springfield VA 22152-2354. 703/866-0020. Fax: 703/866-3526. E-mail address: info@astronautical.org. Offers conferences for members and scholarships for students.

AMERICAN INSTITUTE OF AERONAUTICS AND ASTRONAUTICS, INC.
1801 Alexander Bell Drive, Suite 500, Reston VA 20191-4344. 703/264-7500. Toll-free phone: 800/NEW-AIAA. Fax: 703/264-7551. World Wide Web address: http://www.aiaa.org. Membership required. Publishes six journals and books. The Website provides information on employment opportunities, resume services, aerospace news, career placement services, continuing education resources, and a mentor program.

NATIONAL AERONAUTIC ASSOCIATION
1815 North Fort Myer Drive, Suite 700, Arlington VA 22209. 703/527-0226. World Wide Web address: http://www.naa.ycg.org. Publishes a magazine. Membership required.

PROFESSIONAL AVIATION MAINTENANCE ASSOCIATION
636 Eye Street NW, Suite 300, Washington DC 20001-3736. 202/216-9220. World Wide Web address: http://www.pama.org. Conducts local and national seminars; publishes industry news journals; and addresses governmental issues. Members have access to the Worldwide Membership Directory.

Visit our exciting job and career site at http://www.careercity.com

APPAREL, FASHION, AND TEXTILES

Employment in the apparel and textiles industry has been hurt by advances in labor-saving technology. Computer-controlled cutters, semi-automatic sewing machines, and automated material handling systems continue to reduce the need for apparel workers. However, positions are still available due to the industry's high turnover rate.

Increased overseas production of textiles has also decreased the need for domestic workers who perform sewing functions. In fact, the U.S. Department of Labor estimates that imports now comprise 50 percent of U.S. apparel consumption, a figure that will increase as the North American Free Trade Agreement (NAFTA) becomes fully implemented. The industry has responded by attempting to develop niche markets, strong brand names, and faster customer response systems, according to Monthly Labor Review. *Despite these efforts, over 1 million U.S. textile and apparel jobs were eliminated between 1973 and 1997, and the U.S. Department of Labor expects employment to decline steadily through the year 2006.*

FARIBAULT WOOLEN MILL COMPANY
P.O. Box 369, Faribault MN 55021. 507/334-6444. **Contact:** Human Resources Department. **Description:** Manufactures wool blankets.

S.B. FOOT TANNING COMPANY
805 Bench Street, Red Wing MN 55066. 651/388-4731. **Contact:** Jerry Dietzman, Human Resources Manager. **Description:** S.B. Foot Tanning Company specializes in leather tanning and finishing services. **Common positions include:** Accountant/Auditor; Blue-Collar Worker Supervisor; Customer Service Representative; Industrial Engineer; Industrial Production Manager; Purchasing Agent/Manager. **Educational backgrounds include:** Business Administration; Chemistry; Liberal Arts. **Benefits:** 401(k); Disability Coverage; Investment Plan; Life Insurance; Medical Insurance; Pension Plan; Savings Plan; Tuition Assistance. **Special programs:** Internships. **Corporate headquarters location:** This Location. **Parent company:** Red Wing Shoe Company. **Operations at this facility include:** Administration; Manufacturing; Research and Development; Sales; Service.

FUTURE PRODUCTS INC.
2100 Minnesota Avenue, Benson MN 56215. 320/843-4614. **Contact:** Don Lenz, Human Resources. **E-mail address:** futureproducts@willmar.com. **Description:** Manufactures sewing and embroidery products.

JP&A MINNESOTA
3401 Spring Street NE, Minneapolis MN 55413. 612/331-3300. **Contact:** Office Manager. **Description:** Manufactures athletic outerwear and other apparel.

KNITCRAFT
4020 West Sixth Street, Winona MN 55987. 507/454-1163. **Contact:** Human Resources. **Description:** Knits men's and women's sweaters.

LAKESHIRTS, INC.
750 Randolph Road, P.O. Box 52, Detroit Lakes MN 56502. 218/847-2171. **Contact:** Human Resources Department. **Description:** Lakeshirts specializes in embroidering and screenprinting T-shirts.

PREMIUMWEAR, INC.
5500 Feltl Road, Minnetonka MN 55343. 612/979-1700. **Contact:** Tom Gleason, CEO. **World Wide Web address:** http://www.premiumwear.com. **Description:** A manufacturer of women's clothing.

RED WING SHOE COMPANY
314 Main Street, River Front Center, Red Wing MN 55066. 651/388-8211. **Contact:** Vice President of Human Resources. **World Wide Web address:** http://www.redwing.com. **Description:** A manufacturer of men's footwear.

WINONA KNITTING MILLS
902 East Second Street, Winona MN 55987. 507/454-4381. **Contact:** Mary Hazelton, Human Resources. **World Wide Web address:** http://www.hamp.com. **Description:** Knits men's sweaters. **Parent company:** Hampshire Group, Limited (Anderson SC).

For more information on career opportunities in the apparel, fashion, and textiles industries:

Associations

AMERICAN APPAREL MANUFACTURERS ASSOCIATION
2500 Wilson Boulevard, Suite 301, Arlington VA 22201. 703/524-1864. World Wide Web address: http://www.americanapparel.org. American Apparel Manufacturers Association publishes numerous magazines, newsletters, and bulletins for the benefit of employees in the apparel manufacturing industry.

AMERICAN TEXTILE MANUFACTURERS INSTITUTE
Office of the Chief Economist, 1130 Connecticut Avenue, Suite 1200, Washington DC 20036. 202/862-0500. Fax: 202/862-0570. World Wide Web address: http://www.atmi.org. The national trade association for the domestic textile industry. Members are corporations only.

THE FASHION GROUP INTERNATIONAL, INC.
597 Fifth Avenue, 8th Floor, New York NY 10017. 212/593-1715. World Wide Web address: http://www.fgi.org. The Fashion Group International is a nonprofit organization for professional women in the fashion industries (apparel, accessories, beauty, and home). Offers career counseling workshops 18 times each year.

INTERNATIONAL ASSOCIATION OF CLOTHING DESIGNERS
475 Park Avenue South, 9th Floor, New York NY 10016. 212/685-6602. Fax: 212/545-1709.

Directories

AAMA DIRECTORY
American Apparel Manufacturers Association, 2500 Wilson Boulevard, Suite 301, Arlington VA 22201. 703/524-1864. A directory of publications distributed by the American Apparel Manufacturers Association.

APPAREL TRADES BOOK
Dun & Bradstreet Inc., One Diamond Hill Road, Murray Hill NJ 07974. 908/665-5000.

FAIRCHILD'S MARKET DIRECTORY OF WOMEN'S AND CHILDREN'S APPAREL
Fairchild Publications, 7 West 34th Street, New York NY 10001. 212/630-4000.

Magazines

ACCESSORIES
Business Journals, 50 Day Street, P.O. Box 5550, Norwalk CT 06854. 203/853-6015.

AMERICA'S TEXTILES INTERNATIONAL
Billiam Publishing, 555 North Pleasantburg Drive, Suite 132, Greenville SC 29607. 864/242-5300.

APPAREL INDUSTRY MAGAZINE
Shore Verone Inc., 6255 Barfield Road, Suite 200, Atlanta GA 30328-4300. 404/252-8831. World Wide Web address: http://www.aimagazine.com.

BOBBIN MAGAZINE
Bobbin Publishing Group, P.O. Box 1986, 1110 Shop Road, Columbia SC 29202. 803/771-7500.

TEXTILE HILIGHTS
American Textile Manufacturers Institute, Office of the Chief Economist, 1130 Connecticut Avenue NW, Washington DC 20036. A quarterly publication. Subscriptions: $125.00 per year (domestic); $200.00 per year (international).

WOMEN'S WEAR DAILY (WWD)
Fairchild Publications, 7 West 34th Street, New York NY 10001. 212/630-4000. World Wide Web address: http://www.fairchildpub.com.

Online Services

THE INTERNET FASHION EXCHANGE
http://www.fashionexch.com. An excellent site for those industry professionals interested in apparel and retail. The extensive search engine allows you to search by job title, location, salary, product line, industry, and whether you want a permanent, temporary, or freelance position. The Internet Fashion Exchange also offers career services such as recruiting and outplacement firms that place fashion and retail professionals.

Visit our exciting job and career site at http://www.careercity.com

ARCHITECTURE, CONSTRUCTION, AND ENGINEERING

Building on its success of the mid-90's, the construction industry is flourishing. The Federal Reserve Board notes that new and existing home sales are strong in most areas of the U.S., and that construction may only be limited by a shortage of workers. Approximately 7.1 million workers were employed in the industry in 1997, a record year according to U.S. Industry and Trade Outlook 1998.

For jobseekers who choose construction, the best opportunities will be in projects at electric utilities, educational structures, and water supply facilities. In 1998, housing starts were expected to total 1.6 million, versus 1.5 million in 1997. Construction is likely to remain strongest in the Midwest and the South. Building trade workers such as architects, concrete masons, and sheet metal workers will see only average growth in their industries through 2005.

In engineering, the best opportunities through 2005 are in the civil, industrial, and electrical sectors. Aerospace engineers will continue to face fierce competition and chemical engineers will have more opportunities with companies focusing on the development of specialty chemicals.

ADOLFSON AND PETERSON INC.
6701 West 23rd Street, St. Louis Park MN 55426. 612/544-1561. **Contact:** Personnel. **World Wide Web address:** http://www.adolfsonpeterson.com. **Description:** A construction company.

ANDERSEN CORPORATION
100 Fourth Avenue North, Bayport MN 55003. 651/439-5150. **Contact:** Personnel Department. **World Wide Web address:** http://www.andersenwindows.com. **Description:** Manufactures windows and doors.

ARCHITECTURE TECHNOLOGY CORPORATION
P.O. Box 24344, Minneapolis MN 55424. 612/935-2035. **Fax:** 612/829-5871. **Contact:** Ken Thurber, President. **World Wide Web address:** http://www.atcorp.com. **Description:** An architectural consulting firm.

ARCON CONSTRUCTION COMPANY
43425 Frontage Road, P.O. Box 159, Harris MN 55032. 651/674-4474. **Contact:** Controller/Secretary. **Description:** A contracting firm specializing in highway and street construction.

BOR-SON CONSTRUCTION INC.
2001 Killebrew Drive, Suite 141, Bloomington MN 55425. 612/854-8444. **Contact:** President. **Description:** A regional construction firm.

CERTAINTEED CORPORATION
3303 Fourth Avenue East, Shakopee MN 55379. 612/445-6450. **Contact:** Human Resources. **World Wide Web address:** http://www.certainteed.com. **Description:** Manufactures shingles.

CRYSTAL CABINET WORKS
1100 Crystal Drive, Princeton MN 55371. 612/389-4187. **Contact:** Human Resources. **World Wide Web address:** http://www.ccworks.com. **Description:** A manufacturer of custom-made kitchen cabinets.

DURA SUPREME
300 Dura Drive, Howard Lake MN 55349. 320/543-3872. **Contact:** Louise Erickson, Human Resources Manager. **Description:** Manufactures cabinets. **Common positions include:**

Accountant/Auditor; Buyer; Computer Programmer; Credit Manager; Draftsperson; Electrician; Human Resources Manager; Industrial Engineer; Industrial Production Manager; Quality Control Supervisor. **Educational backgrounds include:** Engineering; Marketing. **Benefits:** 401(k); Dental Insurance; Disability Coverage; Employee Discounts; Life Insurance; Medical Insurance. **Special programs:** Internships. **Corporate headquarters location:** This Location. **Operations at this facility include:** Administration; Manufacturing. **Listed on:** Privately held. **Number of employees at this location:** 300.

EGAN MECHANICAL CONTRACTORS INC.
7100 Medicine Lake Road, Minneapolis MN 55427. 612/544-4131. **Contact:** Controller. **Description:** Mechanical and electrical contractors specializing in commercial and industrial projects.

ELLERBE BECKET
800 LaSalle Avenue, Minneapolis MN 55402-2014. 612/376-2000. **Fax:** 612/376-2390. **Recorded jobline:** 612/376-2069. **Contact:** Human Resources. **World Wide Web address:** http://www. ellerbebecket.com. **Description:** An architectural and engineering firm. Ellerbe Becket is engaged in the design of industrial, commercial, corporate, public assembly, educational, and medical buildings nationwide. Founded in 1908. **NOTE:** The company offers entry-level positions. **Common positions include:** Administrative Assistant; Architect; Civil Engineer; Draftsperson; Electrical/Electronics Engineer; Mechanical Engineer. **Educational backgrounds include:** Architecture; Engineering. **Benefits:** 401(k); Dental Insurance; Disability Coverage; Employee Discounts; Life Insurance; Medical Insurance. **Corporate headquarters location:** This Location. **Operations at this facility include:** Administration; Divisional Headquarters. **Annual sales/revenues:** More than $100 million. **Number of employees at this location:** 425. **Number of employees nationwide:** 700.

GAF MATERIALS CORPORATION
50 Lowry Avenue North, Minneapolis MN 55411. 612/529-9121. **Contact:** Human Resources. **World Wide Web address:** http://www.gaf.com. **Description:** GAF Materials Corporation manufactures roofing materials. **Common positions include:** Accountant/Auditor; Industrial Engineer; Industrial Production Manager; Quality Control Supervisor. **Educational backgrounds include:** Accounting; Business Administration; Engineering; Finance. **Benefits:** Dental Insurance; Disability Coverage; Life Insurance; Medical Insurance; Pension Plan; Tuition Assistance. **Corporate headquarters location:** Wayne NJ. **Operations at this facility include:** Administration; Manufacturing.

GENERAL RESOURCE CORPORATION
201 Third Street South, Hopkins MN 55343. 612/933-7474. **Fax:** 612/933-9777. **Contact:** Ms. C.J. Bollhoefer, Personnel Director. **Description:** Manufactures ventilating, dust collection, and heating equipment. **Common positions include:** Accountant/Auditor; Administrative Worker/Clerk; Advertising Clerk; Applications Engineer; Buyer; Computer Operator; Designer; Draftsperson; Food Scientist/Technologist; Machinist; Mechanical Engineer; Purchasing Agent/Manager; Receptionist; Sales Engineer; Secretary; Sheet-Metal Worker; Technician; Transportation/Traffic Specialist; Typist/Word Processor; Welder. **Educational backgrounds include:** Accounting; Business Administration; Communications; Engineering; Finance; Marketing. **Benefits:** Disability Coverage; Life Insurance; Medical Insurance; Profit Sharing; Tuition Assistance. **Corporate headquarters location:** This Location. **Subsidiaries include:** Air Purification Methods, Inc., which produces air pollution control systems; Fluidizer, Inc., which designs and manufactures systems and equipment for the conveying and storage, vacuum clean up, and ship and barge loading and unloading of bulk materials and commodities; Ammerman, Inc., which produces roof ventilators, industrial fans, and auto exhaust ventilator systems; Isomatic Corporation, which produces standard and custom industrial components; and Marshall Labs Inc., which is engaged in the spray-drying of food products and pharmaceutical products. **Operations at this facility include:** Research and Development; Sales; Service.

HANS HAGEN HOMES
941 NE Hillwind Road, Suite 300, Fridley MN 55432. 612/572-9455. **Contact:** Marie Reese, Personnel Director. **World Wide Web address:** http://www.hanshagenhomes.com. **Description:** A construction company specializing in town houses and single-family homes.

HAMMEL GREEN & ABRAHAMSON, INC.
1201 Harmon Place, Minneapolis MN 55403. 612/337-4100. **Contact:** Sandy Parsley, Personnel Director. **World Wide Web address:** http://www.hga.com. **Description:** An architectural engineering firm.

HEAT-N-GLO CORPORATION
6665 Highway West 13, Savage MN 55378. 612/890-8367. **Contact:** Michael Mady, Human Resources. **World Wide Web address:** http://www.heatnglo.com. **Description:** Operates a network of dealers who install fireplaces in local residences. **Corporate headquarters location:** This Location.

HUNT ELECTRIC CORPORATION
2300 Territorial Road, St. Paul MN 55114. 651/646-2911. **Contact:** Jim Kranz, Personnel. **Description:** A commercial electrical contracting company.

INSITUFORM CENTRAL, INC.
12450 Wayzata Boulevard, Suite 224, Minnetonka MN 55305. 612/835-1006. **Contact:** Bob Ratz, Sales Manager. **Description:** Insituform Central is involved in sewer pipeline improvement. **Parent company:** Insituform Mid-America, Inc. uses various trenchless technologies for rehabilitation, new construction, and improvements of pipeline systems, including sewers, gas lines, industrial waste lines, water lines, and oil field, mining, and industrial process pipelines. The company's trenchless technologies require little or no excavation and eliminate the need to replace deteriorating pipe.

GUSTAVE A. LARSON COMPANY
DEALER PRODUCTS GROUP
13200 10th Avenue North, Plymouth MN 55441. 612/546-7175. **Contact:** Randy Green, Product Manager. **World Wide Web address:** http://www.galarson.com. **Description:** A wholesaler of heating and air conditioning systems. **Common positions include:** Administrator; Manufacturer's/Wholesaler's Sales Rep.; Mechanical Engineer. **Educational backgrounds include:** Business Administration; Engineering; Marketing. **Benefits:** Dental Insurance; Disability Coverage; Employee Discounts; Life Insurance; Medical Insurance; Pension Plan; Savings Plan; Tuition Assistance. **Corporate headquarters location:** St. Louis MO. **Operations at this facility include:** Sales.

LESTER BUILDING SYSTEMS
1111 Second Avenue South, Lester Prairie MN 55354. 320/395-2531. **Contact:** Human Resources. **World Wide Web address:** http://www.lesterbuildingsystems.com. **Description:** A manufacturer and retailer of pre-engineered wood-frame buildings. **Common positions include:** Architectural Engineer; Civil Engineer; Draftsperson. **Educational backgrounds include:** Business Administration; Engineering. **Benefits:** Dental Insurance; Disability Coverage; Employee Discounts; Life Insurance; Medical Insurance; Pension Plan; Profit Sharing; Savings Plan; Tuition Assistance. **Corporate headquarters location:** Kansas City MO. **Parent company:** Butler Manufacturing Company.

McGOUGH CONSTRUCTION COMPANY
2737 North Fairview Avenue, St. Paul MN 55113. 651/633-5050. **Contact:** Tom Nonnemacher, Executive Vice President. **World Wide Web address:** http://www.mcgough.com. **Description:** A contractor specializing in industrial buildings and warehouses.

McQUAY INTERNATIONAL
P.O. Box 1551, Minneapolis MN 55440. 612/553-5330. **Contact:** Gary Boyd, Vice President of Human Resources. **World Wide Web address:** http://www.mcquay.com. **Description:** This location houses administrative offices only. Overall, McQuay is an international company that engineers, manufactures, sells, and services commercial heating, ventilating, and air conditioning equipment. **Common positions include:** Accountant/Auditor; Draftsperson; Electrical/Electronics Engineer; Mechanical Engineer. **Educational backgrounds include:** Accounting; Engineering. **Benefits:** Dental Insurance; Disability Coverage; Employee Discounts; Life Insurance; Medical Insurance; Pension Plan; Reimbursement Accounts; Savings Plan; Tuition Assistance. **Operations at this facility include:** Divisional Headquarters.

MEDALLION KITCHENS OF MINNESOTA
180 Industrial Boulevard, Waconia MN 55387. 612/442-5171. **Contact:** Human Resources. **Description:** Manufactures fine wood kitchen cabinets.

MILLER ARCHITECTS AND BUILDERS
P.O. Box 1228, St. Cloud MN 56302. 320/251-4109. **Physical address:** 3335 West St. Germain, St. Cloud MN 56301. **Contact:** Personnel Department. **E-mail address:** mab@cloudnet.com. **Description:** A construction contractor.

M.A. MORTENSON COMPANY
P.O. Box 710, Minneapolis MN 55440. 612/522-2100. **Fax:** 612/522-2278. **Contact:** Maritza Dejesus, Human Services Director. **Description:** A construction company. **Common positions include:** Accountant/Auditor; Attorney; Blue-Collar Worker Supervisor; Construction and Building Inspector; Construction Contractor; Cost Estimator; Systems Analyst. **Educational backgrounds include:** Accounting; Business Administration; Computer Science; Engineering; Marketing. **Benefits:** 401(k); Dental Insurance; Disability Coverage; Life Insurance; Medical Insurance; Pension Plan; Profit Sharing; Tuition Assistance. **Special programs:** Internships. **Corporate headquarters location:** This Location. **Other U.S. locations:** CA; CO; HI; WI. **Operations at this facility include:** Administration; Divisional Headquarters.

NEW MECH COMPANIES
1633 Eustis Street, St. Paul MN 55108. 651/645-0451. **Contact:** Wayne Henquinet, Personnel Manager. **Description:** A heating, plumbing, and air conditioning contractor involved primarily in large commercial or government projects.

NORCRAFT COMPANIES, INC.
3020 Denmark Avenue, Suite 100, Eagan MN 55121. 651/234-3300. **Contact:** Brenda Lee Lally, Manager of Benefits & Payroll. **World Wide Web address:** http://www.norcraftco.com. **Description:** Manufactures fine wood kitchen cabinets. **Corporate headquarters location:** This Location. **Other U.S. locations:** Newton KS; Cottonwood MN.

PCI (PROGRESSIVE CONTRACTORS INC.)
P.O. Box 416, St. Michael MN 55376-0416. 612/497-6100. **Contact:** Human Resources. **Description:** A contractor specializing in highway and street construction.

PACESETTER
1110 New Brighton Boulevard, Minneapolis MN 55413. 651/636-0050. **Contact:** Personnel Department. **World Wide Web address:** http://www.pacesetter.com. **Description:** Manufactures and sells a wide variety of home improvement products including windows and cabinet refacing.

PARK CONSTRUCTION COMPANY
7900 Beech Street NE, Minneapolis MN 55432. 612/786-9800. **Contact:** Personnel. **Description:** A contractor specializing in the construction of bridges and tunnels.

RYAN COMPANIES U.S., INC.
900 Second Avenue South, Suite 700, Minneapolis MN 55402. 612/336-1200. **Recorded jobline:** 612/336-1200x360. **Contact:** James Nahrgang, Director of Human Resources. **World Wide Web address:** http://www.ryancompanies.com. **Description:** Designs and builds commercial projects including corporate office, manufacturing, industrial, project distribution, high-tech, medical, and retail buildings. **Corporate headquarters location:** This Location.

ST. PAUL LINOLEUM & CARPET COMPANY
2956 Center Court, Eagan MN 55121. 612/686-7770. **Contact:** Clemment J. Commers, Owner/President. **Description:** A floor covering contractor and acoustical products distributor.

TRUSS MANUFACTURING COMPANY
P.O. Box 119, Albertville MN 55301. 612/497-3324. **Contact:** Dan Crocker, General Manager. **Description:** Manufactures structural wood members.

WOODCRAFT INDUSTRIES
525 Lincoln Avenue SE, St. Cloud MN 56304-1023. 320/252-1503. **Contact:** Human Resources. **Description:** A manufacturer of wooden cabinet and furniture components.

Note: Because addresses and telephone numbers of smaller companies can change rapidly, we recommend you call each company to verify the information below before inquiring about job opportunities. Mass mailings are not recommended.

Additional small employers:

ARCHITECTURAL SERVICES

Cunningham Group
201 Main St SE, Ste 325,
Minneapolis MN 55414-2139.
612/379-3400.

KKE Architects
300 1st Ave N, Ste 500,
Minneapolis MN 55401-1648.
612/339-4200.

RSP Architects Ltd.
120 1st Avenue North,

Minneapolis MN 55401-1415.
612/339-0313.

Setter Leach & Lindstrom Inc.
730 2nd Ave S, Ste 1100,
Minneapolis MN 55402-2455.
612/338-8741.

BRIDGE, TUNNEL, AND HIGHWAY CONSTRUCTION

Lunda Construction Company
15601 Clayton Ave E, Rosemount MN 55068-2055. 651/437-9666.

CARPENTRY AND FLOOR WORK

Consolidated Building Corp.
16935 Gerdine Path W, Rosemount MN 55068-5113. 612/759-9313.

Renewal by Andersen
1700 Buerkle Rd, White Bear Lake MN 55110-5249. 651/430-7255.

Tappe Construction Co.
PO Box 377, Savage MN 55378-0377. 612/445-9090.

CONCRETE WORK

Jesco Inc.
PO Box 390197, Minneapolis MN 55439-0197. 612/944-7700.

Manor Concrete Construction
4370 Naber Avenue NE, St. Michael MN 55376-9483. 612/497-5420.

ELECTRICAL WORK

Adair Electric Co.
204 16th St SE, Rochester MN 55904-7911. 507/289-7696.

Collins Electrical Construction Co.
278 State St, St. Paul MN 55107-1611. 651/224-2833.

Collisys
4990 Highway 169 N, Minneapolis MN 55428-4026. 612/535-6000.

Elliott Contracting Corp.
2901 Louisiana Ave N, Minneapolis MN 55427-2914. 612/797-0890.

Gephart Electric Co. Inc.
3550 Labore Rd, Ste 11, White Bear Lake MN 55110-5113. 651/484-4900.

Hanson Electric of Bemidji
PO Box 1626, Bemidji MN 56619-1626. 218/751-5833.

Muska Electric Co.
1985 Oakcrest Ave, Roseville MN 55113-2605. 651/636-5820.

Parsons Electric Co.
5960 Main St NE, Fridley MN 55432-5496. 612/571-8000.

Premier Electrical Corporation
4401 85th Ave North, Minneapolis MN 55443-1937. 612/424-6551.

Security Services Group LLC
4600 W 77th St, Minneapolis MN 55435-4909. 612/897-0094.

Sterling Electric
2817 Lyndale Ave S, Minneapolis MN 55408-2109. 612/872-7300.

ENGINEERING SERVICES

Abe Mathews Engineering Co.
PO Box 1338, Hopkins MN 55345-0338. 612/832-2832.

Braun Intertec Corporation
1345 Northland Dr, Mendota Heights MN 55120-1141. 612/683-8700.

Braun Intertec Corporation
PO Box 39108, Minneapolis MN 55439-0108. 612/941-5600.

BRW Group Inc.
700 S 3rd St, Minneapolis MN 55415-1130. 612/370-0700.

Dacon Engineering & Service Co.
4915 W 35th St, Ste 101, Minneapolis MN 55416-2643. 612/920-8040.

DDI
14264 23rd Avenue North, Plymouth MN 55447-4910. 612/550-1138.

OSM & Associates
5775 Wayzata Blvd, Ste 300, Minneapolis MN 55416-1235. 612/595-5775.

RC Consultants Inc.
2520 Larpenteur Ave W, Roseville MN 55113-5264. 651/645-8576.

SEH
3535 Vadnais Center Dr, White Bear Lake MN 55110-5196. 651/490-2000.

Simons Engineering Inc.
800 Marquette Avenue, Minneapolis MN 55402-2812. 612/332-8326.

SRF Consulting Group Inc.
1 Carlson Pkwy, Ste 150, Plymouth MN 55447-4453. 612/475-0010.

TE Ibberson Company
828 Fifth Street South, Hopkins MN 55343-7752. 612/938-7007.

GENERAL CONTRACTORS

Larry D. Barnabo Builders Inc.
8164 Arthur St NE, Fridley MN 55432-2131. 612/717-3990.

GENERAL INDUSTRIAL CONTRACTORS

JA Jones Construction Co.
PO Box 4178, Hastings MN 55033-7178. 651/480-3922.

MA Mortenson Company
4559 W Highway 2, Grand Rapids MN 55744-9625. 218/328-6265.

Met-Con Construction Inc.
PO Box 427, Faribault MN 55021-0427. 507/332-2266.

Opus Corporation
PO Box 59110, Minneapolis MN 55459. 612/936-4444.

Oscar J. Boldt Construction Co.
PO Box 287, Cloquet MN 55720-0287. 218/879-1293.

Sheehy Construction Co.
PO Box 64570, St. Paul MN 55164-0570. 651/488-6691.

Witcher Construction Co.
PO Box 581549, Minneapolis MN 55458-1549. 612/830-9000.

MISC. SPECIAL TRADE CONTRACTORS

A&M Business Interior Services
2700 Winter St NE, Minneapolis MN 55413-2945. 612/627-1600.

Brin Northwestern Glass
2300 N 2nd St, Minneapolis MN 55411-2209. 612/529-9671.

Harmon Contract Inc.
2400 Minnehaha Ave, Minneapolis MN 55404-4116. 612/721-6393.

Harmon Contract Inc.
2001 Killebrew Dr, Ste 400, Minneapolis MN 55425-1887. 612/851-9949.

Harmon Contract Inc.
1620 Broadway St NE, Minneapolis MN 55413-2617. 612/331-4300.

PLUMBING, HEATING, AND A/C

Albers Mechanical Services
200 Plato Blvd W, St. Paul MN 55107-2045. 651/224-5428.

Himec Inc.
PO Box 4700, Rochester MN 55903-4700. 507/281-4000.

Metropolitan Mechanical Contractors
7340 Washington Ave S, Eden Prairie MN 55344-3514. 612/941-7010.

Plaas Incorporated
1427 Old West Main St, Red Wing MN 55066-2162. 651/388-8881.

PLUMBING, HEATING, AND A/C EQUIPMENT WHOLESALE

Goodin Company
PO Box 9326, Minneapolis MN 55440-9326. 612/588-7811.

SCS Company
6363 Highway 7, Minneapolis MN 55416-2346. 612/929-1377.

ROAD CONSTRUCTION

CS McCrossan Inc.
PO Box 1240, Osseo MN 55311-6240. 612/425-4167.

ROOFING, SIDING, AND SHEET METAL WORK

Berwald Roofing Co.
2440 Charles St N, Maplewood MN 55109-3013. 651/777-7411.

Dalco Roofing & Sheet Metal
15525 32nd Ave N, Plymouth MN 55447-1453. 612/559-0222.

Globe Building Materials Inc.
1120 Seventh Street East, St. Paul MN 55106-3954. 651/776-2793.

United Sheet Metal
520 Front Ave, St. Paul MN 55117-4707. 651/487-1061.

WHV Roofing
PO Box 77, Winona MN 55987-0077. 507/452-2064.

For more information on career opportunities in architecture, construction, and engineering:

Associations

AACE INTERNATIONAL: THE ASSOCIATION FOR ADVANCEMENT OF COST ENGINEERING
209 Prairie Avenue, Suite 100, Morgantown WV 26505. 304/296-8444. Toll-free phone: 800/858-2678. Fax: 304/291-5728. World Wide Web address: http://www.aacei.org. A membership organization which offers *Cost Engineering*, a monthly magazine; employment referral services; technical reference information and assistance; insurance; and a certification program accredited by the Council of Engineering Specialty Boards. Toll-free number provides information on scholarships for undergraduates.

ASM INTERNATIONAL: THE MATERIALS INFORMATION SOCIETY
9639 Kinsman Road, Materials Park OH 44073. 440/338-5151. World Wide Web address: http://www. asm-intl.org. Gathers, processes, and disseminates technical information to foster the understanding and application of engineered materials.

AMERICAN ASSOCIATION OF ENGINEERING SOCIETIES
1111 19th Street NW, Suite 403, Washington DC 20036-3690. 202/296-2237. World Wide Web address: http://www.aaes.org. A multidisciplinary organization of professional engineering societies. Publishes reference works, including *Who's Who in Engineering*, *International Directory of Engineering Societies*, and the *Thesaurus of Engineering and Scientific Terms*, as well as statistical reports from studies conducted by the Engineering Workforce Commission.

AMERICAN CONSULTING ENGINEERS COUNCIL
1015 15th Street NW, Suite 802, Washington DC 20005. 202/347-7474. Fax: 202/898-0068. World Wide Web address: http://www.acec.org. A national organization of more than 5,000 member firms. Offers *Last Word*, a weekly newsletter; *American Consulting Engineer* magazine; life and health insurance programs; books, manuals, video- and audiotapes, and contract documents; conferences and seminars; and voluntary peer reviews.

AMERICAN INSTITUTE OF ARCHITECTS
1735 New York Avenue NW, Washington DC 20006. 202/626-7300. Toll-free phone: 800/365-2724. World

Wide Web address: http://www.aia.org. Contact toll-free number for brochures.

AMERICAN INSTITUTE OF CONSTRUCTORS
1300 North 17th Street, Suite 830, Arlington VA 22209. 703/812-2021. World Wide Web address: http://www.aicnet.org.

AMERICAN SOCIETY FOR ENGINEERING EDUCATION
1818 N Street NW, Suite 600, Washington DC 20036. 202/331-3500. World Wide Web address: http://www. asee.org. American Society for Engineering Education publishes magazines and journals including the *Journal of Engineering Education*.

AMERICAN SOCIETY OF CIVIL ENGINEERS
1801 Alexander Bell Drive, Reston VA 20191-4400. 703/295-6300. World Wide Web address: http://www. asce.org. A membership organization which offers subscriptions to *Civil Engineering* magazine and *ASCE News*, discounts on various other publications, seminars, video- and audiotapes, specialty conferences, an annual convention, group insurance programs, and pension plans.

AMERICAN SOCIETY OF HEATING, REFRIGERATING AND AIR CONDITIONING ENGINEERS
1791 Tullie Circle NE, Atlanta GA 30329. 404/636-8400. Fax: 404/321-5478. World Wide Web address: http://www.ashrae.org. A society of 50,000 members which offers handbooks, a monthly journal, a monthly newspaper, discounts on other publications, group insurance, continuing education, and registration discounts for meetings, conferences, seminars, and expositions.

AMERICAN SOCIETY OF LANDSCAPE ARCHITECTS
636 Eye Street NW, Washington DC 20001. 202/898-2444. World Wide Web address: http://www.asla.org. Check out the Website's Joblink for listings of employment opportunities.

AMERICAN SOCIETY OF MECHANICAL ENGINEERS
3 Park Avenue, New York NY 10016. 212/591-7722. World Wide Web address: http://www.asme.org. American Society of Mechanical Engineers handles educational materials for certified engineers, as well as scholarships.

AMERICAN SOCIETY OF NAVAL ENGINEERS
1452 Duke Street, Alexandria VA 22314. 703/836-6727. World Wide Web address: http://www.jhuapl.edu/ASNE. Holds symposiums based on technical papers. Publishes a journal and newsletter bimonthly.

AMERICAN SOCIETY OF PLUMBING ENGINEERS
3617 Thousand Oaks Boulevard, Suite 210, Westlake CA 91362-3649. 805/495-7120. Provides technical and educational information.

AMERICAN SOCIETY OF SAFETY ENGINEERS
1800 East Oakton Street, Des Plaines IL 60018-2187. 847/699-2929. Jobline service available at ext. 243. Fax: 847/768-3434. World Wide Web address: http://www.asse.org. A membership organization offering *Professional Safety,* a monthly journal; educational seminars; an annual professional development conference and exposition; technical publications; certification preparation programs; career placement services; and group and liability insurance programs.

ASSOCIATED BUILDERS AND CONTRACTORS
1300 North 17th Street, 8th Floor, Arlington VA 22209. 703/812-2000. World Wide Web address: http://www.abc.org. Sponsors annual career fair.

ASSOCIATED GENERAL CONTRACTORS OF AMERICA, INC.
1957 E Street NW, Washington DC 20006. 202/393-2040. World Wide Web address: http://www.agc.org. A full-service construction association of subcontractors, specialty contractors, suppliers, equipment manufacturers, and professional firms. Services include government relations, education and training, jobsite services, legal services, and information services.

THE ENGINEERING CENTER (TEC)
One Walnut Street, Boston MA 02108-3616. 617/227-5551. Contact: Abbie Goodman. World Wide Web address: http://www.engineers.org. An association that provides services for many engineering membership organizations.

ILLUMINATING ENGINEERING SOCIETY OF NORTH AMERICA
120 Wall Street, 17th Floor, New York NY 10005-4001. 212/248-5000. World Wide Web address: http://www.iesna.org. An organization for industry professionals involved in the manufacturing, design, specification, and maintenance of lighting systems. Conference held annually. Offers a Technical Knowledge Examination.

JUNIOR ENGINEERING TECHNICAL SOCIETY
1420 King Street, Suite 405, Alexandria VA 22314-2794. 703/548-JETS. Fax: 703/548-0769. E-mail address: jets@nae.edu. World Wide Web address: http://www.asee.org/jets. A nonprofit, educational society promoting interest in engineering, technology, mathematics, and science. Provides information to high school students and teachers regarding careers in engineering and technology.

NATIONAL ACTION COUNCIL FOR MINORITIES IN ENGINEERING
350 Fifth Avenue, Suite 2212, New York NY 10118. 212/279-2626. Offers scholarship programs for students. World Wide Web address: http://www.nacme.org.

NATIONAL ASSOCIATION OF HOME BUILDERS
1201 15th Street NW, Washington DC 20005. 202/822-0200. World Wide Web address: http://www.nahb.com. National Association of Home Builders is a trade association promoting safe and affordable housing. Provides management services and education for members.

NATIONAL ASSOCIATION OF MINORITY ENGINEERING
1133 West Morse Boulevard, Suite 201, Winter Park FL 32789. 407/647-8839.

NATIONAL ELECTRICAL CONTRACTORS ASSOCIATION
3 Bethesda Metro Center, Suite 1100, Bethesda MD 20814. 301/657-3110. World Wide Web address: http://www.necanet.org. Provides information on hiring and trade shows. The association also publishes a magazine called *Electrical Contractor.*

NATIONAL SOCIETY OF BLACK ENGINEERS
1454 Duke Street, Alexandria VA 22314. 703/549-2207. World Wide Web address: http://www.nsbe.org. National Society of Black Engineers is a nonprofit organization run by college students. Offers scholarships, editorials, and magazines.

NATIONAL SOCIETY OF PROFESSIONAL ENGINEERS
1420 King Street, Alexandria VA 22314-2794. 703/684-2800. Call 703/684-2830 for scholarship information for students. Fax: 703/836-4875. World Wide Web address: http://www.nspe.org. A society of over 73,000 engineers. Membership includes the monthly magazine *Engineering Times;* continuing education; scholarships and fellowships; discounts on publications; and health and life insurance programs.

SOCIETY OF AMERICAN REGISTERED ARCHITECTS
303 South Broadway, Suite 322, Tarrytown NY 10591. 914/631-3600. Fax: 914/631-1319. World Wide Web address: http://www.sara-national.org.

SOCIETY OF FIRE PROTECTION ENGINEERS
7315 Wisconsin Avenue, Suite 1225W, Bethesda MD 20814. 301/718-2910. Fax: 301/718-2242. World Wide Web address: http://www.sfpe.org. A professional society which offers members reports, newsletters, *Journal of Fire Protecting Engineering,* insurance programs, short courses, symposiums, tutorials, an annual meeting, and engineering seminars.

Directories

DIRECTORY OF ENGINEERING SOCIETIES
American Association of Engineering Societies, 1111 19th Street NW, Suite 403, Washington DC 20036. 202/296-2237. $185.00. Lists other engineering association members, publications, and convention exhibits.

DIRECTORY OF ENGINEERS IN PRIVATE PRACTICE
National Society of Professional Engineers, 1420 King Street, Alexandria VA 22314-2794. 703/684-2800. $50.00. Lists members and companies.

Magazines

THE CAREER ENGINEER
National Society of Black Engineers, 1454 Duke
Street, Alexandria VA 22314. 703/549-2207.

CHEMICAL & ENGINEERING NEWS
American Chemical Society, 1155 16th Street NW,
Washington DC 20036. 202/872-4600. World Wide
Web address: http://www.acs.org.

COMPUTER-AIDED ENGINEERING
Penton Media, 1100 Superior Avenue, Cleveland OH
44114. 216/696-7000.

EDN CAREER NEWS
Cahners Business Information, 275 Washington
Street, Newton MA 02158. 617/964-3030. World
Wide Web address: http://www.cahners.com.

ENGINEERING TIMES
National Society of Professional Engineers, 1420
King Street, Alexandria VA 22314. 703/684-2800.

NAVAL ENGINEERS JOURNAL
American Society of Naval Engineers, 1452 Duke
Street, Alexandria VA 22314. 703/836-6727.
Subscription: $48.00.

Online Services

ARCHITECTURE AND BUILDING FORUM
Go: Arch. A CompuServe discussion group for
architectural professionals.

**ARCHITECTURE AND LANDSCAPE
ARCHITECTURE JOBS**
http://www.clr.toronto.edu/VIRTUALLIB/jobs.html.
This Website provides job openings for architects and
landscape architects, as well as links to other related
sites.

HOT JOBS! - CONSTRUCTION
http://www.kbic.com/construction.htm. Provides
construction employment opportunities organized by
job title.

P.L.A.C.E.S. FORUM
Keyword: places. A discussion group available to
America Online subscribers who are professionals in
the fields of architecture, construction, and
engineering.

Visit our exciting job and career site at http://www.careercity.com

ARTS AND ENTERTAINMENT/RECREATION

 Diversity is the trend in the entertainment industry. Recently, Business Week reported that media corporations and entertainment powerhouses are trying to gain revenue by creating new divisions. These companies have originated record labels, online services, movie studios, theme parks, and cable networks. As a result, the market is saturated and profits are falling.

A recent study predicted that the average television viewer will gain almost 1,000 channel choices by the time digital compression of television is complete and linking of TVs to the Internet becomes an option. With the creation of new channels comes more competition and as a result, programming costs have hit the roof. In an attempt to ease the sting of losing Seinfeld, *NBC has agreed to pay $13 million for each new episode of* ER *(the network's highest ranking show), versus $2 million per episode in 1997. Advertising costs are rising as well, though not as dramatically. A 30 second spot on* ER *now goes for $565,000, versus $560,000 in 1997. Look for movie makers to create more distinct products that attract consumers in all areas. Fox and Paramount struck a golden iceberg with* Titanic, *which has spawned book tie-ins, a best-selling soundtrack, and a $30 million sale to NBC for the television rights.*

Fans of professional sports continue to spend money on their teams and 1999 will likely be no exception. To retain its contract for Monday Night Football, *ABC will be reportedly paying the National Football League a hard-hitting $550 million per season, as noted in* Fortune. *Major League Baseball has expanded by two more teams and is climbing back from its slump of the mid-'90s with the help of interleague play. The National Hockey League has also begun plans to expand, with four new teams possible by 2000. The National Basketball Association (NBA), however, is facing the possibility of a canceled 1998-99 season due to labor disputes. Prior to the labor disputes, the NBA reportedly inked a television deal with both TNT and NBC for $2.6 billion.*

The U.S. Department of Labor expects employment opportunities for amusement and recreation services to increase by 41 percent between 1996 and 2006. Despite these projections, across much of the industry costs are being cut and joint ventures continue. Therefore, jobseekers with business savvy and a flair for marketing may find some solid opportunities.

BUCK HILL SKI AREA INC.
15400 Buck Hill Road, Burnsville MN 55306. 612/435-7174. **Contact:** Human Resources. **Description:** A ski area.

THE CHILDREN'S THEATRE COMPANY
2400 Third Avenue South, Minneapolis MN 55404. 612/874-0500. **Fax:** 612/874-8199. **Contact:** Human Resources Department. **World Wide Web address:** http://www.childrenstheatre.org. **Description:** Presents approximately six shows each year. In addition to professional theater performances, The Children's Theatre Company offers evening, weekend, and summer acting classes for children.

DULUTH ENTERTAINMENT CONVENTION CENTER
350 Harbor Drive, Duluth MN 55802. 218/722-5573. **Contact:** Human Resources. **Description:** A convention center that hosts a variety of sports and entertainment events.

GUTHRIE THEATER
725 Vineland Place, Minneapolis MN 55403. 612/347-1100. **Contact:** Personnel. **World Wide Web address:** http://www.guthrietheater.org. **Description:** A theater featuring a resident professional repertory company that presents ensemble productions of classical and modern drama.

HOMETIME
DUPLICATION FACTORY
4275 Norex Drive, Chaska MN 55318. 612/448-9912. **Contact:** Plant Manager. **World Wide Web address:** http://www.hometime.com. **Description:** Produces a television show. Duplication Factory (also at this location) is a provider of video duplication services.

K-TEL INTERNATIONAL (USA), INC.
2605 Fernbrook Lane North, Plymouth MN 55447. 612/559-6800. **Contact:** Lindee Weed, Human Resources Director. **World Wide Web address:** http://www.k-tel.com. **Description:** Distributes recorded music products. **Common positions include:** Accountant/Auditor. **Educational backgrounds include:** Accounting. **Benefits:** 401(k); Dental Insurance; Disability Coverage; Employee Discounts; Life Insurance; Medical Insurance; Tuition Assistance. **Corporate headquarters location:** This Location. **Parent company:** K-Tel International, Inc.

LIEBERMAN MUSIC COMPANY
9549 Penn Avenue South, Bloomington MN 55431. 612/887-5299. **Contact:** Human Resources. **Description:** A wholesale record and tape distributor. **Common positions include:** Accountant/Auditor; Branch Manager; Credit Manager; Customer Service Representative; Manufacturer's/Wholesaler's Sales Rep.; Operations/Production Manager. **Educational backgrounds include:** Accounting. **Benefits:** 401(k); Dental Insurance; Disability Coverage; Life Insurance; Medical Insurance; Savings Plan. **Special programs:** Internships. **Corporate headquarters location:** This Location. **Parent company:** LIVE. **Operations at this facility include:** Administration; Sales; Service. **Listed on:** Privately held. **Number of employees at this location:** 60.

MANN THEATRES
704 Hennepin Avenue, Minneapolis MN 55403. 612/332-3303. **Contact:** Human Resources. **Description:** Operates a chain of movie theatres throughout Minnesota. **Corporate headquarters location:** This Location.

THE MINNEAPOLIS INSTITUTE OF ARTS
2400 Third Avenue South, Minneapolis MN 55404. 612/870-3074. **Contact:** Debra Duffy, Human Resources Director. **Description:** An art museum that stresses the collection of master works of art in the areas of painting; sculpture; decorative arts; prints; drawings; photography; textiles; and Asian, African, Oceanic, and Native American arts. Established in 1883.

MINNESOTA TIMBERWOLVES
Target Center, 600 First Avenue North, Minneapolis MN 55403. 612/673-1600. **Contact:** Chris Wright, Vice President of Marketing and Sales. **World Wide Web address:** http://www.timberwolves.com. **Description:** Operates an NBA basketball team.

MINNESOTA TWINS
34 Kirby Puckett Place, Minneapolis MN 55415. 612/375-1366. **Contact:** Raenell Dorn, Human Resources Director. **World Wide Web address:** http://www.mntwins.com. **Description:** Operates a Major League Baseball franchise.

MINNESOTA VIKINGS
9520 Viking Drive, Eden Prairie MN 55344. 612/828-6500. **Contact:** Jeff Diamond, Vice President of Team Operations. **World Wide Web address:** http://www.nfl.com. **Description:** Operates an NFL football team. **Benefits:** 401(k); Dental Insurance; Disability Coverage; Employee Discounts; Life Insurance; Medical Insurance; Pension Plan. **Corporate headquarters location:** This Location.

NORTHWEST TELEPRODUCTIONS
4455 West 77th Street, Minneapolis MN 55435. 612/835-4455. **Contact:** Bob Haak, Operations Supervisor. **World Wide Web address:** http://www.nwtele.com. **Description:** A videotape production service.

SCIENCE MUSEUM OF MINNESOTA
30 East 10th Street, St. Paul MN 55101. 651/221-2558. **Fax:** 651/221-4777. **Recorded jobline:** 651/221-4548. **Contact:** Jody Anderson, Employee Placement Specialist. **Description:** Science

Museum of Minnesota is a private, nonprofit, educational and research institution organized to collect, study, and preserve objects of scientific significance and to interpret the objects, discoveries, and insights of science for the general public through its exhibits and education programs. The museum has exhibits in anthropology, biology, geography, paleontology, technology, cultural history, and natural history. Additionally, the museum houses a collection of over 1.5 million scientific objects and an Omnitheater that produces and distributes OMNIMAX films shown around the world. **NOTE:** Advanced degrees in the natural sciences are required for curatorial positions. **Common positions include:** Biological Scientist; Buyer; Curatorial Specialist; Customer Service Representative; Designer; Editor; Education Administrator; Exhibit Designer; Financial Analyst; Fundraising Specialist; Geographer; Graphic Artist; Human Resources Manager; Interpreter; Library Technician; Marketing Specialist; Public Relations Specialist; Services Sales Representative; Teacher/Professor; Technical Writer/Editor; Wholesale and Retail Buyer; Writer. **Educational backgrounds include:** Accounting; Anthropology; Art/Design; Business Administration; Communications; Computer Science; Finance; Geology; Liberal Arts; Marketing; Mathematics; Paleontology; Physics. **Benefits:** Dental Insurance; Employee Discounts; Life Insurance; Medical Insurance; Pension Plan; Section 125 Plan. **Corporate headquarters location:** This Location. **Operations at this facility include:** Administration. **Number of employees at this location:** 600.

WALKER ART CENTER
725 Vineland Place, Minneapolis MN 55403. 612/375-7600. **Fax:** 612/375-7590. **Recorded jobline:** 612/375-7588. **Contact:** Gary A. White, Manager of Human Resources. **World Wide Web address:** http://www.walkerart.org. **Description:** An international contemporary art museum with exhibition, film/video, and performing arts programming. Walker Art Center also curates the artistic presence in the adjacent, 11-acre Minneapolis Sculpture Garden. **Common positions include:** Accountant/Auditor; Administrator; Carpenter; Curatorial Specialist; Editor; Educational Specialist; Graphic Artist; Human Resources Manager; Marketing Specialist; Program Manager; Secretary; Technician; Visitor Services. **Educational backgrounds include:** Accounting; Art History; Art/Design; Business Administration; Communications; Liberal Arts; Marketing. **Benefits:** Dental Insurance; Disability Coverage; EAP; Employee Discounts; Life Insurance; Medical Insurance; Pension Plan. **Special programs:** Internships. **Corporate headquarters location:** This Location. **Number of employees at this location:** 100.

FREDERICK R. WEISMAN MUSEUM
University of Minnesota, 333 East River Road, Minneapolis MN 55455. 612/625-9494. **Contact:** Rose Blixt, Human Resources. **World Wide Web address:** http://hudson.acad.umn.edu. **Description:** A museum of contemporary American art.

Note: Because addresses and telephone numbers of smaller companies can change rapidly, we recommend you call each company to verify the information below before inquiring about job opportunities. Mass mailings are not recommended.

Additional small employers:

AMUSEMENT AND RECREATION SERVICES

All Seasons Arena
301 Monks Ave, Mankato MN 56001-4981. 507/387-6552.

Buena Vista Ski Area
621 Lake Julia Drive NW, Bemidji MN 56601-7108. 218/243-2231.

Little Six Inc.
2400 Mystic Lake Blvd NW, Prior Lake MN 55372-9004. 612/496-6941.

Nationwide Fun Ltd.
18960 Jaspar St NW, Anoka MN 55303-9638. 612/753-4679.

Palace Bingo & Casino
Rural Route 3, Box 221, Cass Lake MN 56633-8924. 218/335-7000.

Richfield Ice Arena
6700 Portland Avenue, Minneapolis MN 55423-2560. 612/861-9700.

The Connection
11351 Rupp Dr, Burnsville MN 55337-1285. 612/895-8417.

Ticketmaster Corporation
1010 S 7th St, Ste 540, Minneapolis MN 55415-1755. 612/371-2000.

BOTANICAL AND ZOOLOGICAL GARDENS

Minnesota Zoo
13000 Zoo Blvd, Apple Valley MN 55124-4621. 612/431-9200.

ENTERTAINERS AND ENTERTAINMENT GROUPS

Entertainment Themes Inc.
1551 Livingston Ave, St. Paul MN 55118-3416. 651/457-9057.

Minnesota Orchestral Association
1111 Nicollet Mall, Minneapolis MN 55403-2406. 612/371-5600.

GOLF COURSES

Braemar Golf Course
6364 John Harris Dr, Minneapolis MN 55439-2564. 612/941-2072.

Brookview Golf Course
7800 Golden Valley Rd, Minneapolis MN 55427-4508. 612/593-8012.

Majestic Oaks
701 Bunker Lake Blvd N, Anoka
MN 55304-6720. 612/755-2140.
**MOTION PICTURE AND
VIDEO TAPE PRODUCTION
AND DISTRIBUTION**

Avery Pix Inc.
1010 Park Ave, Minneapolis MN
55404-1437. 612/335-3426.

**MUSEUMS AND ART
GALLERIES**

Minnesota Children's Museum
10 7th St W, St. Paul MN 55102-
1104. 651/225-6001.

**PHYSICAL FITNESS
FACILITIES**

Dakota Sport & Fitness
2100 Trail of Dreams NW, Prior
Lake MN 55372. 612/445-9400.

Life Time Fitness
2100 Northdale Blvd NW, Coon
Rapids MN 55433-3005.
612/767-9000.

Life Time Fitness
675 Commons Drive, Woodbury
MN 55125-8880. 651/730-6000.

Northwest Athletic Clubs
5525 Cedar Lake Rd S,
Minneapolis MN 55416-1420.
612/546-8059.

**Scandinavian US Swim &
Fitness**
4239 Winnetka Ave N,
Minneapolis MN 55428-4924.
612/533-0101.

**Scandinavian US Swim &
Fitness**
71 Minnesota Avenue, St. Paul
MN 55117-1737. 651/484-4444.

**Scandinavian US Swim &
Fitness**
4951 West 80th Street,
Minneapolis MN 55437-1128.
612/896-1000.

The Marsh
15000 Minnetonka Blvd,
Minnetonka MN 55345-1506.
612/935-2202.

**THEATRICAL PRODUCERS
AND SERVICES**

Chanhassen Dinner Theatre
PO Box 100, Chanhassen MN
55317-0100. 612/934-1500.

**Great American History
Theatre**
30 10th St E, St. Paul MN 55101-
2205. 651/292-4323.

Just For Kix Precision Dance
PO Box 724, Brainerd MN
56401-0724. 218/829-7107.

Mankato Civic Center
1 Civic Center Plaza,
Mankato MN 56001-7777.
507/389-3000.

Ordway Music Theatre
345 Washington Street, St.
Paul MN 55102-1419. 651/282-
3000.

State Theatre
805 Hennepin Avenue,
Minneapolis MN 55402-1818.
612/339-0075.

For more information on career opportunities in arts, entertainment, and recreation:

Associations

AMERICAN ASSOCIATION OF MUSEUMS
1575 I Street NW, Suite 400, Washington DC 20005.
202/289-1818. Fax: 202/289-6578. World Wide Web
address: http://www.aam-us.org. Publishes *AVISO*, a
monthly newsletter containing employment listings
for the entire country.

AMERICAN CRAFTS COUNCIL
72 Spring Street, New York NY 10012-4019.
212/274-0630. Operates a research library. Publishes
American Crafts magazine.

AMERICAN DANCE GUILD
31 West 21st Street, New York NY 10010. 212/627-
3790. Holds an annual conference with panels,
performances, and workshops. Operates a job listings
service (available at a discount to members).

AMERICAN FEDERATION OF MUSICIANS
1501 Broadway, Suite 600, New York NY 10036.
212/869-1330. World Wide Web address: http://www.
afm.org.

AMERICAN FILM INSTITUTE
2021 North Western Avenue, Los Angeles CA 90027.
323/856-7600. Toll-free phone: 800/774-4AFI. World
Wide Web address: http://www.afionline.org.
Membership is required, and includes a newsletter and
members-only discounts on events, seminars,
workshops, and exhibits.

AMERICAN MUSIC CENTER
30 West 26th Street, Suite 1001, New York NY
10010-2011. 212/366-5260. Fax: 212/366-5265.
World Wide Web address: http://www.amc.net. A
nonprofit research and information center for
contemporary music and jazz. Provides information
services and grant programs.

**AMERICAN SOCIETY OF COMPOSERS,
AUTHORS, AND PUBLISHERS (ASCAP)**
One Lincoln Plaza, New York NY 10023. 212/621-
6000. World Wide Web address: http://www.ascap.
com. A membership association which licenses
members' work and pays members' royalties. Offers
showcases and educational seminars and workshops.
The society also has an events hotline: 212/621-6485.

**AMERICAN SYMPHONY ORCHESTRA
LEAGUE**
1156 15th Street NW, Suite 800, Washington DC
20005. 202/776-0212. World Wide Web address:
http://www.symphony.org.

**AMERICAN ZOO AND AQUARIUM
ASSOCIATION**
8403 Colesville Road, Suite 710, Silver Spring MD
20910. 301/562-0777. E-mail address: azaoms@aol.
com. World Wide Web address: http://www.aza.org.
Publishes a monthly newspaper with employment
opportunities for members.

AMERICANS FOR THE ARTS
One East 53rd Street, 2nd Floor, New York NY
10022. 212/223-2787. World Wide Web address:
http://www.artsusa.org. A nonprofit organization for
the literary, visual, and performing arts. Supports K-
12 education and promotes public policy through
meetings, forums, and seminars.

**ASSOCIATION OF INDEPENDENT VIDEO
AND FILMMAKERS**
304 Hudson Street, 6th Floor, New York NY 10013.
212/807-1400. World Wide Web address: http://www.
aivf.org.

**THE CENTER FOR THE STUDY OF SPORT IN
SOCIETY**
360 Huntington Avenue, Suite 161 CP, Boston MA
02115. 617/373-4025. World Wide Web address:

http://www.sportinsociety.org. Develops programs and provides publications on the interaction of sports and society.

NATIONAL ARTISTS' EQUITY ASSOCIATION
P.O. Box 28068, Central Station, Washington DC 20038-8068. 202/628-9633. A national, nonprofit organization dedicated to improving economic, health, and legal conditions for visual artists.

NATIONAL ENDOWMENT FOR THE ARTS
1100 Pennsylvania Avenue NW, Washington DC 20506. 202/682-5400. World Wide Web address: http://www.arts.endow.gov.

NATIONAL RECREATION AND PARK ASSOCIATION
22377 Belmont Ridge Road, Ashburn VA 20148. 703/858-0784. Fax: 703/858-0794. World Wide Web address: http://www.nrpa.org. A national, nonprofit service organization. Offers professional development and training opportunities in recreation, parks, and leisure services. Publishes a newsletter and magazine that offer employment opportunities for members only.

PRODUCERS GUILD OF AMERICA
400 South Beverly Drive, Suite 211, Beverly Hills CA 90212. 310/557-0807. Fax: 310/557-0436. World Wide Web address: http://www.producersguild.com. Membership is required, and includes credit union access; subscription to *P.O.V. Magazine* and the association newsletter; attendance at the organization's annual Golden Laurel Awards and other events; and special screenings of motion pictures at the time of the Academy Awards.

Directories

ARTIST'S AND GRAPHIC DESIGNER'S MARKET
Writer's Digest Books, 1507 Dana Avenue, Cincinnati OH 45207. 513/531-2222.

BLACK BOOK ILLUSTRATION
The Black Book, 10 Astor Place, 6th Floor, New York NY 10003. 212/539-9800. World Wide Web address: http://www.blackbook.com.

BLACK BOOK PHOTOGRAPHY
The Black Book, 10 Astor Place, 6th Floor, New York NY 10003. 212/539-9800. World Wide Web address: http://www.blackbook.com.

PLAYERS GUIDE
165 West 46th Street, Suite 1305, New York NY 10036. 212/869-3570.

ROSS REPORTS TELEVISION AND FILM
BPI Communications, Inc., 1515 Broadway, 14th Floor, New York NY 10036-8986. 212/764-7300.

Magazines

AMERICAN CINEMATOGRAPHER
American Society of Cinematographers, 1782 North Orange Drive, Hollywood CA 90028. 213/969-4333. World Wide Web address: http://www.cinematographer.com.

ARTFORUM
65 Bleecker Street, 13th Floor, New York NY 10012. 212/475-4000. World Wide Web address: http://www.artforum.com.

AVISO
American Association of Museums, 1575 Eye Street NW, Suite 400, Washington DC 20005. 202/289-1818.

BACK STAGE
Billboard Publications, Inc., 1515 Broadway, New York NY 10036-8986. 212/764-7300. World Wide Web address: http://www.backstage.com.

BILLBOARD
Billboard Publications, Inc., 1515 Broadway, New York NY 10036-8986. 212/764-7300. World Wide Web address: http://www.billboard.com.

CRAFTS REPORT
300 Water Street, Box 1992, Wilmington DE 19899. 302/656-2209. World Wide Web address: http://www.craftsreport.com.

DRAMA-LOGUE
P.O. Box 38771, Los Angeles CA 90038. 213/464-5079.

HOLLYWOOD REPORTER
5055 Wilshire Boulevard, 6th Floor, Los Angeles CA 90036. 213/525-2000. World Wide Web address: http://www.hollywoodreporter.com.

VARIETY
245 West 17th Street, 5th Floor, New York NY 10011. 212/337-7001. Toll-free phone: 800/323-4345.

WOMEN ARTIST NEWS
300 Riverside Drive, New York NY 10025. 212/666-6990.

Online Services

AMERICAN CAMPING ASSOCIATION
http://www.aca-camps.org. Provides listings of jobs at day and overnight camps for children and adults with special needs.

ARTJOB
Gopher://gopher.tmn.com/11/Artswire/artjob. Provides information on jobs, internships, and conferences in theater, dance, opera, and museums. This site is only accessible through America Online.

COOLWORKS
http://www.coolworks.com. Provides links to 22,000 job openings in national parks, summer camps, ski areas, river areas, ranches, fishing areas, cruise ships, and resorts. This site also includes information on volunteer openings.

VISUAL NATION ARTS JOBS LINKS
http://fly.hiwaay.net/%7Edrewyor/art_job.html. Provides links to other sites that post arts and academic job openings and information.

AUTOMOTIVE

In the face of fierce worldwide competition, automotive manufacturers have been forced to lower car prices, grant low interest-rate financing, and offer better deals on leasing. With consumer confidence relatively high, there is a strong buyer's market, but according to Business Week, *auto consumers are also more discriminating than ever.*

Nineteen ninety-eight was a big year for the automotive industry. General Motors survived one of the worst strikes of its 91 year history, resulting in huge financial losses and the delayed introduction of new models. The industry as a whole continues to shift more production to Mexico, where auto production was at 1.5 million in 1998, and is estimated to reach 2.2 million by 2001 as the North American Free Trade Agreement (NAFTA) becomes fully implemented. Nineteen ninety-eight also saw the birth of DaimlerChrysler, the international partnership between Chrysler Corporation and Daimler Benz. It is expected that other automotive companies will follow suit in efforts to trim costs and share resources. Ford, for example, was recently outbid by Hyundai in the sale of Korea's troubled Kia Motors Corporation.

Despite the General Motors strike, industry profits were up 141 percent for the first two quarters of 1998 as compared to the same period of 1997.

CENTURY MANUFACTURING COMPANY
9231 Penn Avenue South, Minneapolis MN 55431. 612/884-3211. **Toll-free phone:** 800/328-2921. **Fax:** 612/886-6405. **Contact:** James Karlin, Human Resources Generalist. **E-mail address:** jekhr@yahoo.com. **World Wide Web address:** http://www.century.com. **Description:** Manufactures battery chargers and testers, portable power supplies, automotive refrigerant and coolant recyclers, arc and MIG welders, plasma cutters, and welding accessories. Brand names include Century, Solar, Booster Pac, Viper, and Cobra. Century Manufacturing serves the automotive aftermarket and retail channels for professional and do-it-yourself automotive and body repair. **NOTE:** Entry-level positions and second and third shifts are offered. **Common positions include:** Administrative Assistant; Computer Operator; Design Engineer; Manufacturing Engineer; Mechanical Engineer; MIS Specialist; Sales Manager; Sales Representative. **Benefits:** 401(k); Dental Insurance; Disability Coverage; Employee Discounts; Flexible Schedule; Job Sharing; Life Insurance; Medical Insurance; Pension Plan; Profit Sharing; Public Transit Available; Savings Plan; Tuition Assistance. **Special programs:** Internships; Co-ops; Summer Jobs. **Internship information:** Internships are offered in the areas of engineering and marketing. **Other U.S. locations:** Bloomington MN; Pierre SD. **International locations:** St. Jean-sur-Richelieu, Quebec, Canada. **Parent company:** Pentair, Inc. (St. Paul MN) is a diversified industrial manufacturer comprised of nine businesses which serve the construction, woodworking, electronics, water conditioning, automotive, and industrial markets. Primary products are electrical and electronic closures, professional tools and equipment, and water and fluid technologies. The company has 54 locations in North America, Europe, and Asia. **President:** Steve Bentson. **Annual sales/revenues:** $51 - $100 million. **Number of employees at this location:** 320. **Number of employees worldwide:** 445.

CRYSTEEL MANUFACTURING
P.O. Box 178, Lake Crystal MN 56055-0178. 507/726-2728. **Contact:** Human Resources. **World Wide Web address:** http://www.crysteel.com. **Description:** Manufactures truck bodies and hoists.

FEDERAL-MOGUL CORPORATION
520 North Eighth Street, Lake City MN 55041. 651/345-4543. **Contact:** Tom Heimer, Human Resources. **Description:** Manufactures engine components and transportation products.

FORD MOTOR COMPANY
TWIN CITIES ASSEMBLY PLANT
966 South Mississippi River Boulevard, St. Paul MN 55116. 651/699-1321. **Contact:** Personnel. **World Wide Web address:** http://www.tcap.ba.ford.com. **Description:** This location is an

automobile assembly plant. Overall, Ford Motor Company is engaged in the design, development, manufacture, and sale of cars, trucks, tractors, and related components and accessories. Ford is also one of the largest providers of financial services in the United States. The company has manufacturing, assembly, and sales affiliates in 29 countries outside the United States. The company's two core businesses are the Automotive Group and the Financial Services Group (Ford Credit, The Associates, USL Capital, and First Nationwide). Ford is also engaged in a number of other businesses, including electronics, glass, electrical and fuel-handling products, plastics, climate control systems, automotive service and replacement parts, vehicle leasing and rental, and land development. **Corporate headquarters location:** Dearborn MI. **Number of employees worldwide:** 300,000.

LUCAS BODY SYSTEMS
P.O. Box 5649, Winona MN 55987. 507/457-3750. **Fax:** 507/454-5977. **Contact:** Human Resources. **Description:** A full-service contract manufacturer of switches and controls, primarily for the automotive industry. Lucas Body Systems operates eight facilities. **Common positions include:** Accountant/Auditor; Blue-Collar Worker Supervisor; Buyer; Computer Operator; Computer Programmer; Cost Estimator; Credit Clerk and Authorizer; Customer Service Representative; Department Manager; Designer; Dispatcher; Draftsperson; Electrical/Electronics Engineer; Employment Interviewer; Financial Manager; Human Resources Manager; Industrial Engineer; Manufacturer's/Wholesaler's Sales Rep.; Marketing Manager; Mechanical Engineer; Millwright; Payroll Clerk; Postal Clerk/Mail Carrier; Purchasing Agent/Manager; Quality Control Supervisor; Receptionist; Software Engineer; Systems Analyst; Tool and Die Maker; Transportation/Traffic Specialist; Truck Driver; Typist/Word Processor. **Educational backgrounds include:** Accounting; Art/Design; Business Administration; Computer Science; Engineering; Finance; Marketing; Physics. **Special programs:** Internships. **Other U.S. locations:** Southfield MI; Rushford MN; Stewartville MN; Ettrick WI; Galesville WI. **Parent company:** Guy F. Atkinson. **Operations at this facility include:** Administration; Research and Development; Sales; Service. **Listed on:** NASDAQ. **Number of employees at this location:** 200. **Number of employees nationwide:** 1,400.

PAM COMPANIES
1105 Xenium Lane North, Suite 100, Plymouth MN 55441. 612/591-5827. **Contact:** Personnel. **World Wide Web address:** http://www.pam-companies.com. **Description:** Distributes automotive parts to retailers and wholesalers. **Corporate headquarters location:** Sioux Falls SD. **Other U.S. locations:** Denver CO; Council Bluffs IA; Boise ID; Fargo ND; Salt Lake City UT. **Listed on:** Privately held. **Number of employees nationwide:** 325.

SHELDAHL INC.
1150 Sheldahl Road, Northfield MN 55057. 507/663-8000. **Contact:** Mr. B.M. Brumbaugh, Vice President of Human Resources. **World Wide Web address:** http://www.sheldahl.com. **Description:** Manufactures flexible plastic circuitry for automotive use.

UNIVERSAL CO-OP INC.
P.O. Box 460, Minneapolis MN 55440. 612/854-0800. **Physical address:** 7801 Metro Park, Bloomington MN 55425. **Contact:** Bryan Morrison, Vice President of Human Resources. **World Wide Web address:** http://www.ucoop.com. **Description:** A wholesaler of automotive parts and supplies.

Note: Because addresses and telephone numbers of smaller companies can change rapidly, we recommend you call each company to verify the information below before inquiring about job opportunities. Mass mailings are not recommended.

Additional small employers:

AUTOMOTIVE REPAIR SHOPS

Harmon Glass Company
4000 Olson Memorial Hwy,
Crystal MN 55422-5351.
612/521-5100.

Pro Stop Truck Service Inc.
2811 Highway 55, St. Paul MN
55121-1406. 612/452-8137.

Waldoch Crafts
13621 Lake Drive NE, Forest
Lake MN 55025-9444. 651/464-
1559.

INDUSTRIAL VEHICLES AND MOVING EQUIPMENT

Valley Craft Inc.
2001 South Highway 61, Lake
City MN 55041-9555. 651/345-
3386.

MOTOR VEHICLE EQUIPMENT WHOLESALE

Allstate Sales Corporation
558 Villuame Avenue, South St.
Paul MN 55075-2445. 651/455-
6500.

**Auto Dealers Exchange
Minneapolis LLC**
PO Box 360, Maple Grove MN
55369-0360. 612/428-8777.

Chesley Freightliner Truck Sales
PO Box 130370, St. Paul MN 55113-0004. 651/636-3400.

Mid-State Auto Auction Inc.
PO Box 100, New York Mills MN 56567-0100. 218/385-3777.

NAPA Auto Parts
PO Box 26250, Minneapolis MN 55426-0250. 612/929-1635.

MOTOR VEHICLES AND EQUIPMENT

Dana Corporation, Spicer Off-Highway Axle Division
PO Box 47520, Minneapolis MN 55447-0520. 612/559-0989.

Eaton Hydraulics
15151 Highway 5, Eden Prairie MN 55344-2018. 612/937-9800.

Horton Inc.
PO Box 9455, Minneapolis MN 55440-9455. 612/331-5931.

Lucas Body Systems
PO Box 708, Rushford MN 55971-0708. 507/864-7753.

Lund International Holdings
911 Lund Blvd, Anoka MN 55303-1090. 612/576-4200.

McNeilus Truck and Manufacturing
PO Box 70, Dodge Center MN 55927-0070. 507/374-6321.

Microtron Inc.
1200 Washington Ave N, Minneapolis MN 55401-1037. 612/338-2580.

New Flyer of America Incorporated
214 5th Ave SW, Crookston MN 56716-2118. 218/281-5752.

North Star Plating Company
PO Box 04, Brainerd MN 56401-3106. 218/829-6324.

St. James Automotive Corporation
240 15th Street South, St. James MN 56081-2437. 507/375-3559.

For more information on career opportunities in the automotive industry:

Associations

AMERICAN AUTOMOBILE MANUFACTURERS ASSOCIATION
1401 H Street NW, Suite 900, Washington DC 20005. 202/326-5500. Fax: 202/326-5567. World Wide Web address: http://www.aama.com. A trade association. Sponsors research projects, distributes publications, and reviews social and public policies pertaining to the motor vehicle industry and its customers.

ASSOCIATION OF INTERNATIONAL AUTOMOBILE MANUFACTURERS, INC.
1001 North 19th Street, Suite 1200, Arlington VA 22209. 703/525-7788. World Wide Web address: http://www.aiam.org.

AUTOMOTIVE SERVICE ASSOCIATION
P.O. Box 929, Bedford TX 76095. 817/283-6205. World Wide Web address: http://www.asashop.org. Works with shops to find workers. Publishes a monthly magazine with classified advertisements.

AUTOMOTIVE SERVICE INDUSTRY ASSOCIATION
25 Northwest Point Boulevard, Suite 425, Elk Grove Village IL 60007-1035. 847/228-1310. World Wide Web address: http://www.aftmkt.com/asia. Members are manufacturers and distributors of automobile replacement parts. Sponsors a trade show. Publishes educational guidebooks and training manuals.

Directories

AUTOMOTIVE NEWS MARKET DATA BOOK
Crain Communications, Automotive News, 1400 Woodbridge Avenue, Detroit MI 48207-3187. 313/446-6000.

WARD'S AUTOMOTIVE YEARBOOK
Ward's Communications, Inc., 3000 Town Center, Suite 2750, Southville MI 48075. 248/357-0800. World Wide Web address: http://www.wardsauto.com.

Magazines

AUTOMOTIVE INDUSTRIES
Cahners Business Information, 201 King of Prussia Road, Radnor PA 19089. 610/964-4000.

AUTOMOTIVE NEWS
Crain Communications, 1400 Woodbridge Avenue, Detroit MI 48207-3187. 313/446-6000.

WARD'S AUTO WORLD
WARD'S AUTOMOTIVE REPORTS
Ward's Communications, Inc., 3000 Town Center, Suite 2750, Southville MI 48075. 248/357-0800. World Wide Web address: http://www.wardsauto.com.

BANKING/SAVINGS AND LOANS

Though the banking industry is expected to experience 10 to 20 percent job growth through 2006, it is still plagued by uncertainty heading into 2000. Mergers and acquisitions continue to be the norm, as in the case of the mega-merger between Citicorp and Travelers Group, with combined assets in excess of $700 billion. The Asian crisis continues to loom abroad, and the Year 2000 computer glitch is causing concerns for many banks. Although most banks remain unscathed and continue to prosper, some are still losing ground to security houses and financial divisions of large corporations. According to Standard & Poor, the industry saw a 15 percent increase in profits in the second quarter of 1998 from the second quarter of 1997, as well as an increase in profit margins.

An increasing number of smaller banks are finding the mega-mergers to be good for business. More and more consumers are choosing to take their money out of banking conglomerates and are giving their business to smaller, more personalized community banks. In fact, Business Week reports that even analysts in the field are beginning to lose faith in the promised efficiency of the mega-mergers of 1997.

One successful banking trend is automation. Automated teller machines (ATMs) will begin to offer more services including check cashing and printouts of account information. Jobseekers will find less opportunities as bank tellers and more opportunities as call center customer service representatives. The Bureau of Labor Statistics expects bank tellers to lose 152,000 jobs by 2005 and projects numerous layoffs for bank office workers and managers.

AGRIBANK, FCB
375 Jackson Street, St. Paul MN 55101. 651/282-8800. **Contact:** Human Resources Manager. **World Wide Web address:** http://www.mainstreet-usa.com. **Description:** A banking institution serving the states of Arkansas, Illinois, Missouri, Michigan, Wisconsin, Minnesota, and North Dakota. **Common positions include:** Accountant/Auditor; Attorney; Financial Analyst. **Benefits:** Dental Insurance; Disability Coverage; Life Insurance; Medical Insurance; Pension Plan; Savings Plan; Tuition Assistance. **Corporate headquarters location:** This Location.

BREMER FINANCIAL SERVICES INC.
445 Minnesota Street, Suite 2000, St. Paul MN 55101. 651/227-7621. **Contact:** Sandra Emmen, Human Resources. **Description:** A bank holding company. **Subsidiaries include:** First American Bank operates banking locations in Minnesota, North Dakota, and Wisconsin.

FEDERAL RESERVE BANK OF MINNEAPOLIS
P.O. Box 291, Minneapolis MN 55480-0291. 612/204-5000. **Fax:** 612/204-5339. **Contact:** Human Resources. **Description:** One of 12 regional Federal Reserve banks that, along with the Federal Reserve Board of Governors in Washington DC and the Federal Open Market Committee, form the Federal Reserve System. As the nation's central bank, the Federal Reserve System is charged with three major responsibilities: monetary policy, banking supervision and regulation, and processing payments. **Common positions include:** Accountant/Auditor; Computer Programmer; Economist; Financial Analyst; Human Resources Manager; Management Analyst/Consultant; Systems Analyst. **Educational backgrounds include:** Accounting; Business Administration; Computer Science; Economics; Finance. **Benefits:** Dental Insurance; Disability Coverage; Life Insurance; Medical Insurance; Savings Plan; Tuition Assistance. **Operations at this facility include:** Administration; Regional Headquarters; Research and Development. **Number of employees at this location:** 1,150.

MARQUETTE BANCSHARES
1650 West 82nd Street, Suite 400, Bloomington MN 55431. 612/948-5611. **Contact:** Deborah Feehan, Vice President of Human Resources. **World Wide Web address:** http://www. marquette.com. **Description:** Marquette Bancshares is a bank holding company affiliated with 32 banks throughout the Midwest. **Corporate headquarters location:** This Location.

NATIONAL CITY BANK OF MINNEAPOLIS
651 Nicollet Mall, Minneapolis MN 55402. 612/904-8306. **Contact:** Personnel Director. **Description:** A banking institution. **Parent company:** National City Bancorporation.

NORWEST BANK
400 West Main Street, Marshall MN 56258. 507/532-4405. **Contact:** Human Resources. **World Wide Web address:** http://www.norwest.com. **Description:** A full-service bank offering corporate and community banking services, credit card products, trusts, investment services, and insurance. **Parent company:** Norwest Corporation (Minneapolis MN) is one of the largest domestic bank holding companies operating 583 branches in 15 western states. The company offers corporate and community banking services, credit card products, trust and investment services, and insurance. Its subsidiaries provide consumer financial, commercial financial, mortgage banking, venture capital, and data processing services, operating more than 2,660 branches and affiliates in all 50 states, Canada, and foreign countries.

NORWEST BANK
P.O. Box 488, Duluth MN 55802. 218/723-2600. **Contact:** Human Resources. **World Wide Web address:** http://www.norwest.com. **Description:** A full-service bank offering corporate and community banking services, credit card products, trusts, investment services, and insurance. **Parent company:** Norwest Corporation (Minneapolis MN) is one of the largest domestic bank holding companies operating 583 branches in 15 western states. The company offers corporate and community banking services, credit card products, trust and investment services, and insurance. Its subsidiaries provide consumer financial, commercial financial, mortgage banking, venture capital, and data processing services, operating more than 2,660 branches and affiliates in all 50 states, Canada, and foreign countries.

NORWEST CORPORATION
Northstar East Building, Suite 1300, 608 Second Avenue South, Minneapolis MN 55479-2118. 612/667-1234. **Contact:** Human Resources. **World Wide Web address:** http://www.norwest.com. **Description:** One of the largest domestic bank holding companies operating 583 branches in 15 western states. The company offers corporate and community banking services, credit card products, trust and investment services, and insurance. Its subsidiaries provide consumer financial, commercial financial, mortgage banking, venture capital, and data processing services, operating more than 2,660 branches and affiliates in all 50 states, Canada, and foreign countries. **Corporate headquarters location:** This Location. **Listed on:** New York Stock Exchange.

RICHFIELD BANK & TRUST
6625 Lyndale Avenue South, Richfield MN 55423. 612/798-3364. **Fax:** 612/798-3191. **Recorded jobline:** 612/798-3222. **Contact:** Human Resources. **Description:** One location of a chain of banks located throughout the Twin Cities metropolitan area. Founded in 1947. **Other area locations:** Bloomington MN; Burnsville MN; Chanhassen MN; Edina MN. **Number of employees nationwide:** 250.

U.S. BANK
601 Second Avenue South, Minneapolis MN 55402. 612/973-1111. **Contact:** Robert Sayer, Human Resources Director. **Description:** A bank. **Parent company:** U.S. Bancorp is one of the largest bank holding companies in the Northwest.

Note: Because addresses and telephone numbers of smaller companies can change rapidly, we recommend you call each company to verify the information below before inquiring about job opportunities. Mass mailings are not recommended.

Additional small employers:

COMMERCIAL BANKS

Firstar Bank
2818 Como Ave SE, Minneapolis MN 55414-2825. 612/625-9500.

Firstar Bank of Minnesota NA
1550 E 79th St, Minneapolis MN 55425-1139. 612/854-2211.

Liberty State Bank
PO Box 64075, St. Paul MN 55164-0075. 651/646-8681.

Marquette Bank NA
PO Box 1000, Minneapolis MN
55480-1000. 612/661-3900.

Merchants National Bank of Winona
PO Box 248, Winona MN 55987-0248. 507/457-1100.

Mid America Bank
175 W Lafayette Frontage Rd, St. Paul MN 55107. 651/227-0881.

Norwest Bank Minnesota NA
55 5th St E, St. Paul MN 55101-2701. 651/291-2211.

Zapp Bank NA
PO Box 887, St. Cloud MN
56302-0887. 320/251-7110.

CREDIT UNIONS

IBM Mid America Employees Federal Credit Union
PO Box 5949, Rochester MN
55903-5949. 507/288-3425.

NWA Federal Credit Union
4 Appletree Sq, Minneapolis MN
55425-1641. 612/726-2073.

US Federal Credit Union
2772 E 82nd St, Minneapolis MN
55425-1365. 612/794-4700.

OFFICES OF BANK HOLDING COMPANIES

FSF Financial Corp.
201 Main St S, Hutchinson MN
55350-2508. 320/234-4500.

SAVINGS INSTITUTIONS

American Express Trust Co.
PO Box 534, Minneapolis MN
55440-0534. 612/671-2992.

For more information on career opportunities in the banking/savings and loans industry:

Associations

AMERICA'S COMMUNITY BANKERS
900 19th Street NW, Suite 400, Washington DC 20006. 202/857-3100. World Wide Web address: http://www.acbankers.org. America's Community Bankers is a trade association representing the expanded thrift industry. Membership is limited to institutions.

AMERICAN BANKERS ASSOCIATION
1120 Connecticut Avenue NW, Washington DC 20036. 202/663-5221. World Wide Web address: http://www.aba.com. American Bankers Association provides banking education and training services, sponsors industry programs and conventions, and publishes articles, newsletters, and the *ABA Service Member Directory*.

Directories

AMERICAN BANK DIRECTORY
Thomson Financial Publications, 4709 West Golf Road, Skokie IL 60076. Toll-free phone: 800/321-3373.

AMERICAN SAVINGS DIRECTORY
Thomson Financial Publications, 4709 West Golf Road, Skokie IL 60076. Toll-free phone: 800/321-3373.

MOODY'S BANK AND FINANCE MANUAL
Moody's Investors Service, Inc., 99 Church Street, 1st Floor, New York NY 10007-2701. 212/553-0300. World Wide Web address: http://www.moodys.com.

RANKING THE BANKS/THE TOP NUMBERS
American Banker, Inc., One State Street Plaza, New York NY 10004. 212/803-6700. World Wide Web address: http://www.americanbanker.com.

Magazines

ABA BANKING JOURNAL
American Bankers Association, 1120 Connecticut Avenue NW, Washington DC 20036. 202/663-5221. World Wide Web address: http://www.aba.com.

BANKERS MAGAZINE
Faulkner & Gray, 11 Penn Plaza, New York NY 10001. Toll-free phone: 800/200-8963.

BANKING STRATEGIES
Bank Administration Institute, One North Franklin, Suite 1000, Chicago IL 60606. Toll-free phone: 800/224-9889. World Wide Web address: http://www.bai.org.

JOURNAL OF LENDING AND CREDIT RISK MANAGEMENT
Robert Morris Associates, 1650 Market Street, Suite 2300, Philadelphia PA 19103. 215/446-4000.

Online Services

JOBS FOR BANKERS
http://www.bankjobs.com. This site provides access to a database of over 9,000 banking-related job openings. Jobs for Bankers is run by Careers, Inc. This Website also includes a resume database.

JOBS IN COMMERCIAL BANKING
http://www.cob.ohio-state.edu/dept/fin/jobs/commbank.htm. Provides information and resources for jobseekers looking to work in the field of commercial banking.

NATIONAL BANKING NETWORK: RECRUITING FOR BANKING AND FINANCE
http://www.banking-financejobs.com. Offers a searchable database of job openings in banking and financial services. The database is searchable by region, keyword, and job specialty.

BIOTECHNOLOGY, PHARMACEUTICALS, AND SCIENTIFIC R&D

The forecast is bright for the biotechnology industry, with the advent of new technologies in drug research and a heightened demand for prescription drugs of all types. As noted in The Wall Street Journal *and* The New York Times, *biotechnology and pharmaceutical companies, such as Amgen Inc. and Pharmacia & Upjohn, were experiencing strong earnings during the latter half of 1998. According to the Bureau of Labor Statistics, biological and medical scientists in particular can expect a 21 to 35 percent increase in the number of jobs through 2006. However, a large portion of research money comes from the federal government, funding which is expected to decline in coming years.*

Large drug companies are preparing to release a plethora of new products and continue to face competition from generic drug makers. Advances in genetic research offer promising new developments, but capitalizing on them requires significant investment. Therefore, those companies with bigger research budgets currently dominate. However, a trend is developing whereby large drug companies form partnerships with smaller biotechnology firms that provide them with research services. Often, these partnerships allow a drug to move through the development process faster, thereby gaining FDA approval much sooner.

Among the industry leaders in breakthrough drug development is Merck & Company, Inc., which plans to introduce new painkillers; antidepressants; and drugs for arthritis, male pattern baldness, and asthma. Analysts project that Merck's new asthma drug, Singulair, could reap $1.5 billion in sales within the next three years. Other drug manufacturers anticipate new drugs for hepatitis-B as well as new AIDS drug combinations. In addition, drug-delivery companies are working to improve the ways in which drugs are absorbed by the body.

APOTHECARY PRODUCTS
11531 Rupp Drive, Burnsville MN 55337. 612/890-1940. **Contact:** Human Resources. **Description:** Manufactures pharmaceutical products for compounding.

BECKMAN COULTER
1000 Lake Hazeltine Drive, Chaska MN 55318-1084. 612/448-4848. **Contact:** Human Resources Manager. **World Wide Web address:** http://www.beckman.com. **Description:** A manufacturer of diagnostic test kits. **Common positions include:** Accountant/Auditor; Biological Scientist; Chemist; Electrical/Electronics Engineer; General Manager; Manufacturer's/Wholesaler's Sales Rep.; Marketing Specialist; Mechanical Engineer; Quality Control Supervisor; Systems Analyst. **Benefits:** Dental Insurance; Disability Coverage; Employee Discounts; Life Insurance; Medical Insurance; Pension Plan; Savings Plan; Tuition Assistance. **Operations at this facility include:** Administration; Manufacturing; Research and Development; Sales; Service.

CENTER FOR DIAGNOSTIC IMAGING
5775 Wayzata Boulevard, Suite 190, Minneapolis MN 55416. 612/541-1840. **Contact:** Human Resources. **Description:** A diagnostic laboratory performing CAT scans and MRIs.

CIMA LABS INC.
10000 Valley View Road, Eden Prairie MN 55344. 612/947-8700. **Fax:** 612/947-8770. **Contact:** Ron Gay, Human Resources. **Description:** Develops, formulates, and manufactures a pharmaceutical drug delivery system. The company's main product is a fast-dissolving tablet for

individuals who have difficulty swallowing pills. Founded in 1986. **NOTE:** Entry-level positions are offered. **Corporate headquarters location:** This Location. **Listed on:** NASDAQ. **Stock exchange symbol:** CIMA. **Annual sales/revenues:** $5 - $10 million. **Number of employees at this location:** 70.

DIASORIN
1990 Industrial Boulevard, P.O. Box 285, Stillwater MN 55082. 651/439-9710. **Contact:** Human Resources. **World Wide Web address:** http://www.incstar.com. **Description:** DiaSorin manufactures medical testing kits.

IMMUNOCHEMISTRY TECHNOLOGIES, LLC
9401 James Avenue South, Suite 155, Bloomington MN 55431. 612/888-8788. **Toll-free phone:** 800/829-3194. **Contact:** Sally Hed, Vice President of Marketing. **World Wide Web address:** http://www.mm.com/ichem. **Description:** Develops, manufactures, and optimizes custom-designed immunoassays in kit form. Immunochemistry Technologies also provides protein purification, modification, and conjugation services, as well as antibody production. Founded in 1994. **NOTE:** The company offers entry-level positions. **Common positions include:** Biochemist; Biological Scientist; Chemist; Clinical Lab Technician; Market Research Analyst. **Educational backgrounds include:** Biology; Business Administration; Chemistry; Marketing. **Benefits:** Medical Insurance. **Special programs:** Internships; Apprenticeships. **Corporate headquarters location:** This Location. **Listed on:** Privately held. **President:** Gary L. Johnson. **Annual sales/revenues:** Less than $5 million. **Number of employees at this location:** 15.

MEDTOX LABORATORIES
402 West County Road D, St. Paul MN 55112-3522. 651/636-7466. **Contact:** Human Resources. **World Wide Web address:** http://www.medtox.com. **Description:** A drug testing and toxicology laboratory.

NOVARTIS NUTRITION
P.O. Box 370, Minneapolis MN 55440. **Contact:** Human Resources. **World Wide Web address:** http://www.novartis.com. **Description:** Manufactures medical supplements, nutritional supplements, food service products, and weight management systems for medical and institutional businesses.

PADDOCK LABORATORIES, INC.
3940 Quebec Avenue North, Minneapolis MN 55427. 612/546-4676. **Toll-free phone:** 800/328-5113. **Fax:** 612/546-4842. **Contact:** Human Resources. **World Wide Web address:** http://www.paddocklabs.com. **Description:** Manufactures generic pharmaceuticals.

PROTEIN DESIGN LABS, INC.
3955 Annapolis Lane, Plymouth MN 55447. 612/551-1778. **Contact:** Human Resources. **World Wide Web address:** http://www.pdl.com. **Description:** Researches biological pharmaceuticals.

R&D SYSTEMS
TECHNE CORPORATION
614 McKinley Place NE, Minneapolis MN 55413. 612/379-2956. **Toll-free phone:** 800/328-2400. **Contact:** Lea Simoane, Human Resources Manager. **World Wide Web address:** http://www.rndsystems.com. **Description:** R&D Systems is a supplier of cytokine and related reagents to research institutions. **Corporate headquarters location:** This Location. **Parent company:** Techne Corporation (also at this location) is a holding company whose subsidiaries manufacture hematology control products, biotech products, and biological products. **Number of employees at this location:** 190.

SMITHKLINE BEECHAM CLINICAL LABORATORIES
P.O. Box 629, Minneapolis MN 55440. 651/635-1500. **Physical address:** 600 West County Road D, New Brighton MN 55112. **Contact:** Human Resources. **World Wide Web address:** http://www.sb.com. **Description:** One of the largest clinical laboratories in North America, providing a broad range of clinical laboratory services to more than 50,000 health care and industry clients. The company offers and performs 1,500 tests on blood, urine, and other bodily fluids and tissues to provide information for health and well-being. SmithKline Beecham Clinical Laboratories was among the first to receive certification from the U.S. government's National Institute on Drug Abuse. The company operates 24 laboratories throughout the U.S., as well as an additional 300 testing sites and specimen collection centers to support these labs. Labs are staffed by certified technologists, including more than 200 physicians and Ph.D.s. The company performs more than 56 million tests a year. Clients include physicians, hospitals, clinics, dialysis centers, pharmaceutical companies, and corporations. **Parent company:** SmithKline Beecham Corporation

is a health care company engaged in the research, development, manufacture, and marketing of ethical pharmaceuticals, animal health products, ethical and proprietary medicines, and eye care products. In addition to SmithKline Beecham Clinical Laboratories, the company's principal divisions include SmithKline Beecham Pharmaceuticals, SmithKline Beecham Animal Health, and SmithKline Beecham Consumer Healthcare. The company is also engaged in many other aspects of the health care field including the production of medical and electronic instruments. SmithKline Beecham Corporation manufactures proprietary medicines through its subsidiary, Menley & James Laboratories, including such products as Contac Cold Capsules, Sine-Off sinus medicine, Love cosmetics, and Sea & Ski outdoor products.

SOLVAY PHARMACEUTICALS
P.O. Box 370, Baudette MN 56623. 218/634-1866. **Contact:** Human Resources. **World Wide Web address:** http://www.solvay.com. **Description:** This location develops a variety of prescription pharmaceuticals used to treat psychiatric, hormonal, and gastrointestinal disorders. **Other U.S. locations:** Marietta GA.

UPSHER-SMITH LABORATORIES
14905 23rd Avenue North, Minneapolis MN 55447. 612/475-3023. **Contact:** Human Resources. **Description:** Manufactures prescription and nonprescription pharmaceuticals.

VIROMED LABORATORIES
6101 Blue Circle Drive, Minneapolis MN 55343-9108. 612/931-0077. **Contact:** Jeanne Kokx, Human Resources Department. **Description:** A medical laboratory that provides testing services for hospitals.

For more information on career opportunities in biotechnology, pharmaceuticals, and scientific R&D:

Associations

AMERICAN ASSOCIATION FOR CLINICAL CHEMISTRY
2101 L Street NW, Suite 202, Washington DC 20037-1526. 202/857-0717. Toll-free phone: 800/892-1400. World Wide Web address: http://www.aacc.org. International scientific/medical society of individuals involved with clinical chemistry and other clinical lab science-related disciplines.

AMERICAN ASSOCIATION OF COLLEGES OF PHARMACY
1426 Prince Street, Alexandria VA 22314-2841. 703/739-2330. World Wide Web address: http://www. aacp.org. An organization composed of all U.S. pharmacy colleges and over 2,000 school administrators and faculty members. Career publications include *Shall I Study Pharmacy?*, *Pharmacy: A Caring Profession*, and *A Graduate Degree in the Pharmaceutical Sciences: An Option For You?*

AMERICAN ASSOCIATION OF PHARMACEUTICAL SCIENTISTS
1650 King Street, Suite 200, Alexandria VA 22314-2747. 703/548-3000. World Wide Web address: http://www.aaps.org.

THE AMERICAN COLLEGE OF CLINICAL PHARMACY (ACCP)
3101 Broadway, Suite 380, Kansas City MO 64111. 816/531-2177. World Wide Web address: http://www. accp.com. Operates ClinNet jobline at 412/648-7893 for members only.

AMERICAN PHARMACEUTICAL ASSOCIATION
2215 Constitution Avenue NW, Washington DC 20037-2985. 202/628-4410. World Wide Web address: http://www.aphanet.org.

AMERICAN SOCIETY FOR BIOCHEMISTRY AND MOLECULAR BIOLOGY
9650 Rockville Pike, Bethesda MD 20814-3996. 301/530-7145. Fax: 301/571-1824. World Wide Web address: http://www.faseb.org/asbmb. A nonprofit scientific and educational organization whose primary scientific activities are in the publication of the *Journal of Biological Chemistry* and holding an annual scientific meeting. Also publishes a career brochure entitled *Unlocking Life's Secrets: Biochemistry and Molecular Biology*.

AMERICAN SOCIETY OF HEALTH-SYSTEM PHARMACISTS
7272 Wisconsin Avenue, Bethesda MD 20814. 301/657-3000. World Wide Web address: http://www. ashp.org. Provides pharmaceutical education. Updates pharmacies on current medical developments. Offers a service for jobseekers for a fee.

BIOTECHNOLOGY INDUSTRY ORGANIZATION (BIO)
1625 K Street NW, Suite 1100, Washington DC 20006-1604. 202/857-0244. Fax: 202/857-0237. World Wide Web address: http://www.bio.org. Represents agriculture, biomedical, diagnostic, food, energy, and environmental companies. Publishes a profile of the U.S. biotechnology industry.

INTERNATIONAL SOCIETY FOR PHARMACEUTICAL ENGINEERING
3816 West Linebaugh Avenue, Suite 412, Tampa FL 33624. 813/960-2105. World Wide Web address: http://www.ispe.org.

NATIONAL PHARMACEUTICAL COUNCIL
1894 Preston White Drive, Reston VA 20191. 703/620-6390. Fax: 703/476-0904. National Pharmaceutical Council is an organization of research-based pharmaceutical companies.

Directories

DRUG TOPICS RED BOOK
Medical Economics Company, 5 Paragon Drive,
Montvale NJ 07645. 201/358-7200.

Magazines

PHARMACEUTICAL ENGINEERING
International Society for Pharmaceutical Engineering,
3816 West Linebaugh Avenue, Suite 412, Tampa FL
33624. 813/960-2105. World Wide Web address:
http://www.ispe.org.

Online Services

MEDZILLA
E-mail address: info@medzilla.com. World Wide
Web address: http://www.medzilla.com. Lists job
openings for professionals in the fields of
biotechnology, health care, medicine, and science
related industries.

Visit our exciting job and career site at http://www.careercity.com

BUSINESS SERVICES AND NON-SCIENTIFIC RESEARCH

 Standard & Poor *forecasted 7.5 percent growth across the board for the business services industry in 1998. This sector covers a broad range of services, from adjustment and collection to data processing. While the outlook varies depending on the service, in general, the business services sector is among the fastest-growing in the nation. In fact, the Bureau of Labor Statistics expects computer and data processing services to be the fastest-growing industry through 2006.*

Steady consolidation across many industries continued to result in a greater need for services in 1998, from temporary help to consulting and engineering services. Security firms expect a significant boost in employment through the year 2005, due to increased concern about crime and vandalism, and the surge in commercial use of sophisticated computer equipment and guards trained to operate such equipment.

AMERIPRIDE SERVICES
47 South Ninth Street, Minneapolis MN 55402. 612/371-4200. **Contact:** Bob Tabolich, Personnel Director. **World Wide Web address:** http://www.ameripride.com. **Description:** A linen and uniform rental and supply company.

THE BARBERS
HAIRSTYLING FOR MEN & WOMEN, INC.
300 Industrial Boulevard NE, Minneapolis MN 55413. 612/331-8500. **Contact:** Donna Hazelton, Vice President of Human Resources. **Description:** A franchiser of Cost Cutters and City Looks beauty salons. The Barbers also owns corporate salons. **Common positions include:** Accountant/Auditor; Buyer; Computer Programmer; Cosmetologist; Credit Manager; Customer Service Representative; Draftsperson; Financial Analyst; Human Resources Manager; Purchasing Agent/Manager. **Educational backgrounds include:** Accounting; Business Administration; Cosmetology; Finance; Marketing. **Benefits:** 401(k); Dental Insurance; Disability Coverage; Employee Discounts; Life Insurance; Medical Insurance; Profit Sharing; Tuition Assistance. **Corporate headquarters location:** This Location. **Operations at this facility include:** Administration; Sales. **Listed on:** NASDAQ. **Number of employees at this location:** 75. **Number of employees nationwide:** 300.

CERIDIAN CORPORATION
8100 34th Avenue South, Bloomington MN 55425. 612/853-8100. **Contact:** Human Resources. **World Wide Web address:** http://www.ceridian.com. **Description:** Provides payroll processing and other employer services, media and market research, and network services to business customers worldwide. Ceridian Corporation also provides technology-based services and products to government customers worldwide. **Corporate headquarters location:** This Location. **Subsidiaries include:** Arbitron Company, a full-service media and marketing information firm serving customers in broadcast advertising; Ceridian Employer Services, which provides information management and data processing services that help customers accomplish functions related to the employment, compensation, and management of their workforces; and Ceridian Network Services, providing services based on computer and network technologies.

DATA RECOGNITION CORPORATION
5900 Baker Road, Minnetonka MN 55345. 612/935-5900. **Fax:** 612/945-7301. **Recorded jobline:** 612/945-7354. **Contact:** Tara Gundacker, Human Resources. **World Wide Web address:** http://www.drc-mn.com. **Description:** Processes educational tests and surveys. **NOTE:** Entry-level positions and second and third shifts are offered. **Common positions include:** Account Manager; Accountant/Auditor; Administrative Assistant; Blue-Collar Worker Supervisor; Computer Operator; Computer Programmer; Controller; Customer Service Representative; Finance Director; Human Resources Manager; Marketing Manager; Operations Manager; Project Manager; Sales Representative; Secretary; Typist/Word Processor. **Educational backgrounds include:** Accounting; Computer Science; Finance. **Benefits:** 401(k); Dental Insurance; Disability Coverage;

Life Insurance; Medical Insurance; Public Transit Available; Savings Plan; Tuition Assistance. **Special programs:** Internships. **Corporate headquarters location:** This Location. **Listed on:** Privately held. **Number of employees at this location:** 150.

DYNAMARK, INC.
4295 Lexington Avenue North, St. Paul MN 55126. 651/482-8593. **Contact:** Human Resources. **World Wide Web address:** http://www.dynamark.com. **Description:** Dynamark, Inc. provides data processing, database management, and personalized printing services to organizations engaged in direct marketing. **Parent company:** Fair, Isaac and Company is a leading developer of data management systems and services for the consumer credit, personal lines insurance, and direct marketing industries. Fair, Isaac employs various tools such as database enhancement software, predictive modeling, adaptive control, and systems automation.

G&K SERVICES INC.
5995 Opus Parkway, Suite 500, Minnetonka MN 55343. 612/912-5500. **Contact:** Erin Daniels, Human Resources. **World Wide Web address:** http://www.gkcares.com. **Description:** A linen supply service. **Corporate headquarters location:** This Location.

MARSDEN BUILDING MAINTENANCE COMPANY
1717 University Avenue, St. Paul MN 55104. 651/641-1717. **Fax:** 651/523-6629. **Contact:** Patricia Thomas, Human Resources Manager. **Description:** Marsden Building Maintenance Company provides contract janitorial services. **Common positions include:** Automotive Mechanic; Blue-Collar Worker Supervisor; Computer Programmer; Heating/AC/Refrigeration Technician; Human Resources Manager; Management; Management Trainee; Operations/ Production Manager; Security Officer. **Educational backgrounds include:** Accounting; Business Administration; Communications; Computer Science; Liberal Arts. **Benefits:** 401(k); Dental Insurance; Medical Insurance; Performance Bonus. **Corporate headquarters location:** This Location. **Other U.S. locations:** Des Moines IA.

PINKERTON SECURITY & INVESTIGATION SERVICES
7300 France Avenue South, Suite 130, Edina MN 55435. 612/831-7143. **Contact:** Human Resources Department. **World Wide Web address:** http://www.pinkerton.com. **Description:** This location is a district office of the international investigation and security company. Overall, Pinkerton Security & Investigative Services offers a full range of specialized protective services including premier property/high-rise services, health care/hospital services, special event services, ATM services, and patrol services. The company also provides thousands of companies worldwide with investigation services, threat assessment services, and executive protection. **Common positions include:** Administrative Worker/Clerk; Investigator; Security Officer. **Educational backgrounds include:** High School Diploma/GED. **Benefits:** Employee Discounts. **Corporate headquarters location:** Encino CA. **Other U.S. locations:** Santa Ana CA; Denver CO; Atlanta GA; Las Vegas NV; El Paso TX; Appleton WI. **International locations:** Worldwide. **Operations at this facility include:** Administration; Divisional Headquarters; Sales; Service. **Listed on:** NASDAQ. **Number of employees at this location:** 300. **Number of employees nationwide:** 47,000.

QUESTAR DATA SYSTEMS, INC.
2905 West Service Road, Eagan MN 55121. 651/688-0089. **Toll-free phone:** 800/959-8755. **Fax:** 651/688-0689. **Recorded jobline:** 651/683-4750. **Contact:** Human Resources Department. **World Wide Web address:** http://www.questarweb.com. **Description:** Questar Data Systems, Inc. is a full-service survey research and consulting firm that works with clients to develop, conduct, and analyze surveys in the areas of public sector research, organizational consulting, and service quality research. **NOTE:** The company offers entry-level positions. **Common positions include:** Account Representative; Administrative Assistant; Computer Programmer; Customer Service Representative; Marketing Specialist; MIS Specialist; Project Manager; Quality Control Supervisor; Sales Representative; Systems Analyst; Technical Writer/Editor; Typist/Word Processor. **Educational backgrounds include:** Business Administration; Computer Science; Marketing; Mathematics; Social Science. **Benefits:** 401(k); Dental Insurance; Disability Coverage; Employee Discounts; Life Insurance; Medical Insurance; Profit Sharing; Tuition Assistance. **Corporate headquarters location:** This Location. **Listed on:** Privately held. **Annual sales/revenues:** $11 - $20 million. **Number of employees at this location:** 170.

REGIS CORPORATION
7201 Metro Boulevard, Minneapolis MN 55439. 612/947-7777. **Contact:** Human Resources. **Description:** Operates a chain of beauty salons.

SCICOM DATA SERVICES

10101 Bren Road East, Minnetonka MN 55343. 612/933-4200. **Contact:** John Honzl, Vice President of Finance. **World Wide Web address:** http://www.scicom.com. **Description:** Provides document and mail processing services, marketing publication services, and information management.

Note: Because addresses and telephone numbers of smaller companies can change rapidly, we recommend you call each company to verify the information below before inquiring about job opportunities. Mass mailings are not recommended.

Additional small employers:

ADJUSTMENT AND COLLECTION SERVICES

Chex Systems Collection Agency
1550 E 79th St, Ste 700, Minneapolis MN 55425-3101. 612/854-3422.

Diversified Adjustment Services Inc.
PO Box 32145, Minneapolis MN 55432-0145. 612/780-1042.

Metro Collections
PO Box 59207, Minneapolis MN 55459-0207. 612/944-7575.

Risk Management Alternatives
1500 Commerce Dr, Mendota Heights MN 55120-1023. 651/234-1184.

CREDIT REPORTING SERVICES

Equifax Credit Information Services
PO Box 1142, Minneapolis MN 55440-1142. 612/591-9214.

DETECTIVE, GUARD, AND ARMORED CAR SERVICES

American Commercial Security Services
13220 County Road 6, Plymouth MN 55441-3832. 612/550-9787.

American Security Corporation
1717 University Avenue W, St. Paul MN 55104-3613. 651/644-1155.

Burns International Security Services
1350 Energy Lane, Ste 205, St. Paul MN 55108-5254. 651/644-7000.

General Security Services
9110 Meadowview Rd, Minneapolis MN 55425-2458. 612/858-5000.

Globe Airport Security Services
4300 Glumack Dr, Rm 2459, St. Paul MN 55111-3002. 612/725-6423.

Hannon Security Services Inc.
9036 Grand Ave S, Minneapolis MN 55420-3634. 612/881-5865.

Retail Merchandising Services Inc.
12935 16th Ave N, Plymouth MN 55441-4560. 612/553-7732.

Stanley Smith Security Inc.
1611 County Road B W, Roseville MN 55113-4053. 612/844-0268.

SECURITY SYSTEMS SERVICES

ADT Security Services Inc.
2561 Territorial Rd, St. Paul MN 55114-1500. 651/917-0000.

Avalon Security Corporation
9697 East River Road, Coon Rapids MN 55433-5514. 612/755-9133.

Floyd Total Security
9036 Grand Avenue S, Minneapolis MN 55420-3634. 612/881-5625.

General Security Services
1610 Maple Grove Rd, Duluth MN 55811-1868. 218/726-1606.

For more information on career opportunities in miscellaneous business services and non-scientific research:

Associations

AMERICAN SOCIETY OF APPRAISERS
P.O. Box 17265, Washington DC 20041. 703/478-2228. Toll-free phone: 800/ASA-VALU. Fax: 703/742-8471. World Wide Web address: http://www.appraisers.org. An international, nonprofit, independent appraisal organization. ASA teaches, tests, and awards designations.

EQUIPMENT LEASING ASSOCIATION OF AMERICA
4301 North Fairfax Drive, Suite 550, Arlington VA 22203. 703/527-8655. World Wide Web address: http://www.elaonline.com.

NATIONAL ASSOCIATION OF PERSONNEL SERVICES
3133 Mt. Vernon Avenue, Alexandria VA 22305.
703/684-0180. Fax: 703/684-0071. World Wide Web address: http://www.napsweb.org. Provides federal legislative protection, education, certification, and business products and services to its member employment service agencies.

Online Services

INTERNET BUSINESS OPPORTUNITY SHOWCASE
http://www.clark.net./pub/ibos/busops.html. This Website offers links to franchise, small business, and related opportunities.

PLANT MAINTENANCE RESOURCE CENTER
http://www.plant-maintenance.com. A great resource for maintenance professionals offering links to maintenance consultants and vendors; information on conferences; and articles on maintenance.

Visit our exciting job and career site at http://www.careercity.com

CHARITIES AND SOCIAL SERVICES

 Charitable health organizations have come into the spotlight in recent years. The American Heart Association, the Arthritis Foundation, and the American Lung Association have all offered their names (for a fee) to promote the sale of brand name products. Many think that the charities are risking their reputations by choosing one product over another. Even with this controversy, there is still a growing need for professionals to work in charitable organizations. The industry faces a high turnover rate and opportunities are plentiful.

The need for qualified social workers continues to grow as the older population in need of such services increases. Other factors leading to increasing job opportunities include growth of the overall population; an increase in crime rates and juvenile delinquency; a growing number of mentally ill, AIDS patients, and families in crisis; and the need for more social workers to admisnister discharge plans at medical facilities.

ABILITY BUILDING CENTER (ABC)
P.O. Box 6938, Rochester MN 55903. 507/281-6262. **Physical address:** 1911 NW 14th Street, Rochester MN. **Contact:** Human Resources. **Description:** Assists people with disabilities in finding employment.

INDUSTRIES INC.
500 South Walnut, Mora MN 55051. 320/679-2354. **Contact:** Human Resources. **Description:** Provides job training and placement services for individuals who are mentally challenged.

LIGHTHOUSE FOR THE BLIND
4505 West Superior Street, Duluth MN 55807. 218/624-4828. **Contact:** Human Resources. **Description:** Provides sight-impaired and blind people with rehabilitative services, such as Braille instruction and teaching daily living skills.

MANKATO REHABILITATION CENTER (MRCI)
15 Map Drive, Mankato MN 56001. 507/386-5600. **Fax:** 507/345-5991. **Contact:** Human Resources. **Description:** A sheltered workshop for mentally and physically challenged individuals.

OCCUPATIONAL DEVELOPMENT CENTER
245 Fifth Avenue SW, Crookston MN 56716. 218/281-3326. **Contact:** Human Resources. **Description:** Provides disabled people with an environment where they can enhance job skills, and aids them in finding employment.

AMHERST H. WILDER FOUNDATION
919 Lafond Avenue, St. Paul MN 55104. 651/642-4000. **Fax:** 651/642-4068. **Contact:** Jennifer Hawkins, Human Resources. **World Wide Web address:** http://www.wilder.org. **Description:** A nonprofit, human services foundation operating over 100 programs serving people in need. **NOTE:** Entry-level positions are offered. **Common positions include:** Counselor; Human Service Worker; Licensed Practical Nurse; Occupational Therapist; Physical Therapist; Preschool Worker; Psychologist; Registered Nurse; Social Worker; Teacher Aide. **Educational backgrounds include:** Social Work. **Benefits:** Dental Insurance; Disability Coverage; Life Insurance; Medical Insurance; Pension Plan; Savings Plan; Tuition Assistance. **Special programs:** Internships. **Corporate headquarters location:** This Location. **Operations at this facility include:** Administration; Divisional Headquarters; Regional Headquarters; Service. **Number of employees at this location:** 1,300.

Note: Because addresses and telephone numbers of smaller companies can change rapidly, we recommend you call each company to verify the information below before inquiring about job opportunities. Mass mailings are not recommended.

Additional small employers:

MISC. SOCIAL SERVICES

Association of the Deaf
2430 8th St S #44, Moorhead MN
56560-4443. 218/291-1120.

Cedar Valley Conservation Club
PO Box 502, Austin MN 55912-0502. 507/433-4937.

Commonbond Communities
328 Kellogg Blvd W, St. Paul
MN 55102-1900. 651/291-1750.

East Side Neighborhood Services
92 Saint Mary's Ave SE,
Minneapolis MN 55414-3459.
612/331-8676.

Easter Seal Society of Minnesota
2543 Como Ave, St. Paul MN
55108-1216. 651/646-2591.

MCDA
105 5th Ave S, Ste 200,

Minneapolis MN 55401-2521.
612/673-5095.

United Way of Minneapolis Area
404 South Eighth Street,
Minneapolis MN 55404-1027.
612/340-7400.

Western Community Action Inc.
PO Box 207, Jackson MN 56143-0207. 507/847-2632.

For more information on career opportunities in charities and social services:

Associations

ALLIANCE FOR CHILDREN AND FAMILIES
11700 West Lake Park Drive, Park Place, Milwaukee
WI 53224. 414/359-1040. World Wide Web address:
http://www.fsanet.org. Membership required.

AMERICAN COUNCIL OF THE BLIND
1155 15th Street NW, Suite 720, Washington DC
20005. 202/467-5081. World Wide Web address:
http://www.acb.org. Membership required. Offers an
annual conference, a monthly magazine, and
scholarships.

CAREER OPPORTUNITIES
1575 I Street NW, Suite 1190, Washington DC
20005-1168. 202/408-7900. Fax: 202/408-7907.
World Wide Web address: http://www.careeropps.
com. Publishes *CEO Update*, a bimonthly newsletter
which lists job openings at associations and nonprofit
organizations with salaries of at least $50,000 per
year.

NATIONAL ASSOCIATION OF SOCIAL WORKERS
750 First Street NE, Suite 700, Washington DC
20002-4241. 202/408-8600. World Wide Web
address: http://www.naswdc.org.

NATIONAL COUNCIL ON FAMILY RELATIONS
3989 Central Avenue NE, Suite 550, Minneapolis MN
55421. 612/781-9331. Fax: 612/781-9348.
Membership required. Publishes two quarterly
journals. Offers an annual conference and newsletters.

NATIONAL FEDERATION OF THE BLIND
1800 Johnson Street, Baltimore MD 21230. 410/659-9314. World Wide Web address: http://www.nfb.org.
Membership of 50,000 in 600 local chapters.
Publishes a monthly magazine.

NATIONAL MULTIPLE SCLEROSIS SOCIETY
733 Third Avenue, New York NY 10017. 212/986-3240. Toll-free phone: 800/344-4867. World Wide
Web address: http://www.nmss.org. Publishes a
quarterly magazine.

NATIONAL ORGANIZATION FOR HUMAN SERVICE EDUCATION
Brookdale Community College, 765 Newman Springs
Road, Lyncroft NJ 07738. 732/842-1900x546.

Online Services

AMERICAN CAMPING ASSOCIATION
World Wide Web address: http://www.aca-camps.org.
Provides listings of jobs at day and overnight camps
for children and adults with special needs.

COOLWORKS
World Wide Web address: http://www.coolworks.
com. This Website includes information on volunteer
openings. The site also provides links to 22,000 job
openings in national parks, summer camps, ski areas,
river areas, ranches, fishing areas, cruise ships, and
resorts.

NONPROFIT JOBS
World Wide Web address: http://www.philanthropy-journal.org. The *Philanthropy Journal*'s site lists jobs
in nonprofit associations and philanthropic
occupations.

Visit our exciting job and career site at http://www.careercity.com

CHEMICALS/RUBBER AND PLASTICS

Growth in the chemicals industry should be rather weak overall, but some sectors are expected to fare better than others. Since 1996, the industry has done poorly in terms of growth, trade, and earnings, according to the U.S. Department of Commerce. Standard & Poor *reported a 7 percent drop in profits for the chemical industry through the first half of 1998 from the first half of 1997, and profit margins were down as well.*

One of the major consumers of chemicals -- the electrical products sector -- has seen a sharp decline in profits through the first half of 1998. Conversely, two other major industrial consumers -- the housing and automotive industries -- are doing well. Jobseekers with chemical engineering backgrounds will likely find opportunities with specialty chemicals, pharmaceuticals, and plastics manufacturers.

The demand for and production of plastics continues to grow, most notably in the automotive industry. Additionally, industrial use of rubber will expand as the demand for synthetic rubber by the automotive industry increases.

APPLIED COATING TECHNOLOGY INC.
2411 Pilot Knob Road, Mendota Heights MN 55120. 612/454-7777. **Contact:** Human Resources. **Description:** Engaged in silk screening and powder painting.

ASHLAND CHEMICAL COMPANY
ASHLAND ENVIRONMENTAL SERVICES
4401 Valley Industrial Road, Shakopee MN 55379. 612/403-5180. **Contact:** District Manager. **World Wide Web address:** http://www.ashchem.com. **Description:** This location is a distribution center. Overall, Ashland Chemical Company manufactures industrial chemicals and solvents. Ashland Environmental Services (also at this location) provides hazardous waste removal services. **Corporate headquarters location:** Dublin OH. **Parent company:** Ashland Oil Company, Inc.

BROOKDALE PLASTICS INC.
9909 South Shore Drive, Plymouth MN 55441. 612/797-1000. **Toll-free phone:** 800/383-7092. **Fax:** 612/797-5252. **Contact:** Pat Stankovitch, Human Resources. **E-mail address:** brkdale@aol. com. **Description:** Manufactures plastic packing and display products through vacuum-forming and thermoforming processes. Founded in 1963. **NOTE:** The company offers entry-level positions. **Common positions include:** Accountant/Auditor; Administrative Assistant; Applications Engineer; Blue-Collar Worker Supervisor; Buyer; Controller; Customer Service Representative; Design Engineer; Draftsperson; Human Resources Manager; Marketing Manager; Production Manager; Purchasing Agent/Manager; Quality Control Supervisor; Sales Manager; Sales Representative; Secretary. **Educational backgrounds include:** Accounting; Business Administration; Engineering; Finance; Marketing. **Benefits:** 401(k); Daycare Assistance; Dental Insurance; Disability Coverage; Life Insurance; Medical Insurance; Pension Plan; Profit Sharing; Tuition Assistance. **Special programs:** Internships. **Corporate headquarters location:** This Location. **Parent company:** Ameristar Packaging. **Listed on:** Privately held. **Annual sales/revenues:** $5 - $10 million. **Number of employees at this location:** 45.

CARDINAL PACKAGING COMPANY
834 North Seventh Street, Minneapolis MN 55411. 612/332-2100. **Contact:** Phil Boeke, Human Resources. **Description:** Manufactures plastic containers, including ice cream buckets and cups.

CARLISLE PLASTICS, INC.
1401 West 94th Street, Minneapolis MN 55431. 612/884-7281. **Contact:** Ben Crockett, Director of Human Resources. **World Wide Web address:** http://www.carlisle-plastics.com. **Description:** As part of the Plastic Films Group, this location manufactures and markets plastic products including Film-Gard brand plastic sheeting; a full line of sheeting products including construction film for building and remodeling; do-it-yourself products such as drop cloths and landscape films; and agricultural products for farm applications. Carlisle also manufactures Ruffies brand trash bags, Sure Strength high-density plastic trash bags, Color Scents trash bags, Shop Sak heavy-duty clean-

up bags, business and specialty bags, Christmas tree disposable bags, Eco-Choice concentrated high-density plastic trash bags with 33.3 percent recycled plastic content, and the Ultra-Flex proprietary formula of high-density plastic trash bags. In addition, Carlisle also makes private label products including garbage, waste, and tall kitchen household bags; lawn and leaf bags; sandwich bags; and reclosable bags. **Common positions include:** Accountant/Auditor; Buyer; Computer Programmer; Customer Service Representative; Financial Analyst; General Manager; Human Resources Manager; Manager of Information Systems; Manufacturing Engineer; Marketing Specialist; Plant Manager; Production Manager; Sales Representative; Systems Analyst. **Educational backgrounds include:** Accounting; Business Administration; Engineering; Liberal Arts. **Benefits:** 401(k); Dental Insurance; Disability Coverage; Life Insurance; Medical Insurance; Tuition Assistance. **Corporate headquarters location:** Phoenix AZ. **Parent company:** Tyco International, Ltd. **Operations at this facility include:** Divisional Headquarters; Manufacturing; Sales. **Listed on:** New York Stock Exchange. **Number of employees at this location:** 150. **Number of employees nationwide:** 2,100.

COLOR SPECIALTIES INC.
6405 Cedar Avenue, Richfield MN 55423. 612/861-1555. **Contact:** Personnel Manager. **Description:** A manufacturer and distributor of chemicals, bonds, and dyes used in automobile refinishing. **Special programs:** Training.

CONKLIN COMPANY
P.O. Box 155, Shakopee MN 55379. 612/445-6010. **Contact:** Human Resources. **World Wide Web address:** http://www.conklin.com. **Description:** Manufactures lubricants, fertilizers, and cleaning products.

CYTEC FIBERITE INC.
501 West Third Street, Winona MN 55987. 507/452-8038. **Fax:** 507/452-8195. **Contact:** Donald Schneider, Employee Resources Manager. **World Wide Web address:** http://www.cytcc.com. **Description:** A manufacturer of plastic molding compounds. **NOTE:** The company offers entry-level positions as well as second and third shifts. **Common positions include:** Account Representative; Accountant; Buyer; Chemical Engineer; Chemist; Controller; Customer Service Representative; Design Engineer; Draftsperson; Electrical/Electronics Engineer; Electrician; General Manager; Human Resources Manager; Manufacturing Engineer; Marketing Specialist; MIS Specialist; Occupational Therapist; Sales Representative; Secretary. **Educational backgrounds include:** Accounting; Business Administration; Chemistry; Engineering. **Benefits:** 401(k); Dental Insurance; Disability Coverage; Flexible Schedule; Life Insurance; Medical Insurance; Pension Plan; Savings Plan; Tuition Assistance. **Special programs:** Internships; Training. **Corporate headquarters location:** Tempe AZ. **Other U.S. locations:** Orange CA; Delano PA; Greenville TX. **Parent company:** Cytec Industries. **General Manager:** William Wood. **Plant Manager:** Scott Jackels. **Number of employees at this location:** 250.

DAYCO PRODUCTS
4079 Pepin Avenue, Red Wing MN 55066. 651/388-0771. **Contact:** Becky Turner, Director of Personnel. **Description:** A manufacturer of rubber belts for the automotive and machinery industries.

DIVERSIFOAM PRODUCTS
9091 County Road 50, Rockford MN 55373. 612/477-5854. **Contact:** Carl Mura, Personnel Director. **World Wide Web address:** http://www.diversifoam.com. **Description:** A manufacturer of polystyrene insulation and protective packaging. **Corporate headquarters location:** This Location. **Operations at this facility include:** Administration; Manufacturing.

EPC/LOUDON
1020 East Maple Avenue, Mora MN 55051. 320/679-3232. **Contact:** Karleen Crocker, Human Resources Manager. **Description:** Produces custom injection-molded plastics. **Common positions include:** Accountant/Auditor; Buyer; Credit Manager; Human Resources Manager; Industrial Engineer; Manufacturer's/Wholesaler's Sales Rep.; Mechanical Engineer; Purchasing Agent/Manager. **Educational backgrounds include:** Engineering. **Benefits:** Dental Insurance; Disability Coverage; Life Insurance; Medical Insurance; Savings Plan; Tuition Assistance. **Corporate headquarters location:** London. **Operations at this facility include:** Manufacturing; Sales.

H.B. FULLER COMPANY
P.O. Box 64683, St. Paul MN 55164-0683. 651/481-4600. **Fax:** 651/236-5100. **Contact:** Human Resources Department. **World Wide Web address:** http://www.hbfuller.com. **Description:** A worldwide manufacturer of adhesives, sealants, coatings, and specialty chemicals. **Common**

positions include: Accountant/Auditor; Attorney; Chemical Engineer; Chemist; Computer Programmer; Customer Service Representative; Industrial Production Manager; Manufacturer's/ Wholesaler's Sales Rep. **Educational backgrounds include:** Accounting; Chemistry; Engineering; Finance. **Benefits:** 401(k); Daycare Assistance; Dental Insurance; Disability Coverage; Life Insurance; Medical Insurance; Pension Plan; Profit Sharing; Tuition Assistance. **Special programs:** Internships. **Corporate headquarters location:** This Location. **Other U.S. locations:** Nationwide. **Annual sales/revenues:** More than $100 million. **Number of employees at this location:** 300. **Number of employees nationwide:** 2,000. **Number of employees worldwide:** 6,000.

INTERPLASTIC CORPORATION
1225 Willow Lake Boulevard, Vadnais Heights MN 55110. 651/481-6860. **Contact:** Carole Arndt, Human Resources Manager. **Description:** Produces synthetic resins and companion items, polyethylene containers, and sheet molding compound. **Common positions include:** Accountant/Auditor; Budget Analyst; Buyer; Chemical Engineer; Chemist; Clinical Lab Technician; Computer Programmer; Credit Manager; Customer Service Representative; Financial Analyst; Human Resources Manager; Mechanical Engineer; Operations/Production Manager; Paralegal. **Educational backgrounds include:** Accounting; Chemistry; Engineering; Marketing. **Benefits:** 401(k); Dental Insurance; Disability Coverage; Life Insurance; Medical Insurance; Profit Sharing; Tuition Assistance. **Corporate headquarters location:** This Location. **Operations at this facility include:** Administration; Sales. **Listed on:** Privately held. **Number of employees at this location:** 60. **Number of employees nationwide:** 350.

McKECHNIE PLASTIC COMPONENTS
7309 West 27th Street, St. Louis Park MN 55426. 612/929-3312. **Fax:** 612/929-8404. **Contact:** Human Resources Department. **World Wide Web address:** http://www.mckechnie.com. **Description:** A manufacturer of plastic injection molding. **Common positions include:** Accountant/Auditor; Biomedical Engineer; Blue-Collar Worker Supervisor; Buyer; Customer Service Manager; Customer Service Representative; Designer; Human Resources Manager; Industrial Engineer; Mechanical Engineer; Meteorologist; Operations/Production Manager; Quality Control Supervisor; Sales Representative. **Benefits:** 401(k); Dental Insurance; Disability Coverage; Life Insurance; Medical Insurance; Tuition Assistance. **Corporate headquarters location:** This Location.

MINNESOTA RUBBER
3630 Wooddale Avenue, St. Louis Park MN 55416. 612/927-1400. **Contact:** John Camp, Director of Human Resources. **World Wide Web address:** http://www.mnrubber.com. **Description:** Produces precision-molded rubber and plastic parts. **Common positions include:** Accountant/ Auditor; Advertising Clerk; Blue-Collar Worker Supervisor; Chemist; Computer Programmer; Credit Manager; Customer Service Representative; Department Manager; Draftsperson; General Manager; Human Resources Manager; Industrial Engineer; Manufacturer's/Wholesaler's Sales Rep.; Mechanical Engineer; Operations/Production Manager; Purchasing Agent/Manager; Quality Control Supervisor; Systems Analyst. **Benefits:** Dental Insurance; Disability Coverage; Life Insurance; Medical Insurance; Profit Sharing; Savings Plan; Tuition Assistance. **Corporate headquarters location:** This Location. **Parent company:** Quadion Corporation. **Operations at this facility include:** Administration; Divisional Headquarters; Manufacturing; Regional Headquarters; Research and Development; Sales; Service.

NOVUS
10425 Hampshire Avenue South, Minneapolis MN 55438. 612/944-8000. **Fax:** 612/944-2542. **Contact:** Sylvia MacFarland, Manager of Administrative Services. **World Wide Web address:** http://www.novuswsr.com. **Description:** Formulates resins and injects them into stone-damaged windshields for repair. Novus has franchised this process and it is available throughout the United States, Canada, and several foreign countries. The company also manufactures and sells a plastic polish. **Common positions include:** Accountant/Auditor; Administrative Manager; Attorney; Blue-Collar Worker Supervisor; Buyer; Chemist; Clerical Supervisor; Credit Manager; Customer Service Representative; Designer; Industrial Production Manager; Mechanical Engineer; Operations/Production Manager; Paralegal; Purchasing Agent/Manager; Quality Control Supervisor; Systems Analyst. **Educational backgrounds include:** Business Administration; Marketing. **Benefits:** 401(k); Dental Insurance; Disability Coverage; Life Insurance; Medical Insurance; Profit Sharing; Tuition Assistance. **Corporate headquarters location:** This Location. **Parent company:** TCGI. **Operations at this facility include:** Administration; Divisional Headquarters; Manufacturing; Research and Development; Sales; Service. **Listed on:** Canadian Stock Exchange. **Number of employees at this location:** 50.

PLASTECH RESEARCH INC.
P.O. Box 7, Rush City MN 55069. 320/358-4771. **Physical address:** 920 Field Avenue South, Rush City MN 55069. **Fax:** 320/407-5612. **Contact:** Pam McLain, Personnel Manager. **Description:** A manufacturer of assorted plastic products including injection moldings. **Common positions include:** Blue-Collar Worker Supervisor; Computer Programmer; Industrial Engineer; Mechanical Engineer. **Educational backgrounds include:** Engineering. **Special programs:** Internships. **Corporate headquarters location:** This Location. **Other U.S. locations:** Albuquerque NM. **Operations at this facility include:** Administration; Manufacturing. **Listed on:** Privately held. **Number of employees at this location:** 450.

PLASTIC PRODUCTS INC.
30355 Akerson Street, Lindstrom MN 55045. 651/257-5980. **Contact:** Jacquie Stendahl, Personnel. **Description:** A plastics company producing a wide range of injection-molded products. **Number of employees at this location:** 200.

RTI PLASTICS
4400 McMenemy Street, Vadnais Heights MN 55127. 651/490-0007. **Contact:** Human Resources. **World Wide Web address:** http://www.rtihearing.com. **Description:** A manufacturer of injection-molded plastic products, including components for hearing aids for the health care industry. **NOTE:** Jobseekers should contact Shelly Walberg at Human Resources, 1260 Red Fox Road, Arden Hills MN 55112. **Corporate headquarters location:** Arden Hills MN.

RTP COMPANY
MILLER WASTE MILLS
580 East Front Street, Winona MN 55987. 507/454-6900. **Contact:** Human Resources. **World Wide Web address:** http://www.rtpcompany.com. **Description:** Manufactures reinforced and modified thermoplastics. **Parent company:** Miller Waste Mills (also at this location).

3M COTTAGE GROVE
P.O. Box 33131, St. Paul MN 55133. 651/458-2000. **Physical address:** 10746 Innovation Road, Cottage Grove MN 55016-4600. **Contact:** Human Resources Manager. **World Wide Web address:** http://www.3m.com. **Description:** This location manufactures photographic chemicals and supplies. Overall, 3M manufactures products in three sectors: Industrial and Consumer; Information, Imaging, and Electronic; and Life Sciences. The Industrial and Consumer Sector includes a variety of products under brand names including 3M, Scotch, Post-it, Scotch-Brite, and Scotchgard. The Information, Imaging, and Electronic Sector is a leader in several high-growth global industries including telecommunications, electronics, electrical, imaging, and memory media. The Life Sciences Sector serves two broad market categories: health care, and traffic and personal safety. In the health care market, 3M is a leading provider of medical and surgical supplies, drug delivery systems, and dental products; in traffic and personal safety, 3M is a leader in products for transportation safety, worker protection, vehicle and sign graphics, and out-of-home advertising. **Corporate headquarters location:** St. Paul MN. **Listed on:** Amsterdam Stock Exchange; Chicago Stock Exchange; Frankfurt Stock Exchange; New York Stock Exchange; Pacific Stock Exchange; Paris Stock Exchange; Swiss Stock Exchange; Tokyo Stock Exchange.

UFE INC.
P.O. Box 7, Stillwater MN 55082-0007. 651/351-4127. **Physical address:** 1850 South Greeley Street, Stillwater MN 55082. **Fax:** 651/351-4287. **Recorded jobline:** 651/351-4397. **Contact:** Ms. Carmen Robb, Staffing Manager. **Description:** UFE Inc. is a leader in the design and production of precision molded plastic components. Founded in 1953. **NOTE:** The company offers entry-level positions. **Common positions include:** Administrative Assistant; Computer Programmer; Systems Analyst. **Educational backgrounds include:** Business Administration; Computer Science; Engineering. **Benefits:** 401(k); Dental Insurance; Disability Coverage; Employee Discounts; Financial Planning Assistance; Life Insurance; Medical Insurance; Profit Sharing; Tuition Assistance. **Special programs:** Internships; Apprenticeships; Training; Co-ops. **Corporate headquarters location:** This Location. **Other U.S. locations:** El Paso TX; Dresser WI; River Falls WI. **Operations at this facility include:** Administration; Manufacturing; Regional Headquarters; Research and Development; Sales; Service. **Listed on:** Privately held. **Annual sales/revenues:** $51 - $100 million. **Number of employees at this location:** 200. **Number of employees worldwide:** 800.

THE VALSPAR CORPORATION
P.O. Box 1461, Minneapolis MN 55440. 612/332-7371. **Physical address:** 1101 South Third Street, Minneapolis MN. **Contact:** Lisa Van Arman, Human Resources. **Description:** Manufactures paints, varnishes, lacquers, and related products through 22 manufacturing locations. **Common positions include:** Accountant/Auditor; Administrator; Blue-Collar Worker Supervisor;

Buyer; Chemical Engineer; Chemist; Computer Programmer; Credit Manager; Customer Service Representative; Financial Analyst; General Manager; Human Resources Manager; Industrial Production Manager; Manufacturer's/Wholesaler's Sales Rep.; Mechanical Engineer; Operations/ Production Manager; Purchasing Agent/Manager; Systems Analyst. **Educational backgrounds include:** Accounting; Business Administration; Chemistry; Computer Science; Engineering; Finance; Marketing. **Benefits:** 401(k); Daycare Assistance; Dental Insurance; Disability Coverage; Employee Discounts; Life Insurance; Medical Insurance; Pension Plan; Profit Sharing; Savings Plan; Stock Option; Tuition Assistance. **Special programs:** Internships. **Corporate headquarters location:** This Location. **Operations at this facility include:** Administration; Research and Development; Sales; Service. **Listed on:** New York Stock Exchange. **Number of employees nationwide:** 2,500.

VIRATEC THIN FILMS, INC.

2150 Airport Drive, Faribault MN 55021. 507/334-0051. **Fax:** 507/334-0059. **Contact:** Human Resources. **World Wide Web address:** http://www.viratec.com. **Description:** Designs and manufactures high-performance, optical, thin film coatings on both glass and plastic. Founded in 1988. **Corporate headquarters location:** This Location. **Other U.S. locations:** San Diego CA. **Parent company:** Apogee Enterprises, Inc.

Note: Because addresses and telephone numbers of smaller companies can change rapidly, we recommend you call each company to verify the information below before inquiring about job opportunities. Mass mailings are not recommended.

Additional small employers:

ADHESIVES AND SEALANTS

3M Industrial Tape & Specialty Division
2208E 4th St, St. Paul MN 55110-3011. 651/733-1237.

HB Fuller Company
3530 Lexington Ave N, Shoreview MN 55126-8002. 651/481-1588.

CLEANING, POLISHING, AND SANITATION PREPARATIONS

Ecolab Inc.
840 Sibley Hwy, St. Paul MN 55118-1708. 651/451-5667.

PAINTS, VARNISHES, AND RELATED PRODUCTS

HB Fuller Company
2900 Granada Ln N, St. Paul MN 55128-3607. 651/481-9558.

PLASTIC MATERIALS, SYNTHETICS, AND ELASTOMERS

Precision Associates Inc.
740 Washington Ave N, Minneapolis MN 55401-1110. 612/333-7464.

PLASTIC PRODUCTS

Acrotech Midwest Inc.
PO Box 220, Crosby MN 56441-0220. 218/546-5115.

Amcon
5360 Main St NE, Minneapolis MN 55421-1100. 612/574-1044.

Bedford Industries
PO Box 39, Worthington MN 56187-0039. 507/376-4136.

Conwed Plastics
760 770 29th Ave SE, Minneapolis MN 55414. 612/623-1700.

Donnelly Custom Manufacturing Co.
105 Donovan Dr, Alexandria MN 56308-8531. 320/762-2396.

Dyneon LLC
6744 33rd St N, St. Paul MN 55128-3623. 651/733-3295.

Emplast Inc.
233 Industrial Blvd, Waconia MN 55387-1735. 612/975-3500.

Filmtec Corporation
5230 W 73rd St, Minneapolis MN 55439-2204. 612/835-5475.

General Pattern Co. Inc.
3075 84th Ln NE, Minneapolis MN 55449-7215. 612/780-3518.

Genova Minnesota
500 12th St NW, Faribault MN 55021-3743. 507/332-7421.

Holm Industries Inc.
PO Box 187, New Ulm MN 56073-0187. 507/354-3191.

Hood Flexible Packaging
3080 Long Lake Rd, Roseville MN 55113-1050. 651/636-2500.

Illbruck Inc.
3800 Washington Ave N,

Minneapolis MN 55412-2142. 612/521-3555.

Intek Plastics Inc.
800 10th St E, Hastings MN 55033-2217. 651/437-7700.

Juno Inc.
106 Donovan Dr, Alexandria MN 56308-8531. 320/763-6684.

Lakeland Tool and Engineering Inc.
2939 6th Ave, Anoka MN 55303-1144. 612/422-8866.

McKechnie Tooling and Engineering
501 Prairie Ave W, Staples MN 56479-3253. 218/894-1218.

Nordic Ware
5005 Highway 7, Minneapolis MN 55416-2256. 612/920-2888.

Northern Contours Inc.
409 S Robert St, Fergus Falls MN 56537-3137. 218/736-2973.

Olsen Tool and Plastics Inc.
4060 Norex Dr, Chaska MN 55318-3000. 612/448-7892.

Pawnee Rotational Molding LP
PO Box 147, Maple Plain MN 55359-0147. 612/479-3160.

Pearl Baths Inc.
9224 73rd Ave N, Minneapolis MN 55428-1111. 612/424-3335.

Perfecseal Inc.
1301 3rd Ave, Mankato MN 56001-2903. 507/625-1131.

Phoenix Industries
PO Box 455, Crookston MN
56716-0455. 218/281-2065.

Plastic Products Inc.
610 S Old Highway 18, Princeton
MN 55371-2131. 612/389-3683.

Reo Plastics Inc.
11850 93rd Ave N, Maple Grove
MN 55369-3633. 612/425-4171.

S&W Plastics Inc.
10206 Crosstown Cir, Eden
Prairie MN 55344-3304. 612/942-
7760.

Satellite Industries Inc.
2530 Xenium Ln N, Plymouth
MN 55441-3610. 612/553-1900.

SPM Minneapolis
9300 52nd Ave N, Minneapolis
MN 55428-4022. 612/537-8587.

STI Plastics
5338 Shoreline Dr, Mound MN
55364-1630. 612/472-3600.

Ultra Pac Inc.
21925 Industrial Blvd, Rogers
MN 55374-9575. 612/428-8340.

Wirsbo Company
5925 148th St W, Apple Valley
MN 55124-8197. 612/891-2000.

PRINTING INK

Flint Ink Corporation
245 Marie Ave E, St. Paul MN
55118-4007. 651/455-1261.

RUBBER PRODUCTS

Anagram International Inc.
7700 Anagram Dr, Eden Prairie
MN 55344-7305. 612/949-5600.

Stearns Inc.
PO Box 340, Carlton MN 55718-
0340. 218/384-4201.

Stern Rubber Company
PO Box 69, Staples MN 56479-
0069. 218/894-3898.

**SOAP AND OTHER
DETERGENTS**

Ecolab Inc.
940 Lone Oak Rd, St. Paul MN
55121-2214. 612/452-1460.

Softsoap Enterprises Inc.
134 Columbia Ct, Chaska MN
55318-2304. 612/448-4799.

**UNSUPPORTED PLASTIC
PRODUCTS**

**American National Can
Company**
150 26th Ave SE, Minneapolis
MN 55414-3434. 612/378-3300.

Armin Plastics
PO Box 978, Fairmont MN
56031-0978. 507/238-4281.

Atlantis Plastics Inc.
PO Box 4309, Mankato MN
56002-4309. 507/386-4420.

Rexam Medical Packaging
8235 220th St W, Lakeville MN
55044-9013. 612/469-5461.

Strongwell
1610 Highway 52 S, Chatfield
MN 55923-9757. 507/867-3479.

Up North Plastics Inc.
9480 Jamaica Ave S, Cottage
Grove MN 55016-3906. 651/459-
7339.

For more information on career opportunities in the chemicals/rubber and plastics industries:

Associations

**AMERICAN ASSOCIATION FOR CLINICAL
CHEMISTRY**
2101 L Street NW, Suite 202, Washington DC 20037-
1526. 202/857-0717. Toll-free phone: 800/892-1400.
World Wide Web address: http://www.aacc.org.
International scientific/medical society of individuals
involved with clinical chemistry and other clinical lab
science-related disciplines.

AMERICAN CHEMICAL SOCIETY
Career Services, 1155 16th Street NW, Washington
DC 20036. 202/872-4600. World Wide Web address:
http://www.acs.org.

**AMERICAN INSTITUTE OF CHEMICAL
ENGINEERS**
3 Park Avenue, New York NY 10016. 212/591-7338.
Toll-free phone: 800/242-4363. World Wide Web
address: http://www.aiche.org. Provides leadership in
advancing the chemical engineering profession as it
meets the needs of society.

**CHEMICAL MANAGEMENT & RESOURCES
ASSOCIATION**
1255 23rd Street NW, Washington DC 20037.
202/452-1620. Engaged in marketing, marketing
research, business development, and planning for the
chemical and allied process industries. Provides
technical meetings, educational programs, and
publications to members.

**CHEMICAL MANUFACTURERS
ASSOCIATION**
1300 Wilson Boulevard, Arlington VA 22209.
703/741-5000. World Wide Web address: http://www.
cmahq.com. A trade association that develops and

implements programs and services and advocates
public policy that benefits the industry and society.

THE ELECTROCHEMICAL SOCIETY
10 South Main Street, Pennington NJ 08534. 609/737-
1902. An international educational society dealing
with electrochemical issues. Also publishes monthly
journals.

SOAP AND DETERGENT ASSOCIATION
475 Park Avenue South, New York NY 10016.
212/725-1262. World Wide Web address: http://www.
sdahq.org. A trade association and research center.

SOCIETY OF PLASTICS ENGINEERS
P.O. Box 403, Brookfield CT 06804-0403. 203/775-
0471. World Wide Web address: http://www.4spe.org.
Dedicated to helping members attain higher
professional status through increased scientific,
engineering, and technical knowledge.

**THE SOCIETY OF THE PLASTICS INDUSTRY,
INC.**
1801 K Street NW, Suite 600K, Washington DC
20006. 202/974-5200. Promotes the development of
the plastics industry and enhances public
understanding of its contributions while meeting the
needs of society.

Directories

CHEMICAL INDUSTRY DIRECTORY
State Mutual Book and Periodical Service, Order
Department, 17th Floor, 521 Fifth Avenue, New York
NY 10175. 516/537-1104.

CHEMICALS DIRECTORY
Cahners Business Information, 275 Washington
Street, Newton MA 02458. 617/964-3030.

DIRECTORY OF CHEMICAL ENGINEERING CONSULTANTS
American Institute of Chemical Engineers, 3 Park Avenue, New York NY 10016. 212/591-7338. Toll-free phone: 800/242-4363. World Wide Web address: http://www.aiche.org.

DIRECTORY OF CHEMICAL PRODUCERS
SRI International, 333 Ravenswood Avenue, Menlo Park CA 94025. 650/895-2000. World Wide Web address: http://www.sri.com.

Magazines

CHEMICAL & ENGINEERING NEWS
American Chemical Society, 1155 16th Street NW, Washington DC 20036. 202/872-4600. World Wide Web address: http://www.pubs.acs.org/cen.

CHEMICAL WEEK
888 Seventh Avenue, 26th Floor, New York NY 10106. 212/621-4900. World Wide Web address: http://www.chemweek.com.

Visit our exciting job and career site at http://www.careercity.com

COMMUNICATIONS: TELECOMMUNICATIONS AND BROADCASTING

The telecommunications industry continued to evolve in 1998, with consolidation and intense competition between local and long-distance carriers. In reaction to price drops and increased competition across all segments of the industry, mergers and acquisitions have been an industry trend. The proposed mega-merger of AT&T and TCI is an attempt to pool the resources of one of the nation's telephone giants with a leading cable company.

The Telecommunications Act of 1996, coupled with promising new wireless technology, opened the door for major long-distance companies to break into the local phone market within their respective regions, which proved a very costly venture. However, a federal court decision to limit the FCC's regulation over long-distance carriers should give businesses more power over prices and the freedom to enter new territories.

Competition has increased in the wireless communications industry, which has resulted in lower prices for wireless minutes. According to Business Week, *the number of wireless subscribers increased from 144.2 million in 1996 to 213.7 million in 1997. Despite the increase in subscribers, it is unlikely smaller wireless operators will fare well amidst the price wars of the larger operators.*

Internet technologies continue to transform the telecommunications industry as companies begin to offer long-distance and fax services over the Internet. According to Action Information Services, these services will produce $1 billion in revenues by 2001, although companies must satisfy customers' demands for increasingly faster Internet access.

E.F. JOHNSON COMPANY
603 West Travelers Trail, Burnsville MN 55337. 612/882-5500. **Contact:** Human Resources Manager. **World Wide Web address:** http://www.transcrypt.com. **Description:** This location is a sales office. Overall, E.F. Johnson Company is engaged in the design and production of two-way radio communications equipment and data telemetry. **Common positions include:** Accountant/Auditor; Buyer; Computer Programmer; Customer Service Representative; Electrical/Electronics Engineer; Mechanical Engineer; Services Sales Representative; Software Engineer. **Educational backgrounds include:** Computer Science; Engineering. **Benefits:** 401(k); Dental Insurance; Disability Coverage; Life Insurance; Medical Insurance; Profit Sharing; STD/LTD Coverage; Tuition Assistance. **Corporate headquarters location:** Lincoln NE. **Other U.S. locations:** Waseca MN. **Parent company:** Transcrypt International. **Operations at this facility include:** Divisional Headquarters. **Listed on:** Privately held. **Number of employees at this location:** 90. **Number of employees nationwide:** 600.

E.F. JOHNSON COMPANY
299 Johnson Avenue, Waseca MN 56093. 507/835-6222. **Contact:** Human Resources. **World Wide Web address:** http://www.transcrypt.com. **Description:** Manufactures two-way radio communications equipment and data telemetry. **Corporate headquarters location:** Lincoln NE. **Parent company:** Transcrypt International. **Number of employees nationwide:** 600.

KSTP-TV
HUBBARD BROADCASTING, INC.
3415 University Avenue SE, St. Paul MN 55114. 651/646-5555. **Contact:** Human Resources. **Description:** A television station affiliated with the ABC network. **Common positions include:** Editor; Engineer; Graphic Artist; Production Assistant; Sales Representative. **Parent company:** Hubbard Broadcasting, Inc. (also at this location).

NORSTAN COMMUNICATIONS
5101 Shady Oak Road, Minnetonka MN 55343-4100. 612/352-4000. **Contact:** Human Resources. **World Wide Web address:** http://www.norstan.com. **Description:** Provides voice, data, videoconferencing, and telecommunications services to businesses.

SPRINT UNITED TELEPHONE COMPANY
343 East 82nd Street, Chaska MN 55318. 612/448-8200. **Recorded jobline:** 800/725-6540. **Contact:** Human Resources. **World Wide Web address:** http://www.sprint.com. **Description:** A diversified telecommunications company with a nationwide, all-digital, fiberoptic network. Sprint's divisions provide global long-distance voice, data, and video products and services; local telephone services in 19 states; and cellular operations that serve 42 metropolitan markets and more than 50 rural areas. **NOTE:** Sprint's Staff Associate Program is a two- to three-year developmental program designed to ensure an influx of individuals who have the capability to assume middle- to upper-level management positions within the corporation. Each candidate should have the opportunity to experience at least three of the following departments: Finance, Information Systems, Marketing, Network Operations, Customer Service, and International. Staff Associates are hired into one of three specific tracks: Financial, Technological, or General Management. Students should contact their placement offices regarding on-campus interviews. Please send resumes to Sprint Corporation, Human Resources, 5454 West 110th Street, Overland Park KS 66211. **Corporate headquarters location:** Westwood KS. **Other U.S. locations:** Nationwide. **Parent company:** Sprint Corporation. **Number of employees nationwide:** 55,000.

U S WEST COMMUNICATIONS
200 South Fifth Street, Suite 110, Minneapolis MN 55402. 612/663-4161. **Toll-free phone:** 800/879-4357. **Contact:** Director of Personnel. **Description:** A telecommunications company that provides a full range of connection solutions to more than 25 million business, government, and residential customers in 14 western and midwestern states. **Corporate headquarters location:** Denver CO. **Parent company:** U S WEST is a telecommunications company with several divisions. U S WEST's Marketing Resources Group connects buyers and sellers through telephone directories, database marketing, and new multimedia services. The Multimedia Group manages U S WEST's entry into domestic broadband markets outside the region served by U S WEST Communications. Working with local partners, U S WEST International and Business Development Group provides advanced communications and entertainment services to more than 1.8 million customers in 15 rapidly expanding markets around the world.

VALUEVISION INTERNATIONAL
6740 Shady Oak Road, Eden Prairie MN 55344. 612/947-5200. **Contact:** Ray Campbell, Director of Human Resources. **World Wide Web address:** http://www.vvtv.com. **Description:** Operates a home shopping channel on cable television.

WCCO-TV
90 South 11th Street, Minneapolis MN 55403. 612/330-2400. **Contact:** Greg Keck, Director of Broadcast Operations. **World Wide Web address:** http://www.wcco.com. **Description:** WCCO-TV is a television broadcasting company affiliated with the CBS network. **Common positions include:** Accountant/Auditor; Broadcast Engineer; Credit Manager; Editor; Photographer/Camera Operator; Reporter; Services Sales Representative. **Educational backgrounds include:** Broadcasting. **Benefits:** Dental Insurance; Disability Coverage; Employee Discounts; Life Insurance; Medical Insurance; Pension Plan; Profit Sharing; Savings Plan. **Corporate headquarters location:** New York NY. **Parent company:** CBS, Inc. **Number of employees at this location:** 200.

WILLIAMS COMMUNICATIONS SOLUTIONS
5929 Baker Road, Suite 440, Minnetonka MN 55345. 612/933-5331. **Contact:** Personnel Department. **World Wide Web address:** http://www.wilcomsol.com. **Description:** Williams Communications Solutions integrates business communications systems and services enterprise networks for voice, video, and data applications. **Common positions include:** Branch Manager; Manufacturer's/Wholesaler's Sales Rep.; Telephone Technician. **Benefits:** Dental Insurance; Life Insurance; Medical Insurance; Pension Plan; Profit Sharing; Tuition Assistance. **Corporate headquarters location:** Houston TX. **Operations at this facility include:** Sales; Service. **Listed on:** New York Stock Exchange.

Note: Because addresses and telephone numbers of smaller companies can change rapidly, we recommend you call each company to verify the information below before inquiring about job opportunities. Mass mailings are not recommended.

Additional small employers:

CABLE/PAY TELEVISION SERVICES

MediaOne Inc.
214 4th St E, St. Paul MN 55101-
1481. 651/224-2697.

Meredith Cable
934 Woodhill Dr, Roseville MN
55113-2012. 651/483-3233.

COMMUNICATIONS EQUIPMENT

A-Tek North
PO Box 403, Brainerd MN
56401-0403. 218/829-1481.

ADC Solitra
PO Box 157, Hutchinson MN
55350-0157. 320/587-6498.

ADC Telecommunications Inc.
11311 K-Tel Dr, Hopkins MN
55343-8869. 612/936-8335.

ADC Telecommunications Inc.
1100 N 4th St, Le Sueur MN
56058-1419. 507/665-6281.

CSI Suttle
PO Box 777, Hector MN 55342-
0777. 320/848-6671.

Lucent Technologies Inc.
1650 W 82nd St, Ste 500,
Bloomington MN 55431-1457.
612/885-4645.

TCM
PO Box 33225, St. Paul MN
55133-3225. 651/733-0981.

Telex Communications Inc.
PO Box 125, Blue Earth MN
56013-0125. 507/526-3205.

MISC. COMMUNICATIONS SERVICES

Conus Communications LP
3415 University Ave W, St. Paul
MN 55114-1019. 651/642-4645.

RADIO BROADCASTING STATIONS

KQRS 92.5
917 Lilac Dr N, Crystal MN
55422-4615. 612/545-5601.

Minnesota Public Radio
45 7th St E, St. Paul MN 55101-
2202. 651/290-1500.

WCCO-AM
625 2nd Ave S, Minneapolis MN
55402-1912. 612/370-0611.

WMMR
300 Washington Ave SE,
Minneapolis MN 55455-0396.
612/625-5926.

TELEPHONE COMMUNICATIONS

Arvig Enterprises Inc.
150 2nd Ave SW, Perham MN
56573-1409. 218/346-4200.

Cellular 2000
PO Box 2000, Alexandria MN
56308-2000. 320/762-2000.

Frontier Communications
PO Box 1527, Burnsville MN
55337-0527. 612/435-3600.

MCI Telecommunications Corp.
5500 Wisetta Blvd, Minneapolis
MN 55416. 612/591-0705.

Means Inc.
10300 6th Avenue North,
Plymouth MN 55441-6371.
612/230-4100.

U S WEST Communications
4700 Welcome Ave N,
Minneapolis MN 55429-3518.
612/536-2070.

U S WEST Communications Inc.
5910 Shingle Creek Pkwy,
Brooklyn Center MN 55430-
2319. 612/569-2441.

U S WEST Direct
6300 Shingle Creek Pkwy,
Brooklyn Center MN 55430-
2124. 612/585-2000.

U S WEST Inc.
600 Stinson Blvd, Minneapolis
MN 55413-2620. 612/664-3917.

US Link Long Distance
PO Box 327, Pequot Lakes MN
56472-0327. 218/568-4000.

Vista Communications
14450 Burnhaven Dr, Burnsville
MN 55306-6125. 612/435-3133.

TELEVISION BROADCASTING STATIONS

KARE-11
8811 Olson Memorial Hwy,
Minneapolis MN 55427-4762.
612/546-1111.

KTCA-TV
172 4th St E, St. Paul MN 55101-
1400. 651/222-1717.

For more information on career opportunities in the communications industries:

Associations

ACADEMY OF TELEVISION ARTS & SCIENCES
5220 Lankershim Boulevard, North Hollywood CA
91601. 818/754-2800. World Wide Web address:
http://www.emmys.org.

AMERICAN DISC JOCKEY ASSOCIATION
297 Route 72 West, Suite C-120, Manahawkin NJ
08050-2980. 609/978-2180. World Wide Web
address: http://www.adja.org. A membership
organization for professional disc jockeys that
publishes a newsletter of current events and new
products.

AMERICAN WOMEN IN RADIO AND TELEVISION, INC.
1650 Tysons Boulevard, Suite 200, McLean VA
22102. 703/506-3290. World Wide Web address:
http://www.awrt.org. A national, nonprofit
professional organization for the advancement of
women who work in electronic media and related

fields. Services include *News and Views,* a fax
newsletter transmitted biweekly to members;
Careerline, a national listing of job openings available
to members only; and the AWRT Foundation, which
supports charitable and educational programs and
annual awards.

THE COMPETITIVE TELECOMMUNICATIONS ASSOCIATION (COMPTEL)
1900 M Street NW, Suite 800, Washington DC
20036. 202/296-6650. World Wide Web address:
http://www.comptel.org. A national association
providing a wide variety of resources including
telecommunications trade shows.

INTERNATIONAL TELEVISION ASSOCIATION
6311 North O'Connor Road, Suite 230, Irving TX
75309. 972/869-1112. World Wide Web address:
http://www.itva.org. Membership required.

NATIONAL ASSOCIATION OF BROADCASTERS
1771 N Street NW, Washington DC 20036. 202/429-5300, ext. 5490. Fax: 202/429-5343. World Wide Web address: http://www.nab.org. Provides employment information.

NATIONAL CABLE TELEVISION ASSOCIATION
1724 Massachusetts Avenue NW, Washington DC 20036-1969. 202/775-3669. Fax: 202/775-3695. World Wide Web address: http://www.ncta.com. A trade association. Publications include *Cable Television Developments, Secure Signals,* and *Kids and Cable*.

PROMAX INTERNATIONAL
2029 Century Park East, Suite 555, Los Angeles CA 90067. 310/788-7600. Fax: 310/788-7616. A nonprofit organization for radio, film, television, video, and other broadcasting professionals. Ask for the jobline.

U.S. TELEPHONE ASSOCIATION
1401 H Street NW, Suite 600, Washington DC 20005-2136. 202/326-7300. World Wide Web address: http://www.usta.org. A trade association for local telephone companies.

Magazines

BROADCASTING AND CABLE
Broadcasting Publications Inc., 1705 DeSales Street NW, Washington DC 20036. 202/659-2340.

Online Services

BROADCAST PROFESSIONALS FORUM
Go: BPForum. A CompuServe discussion group for professionals in radio and television.

CPB JOBLINE
http://www.cpb.org/jobline/index.html. The Corporation for Public Broadcasting, a nonprofit company, operates this site which provides a list of job openings in the public radio and television industries.

JOURNALISM FORUM
Go: Jforum. A CompuServe discussion group for journalists in print, radio, or television.

ON-LINE DISC JOCKEY ASSOCIATION
http://www.odja.com. Provides members with insurance, Internet advertising, a magazine, and networking resources. This site also posts job opportunities.

Visit our exciting job and career site at http://www.careercity.com

COMPUTER HARDWARE, SOFTWARE, AND SERVICES

As the computer industry's expansion continues to gain strength in a diverse and competitive marketplace, a plethora of new products and services will open up even more opportunities for employment into the next decade. The Bureau of Labor Statistics projects that through 2006 four of the ten fastest-growing occupations will be in the computer field, from desktop publishers, with an anticipated growth rate of 74 percent, to various computer scientists, with an anticipated growth rate of 118 percent. The number of computer repair positions will increase with rising hardware sales, and computer programmers will be in high demand as companies strive to keep up with technology and upgrade systems. Projections also indicate an additional 520,000 systems analysts positions by 2006. Computer operators, however, will see a decline in opportunities due to automation and advances in user-friendly software.

The demand for software, particularly for education, entertainment, and communications, increased by 12 percent in 1997, and had increased by 3 percent through the first two quarters of 1998. Internet-related software sales are expected to double each year through 2000, according to the U.S. Department of Labor.

In 1998, Microsoft, though still a software powerhouse, was bumped out by SAP as the leading software company. Microsoft continues to fight off anti-trust accusations brought by the U.S. Department of Justice. Intel, having derived much success from its Pentium chips, has started to lose market share to chips such as the AMD K6, a leading alternative used in the booming sub-$1,000 computer market. Apple hit it big in 1998 with the introduction of the iMac, which drove the company's market share from 6.8 percent to 13.5 percent.

Telephone and cable companies are investing in new technologies, including ASDL (asynchronous digital subscriber line), that promise to link users to the Internet up to 200 times faster than traditional modems. According to Dataquest Inc., 80 percent of the nation's households will have these fast-access technologies available by 2001.

Mainframe programmers and consultants are being actively hired to correct the "Year 2000 problem" and will likely stay in demand after the January 2000 deadline. Personnel who can read old programming codes are needed, and many qualified workers from other segments of the computer industry are leaving their current jobs to work as Year 2000 consultants.

AMERICABLE INC.
7450 Flying Cloud Drive, Eden Prairie MN 55344. 612/942-3800. **Contact:** Human Resources Recruiter. **World Wide Web address:** http://www.americable.com. **Description:** Supplies businesses with networking hardware and software.

ANALYSTS INTERNATIONAL CORPORATION (AiC)
7615 Metro Boulevard, Minneapolis MN 55439. 612/835-5900. **Toll-free phone:** 800/800-5044. **Contact:** Senior Staffing Assistant. **World Wide Web address:** http://www.analysts.com.

Description: AiC is an international computer consulting firm. The company assists clients in a variety of industries develop systems using different programming languages and software. This involves systems analysis, design, and development. **NOTE:** A minimum of one to two years of programming experience is required. Please send resumes to 8200 Normandale Boulevard, Minneapolis MN 55437. 612/897-4590. **Common positions include:** Computer Programmer; Management Analyst/Consultant; Software Engineer; Systems Analyst; Technical Writer/Editor. **Educational backgrounds include:** Business Administration; Computer Science; Engineering; Mathematics. **Benefits:** 401(k); Dental Insurance; Disability Coverage; Employee Discounts; Life Insurance; Medical Insurance; Pension Plan; Profit Sharing; Savings Plan; Tuition Assistance. **Corporate headquarters location:** This Location. **Other U.S. locations:** Nationwide. **Operations at this facility include:** Administration; Sales; Service. **Listed on:** NASDAQ. **Stock exchange symbol:** ANALY. **Annual sales/revenues:** More than $100 million. **Number of employees at this location:** 400. **Number of employees nationwide:** 2,700. **Number of employees worldwide:** 4,600.

APERTUS CARLETON CORPORATION
7275 Flying Cloud Drive, Eden Prairie MN 55344. 612/828-0300. **Toll-free phone:** 800/328-3998. **Contact:** Lori Cocking, Director of Human Resources. **World Wide Web address:** http://www.apertus.com. **Description:** Apertus Carleton Corporation is a multi-product software development company that provides organizations with cost-effective network integration solutions. The company's products include network gateways, communications software, data integration tools, and system management products. Founded in 1979. **Common positions include:** Computer Programmer; Software Engineer; Technical Writer/Editor. **Educational backgrounds include:** Computer Science. **Benefits:** 401(k); Dental Insurance; Disability Coverage; Life Insurance; Medical Insurance; Tuition Assistance. **Other U.S. locations:** El Toro CA; Atlanta GA; New York NY; Dallas TX. **International locations:** Germany; United Kingdom. **Listed on:** NASDAQ. **Annual sales/revenues:** $21 - $50 million. **Number of employees at this location:** 165.

APPLIED STATISTICS, INC.
2055 White Bear Avenue, Maplewood MN 55109. 651/481-0202. **Fax:** 651/773-4930. **Contact:** Personnel Manager. **World Wide Web address:** http://www.appliedstatistics.com. **Description:** Develops software for the Windows operating system utilizing Microsoft Visual C++. **Common positions include:** Administrative Assistant; Administrative Manager; Computer Programmer; Sales Engineer; Sales Manager; Software Engineer. **Educational backgrounds include:** Computer Science; Engineering. **Benefits:** 401(k); Dental Insurance; Medical Insurance; Tuition Assistance. **Corporate headquarters location:** This Location. **Listed on:** Privately held. **Annual sales/revenues:** $5 - $10 million. **Number of employees at this location:** 50.

ARTESYN TECHNOLOGIES
1425 East Bridge Street, Redwood Falls MN 56283. 507/637-2966. **Contact:** Sheila Stage, Human Resources. **World Wide Web address:** http://www.artesyn.com. **Description:** Manufactures and repairs power supplies for computer applications.

BANKERS SYSTEMS, INC.
6815 Sauckview Drive, St. Cloud MN 56303. 320/251-3060. **Contact:** Human Resources Department. **World Wide Web address:** http://www.bankerssystems.com. **Description:** Develops marketing, operations, regulatory compliance, and training software for the financial services industry.

BELOS MEDICAL INFORMATICS
10900 Red Circle Drive, Suite 100, Minnetonka MN 55343. 612/939-2200. **Contact:** Director of Human Resources. **World Wide Web address:** http://www.belos.com. **Description:** Develops and markets clinical database programs to the medical industry.

CIBER, INC.
1915 Highway 52 North, Suite 105, Rochester MN 55901. 507/280-9267. **Fax:** 507/280-0833. **Contact:** Recruiter. **World Wide Web address:** http://www.ciber.com. **Description:** Ciber provides major corporations with computer consulting services covering a wide range of areas including networking, systems integration, and software.

CIM SOFTWARE CORPORATION
5735 Lindsay Street, Minneapolis MN 55422. 612/544-1752. **Contact:** Human Resources. **World Wide Web address:** http://www.cimsoftware.com. **Description:** Develops networking software for systems integration.

COMPUTER NETWORK TECHNOLOGY CORPORATION
6500 Wedgewood Road, Maple Grove MN 55311-3640. 612/550-8000. **Contact:** Human Resources. **World Wide Web address:** http://www.cnt.com. **Description:** Designs, manufactures, markets, and supports channel networking products that enable the high-speed transmission of information among local and geographically dispersed computing systems, primarily IBM and IBM-compatible, as well as related peripheral devices. **Common positions include:** Accountant/Auditor; Budget Analyst; Buyer; Electrical/Electronics Engineer; Financial Analyst; Software Engineer; Technical Writer/Editor. **Educational backgrounds include:** Business Administration; Computer Science; Liberal Arts. **Benefits:** 401(k); Daycare Assistance; Dental Insurance; Disability Coverage; Employee Discounts; Life Insurance; Medical Insurance; Profit Sharing; Tuition Assistance. **Corporate headquarters location:** This Location. **Operations at this facility include:** Administration; Manufacturing; Research and Development. **Number of employees at this location:** 300. **Number of employees nationwide:** 400.

CONTROL DATA SYSTEMS, INC.
4201 Lexington Avenue North, Arden Hills MN 55126. 651/415-2999. **Contact:** Katy Adams, Vice President of Human Resources. **E-mail address:** info@cdc.com. **World Wide Web address:** http://www.cdc.com. **Description:** Control Data Systems provides a wide range of services that include design consulting, program management, application development, network integration, and life cycle support. An independent company since 1992, Control Data Systems develops two network infrastructure solutions: message integration (designing and building messaging solutions for large corporations and government institutions that want widely dispersed users and applications to exchange information) and product data management (the company's consultants use the workflow, product configuration, and imaging capabilities of the Metaphase concurrent engineering software to help manufacturers track design and tooling data from initial sketches on a CAD terminal to the final checkout on the assembly line floor). **Common positions include:** Computer Programmer; Industrial Engineer; Services Sales Representative; Software Engineer; Systems Analyst. **Educational backgrounds include:** Computer Science; Engineering; Mathematics. **Benefits:** 401(k); Dental Insurance; Disability Coverage; Employee Discounts; Life Insurance; Medical Insurance; Profit Sharing; Savings Plan; Tuition Assistance. **Special programs:** Internships. **Corporate headquarters location:** This Location. **Other U.S. locations:** Nationwide. **Operations at this facility include:** Administration; Divisional Headquarters; Regional Headquarters; Sales; Service. **Number of employees at this location:** 700. **Number of employees nationwide:** 2,800.

DIGI INTERNATIONAL INC.
11001 Bren Road East, Minnetonka MN 55343. 612/912-3444. **Contact:** Human Resources. **World Wide Web address:** http://www.dgii.com. **Description:** Provides data communications hardware and software that enable connectivity solutions for multi-user environments, remote access, and LAN connectivity markets. These products support most major microcomputer and workstation architectures and most popular single- and multi-user systems. Digi International also provides cross-platform compatibility and software and technical support services. The company's products are marketed to a broad range of worldwide distributors, system integrators, value-added resellers, and OEMs. In July 1998, Digi International announced plans to acquire ITK International (Germany) and Central Data Corporation (Champaign IL). **Corporate headquarters location:** This Location. **International locations:** Worldwide. **Listed on:** NASDAQ. **Stock exchange symbol:** DGII.

EXi CORPORATION
2345 Rice Street, Suite 230, Roseville MN 55113. 651/490-5700. **Fax:** 651/490-9760. **Contact:** Mark Dembouski, Technical Resource Coordinator. **E-mail address:** info@exicorp.com. **World Wide Web address:** http://www.exicorp.com. **Description:** Exi Corporation provides technology-based consulting solutions in the areas of business applications development, network architecture and security, and software engineering. Founded in 1992. **NOTE:** Entry-level positions are offered. **Common positions include:** Applications Engineer; Computer Programmer; Computer Scientist; Computer Technical Support; Computer Technician; Network/Systems Administrator; Software Engineer; SQL Programmer. **Educational backgrounds include:** C/C++; HTML; Internet Development; Java; MCSE; Software Development; Software Technical Support. **Benefits:** 401(k); Casual Dress - Daily; Dental Insurance; Disability Coverage; Employee Discounts; Financial Planning; Flexible Schedule; Life Insurance; Medical Insurance; Profit Sharing; Public Transit Available; Telecommuting; Tuition Assistance. **Special programs:** Training. **Corporate headquarters location:** Newport Beach CA. **International locations:** Australia; England. **Operations at this facility include:** Regional Headquarters. **Annual sales/revenues:** More than $100 million. **Number of employees at this location:** 125. **Number of employees nationwide:** 2,600. **Number of employees worldwide:** 3,000. **Number of projected hires for 1999 - 2000 at this location:** 55.

FOURTH SHIFT CORPORATION
Two Meridian Crossings, Minneapolis MN 55423. 612/851-1500. **Contact:** Human Resources. **World Wide Web address:** http://www.fs.com. **Description:** Develops and markets manufacturing software.

FUJIKURA RICHARD MANUFACTURING COMPANY INC.
6250 Bury Drive, Eden Prairie MN 55346. 612/934-3000. **Contact:** Human Resources. **Description:** Manufactures components for computer disk drives.

GE CAPITAL IT SOLUTIONS
10200 51st Avenue North, Minneapolis MN 55442. 612/557-2500. **Fax:** 612/551-5566. **Contact:** Human Resources Manager. **World Wide Web address:** http://www.gecits.ge.com. **Description:** A reseller of CPUs, monitors, various drives, and peripherals. At this location, the company also provides technical support. Overall, GE Capital IT Solutions is a nationwide provider of computer products and services to commercial, governmental, and educational users. The company's products and services range from procurement to value-added systems including systems integration, networking services, support, maintenance, facilities management and outsourcing, software and business consulting services, and rental services. GE Capital IT Solutions markets its computer products and business services through its offices in approximately 70 cities throughout the country. **Special programs:** Internships. **Number of employees at this location:** 275.

HBO & COMPANY (HBOC)
2700 Snelling Avenue North, 4th Floor, Roseville MN 55113. 651/697-5900. **Contact:** Human Resources. **World Wide Web address:** http://www.hboc.com. **Description:** Develops scheduling systems software for the health care industry.

HAGEN SYSTEMS INC.
6438 City West Parkway, Eden Prairie MN 55344. 612/944-6865. **Contact:** Clarice Garborg, Human Resources. **World Wide Web address:** http://www.hagensys.com. **Description:** Develops management software for the graphic arts industry.

HEALTH OUTCOME MANAGEMENT INC.
2331 University Avenue SE, Minneapolis MN 55414. 612/378-3053. **Contact:** Human Resources. **World Wide Web address:** http://www.homi.com. **Description:** Develops, markets, and maintains software for health care providers, including long-term care facilities, retail pharmacies, and hospitals.

HEALTH SYSTEMS INTEGRATION INC.
8009 34th Avenue South, Bloomington MN 55425. 612/851-9696. **Fax:** 612/858-7905. **Contact:** Human Resources. **World Wide Web address:** http://www.health-systems.com. **Description:** A designer and developer of software for the health care industry. Founded in 1977. **Common positions include:** Account Manager; Accountant/Auditor; Administrative Assistant; Chief Financial Officer; Claim Representative; Clerical Supervisor; Computer Programmer; Customer Service Representative; Database Manager; Financial Analyst; Human Resources Manager; Marketing Specialist; MIS Specialist; Operations/Production Manager; Project Manager; Sales Executive; Sales Representative; Secretary; Software Engineer; Systems Analyst; Technical Writer/Editor. **Educational backgrounds include:** Business Administration; Computer Science; Finance; Health Care; Marketing. **Benefits:** 401(k); Dental Insurance; Disability Coverage; Life Insurance; Medical Insurance. **Corporate headquarters location:** This Location. **Other U.S. locations:** Reston VA. **Parent company:** CompuCare. **Listed on:** Privately held. **Number of employees at this location:** 350.

HUTCHINSON TECHNOLOGY
40 West Highland Park, Hutchinson MN 55350. 320/587-1962. **Fax:** 320/587-1290. **Contact:** Human Resources. **World Wide Web address:** http://www.htch.com. **Description:** A manufacturer of precision spring components for disk drives. **Common positions include:** Chemical Engineer; Design Engineer; Electrical/Electronics Engineer; Industrial Engineer; Mechanical Engineer. **Educational backgrounds include:** Engineering. **Benefits:** 401(k); Dental Insurance; Disability Coverage; Life Insurance; Medical Insurance; Profit Sharing; Tuition Assistance. **Special programs:** Internships. **Corporate headquarters location:** This Location. **Other U.S. locations:** Sioux Falls SD; Eau Claire WI. **Operations at this facility include:** Administration; Manufacturing; Research and Development; Sales. **Listed on:** NASDAQ.

IBM CORPORATION
3605 Highway 52 North, Rochester MN 55901-7829. 507/253-4011. **Toll-free phone:** 800/796-9876. **Contact:** IBM Staffing Services. **World Wide Web address:** http://www.us.ibm.com.

Description: This location is a manufacturing facility. Overall, IBM is a developer, manufacturer, and marketer of advanced information processing products including computers and microelectronic technology, software, networking systems, and information technology-related services. **NOTE:** Jobseekers should send resumes to IBM Staffing Services, Department 1DP, Building 051, P.O. Box 12195, Research Triangle Park NC 27709-2195. **Common positions include:** Chemical Engineer; Computer Operator; Computer Programmer; Data Entry Clerk; Electrical/Electronics Engineer; Manufacturing Engineer; Mechanical Engineer; Sales Representative; Secretary; Software Engineer; Systems Analyst; Technical Writer/Editor; Technician.

IMAGE SYSTEMS CORPORATION
6103 Blue Circle Drive, Minnetonka MN 55343. 612/935-1171. **Fax:** 612/935-1386. **Contact:** Laura Sorensen, Manager of Human Resources. **E-mail address:** lauras@imagesystemscorp.com. **World Wide Web address:** http://www.imagesystemscorp.com. **Description:** Designs and manufactures high-resolution computer monitors. Applications include medical and document imaging and air traffic control. **NOTE:** The company offers second and third shifts. **Company slogan:** You'll like what you see! **Common positions include:** Design Engineer; Electrical/Electronics Engineer; Electronics Technician; Industrial Engineer; Manufacturing Engineer; Quality Control Supervisor. **Educational backgrounds include:** Business Administration; Engineering. **Benefits:** 401(k); Disability Coverage; Medical Insurance. **Special programs:** Internships. **Corporate headquarters location:** This Location. **Listed on:** NASDAQ. **Stock exchange symbol:** IMSG. **Annual sales/revenues:** $5 - $10 million. **Number of employees at this location:** 40.

IMATION CORPORATION
One Imation Place, Oakdale MN 55128-3414. 651/704-4000. **Toll-free phone:** 888/466-3456. **Fax:** 800/537-4675. **Contact:** Staffing Specialist. **E-mail address:** info@imation.com. **World Wide Web address:** http://www.imation.com. **Description:** A global technology solutions company offering systems, products, and services for the handling, storage, transmission, and use of information. Businesses include data storage products, medical imaging and photo products, printing and publishing systems, and customer support technologies and document imaging. Imation is an independent spin-off of 3M's data storage and imaging businesses. **Corporate headquarters location:** This Location. **Listed on:** Chicago Stock Exchange; New York Stock Exchange. **Stock exchange symbol:** IMN. **Annual sales/revenues:** More than $100 million. **Number of employees worldwide:** 10,000.

INFORMATION ADVANTAGE INC.
7905 Golden Triangle Drive, Suite 190, Eden Prairie MN 55344. 612/833-3700. **Contact:** Human Resources Department. **Description:** Information Advantage is a developer of enterprise online analytical processing software used by companies in a variety of industries including finance, government, health care, insurance, manufacturing, retail, and telecommunications. The company's primary product is DecisionSuite, a business decision-making program. Founded in 1991. **Corporate headquarters location:** This Location. **Listed on:** NASDAQ. **Stock exchange symbol:** IACO.

INNOVEX
530 11th Street South, Hopkins MN 55343. 612/938-4155. **Contact:** Human Resources. **Description:** Manufactures lead wire assemblies for heads of computer hard drives. **Corporate headquarters location:** This Location.

JASC SOFTWARE
P.O. Box 44997, Eden Prairie MN 55344. 612/930-9800. **Fax:** 612/930-9172. **Contact:** Kevin Kiloran, Controller. **E-mail address:** jobs@jasc.com. **World Wide Web address:** http://www.jasc.com. **Description:** A developer of Windows-based graphics and multimedia software. Jasc's product line includes Paint Shop Pro, Jasc Media Center, and Professional Capture Systems. Founded in 1991. **Common positions include:** Computer Programmer; Software Engineer. **Benefits:** 401(k); Dental Insurance; Disability Coverage; Financial Planning Assistance; Life Insurance; Medical Insurance; Profit Sharing; Tuition Assistance; Vision Insurance. **Special programs:** Internships. **Annual sales/revenues:** $5 - $10 million.

KENNSCO INC.
14700 28th Avenue North, Plymouth MN 55447. 612/559-5100. **Toll-free phone:** 800/358-5574. **Contact:** Katy Bentrott, Vice President of Field Engineering. **Description:** Sells and services PC, LAN, and WAN equipment. Founded in 1974. **NOTE:** Entry-level positions are offered. **Common positions include:** Account Manager; Account Representative; Accountant; Adjuster; Administrative Assistant; Administrative Manager; Branch Manager; Buyer; Electrical/Electronics

Engineer; MIS Specialist; Operations Manager; Project Manager; Sales Executive; Sales Manager; Sales Representative. **Benefits:** 401(k); Dental Insurance; Disability Coverage; Flexible Schedule; Life Insurance; Medical Insurance; Profit Sharing; Tuition Assistance. **Corporate headquarters location:** This Location. **Listed on:** Privately held. **Annual sales/revenues:** $21 - $50 million. **Number of employees at this location:** 80. **Number of employees nationwide:** 200.

LASER DESIGN INC.
9401 James Avenue South, Suite 162, Minneapolis MN 55431. 612/884-9648. **Contact:** Human Resources. **World Wide Web address:** http://www.laserdesign.com. **Description:** Designs software for three-dimensional laser digitizers.

LAWSON SOFTWARE
1300 Godward Street, Minneapolis MN 55413. 612/379-2633. **Contact:** Human Resources. **World Wide Web address:** http://www.lawson.com. **Description:** Creates financial software for procurement departments.

THE LEARNING COMPANY
6160 Summit Drive North, Brooklyn Center MN 55430. 612/569-1500. **Contact:** Human Resources Department. **World Wide Web address:** http://www.learningco.com. **Description:** This location develops software and maintains a sales and marketing team. Overall, The Learning Company uses emerging technologies to create a system of easy-to-use software products that help build important lifelong learning and communication skills. Most of the company's products are available in home editions, and certain products are also available in school editions, which include network, site license, and stand-alone configurations. Product families include the Rabbit Family (ages three to seven), the Treasure Family (ages six to eight), the Writing Tools Family (ages eight and up) and the Children's Writing & Publishing Center, and The Foreign Languages Family (ages 15 and up).

LEGAL DECISIONS SYSTEMS INC. (LDSi)
2021 East Hennepin Avenue, Suite LL-30, Minneapolis MN 55413. 612/378-1108. **Contact:** Jerry Snyder, President. **Description:** Provides computer consulting services and support for networks and applications.

LOCKHEED MARTIN TACTICAL DEFENSE SYSTEMS
P.O. Box 64525, St. Paul MN 55164-0525. 651/456-2222. **Physical address:** 3333 Pilot Knob Road, Eagan MN. **Contact:** Human Resources. **Description:** This location designs computer systems for the defense industry. Overall, Lockheed Martin Tactical Defense Systems designs and builds 16-bit and 32-bit technical computing systems used in mil-spec environments. Applications include electronic warfare, signal intelligence, radar, sonar, and imaging where digital signal processing or general purpose computing is required. The company also provides systems engineering, software development tools, rugged computer systems, and integrated workstations of commercial architectures for proof-of-concept program phases.

MAGNETIC DATA INC.
6754 Shady Oak Road, Eden Prairie MN 55344. 612/941-0453. **Contact:** Ms. Teri Berndt, Human Resources Manager. **Description:** Refurbishes computer parts.

MANAGEMENT GRAPHICS INC.
1401 East 79th Street, Minneapolis MN 55425. 612/854-1220. **Contact:** Human Resources. **World Wide Web address:** http://www.mgi.com. **Description:** Develops graphics systems for computers and applicable software.

METAFILE INFORMATION SYSTEMS INC.
4131 Highway 52 North, Suite B221, Rochester MN 55901. 507/286-9232. **Contact:** Human Resources. **World Wide Web address:** http://www.metafileweb.com. **Description:** Develops fundraising, imaging, and storage software.

METAMOR ITS
105 Fifth Avenue South, Suite 300, Minneapolis MN 55401-2535. 612/630-9100. **Contact:** Human Resources. **World Wide Web address:** http://www.metamor-its.com. **Description:** A full-service computer consulting firm. **Parent company:** Metamor Worldwide, Inc.

MINDSHARP LEARNING CENTERS
3800 West 80th Street, Suite 1155, Bloomington MN 55431. 612/893-7555. **Fax:** 612/893-7550. **Contact:** Manager. **World Wide Web address:** http://www.mindsharp.com. **Description:**

Provides computer training courses both on-site and in offices of client companies. **Other area locations:** Bloomington MN; St. Paul MN.

MOORE DATA MANAGEMENT SERVICES
MOORE GRAPHICS SERVICES
2117 West River Road North, Minneapolis MN 55411. 612/588-7200. **Contact:** Human Resources. **Description:** A primary provider of online computer services to the real estate industry. This location also houses Moore Graphics Services, which provides commercial printing and electronic, on-demand, and database publishing to *Fortune* 500 companies. **Corporate headquarters location:** This Location. **Other U.S. locations:** Nationwide. **Parent company:** Moore Corporation. **Operations at this facility include:** Manufacturing. **Listed on:** New York Stock Exchange. **Number of employees nationwide:** 1,200.

MULTI-TECH SYSTEMS INC.
2205 Woodale Drive, Mounds View MN 55112. 612/785-3500. **Contact:** Human Resources. **World Wide Web address:** http://www.multi-tech.com. **Description:** Manufactures modems and provides data communication services.

NATIONAL COMPUTER SYSTEMS (NCS)
4401 West 76th Street, Edina MN 55435. 612/830-7600. **Contact:** Betsy Shober, Human Resources Director. **World Wide Web address:** http://www.ncs.com. **Description:** Manufactures scanners and collects data. **Corporate headquarters location:** Eden Prairie MN. **Other U.S. locations:** Mesa AZ; Laguna Hills CA; Iowa City IA. **Listed on:** NASDAQ. **Number of employees nationwide:** 3,000.

NATIONAL COMPUTER SYSTEMS (NCS)
11000 Prairie Lakes Drive, Eden Prairie MN 55344. 612/829-3000. **Toll-free phone:** 800/431-1421. **Contact:** Craig Mullin, Director of Sourcing and Staffing. **E-mail address:** info@ncs.com. **World Wide Web address:** http://www.ncs.com. **Description:** A global information services company providing software, service, and systems for the collection, management, and interpretation of data. **NOTE:** The company offers entry-level positions. **Common positions include:** Account Manager; Applications Engineer; Computer Programmer; Database Manager; Financial Analyst; Internet Services Manager; Project Manager; Systems Analyst; Systems Engineer; Systems Manager; Webmaster. **Educational backgrounds include:** Accounting; Computer Science; Engineering; Mathematics; Software Development; Software Tech. Support. **Benefits:** 401(k); Dental Insurance; Disability Coverage; Flexible Schedule; Life Insurance; Medical Insurance; Tuition Assistance. **Special programs:** Internships. **Corporate headquarters location:** This Location. **Other U.S. locations:** Mesa AZ; Laguna Hills CA; Iowa City IA; Edina MN. **Listed on:** NASDAQ. **Annual sales/revenues:** More than $100 million. **Number of employees nationwide:** 3,000.

NETWORK COMPUTING SERVICES, INC.
1200 Washington Avenue South, Minneapolis MN 55415. 612/337-0200. **Contact:** Personnel Department. **World Wide Web address:** http://www.networkcs.com. **Description:** Rents supercomputers to other companeis for inhouse use.

NORSTAN CONSULTING
7101 Metro Boulevard, Minneapolis MN 55439. 612/944-0181. **Contact:** Human Resources. **World Wide Web address:** http://www.norstan.com. **Description:** Offers computer consulting services to a variety of businesses. **Corporate headquarters location:** Minnetonka MN. **Parent company:** Norstan, Inc.

PC SOLUTIONS
3839 Washington Avenue North, Minneapolis MN 55412. 612/588-7501. **Contact:** Jim Clymer, Controller. **Description:** Custom designs, distributes, installs, and maintains networking systems, primarily for corporate customers.

PLASMON IDE
9625 West 76th Street, Suite 100, Eden Prairie MN 55344. 612/946-4100. **Contact:** Human Resources. **World Wide Web address:** http://www.plasmon.com. **Description:** Engaged in the manufacture of optical and media storage products.

ROVACK
P.O. Box 858, Lake Elmo MN 55042. 651/779-9444. **Physical address:** 3549 Lake Elmo Avenue North, Lake Elmo MN. **Contact:** Greg Walker, Director of Operations. **World Wide Web address:** http://www.rovack.com. **Description:** Develops software for the health care community.

Common positions include: Computer Programmer; Customer Service Representative; Services Sales Representative; Software Engineer; Systems Analyst. **Educational backgrounds include:** Accounting; Business Administration; Communications; Computer Science; Marketing. **Benefits:** Dental Insurance; Disability Coverage; Employee Discounts; Life Insurance; Medical Insurance; Profit Sharing. **Corporate headquarters location:** This Location. **Operations at this facility include:** Administration; Divisional Headquarters; Manufacturing; Regional Headquarters; Research and Development; Sales; Service. **Listed on:** Privately held. **Number of employees at this location:** 30.

SEAGATE TECHNOLOGY
7801 Computer Avenue South, Bloomington MN 55435-5489. 612/844-8000. **Fax:** 612/844-7008. **Contact:** John Rotty, Senior Director of Human Resources. **World Wide Web address:** http://www.seagate.com. **Description:** This location is a manufacturing facility. Overall, Seagate Technology is a designer and manufacturer of data storage devices and related products including hard disk drives, tape drives, software, and systems for many different computer-related applications and operating systems. These products include 2.5 and 3.5 inch drives with memory storage capacity between 150 megabytes and one gigabyte. The company sells its products primarily through a sales force to OEMs (original equipment manufacturers) and through non-affiliated distributors. **Common positions include:** Chemical Engineer; Mechanical Engineer; Software Engineer; Systems Analyst. **Educational backgrounds include:** Chemistry; Computer Science; Engineering; Physics. **Benefits:** 401(k); Dental Insurance; Disability Coverage; Employee Discounts; Life Insurance; Medical Insurance; Profit Sharing; Tuition Assistance. **Special programs:** Training. **Corporate headquarters location:** Scotts Valley CA. **Other U.S. locations:** OK. **Annual sales/revenues:** More than $100 million. **Number of employees at this location:** 3,500. **Number of employees nationwide:** 89,000.

SHOWCASE CORPORATION
4131 Highway 52 North, Suite G-111, Rochester MN 55901. 507/288-5922. **Contact:** Human Resources Department. **World Wide Web address:** http://www.showcasecorp.com. **Description:** Develops software designed to access AS/400 systems. ShowCase's main product is STRATEGY.

SILICON GRAPHICS, INC.
655 Lone Oak Drive, Eagan MN 55121. 612/452-6650. **Contact:** Carolyn Harrington, Personnel Director. **World Wide Web address:** http://www.sgi.com. **Description:** This location manufactures supercomputers. Overall, Silicon Graphics manufactures a family of workstation and server systems that are used by engineers, scientists, and other creative professionals to develop, analyze, and simulate complex, three-dimensional objects. Systems include Onyx, IRIS, Indigo, and Challenge, and all use RISC processors in their circuitry. **Corporate headquarters location:** Mountain View CA.

SOFTWARE AG AMERICAS
1650 West 82nd Street, Suite 750, Bloomington MN 55431. 612/888-4404. **Contact:** Recruiting. **World Wide Web address:** http://www.sagafyi.com. **Description:** This location develops some software products and serves as a regional sales office for Software AG Americas. **Corporate headquarters location:** Reston VA. **International locations:** Germany.

STORAGE TECHNOLOGY CORPORATION
60 South Sixth Street, Suite 3210, Minneapolis MN 55428. 612/339-6161. **Toll-free phone:** 800/248-8777. **Contact:** Human Resources. **World Wide Web address:** http://www.stortek.com. **Description:** This location is a sales and technical support office. Overall, Storage Technology Corporation manufactures high-performance computer information storage and retrieval systems for mainframe and mid-frame computers and networks. Products include automated cartridge systems, random access subsystems, and fault-tolerant disk arrays. The company also distributes equipment; sells new peripherals, software, and hardware; and offers support services. **Corporate headquarters location:** Louisville CO. **Listed on:** New York Stock Exchange.

STORAGETEK NETWORK SYSTEMS GROUP
7600 Boone Avenue North, Minneapolis MN 55428. 612/424-4888. **Contact:** Human Resources Manager. **Description:** A data telecommunications firm specializing in the local networking of mainframe computers and subsystems. **Number of employees at this location:** 1,000.

SUNRISE INTERNATIONAL LEASING
5500 Wayzata Boulevard, Suite 725, Golden Valley MN 55416. 612/593-1904. **Contact:** Linda Taube, Human Resources Manager. **Description:** Leases computers.

TECH SQUARED
5198 West 76th Street, Edina MN 55439. 612/832-5622. **Contact:** Human Resources Department. **World Wide Web address:** http://www.dtpdirect.com. **Description:** Tech Squared is a computer distributor that sells computers, scanners, monitors, and other desktop publishing-related hardware. Most of the company's business is generated through the company's catalog, DTP Direct.

TRANSITION NETWORKS
6475 City West Parkway, Minneapolis MN 55344. 612/941-7600. **Fax:** 612/941-2322. **Contact:** Human Resources Department. **E-mail address:** info@transition.com. **World Wide Web address:** http://www.transition.com. **Description:** Transition Networks is a manufacturer of computer networking hardware, including StackMaster Pro SPS 2000 static port switching hubs; SwitchMaster Ethernet bridge/switch products; StackMaster Ethernet stackable, manageable hubs; Ethernet hubs, transceivers, and media converters; Twinax/3X-AS400 baluns and active hubs; and Token Ring stackable hubs, repeaters, and media filters. **Corporate headquarters location:** This Location.

TREEV
8009 34th Avenue South, Suite 125, Bloomington MN 55425. 612/854-6109. **Contact:** Human Resources. **World Wide Web address:** http://www.treev.com. **Description:** This location is a sales office. Overall, Treev manufactures networking software, sells the applicable hardware, and offers technical assistance.

TRICORD SYSTEMS INC.
2905 Northwest Boulevard, Suite 20, Plymouth MN 55441. 612/557-9005. **Contact:** Human Resources Department. **Description:** Tricord Systems is a manufacturer of computer servers and related equipment.

TRIMIN SYSTEMS INC.
3030 Center Point Drive, Suite 100, Roseville MN 55113. 651/636-7667. **Contact:** Human Resources. **World Wide Web address:** http://www.triminsystems.com. **Description:** Develops and markets manufacturing software.

UNISYS CORPORATION
3199 Pilot Knob Road, Eagan MN 55121. 612/687-2200. **Contact:** Human Resources Department. **World Wide Web address:** http://www.unisys.com. **Description:** This location performs marketing and customer service functions. Overall, Unisys Corporation is a provider of information services, technology, and software. Unisys specializes in developing business critical solutions based on open information networks. The company's enabling software team creates a variety of software projects which facilitate the building of user applications and the management of distributed systems. The company's platforms group is responsible for UNIX operating systems running across a wide range of multiple processor server platforms, including all peripheral and communication drivers. The Unisys commercial parallel processing team develops microkernel-based operating systems, I/O device drivers, ATM hardware, diagnostics, and system architectures. The system management group is chartered with the overall management of development programs for UNIX desktop and entry-server products. **Corporate headquarters location:** Blue Bell PA. **Operations at this facility include:** Customer Service; Marketing. **Number of employees worldwide:** 49,000.

WINNEBAGO SOFTWARE COMPANY
457 East South Street, P.O. Box 430, Caledonia MN 55921. 507/724-5411. **Contact:** Nancy Hager, Vice President of Administration. **World Wide Web address:** http://www.winnebago.com. **Description:** A developer of software for libraries. Winnebago Software Company's products are used by librarians as well as by library patrons.

XATA CORPORATION
151 East Cliff Road, Suite 10, Burnsville MN 55337. 612/894-3680. **Fax:** 612/894-2463. **Contact:** Human Resources. **E-mail address:** info@xata.com. **World Wide Web address:** http://www. xata.com. **Description:** Manufactures onboard computers and software for the transportation and logistics segments of the fleet trucking industry. Founded in 1985. **Educational backgrounds include:** Engineering; Software Development; Transportation/Logistics. **Benefits:** 401(k); Dental Insurance; Disability Coverage; Life Insurance; Medical Insurance; Pension Plan; Profit Sharing. **Office hours:** Monday - Friday, 7:30 a.m. - 5:30 p.m. **Corporate headquarters location:** This Location. **Other U.S. locations:** Peoria IL. **Listed on:** NASDAQ. **Stock exchange symbol:** XATA. **CEO/President:** Dennis Johnson. **Number of employees at this location:** 75. **Number of employees nationwide:** 90.

ZH COMPUTER, INC.
7600 Frances Avenue South, Suite 550, Minneapolis MN 55435-5939. 612/844-0915. **Fax:** 612/844-9025. **Contact:** Judy Brown-Wescott, Human Resources. **E-mail address:** scidev@ zhcomp.com. **World Wide Web address:** http://www.zhcomputer.com. **Description:** A developer of software and products specializing in the application of advanced science and mathematics.

Note: Because addresses and telephone numbers of smaller companies can change rapidly, we recommend you call each company to verify the information below before inquiring about job opportunities. Mass mailings are not recommended.

Additional small employers:

COMPUTER MAINTENANCE AND REPAIR

Expresspoint Technology Services
7101 31st Ave N, Minneapolis MN 55427-2848. 612/591-0009.

Wang Laboratories Inc.
19011 Lake Dr E, Chanhassen MN 55317-9322. 612/906-6000.

COMPUTER MANUFACTURERS

Compaq Computer Corporation
2051 Killebrew Dr, Ste 100, Minneapolis MN 55425-1894. 612/851-2003.

General Dynamics Information Systems
8800 Queen Avenue S, Bloomington MN 55431-1908. 612/921-6097.

Micro Dynamics Corporation
PO Box 71, Montevideo MN 56265-0071. 320/269-5521.

Pemstar Inc.
2535 Highway 14 West, Rochester MN 55901-7596. 507/288-6720.

Plexus/NEI
1700 93rd Ln NE, Minneapolis MN 55449-4326. 612/785-9717.

Rosemount Control Systems
12000 Portland Avenue, Burnsville MN 55337-1522. 612/895-2000.

Siemens
7225 Northland Dr N, Minneapolis MN 55428-1516. 612/536-4100.

COMPUTER PERIPHERAL EQUIPMENT MANUFACTURERS

BH Electronics Inc.
604 Michigan Rd, Marshall MN 56258-2734. 507/532-3211.

Bit-3 Computer Corporation
1284 Corp Center Dr, St. Paul MN 55121. 612/905-4700.

CSP Inc.
14305 21st Ave N, Plymouth MN 55447-4695. 612/476-6866.

Digi International
10000 W 76th St, Eden Prairie MN 55344-3767. 612/943-1055.

Fieldworks Inc.
7631 Anagram Drive, Eden Prairie MN 55344-7310. 612/974-7000.

Kavouras Inc.
11400 Rupp Dr, Burnsville MN 55337-1279. 612/895-9515.

National Computer Systems
PO Box 21690, St. Paul MN 55121. 612/683-6000.

Netstar Inc.
10250 Valley View Rd, Eden Prairie MN 55344-3540. 612/943-8990.

Schott Corporation
604 E Erie Rd, Marshall MN 56258-2704. 507/532-3201.

COMPUTER PROCESSING AND DATA PREPARATION SERVICES

Adia Information Technologies
2051 Killebrew Dr, Ste 307, Minneapolis MN 55425-1896. 612/853-7823.

APS Services Inc.
PO Box 1559, St. Cloud MN 56302-1559. 320/654-8442.

Automatic Data Processing
8100 Cedar Ave S, Minneapolis MN 55425-1801. 612/854-1700.

Benchmark Media Services Inc.
5353 Nathan Ln North, Minneapolis MN 55442-1952. 612/553-9300.

Data Input Services Corp.
9555 James Ave S, Ste 270, Bloomington MN 55431-2547. 612/881-7000.

Keane Inc.
4131 Highway 52 N, Rochester MN 55901-0144. 507/281-8500.

National Business Systems
2905 W Service Rd, St. Paul MN 55121-1295. 612/688-0202.

Ontrack Data International
6321 Bury Dr, Ste 13-21, Eden Prairie MN 55346-1739. 612/937-1107.

Primenet Marketing Services
PO Box 21800, St. Paul MN 55121-0800. 612/405-4000.

Questpoint
1350 Energy Ln, Ste 200, St. Paul MN 55108-5254. 651/644-8898.

Sungard Financial Systems Inc.
601 2nd Ave S, Hopkins MN 55343-7779. 612/935-3300.

COMPUTER RENTAL AND LEASING

Comdisco Inc.
5468 Feltl Rd, Ste 200, Minnetonka MN 55343-7982. 612/938-5071.

COMPUTER SOFTWARE, PROGRAMMING, AND SYSTEMS DESIGN

Achieve Healthcare Information Systems
5501 Green Valley Dr, Minneapolis MN 55437-1003. 612/831-2300.

Adaytum Software Inc.
2001 Killebrew Dr #360, Minneapolis MN 55425-1865. 651/698-7624.

American Software
PO Box 240666, St. Paul MN 55124-0666. 612/440-8669.

B-Tree Systems
5929 Baker Rd, Ste 475, Minnetonka MN 55345-5955. 612/936-7887.

Berkley Information Services
10 Round Wind Rd, Luverne MN 56156. 507/283-9195.

Bindco Corporation
11900 Wayzata Boulevard,
Hopkins MN 55305-2031.
612/513-0193.

Bindco Corporation
6523 James Ave N, Brooklyn
Center MN 55430-1728. 612/561-
6775.

Born Information Services
294 Grove Ln E, Ste 100,
Wayzata MN 55391-1600.
612/404-4000.

Camax
7851 Metro Pkwy, Minneapolis
MN 55425-1524. 612/854-5300.

Centron Company Inc.
6455 City West Pkwy, Eden
Prairie MN 55344-3246. 612/829-
2800.

Ciber, Inc.
5353 Wayzata Blvd, Ste 400,
Minneapolis MN 55416-1333.
612/591-6100.

CICS
8100 26th Ave S, Ste 160,
Minneapolis MN 55425-1304.
612/854-3600.

CNT
605 Highway 169 N, Ste 800,
Plymouth MN 55441-6463.
612/797-6000.

Coda Music Technology Inc.
6210 Bury Dr, Eden Prairie MN
55346-1718. 612/937-9611.

Comdisco Network Services
5500 Feltl Rd, Hopkins MN
55343-7920. 612/931-9966.

Computer Horizons Corp.
431 S 7th St, Ste 2545,
Minneapolis MN 55415-1855.
612/337-8181.

Computer People Unlimited
608 2nd Ave S, Ste 585,
Minneapolis MN 55402-1911.
612/338-3001.

Compuware Corporation
6700 France Avenue S,
Minneapolis MN 55435-1902.
612/925-5900.

Connectivity Systems Inc.
3500 Holly Ln N, Ste 60,
Plymouth MN 55447-1284.
612/509-6600.

CWC
PO Box 4459, Mankato MN
56002-4459. 507/388-0500.

CWC
7401 Metro Blvd, Ste 200,
Minneapolis MN 55439-3030.
612/830-1339.

Cycle Software Services
8711 Lyndale Ave S,
Minneapolis MN 55420-2737.
612/884-6677.

**Dairyland Computers &
Consulting Co.**
PO Box 156, Glenwood MN
56334-0156. 320/634-5331.

Data Collection Systems Inc.
7555 Market Place Dr, Eden
Prairie MN 55344-3637. 612/947-
4088.

Datasource Hagen
5051 Highway 7, Minneapolis
MN 55416-2256. 612/844-1400.

DDS
80 S 8th St, Ste 1700,
Minneapolis MN 55402-2110.
612/332-5200.

Development Resource Group
7295 Silver Lake Rd, St. Paul
MN 55112-4446. 612/783-7878.

Disc Computer Systems
3055 Old Highway 8,
Minneapolis MN 55418-2500.
612/782-2450.

Help Systems Inc.
6101 Baker Rd, Ste 210,
Minnetonka MN 55345-5959.
612/933-0609.

Ideas
3500 Yankee Dr, Ste 350, St.
Paul MN 55121-1632. 612/905-
3200.

Inacom Information Systems
10300 Valley View Rd, Eden
Prairie MN 55344-3546. 612/946-
1100.

Inasyst Inc.
12224 Nicollet Avenue,
Burnsville MN 55337-1649.
612/890-1556.

Infinite Graphics Inc.
4611 East Lake Street,
Minneapolis MN 55406-2305.
612/721-6283.

Interactive Dataworks
8009 34th Ave S, Ste 1000,
Minneapolis MN 55425-1616.
612/814-2300.

Intercim
501 Highway 13 E, Burnsville
MN 55337-2884. 612/894-9010.

Intranet Solutions Inc.
8091 Wallace Road, Eden Prairie
MN 55344-2224. 612/903-2000.

ISI Systems Inc.
12450 Wayzata Blvd #121,
Minneapolis MN 55416. 612/542-
8601.

Job Boss Software Incorporated
7701 York Ave S, Ste 350,
Minneapolis MN 55435-5832.
612/831-7182.

**Magenic Technologies
Incorporated**
600 Highway 169 S, Ste 701,
Minneapolis MN 55426-1211.
612/512-7800.

**Micro Voice Applications
Incorporated**
100 S 5th St, Ste 1800,
Minneapolis MN 55402-1215.
612/373-9300.

Omni Resources Inc.
2051 Killebrew Dr, Ste 315,
Minneapolis MN 55425-1896.
612/851-3090.

Orion Consulting Inc.
880 Sibley Memorial Hwy, St.
Paul MN 55118-1736. 651/450-
1600.

Parametric Technology
8500 Normandale Lake Blvd,
Minneapolis MN 55437. 612/820-
0026.

Perigee Communications
10 2nd St NE, Ste 400,
Minneapolis MN 55413-2270.
612/379-0703.

PLATINUM technology inc.
11095 Viking Dr #125, Eden
Prairie MN 55344-7223. 612/906-
1590.

PRA Solutions LLC
333 S Seventh Street,
Minneapolis MN 55402-2414.
612/317-7501.

Programming Alternatives
7701 France Ave S, Ste 100,
Minneapolis MN 55435-5297.
612/922-1103.

Quikpages Inc.
12 N 12th St, Ste 400,
Minneapolis MN 55403-1331.
612/317-5100.

Racotek Inc.
7301 Ohms Ln, Ste 200,
Minneapolis MN 55439-2335.
612/832-9800.

**Rainier Technology
Incorporated**
1660 Highway 100 S,
Minneapolis MN 55416-1529.
612/595-8895.

Renaissance Worldwide
2850 Metro Dr, Ste 100,
Minneapolis MN 55425-1405.
612/851-3160.

Response Inc.
120 1st St NE, Rochester MN
55906-3717. 507/281-5005.

ROI Systems Inc.
435 Ford Rd, Ste 700,
Minneapolis MN 55426-4913.
612/595-0500.

Safenet Software Inc.
10125 Crosstown Cir, Eden
Prairie MN 55344-3319. 612/996-
0995.

SAP America Inc.
60 S 6th St, Ste 3530,
Minneapolis MN 55402-4401.
612/359-5000.

**Shared Resource Management
Inc.**
3550 Lexington Ave N,
Shoreview MN 55126-8048.
651/486-0417.

SSA Minneapolis
1000 Boone Ave N, Ste 500,
Minneapolis MN 55427-4474.
612/797-8700.

St. Paul Software Inc.
1450 Energy Park Dr, St. Paul
MN 55108-5227. 651/603-4400.

Stratagem Inc.
10201 Wayzata Blvd, Hopkins
MN 55305-5507. 612/542-8910.

Super Solutions Corporation
10100 Viking Dr, Ste 100, Eden
Prairie MN 55344-7255. 612/942-
6297.

Systems Group Inc.
80 S 8th St, Ste 3620,
Minneapolis MN 55402-2217.
612/349-9300.

Tech-Pro Inc.
3000 Centre Pointe Drive,
Roseville MN 55113-1122.
612/781-3216.

Techknowledge Inc.
1000 Shelard Pkwy, Ste 360,
Minneapolis MN 55426-4933.
612/545-0980.

Transcape
10800 Lyndale Ave S,
Minneapolis MN 55420-5614.
612/885-7287.

Unimax Systems Corporation
430 1st Ave N, Ste 790,
Minneapolis MN 55401-1738.
612/341-0946.

Wam Net International
6100 West 110th St, Minneapolis
MN 55438-2664. 612/886-5100.

**COMPUTERS AND
RELATED EQUIPMENT**

IBM Corp.
650 3rd Ave S, Ste 1100,
Minneapolis MN 55402-4300.
612/397-5356.

**MISC. COMPUTER
RELATED SERVICES**

**Advanced Duplication Services
Inc.**
14505 21st Ave N, Ste 228,
Plymouth MN 55447-5602.
612/473-0992.

**Computer Petroleum
Corporation**
30 7th St E, St. Paul MN 55101-
4914. 651/225-9550.

CSC Consulting Inc.
5500 Wayzata Blvd, Minneapolis
MN 55416-1241. 612/593-1122.

Data Base Ideas Inc.
6200 Shingle Creek Pkwy,
Brooklyn Center MN 55430-
2128. 612/561-4990.

Entex Information Services
1000 Boone Avenue N,

Minneapolis MN 55427-4466.
612/797-0068.

Gartner Group Learning Inc.
10729 Bren Rd E, Hopkins MN
55343-9056. 612/930-0330.

Harmonic Systems Inc.
701 4th Ave S, Ste 320,
Minneapolis MN 55415-1600.
612/672-9330.

Keane Inc.
2901 Metro Dr, Ste 525,
Minneapolis MN 55425-1559.
612/851-3200.

Rimage Services Group
9701 Penn Ave S, Ste 101,
Bloomington MN 55431-2544.
612/881-4207.

Servicenet
333 S 7th St, Ste 500,
Minneapolis MN 55402-2414.
612/317-7777.

Skamp Corporation
6462 City West Pkwy, Eden
Prairie MN 55344-7734. 612/941-
0696.

Soft Link Inc.
2375 Ariel Street North,
Maplewood MN 55109-2248.
651/776-7963.

Talus Group Inc.
1550 Utica Ave S, Ste 555,
Minneapolis MN 55416-5305.
612/544-2526.

Teltech
2850 Metro Dr, Ste 600,
Minneapolis MN 55425-1589.
612/851-7500.

Whittman-Hart Inc.
5700 Smetana Dr, Ste 300,
Hopkins MN 55343-9686.
612/945-0944.

For more information on career opportunities in the computer industry:

<u>Associations</u>

AMERICAN INTERNET ASSOCIATION
World Wide Web address: http://www.amernet.org.
A nonprofit association providing assistance in the use
of the Internet. Membership required.

**ASSOCIATION FOR COMPUTING
MACHINERY**
1515 Broadway, 17th Floor, New York NY 10036.
212/869-7440. World Wide Web address: http://www.
acm.org. An association dedicated to the field of
information technology. Also offers a variety of
related publications. Membership required.

**ASSOCIATION FOR MULTIMEDIA
COMMUNICATIONS**
P.O. Box 10645, Chicago IL 60610. 312/409-1032. E-
mail address: amc@amcomm.org. World Wide Web

address: http://www.amcomm.org. A multimedia and
Internet association.

ASSOCIATION FOR WOMEN IN COMPUTING
41 Sutter Street, Suite 1006, San Francisco CA 94104.
415/905-4663. E-mail address: awc@awe.org. World
Wide Web address: http://www.awc-hq.org. A
nonprofit organization promoting women in
computing professions.

**ASSOCIATION OF INTERNET
PROFESSIONALS**
1301 Fifth Avenue, Suite 3300, Seattle WA 98101. E-
mail address: info@associp.org. World Wide Web
address: http://www.associp.org. A nonprofit trade
association providing a forum for Internet users and
professionals.

BLACK DATA PROCESSING ASSOCIATES
1111 14th Street NW, Suite 700, Washington DC
20005-5603. Toll-free phone: 800/727-BDPA. E-mail
address: nbdpa@bdpa.org. World Wide Web address:
http://www.bdpa.org. An organization of information
technology professionals serving the minority
community.

**THE CENTER FOR SOFTWARE
DEVELOPMENT**
111 West St. John, Suite 200, San Jose CA 95113.
408/494-8378. E-mail address: info@center.org.
World Wide Web address: http://www.center.org. A
nonprofit organization providing technical and
business resources for software developers.

**COMMERCIAL INTERNET EXCHANGE
ASSOCIATION (CIX)**
1041 Sterling Road, Suite 104A, Herndon VA 20170.
703/709-8200. E-mail address: helpdesk@cix.org.
World Wide Web address: http://www.cix.org. A
nonprofit trade association of data internetworking
service providers.

HTML WRITERS GUILD
World Wide Web address: http://www.hwg.org. An
international organization of Web page writers and
Internet professionals.

**INFORMATION TECHNOLOGY
ASSOCIATION OF AMERICA**
1616 North Fort Myer Drive, Suite 1300, Arlington
VA 22209. 703/522-5055. World Wide Web address:
http://www.itaa.org.

INTERNET ALLIANCE
1825 Eye Street, Suite 400, P.O. Box 65782,
Washington DC 20035. 202/955-8091. World Wide
Web address: http://www.isa.net.

MULTIMEDIA DEVELOPMENT GROUP
520 Third Street, Suite 257, San Francisco CA 94107.
415/512-3556. Fax: 415/512-3569. E-mail address:
geninfo@mdg.org. A nonprofit trade association
dedicated to the business and market development of
multimedia companies.

THE OPEN GROUP
29-B Montvale Avenue, Woburn MA 01801.
781/376-8200. World Wide Web address: http://www.
opengroup.org. A consortium concerned with open
systems technology in the information systems
industry. Membership required.

**SOCIETY FOR INFORMATION
MANAGEMENT**
401 North Michigan Avenue, Chicago IL 60611-4267.
312/644-6610. E-mail address: info@simnet.org.
World Wide Web address: http://www.simnet.org. A
forum for information technology professionals.

SOFTWARE FORUM
953 Industrial Avenue, Suite 117, Palo Alto CA
94303. 650/856-3706. E-mail address: info@
softwareforum.org. World Wide Web address:
http://www.softwareforum.org. An independent,
nonprofit organization for software industry
professionals.

SOFTWARE PUBLISHERS ASSOCIATION
1730 M Street NW, Suite 700, Washington DC
20036. 202/452-1600. World Wide Web address:
http://www.spa.org.

**SOFTWARE SUPPORT PROFESSIONALS
ASSOCIATION**
11858 Bernardo Plaza Court, Suite 101C, San Diego
CA 92128. Toll-free phone: 877/ASK-SSPA. World
Wide Web address: http://www.sspa-online.com. A
forum for service and support professionals in the
software industry.

USENIX ASSOCIATION
2560 Ninth Street, Berkeley CA 94710. 510/528-
8649. World Wide Web address: http://www.usenix.
org. An advanced computing systems professional
association for engineers, systems administrators,
scientists, and technicians.

WORLD WIDE WEB TRADE ASSOCIATION
World Wide Web address: http://www.web-star.com/
wwwta.html. An association promoting responsible
use of the World Wide Web.

Magazines

COMPUTER-AIDED ENGINEERING
Penton Media, 1100 Superior Avenue, Cleveland OH
44114. 216/696-7000. World Wide Web address:
http://www.penton.com/cae.

DATA COMMUNICATIONS
McGraw-Hill, 3 Park Avenue, 31st Floor, New York
NY 10013. 212/512-2000.

DATAMATION
Earthweb Inc., 10 Post Office Square, Suite 600
South, Boston MA 02109. 617/988-2767. World Wide
Web address: http://www.datamation.com.

IDC REPORT
International Data Corporation, 5 Speen Street,
Framingham MA 01701. 508/872-8200.

Online Services

COMPUTER CONSULTANTS
Go: Consult. A CompuServe discussion group for
computer professionals interested in networking and
business development.

COMPUTERWORLD
http://www.computerworld.com. A weekly online
newspaper for information sciences professionals.
Features the latest news and employment
opportunities. *Computerworld* conducts a job search
by skills, job level (entry-level or experienced), job
title, company, and your choice of three cities and
three states. One feature of this site is "Career
Central," a service which e-mails you when a job
matches the skills you have submitted online. This site
also has corporate profiles, an events calendar,
Computerworld's publications, an index of graduate
schools, and other informative and educational
resources.

IT JOBS
http://www.internet-solutions.com/itjobs/us/usselect.
htm. This Website provides links to companies that
have job openings in the information technology
industry.

JOBSERVE
http://www.jobserve.com. Provides information on job
openings in the field of information technology for
companies throughout Europe. The site also offers
links to numerous company Web pages, resume
posting services, and a directory of recruiters.

SELECTJOBS
http://www.selectjobs.com. Post a resume and search the job database by region, discipline, special requirements, and skills on *SelectJOBS*. Once your search criteria has been entered, this site will automatically e-mail you when a job opportunity matches your requests.

THE SOFTWARE JOBS HOMEPAGE
http://www.softwarejobs.com. This Website offers a searchable database of openings for jobseekers looking in the software industry. The site is run by Allen Davis & Associates.

EDUCATIONAL SERVICES

 *Job prospects remain favorable in educational services, due to a healthy demand for qualified teachers at all levels. The U.S. Department of Labor projects that over the next 10 years, more than 2 million teachers will retire. Demand will be strong for elementary and secondary teachers, college and university faculty, education administrators, school counselors, kindergarten teachers, and teacher assistants. Special education teachers are still in strong demand, with a 56 percent projected increase in openings through 2005. According to the U.S. Department of Education, a need for additional educators in the areas of bilingual education, math, and science is likely.*

It is estimated that national high school enrollment will increase 11 percent by 2008. As the enrollment swells in elementary and secondary schools, and at higher learning institutions, operating costs will rise significantly as well. Among the cost pressures schools face are the implementation of computer technology in the classroom and curriculum changes.

According to Business Week, *colleges and universities under fiscal constraints are struggling to meet the challenges of sustaining a high level of teaching and curricula without increasing tuition to the point that they are not affordable for the majority of students. For their part, some states (such as Massachusetts) are currently implementing programs that require teachers to pass aptitude tests, in efforts of improving the quality of education.*

AUGSBURG COLLEGE
2211 Riverside Avenue, CB 79, Minneapolis MN 55454. 612/330-1000. **Recorded jobline:** 612/330-1317. **Contact:** Marquitta Frost, Staffing Manager. **World Wide Web address:** http://www.augsburg.edu. **Description:** A private, four-year college with graduate programs in education, leadership, and sociology.

CARLETON COLLEGE
One North College Street, Northfield MN 55057. 507/646-4000. **Contact:** Human Resources. **World Wide Web address:** http://www.carleton.edu. **Description:** A private, four-year, liberal arts college.

CENTURY COLLEGE
3300 Century Avenue, White Bear Lake MN 55110. 651/779-3200. **Contact:** Betty Mayer, Human Resources Director. **World Wide Web address:** http://www.century.cc.mn.us. **Description:** A community college offering Associate in Art, Associate in Science, and Associate in Applied Science degrees, as well as diplomas and certificates.

COLLEGE OF SAINT BENEDICT
37 College Avenue South, St. Joseph MN 56374. 320/363-5011. **Contact:** Herb Trenz, Director of Human Resources. **World Wide Web address:** http://www.csbsju.edu. **Description:** A private, four-year, liberal arts college for women.

HAMLINE UNIVERSITY
1536 Hewitt Avenue, St. Paul MN 55104. 651/523-2800. **Recorded jobline:** 651/523-3046. **Contact:** Dixie Lindsley, Director of Human Resources. **World Wide Web address:** http://www.hamline.edu. **Description:** A private, Methodist university. Hamline also has a law school and offers graduate programs to the doctoral level.

INVER HILLS COMMUNITY COLLEGE
2500 80th Street East, Inver Grove Heights MN 55076-3209. 651/450-8500. **Contact:** Human Resources. **World Wide Web address:** http://www.ih.cc.mn.us. **Description:** A state community

college offering Associate in Science and Associate in Applied Science degrees, as well as vocational certificates.

MACALESTER COLLEGE
1600 Grand Avenue, St. Paul MN 55105. 651/696-6000. **Fax:** 651/696-6612. **Contact:** Ms. Terry Bailey, Human Resources Representative. **World Wide Web address:** http://www.macalester.edu. **Description:** A private, four-year, liberal arts college. **Common positions include:** Accountant/ Auditor; Administrative Assistant; Counselor; Education Administrator; Geologist/Geophysicist; Human Resources Manager; Librarian; Licensed Practical Nurse; Psychologist; Registered Nurse; Secretary. **Educational backgrounds include:** Accounting; Art/Design; Biology; Business Administration; Chemistry; Communications; Computer Science; Economics; Finance; Geology; Health Care; Liberal Arts; Mathematics. **Benefits:** 403(b); Dental Insurance; Disability Coverage; Employee Discounts; Financial Planning Assistance; Flexible Schedule; Job Sharing; Life Insurance; Medical Insurance; Pension Plan; Telecommuting; Tuition Assistance.

MINNESOTA STATE UNIVERSITY MANKATO
Human Resources Box 47, P.O. Box 8400, Mankato MN 56002-8400. 507/389-2191. **Contact:** Human Resources. **World Wide Web address:** http://www.mankato.msus.edu. **Description:** A four-year, state university offering undergraduate and graduate degrees in arts and humanities; business; education; nursing; science, engineering, and technology; and social and behavioral sciences. Approximately 12,000 students attend Minnesota State University Mankato.

MOORHEAD STATE UNIVERSITY
1104 Seventh Avenue South, Moorhead MN 56563. 218/236-2158. **Contact:** Human Resources. **World Wide Web address:** http://www.moorhead.msus.edu. **Description:** A four-year, state university offering bachelor's and master's degrees in over 100 majors, as well as pre-professional programs in 20 disciplines. Approximately 6,400 students attend Moorhead State University.

NORMANDALE COMMUNITY COLLEGE
9700 France Avenue South, Bloomington MN 55431. 612/832-6000. **Contact:** Director of Human Resources. **Description:** A two-year community college.

ST. CLOUD STATE UNIVERSITY
720 Fourth Avenue South, St. Cloud MN 56301. 320/255-3203. **Contact:** Human Resources. **World Wide Web address:** http://www.stcloudstate.edu. **Description:** A four-year state university.

SOUTHWEST STATE UNIVERSITY
1501 State Street, Marshall MN 56258. 507/537-7021. **Contact:** Personnel Services Manager. **Description:** A four-year, state university with 2,400 students. The university offers graduate programs in education and management.

TESSERACT GROUP
3800 West 80th Street, Suite 1400, Minneapolis MN 55431. 612/832-0092. **Contact:** Nicole Manderscheid, Human Resources Coordinator. **Description:** Owns, operates, and consults with private schools and seeks to establish contracts to operate public charter schools.

UNIVERSITY OF MINNESOTA DULUTH
10 University Drive, Duluth MN 55812. 218/726-7106. **Contact:** Human Resources. **World Wide Web address:** http://www.d.umn.edu. **Description:** A branch of the four-year, state university offering undergraduate and graduate degrees. **Corporate headquarters location:** Minneapolis MN.

UNIVERSITY OF MINNESOTA MORRIS
600 East Fourth Street, Behmler Hall, Morris MN 56267. 320/589-6021. **Contact:** Sarah Mattson, Office of the Chancellor. **Description:** A public, liberal arts college offering bachelor's degrees and pre-professional programs. **Corporate headquarters location:** Minneapolis MN. **Number of employees at this location:** 380.

UNIVERSITY OF MINNESOTA TWIN CITIES
319 15th Avenue SE, Room 200, Donhowe Building, Minneapolis MN 55455. 612/625-3861. **Fax:** 612/624-6037. **Contact:** Nan Wilhelmson, Director of Staffing and Employment. **World Wide Web address:** http://www.umn.edu/ohr/jobs. **Description:** A four-year, state university offering 161 bachelor's degrees, 218 master's degrees, 114 doctoral degrees, and five professional degrees. **Common positions include:** Accountant/Auditor; Administrative Manager; Agricultural Scientist; Attorney; Biological Scientist; Chemist; Clerical Supervisor; Computer Programmer; Counselor;

Customer Service Representative; Dental Assistant/Dental Hygienist; Editor; Human Resources Manager; Library Technician; Medical Records Technician; Pharmacist; Physical Therapist; Physician; Physicist; Public Relations Specialist; Purchasing Agent/Manager; Radiological Technologist; Real Estate Agent; Registered Nurse; Restaurant/Food Service Manager; Science Technologist; Systems Analyst; Teacher/Professor; Transportation/Traffic Specialist; Veterinarian. **Educational backgrounds include:** Accounting; Art/Design; Business Administration; Chemistry; Communications; Computer Science; Health Care. **Benefits:** Dental Insurance; Disability Coverage; Life Insurance; Medical Insurance; Pension Plan; Tuition Assistance. **Corporate headquarters location:** This Location. **Operations at this facility include:** Administration; Research and Development; Service.

UNIVERSITY OF ST. THOMAS
Mail Number AQU217, 2115 Summit Avenue, St. Paul MN 55105. 651/962-6510. **Contact:** Human Resources. **World Wide Web address:** http://www.hr.stthomas.edu. **Description:** A private, four-year, liberal arts college.

WINONA STATE UNIVERSITY
P.O. Box 5838, Winona MN 55987-5838. 507/457-5000. **Contact:** Tess Kruger, Director of Human Resources. **World Wide Web address:** http://www.winona.msus.edu. **Description:** A four-year, state university offering undergraduate, graduate, and pre-professional programs through Winona State University's five colleges: business, education, liberal arts, nursing and health sciences, and science and engineering. Approximately 7,200 students attend the university.

Note: Because addresses and telephone numbers of smaller companies can change rapidly, we recommend you call each company to verify the information below before inquiring about job opportunities. Mass mailings are not recommended.

Additional small employers:

BUSINESS, SECRETARIAL, AND DATA PROCESSING SCHOOLS

TRO Learning Inc.
4660 West 77th Street, Minneapolis MN 55435-4911. 612/832-1000.

CHILD DAYCARE SERVICES

Kids Come First Children's Center
1818 Greenview Pl SW, Rochester MN 55902-1076. 507/281-8953.

Playworks
2200 Trail of Dreams NW, Prior Lake MN 55372-1057. 612/445-7529.

Shakopee Head Start Inc.
1257 Marschall Rd, Ste 100, Shakopee MN 55379-2854. 612/496-2125.

Southwest YMCA Child Care
550 Opperman Dr, St. Paul MN 55123-1337. 612/456-5437.

COLLEGES, UNIVERSITIES, AND PROFESSIONAL SCHOOLS

Bemidji State University
1500 Birchmont Dr NE, Bemidji MN 56601-2600. 218/755-2000.

College of St. Scholastica Inc.
1200 Kenwood Ave, Duluth MN 55811-4199. 218/723-6042.

Concordia University St. Paul
275 Syndicate St N, St. Paul MN 55104-5436. 651/641-8278.

Crown College
6425 County Road 30, St. Bonifacius MN 55375-9002. 612/446-4121.

Dakota County Technical College
1300 145th Street East, Rosemount MN 55068-2932. 612/423-8000.

Gustavus Adolphus College
800 W College Ave, St. Peter MN 56082-1485. 507/933-8000.

Martin Luther College
1995 Luther Ct, New Ulm MN 56073-3965. 507/354-8221.

Metropolitan State University
700 7th St E, St. Paul MN 55106-5003. 651/772-7777.

North Central Bible College
910 Elliot Ave, Minneapolis MN 55404-1322. 612/332-3491.

Northwestern College of Chiropractics
2501 W 84th St, Bloomington MN 55431-1602. 612/888-4777.

Pillsbury Baptist Bible College
315 S Grove Ave, Owatonna MN 55060-3068. 507/451-2710.

Riverland Community College
2200 Tech Dr, Albert Lea MN 56007-3402. 507/373-0656.

St. John's University
PO Box 5000, Collegeville MN 56321-5000. 320/363-3166.

St. Mary's University
700 Terrace Hts, Winona MN 55987-1321. 507/452-4430.

St. Mary's University
2510 Park Ave, Minneapolis MN 55404-4403. 612/874-9877.

St. Olaf College
1520 St. Olaf Ave, Northfield MN 55057-1574. 507/646-2222.

University of Minnesota Crookston
2900 University Ave, Crookston MN 56716-5000. 218/281-6510.

William Mitchell College of Law
875 Summit Ave, St. Paul MN 55105-3030. 651/227-9171.

ELEMENTARY AND SECONDARY SCHOOLS

Albany High School
PO Box 330, Albany MN 56307-0330. 320/845-2161.

Andersen Open Elementary School
1098 Andersen Ln, Minneapolis MN 55407-1109. 612/627-2295.

Anoka Senior High School
3939 7th Ave, Anoka MN 55303-1261. 612/506-6200.

Anoka-Hennepin Independent School District
11299 Hanson Blvd NW, Coon Rapids MN 55433-3715. 612/506-1000.

Anoka-Hennepin Independent School District
625 109th Ave N, Champlin MN 55316. 612/493-8600.

Austin Senior High School
301 3rd St NW, Austin MN 55912-3128. 507/433-0401.

Becker Junior Senior High School
12000 Hancock St, Becker MN 55308-9561. 612/261-4501.

Bemidji Middle School
1910 Middle School Ave NW, Bemidji MN 56601-5500. 218/759-3210.

Bemidji Senior High School
201 15th St NW, Bemidji MN 56601-3865. 218/759-3135.

Bendix Elementary School
PO Box 190, Annandale MN 55302-0190. 320/274-8218.

Benjamin Mays Elementary School
560 Concordia Ave, St. Paul MN 55103-2443. 651/293-8730.

Bishop Elementary School
406 36th Ave NW, Rochester MN 55901-7541. 507/281-6063.

Black Hawk Middle School
1540 Deerwood Dr, Eagan MN 55122-1834. 612/683-8521.

Blackduck Independent School District
PO Box N, Blackduck MN 56630-0342. 218/835-5200.

Blaine Senior High School
12555 University Ave N, Minneapolis MN 55434-2108. 612/422-5800.

Blake School
511 Kenwood Pkwy, Minneapolis MN 55403-1135. 612/377-1245.

Bloomington Public School District
8900 Portland Ave, Minneapolis MN 55420-2919. 612/885-8450.

Blue Earth Elementary School
315 E 6th St, Blue Earth MN 56013-2006. 507/526-3188.

Brainerd High School
702 S 5th St, Brainerd MN 56401-4019. 218/828-5255.

Breck School
123 Ottawa Ave N, Crystal MN 55422-5124. 612/377-5000.

Breckenridge High School
710 13th St N, Breckenridge MN 56520-1317. 218/643-2694.

Brooklyn Center High School
6500 Humboldt Ave N, Brooklyn Center MN 55430-1800. 612/561-2120.

Brooklyn Junior High School
7377 Noble Ave N, Minneapolis MN 55443-3312. 612/566-6893.

Bryn Mawr Primary School
252 Upton Ave S, Minneapolis MN 55405-1944. 612/627-7180.

Buffalo High School
877 Bison Blvd, Buffalo MN 55313-4322. 612/682-8100.

Burnsville Eagan Savage School District
100 River Ridge Ct, Burnsville MN 55337-1613. 612/707-2000.

Cambridge Elementary School
310 Elm St N, Cambridge MN 55008-1079. 612/689-1670.

Cass Lake Independent School District
Rural Route 3, Box 4, Cass Lake MN 56633-8900. 218/335-2204.

Central High School
2451 Eagle Ridge Dr, Red Wing MN 55066-7444. 651/385-4500.

Central High School
800 E Central Entrance, Duluth MN 55811-5541. 218/722-6343.

Central High School
275 Lexington Pkwy N, St. Paul MN 55104-5402. 651/293-8700.

Central High School
400 Maple Ave E, Mora MN 55051-1334. 320/679-3560.

Central Middle School
8025 School Rd, Eden Prairie MN 55344-2234. 612/975-7300.

Chaska High School
545 Pioneer Trl, Chaska MN 55318-1153. 612/361-5470.

Chaska Middle School
1600 Park Ridge Dr, Chaska MN 55318-2806. 612/448-8700.

Chippewa Middle School
5000 Hodgson Rd, Shoreview MN 55126-1226. 651/483-6635.

Cleveland Middle School
1000 Walsh St, St. Paul MN 55106-3122. 651/293-8880.

Columbia Heights Public Schools
1400 49th Ave NE, Minneapolis MN 55421-1939. 612/586-6505.

Como Park High School
740 Rose Ave W, St. Paul MN 55117-4042. 651/293-8800.

Coon Rapids Junior High School
11600 Raven St NW, Coon Rapids MN 55433-3011. 612/422-5400.

Dakota Hills Middle School
4183 Braddock Trl, St. Paul MN 55123-1575. 612/683-6800.

Dassel Cokato Middle School
PO Box Q, Cokato MN 55321-0287. 320/286-6321.

Dawson Boyd High School
848 Chestnut St, Dawson MN 56232-2224. 320/769-2955.

Denfield High School
4405 W 4th St, Duluth MN 55807. 218/624-4833.

Dilworth Glendon Felton School
113 Main St, Dilworth MN 56529. 218/287-2371.

Discovery School
700 7th St S, Waite Park MN 56387-1512. 320/251-7770.

Dowling Elementary School
3900 W River Pkwy, Minneapolis MN 55406-3612. 612/627-2732.

Duluth Public Schools
215 N 1st Ave E, Duluth MN 55802-2058. 218/723-4150.

Eagan High School
4185 Braddock Trl, St. Paul MN 55123-1575. 612/683-6900.

Earle Brown Elementary School
5900 Humboldt Ave N, Brooklyn Center MN 55430-2639. 612/561-4480.

East Consolidated Elementary School
409 Case Ave, St. Paul MN 55101-4051. 651/293-8685.

East Elementary School
600 Columbia Ave, Morris MN 56267-1230. 320/589-1250.

East High School
2900 E 4th St, Duluth MN 55812.
218/724-8827.

Eden Prairie High School
17185 Valley View Rd, Eden
Prairie MN 55346-4252. 612/975-
8000.

Edina Public Schools
5701 Normandale Rd, Edina MN
55424-2400. 612/928-2500.

Edina Senior High School
6754 Valley View Rd,
Minneapolis MN 55439-1761.
612/947-1900.

Edison High School
700 22nd Ave NE, Minneapolis
MN 55418-3602. 612/627-2982.

**Edward D. Neill Elementary
School**
6600 27th Ave N, Minneapolis
MN 55427-3042. 612/545-3747.

**Elk River Area Senior High
School**
900 School St, Elk River MN
55330-1336. 612/441-1390.

Ellis Middle School
1700 4th Ave SE, Austin MN
55912-4221. 507/433-7093.

Epiphany School
11001 Hanson Blvd NW, Coon
Rapids MN 55433-4142.
612/754-1750.

Eveleth-Gilbert Public Schools
801 Jones St, Eveleth MN 55734-
1633. 218/744-4380.

Expo Magnet School
540 Warwick St, St. Paul MN
55116-1538. 651/290-8384.

Fairmont High School
900 Johnson St, Fairmont MN
56031-4502. 507/238-4411.

Falls High School
1515 11th Ave, International MN
56649-3618. 218/283-2571.

Faribault Public Schools
PO Box 618, Faribault MN
55021-0618. 507/333-6000.

Farmington High School
800 Denmark Avenue,
Farmington MN 55024-9002.
612/463-6501.

Farmington Middle School
4200 208th St W, Farmington
MN 55024-8812. 612/463-6560.

Fergus Falls Middle School
601 Randolph Avenue, Fergus
Falls MN 56537-1669. 218/736-
5601.

Fergus Falls Senior High School
502 Friberg Ave, Fergus Falls
MN 56537-2280. 218/736-6971.

**Foley Intermediate Elementary
School**
PO Box 297, Foley MN 56329-
0297. 320/968-6251.

Folwell Middle School
3611 20th Ave S, Minneapolis
MN 55407-2901. 612/627-2604.

Forest Lake Senior High School
6101 Scandia Trl N, Forest Lake
MN 55025-2630. 651/464-9200.

Fridley Middle School
6100 Moore Lake Dr W, Fridley
MN 55432-5602. 612/571-6000.

Galtier Elementary School
1317 Charles Ave, St. Paul MN
55104-2519. 651/293-8710.

Gaylord Elementary School
PO Box 356, Gaylord MN 55334-
0356. 507/237-5511.

**Groveland Park Elementary
School**
2045 Saint Clair Ave, St. Paul
MN 55105-1651. 651/293-8760.

**Hancock Hamline University
Magnet School**
1599 Englewood Ave, St. Paul
MN 55104-1224. 651/293-8715.

Harding High School
1540 6th St E, St. Paul MN
55106-4806. 651/293-8900.

**Hastings Independent School
District**
9th & Vermillion St, Hastings
MN 55033. 651/437-6111.

Hawley Public School
PO Box 608, Hawley MN 56549-
0608. 218/483-3555.

**Hazel Park Academy Middle
School**
1140 White Bear Ave N, St. Paul
MN 55106-3004. 651/293-8920.

**Henry Sibley Senior High
School**
1897 Delaware Ave, St. Paul MN
55118-4338. 612/681-2350.

Hibbing Senior High School
800 E 21st St, Hibbing MN
55746-1803. 218/263-3675.

**Hopkins North Junior High
School**
10700 Cedar Lake Rd, Hopkins
MN 55305-3361. 612/988-4800.

**Hopkins West Junior High
School**
3830 Baker Rd, Hopkins MN
55305-4900. 612/988-4400.

**Howard Lake-Waverly
Secondary School**
PO Box 708, Howard Lake MN
55349-0708. 320/543-3471.

**Hubert Olson Junior High
School**
4551 W 102nd St, Minneapolis
MN 55437-2610. 612/844-2900.

Humboldt Senior High School
30 Baker St E, St. Paul MN
55107-2966. 651/293-8600.

Hutchinson Middle School
1365 S Grade Rd SW,
Hutchinson MN 55350-9005.
320/587-2854.

Hutchinson Senior High School
1200 Roberts Road SW,
Hutchinson MN 55350-2145.
320/587-3797.

**Inver Grove Heights Middle
School**
8167 Cahill Avenue, South St.
Paul MN 55076-3236. 651/457-
7220.

Irondale High School
2425 Long Lake Rd, St. Paul MN
55112-5267. 612/786-5200.

Jackson High School
1128 North Hwy, Jackson MN
56143-1075. 507/847-5310.

Jefferson School
318 South Payne Street, New
Ulm MN 56073-3272. 507/359-
8460.

Jefferson Senior High School
4001 W 102nd St, Minneapolis
MN 55437-2602. 612/844-5000.

Jenny Lind Elementary School
5025 Bryant Ave N, Brooklyn
Center MN 55430-3500. 612/627-
2973.

JF Kennedy High School
9701 Nicollet Ave, Minneapolis
MN 55420-4448. 612/885-7800.

**John Adams Junior High
School**
1525 31st St NW, Rochester MN
55901-1436. 507/285-8840.

**John Marshall Senior High
School**
1510 14th St NW, Rochester MN
55901-0244. 507/285-8681.

Johnson Senior High School
1349 Arcade St, St. Paul MN
55106-1801. 651/293-8890.

**Joseph Nicollet Junior High
School**
400 E 134th St, Burnsville MN
55337-4010. 612/707-2600.

Kellogg Middle School
503 17th St NE, Rochester MN
55906-4216. 507/285-8701.

Kennedy Elementary School
824 W 7th St, Willmar MN
56201. 320/235-4419.

**Kerkhoven-Murdock-Sunburg
School District**
PO Box 168, Kerkhoven MN
56252-0168. 320/264-1411.

Lake of The Woods School
PO Box 310, Baudette MN
56623-0310. 218/634-2735.

**Lincoln Center Elementary
School**
357 9th Ave N, South St. Paul
MN 55075-1907. 651/457-9426.

Lincoln Elementary School
510 Lincoln Ave NW, Faribault
MN 55021-4722. 507/334-5525.

Lincoln Elementary School
204 Willow St E, Detroit Lakes
MN 56501-4004. 218/847-4123.

Lincoln Park K-8 School
2427 W 4th St, Duluth MN
55806-1505. 218/722-3935.

Linwood Elementary School
1023 Osceola Ave, St. Paul MN
55105-3233. 651/293-6606.

Little Falls Senior High School
1001 5th Ave SE, Little Falls MN
56345-3357. 320/632-2921.

**Long Prairie-Grey Eagle
Secondary School**
205 2nd St S, Long Prairie MN
56347-1603. 320/732-2194.

**Longfellow Magnet Elementary
School**
318 Moore St, St. Paul MN
55104-5152. 651/293-8725.

Luverne Elementary School
PO Box 278, Luverne MN 56156.
507/283-4497.

Luverne Public Schools
709 N Kniss Ave, Luverne MN
56156-1229. 507/283-8088.

Mahnomen Elementary School
PO Box 319, Mahnomen MN
56557-0319. 218/935-2581.

**Mankato West Junior Senior
High School**
PO Box 8713, Mankato MN
56002-8713. 507/387-3461.

**Maple Grove Junior High
School**
7000 Hemlock Ln N, Maple
Grove MN 55369-5572. 612/425-
4500.

Maple Lake Public School
PO Box 820, Maple Lake MN
55358-0820. 320/963-3171.

Maplewood Middle School
2410 Holloway Ave E,
Maplewood MN 55109-4006.
651/770-4691.

Marshall School
1215 Rice Lake Rd, Duluth MN
55811-2160. 218/727-7266.

**Maxfield Magnet Elementary
School**
380 Victoria St N, St. Paul MN
55104-4849. 651/293-8680.

McArthur Elementary School
727 N Central Ave, Duluth MN
55807-1304. 218/628-0265.

**Menahga Independent School
District**
PO Box 160, Menahga MN
56464-0160. 218/564-4141.

Minneapolis Public Schools
807 Broadway St NE,
Minneapolis MN 55413-2332.
612/627-2050.

**Minnesota Center for Arts
Education**
6125 Olson Memorial Hwy,
Crystal MN 55422-4918.
612/591-4748.

**Minnesota State Academy for
the Deaf**
PO Box 308, Faribault MN
55021-0308. 507/332-5400.

Minnetonka Junior High School
17000 Lake Street Ext,
Minnetonka MN 55345-2530.
612/935-8601.

Minnetonka Senior High School
18301 Highway 7, Minnetonka
MN 55345-4114. 612/470-3500.

Monroe Elementary School
810 Palace Ave, St. Paul MN
55102-3435. 651/293-8690.

Monticello Public School
PO Box 897, Monticello MN
55362-0897. 612/295-5184.

Moorhead Junior High School
2020 11th St S, Moorhead MN
56560-3676. 218/299-6290.

Moorhead Senior High School
2300 4th Ave S, Moorhead MN
56560-3269. 218/299-6317.

Moreland Elementary School
217 Moreland Ave W, St. Paul
MN 55118-2144. 651/455-8681.

Mounds Park Academy
2051 Larpenteur Ave E,

Maplewood MN 55109-4717.
651/777-2555.

Mounds View High School
1900 Lake Valentine Rd, St. Paul
MN 55112-2841. 651/633-4031.

Mountain Lake Public Schools
PO Box 400, Mountain Lake MN
56159-0400. 507/427-2325.

**New London-Spicer Junior
Senior High School**
PO Box 430, New London MN
56273-0430. 320/354-2255.

**New Richland-Hartland
Independent School District**
PO Box 427, New Richland MN
56072-0427. 507/465-3205.

New Ulm Senior High School
414 S Payne St, New Ulm MN
56073-3273. 507/359-8420.

North Community High School
1500 James Ave N, Minneapolis
MN 55411-3161. 612/627-2778.

North High School
2416 11th Ave E, Maplewood
MN 55109-2200. 651/770-4703.

**North Intermediate Elementary
School**
815 N 9th St, St. Peter MN
56082-1278. 507/931-3260.

**North St. Paul Maplewood
Oakdale School**
1801 Beebe Rd, Maplewood MN
55109-4801. 651/770-4601.

North Star Community School
2410 Girard Ave N, Minneapolis
MN 55411-2057. 612/627-2961.

North View Junior High School
5869 69th Ave N, Minneapolis
MN 55429-1508. 612/566-6220.

Northdale Junior High School
11301 Dogwood St NW,
Minneapolis MN 55448-2420.
612/422-5650.

Northeast Middle School
2955 Hayes St NE, Minneapolis
MN 55418-2227. 612/627-3042.

Oak Grove Intermediate School
1300 W 106th St, Bloomington
MN 55431-4152. 612/885-7301.

**Oak Hill Community
Elementary School**
2600 County Road 136, St. Cloud
MN 56301-9016. 320/251-7936.

**Oak Point Intermediate
Elementary School**
13400 Staring Lake Pkwy, Eden
Prairie MN 55347-1800. 612/975-
7600.

Ogilvie Independent School District
333 School Dr, Ogilvie MN 56358-9019. 320/272-4431.

Osseo Area Public Schools
11200 93rd Ave N, Osseo MN 55369-3669. 612/391-7000.

Osseo Junior High School
10223 93rd Ave N, Osseo MN 55369-4114. 612/425-2422.

Owatonna Senior High School
333 E School St, Owatonna MN 55060-3024. 507/451-4712.

Oxbow Creek Elementary School
6050 109th Ave N, Champlin MN 55316-3463. 612/493-4171.

Patrick Henry High School
2020 43rd Ave N, Minneapolis MN 55412-1636. 612/627-2897.

Pequot Lakes Independent School District
PO Box 368, Pequot Lakes MN 56472-0368. 218/568-4996.

Pine Island Secondary School
PO Box 398, Pine Island MN 55963-0398. 507/356-8326.

Pine River Backus School District
PO Box 610, Pine River MN 56474-0610. 218/587-4720.

Pinewood Elementary School
PO Box 897, Monticello MN 55362-0897. 612/295-5164.

Plainview Secondary School
500 W Broadway, Plainview MN 55964-1031. 507/534-3128.

Plymouth Middle School
10011 36th Ave N, Plymouth MN 55441-2441. 612/504-7100.

Prairie View Elementary School
17255 Peterborg Rd, Eden Prairie MN 55346-3543. 612/975-8800.

Prosperity Heights Elementary School
1305 Prosperity Ave, St. Paul MN 55106-2124. 651/293-8695.

Ramsey Fine Arts Elementary School
1 W 49th St, Minneapolis MN 55409-2526. 612/627-2540.

Ramsey Junior High School
1700 Summit Ave, St. Paul MN 55105-1832. 651/293-8860.

Randolph Heights Elementary School
348 Hamline Ave S, St. Paul MN 55105-2408. 651/293-8780.

Richfield High School
7001 Harriet Ave, Minneapolis MN 55423-3061. 612/798-6100.

Robbinsdale Area Schools
4148 Winnetka Ave N, Minneapolis MN 55427-1210. 612/504-8000.

Robbinsdale Armstrong High School
10635 36th Ave N, Plymouth MN 55441-2410. 612/504-8800.

Robbinsdale Cooper High School
8230 47th Ave N, Minneapolis MN 55428-4511. 612/504-8500.

Rochester Montessori School
1801 9th Ave SE, Rochester MN 55904-5473. 507/281-6076.

Rochester School District
615 7th St SW, Rochester MN 55902-2052. 507/285-8294.

Roosevelt Elementary School
510 11th Ave, Detroit Lakes MN 56501-2800. 218/847-1106.

Roosevelt Middle School
650 Main St NE, Minneapolis MN 55434-3134. 612/422-5450.

Roosevelt Senior High School
4029 28th Ave S, Minneapolis MN 55406-3118. 612/627-2658.

Roseau School
509 3rd St NE, Roseau MN 56751-1113. 218/463-2770.

Roseville Area High Schools
1240 County Road B2 W, Roseville MN 55113-4338. 651/635-1660.

Rossman Elementary School
1221 Rossman Ave, Detroit Lakes MN 56501-3826. 218/847-9268.

Sanford Middle School
3524 42nd Ave S, Minneapolis MN 55406-2813. 612/627-2720.

Sauk Centre Independent School District
903 State Rd, Sauk Centre MN 56378-1672. 320/352-2284.

Scott Highlands Middle School
14011 Pilot Knob Rd, Apple Valley MN 55124-6602. 612/423-7581.

South Elementary School
1405 S 7th St, St. Peter MN 56082-1506. 507/931-2754.

South St. Paul High School
700 2nd St N, South St. Paul MN 55075-2062. 651/457-9401.

South View Middle School
4725 S View Ln, Edina MN 55424-1541. 612/928-2700.

Spring Lake Park High School
8001 Able St NE, Fridley MN 55432-2059. 612/786-5571.

St. David's School
3395 Plymouth Rd, Hopkins MN 55305-3765. 612/939-0396.

St. Francis Senior High School
3325 Bridge St NW, St. Francis MN 55070-9732. 612/753-2800.

St. Louis Park School District
6425 W 33rd St, St. Louis Park MN 55426-3403. 612/928-6000.

St. Paul Academy Summit School
1712 Randolph Ave, St. Paul MN 55105-2159. 651/698-2451.

St. Paul Public School District
360 Colborne St, St. Paul MN 55102-3228. 651/293-5100.

St. Peter Middle/High School
100 Lincoln Dr, St. Peter MN 56082-1332. 507/931-4210.

Staples-Motley Senior High School
PO Box 247, Staples MN 56479-0247. 218/894-2430.

Stillwater Junior High School
110 Pine St E, Stillwater MN 55082-5109. 651/351-6905.

Sullivan Elementary School
3100 E 28th St, Minneapolis MN 55406-1601. 612/627-7100.

Tanglen Elementary School
10901 Hillside Lane West, Hopkins MN 55305-2577. 612/988-4900.

Twin Bluff Middle School
2120 Twin Bluff Rd, Red Wing MN 55066-3009. 651/388-7144.

Valley Middle School
900 Garden View Dr, Apple Valley MN 55124-7113. 612/431-8300.

Valley View Middle School
6750 Valley View Rd, Minneapolis MN 55439-1761. 612/947-1800.

Vandenberg Junior High School
948 Proctor Ave, Elk River MN 55330-2417. 612/241-3450.

Wabasha High School
2113 Hiawatha Dr E, Wabasha MN 55981-1781. 651/565-4537.

Warren School District
224 E Bridge Ave, Warren MN
56762-1533. 218/745-4636.

Waseca Public Schools
501 E Elm Ave, Waseca MN
56093-3360. 507/835-2500.

Waseca School District
605 7th St NE, Waseca MN
56093-3210. 507/835-2248.

Washburn Senior High School
201 W 49th St, Minneapolis MN
55409-2530. 612/627-2323.

**Waterville & Elysian Public
Schools**
500 Paquin St E, Waterville MN
56096-1533. 507/362-4432.

**Waubun Independent School
District**
PO Box 98, Waubun MN 56589-
0098. 218/473-2171.

Wayzata High School
305 Vicksburg Ln N, Plymouth
MN 55447-3941. 612/476-3000.

**Webster Magnet Elementary
School**
707 Holly Ave, St. Paul MN
55104-7126. 651/293-8625.

**Webster Open Elementary
School**
425 5th St NE, Minneapolis MN
55413-2117. 612/627-2312.

**White Bear Lake High School
North**
5040 Bald Eagle Ave, White Bear
Lake MN 55110-6618. 651/653-
2915.

**White Bear Lake High School
South**
3551 McKnight Rd N, White
Bear Lake MN 55110-5575.
651/773-6204.

**William Byrne Elementary
School**
11608 River Hills Dr, Burnsville
MN 55337-3276. 612/895-7292.

Willmar Senior High School
2701 30th St NE, Willmar MN
56201-9192. 320/231-8300.

Willow Creek Middle School
2425 11th Ave SE, Rochester MN
55904-5699. 507/285-8876.

Windom Public Schools
PO Drawer C177, Windom MN
56101-0177. 507/831-4881.

Winona Senior High School
901 Gilmore Ave, Winona MN
55987-2526. 507/454-9500.

Woodland Transition School
201 Clover St, Duluth MN
55812-1104. 218/724-8868.

**Zachary Lane Elementary
School**
4350 Zachary Lane N,
Minneapolis MN 55442-2802.
612/559-2737.

JUNIOR COLLEGES AND TECHNICAL INSTITUTES

**Anoka-Ramsey Community
College**
11200 Mississippi Blvd NW,
Coon Rapids MN 55433-3470.
612/427-2600.

Cambridge Community College
300 Polk St S, Cambridge MN
55008-5706. 612/689-7000.

**Eden Prairie-Hennepin
Technical College**
9200 Flying Cloud Dr, Eden
Prairie MN 55347-2601. 612/944-
2222.

**Minneapolis Community
Technical College**
1501 Hennepin Avenue,
Minneapolis MN 55403-1710.
612/341-7000.

Minneapolis Technical Institute
1415 Hennepin Ave, Minneapolis
MN 55403-1712. 612/370-9400.

**North Hennepin Community
College**
7411 85th Avenue N,
Minneapolis MN 55445-2231.
612/424-0950.

**Northland Community
Technical College**
1101 Highway 1 E, Thief River
Falls MN 56701-2537. 218/681-
0701.

Ridgewater College
2101 15th Ave NW, Willmar MN
56201-6501. 320/235-5114.

Ridgewater College
2 Century Ave SE, Hutchinson
MN 55350-3100. 320/587-3636.

Riverland Community College
1600 8th Ave NW, Austin MN
55912-1400. 507/433-0505.

Riverland Technical College
1900 8th Ave NW, Austin MN
55912-1473. 507/433-0600.

**Rochester Community
Technical College**
851 30th Ave SE, Rochester MN
55904-4915. 507/285-7215.

St. Cloud Technical College
1540 Northway Dr, St. Cloud MN
56303-1240. 320/654-5000.

St. Paul Technical College
235 Marshall Ave, St. Paul MN
55102-1807. 651/221-1300.

Willmar Community College
PO Box 797, Willmar MN 56201-
0797. 320/231-5134.

VOCATIONAL SCHOOLS

Brown Institute
1440 Northland Dr, Mendota
Heights MN 55120-1004.
612/905-3400.

**Hibbing Technical Community
College**
1515 E 25th St, Hibbing MN
55746-3354. 218/262-7200.

For more information on career opportunities in educational services:

Associations

**AMERICAN ASSOCIATION FOR HIGHER
EDUCATION**
One DuPont Circle, Suite 360, Washington DC
20036. 202/293-6440. World Wide Web address:
http://www.aahe.org.

**AMERICAN ASSOCIATION OF SCHOOL
ADMINISTRATORS**
1801 North Moore Street, Arlington VA 22209.
703/528-0700. Fax: 703/841-1543. World Wide Web
address: http://www.aasa.org. An organization of
school system leaders. Membership includes a
national conference on education; programs and

seminars; *The School Administrator*, a monthly
magazine; *Leadership News*, a monthly newspaper;
Leader's Edge, *Back Fence*, and *Edge City*, quarterly
publications; and a catalog of other publications and
audiovisuals.

AMERICAN FEDERATION OF TEACHERS
555 New Jersey Avenue NW, Washington DC 20001.
202/879-4400. World Wide Web address:
http://www.aft.org.

**COLLEGE AND UNIVERSITY PERSONNEL
ASSOCIATION**
1233 20th Street NW, Suite 301, Washington DC

20036. 202/429-0311. World Wide Web address: http://www.cupa.org. Membership required.

NATIONAL ASSOCIATION FOR COLLEGE ADMISSION COUNSELING
1631 Prince Street, Alexandria VA 22314. 703/836-2222. World Wide Web address: http://www.nacac.com. An education association of school counselors and admissions officers who assist students in making the transition from high school to post-secondary education.

NATIONAL ASSOCIATION OF BIOLOGY TEACHERS
11250 Roger Bacon Drive, Suite 19, Reston VA 20190. 703/471-1134. Toll-free phone: 800/406-0775. Fax: 703/435-5582. E-mail address: office@nabt.com. World Wide Web address: http://www.nabt.org. A professional organization for biology and life science educators.

NATIONAL ASSOCIATION OF COLLEGE AND UNIVERSITY BUSINESS OFFICERS
2501 M Street NW, Suite 400, Washington DC 20037-1308. 202/861-2500. World Wide Web address: http://www.nacubo.org. National Association of College and University Business Officers is an association for those involved in the financial administration and management of higher education. Membership required.

NATIONAL COMMISSION FOR COOPERATIVE EDUCATION (NCCE)
360 Huntington Avenue, Suite 384 CP, Boston MA 02115-3770. 617/373-3770. E-mail address: ncce@lynx.neu.edu. Offers free information to students interested in learning more about cooperative education programs.

NATIONAL SCIENCE TEACHERS ASSOCIATION
1840 Wilson Boulevard, Arlington VA 22201-3000. 703/243-7100. World Wide Web address: http://www.nsta.org. National Science Teachers Association is an organization committed to the improvement of science education at all levels, preschool through college. Publishes five journals, a newspaper, and a number of special publications. Also conducts national and regional conventions.

NATIONAL SOCIETY FOR EXPERIENTIAL EDUCATION (NSEE)
3509 Haworth Drive, Suite 207, Raleigh NC 27609-7299. 919/787-3263. E-mail address: info@nsee.org. World Wide Web address: http://www.nsee.org. National Society for Experimental Education is a membership organization offering publications, conferences, and a resource center. Among the society's publications is *The Experienced Hand: A Student Manual for Making the Most of an Internship.*

Books

HOW TO GET A JOB IN EDUCATION
Adams Media Corporation, 260 Center Street, Holbrook MA 02343. 781/767-8100. World Wide Web address: http://www.adamsmedia.com.

Directories

WASHINGTON EDUCATION ASSOCIATION DIRECTORY
Council for Advancement and Support of Education, 1307 New York Avenue, Suite 1000, Washington DC 20005-4701. 202/328-5900. World Wide Web address: http://www.case.org.

Online Services

ACADEMIC EMPLOYMENT NETWORK
http://www.academploy.com. This site offers information for the educational professional. It allows you to search for positions using keywords or location. It also has information on other sites of interest, educational products, certification requirements by state, and relocation services.

THE CHRONICLE OF HIGHER EDUCATION
http://chronicle.com/jobs. This Website provides job listings from the weekly published newspaper *The Chronicle of Higher Education.* Besides featuring articles from the paper, this site also offers employment opportunities. You can search for information by geographic location, type of position, and teaching fields.

EDUCATION & INSTRUCTION JOBS
http://csueb.sfsu.edu/jobs/educationjobs.html. Offers a long list of links to other sites around the country that provide job openings and information for jobseekers looking in education. This site is part of the California State University Employment Board.

EDUCATION FORUM
Go: Edforum. This CompuServe discussion group is open to educators of all levels.

JOBWEB SCHOOL DISTRICTS SEARCH
http://www.jobweb.org/search/schools. Provides a search engine for school districts across the country. The site is run by the National Association of Colleges and Employers and it also provides information on colleges and career fairs.

THE TEACHER'S LOUNGE
Keyword: teacher's lounge. An America Online discussion group for teachers of kindergarten through the twelfth grade.

VISUAL NATION ARTS JOBS LINKS
http://fly.hiwaay.net/%7Edrewyor/art_job.html. Provides links to other sites that post academic and arts job openings and information.

ELECTRONIC/INDUSTRIAL ELECTRICAL EQUIPMENT

Intense international competition is prompting the U.S. electronics industry to become more globalized. Companies are being forced to seek less expensive materials and labor. Standard & Poor reported a 92 percent decrease in second quarter 1998 profits for the electrical and electronics industry, and second quarter industry profit margins dropped from 9.9 percent in 1997 to 0.7 percent in 1998. The Bureau of Labor Statistics expects growth in non-manufacturing jobs, and well as positions for electrical consultants. Electrical assemblers, on the other hand, will see a decline in the number of positions through 2006.

U.S. Industry and Trade Outlook 1998 projects the best opportunities for jobseekers to be in the production of analog and memory ICs, microcomponents, and discrete semiconductors. Industry analysts worldwide predict that semiconductor markets will grow at an approximate rate of 15 percent annually through 2005. The outlook for the switchgear sector is highly favorable. U.S. electric utilities are expected to spend more than $300 million to automate power substations by 2000, and shipments of switchgear are forecasted to grow at an average rate of 4 to 5 percent through 2000.

ADC TELECOMMUNICATIONS
P.O. Box 1101, Minneapolis MN 55440-1101. 612/835-6800. **Contact:** Human Resources. **World Wide Web address:** http://www.adc.com. **Description:** Supplies voice, video, and data systems for high-speed transmissions. ADC Telecommunications serves the broadcast, cable television, Internet, telephone, and wireless communications industries worldwide. **Common positions include:** Design Engineer; Electrical/Electronics Engineer; Marketing Specialist; Mechanical Engineer; Sales Representative. **Corporate headquarters location:** Minnetonka MN. **Listed on:** NASDAQ.

ABELCONN
9210 Science Center Drive, Minneapolis MN 55428. 612/533-3533. **Contact:** Donna Sauter, Human Resources. **Description:** This location houses administrative offices. Overall, AbelConn is a manufacturer of electronic connectors, circuit boards, and other electronic products. **Other U.S. locations:** Cokato MN. **Number of employees at this location:** 35.

ABELCONN
400 Cokato Street, Cokato MN 55321. 320/286-2138. **Contact:** Human Resources. **Description:** A manufacturer of electronic connectors, circuit boards, and other electronic products. **Other U.S. locations:** Minneapolis MN.

ADVANCED FLEX, INC.
15115 Minnetonka Industrial Road, Minnetonka MN 55345. 612/930-4800. **Contact:** Donna Johnson, Corporate Manager of Human Resources. **World Wide Web address:** http://www. flex.advflex.com. **Description:** Manufactures printed circuit boards. **Common positions include:** Chemical Engineer; Electrical/Electronics Engineer. **Benefits:** 401(k); Dental Insurance; Disability Coverage; Life Insurance; Medical Insurance; Profit Sharing; Tuition Assistance. **Other U.S. locations:** Chaska MN. **Listed on:** Privately held. **Number of employees at this location:** 220. **Number of employees nationwide:** 300.

ALTRON INC.
6700 Industry Avenue NW, Anoka MN 55303. 612/427-7735. **Contact:** Personnel Department. **World Wide Web address:** http://www.altronmfg.com. **Description:** Engaged in circuit board assembly, wiring, and harnessing.

AULT INC.
7300 Boone Avenue North, Minneapolis MN 55428. 612/493-1900. **Fax:** 612/493-1911. **Contact:** Judy Sand, Benefits and Compensation Administrator. **World Wide Web address:** http://www. aultinc.com. **Description:** A designer, manufacturer, and marketer of power conversion products for the OEM market. **NOTE:** Entry-level positions are offered. **Common positions include:** Accountant/Auditor; Buyer; Computer Programmer; Customer Service Representative; Design Engineer; Draftsperson; Electrical/Electronics Engineer; Human Resources Manager; Industrial Engineer; Mechanical Engineer; Operations/Production Manager; Systems Analyst; Typist/Word Processor. **Educational backgrounds include:** Accounting; Business Administration; Computer Science; Engineering; Finance; Marketing. **Benefits:** 401(k); Dental Insurance; Disability Coverage; Life Insurance; Medical Insurance; Profit Sharing; Savings Plan; Stock Option; Tuition Assistance. **Corporate headquarters location:** This Location. **Operations at this facility include:** Administration; Divisional Headquarters; Manufacturing; Research and Development; Sales. **Listed on:** NASDAQ. **Stock exchange symbol:** AULT. **Annual sales/revenues:** $21 - $50 million. **Number of employees at this location:** 145.

BMC INDUSTRIES INC.
One Meridian Crossing, Suite 850, Richfield MN 55423. 612/851-6000. **Contact:** Human Resources. **World Wide Web address:** http://www.bmcind.com. **Description:** Manufactures aperture masks for color cathode-ray tubes, through its Precision Imaged Products business segment; and supplies corrective eyeglass lenses to ophthalmic laboratories and retail eyewear chains, through its Optical Products division.

BANNER ENGINEERING CORPORATION
9714 10th Avenue North, Minneapolis MN 55441-5019. 612/544-3164. **Contact:** Human Resources. **World Wide Web address:** http://www.baneng.com. **Description:** Designs and manufactures photo-electric control systems.

CIPRICO, INC.
2800 Campus Drive, Suite 60, Plymouth MN 55441. 612/551-4000. **Contact:** Jeanne Vincill, Director of Human Resources. **World Wide Web address:** http://www.ciprico.com. **Description:** A designer and manufacturer of intelligent disk and tape controller boards.

CYBEROPTICS
5900 Golden Hills Drive, Minneapolis MN 55416. 612/542-5000. **Contact:** Human Resources. **World Wide Web address:** http://www.cyberoptics.com. **Description:** Designs, develops, and manufactures intelligent, laser-based sensor systems that are used for quality control electronic inspections and other related applications. **Corporate headquarters location:** This Location.

DRS AHEAD TECHNOLOGY
3550 Annapolis Lane North, Suite 60, Plymouth MN 55447. 612/519-9129. **Contact:** Human Resources. **World Wide Web address:** http://www.drs.com. **Description:** A producer of magnetic recording heads for the information processing industry. **Common positions include:** Accountant/Auditor; Actuary; Buyer; Ceramics Engineer; Computer Programmer; Computer-Aided Designer; Credit Manager; Customer Service Representative; Department Manager; Electrical/Electronics Engineer; General Manager; Industrial Engineer; Industrial Production Manager; Manufacturer's/Wholesaler's Sales Rep.; Mechanical Engineer; Metallurgical Engineer; Operations/Production Manager; Purchasing Agent/Manager; Quality Control Supervisor; Systems Analyst; Technical Writer/Editor. **Educational backgrounds include:** Accounting; Business Administration; Chemistry; Economics; Engineering; Finance; Marketing; Mathematics; Metallurgy; Physics. **Benefits:** 401(k); Dental Insurance; Disability Coverage; Life Insurance; Medical Insurance; Tuition Assistance. **Corporate headquarters location:** This Location. **Operations at this facility include:** Administration; Financial Offices; Manufacturing; Research and Development.

DETECTOR ELECTRONIC CORPORATION
6901 West 110th Street, Bloomington MN 55438. 612/941-5665. **Fax:** 612/829-8745. **Contact:** Dee Possin, Human Resources Supervisor. **World Wide Web address:** http://www.detronics.com. **Description:** An international leader in manufacturing electronic flame and gas detection equipment and systems. **Common positions include:** Accountant/Auditor; Administrator; Assembly Worker; Blue-Collar Worker Supervisor; Buyer; Computer Programmer; Credit Manager; Customer Service Representative; Department Manager; Draftsperson; Electrical/Electronics Engineer; Human Resources Manager; Industrial Engineer; Manufacturer's/Wholesaler's Sales Rep.; Marketing Specialist; Mechanical Engineer; Operations/Production Manager; Purchasing Agent/Manager; Quality Control Supervisor; Systems Analyst; Technical Writer/Editor. **Educational backgrounds include:** Accounting; Business Administration;

Communications; Computer Science; Engineering; Finance; Liberal Arts; Marketing; Mathematics. **Benefits:** 401(k); Dental Insurance; Disability Coverage; Employee Discounts; Life Insurance; Medical Insurance; Pension Plan; Tuition Assistance. **Corporate headquarters location:** This Location. **Parent company:** Williams Holdings, Ltd. **Number of employees at this location:** 240. **Number of employees nationwide:** 260.

DIGITAL BIOMETRICS, INC.
5600 Rowland Road, Suite 205, Minnetonka MN 55343. 612/932-0888. **Contact:** Human Resources. **Description:** A manufacturer of computerized fingerprint identification systems.

FSI INTERNATIONAL
322 Lake Hazeltine Drive, Chaska MN 55318. 612/448-5440. **Contact:** Brenda Kubesh, Human Resources Representative. **World Wide Web address:** http://www.fsi-intl.com. **Description:** A worldwide leader in producing automated silicon wafer processing equipment used by semiconductor manufacturers. The company offers three types of products: microlithography clusters, surface conditioning products, and chemical management systems. Microlithography clusters apply and develop photosensitive materials on the surface of silicon wafers. Surface conditioning products are used for preparing silicon wafers for the processing of integrated circuits. Chemical management systems are used by semiconductor manufacturers for purposes such as the controlled distribution and conditioning of chemicals throughout a semiconductor manufacturing facility and the blending of concentrated chemicals with deionized water. **Common positions include:** Customer Service Representative; Electrical/Electronics Engineer; Mechanical Engineer; Process Engineer. **Educational backgrounds include:** Chemistry; Engineering. **Benefits:** Disability Coverage; Life Insurance; Medical Insurance; Pension Plan; Profit Sharing; Tuition Assistance. **Corporate headquarters location:** This Location. **Subsidiaries include:** Vinylglass, Ltd. and Applied Chemical Solutions (ACS), both of which produce chemical management products for semiconductor manufacturers. **Operations at this facility include:** Administration; Manufacturing; Research and Development; Sales; Service.

GOPHER ELECTRONICS COMPANY
222 Little Canada Road, St. Paul MN 55117. 651/490-4900. **Toll-free phone:** 800/592-9519. **Fax:** 651/490-4911. **Contact:** Doug Beutel, Human Resources. **E-mail address:** info@gopherelectronics.com. **World Wide Web address:** http://www.gopherelectronics.com. **Description:** Distributes passive and electromechanical components.

HEI INC.
P.O. Box 5000, Victoria MN 55386-5000. 612/443-2500. **Contact:** Jerald Mortenson, Director of Human Resources. **World Wide Web address:** http://www.heii.com. **Description:** Manufactures microelectronic components for use in products including hearing aids and medical instruments.

HOFFMAN ENGINEERING
900 Ehlen Drive, Anoka MN 55303. 612/421-2240. **Contact:** Kent Vesper, Vice President. **World Wide Web address:** http://www.hoffmanonline.com. **Description:** Manufactures and distributes electrical and electronic enclosures. **Common positions include:** Accountant/Auditor; Attorney; Buyer; Computer Programmer; Draftsperson; General Manager; Human Resources Manager; Marketing Specialist; Mechanical Engineer; Metallurgical Engineer; Systems Analyst; Technical Writer/Editor; Transportation/Traffic Specialist. **Educational backgrounds include:** Accounting; Business Administration; Communications; Computer Science; Engineering. **Benefits:** Dental Insurance; Disability Coverage; Employee Discounts; Life Insurance; Medical Insurance; Pension Plan; Profit Sharing; Savings Plan; Tuition Assistance. **Corporate headquarters location:** This Location. **Operations at this facility include:** Administration; Divisional Headquarters; Manufacturing; Regional Headquarters; Research and Development; Sales; Service.

HONEYWELL INC.
P.O. Box 524, Minneapolis MN 55440. 612/951-0022. **Contact:** Staffing Manager. **World Wide Web address:** http://www.honeywell.com. **Description:** A global leader in providing control components, products, systems, and services for homes and buildings, space and aviation, industrial processes, and manufacturing applications. **Common positions include:** Accountant/Auditor; Administrator; Attorney; Chemical Engineer; Computer Programmer; Credit Manager; Customer Service Representative; Dietician/Nutritionist; Electrical/Electronics Engineer; Financial Analyst; Human Resources Manager; Mechanical Engineer; Software Engineer. **Educational backgrounds include:** Accounting; Business Administration; Computer Science; Engineering; Finance. **Benefits:** 401(k); Daycare Assistance; Dental Insurance; Disability Coverage; Life Insurance; Medical Insurance; Pension Plan; Tuition Assistance. **Special programs:** Internships. **Corporate headquarters location:** This Location. **Other U.S. locations:** Phoenix AZ; Clearwater FL; Freeport IL; Albuquerque NM. **Operations at this facility include:** Administration;

Manufacturing; Research and Development. **Listed on:** New York Stock Exchange. **Number of employees nationwide:** 52,000.

ION CORPORATION
1507 South Sixth Street, Hopkins MN 55343. 612/936-9490. **Fax:** 612/936-7527. **Contact:** Human Resources. **Description:** Manufactures electronic products including circuitboards, cables, and harnesses. **Educational backgrounds include:** Engineering. **Benefits:** Dental Insurance; Life Insurance; Medical Insurance; Section 125 Plan. **Corporate headquarters location:** This Location. **Operations at this facility include:** Administration; Manufacturing; Sales. **Number of employees at this location:** 100.

MTS SYSTEMS CORPORATION
14000 Technology Drive, Eden Prairie MN 55344. 612/937-4000. **Contact:** Bruce Hebeisen, Human Resources Manager. **World Wide Web address:** http://www.mts.com. **Description:** Manufactures electronic instruments, hydraulic devices, and mechanical testing and analysis instruments.

MANUFACTURERS SERVICES
4300 Round Lake Road, Arden Hills MN 55112. 651/604-2400. **Contact:** Sue Bergman, Human Resources. **Description:** A manufacturer of circuit boards and other electronics products.

MICRO COMPONENT TECHNOLOGY INC.
2340 West County Road C, St. Paul MN 55113-2528. 651/697-4000. **Contact:** Personnel Department. **World Wide Web address:** http://www.mct.com. **Description:** Manufactures instruments for the measuring and testing of electricity and electrical signals.

MIDWEST ELECTRIC PRODUCTS, INC.
P.O. Box 910, Mankato MN 56002-0910. 507/625-4414. **Contact:** Human Resources. **World Wide Web address:** http://www.midwestelectric.com. **Description:** A manufacturer of outdoor waterproof and weatherproof electrical equipment, including junction boxes, meter sockets, power outlets, RV products, and transfer switches. **Corporate headquarters location:** This Location.

PHYSICAL ELECTRONICS, INC.
6509 Flying Cloud Drive, Eden Prairie MN 55344. 612/828-6100. **Contact:** Human Resources. **World Wide Web address:** http://www.phi.com. **Description:** Manufacturers of electronic instruments, including surface analysis equipment. **Common positions include:** Accountant/Auditor; Buyer; Customer Service Representative; Designer; Electrical/Electronics Engineer; Human Resources Manager; Mechanical Engineer; Physicist; Science Technologist; Software Engineer; Technical Writer/Editor. **Educational backgrounds include:** Accounting; Business Administration; Chemistry; Computer Science; Engineering; Physics. **Benefits:** 401(k); Daycare Assistance; Dental Insurance; Disability Coverage; Employee Discounts; Life Insurance; Medical Insurance; Pension Plan; Profit Sharing; Savings Plan; Tuition Assistance. **Corporate headquarters location:** This Location. **Operations at this facility include:** Administration; Manufacturing; Research and Development; Sales; Service. **Listed on:** Privately held. **Number of employees at this location:** 300.

SCHOTT CORPORATION
218 North Jefferson, Route 1, Box 400, Minneota MN 56264. 507/872-6103. **Contact:** Human Resources. **World Wide Web address:** http://www.schottcorp.com. **Description:** A manufacturer of electronic transformers.

TSI INC.
P.O. Box 64394, St. Paul MN 55164. 651/483-0900. **Contact:** Haakon Oksnevad, Human Resources Manager. **Description:** Engaged in the production of particle research instruments, wire-hot film anemometry, laser velocimetry, and mass flow transconductors.

TELEX COMMUNICATIONS INC.
9600 Aldrich Avenue South, Minneapolis MN 55420. 612/884-4051. **Contact:** Kathy Curran, Personnel Director. **World Wide Web address:** http://www.telex.com. **Description:** Manufactures electronic components for intercom systems and related communications products. **Corporate headquarters location:** This Location. **Other U.S. locations:** Nationwide.

TELEX COMMUNICATIONS INC.
1720 East 14th Street, Glencoe MN 55336. 320/864-3177. **Fax:** 320/864-3225. **Contact:** Judy Graupmann, Human Resources Manager. **World Wide Web address:** http://www.telex.com. **Description:** Manufactures electronic components for intercom systems and related

communications products. **Common positions include:** Buyer; Clerical Supervisor; Computer Programmer; Customer Service Representative; Electrical/Electronics Engineer; Human Resources Manager; Mechanical Engineer; Operations/Production Manager; Purchasing Agent/Manager; Quality Control Supervisor. **Educational backgrounds include:** Business Administration; Computer Science; Engineering. **Benefits:** 401(k); Dental Insurance; Disability Coverage; Employee Discounts; Life Insurance; Medical Insurance; Pension Plan; Savings Plan; Tuition Assistance. **Special programs:** Internships. **Corporate headquarters location:** Minneapolis MN. **Other U.S. locations:** Nationwide. **Operations at this facility include:** Manufacturing; Service. **Listed on:** Privately held. **Number of employees at this location:** 300.

THE TRANE COMPANY
BUILDING AUTOMATION SYSTEMS DIVISION
4833 White Bear Parkway, St. Paul MN 55110. 651/407-4000. **Contact:** Sandra Fellman, Human Resources Process Owner. **E-mail address:** sfellman@trane.com. **World Wide Web address:** http://www.trane.com. **Description:** Manufactures and markets computerized energy automation systems used in commercial industries. **Common positions include:** Accountant/Auditor; Buyer; Computer Programmer; Credit Manager; Department Manager; Draftsperson; Electrical/Electronics Engineer; Financial Analyst; Human Resources Manager; Marketing Specialist; Operations/Production Manager; Purchasing Agent/Manager; Quality Control Supervisor; Systems Analyst. **Educational backgrounds include:** Accounting; Computer Science; Engineering. **Benefits:** Dental Insurance; Disability Coverage; Employee Discounts; Life Insurance; Medical Insurance; Pension Plan; Savings Plan; Tuition Assistance. **Corporate headquarters location:** Piscataway NJ. **Parent company:** American Standard, Inc. **Operations at this facility include:** Administration; Divisional Headquarters; Financial Offices; Manufacturing; Policy Development; Sales; Service.

VTC INC.
2800 East Old Shakopee Road, Bloomington MN 55425. 612/853-5100. **Contact:** Robert Rousseau, Director of Human Resources. **World Wide Web address:** http://www.vtc.com. **Description:** A manufacturer of semiconductors and integrated circuits. **Listed on:** Privately held.

Note: Because addresses and telephone numbers of smaller companies can change rapidly, we recommend you call each company to verify the information below before inquiring about job opportunities. Mass mailings are not recommended.

Additional small employers:

AEROSPACE AND/OR NAUTICAL SYSTEMS AND INSTRUMENTS

SL-Montevideo Technology Inc.
2002 Black Oak Ave,
Montevideo MN 56265-2400.
320/269-6562.

ELECTRIC LIGHTING AND WIRING EQUIPMENT

Electric Cords Inc.
5350 Highway 61 N, White Bear Lake MN 55110-2375. 651/426-7958.

Hoffman Enclosures Inc.
6530 James Ave N, Brooklyn Center MN 55430-1710. 612/566-9490.

Minnesota Wire & Cable Co.
1835 Energy Park Dr, St. Paul MN 55108-2721. 651/642-1800.

ELECTRICAL ENGINE EQUIPMENT

Westling Manufacturing Co.
705 Hwy 18, Princeton MN 55371. 612/389-4440.

ELECTRICAL EQUIPMENT WHOLESALE

Graybar Electric Company Inc.
PO Box 160, Minneapolis MN 55440-0160. 612/721-3545.

Security Link
43 Main St SE, Ste 303,
Minneapolis MN 55414-1032.
612/673-6400.

United Electric Company
601 Lakeview Point Dr, St. Paul MN 55112-3494. 651/582-3900.

ELECTRICAL EQUIPMENT, MACHINERY, AND SUPPLIES

American Farmworks
PO Box 6117, Rochester MN 55903-6117. 507/288-7777.

ITI
2266 2nd St N, Maplewood MN 55109-2914. 651/777-2690.

Lumonics
6690 Shady Oak Rd, Eden Prairie MN 55344-3200. 612/941-9530.

ELECTRICAL INDUSTRIAL APPARATUS

EMC
1365 Park Rd, Chanhassen MN 55317-9527. 612/474-1116.

I Corp.
4929 Boone Ave N, Minneapolis MN 55428-4031. 612/535-6800.

ITT Cannon Switch Products
8081 Wallace Rd, Eden Prairie MN 55344-2224. 612/934-4400.

Turck Inc.
5000 Fernbrook Ln N,
Minneapolis MN 55446-3482.
612/553-7300.

ELECTRONIC COILS AND TRANSFORMERS

3M Filtration Products
2465 Lexington Ave S #60,
Mendota Heights MN 55120-1218. 651/733-9733.

Precision Inc.
1800 Freeway Blvd, Brooklyn Center MN 55430-1708. 612/561-6880.

ELECTRONIC COMPONENTS AND ACCESSORIES

Buckbee Mears
245 6th St E, St. Paul MN 55101-1918. 651/228-6400.

Hibbing Electronics Corp.
PO Box 129, Hibbing MN 55746-0129. 218/263-8971.

Holaday Circuits Inc.
11126 Bren Rd W, Hopkins MN 55343-9074. 612/933-3303.

Johnson Matthey Advanced Circuits
560 16th Ave S, Hopkins MN 55343-7825. 612/935-5695.

Johnson Matthey Advanced Circuits
15102 Minnetonka Industrial, Minnetonka MN 55345-2111. 612/930-8000.

Johnson Matthey Semiconductor Packages
3965 Meadowbrook Rd, St. Louis Park MN 55426-4505. 612/931-1300.

PDI
14755 27th Avenue North, Plymouth MN 55447-4809. 612/553-9838.

Shafer Electronics Co.
PO Box 68, Shafer MN 55074-0068. 651/257-5332.

Universal Circuits Incorporated
200 Centennial Drive, Buffalo MN 55313-9000. 612/682-0019.

Universal Circuits Incorporated
8860 Zachary Lane North, Maple Grove MN 55369-4524. 612/424-3788.

ELECTRONIC CONNECTORS

Johnson Components Inc.
299 Johnson Avenue SW, Waseca MN 56093-2539. 507/835-4886.

ELECTRONIC PARTS AND EQUIPMENT WHOLESALE

ADC Telecommunications Inc.
1087 Park Pl, Shakopee MN 55379-1889. 612/403-1900.

Cady Communications Inc.
3200 Harbor Ln N, Plymouth MN 55447-5236. 612/553-1001.

Collins Communication Systems Co.
2920 Centre Pointe Dr, Roseville MN 55113-1122. 651/634-1800.

ESI Communications North
5959 Baker Rd, Ste 390, Minnetonka MN 55345-5996. 612/835-2500.

IOS
6701 W 110th Street, Minneapolis MN 55438-2648. 612/947-5810.

Vaughn Communications Inc.
5050 W 78th Street, Bloomington MN 55435-5411. 612/832-3200.

MISC. ELECTRONIC COMPONENTS

Aerospace Systems Company
1007 E 10th St, Fairmont MN 56031-3728. 507/235-3355.

Artesyn Technologies
7575 Market Place Dr, Eden Prairie MN 55344-3637. 612/941-1100.

EMD Associates
4065 Theurer Blvd, Winona MN 55987-1537. 507/452-8932.

Innovex Inc.
1602 Benson Rd, Montevideo MN 56265-3002. 320/269-5588.

Nortek Systems
PO Box 84, Merrifield MN 56465-0084. 218/765-3151.

Nortek Systems Inc.
4050 Norris Ct NW, Bemidji MN 56601-8712. 218/751-0110.

Taytronics
430 Ritt St, St. Peter MN 56082-1603. 507/931-1406.

Tower Electronics Inc.
281 Commerce Cir S, Fridley MN 55432-3106. 612/571-3737.

SEMICONDUCTORS AND RELATED DEVICES

Cypress Minnesota
2401 E 86th St, Minneapolis MN 55425-2704. 612/851-5200.

Datakey Inc.
407 West Travelers Trl, Burnsville MN 55337-2554. 612/890-6850.

Litchfeld Precision Components
1 N Precision Dr, Litchfield MN 55355-2610. 320/693-2891.

SWITCHGEAR AND SWITCHBOARD APPARATUS

Bergquist Company
Rural Route 3, Box 926, Bigfork MN 56628-9511. 218/743-1200.

Bureau Electronics Group
3311 Broadway St NE, Minneapolis MN 55413-1745. 612/623-0900.

Onan Corporation
922 Swift St, St. Peter MN 56082-1844. 507/931-2700.

For more information on career opportunities in the electronic/industrial electrical equipment industry:

<u>Associations</u>

AMERICAN CERAMIC SOCIETY
P.O. Box 6136, Westerville OH 43086-6136. 614/890-4700. World Wide Web address: http://www.acers.org. Provides ceramics industry information. Membership required.

ELECTROCHEMICAL SOCIETY
10 South Main Street, Pennington NJ 08534. 609/737-1902. World Wide Web address: http://www.electrochem.org. An international society which holds bi-annual meetings internationally and periodic meetings through local sections.

ELECTRONIC INDUSTRIES ASSOCIATION
2500 Wilson Boulevard, Arlington VA 22201.

703/907-7500. World Wide Web address: http://www.eia.org.

ELECTRONICS TECHNICIANS ASSOCIATION
602 North Jackson Street, Greencastle IN 46135. 765/653-4301. World Wide Web address: http://www.eta-sda.com. Offers published job-hunting advice from the organization's officers and members. Also offers educational material and certification programs.

FABLESS SEMICONDUCTOR ASSOCIATION
Three Lincoln Centre, 5430 LBJ Freeway, Suite 280, Dallas TX 75240. 972/866-7579. Fax: 972/239-2292. World Wide Web address: http://www.fsa.org.

INSTITUTE OF ELECTRICAL AND ELECTRONICS ENGINEERS (IEEE)
345 East 47th Street, New York NY 10017. 212/705-

7900. Toll-free customer service line: 800/678-4333. World Wide Web address: http://www.ieee.org.

INTERNATIONAL SOCIETY OF CERTIFIED ELECTRONICS TECHNICIANS
2708 West Berry Street, Fort Worth TX 76109. 817/921-9101. World Wide Web address: http://www. iscet.org.

NATIONAL ELECTRONICS SERVICE DEALERS ASSOCIATION
2708 West Berry Street, Fort Worth TX 76109. 817/921-9061. World Wide Web address: http://www. nesda.com. National Electronics Service Dealers Association provides newsletters and directories to members.

SEMICONDUCTOR EQUIPMENT AND MATERIALS INTERNATIONAL
805 East Middlefield Road, Mountain View CA 94043-4080. 650/964-5111. E-mail address: semihq@ semi.org. World Wide Web address: http://www.semi. org. An international trade association concerned with the semiconductor and flat-panel display industries. Membership required.

ENVIRONMENTAL AND WASTE MANAGEMENT SERVICES

The United States is the world's largest producer and consumer of environmental goods and services. The industry continues to expand as a result of increasing public concern for the environment and the passing of both the Clean Air and Clean Water Acts. Global environmental revenues are expected to increase 33 percent by 2000. Jobseekers may look to private businesses for environmental jobs, as more and more companies start to self-regulate. Environmental jobs with the government, such as environmental inspectors and compliance officers, are subject to slow growth. However, once obtained, government jobs usually hold a great deal of security.

Solid waste management remains the largest of the environmental business segments. USA Waste acquired the industry leader, Waste Management, and is now left with Browning-Ferris as a main competitor. Another significant environmental segment is hazardous/toxic waste. In 1998, the Texas Natural Resource Conservation Commission denied a request to store nuclear waste from outside the state's borders. This is an issue that will continue to gain attention, as more states are faced with storing hazardous waste. Job opportunities will continue to be found primarily in the areas of environmental protection, natural resources, and education.

AERATION INDUSTRIES INTERNATIONAL
P.O. Box 59144, Minneapolis MN 55459. 612/448-6789. **Physical address:** 4100 Peavey Road, Chaska MN 55318. **Contact:** Marlene Miller, Personnel Department. **Description:** A world leader in restoring lakes, rivers, and harbors, as well as wastewater treatment and aquaculture.

APPLIANCE RECYCLING CENTER OF AMERICA, INC.
7400 Excelsior Boulevard, Minneapolis MN 55426. 612/930-9000. **Contact:** Human Resources Manager. **Description:** Provides a full range of environmentally sound appliance collection, processing, and recycling services and reclaims hazardous substances for reuse. **Number of employees at this location:** 280.

BROWNING-FERRIS INDUSTRIES, INC. (BFI)
9813 Flying Cloud Drive, Eden Prairie MN 55347-4005. 612/941-5174. **Contact:** Human Resources. **World Wide Web address:** http://www.bfi.com. **Description:** Engaged primarily in the collection and disposal of solid waste for commercial, industrial, and residential customers. Services provided by BFI include landfill services, waste-to-energy programs, hazardous waste removal, and liquid waste removal. The company has operations at more than 500 facilities worldwide.

DELTA ENVIRONMENTAL CONSULTANTS, INC.
2770 Cleveland Avenue North, Roseville MN 55113. 651/639-9449. **Contact:** Human Resources. **Description:** An environmental consulting firm.

LEGGETTE BRASHEARS & GRAHAM
1210 West County Road E, Suite 700, St. Paul MN 55112. 651/490-1405. **Contact:** Kevin Powers, Vice President. **Description:** A consulting company that tests soil and groundwater samples and recommends environmentally sound clean-up procedures.

MAXIM TECHNOLOGIES, INC.
662 Cromwell Avenue, St. Paul MN 55114. 651/645-3601. **Contact:** Human Resources. **Description:** Provides environmental consulting, geotechnical engineering, specialty testing, and chemistry services from 54 offices in 20 states. **Common positions include:** Chemist; Civil

Engineer; Environmental Engineer; Geologist/Geophysicist; Metallurgical Engineer. **Educational backgrounds include:** Chemistry; Engineering; Geology. **Benefits:** Dental Insurance; Disability Coverage; Life Insurance; Medical Insurance; Savings Plan. **Corporate headquarters location:** Dallas TX. **Operations at this facility include:** Administration; Sales; Service. **Listed on:** Privately held. **Annual sales/revenues:** $51 - $100 million. **Number of employees at this location:** 1,000.

URS GREINER WOODWARD CLYDE
6465 Wayzata Boulevard, Suite 660, Minneapolis MN 55426. 612/593-5650. **Contact:** Jean Meyer, Human Resources. **World Wide Web address:** http://www.urscorp.com. **Description:** Engaged in environmental engineering.

WASTE MANAGEMENT
12448 Pennsylvania Avenue, Savage MN 55378. 651/423-8837. **Contact:** Human Resources. **World Wide Web address:** http://www.wastemanagement.com. **Description:** An international provider of comprehensive waste management services, as well as engineering and construction, industrial, and related services, with operations in 19 countries. **Corporate headquarters location:** Oak Brook IL. **Number of employees nationwide:** 67,200.

WESTERN LAKE SUPERIOR SANITARY DISTRICT
2626 Courtland Street, Duluth MN 55806. 218/722-3336. **Contact:** Personnel. **Description:** Operates a landfill and collects household hazardous waste.

For more information on career opportunities in environmental and waste management services:

Associations

AIR & WASTE MANAGEMENT ASSOCIATION
One Gateway Center, 3rd Floor, Pittsburgh PA 15222. 412/232-3444. World Wide Web address: http://www. awma.org. A nonprofit, technical and educational organization providing a neutral forum where all points of view regarding environmental management issues can be addressed.

AMERICAN ACADEMY OF ENVIRONMENTAL ENGINEERS
130 Holiday Court, Suite 100, Annapolis MD 21401. 410/266-3311. World Wide Web address: http://www. enviro-engrs.org. Publishes *Environmental Engineer*, a quarterly magazine addressing policies and technical issues.

ENVIRONMENTAL INDUSTRY ASSOCIATIONS
4301 Connecticut Avenue NW, Suite 300, Washington DC 20008. 202/244-4700. World Wide Web address: http://www.envasns.org.

INSTITUTE OF CLEAN AIR COMPANIES
1660 L Street NW, Suite 1100, Washington DC 20036. 202/457-0911. World Wide Web address: http://www.icac.com. A national association of companies involved in stationary source air pollution control.

MINNESOTA ENVIRONMENTAL INITIATIVE
2420 Rand Tower, 527 Marquette Avenue South, Minneapolis MN 55402. 612/334-3388. A nonprofit environmental educational organization that attempts to integrate government and environmental groups by providing a variety of workshops and educational seminars for environmental, government, and business professionals.

Magazines

JOURNAL OF AIR AND WASTE MANAGEMENT ASSOCIATION
One Gateway Center, 3rd Floor, Pittsburgh PA 15222. Toll-free phone: 800/275-5851. World Wide Web address: http://www.awma.org.

Online Services

ECOLOGIC
http://www.eng.rpi.edu/dept/union/pugwash/ecojobs. htm. This Website provides links to a variety of environmental job resources. This site is run by the Rensselaer Student Pugwash.

ENVIRONMENTAL JOBS SEARCH PAGE/UBIQUITY
http://ourworld.compuserve.com/homepages/ubikk/ env4.htm. This Website includes internships, tips, and links to other databases of environmental job openings.

INTERNATIONAL & ENVIRONMENTAL JOB BULLETINS
http://www.sas.upenn.edu/African_Studies/ Publications/International_Environmental_16621. html. Provides a wealth of information on bulletins, magazines, and resources for jobseekers who are looking to get into the environmental field. Most of these resources are on a subscription basis and provide job openings and other information. This information was compiled by Dennis F. Desmond.

LINKS TO SOURCES OF INFORMATION ON ENVIRONMENTAL JOBS
http://www.utexas.edu/ftp/student/scb/joblinks.html. Provides links to numerous sites that offer job openings and information in the environmental field. The site is run by the University of Texas at Austin.

Visit our exciting job and career site at http://www.careercity.com

FABRICATED/PRIMARY METALS AND PRODUCTS

The fabricated metals industry is on the rebound after a rough time in the early '90s. However, according to the Federal Reserve, the industry still suffers occasional setbacks, among them the decrease in steel production during the latter half of 1998. Steel production fell approximately 9 percent between January and September of 1998, due in large part to an increase in imports.

Standard & Poor data indicated a 3 percent gain in sales for the steel industry, coupled with a 9 percent loss in profits for the first two quarters of 1998. The aluminum segment saw a 2 percent gain in sales for the same period, with a 23 percent decrease in profits.

As of September 1998, U.S. industrial production was 128 percent higher than at the same point in 1992. The transportation sector is expected to increase demand for metal castings, and commercial aircraft deliveries will still have a heavy reliance on plate products.

A&B TOOL AND GAGE CORPORATION
2025 105th Avenue NE, Blaine MN 55449. 612/784-5330. **Contact:** Daniel M. Bjorn, President. **Description:** Manufactures metal stampings, tools, dies, jigs, fixtures, and special machinery. The company is also engaged in machine work.

BERMO INC.
4501 Ball Road NE, Circle Pines MN 55014. 612/786-7676. **Contact:** Human Resources. **World Wide Web address:** http://www.bermo.com. **Description:** A manufacturer of sheet metals, metal stampings, and injection-molded parts.

CMS HARTZELL, INC.
P.O. Box 64529, St. Paul MN 55164-0529. 651/646-9456. **Contact:** Human Resources. **World Wide Web address:** http://www.cmshartzell.com. **Description:** A manufacturer of aluminum die castings.

CRENLO, INC.
1600 Fourth Avenue NW, Rochester MN 55901. 507/287-3610. **Contact:** Wayne DeBruin, Director of Industrial Relations. **Description:** A manufacturer of metal fabrications ranging from simple sheet metal panels to large, complex weldings. Crenlo is also a supplier of off-highway vehicle cabs, electronic cabinets, metal enclosures, and subcontract metal fabrications. Founded in 1951. **Common positions include:** Accountant/Auditor; Blue-Collar Worker Supervisor; Buyer; Computer Programmer; Draftsperson; Electrical/Electronics Engineer; Human Resources Manager; Industrial Engineer; Mechanical Engineer; Operations/Production Manager; Purchasing Agent/Manager; Quality Control Supervisor; Registered Nurse; Software Engineer; Systems Analyst; Transportation/Traffic Specialist. **Educational backgrounds include:** Accounting; Business Administration; Computer Science; Engineering; Finance; Marketing. **Benefits:** 401(k); Dental Insurance; Disability Coverage; Employee Discounts; Life Insurance; Medical Insurance; Pension Plan; Profit Sharing; Tuition Assistance. **Special programs:** Internships. **Corporate headquarters location:** This Location. **Operations at this facility include:** Administration; Manufacturing; Research and Development; Sales; Service. **Number of employees at this location:** 875.

DALSIN INDUSTRIES INC.
9111 Grand Avenue South, Bloomington MN 55420. 612/881-2260. **Contact:** Larry Schuster, Human Resources. **Description:** A fabricator of metals such as aluminum steel and stainless steel.

EDGECOMB METALS COMPANY
2021 East Hennepin, Minneapolis MN 55413. 612/331-4000. **Contact:** Steve Wright, Personnel. **Description:** Distributors of stainless steel and other metals to industrial clients.

HITCHCOCK INDUSTRIES, INC.
8701 Harriet Avenue South, Minneapolis MN 55420-2787. 612/887-7800. **Contact:** Human Resources. **World Wide Web address:** http://www.hitchcock-ind.com. **Description:** A non-ferrous foundry that manufactures aluminum and magnesium castings for aerospace and industrial companies. Founded in 1916. **Common positions include:** Mechanical Engineer; Metallurgical Engineer. **Corporate headquarters location:** This Location.

LEE STAMPINGS
1750 West 96th Street, Bloomington MN 55431. 612/888-8831. **Contact:** Martha Richardson, Office Manager. **Description:** Produces metal stampings.

M.E. INTERNATIONAL
200 East Carterett Street, Duluth MN 55808. 218/626-2761. **Contact:** Human Resources. **Description:** A foundry that produces steel castings for the mining industry.

METAL-MATIC
629 Second Street SE, Minneapolis MN 55414. 612/378-0411. **Contact:** Human Resources. **Description:** A manufacturer of steel tubing.

NORTH STAR STEEL MINNESOTA
P.O. Box 64189, St. Paul MN 55164. 651/735-2110. **Contact:** Human Resources. **Description:** A manufacturer of steel bars used for roadway construction.

ORLUCK INDUSTRIES
17171 113th Avenue North, Suite B, Maple Grove MN 55369. 612/428-3175. **Contact:** Mark Orluck, President. **Description:** A metalworking shop that performs machining services on a subcontract basis. Orluck Industries formerly operated under the name J&M Metal Fabricating.

PAPER, CALMENSON & COMPANY
P.O. Box 64432, St. Paul MN 55164-0432. 651/628-6358. **Contact:** Human Resources. **Description:** Manufactures fabricated steel products for industrial use. **Common positions include:** Accountant/Auditor; Customer Service Representative; Draftsperson; Human Resources Manager; Manufacturer's/Wholesaler's Sales Rep.; Production Manager. **Benefits:** Dental Insurance; Disability Coverage; Life Insurance; Medical Insurance; Pension Plan; Savings Plan; Tuition Assistance. **Corporate headquarters location:** This Location. **Operations at this facility include:** Administration; Manufacturing; Sales; Service.

PROSPECT FOUNDRY INC.
1225 Winter Street NE, Minneapolis MN 55413-2697. 612/331-9282. **Contact:** Human Resources. **World Wide Web address:** http://www.prospectfoundry.com. **Description:** An iron foundry primarily engaged in the manufacture of gray and ductile iron castings.

SLP MACHINE INC.
1262 McKay Drive, Ham Lake MN 55304. 612/434-3535. **Contact:** Personnel. **Description:** A producer of machined metal parts.

SILGAN CONTAINERS
755 North Prior Avenue, St. Paul MN 55104. 651/643-3200. **Contact:** John Faltesek, Personnel Manager. **Description:** Manufactures metal food cans, aluminum food containers, and convenience ends for food cans.

TOOL PRODUCTS
5100 Boone Avenue North, New Hope MN 55428. 612/536-5520. **Fax:** 612/535-8938. **Contact:** Gregg Peterson, Human Resources Manager. **Description:** Manufactures aluminum die castings. **Common positions include:** Accountant/Auditor; Blue-Collar Worker Supervisor; Buyer; Ceramics Engineer; Customer Service Representative; Department Manager; Draftsperson; Human Resources Manager; Industrial Engineer; Materials Engineer; Mechanical Engineer; Metallurgical Engineer; Quality Control Supervisor. **Educational backgrounds include:** Accounting; Business Administration; Engineering; Marketing; Mathematics. **Benefits:** 401(k); Dental Insurance; Disability Coverage; Life Insurance; Medical Insurance; Pension Plan; Savings Plan; Tuition Assistance. **Corporate headquarters location:** St. Louis Park MN. **Other U.S. locations:** Jackson TN. **Parent company:** Quadion. **Operations at this facility include:** Administration; Divisional Headquarters; Manufacturing; Research and Development; Sales. **Listed on:** Privately held. **Number of employees at this location:** 370. **Number of employees nationwide:** 460.

**VINCENT METALS
A DIVISION OF RIO ALGOM, INC.**
P.O. Box 360, Minneapolis MN 55440. 612/717-9000. **Contact:** John Oldendorf, Director of Human Resources. **Description:** A distributor of ferrous and non-ferrous metals. The company has 15 other locations. **Common positions include:** Accountant/Auditor; Administrator; Blue-Collar Worker Supervisor; Branch Manager; Buyer; Computer Programmer; Credit Manager; Customer Service Representative; Department Manager; Financial Analyst; Human Resources Manager; Management Trainee; Manufacturer's/Wholesaler's Sales Rep.; Marketing Specialist; Metallurgical Engineer; Operations/Production Manager; Purchasing Agent/Manager; Systems Analyst; Transportation/Traffic Specialist. **Educational backgrounds include:** Accounting; Business Administration; Communications; Computer Science; Finance; Liberal Arts; Marketing. **Benefits:** Dental Insurance; Disability Coverage; Life Insurance; Medical Insurance; On-Site Exercise Facility; Pension Plan; Profit Sharing; Savings Plan; Swimming Pool; Tennis Court; Tuition Assistance. **Corporate headquarters location:** This Location. **Operations at this facility include:** Administration; Divisional Headquarters; Regional Headquarters; Sales; Service.

Note: Because addresses and telephone numbers of smaller companies can change rapidly, we recommend you call each company to verify the information below before inquiring about job opportunities. Mass mailings are not recommended.

Additional small employers:

ALUMINUM FOUNDRIES

Dee Inc.
PO Box 627, Crookston MN 56716-0627. 218/281-5811.

Progress Casting
2600 Niagara Ln N, Plymouth MN 55447-4719. 612/557-1000.

COATING, ENGRAVING, AND ALLIED SERVICES

Micom Corporation
475 8th Ave NW, St. Paul MN 55112-3206. 651/636-5616.

DIECASTINGS

Kurt Die Cast
7585 Highway 65 NE, Fridley MN 55432-3544. 612/572-4650.

Le Sueur Inc.
PO Box 149, Le Sueur MN 56058-0149. 507/665-6204.

Progress Casting
1521 E Hawthorne St, Albert Lea MN 56007-3864. 507/373-6487.

QX Inc.
PO Box 278, Hamel MN 55340-0278. 612/478-9878.

St. Paul Metalcraft Inc.
3737 Lexington Ave N, Shoreview MN 55126-2937. 651/483-6641.

Technical Die-Casting Inc.
PO Box 349, Stockton MN 55988-0349. 507/689-2194.

Twin City Die Castings Co.
1070 33rd Ave SE, Minneapolis MN 55414-2707. 651/645-3611.

FABRICATED METAL PRODUCTS

DBI/Sala
3965 Pepin Ave, Red Wing MN 55066-1837. 651/388-8282.

FABRICATED STRUCTURAL METAL PRODUCTS

DCI Inc.
PO Box 1227, St. Cloud MN 56302-1227. 320/252-8200.

General Sheet Metal Corp.
2330 Louisiana Ave N, Minneapolis MN 55427-3631. 612/544-8747.

Jones Metal Products Inc.
3201 3rd Ave, Mankato MN 56001-2725. 507/625-4436.

Kant-Sag
PO Box 80, Montgomery MN 56069-0080. 507/364-7333.

Mercury Minnesota Inc.
PO Box 188, Faribault MN 55021-0188. 507/334-5513.

Modern Tool Inc.
1200 Northdale Blvd NW, Minneapolis MN 55448-3141. 612/754-7337.

MVE Inc.
PO Box 234, New Prague MN 56071-0234. 612/758-4484.

R&M Manufacturing Co.
4838 W 35th St, Minneapolis MN 55416-2610. 612/929-0468.

Sheet Metal Connectors Inc.
5850 Main St NE, Fridley MN 55432-5439. 612/572-0000.

Snappy Air Distribution Products
1011 11th Ave SE, Detroit Lakes MN 56501-3711. 218/847-9258.

Tenere Inc.
10860 60th St N, Stillwater MN 55082-4514. 651/439-7202.

FABRICATED WIRE PRODUCTS

Northern Wire Products Inc.
PO Box 70, St. Cloud MN 56302-0070. 320/252-3442.

Peerless Chain Company
PO Box 5349, Winona MN 55987-0349. 507/457-9100.

Ron-Vik Inc.
800 Colorado Avenue S, Minneapolis MN 55416-1004. 612/545-0276.

IRON AND STEEL FOUNDRIES

Badger Foundry Company
PO Box 1306, Winona MN 55987-7306. 507/452-5760.

Grede Foundries Inc.
5200 Foundry Cir, St. Cloud MN 56303-2032. 320/255-5200.

LTV Steel Company Inc.
PO Box 196, Aurora MN 55705-0196. 218/225-3345.

National Steel Pellet Company
PO Box 217, Keewatin MN 55753-0217. 218/778-6521.

Versa Iron & Machine-Casting
867 Forest St, St. Paul MN 55106-3866. 651/778-3300.

METAL FORGINGS

Sifco Custom Machining Co.
2430 Winnetka Ave N,
Minneapolis MN 55427-3568.
612/544-3511.

NONFERROUS ROLLING AND DRAWING OF METALS

Alexandria Extrusion Company
401 County Road 22 NW,
Alexandria MN 56308-4974.
320/763-6537.

SCREW MACHINE PRODUCTS

Cass Screw Machine Products Co.
4748 France Ave N, Minneapolis
MN 55429-3915. 612/535-0501.

Northwest Automatic Products
501 Royalston Ave, Minneapolis
MN 55405-1542. 612/339-7521.

Roberts Automatic Products
880 Lake Dr E, Chanhassen MN
55317-9341. 612/949-1000.

SMELTING AND REFINING OF NONFERROUS METALS

FFS Inc.
13220 Doyle Path E, Rosemount
MN 55068-2510. 651/437-2815.

WHOLESALE METALS SERVICE CENTERS AND OFFICES

Envirobate Metro
3301 E 26th St, Minneapolis MN
55406-1725. 612/729-1080.

Keelor Steel
5101 Boone Avenue N,
Minneapolis MN 55428-4024.
612/535-1431.

McNeilus Steel Inc.
PO Box 249, Dodge Center MN
55927-0249. 507/374-6336.

Olympic Steel Inc.
625 Xenium Ln N, Plymouth MN
55441-5561. 612/544-7100.

Ryerson Steel
PO Box 619, Minneapolis MN
55440-0619. 612/544-4401.

Una-Clad
1001 Lund Blvd, Anoka MN
55303-1089. 612/576-9595.

For more information on career opportunities in the fabricated/primary metals and products industries:

Associations

ASM INTERNATIONAL: THE MATERIALS INFORMATION SOCIETY
9639 Kinsman Road, Materials Park OH 44073.
440/338-5151. World Wide Web address: http://www.
asm-intl.org. Gathers, processes, and disseminates
technical information to foster the understanding and
application of engineered materials.

THE ALUMINUM ASSOCIATION, INC.
900 19th Street NW, Washington DC 20006. 202/862-
5100. Fax: 202/862-5164. World Wide Web address:
http://www.aluminum.org. A trade association for
U.S. producers of primary aluminum and recyclers.
Member companies operate over 200 plants
throughout the nation.

AMERICAN FOUNDRYMEN'S SOCIETY
505 State Street, Des Plaines IL 60016. 847/824-0181.
World Wide Web address: http://www.afsinc.org.

AMERICAN WELDING SOCIETY
550 NW LeJeune Road, Miami FL 33126. 305/443-
9353. World Wide Web address: http://www.aws.org.

Directories

DIRECTORY OF STEEL FOUNDRIES AND BUYER'S GUIDE
Steel Founders' Society of America, 455 State Street,
Des Plaines IL 60016. 847/299-9160. World Wide
Web address: http://www.sfsa.org.

Magazines

AMERICAN METAL MARKET
350 Hudson Street, New York NY 10014. 212/519-
7550.

IRON & STEEL ENGINEER
Association of Iron and Steel Engineers, 3 Gateway
Center, Suite 1900, Pittsburgh PA 15222-1004.
412/281-6323. World Wide Web address: http://www.
aise.org.

MODERN METALS
Trend Publishing, 625 North Michigan Avenue, Suite
1500, Chicago IL 60611. 312/654-2300.

FINANCIAL SERVICES

Despite the economic turbulence of 1998, the future appears solid for the financial services sector. According to Business Week, *profits for the financial services industry were up 18 percent for the first two quarters of 1998 from the same period of 1997, though profit margins were down. Merrill Lynch & Company* had a strong year in 1997, posting over $1 trillion in customer assets. Attempting to match Merrill Lynch's success, Morgan Stanley and Dean Witter merged and Travelers Group subsidiary Salomon Inc. joined with Smith Barney Holdings Inc. Travelers Group was in the news again in 1998, when it merged with Citicorp, combining resources of more than $700 billion.*

The best opportunities through the end of the decade will be for investment managers, specifically those with experience in high-technology, natural resources, and emerging markets. Mortgage and security brokerages are also showing significant growth, having added 7,000 and 4,000 jobs, respectively, in October 1998.

DAIN RAUSCHER
INTER-REGIONAL FINANCIAL GROUP, INC.
60 South Sixth Street, Minneapolis MN 55402. 612/371-2711. **Contact:** Human Resources. **World Wide Web address:** http://www.dainrauscher.com. **Description:** A financial consulting and securities firm. **Common positions include:** Broker; Financial Analyst; Operations/Production Manager. **Educational backgrounds include:** Accounting; Business Administration; Economics; Finance. **Benefits:** Dental Insurance; Disability Coverage; Employee Discounts; Life Insurance; Medical Insurance; Pension Plan; Profit Sharing; Tuition Assistance. **Corporate headquarters location:** This Location. **Parent company:** Inter-Regional Financial Group, Inc. (also at this location) is a holding company whose subsidiaries provide securities brokerage and investment banking services. The company also provides real estate syndication and property investment services, as well as data processing services. **Operations at this facility include:** Administration; Divisional Headquarters; Regional Headquarters; Research and Development; Sales; Service. **Listed on:** American Stock Exchange; New York Stock Exchange.

GMAC/RESIDENTIAL FUNDING CORPORATION
8400 Normandale Lake Boulevard, Suite 250, Minneapolis MN 55437. 612/832-7000. **Contact:** Cheryl Cresting, Human Resources. **World Wide Web address:** http://www.rfc.com. **Description:** A secondary mortgage provider. **Common positions include:** Accountant/Auditor; Computer Programmer; Customer Service Representative; Department Manager; Financial Analyst; Human Resources Manager; Systems Analyst; Underwriter/Assistant Underwriter. **Educational backgrounds include:** Accounting; Banking; Business Administration; Computer Science; Economics; Finance. **Benefits:** 401(k); Dental Insurance; Disability Coverage; Employee Discounts; Life Insurance; Medical Insurance; Pension Plan; Profit Sharing; Savings Plan; Tuition Assistance. **Special programs:** Internships. **Corporate headquarters location:** This Location. **Parent company:** GMAC Mortgage Corporation. **Operations at this facility include:** Administration; Divisional Headquarters; Regional Headquarters; Sales; Service. **Number of employees nationwide:** 500.

GREEN TREE FINANCIAL CORPORATION
600 Landmark Towers, 345 St. Peter Street, St. Paul MN 55102-1639. 651/293-4887. **Fax:** 651/293-3622. **Recorded jobline:** 651/293-5825. **Contact:** Human Resources. **World Wide Web address:** http://www.gtfc.com. **Description:** Green Tree aggregates and secures conventional manufactured home, motorcycle, and home improvement contracts and sells securities through public offerings and private placements. Green Tree's FHA-insured and VA-guaranteed manufactured home contracts are converted into GNMA certificates and are sold in the secondary market. Green Tree retains the servicing on all contracts. The company also markets homeowners insurance and life insurance to its customers. Founded in 1976. **Common positions include:** Adjuster; Computer Programmer; Credit Manager; Customer Service Representative; Underwriter/Assistant Underwriter. **Educational backgrounds include:** Accounting; Business

Administration; Economics; Finance; Marketing; Mathematics. **Benefits:** 401(k); Dental Insurance; Disability Coverage; Employee Discounts; Life Insurance; Medical Insurance; Pension Plan; Transport. Reimburse; Tuition Assistance. **Special programs:** Internships. **Corporate headquarters location:** This Location. **Listed on:** New York Stock Exchange. **Number of employees at this location:** 1,200. **Number of employees nationwide:** 4,000.

JCPENNEY CREDIT SERVICE CENTER
P.O. Box 947, Minneapolis MN 55440. 612/942-2339. **Contact:** Diane Grund, Personnel Manager. **Description:** A credit card service center operated by the national department store chain. **Common positions include:** Clerical Supervisor; Collector; Customer Service Representative. **Benefits:** 401(k); Dental Insurance; Disability Coverage; Employee Discounts; Life Insurance; Medical Insurance; Pension Plan; Profit Sharing; Savings Plan. **Operations at this facility include:** Regional Headquarters. **Listed on:** New York Stock Exchange. **Number of employees at this location:** 300.

LUTHERAN BROTHERHOOD COMPANY
625 Fourth Avenue South, Minneapolis MN 55415. 612/340-7054. **Contact:** Gwen Martin, Manager of Staffing and Employee Relations. **World Wide Web address:** http://www. luthbro.com. **Description:** A financial institution providing life, health, and disability insurance, in addition to annuities and mutual funds. **Common positions include:** Actuary; Computer Programmer. **Educational backgrounds include:** Computer Science; Mathematics. **Benefits:** Dental Insurance; Disability Coverage; Life Insurance; Medical Insurance; Pension Plan; Tuition Assistance. **Corporate headquarters location:** This Location. **Operations at this facility include:** Administration; Research and Development; Service.

MILLER & SCHROEDER FINANCIAL, INC.
220 South Sixth Street, Suite 300, Minneapolis MN 55402. 612/376-1500. **Contact:** Carol Anderson, Personnel Director. **Description:** A financial services firm engaged in the underwriting and sale of municipal bonds. **Number of employees at this location:** 250.

MINNEAPOLIS GRAIN EXCHANGE
400 South Fourth Street, Suite 150, Minneapolis MN 55415. 612/338-6212. **Contact:** Dee Stitzel, Human Resources Director. **World Wide Web address:** http://www.mgex.com. **Description:** Minneapolis Grain Exchange trades on futures and options contracts.

NORWEST MORTGAGE INC.
800 LaSalle Avenue, Suite 1000, Minneapolis MN 55402. 612/343-3400. **Contact:** Personnel Department. **Description:** A mortgage banking company.

PIPER JAFFRAY
P.O. Box 28, Minneapolis MN 55440-0028. 612/342-6000. **Toll-free phone:** 800/333-6000. **Fax:** 612/342-5743. **Contact:** Lisa Lyrek, Employment Coordinator. **E-mail address:** applicant@ piperjaffray.com. **World Wide Web address:** http://www.piperjaffray.com. **Description:** Piper Jaffray is a securities firm which offers individual investors and businesses a full array of investment services through 73 branch offices in 17 Midwest, Mountain, and Pacific Northwest states. The company also provides capital markets and investment management services. **Common positions include:** Accountant/Auditor; Administrative Assistant; Administrator; Computer Programmer; Financial Analyst; Investment Manager; Mail Distributor; Receptionist. **Educational backgrounds include:** Accounting; Business Administration; Communications; Economics; Finance; Marketing; Mathematics. **Benefits:** 401(k); Dental Insurance; Disability Coverage; ESOP; Life Insurance; Medical Insurance; Paid Sick Child Care; Stock Option; Tuition Assistance. **Special programs:** Internships. **Corporate headquarters location:** This Location. **Operations at this facility include:** Administration; Research and Development; Sales. **Listed on:** New York Stock Exchange. **Number of employees nationwide:** 2,630.

TCF FINANCIAL CORPORATION
TCF BANK F.S.B.
801 Marquette Avenue South, Minneapolis MN 55402. 612/661-8277. **Fax:** 612/332-1753. **Recorded jobline:** 612/661-8989. **Contact:** Human Resources. **Description:** A bank holding company. **Common positions include:** Accountant/Auditor; Branch Manager; Clerical Supervisor; Computer Programmer; Customer Service Representative; Financial Services Sales Representative; Insurance Agent/Broker; Securities Sales Representative; Services Sales Representative; Systems Analyst; Underwriter/Assistant Underwriter. **Educational backgrounds include:** Accounting; Business Administration; Communications; Computer Science; Finance; Liberal Arts. **Benefits:** 401(k); Daycare Assistance; Dental Insurance; Disability Coverage; Life Insurance; Medical Insurance; Pension Plan; Tuition Assistance. **Corporate headquarters location:** This Location.

Other U.S. locations: Oakbrook IL; Ann Arbor MI; Pontiac MI; Milwaukee WI. **Subsidiaries include:** TCF Bank F.S.B. (also at this location) is a thrift and banking institution that operates 184 retail branches in Minnesota, Wisconsin, and Michigan. Other subsidiaries provide consumer lending, insurance, mutual funds, title insurance, and mortgage banking products and services. **Operations at this facility include:** Administration; Divisional Headquarters; Regional Headquarters; Sales; Service. **Listed on:** New York Stock Exchange. **Number of employees at this location:** 2,500. **Number of employees nationwide:** 3,500.

TRAVELERS EXPRESS COMPANY
1550 Utica Avenue South, Minneapolis MN 55416. 612/591-3000. **Toll-free phone:** 800/542-3590. **Contact:** Human Resources Manager. **Description:** Sells money orders and automated dispensers to convenience store chains, grocery store chains, and oil companies with 20 or more outlets.

Note: Because addresses and telephone numbers of smaller companies can change rapidly, we recommend you call each company to verify the information below before inquiring about job opportunities. Mass mailings are not recommended.

Additional small employers:

CREDIT AGENCIES AND INSTITUTIONS

Green Tree Financial
332 Minnesota St, Ste 600, St. Paul MN 55101-1314. 651/292-2000.

Northstar Guarantee Inc.
444 Cedar Street, Ste 1910, St. Paul MN 55101-2133. 651/290-8780.

Norwest Corporation
2360 Pilot Knob Rd, Mendota Heights MN 55120-1116. 612/667-1975.

INVESTMENT ADVISORS

Investment Advisors Inc.
PO Box 357, Minneapolis MN 55440-0357. 612/376-2600.

Voyageur Companies Inc.
90 S 7th St, Ste 4400, Minneapolis MN 55402-4105. 612/376-7000.

LOAN BROKERS

Eduserv Technologies Inc.
85 7th Pl E, Ste 400, St. Paul MN 55101-2199. 651/227-6735.

MORTGAGE BANKERS

Firstar Home Mortgage Corp.
1550 E 79th St, Ste 880, Minneapolis MN 55425-3111. 612/851-8270.

GMAC/Residential Funding Corporation
12600 Whitewater Dr, Minneapolis MN 55437. 612/979-5000.

Great Lakes Mortgage
7550 France Ave S, Ste 340, Minneapolis MN 55435-4765. 612/844-6800.

Knutson Mortgage Corporation
3001 Metro Dr, Ste 400, Minneapolis MN 55425-1541. 612/204-2600.

Norwest Mortgage
3601 Minnesota Dr, Ste 200, Minneapolis MN 55435-5940. 612/844-2200.

Samboy Financial Inc.
2155 Niagara Ln N, Ste 150, Plymouth MN 55447-4654. 612/404-0056.

NONDEPOSIT TRUST FACILITIES

First Trust NA
180 5th St E #200, St. Paul MN 55101-1631. 651/244-5000.

SECURITY BROKERS AND DEALERS

American Express Financial Advisors
6500 City West Pkwy, Eden Prairie MN 55344-7701. 612/943-8055.

Cargill Financial Services Corp.
6000 Clearwater Dr, Hopkins MN 55343-9448. 612/984-3500.

CRI Securities Inc.
2222 Park Ave, Minneapolis MN 55404-3738. 612/872-1300.

Dain Rauscher Corporation
510 Marquette Avenue, Minneapolis MN 55402-1110. 612/607-8507.

John G. Kinnard & Company Inc.
920 2nd Avenue South, Minneapolis MN 55402-3318. 612/370-2700.

MJK Holdings Inc.
5500 Wayzata Blvd, Ste 800, Minneapolis MN 55416-1249. 612/542-6000.

Primevest Financial Services
PO Box 283, St. Cloud MN 56302-0283. 320/656-4300.

Sales Force Companies Inc.
7905 Golden Triangle Dr, Eden Prairie MN 55344-7220. 612/944-1333.

TRUSTS

Family Trust Inc.
1611 County Road B W, Roseville MN 55113-4053. 651/633-4530.

For more information on career opportunities in financial services:

<u>Associations</u>

FINANCIAL EXECUTIVES INSTITUTE
P.O. Box 1938, Morristown NJ 07962-1938. 973/898-4600. World Wide Web address: http://www.fei.org. Fee and membership required. Publishes biennial member directory. Provides member referral service.

INSTITUTE OF FINANCIAL EDUCATION
55 West Monroe Street, Suite 2800, Chicago IL 60603-5014. Toll-free phone: 800/946-0488. World Wide Web address: http://www.theinstitute.com. Institute of Financial Education offers career development programs.

NATIONAL ASSOCIATION OF BUSINESS ECONOMISTS
1233 20th Street NW, Suite 505, Washington DC 20036. 202/463-6223. World Wide Web address: http://www.nabe.com. Offers a newsletter and Website that provide a list of job openings.

NATIONAL ASSOCIATION OF CREDIT MANAGEMENT
8815 Centre Park Drive, Suite 200, Columbia MD 21045-2158. 410/740-5560. World Wide Web address: http://www.nacm.org. Publishes a business credit magazine.

NATIONAL ASSOCIATION OF TAX PRACTITIONERS
720 Association Drive, Appleton WI 54914-1483. Toll-free phone: 800/558-3402. E-mail address: natp@natptax.com. World Wide Web address: http://www.natptax.com. A membership organization that offers newsletters and nationwide workshops.

PUBLIC SECURITIES ASSOCIATION
40 Broad Street, 12th Floor, New York NY 10004. 212/809-7000. Contact: Caroline Binn, extension 427. Publishes an annual report and several newsletters.

SECURITIES INDUSTRY ASSOCIATION
120 Broadway, 35th Floor, New York NY 10271. 212/608-1500. World Wide Web address: http://www. sia.com. Contact: Phil Williams, Membership. Publishes a security industry yearbook. Membership required.

TREASURY MANAGEMENT ASSOCIATION
7315 Wisconsin Avenue, Suite 600-W, Bethesda MD 20814. 301/907-2862. World Wide Web address: http://www.tma-net.org.

Directories

DIRECTORY OF AMERICAN FINANCIAL INSTITUTIONS
Thomson Business Publications, 4709 West Golf Road, 6th Floor, Skokie IL 66076-1253. Sales: 800/321-3373.

MOODY'S BANK AND FINANCE MANUAL
Financial Information Services, 60 Madison Avenue, 6th Floor, New York NY 10010. Toll-free phone: 800/342-5647. World Wide Web address: http://www.moodys.com.

Magazines

BARRON'S: NATIONAL BUSINESS AND FINANCIAL WEEKLY
Barron's, 200 Liberty Street, New York NY 10281. 212/416-2700.

FINANCIAL PLANNING
Securities Data Publishing, 1290 Avenue of the Americas, 36th Floor, New York NY 10004. 212/765-5311.

FUTURES: THE MAGAZINE OF COMMODITIES AND OPTIONS
250 South Wacker Drive, Suite 1150, Chicago IL 60606. Toll-free phone: 888/898-5514. World Wide Web address: http://www.futuresmag.com.

INSTITUTIONAL INVESTOR
488 Madison Avenue, 12th Floor, New York NY 10022. 212/303-3300.

Online Services

FINANCIAL/ACCOUNTING/INSURANCE JOBS PAGE
http://www.nationjob.com/financial. This Website provides a list of financial, accounting, and insurance job openings.

JOBS IN CORPORATE FINANCE
http://www.cob.ohio-state.edu/dept/fin/jobs/corpfin. htm. Provides information and resources for jobseekers looking to work in the field of corporate finance.

NATIONAL BANKING NETWORK: RECRUITING FOR BANKING AND FINANCE
http://www.banking-financejobs.com. Offers a searchable database of job openings in financial services and banking. The database is searchable by region, keyword, and job specialty.

Visit our exciting job and career site at http://www.careercity.com

FOOD AND BEVERAGES/AGRICULTURE

The food and beverages industry constitutes the nation's largest sector of manufacturing, and the demand for processed food and beverages should increase moderately as the market becomes more globalized. With the popularity of pre-cooked meals, supermarkets have increased spending on prepared foods. Standard & Poor *reported a 39 percent increase in food profits for the first two quarters of 1998 versus profits for the same period of 1997, and a 4 percent increase in beverage profits.*

According to Business Week, *about 15 percent of packaged food industry jobs were eliminated between 1996 and 1998. The trend in the packaged food business is toward cutbacks in the number of brands offered as well as fewer coupons for consumers. By reducing the number of brands, food companies are able to spend less money on marketing and focus on top-selling products. General Mills, for example, has eliminated all but its most profitable cereals.*

Overall, the U.S. Department of Labor projects a slow decline in food industry employment through 2005, particularly for those occupations hurt by rising operations costs, including food processors and butchers. Agricultural careers are also expected to decline through 2005. Due to a high turnover rate, food and beverage service worker jobs will be available over the next decade. The dairy sector should see about 3 percent annual growth over the next few years, due mainly to strong demand for reduced-fat milk, natural cheese, and frozen desserts.

ALLIANT FOOD SERVICE
2864 Eagandale Boulevard, Eagan MN 55121. 612/454-6580. **Contact:** Human Resources. **Description:** Distributes food products, equipment and supplies, cleaning chemicals, and disposables to a variety of food service locations such as restaurants, nursing homes, hospitals, and institutional feeders.

AMERICAN CRYSTAL SUGAR COMPANY
101 North Third Street, Moorhead MN 56560. 218/236-4400. **Contact:** Human Resources. **Description:** American Crystal Sugar Company, an agricultural cooperative, processes and markets sugar, sugar beet pulp, molasses, and seed. Customers are primarily American companies in the food processing industry. American Crystal is a partner in Midwest Agri-Commodities with Minn-Dak Farmers Cooperative and Southern Minnesota Beet Sugar Cooperative. The partners produce about 38 percent of sugar beet pulp, 35 percent of sugar beet molasses, and 40 percent of desugared molasses in the United States. In January 1994, American Crystal Sugar Company, Minn-Dak Farmers Cooperative, and Southern Minnesota Beet Sugar Cooperative pooled resources to form United Sugars Corporation, a beet sugar marketing company. **Corporate headquarters location:** This Location. **Other U.S. locations:** Crookston MN; East Grand Forks MN; Drayton ND; Hillsboro ND. **Number of employees nationwide:** 1,100.

AMERICAN FOODS GROUP
5758 Olson Memorial Highway, Minneapolis MN 55422. 612/546-4471. **Contact:** Human Resources. **Description:** This location is the seafood division. Overall, American Foods Group is an area wholesaler of frozen foods. **NOTE:** Please send resumes to Doug Hagen, Chief Financial Officer, 544 Acme Street, Green Bay WI 54302.

ARMOUR SWIFT-ECKRICH INC.
P.O. Box 508, St. James MN 56081. 507/375-3124. **Contact:** Human Resources. **Description:** This location is a meat packaging and processing plant. Overall, Armour Swift-Eckrich produces processed meats, such as bacon, ham, fresh smoked and dry sausage, and luncheon meats, under brand names such as Armour Star, Brown 'N Serve, Butterball, Eckrich, Healthy Choice, and Swift Premium.

BAILEY NURSERIES, INC.
1325 Bailey Road, St. Paul MN 55119. 651/459-9744. **Contact:** Jeff Poferl, Personnel Manager. **World Wide Web address:** http://www.baileynursery.com. **Description:** A large wholesale grower of nursery products including evergreens, trees, shrubs, bedding plants, annuals, and perennials. **Common positions include:** Agricultural Scientist; Horticulturist. **Educational backgrounds include:** Agricultural Science; Horticulture. **Benefits:** 401(k); Dental Insurance; Disability Coverage; Employee Discounts; Life Insurance; Medical Insurance; Pension Plan; Profit Sharing; Savings Plan; Tuition Assistance. **Special programs:** Internships. **Corporate headquarters location:** This Location. **Operations at this facility include:** Administration; Divisional Headquarters; Manufacturing; Research and Development; Sales; Service. **Listed on:** Privately held. **Number of employees at this location:** 210. **Number of employees nationwide:** 400.

CARGILL INC.
P.O. Box 9300, Mail Stop 63, Minneapolis MN 55440. 612/742-7200. **Physical address:** 15407 McGinty Road West, Wayzata MN 55391. **Toll-free phone:** 800/741-7431. **Contact:** Kris Olson, Human Resources. **World Wide Web address:** http://www.cargill.com. **Description:** Cargill, with its subsidiaries and its affiliates, is involved in nearly 50 individual lines of business. The company has more than 130 years of service and international expertise in commodity trading, handling, transporting, processing, and risk management. Cargill is a major trader of grains and oilseeds, as well as a marketer of many other agricultural and non-agricultural commodities. As a transporter, it moves bulk commodities using a network of rail and road systems, inland waterways, and ocean-going routes combining its own fleet and transportation services purchased from outside sources. Cargill is a leader in developing farm products and in supplying them to growers. Agricultural products include a wide variety of feed, seed, fertilizers, and other goods and services needed by producers worldwide. Cargill is also a leader in producing and marketing seed varieties and hybrids. Cargill Central Research (also at this location) is dedicated to developing new agricultural products to address the needs of customers around the world. The company also provides financial and technical services. Cargill's Financial Markets Division supports Cargill and its subsidiaries with financial products and services that address the full spectrum of market conditions. These include financial instrument trading, emerging markets instrument trading, value investing, and money management. Cargill's worldwide food processing businesses supply products ranging from basic ingredients used in food production to recognized name brands. The company also operates a number of industrial businesses including the production of steel, industrial-grade starches, ethanol, and salt products. **NOTE:** The company offers entry-level positions and second and third shifts. **Common positions include:** Account Manager; Account Representative; Accountant; Attorney; Auditor; Biochemist; Buyer; Chemical Engineer; Chemist; Computer Operator; Computer Programmer; Database Manager; Electrical/Electronics Engineer; Environmental Engineer; Food Scientist/Technologist; Human Resources Manager; Management Trainee; Marketing Specialist; Mechanical Engineer; Metallurgical Engineer; MIS Specialist; Operations Manager; Production Manager; Project Manager; Quality Control Supervisor; Sales Manager; Software Engineer; Transportation/Traffic Specialist. **Educational backgrounds include:** Accounting; Business Administration; Chemistry; Computer Science; Economics; Engineering; Finance; Liberal Arts; Software Tech. Support. **Benefits:** 401(k); Dental Insurance; Disability Coverage; Financial Planning Assistance; Life Insurance; Medical Insurance; Pension Plan; Profit Sharing; Public Transit Available; Telecommuting; Tuition Assistance. **Special programs:** Internships; Training; Co-ops; Summer Jobs. **Corporate headquarters location:** This Location. **International locations:** Worldwide. **Listed on:** Privately held. **Annual sales/revenues:** More than $100 million. **Number of employees worldwide:** 80,000.

CENEX HARVEST STATES - LAND O'LAKES
P.O. Box 64089, St. Paul MN 55164-0089. 651/451-5151. **Contact:** Human Resources. **World Wide Web address:** http://www.chslol.com. **Description:** An agricultural cooperative that produces animal feeds, crop protection products, plant food, and seeds, and processes grain. The company is a joint venture between Cenex Harvest States Cooperative and Land O'Lakes, Inc. **Educational backgrounds include:** Accounting; Agricultural Science; Agronomy; Animal Science; Business Administration; Computer Science; Liberal Arts; Marketing. **Benefits:** Dental Insurance; Disability Coverage; Life Insurance; Medical Insurance; Savings Plan; Tuition Assistance. **Corporate headquarters location:** This Location. **Operations at this facility include:** Administration; Sales; Service.

CENEX HARVEST STATES COOPERATIVE
P.O. Box 64796, St. Paul MN 55164. **Toll-free phone:** 800/328-6539. **Contact:** Human Resources Generalist. **Description:** Cenex Harvest States Cooperative is a grain marketing company. **Common positions include:** Accountant/Auditor; Procurement Specialist. **Educational backgrounds include:** Accounting; Business Administration; Finance; Marketing. **Benefits:**

401(k); Dental Insurance; Disability Coverage; Employee Discounts; Life Insurance; Medical Insurance; Pension Plan; Savings Plan; Tuition Assistance. **Special programs:** Internships. **Corporate headquarters location:** This Location. **Operations at this facility include:** Administration. **Number of employees at this location:** 400. **Number of employees nationwide:** 2,800.

CENTRAL LIVESTOCK ASSOCIATION
310 Market Lane, South St. Paul MN 55075. 651/451-1844. **Contact:** Kurt Zimmerman, Human Resources. **Description:** Buys and sells livestock.

CHIQUITA PROCESSED FOODS
900 North Cedar Avenue, Owatonna MN 55060. 507/451-7670. **Contact:** Human Resources. **Description:** A vegetable canning company.

DAHLGREN & COMPANY, INC.
P.O. Box 609, Crookston MN 56716-0609. **Contact:** Human Resources. **Description:** Processes sunflower seeds. **NOTE:** This firm does not accept unsolicited resumes. Please only respond to advertised openings.

DAIRY FARMERS OF AMERICA
1313 North Star Drive, Zumbrota MN 55992. 507/732-5124. **Contact:** Ramona Redfield, Personnel Director. **World Wide Web address:** http://cac.dfamilk.com. **Description:** A producer of cheddar cheese. **Common positions include:** Accountant/Auditor; Blue-Collar Worker Supervisor; Department Manager; Human Resources Manager; Management Trainee; Mechanical Engineer; Operations/Production Manager; Quality Control Supervisor. **Educational backgrounds include:** Accounting; Engineering; Mathematics. **Benefits:** Dental Insurance; Disability Coverage; Life Insurance; Medical Insurance; Pension Plan; Savings Plan. **Corporate headquarters location:** Kansas City KS. **Operations at this facility include:** Manufacturing.

FAIRWAY FOODS, INC.
1111 West Fifth Street, Northfield MN 55057. 507/645-9311. **Contact:** Human Resources. **World Wide Web address:** http://www.fairwayfoods.com. **Description:** A food distribution warehouse which wholesales food to grocery stores in the Midwest.

FARMLAND FOODS
1000 East Main Street, Albert Lea MN 56007. 507/377-4200. **Contact:** David Boss, Human Resources Manager. **World Wide Web address:** http://www.farmland.com. **Description:** Produces ham and bacon.

FAVORITE BRANDS
P.O. Box 28, Round Lake MN 56167. 507/945-8181. **Contact:** Human Resources. **Description:** Manufactures candy.

FLEMING COMPANIES, INC.
3501 Marshall Street NE, Minneapolis MN 55418. 612/782-4419. **Fax:** 612/782-4405. **Recorded jobline:** 612/782-4444. **Contact:** Lois Stevenson, Human Resource Manager. **Description:** Distributes a wide variety of groceries, meats, dairy and delicatessen products, frozen foods, fresh produce, and a variety of general merchandise and related items; provides a full range of support services, such as collateralized long-term financing, merchandising, marketing, and computerized order entry and shelf management systems; operates a dairy facility; owns and operates supermarkets and a bakery; and operates a truck fleet. Founded in 1917. **Common positions include:** Buyer; Computer Operator; Order Clerk; Quality Control Supervisor; Sales Representative; Secretary; Truck Driver; Warehouse Manager. **Educational backgrounds include:** Business Administration. **Benefits:** 401(k); Dental Insurance; Disability Coverage; Life Insurance; Medical Insurance; Pension Plan; Tuition Assistance. **Corporate headquarters location:** Oklahoma City OK. **Listed on:** New York Stock Exchange. **Annual sales/revenues:** More than $100 million. **Number of employees at this location:** 600.

GFI AMERICA
2815 Blaisdell Avenue, Minneapolis MN 55408-2312. 612/872-6262. **Contact:** Human Resources. **Description:** A meat packing and beef processing plant.

GENERAL MILLS, INC.
P.O. Box 1113, Minneapolis MN 55440. 612/540-2311. **Contact:** Jeanne Smith, Recruitment Department. **World Wide Web address:** http://www.genmills.com. **Description:** Produces and markets consumer foods. Food products include Cheerios, Wheaties, and Total cereals; Betty

Crocker desserts, frostings, and baking mixes; Pop Secret microwave popcorn; Gorton's frozen seafood; Yoplait yogurt; Bisquik pancake mix; and Gold Medal flour. General Mills is also engaged in the full-service dinnerhouse restaurant business, operating over 1,000 company-owned Red Lobster and Olive Garden restaurants in North America. Founded in 1928. **Common positions include:** Chemical Engineer; Food Scientist/Technologist; Mechanical Engineer. **Educational backgrounds include:** Accounting; Chemistry; Computer Science; Engineering; Finance; Food Science; Marketing; MBA. **Corporate headquarters location:** This Location. **Other U.S. locations:** Scottsdale AZ; West Chicago IL; Buffalo NY. **Operations at this facility include:** Administration; Research and Development. **Listed on:** New York Stock Exchange. **Number of employees nationwide:** 121,300.

GOLD'N PLUMP POULTRY
P.O. Box 1106, St. Cloud MN 56302. 320/685-3601. **Contact:** Human Resources. **Description:** A poultry processor.

GOLDEN VALLEY MICROWAVE FOODS, INC.
7450 Metro Boulevard, Edina MN 55439. 612/835-6900. **Contact:** Personnel Department. **World Wide Web address:** http://www.gvmf.com. **Description:** A producer of microwave foods including breakfast foods and popcorn. **Other U.S. locations:** IA; OH. **Parent company:** ConAgra, Inc.

GRIST MILL COMPANY
P.O. Box 430, Lakeville MN 55044-0430. 612/469-4981. **Contact:** Human Resources. **World Wide Web address:** http://www.grist-mill.com. **Description:** Produces ready-to-eat cereal and fruit and grain bars.

HEARTLAND FOOD INC.
112 South Sixth Street, Marshall MN 56258. 507/532-4458. **Contact:** Human Resources. **Description:** A turkey processing and packaging plant.

HORMEL FOODS CORPORATION
One Hormel Place, Austin MN 55912-3680. 507/437-5881. **Fax:** 507/437-5171. **Contact:** Michael G. MacLean, Manager of Professional Staffing and Recruitment. **World Wide Web address:** http://www.hormel.com. **Description:** A *Fortune* 500 company, Hormel Foods Corporation is a leading processor and marketer of branded, value-added meat and food products. Principal products of the company are processed meat and food entrees which are sold fresh, frozen, cured, smoked, and cooked; and canned foods including sausages, hams, franks, bacon, luncheon meats, shelf-stable microwaveable entrees, stews, chili, hash, meat spreads, and frozen processed products. The majority of the company's products are sold under the Hormel brand name. Other trademarks include Farm Fresh, Little Sizzlers, Quick Meal, Kid's Kitchen, Chi Chi's, House of Tsang, Mary Kitchen, Dinty Moore, Light & Lean, Chicken by George, Black Label, and SPAM. Founded in 1891. **NOTE:** Second and third shifts are offered. **Common positions include:** Account Manager; Account Representative; Accountant; Administrative Assistant; Administrative Manager; Applications Engineer; Assistant Manager; Attorney; Budget Analyst; Buyer; Chemist; Clerical Supervisor; Clinical Lab Technician; Computer Operator; Computer Programmer; Database Manager; Financial Analyst; Food Scientist/Technologist; General Manager; Human Resources Manager; Industrial Engineer; Librarian; Manufacturing Engineer; Market Research Analyst; Mechanical Engineer; MIS Specialist; Operations Manager; Paralegal; Production Manager; Sales Executive; Sales Manager; Secretary; Systems Analyst; Systems Manager; Video Production Coordinator; Webmaster. **Educational backgrounds include:** Accounting; Business Administration; Chemistry; Communications; Computer Science; Engineering; Marketing. **Benefits:** 401(k); Dental Insurance; Employee Discounts; Flexible Schedule; Life Insurance; Medical Insurance; Pension Plan; Profit Sharing. **Special programs:** Internships. **Corporate headquarters location:** This Location. **Other U.S. locations:** Nationwide. **International locations:** Worldwide. **Subsidiaries include:** Dan's Prize, Inc.; Dubuque Foods; Farm Fresh Catfish Company; Jennie-O Foods. **Listed on:** New York Stock Exchange. **Stock exchange symbol:** HRL. **Annual sales/revenues:** More than $100 million. **Number of employees at this location:** 2,400. **Number of employees nationwide:** 10,500. **Number of employees worldwide:** 12,500. **Number of projected hires for 1998 - 1999 at this location:** 150.

INTERNATIONAL MULTIFOODS
200 East Lake Street, Wayzata MN 55391. 612/340-3300. **Contact:** Human Resources. **World Wide Web address:** http://www.multifoods.com. **Description:** An international processor and distributor of food products. Segments of International Multifoods include U.S. Food Services, which prepares food products for a variety of industries; Canadian Foods, which produces consumer, institutional, and industrial flour, mixes, cereals, and condiments; and Venezuelan

Foods, which provides foods and animal feeds. **Common positions include:** Accountant/Auditor; Computer Programmer; Department Manager; General Manager; Human Resources Manager; Operations/Production Manager; Systems Analyst. **Educational backgrounds include:** Accounting; Business Administration; Computer Science; Finance. **Benefits:** Dental Insurance; Disability Coverage; Employee Discounts; Life Insurance; Medical Insurance; Pension Plan; Profit Sharing; Savings Plan; Tuition Assistance. **Corporate headquarters location:** This Location. **Listed on:** New York Stock Exchange.

INTERSTATE BRANDS CORPORATION
CONTINENTAL BAKING COMPANY
8090 Excelsior Boulevard, Hopkins MN 55343. 612/935-3034. **Contact:** Donna Braun, Personnel Manager. **World Wide Web address:** http://www.irin.com/ibc. **Description:** Manufactures and distributes a line of bread and cake products. **Common positions include:** Retail Sales Worker; Route Sales Representative. **Educational backgrounds include:** Business Administration; Computer Science; Marketing. **Benefits:** Dental Insurance; Disability Coverage; Life Insurance; Medical Insurance; Pension Plan. **Corporate headquarters location:** Kansas City MO. **Operations at this facility include:** Distribution; Sales.

JENNIE-O FOODS INC.
P.O. Box 778, Willmar MN 56201. 320/235-2622. **Fax:** 320/231-7785. **Contact:** Dave Juhlke, Director of Human Resources. **Description:** Processes turkey. Founded in 1949. **NOTE:** The company offers entry-level positions and second and third shifts. **Common positions include:** Account Manager; Administrative Assistant; Assistant Manager; Buyer; Computer Operator; Computer Programmer; Controller; Credit Manager; Draftsperson; Human Resources Manager; Industrial Engineer; Manufacturing Engineer; Marketing Manager; Production Manager; Purchasing Agent/Manager; Quality Control Supervisor; Registered Nurse; Sales Manager; Secretary; Systems Analyst; Veterinarian. **Educational backgrounds include:** Accounting; Business Administration; Engineering; Finance; Marketing. **Benefits:** Employee Discounts; Life Insurance; Medical Insurance; Pension Plan. **Special programs:** Internships. **Corporate headquarters location:** This Location. **Subsidiaries include:** West Central Turkeys. **Parent company:** Hormel Foods Corporation (Austin MN). **Number of employees at this location:** 100. **Number of employees nationwide:** 2,500.

LAND O'LAKES, INC.
P.O. Box 64101, St. Paul MN 55164. 651/481-2222. **Contact:** Human Resources. **World Wide Web address:** http://www.landolakes.com. **Description:** A large agricultural cooperative of farmers and ranchers involved in the processing and distribution of dairy-related food products including deli cheeses, butter, milk, sour cream, yogurt, ice cream, dips, sauces, and butter blends. The company provides management, research, advisory, lobbying, and other farm-related services for its more than 300,000 members. Land O'Lakes has offices in the U.S., West Africa, the Philippines, Jamaica, Eastern Europe, and Asia. Founded in 1921. **Common positions include:** Account Manager; Account Representative; Accountant; Administrative Assistant; Assistant Manager; Attorney; Auditor; Biochemist; Budget Analyst; Buyer; Chemical Engineer; Chemist; Chief Financial Officer; Computer Operator; Computer Programmer; Controller; Credit Manager; Customer Service Representative; Database Manager; Dietician/Nutritionist; Editor; Editorial Assistant; Environmental Engineer; Finance Director; Financial Analyst; Food Scientist/Technologist; Human Resources Manager; Internet Services Manager; Librarian; Managing Editor; Manufacturing Engineer; Marketing Manager; Marketing Specialist; MIS Specialist; Operations Manager; Paralegal; Project Manager; Public Relations Specialist; Purchasing Agent/Manager; Quality Control Supervisor; Sales Executive; Sales Manager; Sales Representative; Secretary; Software Engineer; Systems Analyst; Systems Manager; Telecommunications Manager; Transportation/Traffic Specialist; Typist/Word Processor; Vice President. **Educational backgrounds include:** Accounting; Biology; Chemistry; Computer Science; Engineering; Finance; Liberal Arts; Marketing; Software Development; Software Tech. Support. **Benefits:** 401(k); Dental Insurance; Disability Coverage; Employee Discounts; Financial Planning Assistance; Flexible Schedule; Job Sharing; Life Insurance; Medical Insurance; Pension Plan; Savings Plan; Telecommuting; Tuition Assistance. **Special programs:** Internships. **Corporate headquarters location:** This Location. **Other U.S. locations:** Nationwide. **International locations:** Mexico; Poland. **President/CEO:** John E. Gherty. **Annual sales/revenues:** More than $100 million. **Number of employees at this location:** 5,000.

LUIGINO'S INC.
P.O. Box 16630, Duluth MN 55816. 218/723-5555. **Contact:** Human Resources. **World Wide Web address:** http://www.michelinas.com. **Description:** Produces frozen Italian and Chinese entrees under the brand names Michelina's and Yu Sing.

MALT-O-MEAL
701 West Fifth Street, Northfield MN 55057. 507/645-6681. **Contact:** Human Resources. **World Wide Web address:** http://www.malt-o-meal.com. **Description:** A manufacturer of breakfast cereals.

MARIGOLD FOODS
2929 University Avenue SE, Minneapolis MN 55414. 612/331-3775. **Contact:** Betsy Rausch, Human Resources Director. **Description:** A producer of ice cream and related products. **Common positions include:** Accountant/Auditor; Computer Programmer; Human Resources Manager; Operations/Production Manager. **Educational backgrounds include:** Accounting; Business Administration; Computer Science; Liberal Arts; Marketing. **Benefits:** Dental Insurance; Disability Coverage; Life Insurance; Medical Insurance; Pension Plan; Tuition Assistance. **Corporate headquarters location:** This Location. **Parent company:** Wessanen, Inc. **Operations at this facility include:** Administration; Divisional Headquarters; Manufacturing; Sales.

McGARVEY SUPERIOR COFFEE, INC.
5725 Highway 7, St. Louis Park MN 55416. 612/929-0462. **Contact:** Jeff Kozak, Plant Manager. **Description:** A coffee producer.

McGLYNN BAKERIES, INC.
7350 Commerce Lane NE, Minneapolis MN 55432. 612/574-2222. **Toll-free phone:** 800/624-5966. **Fax:** 612/574-2210. **Contact:** Human Resources. **World Wide Web address:** http://www.mcglynn.com. **Description:** A producer of cookies and other baked goods that operates in three divisions: McGlynn's Retail Bakeries, which operates over 200 locations; Concept 2 Bakers, which produces and markets frozen bakery foods; and DecoPac, which markets cake decorating sets and supplies in the United States and Canada. **Corporate headquarters location:** This Location. **Parent company:** Pillsbury Company manufactures and markets food products for consumer, industrial, and international markets.

METZ BAKING COMPANY
2745 Long Lake Road, Roseville MN 55113. 651/636-8400. **Contact:** Ron Kibiger, Personnel. **Description:** Produces bread and a variety of other wholesale bakery products. **Common positions include:** Accountant/Auditor; General Manager; Industrial Engineer; Services Sales Representative. **Educational backgrounds include:** Accounting; Business Administration; Mathematics. **Benefits:** Dental Insurance; Disability Coverage; Life Insurance; Medical Insurance. **Corporate headquarters location:** Sioux City IA. **Operations at this facility include:** Manufacturing; Sales; Service.

MICHAEL FOODS, INC.
5353 Wayzata Boulevard, Suite 324, Minneapolis MN 55416. 612/546-1500. **Contact:** Human Resources Department. **World Wide Web address:** http://www.michaelfoods.com. **Description:** Processes and distributes food products including dairy, egg, and refrigerated grocery and potato products.

MIDWEST COCA-COLA BOTTLING COMPANY, INC.
2750 Eagandale Boulevard, Eagan MN 55121. 612/454-5460. **Fax:** 612/456-1265. **Recorded jobline:** 612/454-5460x4691. **Contact:** Human Resources. **Description:** A bottling and distribution facility for the international beverage company. **Common positions include:** Accountant/Auditor; Advertising Clerk; Blue-Collar Worker Supervisor; Branch Manager; Buyer; Clerical Supervisor; Computer Programmer; Customer Service Representative; Financial Analyst; General Manager; Human Resources Manager; Management Trainee; Manufacturer's/Wholesaler's Sales Rep.; Public Relations Specialist; Services Sales Representative. **Educational backgrounds include:** Accounting; Business Administration; Communications; Finance; Liberal Arts; Marketing. **Benefits:** 401(k); Dental Insurance; Disability Coverage; Employee Discounts; Life Insurance; Medical Insurance; Pension Plan; Savings Plan; Tuition Assistance. **Other U.S. locations:** Nationwide. **Listed on:** New York Stock Exchange. **Number of employees at this location:** 1,000.

MINNESOTA BREWING COMPANY
882 West Seventh Street, St. Paul MN 55102. 651/228-9173. **Contact:** Kim Egginger, Human Resources. **Description:** A local, regional, and national processor of malt beverages.

NASH FINCH COMPANY
7600 France Avenue South, Edina MN 55435. 612/832-0534. **Contact:** Edgar Timberlake, Personnel Administration. **Description:** Engaged in wholesale distribution, retail distribution, and produce marketing. The wholesale distribution segment supplies products to approximately 5,700

affiliated and independent supermarkets, military bases, convenience stores, and other customers in 31 states. The retail distribution segment consists of approximately 120 company-owned retail stores in 16 states. Nash Finch's corporate stores operate under names such as Econofoods, Sun Mart, Family Thrift Center, Food Folks, and Easter's. Nash DeCamp markets fresh fruits and vegetables to wholesalers and retailers worldwide. **Corporate headquarters location:** This Location. **Listed on:** NASDAQ.

NOVARTIS SEEDS, INC.
P.O. Box 959, Minneapolis MN 55440. 612/593-7333. **Contact:** Human Resources. **World Wide Web address:** http://www.nk.com. **Description:** A researcher, producer, and marketer of agricultural seeds and products. **Common positions include:** Accountant/Auditor; Advertising Clerk; Buyer; Credit Manager; Environmental Engineer; Human Resources Manager; Mechanical Engineer; MIS Specialist; Paralegal; Public Relations Specialist; Purchasing Agent/Manager; Quality Control Supervisor. **Annual sales/revenues:** More than $100 million. **Number of employees at this location:** 125. **Number of employees nationwide:** 650.

OLD DUTCH FOODS
2375 Terminal Road, Roseville MN 55113. 651/633-8810. **Contact:** Human Resources. **Description:** Produces a variety of foods including Old Dutch brand potato chips and other snack items.

PACE DAIRY FOODS
P.O. Box 6818, Rochester MN 55903. 507/288-6315. **Physical address:** 2700 Valleyhigh Drive NW, Rochester MN. **Contact:** Human Resources. **Description:** A chicken processing plant.

PEPSI-COLA COMPANY
CENTRAL DIVISION
1300 East Cliff Road, Burnsville MN 55337. 612/890-8940. **Contact:** Human Resources. **World Wide Web address:** http://www.pepsi.com. **Description:** This location houses administrative offices. Overall, the beverage segment of PepsiCo, Inc. primarily markets its brands worldwide and manufactures concentrates for its brands for sale to franchised bottlers worldwide. This segment also operates bottling plants and distribution facilities of its own located in the U.S. and key international markets; and distributes ready-to-drink Lipton tea products under a joint venture agreement. In addition, under separate distribution and joint venture agreements, the segment distributes certain previously existing, as well as jointly developed, Ocean Spray juice products. **Common positions include:** Accountant/Auditor; Biological Scientist; Blue-Collar Worker Supervisor; Branch Manager; Computer Programmer; Credit Manager; Department Manager; Financial Analyst; Human Resources Manager; Industrial Engineer; Industrial Production Manager; Management Trainee; Manufacturer's/Wholesaler's Sales Rep.; Marketing Specialist; Mechanical Engineer; Operations/Production Manager; Quality Control Supervisor; Transportation/Traffic Specialist. **Educational backgrounds include:** Accounting; Business Administration; Communications; Engineering; Finance; Industrial Relations; Liberal Arts; Marketing. **Benefits:** Dental Insurance; Disability Coverage; Employee Discounts; Life Insurance; Medical Insurance; Pension Plan; Savings Plan; Tuition Assistance. **Corporate headquarters location:** Purchase NY. **Parent company:** PepsiCo, Inc. **Operations at this facility include:** Administration; Manufacturing; Regional Headquarters; Sales; Service. **Listed on:** New York Stock Exchange.

PILLSBURY BAKERIES AND FOODSERVICE, INC.
8000 Audubon Road, Chanhassen MN 55317. 612/474-7444. **Fax:** 612/474-9319. **Contact:** Molly Driscoll, Human Resources. **World Wide Web address:** http://www.pillsbury.com. **Description:** A producer of bakery goods for food service distribution. **Common positions include:** Accountant/Auditor; Blue-Collar Worker Supervisor; Electrician; Food Scientist/Technologist; Human Resources Manager; Industrial Engineer; Industrial Production Manager; Mechanical Engineer; Occupational Therapist; Registered Nurse. **Benefits:** 401(k); Dental Insurance; Disability Coverage; Employee Discounts; Life Insurance; Medical Insurance; Pension Plan; Profit Sharing; Savings Plan; Tuition Assistance. **Corporate headquarters location:** Minneapolis MN. **Other U.S. locations:** Los Angeles CA; Cedar Rapids IA; Eden Prairie MN; Joplin MO; Martel OH. **Parent company:** Grand Metropolitan. **Operations at this facility include:** Administration; Manufacturing; Research and Development. **Number of employees at this location:** 500. **Number of employees nationwide:** 2,500.

THE PILLSBURY COMPANY
200 South Sixth Street, Mail Stop 37A4, Minneapolis MN 55402. 612/330-4966. **Contact:** Lynn Plaschko, Human Resources. **World Wide Web address:** http://www.pillsbury.com. **Description:** Manufactures and markets food products for consumers and industrial customers worldwide.

Common positions include: Accountant/Auditor; Computer Programmer; Financial Analyst; Human Resources Manager; Marketing Specialist; Science Technologist. **Educational backgrounds include:** Accounting; Engineering; Finance; Marketing. **Benefits:** 401(k); Dental Insurance; Disability Coverage; Medical Insurance; Pension Plan; Profit Sharing; Savings Plan; Tuition Assistance. **Special programs:** Internships. **Corporate headquarters location:** This Location. **Parent company:** Grand Metropolitan.

PURINA MILLS, INC.

3901 Hiawatha Avenue South, Minneapolis MN 55406. 612/721-0738. **Fax:** 612/721-0717. **Contact:** General Manager. **World Wide Web address:** http://www.purina.com. **Description:** A feed manufacturing plant specializing in the production of animal and poultry feeds. **NOTE:** Entry-level positions are offered. **Common positions include:** Administrative Assistant; Controller; Customer Service Representative; General Manager; Management Trainee; Manufacturing Engineer; Production Manager; Purchasing Agent/Manager; Quality Control Supervisor; Sales Manager; Secretary; Typist/Word Processor; Veterinarian. **Educational backgrounds include:** Accounting; Business Administration; Computer Science; Economics; Engineering; Finance; Marketing; Nutrition. **Benefits:** 401(k); Dental Insurance; Life Insurance; Medical Insurance; Pension Plan; Tuition Assistance. **Corporate headquarters location:** St. Louis MO. **Other U.S. locations:** Nationwide. **Operations at this facility include:** Administration; Manufacturing; Sales. **Listed on:** Privately held. **Annual sales/revenues:** More than $100 million. **Number of employees at this location:** 100. **Number of employees nationwide:** 2,500.

RALSTON PURINA COMPANY

1380 Corporate Center Curve, Suite 210, Eagan MN 55121. 612/688-2760. **Contact:** Operations Coordinator. **World Wide Web address:** http://www.purina.com. **Description:** This location is a sales office. Overall, Ralston Purina produces a variety of food for people and animals. **Common positions include:** Administrator; Branch Manager; Customer Service Representative; Manufacturer's/Wholesaler's Sales Rep. **Educational backgrounds include:** Marketing. **Benefits:** Dental Insurance; Disability Coverage; Life Insurance; Medical Insurance; Pension Plan; Savings Plan; Tuition Assistance. **Corporate headquarters location:** St. Louis MO. **Operations at this facility include:** Regional Headquarters.

SENECA FOODS CORPORATION

101 West Eighth Street, Glencoe MN 55336. 320/864-3151. **Fax:** 320/864-5779. **Contact:** Human Resources Manager. **World Wide Web address:** http://www.senecafoods.com. **Description:** This location is a vegetable canning plant. Overall, Seneca Foods Corporation's products include canned and frozen vegetables and bottled, canned, and frozen fruit juice drinks. Brand names include Seneca, Libby's, and Tree Sweet. **Common positions include:** Mechanical Engineer; Operations/Production Manager. **Educational backgrounds include:** Engineering; Operations. **Benefits:** Dental Insurance; Disability Coverage; Employee Discounts; Life Insurance; Medical Insurance; Pension Plan; Profit Sharing; Savings Plan; Tuition Assistance. **Corporate headquarters location:** Pittsford NY. **Operations at this facility include:** Manufacturing.

SENECA FOODS CORPORATION

P.O. Box 35, Blue Earth MN 56013. 507/526-2131. **Contact:** Human Resources. **World Wide Web address:** http://www.senecafoods.com. **Description:** This location is a vegetable canning plant. Overall, Seneca Foods Corporation's products include canned and frozen vegetables and bottled, canned, and frozen fruit juice drinks. Brand names include Seneca, Libby's, and Tree Sweet. **Corporate headquarters location:** Pittsford NY.

TOM THUMB FOOD MARKETS, INC.
POLKA DOT DAIRY, INC.

110 East 17th Street, Hastings MN 55033. 651/437-9023. **Fax:** 651/438-2638. **Contact:** Todd Huffman, Director of Human Resources. **Description:** Tom Thumb Food Markets operates an area grocery and convenience store chain. Polka Dot Dairy (also at this location) is a distributor of bottled milk. **Common positions include:** Management Trainee. **Educational backgrounds include:** Accounting; Business Administration; Economics; Finance; Marketing. **Benefits:** Dental Insurance; Disability Coverage; Life Insurance; Medical Insurance; Profit Sharing. **Corporate headquarters location:** This Location. **Operations at this facility include:** Administration; Regional Headquarters; Sales; Service.

TYSON SEAFOOD GROUP

P.O. Box 16147, Duluth MN 55816-0147. 218/628-0365. **Contact:** Human Resources. **Description:** Processes fresh fish. **Parent company:** Tyson Foods is engaged in chicken slaughtering, dressing, cutting, packaging, and de-boning, and is one of the world's largest fully integrated producers, processors, and marketers of poultry-based food products. The company also produces other center-of-the-plate and convenience food items. Products include Tyson Holly Farms Fresh Chicken, Weaver, Louis Kemp Crab, Lobster Delights, Healthy Portion products, Beef Stir Fry, Crab Delights Stir Fry, Chicken Fried Rice Kits, Pork Chops with Cinnamon Apples, Salmon Grill Kits, Fish'n Chips Kits, and Rotisserie Chicken.

Note: Because addresses and telephone numbers of smaller companies can change rapidly, we recommend you call each company to verify the information below before inquiring about job opportunities. Mass mailings are not recommended.

Additional small employers:

ALCOHOL WHOLESALE

Mark VII Distributors Inc.
475 Prior Ave N, St. Paul MN
55104-3420. 651/646-6063.

Quality Wine & Spirits Co.
PO Box 1145, Minneapolis MN
55440. 612/854-8600.

BAKERY PRODUCTS

Baldinger Bakery
PO Box 70125, St. Paul MN
55107. 651/224-5761.

International Multifoods Bakery Division
111 Cheshire Ln, Ste 100,
Hopkins MN 55305-1066.
612/404-7500.

Lakeland Bakeries
PO Box 848, St. Cloud MN
56302-0848. 320/251-9361.

Metz Baking Company
PO Box 501, Fergus Falls MN
56538-0501. 218/736-7571.

Pies Inc.
300 Lake Hazeltine Drive,
Chaska MN 55318-1034.
612/448-2150.

Pillsbury Company
7752 Mitchell Road, Eden
Prairie MN 55344-2014.
612/937-9406.

Vicom
5275 Quincy St, Minneapolis MN
55416. 612/784-3715.

BEVERAGES

American Bottling
553 Fairview Avenue North, St.
Paul MN 55104-1708. 651/645-
0501.

Bernick's Pepsi
PO Box 7008, St. Cloud MN
56302-7008. 320/252-6441.

Bernick's Pepsi
4301 West Michigan Street,
Duluth MN 55807-2770.
218/628-0276.

Pepsi-Cola Bottling Co. of Rochester
PO Box 7130, Rochester MN
55903-7130. 507/288-3772.

Rahr Malting Co.
800 1st Ave W, Shakopee MN
55379-1148. 612/445-1431.

Stroh Brewery Company
PO Box 64115, St. Paul MN
55164-0115. 651/778-3100.

US Distilled Products
1607 12th St S, Princeton MN
55371-2300. 612/389-4903.

Wis-Pak of Mankato
PO Box 3669, Mankato MN
56002-3669. 507/387-6300.

CEREAL BREAKFAST FOODS

Custom Food Processors Inc.
PO Box 158, Blue Earth MN
56013-0158. 507/526-7575.

CHIPS AND SNACKS

Barrel O' Fun Snack Foods Co.
PO Box 230, Perham MN 56573-
0230. 218/346-7000.

Pioneer Snacks Inc.
1802 1st Ave, Mankato MN
56001-3022. 507/388-1661.

CROP FARMS

Big Stone Colony
Rural Route 1, Box 103,
Graceville MN 56240-9734.
320/748-7961.

Metro Farms Inc.
801 Kingsley St, Winsted MN
55395. 320/485-4401.

CROP SERVICES

ConAgra Flour Milling Co.
2005 Vermillion St, Hastings MN
55033-3652. 651/437-3161.

DAIRY PRODUCTS

AMPI
PO Box 98, New Ulm MN
56073-0098. 507/354-2191.

AMPI Rochester
700 1st Ave SE, Rochester MN
55904-6434. 507/282-7401.

Bongards Creameries
13200 County Road 51, Norwood
MN 55368-9525. 612/466-5521.

Dairy Farmers of America
311 1st St N, Winsted MN 55395.
320/485-2131.

Dairy Farmers of America
301 S Buse St, Fergus Falls MN
56537-3272. 218/736-5481.

Foodmaster International LLC
7300 Metro Blvd, Ste 550,
Minneapolis MN 55439-2308.
612/820-0022.

Kohler Mix Specialties Inc.
4041 Highway 61 N, White Bear
Lake MN 55110-4631. 651/426-
1633.

Kraft Foods Inc.
1000 E Kraft Dr, Melrose MN
56352-1456. 320/256-7461.

Kraft Foods Inc.
PO Box 309, New Ulm MN
56073-0309. 507/354-4131.

Land O'Lakes
PO Box 248, Perham MN 56573-
0248. 218/346-4680.

Land O'Lakes
PO Box 738, Pine Island MN
55963-0738. 507/356-8318.

Marigold Dairies Co.
PO Box 309, Rochester MN
55903-0309. 507/282-8691.

Old Home Foods Inc.
370 University Avenue W, St.
Paul MN 55103-2017. 651/228-
9035.

Yoplait USA
PO Box 59145, Minneapolis MN
55459-0145. 612/540-4281.

DOG AND CAT FOOD

Tuffy's
PO Box 190, Perham MN 56573.
218/346-7500.

FLORICULTURE AND NURSERY PRODUCTS

General Andrew's Nursery
PO Box 95, Willow River MN
55795-0095. 218/372-3182.

FOOD PREPARATIONS

Creamette Co.
428 N 1st St, Minneapolis MN
55401-1119. 612/333-4281.

Deli Express
16101 W 78th St, Eden Prairie
MN 55344-5709. 612/937-9440.

La Canasta of Minnesota Inc.
1565 1st Ave NW, St. Paul MN
55112-1948. 651/697-5500.

Tino's Better Baked Pizza
PO Box 57, Young America MN
55397-0057. 612/467-2668.

Watkins Incorporated
PO Box 5570, Winona MN
55987-0570. 507/457-3300.

FOOD WHOLESALE

AMPI
PO Box 1013, Dawson MN
56232-1013. 320/769-2994.

Appert Foods
900 Highway 10 SE, St. Cloud
MN 56304-1807. 320/251-3200.

Beckman Produce Inc.
415 Grove St, St. Paul MN
55101-2418. 651/222-1212.

Bix Fruit Company Inc.
1415 Lorient St, St. Paul MN
55117. 651/487-8000.

CH Robinson
8100 Michell Rd #200, Eden
Prairie MN 55344. 612/937-8500.

International Multifoods
Rosewood Industrial Park, Rice
MN 56367. 320/393-2060.

J&B Wholesale Distributing
PO Box 212, St. Michael MN
55376-0212. 612/497-3913.

JP Food Service
9605 54th Ave N, Minneapolis
MN 55442-1946. 612/559-9494.

Perlman Rocque Company
51 52nd Way NE, Minneapolis
MN 55421-1004. 612/571-6311.

Reinhart Institutional Foods
PO Box 1088, Marshall MN
56258-0888. 507/537-1451.

Rykoff-Sexton Services
PO Box 16184, Minneapolis MN
55416-0184. 612/542-8522.

Source One Inc.
7825 Telegraph Road,
Minneapolis MN 55438-1133.
612/829-0833.

Sysco Minnesota
PO Box 86, Minneapolis MN
55486-0086. 612/785-9000.

Tree of Life Inc.
2077B Ellis Ave, St. Paul MN
55114-1308. 651/646-2981.

Upper Lakes Foods Inc.
801 Industry Ave, Cloquet MN
55720-1635. 218/879-1265.

Westlunds
PO Box 417, South St. Paul MN
55075-0417. 651/450-6000.

Wholesale Produce Supply Co.
752 Kasota Circle SE,
Minneapolis MN 55414-2815.
612/378-2025.

GENERAL FARMS

Spring Prairie Colony
Rural Route 2, Box 201, Hawley
MN 56549-9408. 218/498-0222.

Waymouth Farms Inc.
5300 Boone Ave N, Minneapolis
MN 55428-4054. 612/533-5300.

GRAIN MILL PRODUCTS

ADM Milling Co.
335 Main St SE, Minneapolis MN
55414-2136. 612/627-8000.

Bay State Milling Company
PO Box 188, Winona MN 55987-
0188. 507/452-1770.

Best Brands LLC
1765 Yankee Doodle Rd, St. Paul
MN 55121-1617. 612/454-5850.

ConAgra Grain Companies
PO Box 2910, Minneapolis MN
55402-0910. 612/370-7500.

Minnesota Corn Processors
400 W Erie, Marshall MN 56258.
507/537-2676.

HOGS

MPI Farms
PO Box 279, Amboy MN 56010-
0279. 507/674-3920.

MEAT AND POULTRY PROCESSING

Armour Swift-Eckrich
PO Box 328, Wells MN 56097-
0328. 507/553-6351.

Butterfield Foods Company
PO Box 229, Butterfield MN
56120-0229. 507/956-5103.

Dan's Prize Inc.
810 1st St S, Long Prairie MN
56347-1540. 320/732-6163.

Ellison Meat Company
PO Box 400, Pipestone MN
56164-0400. 507/825-5486.

Huisken Meat Center Inc.
PO Box 38, Chandler MN 56122-
0038. 507/677-2291.

Jennie-O Foods Inc.
123 5th Ave E, Melrose MN
56352. 320/256-4245.

Lloyd's Barbeque Company
1455 Mendota Heights Rd,
Mendota Heights MN 55120-
1002. 612/688-6000.

Long Prairie Packing Company
PO Box 148, Long Prairie MN
56347-0148. 320/732-2171.

Long Prairie Packing Company
425 Concord St S, South St. Paul
MN 55075-2442. 651/455-6611.

Minnesota Beef Industries Inc.
PO Box 308, Buffalo Lake MN
55314-0308. 320/833-5301.

Northern Pride Inc.
PO Box 598, Thief River Falls
MN 56701-0598. 218/681-1201.

Quality Pork Processors
PO Box 369, Austin MN 55912-
0369. 507/433-0300.

Rochester Meats Inc.
1825 7th St NW, Rochester MN
55901-0270. 507/289-0701.

Sunny Fresh Foods Inc.
206 4th St W, Monticello MN
55362-8524. 612/295-5666.

Swift & Company
PO Box 369, Worthington MN
56187-0369. 507/372-2121.

The Turkey Store Company
1116 4th Ave NW, Faribault MN
55021-3724. 507/334-5555.

Tyson Foods Inc.
PO Box 188, Motley MN 56466-
0188. 218/352-6600.

Tyson Foods Inc.
702 E 13th St, Albert Lea MN
56007-3250. 507/377-2526.

West Central Turkeys Inc.
704 N Broadway, Pelican Rapids
MN 56572-4147. 218/863-3131.

POULTRY AND EGGS

Earl B. Olson Farm North Group
409 E Highway 55, Paynesville
MN 56362-2047. 320/243-3764.

Willmar Poultry Company
PO Box 753, Willmar MN 56201-
0753. 320/235-8850.

**PREPARED FEEDS AND
INGREDIENTS FOR
ANIMALS**

Form-A-Feed Inc.
PO Box 9, Stewart MN 55385-
0009. 320/562-2413.

**PRESERVED FRUITS AND
VEGETABLES**

**Arden International Kitchens
LLC**
21150 Hamburg Ave, Lakeville
MN 55044-9032. 612/469-2000.

Bird's Eye
PO Box 4690, Waseca MN
56093-0518. 507/835-1320.

Fairmont Foods of Minnesota
905 E 4th St, Fairmont MN
56031-4014. 507/238-9001.

Faribault Foods Inc.
PO Box 598, Faribault MN
55021-0598. 507/334-5521.

Lakeside Foods
1055 West Broadway,
Plainview MN 55964-1059.
507/534-3141.

**Little Charlie's Convenience
Foods**
115 W College Dr, Marshall MN
56258-1747. 507/532-3241.

Northern Star Co.
3171 5th St SE, Minneapolis MN
55414-3305. 612/339-8981.

RDO Frozen Co.
PO Box 552, Park Rapids MN
56470-0552. 218/732-7252.

Schwans Europe Limited
115 W College Dr, Marshall MN
56258-1747. 507/532-3274.

Tony Down's Foods Co.
PO Box 127, Madelia MN 56062-
0127. 507/642-3203.

SEAFOOD

Morey Fish Co.
PO Box 248, Motley MN 56466-
0248. 218/352-6345.

**SUGAR AND
CONFECTIONERY
PRODUCTS**

American Crystal Sugar Co.
PO Box 600, Crookston MN
56716-0600. 218/281-1993.

**American Crystal Sugar
Company**
PO Box 357, East Grand Forks
MN 56721-0357. 218/773-1131.

Brach & Brock Confections
1000 West Fifth Street, Winona
MN 55987-5123. 507/452-3433.

**Kenny's Candy Company
Incorporated**
PO Box 269, Perham MN 56573-
0269. 218/346-2340.

Pearson Candy Company
PO Box 64459, St. Paul MN
55164-0459. 651/698-0356.

**Southern Minnesota Beet Sugar
Cooperative**
PO Box 500, Renville MN
56284-0500. 320/329-8305.

**TOBACCO AND TOBACCO
PRODUCTS WHOLESALE**

Fritz Company Inc.
1912 Hastings Ave, Newport MN
55055-1542. 651/459-9751.

Reynolds Wholesale
1035 Nathan Lane North,
Plymouth MN 55441-5024.
612/545-3706.

**For more information on career opportunities in the food, beverage, and agriculture
industries:**

Associations

**AMERICAN ASSOCIATION OF CEREAL
CHEMISTS (AACC)**
3340 Pilot Knob Road, St. Paul MN 55121. 612/454-
7250. World Wide Web address: http://www.scisoc.
org/aacc. Dedicated to the dissemination of technical
information and continuing education in cereal
science.

**AMERICAN CROP PROTECTION
ASSOCIATION**
1156 15th Street NW, Suite 400, Washington DC
20005. 202/296-1585. World Wide Web address:
http://www.acpa.org.

AMERICAN FROZEN FOOD INSTITUTE
2000 Corporate Ridge, Suite 1000, McLean VA
22102. 703/821-0770. Fax: 703/821-1350. World
Wide Web address: http://www.affi.com. A national
trade association representing the interests of the
frozen food industry.

**AMERICAN SOCIETY OF AGRICULTURAL
ENGINEERS**
2950 Niles Road, St. Joseph MI 49085-9659.
616/429-0300. World Wide Web address: http://www.
asae.org.

**AMERICAN SOCIETY OF BREWING
CHEMISTS**
3340 Pilot Knob Road, St. Paul MN 55121. 612/454-
7250. World Wide Web address: http://www.scisoc.
org/asbc. Founded in 1934 to improve and bring

uniformity to the brewing industry on a technical
level.

CIES - THE FOOD BUSINESS FORUM
5549 Lee Highway, Arlington VA 22207. 703/534-
8880. World Wide Web address: http://www.ciesnet.
com. A global food business network. Membership is
on a company basis. Members learn how to manage
their businesses more effectively and gain access to
information and contacts.

DAIRY MANAGEMENT, INC.
10255 West Higgins Road, Suite 900, Rosemont IL
60018. 847/803-2000. World Wide Web address:
http://www.dairyinfo.com. A federation of state and
regional dairy promotion organizations that develop
and execute effective programs to increase consumer
demand for U.S.-produced milk and dairy products.

**INTERNATIONAL ASSOCIATION OF FOOD
INDUSTRY SUPPLIERS**
1451 Dolley Madison Boulevard, McLean VA 22101.
703/761-2600. Fax: 703/761-4334. Contact: Dorothy
Brady. E-mail address: info@iafis.org. World Wide
Web address: http://www.iafis.org. A trade
association whose members are suppliers to the food,
dairy, liquid processing, and related industries.

**MASTER BREWERS ASSOCIATION OF THE
AMERICAS (MBAA)**
2421 North Mayfair Road, Suite 310, Wauwatosa WI
53226. 414/774-8558. World Wide Web address:
http://www.mbaa.com. Promotes, advances, improves,
and protects the professional interests of brew and

malt house production and technical personnel. Disseminates technical and practical information.

NATIONAL BEER WHOLESALERS' ASSOCIATION
1100 South Washington Street, Alexandria VA 22314-4494. 703/683-4300. Fax: 703/683-8965. Contact: Karen Craig.

NATIONAL FOOD PROCESSORS ASSOCIATION
1350 I Street NW, Suite 300, Washington DC 20005. 202/639-5900. World Wide Web address: http://www. nfpa-food.org.

NATIONAL SOFT DRINK ASSOCIATION
1101 16th Street NW, Washington DC 20036. 202/463-6732. World Wide Web address: http://www. nsda.org.

USA POULTRY AND EGG EXPORT COUNCIL
2300 West Park Place Boulevard, Suite 100, Stone Mountain GA 30087. 770/413-0006. Fax: 770/413-0007. E-mail address: info@usapeec.org. World Wide Web address: http://www.usapeec.org.

Directories

THOMAS FOOD INDUSTRY REGISTER
Thomas Publishing Company, Five Penn Plaza, New York NY 10001. 212/290-7341. World Wide Web address: http://www.thomaspublishing.com.

Magazines

FROZEN FOOD AGE
Progressive Grocer Associates, 23 Old Kings Highway South, Darien CT 06820. 203/655-1600.

Visit our exciting job and career site at http://www.careercity.com

GOVERNMENT

The government remains the nation's largest employer. Be advised, however, that the number of federal jobs continues to decline. The Defense Department is expected to reduce the size of its workforce through attrition over the next decade. The outlook for state and local government workers is somewhat better. While opportunities vary by state and department, the Bureau of Labor Statistics forecasts a 10 percent increase in state and local positions through 2006, in response to growing populations and community development.

The U.S. Postal Service expected an operating surplus of approximately $500 to $600 million for 1998, though it still has a debt of approximately $4 billion. Forecasters predict that 1999 will be a record year for volume, as the U.S. Postal Service expects to handle nearly 200 billion pieces of mail. In order to remain competitive, the U.S. Postal Service has been looking for ways to increase first-class mail business, which has been sharply reduced by the convenience and efficiency of electronic mail, faxes, and teleconferencing. The U.S. Postal Service Fiscal Year 1999 Plan calls for improved delivery times, an increase in net earnings, and improved worker proficiency.

There will be a growing need for correctional officers and prison guards as many leave due to low salaries and unattractive rural locations. Positions in fire and police departments will be hardest to obtain as the number of candidates exceed new openings.

The Armed Forces are reducing personnel as a result of relative international peace. However, there are still opportunities for persons wishing to enter the military in the late 1990s. These candidates will finish their first enlistments in 2000 when personnel reductions will be complete. It is estimated that there will then be a need for 190,000 enlisted personnel and 15,000 officers to replace retirees and those who have completed their enlistments.

BURNSVILLE, CITY OF
100 Civic Center Parkway, Burnsville MN 55337. 612/895-4400. **Contact:** Jill Hansen, Human Resources. **World Wide Web address:** http://www.burnsville.org. **Description:** Administrative offices of the city of Burnsville. **Common positions include:** Accountant/Auditor; Civil Engineer; Construction and Building Inspector; Emergency Medical Technician; Human Resources Manager. **Educational backgrounds include:** Accounting; Business Administration; Engineering. **Benefits:** Daycare Assistance; Dental Insurance; Disability Coverage; Life Insurance; Medical Insurance; Pension Plan; Tuition Assistance. **Special programs:** Internships. **Operations at this facility include:** Administration; Service. **Number of employees at this location:** 250.

CARVER COUNTY GOVERNMENT CENTER
Administration Building, 600 East Fourth Street, Chaska MN 55318-2173. 612/361-1525. **Fax:** 612/361-1536. **Recorded jobline:** 612/361-1522. **Contact:** Lori Pawelk, Staffing Coordinator. **Description:** The administrative offices of Carver County. **Common positions include:** Accountant; Attorney; Civil Engineer; Clerical Supervisor; Computer Programmer; Controller; Environmental Engineer; Human Resources Manager; MIS Specialist; Paralegal; Psychologist; Registered Nurse; Secretary; Social Worker; Typist/Word Processor. **Educational backgrounds include:** Accounting; Biology; Business Administration; Communications; Computer Science; Economics; Engineering; Finance; Geology; Health Care; Software Tech. Support. **Benefits:** Employee Discounts; Life Insurance; Medical Insurance. **Special programs:** Internships. **Office hours:** Monday - Friday, 8:00 a.m. - 4:30 p.m. **Corporate headquarters location:** This Location. **Operations at this facility include:** Administration.

DEPARTMENT OF HOUSING & URBAN DEVELOPMENT
220 South Second Street, Minneapolis MN 55401. 612/370-3000. **Contact:** Human Resources. **Description:** Acquires foreclosed housing in order to sell it back to the general public. Department of Housing & Urban Development provides mortgage/loan management services, subsidized housing, and assistance to homeless people.

DEPARTMENT OF LABOR & INDUSTRY
443 Lafayette Road North, St. Paul MN 55155. 651/296-6107. **Contact:** Human Resources. **Description:** Sets labor standards and wages, provides workers' compensation, and houses offices for OSHA (Occupational Safety and Health Administration).

U.S. POSTAL SERVICE
Personnel Services, P.O. Box 645004, St. Paul MN 55164-5004. 651/293-3032. **Contact:** Dan Thewis, Senior Personnel Administrator. **Description:** One location of the United States postal service for the city of St. Paul.

Note: Because addresses and telephone numbers of smaller companies can change rapidly, we recommend you call each company to verify the information below before inquiring about job opportunities. Mass mailings are not recommended.

Additional small employers:

ADMINISTRATION OF ECONOMIC PROGRAMS

Department of Administration
50 Sherburne Ave, Rm 200, St. Paul MN 55155-1402. 651/296-1424.

Department of Commerce
133 7th St E, St. Paul MN 55101-2333. 651/296-0670.

Department of Economic Assistance
300 South 6th St A-9, Minneapolis MN 55487-0999. 612/348-3600.

Economic Development Authority
5005 Minnetonka Blvd, Minneapolis MN 55416-2216. 612/920-3000.

Technology Management Bureau
320 Centennial Bldg, Rm 320, St. Paul MN 55155-0001. 651/296-5320.

Trade & Economic Development Department
500 Metro Sq, 121 7th Place E, St. Paul MN 55101. 651/297-1291.

US Small Business Administration
627C Center Ave, Moorhead MN 56560-1923. 218/233-0778.

ADMINISTRATION OF PUBLIC HEALTH PROGRAMS

Department of Health
PO Box 9441, Minneapolis MN 55440-9441. 612/623-5000.

Environmental Health Division
PO Box 59040, Minneapolis MN 55459-0040. 612/627-5100.

FDA District Office
240 Hennepin Ave, Minneapolis MN 55401-1912. 612/334-4100.

Itasca County Health Department
1209 SE 2nd Ave, Grand Rapids MN 55744-3982. 218/327-2847.

Public Health Service
419 Bush St, Red Wing MN 55066-2529. 651/388-0433.

ADMINISTRATION OF SOCIAL AND MANPOWER PROGRAMS

Blue Earth County Human Services
PO Box 8608, Mankato MN 56002-8608. 507/387-8730.

Department of Human Services
444 Lafayette Road North, St. Paul MN 55155-3802. 651/296-6117.

Morrison County Human Services
213 1st Ave SE, Little Falls MN 56345-3100. 320/632-2941.

Ramsey County Human Services
160 Kellogg Blvd East, St. Paul MN 55101-1425. 651/298-5351.

Social Services Department
PO Box 686, Brainerd MN 56401-0686. 218/828-3966.

Social Services Department
PO Box 1148, Virginia MN 55792-1148. 218/749-7118.

State Services for the Blind
390 Robert St N, St. Paul MN 55101-1812. 651/296-3711.

ADMINISTRATION OF VETERANS' AFFAIRS

VA Regional Office
1 Federal Dr, St. Paul MN 55111-4080. 612/726-1454.

COURTS

County Court House
121 W Junius Ave, Fergus Falls MN 56537-2544. 218/739-2271.

Court Administrator Office
208 E Colvin Ave, Warren MN 56762-1693. 218/745-4921.

Court Administrator Office
18 Vine St N, Mora MN 55051-1351. 320/679-1022.

Courthouse
PO Box 8608, Mankato MN 56002-8608. 507/389-8100.

Courthouse
PO Box 757, Worthington MN 56187-0757. 507/372-8263.

Dakota County Courthouse
1590 Highway 55, Hastings MN 55033-2343. 651/438-4418.

Goodhue County Courthouse
509 W 5th St, Red Wing MN 55066-2540. 651/385-3000.

Hennepin County District Court
300 S 6th St, Minneapolis MN 55487-0999. 612/348-3155.

Immigration & Naturalization
1 Federal Dr, Rm 480, St. Paul MN 55111-4080. 612/725-3850.

Judiciary Courts
25 Constitution Ave, St. Paul MN
55155-1500. 651/296-2581.

St. Louis County District Court
100 N 5th Ave W, Duluth MN
55802-1202. 218/726-2436.

**EXECUTIVE, LEGISLATIVE,
AND GENERAL
GOVERNMENT**

Aitkin County Auditor
209 2nd St NW, Aitkin MN
56431-1257. 218/927-7345.

Apple Valley, City of
14200 Cedar Ave, Apple Valley
MN 55124-8546. 612/431-8800.

Auditor's Office
715 4th St, International MN
56649-2438. 218/283-6201.

Bloomington, City of
2215 W Old Shakopee Rd,
Bloomington MN 55431-3033.
612/948-8700.

Brooklyn Center, City of
6301 Shingle Creek Pkwy,
Brooklyn Center MN 55430-
2113. 612/569-3300.

Brooklyn Park, City of
5200 85th Ave N, Minneapolis
MN 55443-4301. 612/424-8000.

Brown, County of
Brown County Courthouse, New
Ulm MN 56073. 507/359-7900.

Cass, County of
PO Box 3000, Walker MN
56484-3000. 218/547-3300.

Chippewa, County of
629 N 11th St, Montevideo MN
56265-1652. 320/269-7447.

Chisago, County of
313 N Main St, Center City MN
55012-9663. 651/257-1300.

Clerk's Office
PO Box 378, Winona MN 55987-
0378. 507/452-8550.

Coon Rapids, City of
11155 Robinson Dr NW, Coon
Rapids MN 55433-3761.
612/755-2880.

Crow Wing, County of
326 Laurel St, Brainerd MN
56401-3585. 218/828-3970.

Crystal, City of
4141 Douglas Dr N, Crystal MN
55422-1609. 612/537-4571.

Dassel, City of
PO Box 391, Dassel MN 55325-
0391. 320/275-2454.

Duluth, City of
411 W 1st St, Duluth MN 55802-
1102. 218/723-3295.

Eagan, City of
3830 Pilot Knob Rd, Eagan MN
55122-1810. 612/681-4600.

Edina, City of
4801 W 50th St, Edina MN
55424-1330. 612/927-8861.

Eveleth, City of
PO Box 401, Eveleth MN 55734-
0401. 218/744-2501.

Fairmont, City of
PO Box 751, Fairmont MN
56031-0751. 507/238-9461.

Fridley, City of
6431 University Ave NE, Fridley
MN 55432-4303. 612/571-3450.

Hennepin, County of
300 S 6th St, Minneapolis MN
55487-0999. 612/348-7574.

Hopkins, City of
1010 1st St S, Hopkins MN
55343-9475. 612/935-8474.

Maple Grove, City of
PO Box 1180, Osseo MN 55311-
6180. 612/494-6000.

Maplewood, City of
1830 County Road B E,
Maplewood MN 55109-2702.
651/770-4501.

McLeod, County of
830 11th St E, Glencoe MN
55336-2200. 320/864-5551.

Mille Lacs, County of
635 2nd St SE, Milaca MN
56353-1305. 320/983-8399.

Minneapolis, City of
350 S 5th St, Minneapolis MN
55415-1316. 612/673-3000.

Minnesota Senate
75 Constitution Ave, St. Paul MN
55155-1601. 651/296-2887.

Minnesota State Auditor
525 Park St, Ste 400, St. Paul MN
55103-2185. 651/296-2551.

Minnetonka, City of
14600 Minnetonka Blvd,
Minnetonka MN 55345-1502.
612/939-8200.

Moorhead, City of
PO Box 779, Moorhead MN
56561-0779. 218/299-5301.

New Hope, City of
4401 Xylon Ave N, Minneapolis
MN 55428-4843. 612/531-5100.

Owatonna, City of
540 W Hills Cir, Owatonna MN
55060-4701. 507/444-4300.

Plymouth, City of
3400 Plymouth Blvd, Plymouth
MN 55447-1448. 612/509-5000.

Ramsey, County of
270 Chester St, St. Paul MN
55107-1207. 651/266-8044.

Red Wing, City of
PO Box 34, Red Wing MN
55066-0034. 651/388-6734.

Renville, County of
500 E Depue Ave, Olivia MN
56277-1473. 320/523-1172.

Rice, County of
320 3rd St NW, Faribault MN
55021-5195. 507/332-6100.

Roseville, City of
2660 Civic Center Dr, Roseville
MN 55113-1815. 651/490-2200.

Scott, County of
428 Holmes St S, Shakopee MN
55379-1300. 612/445-7750.

Shoreview, City of
4600 Victoria St N, Shoreview
MN 55126-5817. 651/484-3353.

South St. Paul, City of
125 3rd Ave N, South St. Paul
MN 55075-2097. 651/450-8737.

St. Paul, City of
555 Cedar St, St. Paul MN
55101-2209. 651/292-7711.

St. Paul, City of
350 Saint Peter St, St. Paul MN
55102-1514. 651/266-9090.

St. Paul, City of
15 Kellgg Blvd W, Ste 240, St.
Paul MN 55102-1614. 651/266-
8500.

Stevens, County of
Court House Bldg, Morris MN
56267. 320/589-1033.

Waseca, County of
307 N State St, Waseca MN
56093-2932. 507/835-0610.

Washington, County of
PO Box 6, Stillwater MN 55082-
0006. 651/439-3220.

Willmar, City of
PO Box 755, Willmar MN 56201-
0755. 320/235-4984.

Woodbury, City of
8301 Valley Creek Rd,
Woodbury MN 55125-2320.
651/739-5972.

Wright, County of
10 2nd St NW, Rm 230, Buffalo
MN 55313-1100. 612/682-3900.

**FINANCE, TAXATION, AND
MONETARY POLICY
BODIES**

Department of Finance
658 Cedar St, Fl 4, St. Paul MN
55155-1603. 651/296-5900.

Department of Revenue
10 River Park Plz, St. Paul MN
55146-0001. 651/296-3781.

Hennepin County Treasurer
300 S 6th St #A-600, Minneapolis
MN 55487-0999. 612/348-4084.

**State Lottery Control
Commission**
2645 Long Lake Rd, Roseville
MN 55113-1117. 651/635-8100.

Treasurer's Office
900 3rd Ave, Windom MN
56101-1627. 507/831-1342.

**HOUSING AND URBAN
DEVELOPMENT
PROGRAMS**

**Housing Redevelopment
Authority**
217 S 3rd St, Minneapolis MN
55401-2112. 612/342-1408.

**St. Cloud Housing &
Redevelopment Authority**
400 2nd St S, St. Cloud MN
56301-3622. 320/259-0849.

**LAND, MINERAL, AND
WILDLIFE CONSERVATION
PROGRAMS**

**Department of Fisheries &
Wildlife**
1980 Fowell Ave, St. Paul MN
55108. 612/624-3600.

**Department of Natural
Resources**
500 Lafayette Rd N, St. Paul MN
55155-4002. 651/296-6157.

**Department of Natural
Resources**
1201 E Highway 2, Grand Rapids
MN 55744-3244. 218/327-4434.

Fish & Wildlife Regional Office
BHW Federal Bldg, 1 Fed Dr, St.
Paul MN 55111. 612/725-3519.

Itasca State Park
HC 5, Box 4, Lake Itasca MN
56460-9701. 218/266-2100.

Marshall Park & Recreation
PO Box 477, Marshall MN
56258-0477. 507/537-6763.

Park Board
400 S 4th St, Ste 200,
Minneapolis MN 55415-1400.
612/661-4800.

Superior National Forest
PO Box 338, Duluth MN 55801-
0338. 218/720-5324.

**PUBLIC ENVIRONMENTAL
QUALITY PROGRAMS**

Mid Continent Ecology Division
6201 Congdon Blvd, Duluth MN
55804-2558. 218/720-5550.

**PUBLIC ORDER AND
SAFETY**

**Arrowhead Regional
Corrections**
100 N 5th Ave W, Ste 319,
Duluth MN 55802-1202.
218/726-2633.

**Brooklyn Park Police
Department**
5400 85th Ave N, Minneapolis
MN 55443-1823. 612/424-8013.

Department of Corrections
1450 Energy Park Dr, St. Paul
MN 55108-5227. 651/642-0200.

**Department of Fire & Safety
Services**
100 11th St E, St. Paul MN
55101-2227. 651/222-0477.

Department of Public Safety
445 Minnesota St, Ste 1000, St.
Paul MN 55101-2128. 651/296-
6642.

FBI
111 Washington Ave S,
Minneapolis MN 55401-2108.
612/376-3200.

FCI Sandstone
Kettle River Rd, Sandstone MN
55072. 320/245-2262.

FCI Waseca
PO Box 1731, Waseca MN
56093-0831. 507/835-8972.

FMC Rochester
PO Box 4600, Rochester MN
55903-4600. 507/287-0674.

FPC Duluth
PO Box 1400, Duluth MN 55814-
1400. 218/722-8634.

Hennepin County Sheriff
350 S 5th St, Minneapolis MN
55415-1316. 612/348-3744.

**Kandiyohi County Sheriff's
Department**
PO Box 936, Willmar MN 56201-
0936. 320/231-6202.

MCF Willow River Moose Lake
1000 Lakeshore Dr, Moose Lake
MN 55767-9449. 218/485-5016.

Minneapolis Fire Department
350 S 5th St, Ste 230,
Minneapolis MN 55415-1314.
612/673-2536.

Minneapolis Police Department
3000 Minnehaha Ave,
Minneapolis MN 55406-1932.
612/673-5703.

Minnesota Correctional Facility
PO Box C, Sauk Centre MN
56378-0500. 320/352-1100.

Minnesota Correctional Facility
PO Box 10, Stillwater MN
55082-0010. 651/779-1400.

Minnesota Correctional Facility
PO Box 55, Stillwater MN
55082-0055. 651/779-2700.

Minnesota Correctional Facility
PO Box B, St. Cloud MN 56302-
1000. 320/240-3000.

Minnesota Correctional Facility
1079 Highway 292, Red Wing
MN 55066-2833. 651/388-7154.

Police Department
411 W 1st St, Fl 1, Duluth MN
55802-1102. 218/723-3434.

**Ramsey County Community
Corrections**
50 Kellgg Blvd W, Ste 650, St.
Paul MN 55102. 651/266-2384.

**Ramsey County Juvenile
Services**
480 Saint Peter St, St. Paul MN
55102-1111. 651/298-6930.

**Ramsey County Sheriff's
Department**
655 County Road E W,
Shoreview MN 55126-7031.
651/481-1307.

Ramsey County Sheriff's Dept.
14 Kellogg Blvd W, St. Paul MN
55102-1633. 651/266-9300.

Sheriff's Department
County Adm Ctr, Rm 14, St.
Cloud MN 56303. 320/656-3900.

St. Paul Police Department
100 11th St E, St. Paul MN
55101-2227. 651/291-1111.

**REGULATION OF
AGRICULTURAL
MARKETING**

**United States Department of
Agriculture**
90 Plato Blvd W, St. Paul MN
55107-2004. 651/297-3219.

United States Department of Agriculture
100 N 6th St, Fl 5, Minneapolis MN 55403-1505. 612/370-2291.

REGULATORY ADMINISTRATION OF TRANSPORTATION

Department of Public Works
3377 Rice St, Shoreview MN 55126-3050. 651/484-9104.

Department of Public Works
419 Burgess St, St. Paul MN 55117-5202. 651/292-6697.

Department of Transportation
PO Box 307, Owatonna MN 55060-0307. 507/455-5800.

Department of Transportation
395 John Ireland Blvd, St. Paul MN 55155-1801. 651/296-3000.

Department of Transportation
PO Box 6177, Rochester MN 55903-6177. 507/285-7350.

Department of Transportation
PO Box 768, Willmar MN 56201-0768. 320/231-5195.

Freeborn County Highway Department
Courthouse, Albert Lea MN 56007. 507/373-8003.

Metro Transit
230 5th St E, St. Paul MN 55101-1672. 651/291-6359.

Minnesota License Bureau
500 Lafayette Rd N, St. Paul MN 55155-4002. 651/296-4507.

Roseville County Transportation Department
1500 County B 2, Roseville MN 55113. 651/582-1000.

UNITED STATES POSTAL SERVICE

Airport Mail Center
5000 Green Ln, St. Paul MN 55111-3020. 651/293-3136.

Anoka Post Office
2168 7th Ave, Anoka MN 55303-1713. 612/421-1114.

Burnsville Post Office
PO Box 9998, Burnsville MN 55337-9998. 612/890-5148.

Mankato Post Office
401 S 2nd St, Mankato MN 56001-3786. 507/625-1781.

Minneapolis-St. Paul Bulk Mail Center
3165 Lexington Ave S, St. Paul MN 55121-2238. 612/681-2131.

St. Paul Post Office
180 Kellogg Blvd E, St. Paul MN 55101-1438. 651/293-3300.

United States Postal Service
9641 Garfield Ave, Minneapolis MN 55420-4214. 612/881-2619.

United States Postal Service
100 S 1st St, Minneapolis MN 55401-2037. 612/349-4970.

For more information about career opportunities in the government:

Online Services

FEDERAL JOB OPPORTUNITIES BOARD
ftp://fjob.opm.gov/jobs. A Telnet bulletin board that allows jobseekers to search for government jobs by department, agency, or state. The site includes information about the application process as well as opportunities overseas.

FEDERAL JOBS CENTRAL
http://www.fedjobs.com. This resourceful site has only one drawback: Its services require a fee. Federal Jobs Central offers a subscription to a 64-page biweekly publication containing over 3,500 job listings; online listings that are accessible by occupation, salary, and location; and a service that pairs you with the job you are seeking.

FEDERAL JOBS DIGEST
http://www.jobsfed.com. An excellent site for jobseekers hoping to work for the government, this site offers over 3,500 opportunities in fields such as engineering, medical, administration, management, secretarial, computer services, and law enforcement. The site also includes employment links to government agencies. For a fee, you can let *FJD*'s matching service perform the job hunt for you.

FEDWORLD
http://www.fedworld.gov. Provides a wealth of information on all aspects of the government. Besides an employment link to federal job opportunities, this site also offers access to all government agencies and many government documents.

JOBS IN GOVERNMENT
http://www.jobsingovernment.com. E-mail address: info@jobsingovernment.com. A helpful search engine for individuals seeking employment in government or the public sector. The site offers profile based searches for thousands of open positions, the ability to post and e-mail resumes, and information about current topics and resources in government.

Visit our exciting job and career site at http://www.careercity.com

HEALTH CARE: SERVICES, EQUIPMENT, AND PRODUCTS

The rising cost of health care in the United States is influencing the move from the traditional fee-for-service plans to more cost-conscious managed care plans. Cost control is also creating a more demanding nation of health care customers who want the most for their money. Cost-cutting improvements in the field are beginning to take shape with the advent of new technology such as the use of telemedicine. This process allows electronic images of X-rays and test results to be transmitted anywhere in the world for further consultation and diagnosis.

Consolidation is still a dominant factor in the industry. Small, independent hospitals are being purchased by large corporations to form multi-hospital enterprises. As these hospitals merge, it is likely that costs will be cut, resources shared, and ultimately jobs eliminated.

Health care services are still a major source of job creation in the economy. That distinction is not expected to change as the elderly population continues to grow faster than the nation's total population. As this segment of the population continues to increase, opportunities in long-term care facilities, home health agencies, and doctors' offices will also continue to expand.

Industry trends point to a stronger demand for primary care physicians, rather than specialists. Non-traditional forms of medicine, such as acupuncture and home-infusion therapy, are gaining acceptance by consumers, as well as insurers, which should create more job opportunities. According to the Bureau of Labor Statistics, five of the ten fastest-growing occupations through 2006 will be health care related, specifically home health aides and occupational therapy assistants. Registered nurses may see as many as 411,000 new positions by 2006, and nurses aides and orderlies may see more than 300,000 new positions. Overall, it is estimated that the health care services industry will grow a vigorous 68 percent by 2006.

ATS MEDICAL, INC.
3905 Annapolis Lane, Suite 105, Minneapolis MN 55447. 612/553-7736. **Fax:** 612/553-1492. **Contact:** Human Resources. **World Wide Web address:** http://www.atsmedical.com. **Description:** Manufactures the ATS open pivot heart valve. **Corporate headquarters location:** This Location. **Subsidiaries include:** ATS Medical, Ltd. (Glasgow, Scotland). **Listed on:** NASDAQ.

ALBANY HOSPITAL MEDICAL CENTER
300 Third Avenue, Albany MN 56307-9363. 320/845-2121. **Contact:** Human Resources. **Description:** A hospital offering acute care services. **NOTE:** Outpatient services are provided at the hospital's clinic, located at 302 Third Avenue, Albany MN.

ALLIED HEALTH ALTERNATIVES, INC.
5401 Gamble Drive, Suite 235, Minneapolis MN 55416. 612/544-1655. **Toll-free phone:** 800/605-1655. **Contact:** Jennifer Fisher, Human Resources Specialist. **Description:** A home health care provider that offers nursing, rehabilitation, and personal care assistance to individuals of all ages. **Common positions include:** Home Health Aide; Licensed Practical Nurse; Registered Nurse. **Educational backgrounds include:** Accounting; Health Care. **Benefits:** 401(k); Medical Insurance. **Office hours:** Monday - Friday, 8:00 a.m. - 4:30 p.m. **Corporate headquarters location:** This Location. **Facilities Manager:** Ronna Coleman.

ALTERNATIVE CHOICE HEALTH SERVICES
2021 Hennepin Avenue, Suite 135, Minneapolis MN 55413. 612/378-1474. **Contact:** Manager. **Description:** A home health care agency.

AMERICAN MEDICAL SYSTEMS
10700 Bren Road West, Minnetonka MN 55343. 612/933-4666. **Contact:** Ms. Chris Berg, Human Resources. **Description:** Manufactures and distributes medical devices for use in the field of neurology. **Common positions include:** Administrator; Biomedical Engineer; Buyer; Customer Service Representative; Human Resources Manager; Mechanical Engineer.

ANGEION CORPORATION
7601 Northland Drive, Brooklyn Park MN 55428. 612/315-2000. **Toll-free phone:** 800/ANG-EION. **Fax:** 612/315-2045. **Contact:** Virginia Minter, Senior Human Resources Generalist. **E-mail address:** hr@angeion.com. **World Wide Web address:** http://www.angeion.com. **Description:** Develops products for arrhythmia management, primarily ventricular tachycardia. Angeion's primary product focus is on an advanced implantable cardioversion defibrillator. The company is also developing a radio frequency catheter ablation system for use in procedures to treat and potentially cure tachycardia. Founded in 1986. **NOTE:** Entry-level positions are offered. **Company slogan:** We measure success in heartbeats. **Common positions include:** Account Manager; Administrative Assistant; Design Engineer; Field Engineer; Manufacturing Engineer; Mechanical Engineer; Production Manager; Secretary; Software Engineer. **Educational backgrounds include:** Business Administration; Computer Science; Engineering. **Benefits:** 401(k); Dental Insurance; Disability Coverage; Life Insurance; Medical Insurance; Tuition Assistance. **Office hours:** Monday - Friday, 8:00 a.m. - 5:00 p.m. **Corporate headquarters location:** This Location. **International locations:** Germany; United Kingdom. **Listed on:** NASDAQ. **Stock exchange symbol:** ANGEION. **CEO:** Whitney McFarlin. **Annual sales/revenues:** Less than $5 million. **Number of employees at this location:** 250.

ARGOSY ELECTRONICS
10300 West 70th Street, Eden Prairie MN 55344. 612/942-9232. **Contact:** Michelle Wegener, Human Resources. **Description:** Manufactures hearing aids.

AUGUSTINE MEDICAL
10393 West 70th Street, Eden Prairie MN 55344. 612/947-1200. **Fax:** 612/947-1400. **Contact:** Carolyn Kassebaum, Human Resources Manager. **Description:** Augustine Medical manufactures convective warming blankets and fluid warmers for the health care industry.

BMC INDUSTRIES INC.
One Meridian Crossing, Suite 850, Richfield MN 55423. 612/851-6000. **Contact:** Human Resources. **World Wide Web address:** http://www.bmcind.com. **Description:** Manufactures aperture masks for color cathode-ray tubes, through its Precision Imaged Products business segment; and supplies corrective eyeglass lenses to ophthalmic laboratories and retail eyewear chains, through its Optical Products division.

BERNAFON-MAICO INC.
9675 West 76th Street, Eden Prairie MN 55344. 612/941-4200. **Contact:** Human Resources. **World Wide Web address:** http://www.bernafon-maico.com. **Description:** A producer of audiometers and hearing aids. **Common positions include:** Accountant/Auditor; Blue-Collar Worker Supervisor; Buyer; Credit Manager; Customer Service Representative; Electrical/Electronics Engineer; General Manager; Manufacturer's/Wholesaler's Sales Rep.; Mechanical Engineer; Operations/Production Manager; Purchasing Agent/Manager; Quality Control Supervisor; Systems Analyst; Technical Writer/Editor. **Educational backgrounds include:** Accounting; Business Administration; Communications; Health Care; Marketing. **Benefits:** 401(k); Dental Insurance; Disability Coverage; Life Insurance; Medical Insurance; Tuition Assistance. **Corporate headquarters location:** This Location. **Parent company:** Oticon. **Operations at this facility include:** Administration; Manufacturing; Research and Development; Sales; Service. **Number of employees at this location:** 105.

BIRD & CRONIN INC.
1200 Trapp Road, Eagan MN 55121. 612/683-1111. **Contact:** Kerry Gleason, Human Resources. **Description:** Manufactures orthopedic softgoods.

CHILDREN'S HEALTHCARE MINNEAPOLIS
2525 Chicago Avenue South, Minneapolis MN 55404. 612/813-6100. **Contact:** Human Resources. **World Wide Web address:** http://www.childrenshc.org. **Description:** A children's hospital and

medical center with 147 beds. Children's Healthcare Minneapolis formerly operated as Minneapolis Children's Medical Center.

CHILDREN'S HEALTHCARE ST. PAUL
345 North Smith Avenue, Suite 121, St. Paul MN 55102. 651/220-6660. **Contact:** Human Resources. **World Wide Web address:** http://www.khan.childrenshc.org. **Description:** A pediatric hospital.

COMMUNITY HOSPITAL & HEALTH CARE CENTER
618 West Broadway, St. Peter MN 56082-1327. 507/931-2200. **Contact:** Human Resources. **Description:** A medical center offering acute care and outpatient services as well as a wide variety of diagnostic testing.

DAHLBERG, INC.
4101 Dahlberg Drive, Golden Valley MN 55422. 612/520-9500. **Contact:** Human Resources. **Description:** A manufacturer of hearing aids and related items. **Common positions include:** Accountant/Auditor; Computer Programmer; Customer Service Representative; Electrical/Electronics Engineer; Financial Analyst; Software Engineer; Systems Analyst; Wholesale and Retail Buyer. **Educational backgrounds include:** Accounting; Business Administration; Computer Science; Engineering; Finance; Marketing. **Benefits:** 401(k); Dental Insurance; Disability Coverage; Life Insurance; Medical Insurance; Tuition Assistance. **Special programs:** Internships. **Corporate headquarters location:** This Location. **Operations at this facility include:** Administration; Divisional Headquarters; Manufacturing; Research and Development; Sales; Service. **Number of employees at this location:** 450. **Number of employees nationwide:** 500.

DAIG CORPORATION
14901 Deveau Place, Minnetonka MN 55345. 612/933-4700. **Fax:** 612/630-9478. **Contact:** Human Resources. **Description:** Daig Corporation produces electrocardiovascular products.

DIAMETRICS MEDICAL, INC.
2658 Patton Road, Roseville MN 55113. 651/639-8035. **Contact:** Human Resources. **World Wide Web address:** http://www.diametrics.com. **Description:** Develops, manufactures, and markets patient-testing kits which enable a range of tests, including blood gas analyses, to be done during emergency air transports and home health care visits.

EMPI, INC.
599 Cardigan Road, St. Paul MN 55126-3965. 651/415-9000. **Fax:** 651/415-7447. **Contact:** Human Resources. **World Wide Web address:** http://www.empi.com. **Description:** Empi, Inc. manufactures and markets products in three areas: incontinence, physical rehabilitation, and orthopedics. Major products include neuromuscular stimulators, braces and splints, drug administering devices, and cervical traction devices. **Corporate headquarters location:** This Location. **Listed on:** NASDAQ. **Stock exchange symbol:** EMPI.

EVEREST MEDICAL CORPORATION
13755 First Avenue North, Suite 500, Minneapolis MN 55441-5454. 612/473-6262. **Fax:** 612/473-6465. **Contact:** Human Resources. **World Wide Web address:** http://www.everestmedical.com. **Description:** Manufactures bipolar laparoscopy instruments. The company is also developing cardiac surgery products. **Corporate headquarters location:** This Location. **Listed on:** NASDAQ. **Stock exchange symbol:** EVMD. **Annual sales/revenues:** $5 - $10 million.

FAIRVIEW HEALTH SERVICES
2450 Riverside Avenue, Minneapolis MN 55454. 612/672-4545. **Fax:** 612/672-6337. **Contact:** Human Resources. **World Wide Web address:** http://www.fairview.org. **Description:** A nonprofit, regionally integrated health care network of primary, specialty, acute, long-term, and home care services. Fairview Health Services includes seven hospitals, over 70 primary and specialty care clinics, 43 senior residences, 24 nursing homes, 20 physical therapy clinics, and 20 retail pharmacies. **NOTE:** Entry-level positions and second and third shifts are offered. **Common positions include:** Accountant; Administrative Assistant; Biomedical Engineer; Blue-Collar Worker Supervisor; Buyer; Certified Nurses Aide; Clerical Supervisor; Clinical Lab Technician; Computer Operator; Computer Programmer; Counselor; Customer Service Representative; Database Manager; Dietician/Nutritionist; EEG Technologist; EKG Technician; Electrician; Emergency Medical Technician; Finance Director; Financial Analyst; Human Resources Manager; Librarian; Licensed Practical Nurse; Medical Records Technician; MIS Specialist; Nuclear Medicine Technologist; Nurse Practitioner; Occupational Therapist; Pharmacist; Physical Therapist; Physician; Psychologist; Public Relations Specialist; Purchasing Agent/Manager;

Radiological Technologist; Registered Nurse; Respiratory Therapist; Secretary; Social Worker; Speech-Language Pathologist; Surgical Technician; Typist/Word Processor. **Educational backgrounds include:** Accounting; Biology; Business Administration; Computer Science; Health Care; Nutrition. **Benefits:** 403(b); Dental Insurance; Disability Coverage; Employee Discounts; Life Insurance; Medical Insurance; Pension Plan; Tuition Assistance. **Special programs:** Internships. **Corporate headquarters location:** This Location. **Parent company:** Fairview Hospitals and Healthcare System. **Operations at this facility include:** Service. **Listed on:** Privately held. **President/CEO:** David R. Page. **Number of employees at this location:** 2,100.

FARIBAULT REGIONAL CENTER
802 Circle Drive, Faribault MN 55021. 507/332-3000. **Contact:** Human Resources. **Description:** A hospital.

GUIDANT CORPORATION
4100 Hamline Avenue North, Mail Stop 270, St. Paul MN 55112. 651/638-4000. **Recorded jobline:** 651/582-2110. **Contact:** Human Resources. **World Wide Web address:** http://www.guidant.com. **Description:** Develops, manufactures, and sells a wide range of products used in the treatment of cardiac arrhythmias. The company's products are both implantable and external electronic devices and accessories that are sold to hospitals and other health care providers worldwide. **Common positions include:** Biomedical Engineer; Electrical/Electronics Engineer; Financial Analyst; Mechanical Engineer; Systems Analyst. **Educational backgrounds include:** Business Administration; Computer Science; Engineering. **Operations at this facility include:** Administration; Manufacturing; Research and Development.

HEALTHSYSTEM MINNESOTA
3800 Park Nicollet Boulevard, St. Louis Park MN 55416. 612/993-1600. **Fax:** 612/993-1638. **Contact:** Dee Spalla, Employment/Employee Labor Relations Director. **E-mail address:** hr@park.hsmnet.com. **World Wide Web address:** http://www.healthsystemminnesota.com. **Description:** Operates Methodist Hospital, a 426-bed, full-service hospital, and Park Nicollet Clinic, one of the largest multispecialty clinics in the United States. The clinic specializes in the treatment of patients with cancer, heart problems, diabetes, and allergies/asthma. **NOTE:** Entry-level positions and second and third shifts are offered. **Common positions include:** Accountant; Administrative Assistant; Budget Analyst; Buyer; Claim Representative; Clerical Supervisor; Clinical Lab Technician; Computer Operator; Computer Programmer; Controller; Counselor; Customer Service Representative; Database Manager; Dietician/Nutritionist; Editor; Editorial Assistant; EEG Technologist; EKG Technician; Emergency Medical Technician; Financial Analyst; Human Resources Manager; Licensed Practical Nurse; Marketing Manager; Marketing Specialist; Medical Records Technician; MIS Specialist; Occupational Therapist; Operations Manager; Pharmacist; Physical Therapist; Physician; Project Manager; Psychologist; Public Relations Specialist; Purchasing Agent/Manager; Quality Control Supervisor; Radiological Technologist; Registered Nurse; Respiratory Therapist; Secretary; Social Worker; Speech-Language Pathologist; Statistician; Surgical Technician; Systems Analyst; Systems Manager; Technical Writer/Editor; Telecommunications Manager; Typist/Word Processor. **Educational backgrounds include:** Accounting; Biology; Business Administration; Computer Science; Finance; Health Care; Liberal Arts; Marketing; Nutrition; Public Relations; Software Development. **Benefits:** 401(k); 403(b); Daycare Assistance; Dental Insurance; Disability Coverage; Employee Discounts; Financial Planning Assistance; Flexible Schedule; Job Sharing; Life Insurance; Medical Insurance; Pension Plan; Public Transit Available; Savings Plan; Telecommuting; Tuition Assistance. **Special programs:** Internships; Summer Jobs; Training. **CEO:** James Reinertson.

IMMANUEL-ST. JOSEPH'S HOSPITAL
P.O. Box 8673, Mankato MN 56002. 507/345-2632. **Fax:** 507/345-2926. **Recorded jobline:** 507/387-8834. **Contact:** Rachel Wood, Human Resources Technician. **Description:** Immanuel-St. Joseph's Hospital serves as south central Minnesota's regional medical center. Specialized care includes birthing suites for expectant mothers; a fully staffed emergency room; the assessment, diagnosis, and treatment of behavioral health problems; a cancer center; home health care; and a hospice for terminally ill patients and their families. **Common positions include:** Laboratory Technician; Physical Therapist; Social Worker. **Educational backgrounds include:** Health Care. **Subsidiaries include:** Waseca Area Memorial Hospital. **Parent company:** Mayo Health Systems. **Number of employees at this location:** 900.

IN HOME HEALTH, INC.
Carlson Center, Suite 500, 601 Carlson Parkway, Suite 500, Minnetonka MN 55305. 612/449-7500. **Fax:** 612/449-7599. **Contact:** Human Resources. **Description:** In Home Health, Inc. provides comprehensive health care and home-making services to clients in their residences.

Services are provided through a network of over 40 offices and 10 infusion pharmacies in more than 15 geographic markets. **Listed on:** NASDAQ. **Stock exchange symbol:** IHHI.

LIFECORE BIOMEDICAL INC.
3515 Lyman Boulevard, Chaska MN 55318. 612/368-4300. **Contact:** Human Resources. **Description:** Manufactures dental products including implants and prosthetics. **Corporate headquarters location:** This Location.

LOSSING ORTHOPEDIC
P.O. Box 6224, Minneapolis MN 55406. 612/724-2669. **Physical address:** 3230 Snelling Avenue South, Minneapolis MN 55406. **Fax:** 612/724-5089. **Contact:** Human Resources. **Description:** A manufacturer of medical supplies, specializing in the production and marketing of back and neck devices. **Common positions include:** Account Manager; Customer Service Representative; Machinist; Precision Assembler; Receptionist; Secretary; Sheet-Metal Worker; Typist/Word Processor. **Benefits:** Dental Insurance; Life Insurance; Medical Insurance. **Operations at this facility include:** Administration; Manufacturing; Sales; Service. **Number of employees at this location:** 15. **Number of employees nationwide:** 60.

MALLINCKRODT, INC.
2800 Northwest Boulevard, Minneapolis MN 55441. 612/694-3500. **Fax:** 612/694-3844. **Contact:** Kathy Henderson, Human Resources Coordinator. **World Wide Web address:** http://www.mallinckrodt.com. **Description:** Develops and manufactures products that diagnose, monitor and treat respiratory disorders. Mallinckrodt's products are used in hospitals and residential settings. **Corporate headquarters location:** St. Louis MO. **Listed on:** NASDAQ. **Number of employees at this location:** 350.

MEDICAL GRAPHICS CORPORATION
350 Oak Grove Parkway, St. Paul MN 55127. 651/484-4874. **Fax:** 651/484-8941. **Contact:** Cheryl Raphael, Human Resources Director. **World Wide Web address:** http://www.medgraph.com. **Description:** A manufacturer of computerized medical testing equipment for the health care industry. Products include diagnostic systems which test and treat lung and heart disorders. **Listed on:** NASDAQ. **Stock exchange symbol:** MGCC.

MEDTRONIC, INC.
7000 Central Avenue NE, Minneapolis MN 55432. 612/574-4000. **Contact:** Human Resources. **World Wide Web address:** http://www.medtronic.com. **Description:** Medtronic is a medical equipment manufacturer. The company's primary products include pacemakers and related support systems, artificial heart valves, and neurological devices. Pacemaker brands include Elite, Activitrax, Minix, Minvet, and Legend. **Common positions include:** Accountant/Auditor; Biomedical Engineer; Electrical/Electronics Engineer; Metallurgical Engineer; Software Engineer. **Educational backgrounds include:** Accounting; Biology; Computer Science; Engineering; Finance; Marketing. **Corporate headquarters location:** This Location. **Operations at this facility include:** Manufacturing; Research and Development. **Listed on:** New York Stock Exchange. **Number of employees at this location:** 3,000. **Number of employees nationwide:** 10,000.

MEDTRONIC, INC.
PROMEON DIVISION
6700 Shingle Creek Parkway, Brooklyn Center MN 55430. 612/514-1000. **Fax:** 612/514-1170. **Contact:** Dave Mentz, Human Resources Director. **World Wide Web address:** http://www.medtronic.com. **Description:** This location manufactures implantable, cardiac pacemakers. Overall, Medtronic is a medical equipment manufacturer. The company's primary products include pacemakers and related support systems, artificial heart valves, and neurological devices. Pacemaker brands include Elite, Activitrax, Minix, Minvet, and Legend. **Corporate headquarters location:** Minneapolis MN. **Listed on:** New York Stock Exchange. **Number of employees nationwide:** 10,000.

MENTOR UROLOGY
1601 West River Road North, Minneapolis MN 55411. 612/588-4685. **Contact:** Charlotte Sebastian, Personnel Director. **World Wide Web address:** http://www.mentor.com. **Description:** A manufacturer and distributor of specialized medical devices and related disposable health care products. Mentor Urology also produces surgical implant products, primarily for urological, plastic, and general surgery. **Number of employees at this location:** 350.

MERCY HOSPITAL
4050 Coon Rapids Boulevard, Coon Rapids MN 55433. 612/421-8888. **Contact:** Human Resources. **Description:** A full-service hospital.

METHODIST HOSPITAL
P.O. Box 650, Minneapolis MN 55440. 612/993-5000. **Physical address:** 6500 Excelsior Boulevard, St. Louis Park MN 55426. **Contact:** Arthur LaPointe, Human Resources Director. **World Wide Web address:** http://www.methodisthospital.com. **Description:** A 426-bed, full-service hospital. **Parent company:** HealthSystem Minnesota (Minneapolis MN) also operates Park Nicollet Clinic, one of the largest multispecialty clinics in the United States. The clinic specializes in the treatment of patients with cancer, heart problems, diabetes, and allergies/asthma.

NORTHERN ITASCA HEALTH CARE CENTER
P.O. Box 258, Bigfork MN 56628. 218/743-4116. **Fax:** 218/743-3559. **Contact:** Faye Reigel, Human Resources Coordinator. **E-mail address:** nihcc@mail.bigfork.net. **World Wide Web address:** http://www.nihcc.com. **Description:** A nonprofit medical facility consisting of a 20-bed hospital, a 40-bed long-term care unit, and 30 apartments attached to an outpatient clinic. The center also offers adult daycare and pharmacy services. **NOTE:** Entry-level positions as well as second and third shifts are offered. **Company slogan:** We've been making healthy neighbors for 60 years. **Common positions include:** Administrative Assistant; Certified Nurses Aide; Chief Financial Officer; Clinical Lab Technician; Environmental Engineer; Human Resources Manager; Licensed Practical Nurse; Medical Records Technician; Occupational Therapist; Pharmacist; Physical Therapist; Purchasing Agent/Manager; Radiological Technologist; Registered Nurse; Social Worker. **Educational backgrounds include:** Health Care. **Benefits:** 403(b); Employee Discounts; Life Insurance; Medical Insurance; Savings Plan. **Special programs:** Training. **Corporate headquarters location:** This Location. **Administrator:** Richard Ash. **Number of employees at this location:** 150.

PATTERSON DENTAL COMPANY
1031 Mendota Heights Road, Mendota Heights MN 55120. 612/686-1600. **Contact:** Mary Martins, Director of Human Resources. **World Wide Web address:** http://www.pattersondental.com. **Description:** Distributes dental supplies and equipment such as X-ray film and solutions, impression and restorative materials, dental chairs, sterilizers, and diagnostic equipment. Patterson Dental Company provides a full range of related services such as dental equipment installation, maintenance, and repair; dental office design; and equipment financing programs. **Number of employees nationwide:** 2,050.

PRESBYTERIAN HOMES OF MINNESOTA
3220 Lake Johanna Boulevard, Arden Hills MN 55112. 651/631-6126. **Fax:** 651/631-6122. **Contact:** Barb Peterson, Human Resources Representative. **Description:** Offers a broad range of residential and support services to the elderly. Services include apartment living, long-term nursing care, and home health respite programs. **NOTE:** Entry-level positions and second and third shifts are offered. **Common positions include:** Certified Nurses Aide; Dietician/Nutritionist; Environmental Engineer; Licensed Practical Nurse; Registered Nurse; Secretary; Social Worker. **Educational backgrounds include:** Health Care. **Benefits:** 403(b); Dental Insurance; Employee Discounts; Life Insurance; Medical Insurance; Pension Plan; Tuition Assistance. **Special programs:** Summer Jobs. **Corporate headquarters location:** This Location. **CEO:** Daniel Lindh. **Number of employees at this location:** 1,500.

RAMSEY CLINIC
640 Jackson Street, St. Paul MN 55101. 651/221-3152. **Toll-free phone:** 800/332-5720. **Fax:** 651/221-1249. **Recorded jobline:** 651/221-1227. **Contact:** Ruth Bremer, Human Resources Representative. **E-mail address:** ruth.n.bremer@healthpartners.com. **Description:** Ramsey Clinic is a multispecialty, outpatient clinic. **Common positions include:** Account Representative; Administrative Assistant; Claim Representative; Clerical Supervisor; Clinical Lab Technician; Computer Operator; Computer Programmer; Counselor; Emergency Medical Technician; Licensed Practical Nurse; Medical Records Technician; MIS Specialist; Psychologist; Registered Nurse; Secretary; Social Worker; Typist/Word Processor. **Educational backgrounds include:** Accounting; Business Administration; Health Care. **Benefits:** 403(b); Dental Insurance; Disability Coverage; Employee Discounts; Life Insurance; Medical Insurance; Pension Plan; Tuition Assistance. **Special programs:** Internships. **Office hours:** Monday - Friday, 8:00 a.m. - 4:30 p.m. **Corporate headquarters location:** This Location. **Number of employees at this location:** 850.

REM-HEALTH, INC.
3101 West 69th Street, Suite 121, Edina MN 55435. 612/926-9808. **Toll-free phone:** 800/896-8814. **Fax:** 612/926-4002. **Contact:** Gloryanne Stone, Human Resources Manager. **Description:** A home health care agency offering private duty nursing care, live-in companions, respiratory therapy, physical therapy, occupational therapy, psychological services, and applied behavior analysis. Founded in 1989. **NOTE:** Entry-level positions and second and third shifts are offered. **Common positions include:** Administrative Assistant; Certified Nurses Aide; Computer Operator;

Licensed Practical Nurse; Occupational Therapist; Physical Therapist; Psychologist; Registered Nurse; Respiratory Therapist; Secretary; Speech-Language Pathologist; Typist/Word Processor. **Educational backgrounds include:** Accounting; Health Care; Liberal Arts. **Benefits:** 401(k); Dental Insurance; Disability Coverage; Flexible Schedule; Life Insurance; Medical Insurance; Profit Sharing. **Special programs:** Summer Jobs; Training. **Corporate headquarters location:** This Location. **Other U.S. locations:** Woodbine IA; Annandale MN; Cokato MN; Maple Lake MN; New Prague MN; St. Paul MN; Madison WI. **Parent company:** REM, Inc. **Listed on:** Privately held. **Administrator:** Pat Shafer. **Annual sales/revenues:** $11 - $20 million. **Number of employees at this location:** 1,000. **Number of projected hires for 1999 - 2000 at this location:** 200.

RESISTANCE TECHNOLOGY, INC.
1260 Red Fox Road, Arden Hills MN 55112. 651/636-9770. **Fax:** 651/636-8944. **Contact:** Cari Sather, Human Resources Coordinator. **World Wide Web address:** http://www.rtihearing.com. **Description:** A worldwide producer of medical hearing products including ultra-miniature volume controls, CIC faceplates, and programmable hearing systems. **NOTE:** Entry-level positions and second and third shifts are offered. **Common positions include:** Account Manager; Accountant/Auditor; Administrative Assistant; Applications Engineer; Buyer; Controller; Credit Manager; Design Engineer; Designer; Electrical/Electronics Engineer; Human Resources Manager; Industrial Engineer; Manufacturing Engineer; Marketing Manager; Mechanical Engineer; MIS Specialist; Operations/Production Manager; Project Manager; Purchasing Agent/Manager; Sales Engineer; Sales Manager; Systems Analyst. **Educational backgrounds include:** Accounting; Business Administration; Computer Science; Engineering; Marketing. **Benefits:** 401(k); Cafeteria Plan; Daycare Assistance; Dental Insurance; Disability Coverage; Employee Discounts; Life Insurance; Medical Insurance; Pension Plan; Tuition Assistance. **Corporate headquarters location:** This Location. **Parent company:** Selas. **Annual sales/revenues:** $21 - $50 million. **Number of employees at this location:** 260.

RICE MEMORIAL HOSPITAL
301 Becker Avenue SW, Willmar MN 56201. 320/235-4543. **Contact:** Human Resources. **Description:** A hospital offering both acute care and outpatient services.

RIDGEVIEW MEDICAL CENTER
500 South Maple Street, Waconia MN 55387-1714. 612/442-2191. **Contact:** Human Resources. **Description:** A medical center with 109 beds offering both acute care and outpatient services.

ROCHESTER METHODIST HOSPITAL
201 West Center Street, Rochester MN 55902-3003. 507/286-7890. **Contact:** Human Resources. **World Wide Web address:** http://www.mayo.edu/rhosp/rmh.html. **Description:** A 794-bed hospital offering acute care and outpatient services through its Epilepsy Monitoring Unit; a perinatal care center for high-risk pregnancies; a psoriasis and dermatology program; an intraoperative radiation surgical suite; transplant programs for bone marrow, kidney, liver, and pancreas diseases; and a women's cancer center. Rochester Methodist Hospital is an affiliate of the Mayo Clinic.

SABER DENTAL STUDIO
6800 Shingle Creek Parkway, Brooklyn Center MN 55430. 612/566-0210. **Contact:** Human Resources Department. **Description:** A dental laboratory. **Benefits:** 401(k); Incentive Plan; Stock Option. **Corporate headquarters location:** Wayland MA. **Other U.S. locations:** Waukesha WI. **Parent company:** National Dentex Corporation is one of the largest operators of dental laboratories in the United States. National Dentex serves an active customer base of approximately 6,200 dentists through its 20 full-service and three branch dental laboratories located in 18 states. These dental laboratories provide a full range of custom-made dental prosthetic appliances, divided into three main groups: restorative products (crowns and bridges); reconstructive products (partial and full dentures); and cosmetic products (porcelain veneers and ceramic crowns). Each lab is operated as a stand-alone facility under the direction of a local manager. All sales and marketing is done through each lab's own direct sales force. **Listed on:** NASDAQ. **Number of employees nationwide:** 840.

ST. BENEDICT'S CENTER
1810 Minnesota Boulevard SE, St. Cloud MN 56304-2416. 320/252-0010x251. **Fax:** 320/651-3238. **Contact:** Stacey Kaufman, Recruitment Coordinator. **Description:** Offers nonprofit health care and housing for older adults. St. Benedict's Center provides nursing services to over 220 individuals who require 24-hour care. Other services available at the center include the Subacute Care Unit, the Special Care Unit, Hospice Care, and Respite Care. The center also operates a retirement community, an assisted living facility, income-based senior housing, a residential center

for those in the early stages of Alzheimer's disease or memory loss, a licensed adult daycare program, home care services, and a senior dining program for the residents of southeast St. Cloud. Founded in 1978. **NOTE:** Entry-level positions and second and third shifts are offered. **Company slogan:** All shall be treated as Christ. **Common positions include:** Administrative Assistant; Blue-Collar Worker Supervisor; Certified Nurses Aide; Dietician/Nutritionist; Licensed Practical Nurse; Registered Nurse; Social Worker; Typist/Word Processor. **Educational backgrounds include:** Health Care; Nutrition. **Benefits:** 403(b); Dental Insurance; Disability Coverage; Financial Planning Assistance; Life Insurance; Medical Insurance; Pension Plan; Public Transit Available; Savings Plan; Tuition Assistance. **Special programs:** Internships; Summer Jobs; Training. **Internship information:** Unpaid internships are offered during the fall and spring. Opportunities are available in Human Resources, working with people suffering from cognitive disorders, and social services. For more information or to volunteer, contact the Volunteer Coordinator. **Office hours:** Monday - Friday, 8:00 a.m. - 4:30 p.m. **Parent company:** St. Cloud Hospital. **Executive Director:** Linda Doerr. **Number of employees at this location:** 525.

ST. CLOUD HOSPITAL
1406 Sixth Avenue North, St. Cloud MN 56303. 320/251-2700. **Contact:** Employment Department. **Description:** A regional medical center offering a variety of medical specialties. **Common positions include:** Dietician/Nutritionist; Laboratory Technician; Licensed Practical Nurse; Radiological Technologist. **Educational backgrounds include:** Health Care. **Benefits:** Daycare Assistance; Dental Insurance; Disability Coverage; Life Insurance; Medical Insurance; Pension Plan; Savings Plan; Tuition Assistance. **Special programs:** Internships. **Operations at this facility include:** Health Care; Service. **Number of employees at this location:** 2,200.

ST. JUDE MEDICAL, INC.
One Lillehei Plaza, St. Paul MN 55117-9983. 651/483-2000. **Fax:** 651/490-4333. **Contact:** Human Resources. **World Wide Web address:** http://www.sjm.com. **Description:** A world leader in the development of heart valves and medical supplies. The company operates through three divisions: the St. Jude Medical Heart Valve Division, which manufactures products for the management of heart valve diseases; Pacesetter, which manufactures cardiac rhythm products; and Daig, which specializes in the manufacture of catheters. **Corporate headquarters location:** This Location. **International locations:** Worldwide. **Listed on:** New York Stock Exchange. **Stock exchange symbol:** STJ. **Number of employees worldwide:** 3,600.

ST. THERESE HOME
8000 Bass Lake Road, New Hope MN 55428. 612/531-5000. **Fax:** 612/531-5004. **Recorded jobline:** 612/531-5401. **Contact:** Jeff Mutz, Director of Human Resources. **Description:** A religious-sponsored, nonprofit organization that provides long-term health care to the elderly. The company consists of a 302-bed care center, 220 units of senior housing, home care services, and a rehabilitation agency. **NOTE:** Entry-level positions and second and third shifts are offered. **Common positions include:** Certified Nurses Aide; Dietician/Nutritionist; Licensed Practical Nurse; Medical Records Technician; Occupational Therapist; Pharmacist; Physical Therapist; Registered Nurse; Social Worker; Speech-Language Pathologist; Typist/Word Processor. **Educational backgrounds include:** Health Care; Nutrition. **Benefits:** 403(b); Dental Insurance; Life Insurance; Medical Insurance; Public Transit Available; Savings Plan; Tuition Assistance. **Special programs:** Internships; Summer Jobs. **Corporate headquarters location:** This Location. **Listed on:** Privately held. **Annual sales/revenues:** $11 - $20 million. **Number of employees at this location:** 600.

SCIMED LIFE SYSTEMS, INC.
One SciMed Place, Maple Grove MN 55311. 612/494-1700. **Fax:** 612/494-2290. **Recorded jobline:** 612/494-5627. **Contact:** Human Resources. **World Wide Web address:** http://www.scimed.com. **Description:** SciMed Life Systems, Inc. develops, manufactures, and markets disposable medical devices principally for the non-surgical diagnosis and treatment of coronary, peripheral, and neurovascular disease. **Common positions include:** Accountant/Auditor; Manufacturing Manager; Mechanical Engineer; Product Manager. **Educational backgrounds include:** Accounting; Engineering; Marketing. **Benefits:** 401(k); Dental Insurance; Disability Coverage; Life Insurance; Medical Insurance; Tuition Assistance. **Corporate headquarters location:** This Location. **Operations at this facility include:** Administration; Manufacturing; Research and Development. **Listed on:** NASDAQ. **Number of employees at this location:** 1,400.

SIMS DELTEC
1265 Grey Fox Road, St. Paul MN 55112-6967. 651/633-2556. **Contact:** Human Resources. **World Wide Web address:** http://www.deltec.com. **Description:** Manufactures medical infusion devices. **Corporate headquarters location:** This Location.

SPECTRASCIENCE
3650 Annapolis Lane North, Suite 101, Minneapolis MN 55447. 612/509-9999. **Contact:** Office Administrator. **Description:** Designs, manufactures, and markets laser-based medical devices for the treatment of heart and blood vessel diseases.

STARKEY LABS
6700 Washington Avenue South, Eden Prairie MN 55344. 612/941-6401. **Contact:** Larry Miller, Human Resources Director. **Description:** A wholesale supplier of surgical and medical supplies.

STEVENS COMMUNITY MEDICAL CENTER
400 East First Street, Morris MN 56267. 320/589-7646. **Fax:** 320/589-3533. **Contact:** Karla Larson, Personnel Director. **Description:** A nonprofit, multi-specialty clinic and hospital serving the west central Minnesota region. Founded in 1951. **Company slogan:** Caring is our reason for being. **Common positions include:** Certified Nurses Aide; Clinical Lab Technician; Counselor; Dietician/Nutritionist; Licensed Practical Nurse; Medical Records Technician; Pharmacist; Physician; Psychologist; Radiological Technologist; Registered Nurse; Respiratory Therapist; Secretary; Social Worker; Surgical Technician. **Educational backgrounds include:** Health Care. **Benefits:** 403(b); Dental Insurance; Disability Coverage; Life Insurance; Medical Insurance; Pension Plan. **Corporate headquarters location:** This Location. **President/CEO:** John Rau. **Number of employees at this location:** 225.

SULZER SPINE-TECH, INC.
7375 Bush Lake Road, Minneapolis MN 55439. 612/832-5600. **Fax:** 612/832-5620. **Contact:** Human Resources. **Description:** Sulzer Spine-Tech, Inc. manufactures spinal implants to help the fusion of vertebrae in order to stabilize the spine. **Listed on:** NASDAQ. **Stock exchange symbol:** SPYN.

SURGIDYNE, INC.
9909 South Shore Drive, Minneapolis MN 55441. 612/595-0665. **Fax:** 612/595-0667. **Contact:** Larry Hanson, Financial Administrator. **Description:** Assembles medical devices and manufactures closed-suction wound drainage products. **Common positions include:** Accountant; Controller; Marketing Manager; Operations Manager; Production Manager; Quality Control Supervisor; Vice President. **Educational backgrounds include:** Accounting; Business Administration; Engineering; Finance; Marketing. **Benefits:** Medical Insurance. **Corporate headquarters location:** This Location. **President:** Vance Fiegel. **Annual sales/revenues:** Less than $5 million. **Number of employees at this location:** 8.

VASAMEDICS
2963 Yorkton Boulevard, St. Paul MN 55117. 651/490-0999. **Fax:** 651/490-0897. **Contact:** Human Resources. **Description:** A wholesale supplier of laser systems for blood flow monitoring.

VISION-EASE LENS
7000 Sunwood Drive, Ramsey MN 55303. 612/576-3930. **Fax:** 612/576-5152. **Contact:** Diane Wilson, Human Resources Manager. **Description:** Manufactures polycarbonate lenses for eyeglasses. **NOTE:** Entry-level positions and second and third shifts are offered. **Common positions include:** Accountant; Administrative Assistant; Auditor; Blue-Collar Worker Supervisor; Chemical Engineer; Controller; Human Resources Manager; Manufacturing Engineer; Mechanical Engineer; Production Manager; Quality Control Supervisor; Secretary; Vice President of Operations. **Educational backgrounds include:** Engineering. **Benefits:** 401(k); Dental Insurance; Disability Coverage; Life Insurance; Medical Insurance; Profit Sharing; Savings Plan; Tuition Assistance. **Special programs:** Internships; Summer Jobs; Training. **Corporate headquarters location:** This Location. **Other U.S. locations:** St. Cloud MN. **Parent company:** BMC Industries. **Listed on:** New York Stock Exchange. **Stock exchange symbol:** BMC. **CEO:** Paul Burke. **Facilities Manager:** Theresa Biggerstaff. **Annual sales/revenues:** More than $100 million. **Number of employees at this location:** 160.

WALMAN OPTICAL COMPANY
801 12th Avenue North, Minneapolis MN 55411. 612/520-6028. **Contact:** Human Resources Department. **Description:** Manufactures ophthalmic products. **Common positions include:** Blue-Collar Worker Supervisor; Branch Manager; Computer Programmer; Credit Manager; Customer Service Representative; Department Manager; Manufacturer's/Wholesaler's Sales Rep.; Operations/Production Manager; Optician; Purchasing Agent/Manager. **Benefits:** 401(k); Dental Insurance; Disability Coverage; Employee Discounts; Life Insurance; Medical Insurance; Pension Plan; Profit Sharing; Savings Plan. **Operations at this facility include:** Administration; Manufacturing; Sales; Service.

WILSON CENTER
P.O. Box 917, Faribault MN 55021. 507/334-5561. **Toll-free phone:** 800/616-5561. **Fax:** 507/334-9208. **Contact:** Sean Canney, Human Resources Director. **World Wide Web address:** http://www.wilsoncenter.com. **Description:** A residential psychiatric facility for children, adolescents, and adults. Founded in 1971. **NOTE:** Entry-level positions and second and third shifts are offered. **Common positions include:** Accountant; Administrative Assistant; Chief Financial Officer; Counselor; Electrician; Human Resources Manager; Licensed Practical Nurse; Medical Records Technician; Occupational Therapist; Physician; Psychologist; Registered Nurse; Secretary; Social Worker; Teacher/Professor; Typist/Word Processor. **Educational backgrounds include:** Health Care; Human Services; Liberal Arts. **Benefits:** 401(k); Dental Insurance; Disability Coverage; Life Insurance; Medical Insurance; Profit Sharing; Savings Plan. **Special programs:** Internships; Summer Jobs; Training. **Corporate headquarters location:** This Location. **Other area locations:** Northfield MN; Rochester MN. **Listed on:** Privately held. **President:** Kevin Mahoney. **Number of employees at this location:** 250.

WINONA HOSPITAL
P.O. Box 5600, Winona MN 55987-0600. 507/454-3650. **Physical address:** 855 Mankato Avenue, Winona MN. **Contact:** Human Resources. **Description:** A hospital offering various social service programs in order to promote the welfare of the community.

X-CEL OPTICAL COMPANY
P.O. Box 420, Sauk Rapids MN 56379. 320/251-8404. **Contact:** Human Resources. **Description:** Manufactures eyeglass lenses.

Note: Because addresses and telephone numbers of smaller companies can change rapidly, we recommend you call each company to verify the information below before inquiring about job opportunities. Mass mailings are not recommended.

Additional small employers:

DOCTORS' OFFICES AND CLINICS

Albert Lea Regional Medical Group
210 N Saint Mary Ave, Albert Lea MN 56007-2463. 507/373-1441.

Allina Health System
PO Box 9310, Minneapolis MN 55440-9310. 612/992-2000.

Allina Medical Group
3055 Old Highway 8, Minneapolis MN 55418-2500. 612/782-5500.

Apple Valley Clinic
15290 Pennock Ln, Apple Valley MN 55124-7163. 612/431-7070.

Boynton Health Service
410 Church St SE, Minneapolis MN 55455-0346. 612/624-4474.

Cambridge Clinic
626 7th Ave SW, Cambridge MN 55008-1916. 612/689-1411.

Cardiodiagnostics Inc.
255 Smith Ave N, Ste 100, St. Paul MN 55102-2518. 651/292-0616.

Centracare Clinic
1200 6th Ave N, St. Cloud MN 56303-2735. 320/252-5131.

Dakota Clinic Ltd.
PO Box 727, Detroit Lakes MN 56502-0727. 218/847-3181.

Duluth Clinic
400 E 3rd St, Duluth MN 55805-1951. 218/722-8364.

East Range Clinics Ltd.
910 N 6th Ave, Virginia MN 55792-2311. 218/741-0150.

Family Physician Health Center
640 Jackson St, St. Paul MN 55101-2502. 651/221-3456.

Fergus Falls Medical Group PA
615 S Mill St, Fergus Falls MN 56537-2738. 218/739-2221.

Fridley Plaza Clinic
6341 University Avenue NE, Fridley MN 55432-4946. 612/572-5700.

HealthPartners
2220 Riverside Ave, Minneapolis MN 55454-1321. 612/371-1610.

HealthPartners
PO Box 1309, Minneapolis MN 55440-1309. 612/883-6000.

Lakeland Dialysis
4310 Nickolet Ave S, Brooklyn Center MN 55430. 612/822-4411.

Lakeview Clinic Ltd.
424 W Highway 5, Waconia MN 55387-1723. 612/442-4461.

Mankato Clinic
PO Box 8674, Mankato MN 56002-8674. 507/625-1811.

Mayo Clinic
200 1st St SW, Rochester MN 55905-0001. 507/284-2511.

Merit Care Clinic Bemidji
1233 34th St NW, Bemidji MN 56601-5112. 218/759-5000.

Mesaba Clinic
1814 14th Ave E, Hibbing MN 55746-1314. 218/262-3441.

Minneapolis Clinic of Neurology Ltd.
4225 Golden Valley Rd, Crystal MN 55422-4215. 612/588-0661.

Mork Clinic
1833 2nd Ave, Anoka MN 55303-2432. 612/421-3680.

Noran Neurological Clinic PA
910 E 26th St, Minneapolis MN 55404-4526. 612/879-1000.

Owatonna Clinic PA
134 Southview, Owatonna MN 55060-3241. 507/451-1120.

Oxboro Clinics
600 W 98th St, Minneapolis MN 55420-4773. 612/881-2651.

Pleasantview Medical Clinic
30 S Behl St, Appleton MN 56208-1616. 320/289-2422.

St. Cloud Medical Group PA
1301 W Saint Germain St, St.
Cloud MN 56301-3456. 320/251-
8181.

St. Paul Clinic
205 Wabasha Street South, St.
Paul MN 55107-1805. 651/293-
8100.

Stillwater Medical Clinic PA
1500 Curve Crest Blvd W,
Stillwater MN 55082-6040.
651/439-1234.

White Bear Lake Clinic
1430 Highway 96 E, White Bear
Lake MN 55110-3653. 651/426-
1980.

Willmar Clinic
101 Willmar Ave SW, Willmar
MN 56201-3556. 320/231-5000.

Winona Clinic Ltd.
420 E Sarnia St, Winona MN
55987-4074. 507/454-3680.

**Worthington Specialty Clinics
PA**
508 10th St, Worthington MN
56187-2343. 507/372-2921.

**HEALTH AND ALLIED
SERVICES**

**Hennepin County Ambulance
Service**
701 Park Ave, Minneapolis MN
55415-1623. 612/347-2141.

Memorial Blood Centers
2304 Park Ave, Minneapolis MN
55404-3712. 612/871-3300.

**St. Paul Regional Blood
Services**
100 Robert St S, St. Paul MN
55107-1411. 651/291-6789.

**HOME HEALTH CARE
SERVICES**

All Home Health
8140 26th Ave S, Ste 100,
Minneapolis MN 55425-1307.
612/881-8968.

Alliance Health Care Inc.
2204 E 117th St, Burnsville MN
55337-1265. 612/882-1030.

Alliance Health Care Inc.
501 Holly Ln, Mankato MN
56001-6800. 507/386-1666.

At Home Services
3931 Coon Rapids Blvd NW,
Coon Rapids MN 55433-2500.
612/427-8341.

Barnabas Health Care Services
1302 Oak St, Brainerd MN
56401-3730. 218/829-0901.

Becklund Home Health Care
8421 Wayzata Blvd, Ste 100, St.
Louis Park MN 55426-1353.
612/544-0315.

Becklund Home Health Care
24174 Greenway Rd N, Forest
Lake MN 55025-9035. 651/982-
9052.

Becklund Home Health Care
1010 S 4th St, Apt 101, St. Peter
MN 56082-1488. 507/931-9755.

Best Care Inc.
3014 University Ave SE,
Minneapolis MN 55414-3316.
612/378-1040.

Caregivers Network Inc.
11208 Minnetonka Mlls Rd,
Hopkins MN 55305-5149.
612/935-5581.

Caremate Corporation
1951 University Ave W, St. Paul
MN 55104-3427. 651/659-0208.

**Good Neighbor Home Health
Care**
555 Edgewood Dr N, Baxter MN
56425-9603. 218/829-9238.

Health Span Hospice
2750 Arthur St, Roseville MN
55113-1303. 651/636-4663.

**Healtheast Optional Care
Systems**
2577 Territorial Rd, St. Paul MN
55114-1500. 651/232-2800.

Home Free
PO Box 20104, Minneapolis MN
55420-0104. 612/881-7590.

Home Health Plus
2250 County Road C W,
Roseville MN 55113-2504.
651/633-6522.

Homecare Specialists
101 E Howard St, Hibbing MN
55746-1733. 218/262-5887.

Integrated Home Care
475 Etna St, Ste 3, St. Paul MN
55106-5845. 651/776-2112.

**Interim Healthcare of Lake
Superior**
330 Canal Park Dr, Duluth MN
55802-2316. 218/722-0053.

**Metropolitan Visiting Nurse
Association**
2021 E Hennepin Ave,
Minneapolis MN 55413-2700.
612/673-2777.

**Moonlight Nursing Care
Incorporated**
1007 E Franklin Ave,
Minneapolis MN 55404-2920.
612/870-7886.

Olsten Corporation
325 S Lake Avenue, Ste 515,
Duluth MN 55802-2323.
218/723-8999.

Prairie River Home Care Inc.
218 Main Street North,
Hutchinson MN 55350-1810.
320/587-5162.

Prairie River Home Care Inc.
244 W Main St, Marshall MN
56258-1340. 507/532-2264.

Quality Home Healthcare Inc.
1020 E 146th St, Ste 111,
Burnsville MN 55337-6756.
612/953-3399.

**Shamrock In-Home Nursing
Care**
900 W 128th St, Ste 120,
Burnsville MN 55337-2456.
612/894-2663.

Unity Family Home Care
815 2nd St SE, Little Falls MN
56345-3505. 320/632-5441.

**Winona County Public Health
Nursing Services**
60 W 3rd St, Winona MN 55987-
3431. 507/457-6400.

**HOSPITALS AND MEDICAL
CENTERS**

Abbott-Northwestern Hospital
800 E 28th St, Minneapolis MN
55407-3723. 612/863-4000.

**AL Vadheim Memorial
Hospital**
PO Box 280, Tyler MN 56178-
0280. 507/247-5521.

**Anoka-Metro Regional
Treatment Center**
3300 4th Ave, Anoka MN 55303-
1161. 612/422-4150.

Austin Medical Center
1000 1st Dr NW, Austin MN
55912-2941. 507/437-4551.

**Bethesda Lutheran Medical
Center**
559 Capitol Blvd, St. Paul MN
55103-2101. 651/232-2000.

Brainerd Medical Center PA
2024 S 6th St, Brainerd MN
56401-4529. 218/828-7100.

Bridges Medical Services
PO Box 233, Ada MN 56510-
0233. 218/784-2561.

Buffalo Hospital
PO Box 609, Buffalo MN 55313-
0609. 612/682-1212.

Cambridge Memorial Hospital
701 Dellwood St S, Cambridge
MN 55008-1920. 612/689-7700.

Cambridge Regional Human Services Center
1235 Highway 293 S, Cambridge MN 55008-9002. 612/689-7200.

Chippewa County-Montevideo Hospital
824 N 11th St, Montevideo MN 56265-1629. 320/269-8877.

Community Memorial Hospital
512 Skyline Blvd, Cloquet MN 55720-1139. 218/879-4641.

Cuyuna Regional Medical Center
320 E Main St, Crosby MN 56441-1645. 218/546-7000.

Douglas County Hospital
111 17th Ave E, Alexandria MN 56308-3703. 320/762-1511.

Fairmont Community Hospital
PO Box 835, Fairmont MN 56031-0835. 507/238-4254.

Fairview Lakes Regional Healthcare
5200 Fairview Blvd, Wyoming MN 55092-8013. 651/982-7000.

Fairview Redwing Health Services
1407 W 4th St, Red Wing MN 55066-2108. 651/388-6721.

Fairview Ridges Hospital
201 E Nicollet Blvd, Burnsville MN 55337-5714. 612/892-2000.

Falls Memorial Hospital
1400 Highway 71, International MN 56649-2154. 218/283-4481.

First Care Medical Services
900 Hilligoss Blvd SE, Fosston MN 56542-1542. 218/435-1133.

Fridley Medical Center
7675 Madison St NE, Fridley MN 55432-2753. 612/785-4500.

Gillette Child Specialty Healthcare
200 University Ave E, St. Paul MN 55101-2507. 651/291-2848.

Glacial Ridge Hospital District
10 4th Ave SE, Glenwood MN 56334-1820. 320/634-4521.

Greater Staples Hospital Care Center
401 Prairie Ave E, Staples MN 56479-3201. 218/894-1515.

Health Unity Hospital
550 Osborne Rd NE, Fridley MN 55432-2718. 612/421-2222.

Hendricks Community Hospital Association
PO Box 106, Hendricks MN 56136-0106. 507/275-3134.

Hennepin County Medical Center
701 Park Ave, Minneapolis MN 55415-1623. 612/347-2121.

Hutchinson Community Hospital
1095 Highway 15, Hutchinson MN 55350-3153. 320/587-2148.

Interstate Medical Center
PO Box 54, Red Wing MN 55066-0054. 651/388-3503.

Itasca Medical Center
126 SE 1st Ave, Grand Rapids MN 55744-3608. 218/326-3401.

Kanabec County Hospital
300 Clark St, Mora MN 55051-1556. 320/679-1212.

Lake Region Hospital
PO Box 728, Fergus Falls MN 56538-0728. 218/736-8000.

Lakeview Hospital
927 Churchill St W, Stillwater MN 55082-6605. 651/439-5330.

Lakewood Care Center
Rural Route 1, Box 2120, Baudette MN 56623. 218/634-2120.

Long Prairie Memorial Hospital & Home
20 9th St SE, Long Prairie MN 56347-1404. 320/732-2141.

Luverne Community Hospital
PO Box 1019, Luverne MN 56156-2519. 507/283-2321.

Mahnomen County Village Hospital
PO Box 396, Mahnomen MN 56557-0396. 218/935-2511.

Meeker County Memorial Hospital
612 South Sibley Avenue, Litchfield MN 55355-3340. 320/693-3242.

Melrose Hospital & Pine Village
11 N 5th Ave W, Melrose MN 56352-1071. 320/256-4231.

Memorial Medical Center
3300 Oakdale Avenue North, Crystal MN 55422-2926. 612/520-5200.

Mercy Hospital & Health Care Center
710 S Kenwood Ave, Moose Lake MN 55767-9405. 218/485-4481.

Mercy Medical Center
PO Box 32839, Minneapolis MN 55432-0839. 612/422-4522.

Mille Lacs Hospital
PO Box A, Onamia MN 56359-0800. 320/532-3154.

Miller-Dwan Medical Center
502 E 2nd St, Duluth MN 55805-1913. 218/727-8762.

North Country Regional Hospital
1100 38th St NW, Bemidji MN 56601-5107. 218/751-5430.

Northwestern Minnesota Health
PO Box 700, Hallock MN 56728-0700. 218/843-3612.

Olmsted Community Hospital
1650 4th St SE, Rochester MN 55904-4717. 507/285-8485.

Olmsted Medical Center
210 9th St SE, Rochester MN 55904-6425. 507/288-3443.

Owatonna Hospital
903 S Oak Ave, Owatonna MN 55060-3200. 507/451-3850.

Park Nicollet Medical Center
3800 Park Nicollet Blvd, Minneapolis MN 55416-2527. 612/993-3123.

Perham Memorial Hospital & Home
665 3rd St SW, Perham MN 56573-1108. 218/346-4500.

Pine Medical Center
109 Court Ave S, Sandstone MN 55072-5120. 320/245-2212.

Pipestone County Medical Center
911 5th Ave SW, Pipestone MN 56164-1054. 507/825-5811.

Princeton Area Hospital
911 Northland Dr, Princeton MN 55371-2172. 612/389-1313.

Queen of Peace Hospital
301 2nd St NE, New Prague MN 56071-1709. 612/758-4431.

Ramsey Medical Center
9055 Springbrook Dr NW, Coon Rapids MN 55433-5841. 612/780-9155.

Red Lake Comprehensive Health Service
PO Box 249, Red Lake MN 56671-0249. 218/679-3316.

Redwood Falls Municipal Hospital
100 Fallwood Rd, Redwood Falls MN 56283-1828. 507/637-2907.

Regina Memorial Hospital
1175 Nininger Rd, Hastings MN 55033-1056. 651/480-4100.

Rice County District One Hospital
631 1st St SE, Faribault MN 55021-6398. 507/334-6451.

Riverwood Healthcare Center
301 Minnesota Avenue South, Aitkin MN 56431-1626. 218/927-2121.

Roseau Area Hospital
715 Delmore Dr, Roseau MN 56751-1534. 218/463-2500.

Shriner's Hospital for Children
2025 East River Road, Minneapolis MN 55414-3604. 612/335-5300.

Sioux Valley Hospital
PO Box 577, New Ulm MN 56073-0577. 507/354-2111.

Sister Kenny Institute
800 E 28th St, Minneapolis MN 55407-3723. 612/863-4457.

St. Elizabeth Hospital of Wabasha
1200 5th Grant Boulevard, Wabasha MN 55981-1042. 651/565-4531.

St. Francis Medical Center & Home
415 Oak Street, Breckenridge MN 56520-1242. 218/643-7501.

St. Francis Regional Medical Center
1455 Saint Francis Ave, Shakopee MN 55379-3374. 612/403-3000.

St. James Health Services
PO Box 460, St. James MN 56081-0460. 507/375-3261.

St. John's Hospital
1575 Beam Ave, Maplewood MN 55109-1126. 651/232-7000.

St. Joseph's Hospital
600 Pleasant Avenue South, Park Rapids MN 56470-1432. 218/732-3311.

St. Luke's Hospital of Duluth
915 E 1st St, Duluth MN 55805-2107. 218/726-5555.

St. Mary's Medical Center
407 E 3rd St, Duluth MN 55805-1950. 218/726-4000.

St. Mary's Regional Health Center
1027 Washington Ave, Detroit Lakes MN 56501-3409. 218/847-5611.

St. Michael's Hospital
425 Elm Street North, Sauk Centre MN 56378-1010. 320/352-2221.

Tri County Hospital Inc.
415 Jefferson Street North, Wadena MN 56482-1264. 218/631-3510.

United Hospital District
PO Box 160, Blue Earth MN 56013-0160. 507/526-3273.

University Medical Center-Mesabi
750 E 34th St, Hibbing MN 55746-2341. 218/262-4881.

University of Minnesota Hospital & Clinic
PO Box 59160, Minneapolis MN 55459-0160. 612/626-3000.

Veterans Affairs Medical Center
1 Veterans Dr, Minneapolis MN 55417-2300. 612/725-2000.

Veterans Affairs Medical Center
4801 8th St N, St. Cloud MN 56303-2015. 320/252-1670.

Virginia Regional Medical Center
901 9th St N, Virginia MN 55792-2325. 218/741-3340.

White Community Hospital
5211 Highway 110, Aurora MN 55705-1522. 218/229-2211.

Willmar Regional Treatment Center
PO Box 1128, Willmar MN 56201-1128. 320/231-5100.

Worthington Regional Hospital
PO Box 997, Worthington MN 56187-0997. 507/372-2941.

Zumbrota Health Care
383 W 5th St, Zumbrota MN 55992-1656. 507/732-5131.

MEDICAL EQUIPMENT

Authorized Hearing Systems
161 Cheshire Ln, Suite 500, Plymouth MN 55441-5465. 612/949-6690.

Avecor Cardiovascular Inc.
7611 Northland Dr N, Minneapolis MN 55428-1088. 612/391-9000.

Bio-Vascular Inc.
2575 University Avenue West, St. Paul MN 55114-1073. 651/603-3700.

Caire Inc.
3505 County Road 42 W, Burnsville MN 55306-3803. 612/882-5000.

Data Sciences International
4211 Lexington Ave N,

Shoreview MN 55126-6164. 651/481-7410.

DBL Labs Inc.
PO Box 280, St. Joseph MN 56374-0280. 320/363-7211.

GN Danavox Inc.
5600 Rowland Rd, Ste 250, Hopkins MN 55343-4315. 612/930-0416.

Hutchinson Tape Manufacturing
905 Highway 22 S, Hutchinson MN 55350-2900. 320/234-4000.

Lake Region Manufacturing Co.
340 Lake Hazeltine Dr, Chaska MN 55318-1034. 612/448-5111.

Medtronic Bio-Medicus Inc.
8299 Central Ave NE, Fridley MN 55432-2023. 612/944-7784.

Medtronic Milaca
PO Box 129, Milaca MN 56353-0129. 320/983-2531.

Microvena Corporation
1861 Buerkle Rd, White Bear Lake MN 55110-5246. 651/777-6700.

Mytee-Lite
230 Eva St, St. Paul MN 55107-1605. 651/291-1400.

Omega Group
PO Box 1288, St. Cloud MN 56302-1288. 320/251-8591.

Pentax Vision Inc.
PO Box 2300, Hopkins MN 55343-2523. 612/935-7716.

Possis Medical Inc.
9055 Evergreen Blvd NW, Coon Rapids MN 55433-5833. 612/780-4555.

Rochester Medical Corporation
1 Rochester Medical Dr NW, Stewartville MN 55976-1647. 507/533-9600.

Starkey Laboratories Inc.
2915 10th St E, Glencoe MN 55336-3325. 320/864-6106.

Technicoat USA
PO Box 1264, St. Cloud MN 56302-1264. 320/255-9787.

Twin City Optical Company
PO Box 267, Minneapolis MN 55440-0267. 612/551-2000.

Urologix Inc.
14405 21st Avenue North, Plymouth MN 55447-4640. 612/475-1400.

MEDICAL EQUIPMENT AND SUPPLIES WHOLESALE

Colwell Systems
1031 Mendota Heights Rd, Mendota Heights MN 55120-1419. 651/686-1600.

GE Medical Systems
5610 Rowland Rd, Ste 160, Hopkins MN 55343-8920. 612/930-5550.

Micro-Tech
PO Box 59124, Minneapolis MN 55459-0124. 612/934-3001.

Sonar Hearing Health
3130 Lexington Ave S, St. Paul MN 55121-2239. 612/405-6443.

NURSING AND PERSONAL CARE FACILITIES

Aicota Healthcare Center
850 2nd St NW, Aitkin MN 56431. 218/927-2164.

Ambassador Good Samaritan Health
8100 Medicine Lake Rd, Minneapolis MN 55427-3404. 612/544-4171.

Apple Valley Health Care Center
14650 Garrett Avenue, Apple Valley MN 55124-7543. 612/431-7700.

Arlington Good Samaritan Center
PO Box 645, Arlington MN 55307-0645. 507/964-2251.

Arrowhead Health Care Center
PO Box 440, Eveleth MN 55734-0440. 218/744-2550.

Arrowhead Health Care Center
PO Box 971, Virginia MN 55792-0971. 218/741-4590.

Ashwood Health Care Center
500 Russell St, Willmar MN 56201-2583. 320/235-3181.

Assumption Home Inc.
715 1st St N, Cold Spring MN 56320-1401. 320/685-3693.

Auburn Manor
501 N Oak St, Chaska MN 55318-2072. 612/448-9303.

Bethany Good Samaritan Village
804 Wright St, Brainerd MN 56401-4441. 218/829-1407.

Bethany Home
1020 Lark St, Alexandria MN 56308-2219. 320/762-1567.

Bethel Care Center
420 Marshall Ave, St. Paul MN 55102-1718. 651/224-2368.

Bethesda Heritage Center
1012 E Third St, Willmar MN 56201. 320/235-9532.

Bethesda Lutheran Care Center
724 19th Ave N, St. Paul MN 55107. 651/232-6000.

Birchwood Health Care Center
604 1st St NE, Forest Lake MN 55025-1202. 651/464-5600.

Bloomington Care Center
9200 Nicollet Ave, Minneapolis MN 55420-3714. 612/881-8676.

Bryn Mawr Health Care Center
275 Penn Ave N, Minneapolis MN 55405-1216. 612/377-4723.

Burns Manor Nursing Home
135 N High Dr NE, Hutchinson MN 55350-1248. 320/587-4919.

Burr Oak Manor
PO Box 429, Austin MN 55912-0429. 507/433-7391.

Cambridge Health Care Center
548 1st Ave W, Cambridge MN 55008-1020. 612/689-2323.

Cedar Pines Nursing Home
3720 23rd Avenue S, Minneapolis MN 55407-3010. 612/724-5495.

Cedarview Nursing Home
1409 S Cedar Ave, Owatonna MN 55060-3919. 507/451-7240.

Central Care Center
1828 Central Ave NE, Minneapolis MN 55418-4541. 612/781-3118.

Central Todd County Care Center
PO Box 38, Clarissa MN 56440-0038. 218/756-3636.

Chosen Valley Care Center Inc.
1102 Liberty St SE, Chatfield MN 55923-1448. 507/867-4220.

Christian Nursing Center
1801 Willmar Ave SW, Willmar MN 56201-2882. 320/235-0050.

City Lakes Transitional Care Center
110 E 18th St, Minneapolis MN 55403-3794. 612/879-2871.

Clarkfield Care Center
805 5th St, Clarkfield MN 56223. 320/669-7561.

Cokato Manor
182 Sunset Avenur North, Cokato MN 55321-9620. 320/286-2158.

Colonial Acres Health Care Center
5825 Saint Croix Avenue N, Crystal MN 55422-4419. 612/544-1555.

Country Manor Health Care
PO Box 120, Sartell MN 56377-0120. 320/253-1920.

Daytons Bluff Community Care Center
324 Johnson Parkway, St. Paul MN 55106-6412. 651/774-9737.

Delano Healthcare Center
433 County Road 30, Delano MN 55328-9000. 612/972-2987.

Ebenezer Hall
2545 Portland Ave S, Minneapolis MN 55404-4406. 612/879-2262.

Edgebrook Rest Center
PO Box 152, Edgerton MN 56128-0152. 507/442-7121.

Elder Care Nursing Service
2025 Nicollet Ave, Ste 201, Minneapolis MN 55404-2552. 612/871-8805.

Extendicare Facilities Incorporated
7505 Country Club Dr, Minneapolis MN 55427-4501. 612/545-0416.

Falls Care Center
1402 Highway 71, International MN 56649-2154. 218/283-4768.

Faribault Manor
1738 Hulett Ave, Faribault MN 55021-2918. 507/334-3918.

Foley Nursing Center
253 Pine St, Foley MN 56329-9000. 320/968-6201.

Frazee Care Center
PO Box 96, Frazee MN 56544-0096. 218/334-4501.

Glenwood Retirement Village
719 2nd St SE, Glenwood MN 56334-1810. 320/634-5131.

Golden Age Health Care Center
1415 County Road B W, Roseville MN 55113-4216. 651/631-1616.

Golden Crest Health Care Center
2413 1st Ave, Hibbing MN 55746-2101. 218/262-1081.

Good Samaritan Center
700 County Rd 14, Albert Lea MN 56007. 507/373-0684.

Good Samaritan Nursing Center
1414 20th St NW, East Grand Forks MN 56721-1042. 218/773-8912.

Good Samaritan Village
PO Box 59, Mountain Lake MN 56159-0059. 507/427-2464.

Green Acres Country Care Center
PO Box 550, North Branch MN 55056-0550. 651/674-7068.

Guardian Angel Health Care Services
400 Evans Ave, Elk River MN 55330-2604. 612/441-1213.

Harry Meyering Center Inc.
PO Box 302, Mankato MN 56002-0302. 507/387-8281.

Haven Homes Health Center
930 16th St W, Hastings MN 55033-3335. 651/437-6176.

Heritage Health Care Center
3420 Heritage Dr, Minneapolis MN 55435-2261. 612/920-9145.

Heritage Manor Health Care Center
321 6th St NE, Chisholm MN 55719-1287. 218/254-5765.

Highland Chateau Healthcare Center
2319 7th St W, St. Paul MN 55116-2813. 651/698-0793.
Highland Manor
405 N Highland Ave, New Ulm MN 56073-2067. 507/359-2026.

Hillcrest Health Care Center
Rural Route 9, Box 3, Mankato MN 56001-8252. 507/387-3491.

Hillcrest Healthcare Retirement Center
15409 Wayzata Blvd, Wayzata MN 55391-1402. 612/473-5466.

Homeward Bound Inc.
4741 Zealand Ave N, Minneapolis MN 55428-4533. 612/535-6171.

Hopkins Care Center
725 2nd Ave S, Hopkins MN 55343-7782. 612/935-3338.

Jackson Good Samaritan Center
601 West St, Jackson MN 56143-1200. 507/847-3100.

Johnson Memorial Health Services
1282 Walnut St, Dawson MN 56232-2333. 320/769-4323.

Jones-Harrison Residence
3700 Cedar Lake Ave,

Minneapolis MN 55416-4240. 612/920-2030.

Juhl Enterprises Inc.
100 Glenoaks Dr, New London MN 56273-9580. 320/354-2231.

Karlstad Memorial Nursing Center
PO Box B, Karlstad MN 56732. 218/436-2161.

La Crescent Healthcare Center
701 Main St, La Crescent MN 55947-1037. 507/895-4445.

Lake Ridge Health Care Center
2727 Victoria St N, St. Paul MN 55113-2040. 651/483-5431.

Lakeside Medical Center Inc.
129 6th Ave E, Pine City MN 55063-1913. 320/629-2542.

Lakeview Methodist Health Care Center
610 Summit Dr, Fairmont MN 56031-2235. 507/235-6606.

Langton Place
1910 County Road D W, St. Paul MN 55112-3503. 651/631-6200.

Leisure Hills Care Center
2801 S Pokegama Ave, Grand Rapids MN 55744-9552. 218/326-3431.

Leisure Hills Care Center
1500 3rd Ave E, Hibbing MN 55746-1462. 218/263-7583.

Lexington Health Center
375 Lexington Pkwy North, St. Paul MN 55104-4604. 651/645-0577.

Luther Haven
1109 E Highway 7, Montevideo MN 56265-1711. 320/269-6517.

Lutheran Care Center Inc.
PO Box 248, Little Falls MN 56345-0248. 320/632-9211.

Lyngblomsten Care Center Inc.
1415 Almond Ave, St. Paul MN 55108-2507. 651/646-2941.

Mahnomen Health Center
PO Box 396, Mahnomen MN 56557-0396. 218/935-2423.

Mala Strana Nursing Home
1001 Columbus Ave N, New Prague MN 56071-2008. 612/758-2511.

Mankato House Health Care
700 James Ave, Mankato MN 56001-4090. 507/345-4631.

Marian Center of St. Paul
200 Earl St, St. Paul MN 55106-6714. 651/771-2914.

Marshall Manor Good Samaritan Center
410 S McKinley St, Warren MN 56762-1433. 218/745-5282.

Martin Luther Manor
1401 E 100th St, Minneapolis MN 55425-2615. 612/888-7751.

Minneota Manor
700 N Monroe St, Minneota MN 56264-9237. 507/872-5300.

Moorhead Health Care Center
2810 2nd Ave N, Moorhead MN 56560-2508. 218/233-7578.

Mount Olivet Careview Home
5517 Lyndale Ave S, Minneapolis MN 55419-1719. 612/827-5677.

New Harmony Care Center
135 Geranium Ave E, St. Paul MN 55117-5007. 651/488-6658.

Nicollet Health Care Center
4429 Nicollet Ave, Minneapolis MN 55409-2034. 612/827-5667.

Norhaven Inc.
1821 University Ave, W1, St. Paul MN 55104-2801. 651/488-6296.

North Ridge Care Center Inc.
5430 Boone Avenue N, Minneapolis MN 55428-3615. 612/536-7000.

North Shore Hospital & Care Center
PO Box 10, Grand Marais MN 55604-0010. 218/387-3040.

Oaklawn Health Care Center
201 Oaklawn Ave, Mankato MN 56001-4729. 507/388-2913.

Olivia Healthcare Center
PO Box 229, Olivia MN 56277-0229. 320/523-1652.

Osseo Care Center
525 2nd St SE, Osseo MN 55369-1603. 612/425-2128.

Owatonna Health Care Center
201 18th St SW, Owatonna MN 55060-3913. 507/451-6800.

Park Nursing & Convalescent Center
3704 Kipling Ave, Minneapolis MN 55416-4820. 612/927-4949.

Park Point Manor
1601 Saint Louis Ave, Duluth MN 55802-2442. 218/727-8651.

Park View Care Center Inc.
200 Park Ln, Buffalo MN 55313-1336. 612/475-1305.

Pine Haven Care Center
210 3rd St NW, Pine Island MN
55963-9139. 507/356-8304.

Pioneer Memorial Care Center
Rural Route 2, Box 148, Erskine
MN 56535-9349. 218/687-2365.

**Pipestone Good Samaritan
Village**
1311 N Hiawatha Avenue,
Pipestone MN 56164-2200.
507/825-5428.

Presbyterian Homes
10030 Newton Ave S,
Bloomington MN 55431-2939.
612/948-3000.

Presbyterian Homes
4497 Shoreline Dr, Maple Plain
MN 55359. 612/471-6000.

Red Wing Health Center
1412 W 4th St, Red Wing MN
55066-2107. 651/388-2843.

Riverside Health Care Center
1712 Hopkins, Hopkins MN
55305-2029. 612/591-1200.

Rose Camilia Company
11800 Xeon Blvd NW,
Minneapolis MN 55448-2061.
612/755-8400.

Rose of Sharon Manor
1000 Lovell Ave, Roseville MN
55113-4419. 651/484-3378.

Sacred Heart Care Center
1200 12th St SW, Austin MN
55912-2619. 507/433-1808.

Saint Anne Hospice Inc.
1347 W Broadway St, Winona
MN 55987-2327. 507/454-3621.

Samaritan Bethany Heights
24 8th St NW, Rochester MN
55901-6817. 507/289-4031.

Shakopee Friendship Manor
1340 3rd Ave W, Shakopee MN
55379-1011. 612/445-4155.

Sholom Home East Inc.
1554 Midway Pkwy, St. Paul MN
55108-2425. 651/646-6311.

Sholom Home West Inc.
3620 Phillips Pkwy, St. Louis
Park MN 55426-3700. 612/935-
6311.

Sleepy Eye Care Center
1105 3rd Ave SW, Sleepy Eye
MN 56085-1857. 507/794-7995.

**Sogge Memorial Good
Samaritan Center**
705 6th St, Windom MN 56101-
1814. 507/831-1788.

**Southview Acres Health Care
Center**
2000 Oakdale Ave, St. Paul MN
55118-4662. 651/451-1821.

St. Anthony Health Center
3700 Foss Rd, Minneapolis MN
55421-4512. 612/788-9673.

St. John Lutheran Home
710 Walnut St, Springfield MN
56087-1100. 507/723-6251.

St. Joseph's Home for Children
1121 E 46th St, Minneapolis MN
55407-3562. 612/827-6241.

St. Lucas Care Center
500 1st St SE, Faribault MN
55021-6346. 507/332-5100.

**St. Luke's Lutheran Care
Center**
1219 S Ramsey St, Blue Earth
MN 56013-2227. 507/526-2184.

St. Mary's Home
1925 Norfolk Ave, St. Paul MN
55116-2667. 651/696-8400.

St. Mary's Villa Inc.
PO Box 397, Pierz MN 56364-
0397. 320/468-6405.

St. Otto's Care Center
920 4th St SE, Little Falls MN
56345-3540. 320/632-9281.

St. Paul's Church Home Inc.
484 Ashland Ave, St. Paul MN
55102-2006. 651/227-8351.

St. Paul's Home
330 Exchange St S, St. Paul MN
55102-2311. 651/227-0336.

Stewartville Care Center
120 4th St NE, Stewartville MN
55976-1212. 507/533-4288.

Stillwater Maple Manor
1119 Owens St N, Stillwater MN
55082-4316. 651/439-7180.

**Summit Manor Health Care
Center**
80 Western Avenue North, St.
Paul MN 55102-2033. 651/227-
8988.

Sunwood Care Center
200 DeKalb St, Redwood Falls
MN 56283. 507/637-5711.

Talahi Care Center
1717 Michigan Avenue SE, St.
Cloud MN 56304-2023. 320/251-
9120.

**Terrace Heights Assisted Living
Apartments**
410 W Main St, Osakis MN
56360-8243. 320/859-2111.

**Thorne Crest Retirement
Center**
1201 Garfield Ave, Albert Lea
MN 56007-3639. 507/373-2311.

Three Links Care Center
815 Forest Ave, Northfield MN
55057-1643. 507/645-6611.

Trevilla of Robbinsdale Inc.
3130 Grimes Avenue North,
Crystal MN 55422-3217.
612/588-0771.

Unicare
445 Galtier St, St. Paul MN
55103-2329. 651/224-1848.

University Health Care Center
22 27th Avenue Southeast,
Minneapolis MN 55414-3102.
612/332-4262.

Valleyview Health Care Center
4061 W 173rd St, Jordan MN
55352-9380. 612/492-6160.

Viewcrest Health Center
3111 Church Pl, Duluth MN
55811-2925. 218/727-8801.

Villa St. Vincent Inc.
516 Walsh St, Crookston MN
56716-2750. 218/281-3424.

**Waconia Good Samaritan
Center**
333 W 5th St, Waconia MN
55387-1720. 612/442-5111.

**Walker Methodist Health
Center**
3737 Bryant Avenue South,
Minneapolis MN 55409-1019.
612/827-5931.

Watkins Home
PO Box 127, Winona MN 55987-
0127. 507/454-4670.

**Wedgewood Health Care
Center**
2060 Upper 55th St E, South St.
Paul MN 55077-1725. 651/451-
1881.

Westwood Health Care Center
7500 West 22nd Street, St. Louis
Park MN 55426-2602. 612/546-
4261.

**Whispering Pines Good
Samaritan Village**
PO Box 29, Pine River MN
56474-0029. 218/587-4423.

Whittier Health Center
321 East 25th Street, Minneapolis
MN 55404-3602. 612/874-1701.

Woodbury Health Care Center
7012 Lake Rd, Woodbury MN
55125-2433. 651/735-6000.

**OFFICES AND CLINICS OF
HEALTH PRACTITIONERS**

Bridge Rehabilitation
4002 London Rd, Duluth MN
55804-2243. 218/525-8299.

Symphony Rehabilitation
13911 Ridgedale Dr, Hopkins
MN 55305-1771. 612/546-5411.

Woodland Centers
PO Box 787, Willmar MN 56201-
0787. 320/235-4613.

RESIDENTIAL CARE

Andrew Home Care
1215 S 9th St, Minneapolis MN
55404-1710. 612/333-0111.

Berkshire Residence
501 2nd St SE, Maple Grove MN
55369-1603. 612/425-3939.

Chris Jensen Nursing Home
2501 Rice Lake Rd, Duluth MN
55811-4819. 218/720-1500.

**Clara City Community Nursing
Home**
PO Box 797, Clara City MN
56222-0797. 320/847-2221.

Crest View Lutheran Home
4444 Reservoir Blvd,
Minneapolis MN 55421-3255.
612/782-1611.

Ebenezer Covenant Home
310 Lake Blvd S, Buffalo MN
55313-1442. 612/682-1434.

Elders Home Inc.
PO Box 188, New York Mills
MN 56567-0188. 218/385-2005.

Elim Nursing Home
101 7th Ave S, Princeton MN
55371-1700. 612/389-1171.

Emmanuel Nursing Home
1415 Madison Ave, Detroit Lakes
MN 56501-4542. 218/847-4486.

Episcopal Church Home Inc.
1879 Feronia Ave, St. Paul MN
55104-3549. 651/646-4061.

Eventide Lutheran Home
1405 7th St S, Moorhead MN
56560-3444. 218/233-7508.

Fair Meadow Nursing Home
PO Box 8, Fertile MN 56540-
0008. 218/945-6194.

Fairview Nursing Home
PO Box 10, Dodge Center MN
55927-0010. 507/374-2578.

Field Crest Nursing Home
PO Box 6A, Hayfield MN 55940-
0006. 507/477-3266.

**Fountain Lake Treatment
Center**
408 Fountain St, Albert Lea MN
56007. 507/373-2384.

Francis Residence
563 Payne Ave, St. Paul MN
55101-4536. 651/771-3578.

Fridley Convalescent Home
7590 Lyric Ln NE, Fridley MN
55432-3251. 612/786-7700.

Golden Oaks Nursing Home
1025 9th Ave S, South St. Paul
MN 55075-3106. 651/455-6615.

Good Shepard Home
PO Box 747, Rushford MN
55971-0747. 507/864-7714.

Grace Home
PO Box 157, Graceville MN
56240-0157. 320/748-7223.

Grandview Christian Home
800 2nd Ave NW, Cambridge
MN 55008-1034. 612/689-1474.

Hammer Residences Inc.
1909 Wayzata Blvd, Wayzata
MN 55391-2047. 612/473-1261,

Haven Homes of Maple Plain
1520 Wyman Ave, Maple Plain
MN 55359-9639. 612/479-1993.

Homestead Nursing Home
1002 Comstock Dr, Deer River
MN 56636-9700. 218/246-2900.

**John Wimmer Memorial
Nursing Home**
405 2nd Ave E, Ada MN 56510-
1103. 218/784-4994.

Lake City Nursing Home
405 W Grant St, Lake City MN
55041-1145. 651/345-5366.

Lake City Nursing Home
205 W Center St, Lake City MN
55041-1609. 651/345-5383.

Lake Shore Inn Nursing Home
108 8th St NW, Waseca MN
56093-1912. 507/835-2800.

Lakeshore Lutheran Home
4002 London Rd, Duluth MN
55804-2243. 218/525-1951.

Lutheran Home Inc.
611 W Main St, Belle Plaine MN
56011-1221. 612/873-2215.

**Lutheran Memorial Nursing
Home**
PO Box 480, Twin Valley MN
56584-0480. 218/584-5181.

Lutheran Retirement Home
Rural Route 3, Box 78, Truman
MN 56088-9804. 507/776-2031.

Madison Lutheran Home Corp.
900 2nd Ave, Madison MN
56256-1006. 320/598-7536.

Minnesota Masonic Home
11501 Masonic Home Dr,
Minneapolis MN 55437-3661.
612/881-8665.

Minnesota Veterans Home
5101 Minnehaha Ave,
Minneapolis MN 55417-1647.
612/721-0600.

Minnesota Veterans Home
45 Banks Blvd, Silver Bay MN
55614-1337. 218/226-6300.

Nelson Knute Memorial Home
420 12th Ave E, Alexandria MN
56308-2612. 320/763-6653.

**Northern Lights Community
Residence**
120 Labree Ave S, Thief River
Falls MN 56701-2819. 218/681-
4240.

Phoenix Residence Inc.
135 Colorado St E, St. Paul MN
55107-2244. 651/227-7655.

Pioneer Retirement Community
1006 S Sheridan Street, Fergus
Falls MN 56537-3518. 218/739-
3361.

Pleasant Manor Nursing Home
PO Box 446, Faribault MN
55021-0446. 507/334-3558.

Prairie Manor Nursing Home
220 3rd St NW, Blooming Prairie
MN 55917-1121. 507/583-4434.

Ramsey Nursing Home
2000 White Bear Ave N,
Maplewood MN 55109-3713.
651/777-7486.

Redeemer Residence Inc.
625 West 31st Street,
Minneapolis MN 55408-2922.
612/827-2555.

REM-Buffalo Inc.
6921 York Ave South,
Minneapolis MN 55435-2517.
612/925-5067.

REM-Southwest Services Inc.
112 N Bruce St, Marshall MN
56258-3902. 507/532-5310.

**Sanford Memorial Nursing
Home**
3410 21st St W, Farmington MN
55024. 612/463-7825.

Shady Lane Nursing Home
Rural Route 2, Box 12BB,
Wadena MN 56482-9214.
218/631-1391.

St. Ann's Supervised Living
Services
1218 Edmund Ave, St. Paul MN
55104-2522. 651/649-0671.

St. Cloud Children's Home
1726 7th Ave S, St. Cloud MN
56301-5711. 320/251-8811.

St. John Lutheran Nursing
Home
901 Luther Pl, Albert Lea MN
56007-1562. 507/373-8226.

St. Olaf Residence Inc.
2912 Fremont Ave N,

Minneapolis MN 55411-1313.
612/522-6561.

Villa St. Francis Nursing
Home
1001 Scotts Ave, Morris MN
56267-1799. 320/589-1133.

SPECIALTY OUTPATIENT
FACILITIES

Life Care Centers of America
1513 Main Street, Eden Prairie
MN 55343-7406. 612/938-4496.

Life Care Centers of America
34 Moreland Avenue East, St.
Paul MN 55118-2416. 651/457-
1195.

Life Care Centers of America
3649 Chicago Avenue,
Minneapolis MN 55407-2603.
612/823-0301.

Polinsky Memorial
Rehabilitation Center
530 E 2nd St, Duluth MN 55805-
1913. 218/725-5300.

For more information on career opportunities in the health care industry:

Associations

ACCREDITING COMMISSION ON
EDUCATION FOR HEALTH SERVICES
ADMINISTRATION
1911 North Fort Myer Drive, Suite 503, Arlington VA
22209. 202/822-8561.

AMBULATORY INFORMATION
MANAGEMENT ASSOCIATION
BAY VALLEY MEDICAL GROUP
27212 Calaroga Avenue, Hayward CA 94545.
510/293-5688. World Wide Web address: http://www.
aim4.org. E-mail address: info@aim4.org.

AMERICAN ACADEMY OF ALLERGY,
ASTHMA, AND IMMUNOLOGY
611 East Wells Street, Milwaukee WI 53202.
414/272-6071. World Wide Web address: http://www.
aaaai.org.

AMERICAN ACADEMY OF FAMILY
PHYSICIANS
8880 Ward Parkway, Kansas City MO 64114.
816/333-9700. World Wide Web address: http://www.
aafp.org. Promotes continuing education for family
physicians.

AMERICAN ACADEMY OF PEDIATRIC
DENTISTRY
211 East Chicago Avenue, Suite 700, Chicago IL
60611-2616. 312/337-2169. World Wide Web
address: http://www.aapd.org.

AMERICAN ACADEMY OF
PERIODONTOLOGY
737 North Michigan Avenue, Suite 800, Chicago IL
60611-2690. 312/573-3218. World Wide Web
address: http://www.perio.org.

AMERICAN ACADEMY OF PHYSICIAN
ASSISTANTS
950 North Washington Street, Alexandria VA 22314-
1552. 703/836-2272. World Wide Web address:
http://www.aapa.org. Promotes the use of physician
assistants.

AMERICAN ASSOCIATION FOR CLINICAL
CHEMISTRY
2101 L Street NW, Suite 202, Washington DC 20037-
1526. 202/857-0717. World Wide Web address:
http://www.aacc.org. A nonprofit association for
clinical, chemical, medical, and technical doctors.

AMERICAN ASSOCIATION FOR
RESPIRATORY CARE
11030 Ables Lane, Dallas TX 75229-4593. 972/243-
2272. World Wide Web address: http://www.aarc.org.
Promotes the art and science of respiratory care, while
focusing on the needs of the patients.

AMERICAN ASSOCIATION OF COLLEGES OF
OSTEOPATHIC MEDICINE
5550 Friendship Boulevard, Suite 310, Chevy Chase
MD 20815. 301/968-4100. World Wide Web address:
http://www.aacom.org. Provides application
processing services for colleges of osteopathic
medicine.

AMERICAN ASSOCIATION OF COLLEGES OF
PODIATRIC MEDICINE
1350 Piccard Drive, Suite 322, Rockville MD 20850.
301/990-7400. World Wide Web address: http://www.
aacpm.org. Provides applications processing services
for colleges of podiatric medicine.

AMERICAN ASSOCIATION OF DENTAL
SCHOOLS
1625 Massachusetts Avenue NW, Suite 600,
Washington DC 20036-2212. 202/667-9433. Fax:
202/667-0642. E-mail address: aads@aads.jhu.edu.
World Wide Web address: http://www.aads.jhu.edu.
Represents all 54 of the dental schools in the U.S. as
well as individual members. This organization works
to expand postdoctoral training and increase the
number of women and minorities in the dental field.

AMERICAN ASSOCIATION OF HEALTHCARE
CONSULTANTS
11208 Waples Mill Road, Suite 109, Fairfax VA
22030. 703/691-2242. World Wide Web address:
http://www.aahc.net.

AMERICAN ASSOCIATION OF HOMES AND
SERVICES FOR THE AGING
901 E Street NW, Suite 500, Washington DC 20004.
202/783-2242. World Wide Web address: http://www.
aahsa.org.

AMERICAN ASSOCIATION OF MEDICAL
ASSISTANTS
20 North Wacker Drive, Suite 1575, Chicago IL
60606. 312/899-1500. World Wide Web address:
http://www.aama-ntl.org.

AMERICAN ASSOCIATION OF NURSE
ANESTHETISTS
222 South Prospect Avenue, Park Ridge IL 60068-

4001. 847/692-7050. World Wide Web address:
http://www.aana.com

**AMERICAN ASSOCIATION OF ORAL AND
MAXILLOFACIAL SURGEONS**
9700 West Bryn Mawr Avenue, Rosemont IL 60018-
5701. 847/678-6200. World Wide Web address:
http://www.aaoms.org.

AMERICAN CHIROPRACTIC ASSOCIATION
1701 Clarendon Boulevard, Arlington VA 22209.
703/276-8800. World Wide Web address: http://www.
amerchiro.org. A national, nonprofit professional
membership organization offering educational
services (through films, booklets, texts, and kits),
regional seminars and workshops, and major health
and education activities that provide information on
public health, safety, physical fitness, and disease
prevention.

**AMERICAN COLLEGE OF HEALTH CARE
ADMINISTRATORS**
325 South Patrick Street, Alexandria VA 22314.
703/739-7900. World Wide Web address: http://www.
achca.org. A professional membership society for
individual long-term care professionals. Sponsors
educational programs, supports research, and
produces a number of publications.

**AMERICAN COLLEGE OF HEALTHCARE
EXECUTIVES**
One North Franklin Street, Suite 1700, Chicago IL
60606-3491. 312/424-2800. World Wide Web
address: http://www.ache.org. Offers credentialing
and educational programs. Publishes *Hospital &
Health Services Administration* (a journal), and
Healthcare Executive (a magazine).

**AMERICAN COLLEGE OF MEDICAL
PRACTICE EXECUTIVES**
104 Inverness Terrace East, Englewood CO 80112-
5306. 303/799-1111. World Wide Web address:
http://www.mgma.com/acmpe.

**AMERICAN COLLEGE OF OBSTETRICIANS
AND GYNECOLOGISTS**
409 12th Street SW, P.O. Box 96920, Washington DC
20090-6920. World Wide Web address: http://www.
acog.org.

**AMERICAN COLLEGE OF PHYSICIAN
EXECUTIVES**
4890 West Kennedy Boulevard, Suite 200, Tampa FL
33609-2575. 813/287-2000. Fax: 813/287-8993.
World Wide Web address: http://www.acpe.org.

AMERICAN DENTAL ASSOCIATION
211 East Chicago Avenue, Chicago IL 60611.
312/440-2500. World Wide Web address: http://www.
ada.org.
**AMERICAN DENTAL HYGIENISTS'
ASSOCIATION**
444 North Michigan Avenue, Suite 3400, Chicago IL
60611. 312/440-8900. World Wide Web address:
http://www.adha.org.

AMERICAN DIETETIC ASSOCIATION
216 West Jackson Boulevard, Suite 800, Chicago IL
60606-6995. 312/899-0040. Toll-free phone: 800/877-
1600. Promotes optimal nutrition to improve public
health and well-being.

**AMERICAN HEALTH INFORMATION
MANAGEMENT ASSOCIATION**
919 North Michigan Avenue, Suite 1400, Chicago IL

60611. 312/787-2672. World Wide Web address:
http://www.ahima.org.

AMERICAN HOSPITAL ASSOCIATION
One North Franklin Street, Chicago IL 60606.
312/422-3000. World Wide Web address: http://www.
aha.org.

AMERICAN MEDICAL ASSOCIATION
515 North State Street, Chicago IL 60610. 312/464-
5000. World Wide Web address: http://www.ama-
assn.org. An organization for medical doctors.

**AMERICAN MEDICAL INFORMATICS
ASSOCIATION**
4915 St. Elmo Avenue, Suite 401, Bethesda MD
20814. 301/657-1291. World Wide Web address:
http://www.amia.org.

AMERICAN MEDICAL TECHNOLOGISTS
710 Higgins Road, Park Ridge IL 60068. 847/823-
5169. World Wide Web address: http://www.amt1.
com.

**AMERICAN MEDICAL WOMEN'S
ASSOCIATION**
801 North Fairfax Street, Suite 400, Alexandria VA
22314. 703/838-0500. Fax: 703/549-3864. E-mail
address: info@amwa-doc.org. World Wide Web
address: http://www.amwa-doc.org. Supports the
advancement of women in medicine.

AMERICAN NURSES ASSOCIATION
600 Maryland Avenue SW, Suite 100W, Washington
DC 20024-2571. 202/554-4444. World Wide Web
address: http://www.nursingworld.org.

**AMERICAN OCCUPATIONAL THERAPY
ASSOCIATION**
4720 Montgomery Lane, P.O. Box 31220, Bethesda
MD 20824-1220. 301/652-2682. Toll-free phone:
800/377-8555. Fax: 301/652-7711. World Wide Web
address: http://www.aota.org.

AMERICAN OPTOMETRIC ASSOCIATION
243 North Lindbergh Boulevard, St. Louis MO 63141.
314/991-4100. Offers publications, discounts, and
insurance programs for members.

**AMERICAN ORGANIZATION OF NURSE
EXECUTIVES**
One North Franklin Street, 34th Floor, Chicago IL
60606. 312/422-2800. World Wide Web address:
http://www.aone.org.

AMERICAN ORTHOPAEDIC ASSOCIATION
6300 North River Road, Suite 300, Rosemont IL
60018. 847/318-7330. World Wide Web address:
http://www.aoassn.org.

**AMERICAN PHYSICAL THERAPY
ASSOCIATION**
111 North Fairfax Street, Alexandria VA 22314.
703/684-2782. World Wide Web address: http://www.
apta.org. Small fee required for information.

**AMERICAN PODIATRIC MEDICAL
ASSOCIATION**
9312 Old Georgetown Road, Bethesda MD 20814-
1698. 301/571-9200. World Wide Web address:
http://www.apma.org.

AMERICAN PSYCHIATRIC ASSOCIATION
World Wide Web address: http://www.psych.org.

Professional association for mental health professionals.

AMERICAN PUBLIC HEALTH ASSOCIATION
1015 15th Street NW, Suite 300, Washington DC 20005. 202/789-5600. World Wide Web address: http://www.apha.org.

AMERICAN SOCIETY OF ANESTHESIOLOGISTS
520 North NW Highway, Park Ridge IL 60068. 847/825-5586. World Wide Web address: http://www.asahq.org.

AMERICAN SPEECH-LANGUAGE-HEARING ASSOCIATION
10801 Rockville Pike, Rockville MD 20852. Toll-free phone: 800/498-2071. World Wide Web address: http://www.asha.org. Professional, scientific, and credentialing association for audiologists, speech-language pathologists, and speech, language, and hearing, scientists.

AMERICAN SUBACUTE CARE ASSOCIATION
1720 Kennedy Causeway, Suite 109, North Bay Village FL 33141. 305/864-0396. World Wide Web address: http://members.aol.com/ascamail/index.htm.

AMERICAN VETERINARY MEDICAL ASSOCIATION
1931 North Meacham Road, Suite 100, Schaumburg IL 60173-4360. 847/925-8070. World Wide Web address: http://www.avma.org. American Veterinary Medical Association provides a forum for the discussion of important issues in the veterinary profession.

ASSOCIATION OF AMERICAN MEDICAL COLLEGES
2450 N Street NW, Washington DC 20037-1126. 202/828-0400. World Wide Web address: http://www.aamc.org.

ASSOCIATION OF MENTAL HEALTH ADMINISTRATORS
60 Revere Drive, Suite 500, Northbrook IL 60062. 847/480-9626.

ASSOCIATION OF UNIVERSITY PROGRAMS IN HEALTH ADMINISTRATION
1110 Vermont Avenue NW, Suite 220, Washington DC 20005. 202/822-8550.

BAYER QUALITY NETWORK
4700 West Lake Avenue, Glenview IL 60025. Toll-free phone: 888/BAYERNET. World Wide Web address: http://www.bayerquality.org. Bayer Quality Network is a cooperative educational forum for health care professionals.

HEALTH CARE INFORMATION AND MANAGEMENT SYSTEMS SOCIETY
230 East Ohio Street, Suite 500, Chicago IL 60611. 312/664-4467. World Wide Web address: http://www.himss.org.

HEALTHCARE FINANCIAL MANAGEMENT ASSOCIATION
2 Westbrook Corporate Center, Suite 700, Westchester IL 60154. 708/531-9600. World Wide Web address: http://www.hfma.org.

NATIONAL ASSOCIATION FOR CHIROPRACTIC MEDICINE
15427 Baybrook Drive, Houston TX 77062. 281/280-8262. World Wide Web address: http://www.chiromed.org.

NATIONAL COALITION OF HISPANIC HEALTH AND HUMAN SERVICES ORGANIZATIONS
1501 16th Street NW, Washington DC 20036. 202/387-5000. World Wide Web address: http://www.cossmho.org. Strives to improve the health and well-being of Hispanic communities throughout the United States.

NATIONAL HOSPICE ORGANIZATION
1901 North Moore Street, Suite 901, Arlington VA 22209. 703/243-5900. World Wide Web address: http://www.nho.org. Educates and advocates for the principles of hospice care to meet the needs of the terminally ill.

NATIONAL MEDICAL ASSOCIATION
1012 10th Street NW, Washington DC 20001. 202/347-1895. World Wide Web address: http://www.nmanet.org.

Magazines

AMERICAN MEDICAL NEWS
American Medical Association, P.O. Box 10945, Chicago IL 60610. 312/670-7827.

HEALTHCARE EXECUTIVE
American College of Health Care Executives, One North Franklin Street, Suite 1700, Chicago IL 60606-3491. 312/424-2800.

MODERN HEALTHCARE
Crain Communications, 740 North Rush Street, Chicago IL 60611. 312/649-5350. World Wide Web address: http://www.modernhealthcare.com.

NURSEFAX
Springhouse Corporation, 1111 Bethlehem Pike, Springhouse PA 19477. 215/646-8700. World Wide Web address: http://www.springnet.com. This is a jobline service designed to be used in conjunction with *Nursing* magazine. Please call to obtain a copy of a magazine or the *Nursing* directory.

Online Services

AMIA/MEDSIG
Go: MedSIG. A CompuServe forum for health care professionals to discuss and exchange information about topics in medicine.

ACADEMIC PHYSICIAN AND SCIENTIST
Gopher://aps.acad-phy-sci.com. A great resource for jobseekers interested in administrative or clinical positions at teaching hospitals.

HEALTH CARE JOBS ONLINE JOB BULLETIN BOARD
http://www.hcjobsonline.com. This Website is for jobseekers who are looking for job opportunities in the health care industry. This site is maintained by Images, Ink.

MEDSEARCH AMERICA
http://www.medsearch.com. Site geared for medical professionals. Medsearch America offers national and international job searches, career forums, a resume builder, resume posting, recruiters' sites, listings of professional associations, and employer profiles. Over 4,000 job openings are posted on Medsearch America.

MEDZILLA
E-mail address: info@medzilla.com. World Wide
Web address: http://www.medzilla.com. Lists job
openings for professionals in the fields of
biotechnology, health care, medicine, and science
related industries.

NURSING NETWORK FORUM
Go: Custom 261. A CompuServe bulletin board for
nurses that provides periodic "live" discussions with
special guests.

**SALUDOS WEB CAREER GUIDE: HEALTH
CARE**
http://www.saludos.com/cguide/hcguide.html.
Provides information for jobseekers looking in the
health care field. The site includes links to several
health care associations and other sites that are
sources of job openings in health care. This site is run
by Saludos Hispanos.

HOTELS AND RESTAURANTS

Employment in the hotel and restaurant industry increased from 1.66 million workers in 1993 to 1.85 million workers in 1998. Hotels are doing considerable business with a shortage of lodging facilities and a relatively strong economy. However, some areas, such as Las Vegas, have actually seen occupancy rates decrease recently. Las Vegas is due to open $3 billion worth of new hotels, geared toward affluent travelers seeking a resort atmosphere. The city has seen the construction of more than 10,000 new rooms since 1997, resulting in supply outweighing demand. U.S. Industry and Trade Outlook 1998 *reports that numerous U.S. cities are banking on the success of business meetings and conventions and are making significant investments in new and expanded convention facilities.*

Jobs are plentiful for candidates with degrees in hotel and restaurant management. Both business and tourism travel are expected to increase, which may again increase the number of hotels. Hotel chains, like many other businesses, continue to consolidate, and there is an increase in the number of economy hotels offering clean, simple accommodations. These two factors combined may ultimately increase competition for hotel management positions, as fewer hotel managers will be needed.

According to a recent report by the National Restaurant Association, 44 percent of every dollar Americans spend on food goes toward dining out. Nine million people are employed in food services and that number is expected to climb to 11 million by 2005. According to Business Week, *Americans are starting to spend more on casual dining and prepared meals, and less at fast food restaurants. Other restaurant chains are seeing strong sales growth, such as Dunkin' Donuts, which expected 1998 sales to reach $200 million for its bagels alone.*

ARBY'S/FRANCHISE ASSOCIATES INC.
5354 Parkdale Drive, Suite 100, Minneapolis MN 55416. 612/593-4243. **Fax:** 612/546-8342. **Recorded jobline:** 612/593-4298. **Contact:** Jenny Taschner, Staffing and Communications Manager. **E-mail address:** fai.tasch@minn.net. **Description:** Operates a franchise of several national restaurant chains, specifically Arby's and Sbarro. **Common positions include:** Assistant Manager; District Manager; General Manager; Management Trainee. **Educational backgrounds include:** Business Administration; Communications; Education; Hospitality/Restaurant; Liberal Arts; Marketing; Psychology. **Benefits:** 401(k); Dental Insurance; Disability Coverage; Employee Discounts; Life Insurance; Medical Insurance; Profit Sharing; Savings Plan; Tuition Assistance. **Corporate headquarters location:** This Location. **Operations at this facility include:** Regional Headquarters.

BEST WESTERN EDGEWATER
2400 London Road, Duluth MN 55812. 218/728-3601. **Contact:** Human Resources. **Description:** A 282-room hotel.

BUFFETS, INC.
dba OLD COUNTRY BUFFET
10260 Viking Drive, Eden Prairie MN 55344. 612/942-9760. **Fax:** 612/903-1356. **Recorded jobline:** 800/388-6506. **Contact:** Tricia Muetzel, Benefits Coordinator. **World Wide Web address:** http://www.buffet.com. **Description:** Operates a chain of high-volume, full-service, buffet-style restaurants. **Common positions include:** Cashier; Chef/Cook/Kitchen Worker; Computer Operator; Computer Programmer; Construction Trade Worker; Draftsperson; Food and

Beverage Service Worker; Management Trainee; Payroll Clerk; Restaurant/Food Service Manager; Secretary; Systems Analyst. **Benefits:** Disability Coverage; Employee Discounts; Life Insurance; Medical Insurance; Profit Sharing; Tuition Assistance. **Corporate headquarters location:** This Location. **Other U.S. locations:** Nationwide. **Operations at this facility include:** Administration. **Listed on:** NASDAQ. **Number of employees at this location:** 150. **Number of employees nationwide:** 16,000.

CARLSON COMPANIES, INC.
CARLSON MARKETING GROUP
P.O. Box 59159, Minneapolis MN 55459-8246. 612/540-5000. **Contact:** Vern Lovstad, Human Resources Department. **World Wide Web address:** http://www.carlson.com. **Description:** A highly diversified corporation doing business through a variety of subsidiaries. Business areas include hotels, restaurant operations, and retail and wholesale travel. Carlson Marketing Group (also at this location) provides a variety of marketing services for sporting events and airlines; incentive programs for employees of other companies; and strategic consulting to help client companies create customer/brand loyalty. **Corporate headquarters location:** This Location. **Number of employees nationwide:** 50,000.

DOUBLETREE GUEST SUITES HOTEL
1101 LaSalle Avenue, Minneapolis MN 55403. 612/332-6800. **Contact:** Human Resources Department. **World Wide Web address:** http://www.doubletree.com. **Description:** An all-suite hotel.

GENERAL MILLS, INC.
P.O. Box 1113, Minneapolis MN 55440. 612/540-2311. **Contact:** Jeanne Smith, Recruitment Department. **World Wide Web address:** http://www.genmills.com. **Description:** Produces and markets consumer foods. Food products include Cheerios, Wheaties, and Total cereals; Betty Crocker desserts, frostings, and baking mixes; Pop Secret microwave popcorn; Gorton's frozen seafood; Yoplait yogurt; Bisquik pancake mix; and Gold Medal flour. General Mills is also engaged in the full-service dinnerhouse restaurant business, operating over 1,000 company-owned Red Lobster and Olive Garden restaurants in North America. Founded in 1928. **Common positions include:** Chemical Engineer; Food Scientist/Technologist; Mechanical Engineer. **Educational backgrounds include:** Accounting; Chemistry; Computer Science; Engineering; Finance; Food Science; Marketing; MBA. **Corporate headquarters location:** This Location. **Other U.S. locations:** Scottsdale AZ; West Chicago IL; Buffalo NY. **Operations at this facility include:** Administration; Research and Development. **Listed on:** New York Stock Exchange. **Number of employees nationwide:** 121,300.

HOLIDAY INN HOTEL & SUITES
200 West First Street, Duluth MN 55802. 218/722-1202x2203. **Fax:** 218/722-0233. **Contact:** Cheryl Dunbar, Personnel Director. **World Wide Web address:** http://www.duluth.com/holidayinn. **Description:** A full-service, 353-room hotel with convention/meeting space and three restaurants. **NOTE:** Entry-level positions, part-time jobs, and second and third shifts are offered. **Common positions include:** Account Representative; Advertising Executive; Auditor; General Manager; Human Resources Manager; Marketing Specialist; Operations Manager; Sales Executive; Sales Manager; Sales Representative. **Educational backgrounds include:** Accounting; Marketing. **Benefits:** 401(k); Employee Discounts; Flexible Schedule; Job Sharing; Life Insurance; Medical Insurance; Pension Plan; Sick Days (10). **Special programs:** Internships; Summer Jobs. **Annual sales/revenues:** Less than $5 million. **Number of employees at this location:** 240.

HYATT REGENCY MINNEAPOLIS
1300 Nicollet Mall, Minneapolis MN 55403. 612/370-1234. **Fax:** 612/370-1463. **Recorded jobline:** 612/370-1202. **Contact:** Employment Manager. **World Wide Web address:** http://www.hyatt.com. **Description:** A downtown hotel with over 500 rooms and suites. Hotel restaurants include Spike's Sports Bar and Grille, and Taxxi, an American bistro. **Common positions include:** Blue-Collar Worker Supervisor; Customer Service Representative; Management Trainee. **Educational backgrounds include:** Business Administration; Hotel Administration. **Benefits:** 401(k); Dental Insurance; Employee Discounts; Life Insurance; Medical Insurance; Savings Plan; Tuition Assistance. **Special programs:** Internships. **Corporate headquarters location:** Chicago IL. **Other U.S. locations:** Nationwide. **Parent company:** Hyatt Hotels Corporation. **Operations at this facility include:** Administration; Sales; Service. **Listed on:** Privately held. **Number of employees at this location:** 335. **Number of employees nationwide:** 40,000.

INTERNATIONAL DAIRY QUEEN INC.
P.O. Box 39286, Minneapolis MN 55439-0286. 612/830-0200. **Physical address:** 7505 Metro Boulevard, Edina MN. **Contact:** Human Resources. **World Wide Web address:** http://www.

dairyqueen.com. **Description:** A restaurant chain specializing in burgers and ice cream. International Dairy Queen operates 11 regional offices. **Benefits:** 401(k); Dental Insurance; Disability Coverage; Life Insurance; Medical Insurance. **Corporate headquarters location:** This Location. **Subsidiaries include:** Karmelkorn Shoppes, Inc.; Orange Julius of America. **Listed on:** NASDAQ. **Number of employees at this location:** 330. **Number of employees nationwide:** 2,450.

LAKES GAMING
130 Cheshire Lane, Minnetonka MN 55305. 612/449-9092. **Contact:** Human Resources Department. **Description:** Lakes Gaming is a casino entertainment company that develops, constructs, and manages land-based and dockside casinos. The company owns and operates Grand Casino Gulfport, which is one of the largest dockside casinos on the Mississippi Gulf Coast, and Grand Casino Biloxi. The company manages Grand Casino Mille Lacs and Grand Casino Hinckley, which are land-based Native American-owned casinos in Minnesota. The company also has entered into agreements to develop, construct, and manage two land-based, Native American-owned casinos in Louisiana and one land-based, Native American-owned gaming facility in Southern California.

MARQUETTE HOTEL
710 Marquette Avenue, Minneapolis MN 55402. 612/332-2351. **Contact:** Ms. Darcy Paul, Personnel Manager. **Description:** A 280-room hotel.

MARRIOTT CITY CENTER HOTEL
30 South Seventh Street, Minneapolis MN 55402. 612/349-4000. **Contact:** Susan Miller, Human Resources Director. **World Wide Web address:** http://www.marriott.com. **Description:** A 31-floor glass tower hotel, linked to the city's skyway system.

MINNEAPOLIS HILTON & TOWERS
1001 Marquette Avenue, Minneapolis MN 55403. 612/397-4807. **Contact:** Wendi Brockhoff, Director of Human Resources. **Description:** An 814-room convention hotel with both full-service and fine dining restaurants. **Common positions include:** Assistant Manager; Customer Service Representative; Guest Services Agent; Restaurant/Food Service Manager. **Educational backgrounds include:** Business Administration. **Benefits:** Dental Insurance; Employee Discounts; Life Insurance; Medical Insurance; Pension Plan; Tuition Assistance. **Special programs:** Internships. **Corporate headquarters location:** Beverly Hills CA. **Other U.S. locations:** Nationwide. **Operations at this facility include:** Administration; Sales; Service. **Number of employees at this location:** 600.

1 POTATO 2, INC.
7000 Bass Lake Road, Suite 200, Crystal MN 55428. 612/537-3833. **Fax:** 612/537-4241. **Contact:** Bob Durand, Vice President of Operations. **World Wide Web address:** http://www.1potato2.com. **Description:** This location houses administrative offices. Overall, 1 Potato 2 operates a chain of restaurants located in shopping mall food courts. **NOTE:** Opportunities include assistance programs for qualified corporate personnel. **Common positions include:** Chef/Cook/Kitchen Worker; Department Manager; District Manager; Restaurant/Food Service Manager. **Benefits:** Franchise Program; Life Insurance; Medical Insurance; Tuition Assistance. **Corporate headquarters location:** This Location. **Number of employees at this location:** 11. **Number of employees nationwide:** 600.

RADISSON HOTEL
505 West Superior Street, Duluth MN 55802. 218/727-8981. **Contact:** Human Resources. **World Wide Web address:** http://www.radisson.com. **Description:** A 268-room hotel.

SIGNATURE DINING
6300 Penn Avenue South, Richfield MN 55423. 612/866-0041. **Contact:** Human Resources Manager. **Description:** This location houses administrative offices. Overall, Signature Dining provides vending machine and cafeteria services. **Educational backgrounds include:** Food Services. **Benefits:** Medical Insurance; Savings Plan. **Corporate headquarters location:** This Location. **Operations at this facility include:** Administration; Sales; Service.

SOFITEL HOTEL
5601 West 78th Street, Bloomington MN 55439. 612/835-1900x7437. **Contact:** Jeanne Bursche, Human Resources Director. **World Wide Web address:** http://www.sofitel.com. **Description:** The first North American location of the French hotel chain, offering 282 rooms.

Note: Because addresses and telephone numbers of smaller companies can change rapidly, we recommend you call each company to verify the information below before inquiring about job opportunities. Mass mailings are not recommended.

Additional small employers:

DRINKING PLACES

First Avenue Night Club
PO Box 2126, Minneapolis MN
55402-0126. 612/338-8388.

EATING PLACES

Al Baker's
3434 Washington Dr, Eagan MN
55122-1303. 612/454-9000.

Applebee's
1335 Town Centre Dr, St. Paul
MN 55123-2309. 651/686-7022.

Applebee's
1018 Meadowlands Drive, St.
Paul MN 55127-2321. 651/429-
9789.

Applebee's
590 West 79th Street, Chanhassen
MN 55317-9563. 612/949-9190.

Applebee's
1900 Adams St, Mankato MN
56001-6802. 507/386-1010.

Applebee's
4190 West Division Street, St.
Cloud MN 56301-3706. 320/251-
8686.

Bella Vita Ristorante
21 4th Ave W, Duluth MN
55802. 218/722-2211.

**Benchwarmer Bob's Sports
Cafe**
251 W Burnsville Pkwy,
Burnsville MN 55337-2510.
612/895-0800.

**Benchwarmer Bob's Sports
Cafe**
8078 Brooklyn Boulevard,
Minneapolis MN 55445-2407.
612/493-2979.

Bennigan's
1800 West 80th Street,
Bloomington MN 55431-1327.
612/881-0013.

**Blackwood Family Grill and
Bar**
612 7th Ave, Two Harbors MN
55616-1454. 218/834-3846.

Bloomington Park Tavern
5221 Viking Dr, Minneapolis MN
55435-5305. 612/844-0335.

California Cafe Bar & Grille
368 South Boulevard,
Minneapolis MN 55425. 612/854-
2233.

Champp's
790 West 66th Street,
Minneapolis MN 55423-2203.
612/861-3333.

Champp's
2401 7th St W, St. Paul MN
55116-2839. 651/698-5050.

Champp's
1734 Adolphus St, St. Paul MN
55117-2303. 651/487-5050.

Champp's
100 North 6th Street,
Minneapolis MN 55403-1505.
612/335-5050.

Chi-Chi's
7717 Nicollet Avenue,
Minneapolis MN 55423-4235.
612/866-3433.

Chili's Grill & Bar
3625 Pilot Knob Rd, Eagan MN
55122-1316. 651/686-5152.

Chili's Grill & Bar
5245 Wayzata Boulevard,
Minneapolis MN 55416-1323.
612/546-7777.

Chili's Grill & Bar
1800 Beam Avenue,
Maplewood MN 55109-1162.
651/773-9501.

Chili's Grill & Bar
4000 Vinewood Ln N,
Minneapolis MN 55442-1733.
612/557-7000.

Chili's Grill & Bar
1840 County Road B2 W,
Roseville MN 55113-2706.
651/633-7718.

Ciatti's
1611 Larpenteur Ave W,
Roseville MN 55113-5702.
651/644-2808.

Cossetta's Italian Deli
211 7th St W, St. Paul MN
55102-2520. 651/222-3476.

Dairy Queen
3574 Shoreline Dr, Wayzata MN
55391-9782. 612/471-7845.

Dakota Cafe
Rural Route 1, Box 420, Morton
MN 56270-9801. 507/644-3000.

Dixie's Bar & Grill
695 Grand Ave, St. Paul MN
55105-3422. 651/222-7345.

Domino's Pizza
PO Box 514, Willernie MN
55090-0514. 651/429-4252.

Domino's Pizza
PO Box 3583, Mankato MN
56002-3583. 507/345-8696.

Emma Krumbee's Restaurant
501 E South St, Belle Plaine MN
56011-2153. 612/873-4334.

Famous Dave's BBQ & Blues
3001 Hennepin Ave, Minneapolis
MN 55408-2647. 612/822-9900.

Figlio
3001 Hennepin Ave, Minneapolis
MN 55408-2647. 612/822-1688.

Freight House Restaurant
305 Water St S, Stillwater MN
55082-5144. 651/439-5718.

Gators
402 E Broadway, Minneapolis
MN 55425-5515. 612/858-8888.

Grandma's Saloon & Deli Inc.
4301 W 80th St, Minneapolis MN
55437-1121. 612/897-0533.

Grandma's Saloon & Grill
522 S Lake Ave, Duluth MN
55802-2310. 218/727-5971.

Grandma's Sports Garden
425 S Lake Ave, Duluth MN
55802-2307. 218/722-4722.

Green Mill Inn
PO Box 608, Brainerd MN
56401-0608. 218/829-1441.

Green Mill Inn
6025 Hudson Rd, Woodbury MN
55125-1005. 651/735-1000.

Green Mill Inn
1342 Grand Ave, St. Paul MN
55105-2203. 651/690-1946.

Green Mill Inn
2705 Annapolis Ln N, Plymouth
MN 55441-3605. 612/553-9000.

Green Mill Inn
2626 Hennepin Ave, Minneapolis
MN 55408-1149. 612/374-2131.

Green Mill Inn
PO Box 1066, St. Cloud MN
56302-1066. 320/259-6455.

Hardee's
819 30th Ave S, Moorhead MN
56560-5005. 218/236-6604.

Hubbell House Inc.
PO Box 98, Mantorville MN
55955-0098. 507/635-2331.

Joe Sensor's Sports Grill & Bar
2350 Cleveland Avenue N,
Roseville MN 55113-2701.
651/631-1781.

K&J Catering Inc.
2546 7th Avenue East,
Maplewood MN 55109-3010.
651/641-0514.

Kozlak's Royal Oak Restaurant
4785 Hodgson Rd, Shoreview
MN 55126-6014. 651/484-8484.

Lincoln del South
4401 West 80th Street,
Minneapolis MN 55437-1122.
612/831-0780.

McCormick's Restaurant
615 Washington Ave SE,
Minneapolis MN 55414-2931.
612/379-8888.

McDonald's
9516 Garfield Ave, Minneapolis
MN 55420-4213. 612/881-8010.

McDonald's
415 Nicollet Mall, Minneapolis
MN 55401-1928. 612/332-5968.

Michael's Restaurant Inc.
15 S Broadway, Rochester MN
55904-3705. 507/288-2020.

Old Country Buffet
14150 Nicollet Ave, Burnsville
MN 55337-5726. 612/435-5831.

Olive Garden
5235 Wayzata Blvd, Minneapolis
MN 55416-1323. 612/544-4423.

Olive Garden
1601 James Cir N, Brooklyn
Center MN 55430-1700. 612/560-
2801.

Olive Garden
1451 County Road 42 W,
Burnsville MN 55306-6200.
612/898-4200.

Olive Garden
150 Coon Rapids Blvd NW,
Coon Rapids MN 55433-5811.
612/786-1089.

Olive Garden
1749 Beam Ave, Maplewood MN
55109-1128. 651/773-0200.

Olive Garden
4701 W 80th St, Minneapolis MN
55437-1125. 612/831-4044.

Olive Garden
1525 County Road C W,
Roseville MN 55113-3103.
651/638-9557.

Palomino
825 Hennepin Ave, Ste 825,
Minneapolis MN 55402-1802.
612/339-3800.

Panino's North Oaks
857 Village Center Dr, St. Paul
MN 55127-3016. 651/486-0296.

Papa John's
5151 Edina Industrial Blvd,
Minneapolis MN 55439-3013.
612/835-7220.

Planet Hollywood
402 S Avenue, Minneapolis MN
55425-5528. 612/854-7827.

Premium Restaurant Company
1625 Queens Dr, Woodbury MN
55125-1559. 651/735-0000.

Prom Catering Company
190 Smith Ave N, St. Paul MN
55102-2535. 651/291-0059.

Red Lobster
1301 County Rd 42, Burnsville
MN 55306. 612/435-2552.

Red Lobster
2925 White Bear Ave N,
Maplewood MN 55109-1314.
651/770-8825.

Red Lobster
2330 Prior Ave N, Roseville MN
55113-2715. 651/636-9800.

Rudolph's Barbecue Inc.
1933 Lyndale Ave S,
Minneapolis MN 55403-3104.
612/871-8855.

Ruttle's of Mankato Inc.
PO Box 3328, Mankato MN
56002-3328. 507/345-4571.

Shorewood Inn
6161 Highway 65 NE, Fridley
MN 55432-5105. 612/571-3444.

South Beach Bar & Grill
323 1st Avenue N 325,
Minneapolis MN 55401-1609.
612/204-0790.

Sunsets on Wayzata Bay Inc.
700 Lake St E, Wayzata MN
55391-1713. 612/473-5253.

Taher Food Services
5570 Smetana Dr, Hopkins MN
55343-9022. 612/945-0505.

Tequilaberry's
133 Coon Rapids Blvd NW,
Coon Rapids MN 55433-5812.
612/780-1850.

TGI Friday's
7730 Normandale Blvd,
Minneapolis MN 55439-3139.
612/831-6553.

TGI Friday's
2480 Fairview Ave N, Roseville
MN 55113-2623. 651/631-1101.

TGI Friday's
5875 Wayzata Blvd, Minneapolis
MN 55416-1202. 612/544-0675.

Tillie's Restaurant
7801 Normandale Blvd,
Minneapolis MN 55435-5304.
612/831-1201.

Tucci Benucch
W-114 W Market, Minneapolis
MN 55425. 612/853-0200.

Village Inn
3600 Hoffman Rd, White Bear
Lake MN 55110-4630. 651/770-
8670.

HOTELS AND MOTELS

Best Western Apache
1517 16th St SW, Rochester MN
55902-1075. 507/289-8866.

**Best Western Country Manor
Inn**
2007 Highway 71 N, Jackson MN
56143-1096. 507/847-3110.

Best Western Garden Inn
1111 Range St, Mankato MN
56003-2214. 507/625-9333.

Best Western Marshall Inn
1500 East College Drive,
Marshall MN 56258-2602.
507/532-3221.

Best Western Northwest
6900 Lakeland Ave N,
Minneapolis MN 55428-1615.
612/566-8855.

**Best Western Red River Inn
LLP**
600 30th Avenue South,
Moorhead MN 56560-4924.
218/233-6171.

Black Bear Casino
1720 Big Lake Rd, Cloquet MN
55720-9702. 218/879-4593.

Crowne Plaza Northstar Hotel
618 2nd Ave S, Minneapolis MN
55402-1901. 612/338-2288.

Days Inn
1901 Killebrew Dr, Minneapolis
MN 55425-1890. 612/854-8400.

Days Inn Minneapolis West
2955 Empire Lane North,
Plymouth MN 55447-5316.
612/559-2400.

Doubletree
2800 West 80th Street,
Bloomington MN 55431-1205.
612/884-4811.

Embassy Suites
425 S 7th St, Ste 8, Minneapolis
MN 55415-1856. 612/333-3111.

Embassy Suites
7901 34th Avenue South,
Minneapolis MN 55425-1605.
612/854-1000.

Embassy Suites
175 10th St E, St. Paul MN
55101-2352. 651/224-5400.

Firefly Creek Casino
PO Box 96, Granite Falls MN
56241-0096. 320/564-2121.

Fond-Du-Luth Gaming Casino
129 E Superior St, Duluth MN
55802-2127. 218/722-0280.

**Fortune Bay Casino Resort
Center**
1430 Bois Forte Rd, Tower MN
55790-8111. 218/753-6400.

Grand Portage Lodge & Casino
PO Box 234, Grand Portage MN
55605-0234. 218/475-2441.

Holiday Inn
2200 Freeway Blvd, Brooklyn
Center MN 55430-1737. 612/566-
8000.

Holiday Inn
1701 4th St NW, Austin MN
55912-1803. 507/433-1000.

Holiday Inn
I-94 McKnight Rd, St. Paul MN
55119. 651/731-2220.

Holiday Inn
PO Box 1104, St. Cloud MN
56302-1104. 320/253-9000.

Holiday Inn Airport
5401 Greenvalley Dr,
Minneapolis MN 55437. 612/831-
8000.

**Holiday Inn Bloomington
Airport**
1201 West 94th St, Bloomington
MN 55431-2323. 612/884-8211.

Holiday Inn Downtown
PO Box 3386, Mankato MN
56002-3386. 507/345-1234.

Holiday Inn Metrodome
1500 Washington Avenue, Big
Lake MN 55309. 612/333-4646.

Holiday Inn of New Ulm
PO Box 597, New Ulm MN
56073-0597. 507/359-2941.

**Holiday Inn Select
International**
3 Appletree Square, Minneapolis
MN 55425-1635. 612/854-9000.

Holiday Inn South
PO Box 815, Rochester MN
55903-0815. 507/288-1844.

Hyatt-Whitney Hotel
150 Portland Avenue,
Minneapolis MN 55401-2531.
612/339-9300.

Minneapolis Airport Marriott
2020 East 79th Street,
Minneapolis MN 55425-1239.
612/854-7441.

**Minneapolis-St. Paul Airport
Hilton**
3800 E 80th St, Minneapolis MN
55425-1658. 612/854-2100.

Mystic Lake Casino
2400 Mystic Lake Blvd NW,
Prior Lake MN 55372-9004.
612/445-6000.

Northern Lights Casino
PO Box 1003, Walker MN
56484-1003. 218/547-2744.

Northland Inn
7000 Northland Drive North,
Minneapolis MN 55428-1502.
612/536-8300.

**Radisson Hotel & Conference
Center**
3131 Campus Drive, Plymouth
MN 55441-2620. 612/559-6600.

Radisson Hotel South
7800 Normandale Blvd,
Minneapolis MN 55439-3159.
612/835-7800.

Radisson Plaza Hotel
150 S Broadway, Rochester MN
55904-6507. 507/281-8000.

**Radisson Plaza Hotel
Minneapolis**
35 South Seventh Street,
Minneapolis MN 55402-1602.
612/339-4900.

Ramada Hotel St. Paul
1870 Old Hudson Rd, St. Paul
MN 55119-4307. 651/735-2330.

Red Wing Hotel Corporation
406 Main St, Red Wing MN
55066-2325. 651/388-2846.

Regal Minneapolis Hotel
1313 Nicollet Mall, Minneapolis
MN 55403-2668. 612/332-6000.

River Road Casino
Rural Route 3, Box 168A, Thief
River Falls MN 56701-9243.
218/681-4062.

Sawmill Inn
2301 S Pokegama Ave, Grand
Rapids MN 55744-9501.
218/326-8501.

Sheraton Airport Inn
2525 East 78th Street,
Bloomington MN 55431.
612/854-1771.

Sheraton Inn Midway
400 Hamline Avenue North, St.
Paul MN 55104-4004. 651/642-
1234.

**Sheraton Minneapolis
Metrodome**
1330 Industrial Blvd NE,
Minneapolis MN 55413-1703.
612/331-1900.

Shooting Star Casino
PO Box 418, Mahnomen MN
56557-0418. 218/935-2711.

The St. Paul Hotel
350 Market St, St. Paul MN
55102-1430. 651/292-9292.

Treasure Island Resort Casino
PO Box 75, Red Wing MN
55066-0075. 651/388-6300.

Wyndham Garden Hotel
4460 W 78th Street Cir,
Minneapolis MN 55435-5416.
612/831-3131.

For more information on career opportunities in hotels and restaurants:

Associations

**AMERICAN HOTEL AND MOTEL
ASSOCIATION**
1201 New York Avenue NW, Suite 600, Washington
DC 20005-3931. 202/289-3100. World Wide Web
address: http://www.ahma.com. Provides lobbying
services and educational programs, maintains and
disseminates industry data, and produces a variety of
publications.

**THE EDUCATIONAL FOUNDATION OF THE
NATIONAL RESTAURANT ASSOCIATION**
250 South Wacker Drive, Suite 1400, Chicago IL
60606. 312/715-1010. World Wide Web address:
http://www.edfound.org. The Educational Foundation
of the National Restaurant Association offers
educational products, including textbooks, manuals,
instruction guides, manager and employee training
programs, videos, and certification programs.

NATIONAL RESTAURANT ASSOCIATION
1200 17th Street NW, Washington DC 20036.
202/331-5900. World Wide Web address: http://www.
restaurant.org. Provides a number of services,
including government lobbying, communications,
research, and information, and operates the
Educational Foundation (see separate address).

Directories

**DIRECTORY OF CHAIN RESTAURANT
OPERATORS**
Lebhar-Friedman, Inc., 425 Park Avenue, New York
NY 10022. 212/756-5000. World Wide Web address:
http://www.lf.com.

**DIRECTORY OF HIGH-VOLUME
INDEPENDENT RESTAURANTS**
Lebhar-Friedman, Inc., 425 Park Avenue, New York
NY 10022. 212/756-5000. World Wide Web address:
http://www.lf.com.

Magazines

**CORNELL HOTEL AND RESTAURANT
ADMINISTRATION QUARTERLY**
Cornell University School of Hotel Administration,
Statler Hall, Ithaca NY 14853-6902. 607/255-9393.
World Wide Web address: http://www.cornell.edu.

HOSPITALITY WORLD
P.O. Box 84108, Seattle WA 98124. 206/362-7125.

NATION'S RESTAURANT NEWS
Lebhar-Friedman, Inc., 3922 Coconut Palm Drive,
Tampa FL 33619. 813/664-6700.

Online Services

COOLWORKS
http://www.coolworks.com. This Website provides
links to 22,000 job openings at resorts, summer
camps, ski areas, river areas, ranches, fishing areas,
and cruise ships. This site also includes information
on volunteer openings.

**HOSPITALITY NET VIRTUAL JOB
EXCHANGE**
http://www.hospitalitynet.nl/job. This site allows
jobseekers to search for job opportunities worldwide
in the hospitality industry including accounting, food
and beverage, marketing and sales, and conference
and banqueting positions. Jobseekers can also post
resume information and a description of the job they
want.

JOBNET: HOSPITALITY INDUSTRY
http://www.westga.edu:80/~coop/joblinks/subject/hos
pitality.html. This Website provides links to job
openings and information for hotels.

INSURANCE

 *Shaped by a changing marketplace of consolidation and competitive pressures, the insurance industry will face a tough year. The industry is highly competitive, and the U.S. Department of Labor forecasts slower than average growth for the industry through 2006. The added use of computers and databases allows more work to be done by fewer agents. Many opportunities will come as a result of people either retiring or switching professions.*

The industry did see a 14 percent rise in profits during the first six months of 1998 versus the same period of 1997, though profit margins were down. The continued drop in the unemployment rate will help this industry, as more people have more income and property which must be managed and insured. Health care and pension benefits, in relation to an aging population, will also require the services of insurance companies, as will the rise in the number of young drivers and their needs for automobile insurance.

ALLINA HEALTH SYSTEM
5601 Smetana Drive, Route 80310, Minnetonka MN 55343. 612/992-2900. **Contact:** Lynda Laskow, Director of Human Resources. **World Wide Web address:** http://www.allina.com. **Description:** A health insurance company.

AMERICAN HARDWARE INSURANCE GROUP
P.O. Box 435, Minneapolis MN 55440. 612/939-4615. **Physical address:** 5995 Opus Parkway, Minnetonka MN. **Toll-free phone:** 800/227-4663. **Fax:** 612/930-7348. **Recorded jobline:** 612/939-4545. **Contact:** Human Resources. **World Wide Web address:** http://www.youknowus. com. **Description:** A property and casualty insurance company. **Common positions include:** Insurance Agent/Broker; Underwriter/Assistant Underwriter. **Educational backgrounds include:** Business Administration; Marketing. **Benefits:** 401(k); Dental Insurance; Disability Coverage; Life Insurance; Medical Insurance; Pension Plan; Tuition Assistance. **Corporate headquarters location:** This Location. **Other U.S. locations:** Nationwide. **Number of employees at this location:** 200. **Number of employees nationwide:** 300.

AON CORPORATION
P.O. Box 1360, Wirth Park Center, Minneapolis MN 55440. 612/520-3000. **Contact:** Department of Human Resources. **World Wide Web address:** http://www.aon.com. **Description:** Aon Corporation is a holding company for insurance brokerage, consulting, and underwriting subsidiaries, which provide risk management solutions for commercial and industrial enterprises, insurance organizations, and individuals worldwide.

BERKLEY ADMINISTRATORS
P.O. Box 59143, Minneapolis MN 55459-0143. 612/544-0311. **Contact:** Human Resources Department. **Description:** Berkley Administrators provides third-party administration for workers' compensation policies.

FEDERATED INSURANCE
P.O. Box 328, Owatonna MN 55060. 507/455-5200. **Fax:** 507/455-5452. **Contact:** Luane Vanderberg, Employment Manager. **World Wide Web address:** http://www.federatedinsurance. com. **Description:** A multiline insurance company specializing in commercial business insurance for small and medium-sized companies. **Common positions include:** Actuary; Claim Representative; Computer Programmer; Underwriter/Assistant Underwriter. **Educational backgrounds include:** Business Administration; Computer Science; Finance; Liberal Arts; Marketing. **Benefits:** Dental Insurance; Disability Coverage; Life Insurance; Medical Insurance; Pension Plan; Savings Plan. **Corporate headquarters location:** This Location. **Other U.S. locations:** Phoenix AZ; Atlanta GA. **Annual sales/revenues:** More than $100 million. **Number of employees nationwide:** 2,700.

THE HARTFORD LIFE AND ANNUITY INSURANCE COMPANY
505 North Highway 169, Plymouth MN 55459. 612/595-4568. **Fax:** 612/595-4635. **Contact:** Human Resources. **World Wide Web address:** http://www.thehartford.com. **Description:** An individual life insurance firm. **Common positions include:** Accountant; Administrative Manager; Advertising Clerk; Attorney; Budget Analyst; Claim Representative; Clerical Supervisor; Computer Operator; Computer Programmer; Customer Service Representative; Financial Analyst; Human Resources Manager; Purchasing Agent/Manager; Secretary; Systems Analyst; Underwriter/Assistant Underwriter. **Educational backgrounds include:** Accounting; Business Administration; Communications; Computer Science; Finance; Liberal Arts; Marketing; Mathematics. **Benefits:** 401(k); Dental Insurance; Disability Coverage; Employee Discounts; Life Insurance; Medical Insurance; Pension Plan; Profit Sharing; Savings Plan; Tuition Assistance. **Corporate headquarters location:** Hartford CT. **Operations at this facility include:** Administration; Divisional Headquarters; Sales; Service. **Listed on:** American Stock Exchange; NASDAQ; New York Stock Exchange. **Number of employees at this location:** 400.

HEALTH RISK MANAGEMENT INC.
10900 Hampshire Avenue South, Bloomington MN 55438. 612/829-3500. **Fax:** 612/829-3664. **Recorded jobline:** 612/829-3695. **Contact:** Karen Davis, Staffing Specialist. **Description:** A medical review company whose operations include managing benefits and health care services for other companies. Founded in 1977. **NOTE:** Entry-level positions are offered. **Common positions include:** Claim Representative; Computer Operator; Computer Programmer; Customer Service Representative; Nurse Practitioner; Secretary; Software Engineer. **Educational backgrounds include:** Business Administration; Health Care; Liberal Arts. **Benefits:** 401(k); Dental Insurance; Employee Discounts; Flexible Schedule; Medical Insurance; Tuition Assistance. **Corporate headquarters location:** This Location. **Other U.S. locations:** Kalamazoo MI; Philadelphia PA; Milwaukee WI. **Subsidiaries include:** Institute for Healthcare Quality. **Listed on:** NASDAQ. **CEO:** Gary McIlroy. **Facilities Manager:** Bill Breening. **Annual sales/revenues:** $51 - $100 million. **Number of employees at this location:** 600. **Number of employees nationwide:** 1,000. **Number of projected hires for 1998 - 1999 at this location:** 100.

LIFEUSA INSURANCE COMPANY
LIFE USA HOLDING, INC.
P.O. Box 59060, Minneapolis MN 55459-0060. 612/546-7386. **Physical address:** 300 South Highway 169, Suite 95, Minneapolis MN. **Contact:** Owner Services. **Description:** LifeUSA Insurance Company provides life insurance and annuities. The company is licensed in all states except New York and contracts over 65,000 independent agents. **Corporate headquarters location:** This Location. **Parent company:** Other subsidiaries of Life USA Holding, Inc. (also at this location) include LifeUSA Marketing, Inc. and LifeUSA Securities, Inc. **Listed on:** NASDAQ. **Stock exchange symbol:** LUSA.

LUTHERAN BROTHERHOOD COMPANY
625 Fourth Avenue South, Minneapolis MN 55415. 612/340-7054. **Contact:** Gwen Martin, Manager of Staffing and Employee Relations. **World Wide Web address:** http://www.luthbro.com. **Description:** A financial institution providing life, health, and disability insurance, in addition to annuities and mutual funds. **Common positions include:** Actuary; Computer Programmer. **Educational backgrounds include:** Computer Science; Mathematics. **Benefits:** Dental Insurance; Disability Coverage; Life Insurance; Medical Insurance; Pension Plan; Tuition Assistance. **Corporate headquarters location:** This Location. **Operations at this facility include:** Administration; Research and Development; Service.

MIDWEST FAMILY MUTUAL INSURANCE COMPANY
P.O. Box 9425, Minneapolis MN 55440. 612/545-6000. **Contact:** Richard Habstritt, Vice President/Controller. **Description:** A multi-line insurance company.

OLD REPUBLIC NATIONAL TITLE INSURANCE COMPANY
400 Second Avenue South, Minneapolis MN 55401. 612/371-1111. **Fax:** 612/371-1133. **Contact:** Cheryl Jones, Senior Vice President of Corporate Personnel. **World Wide Web address:** http://www.oldrepnatl.com. **Description:** A title insurer. **Common positions include:** Accountant/Auditor; Attorney; Branch Manager; Computer Operator; Computer Programmer; Customer Service Representative; Department Manager; Employment Interviewer; General Manager; Human Resources Manager; Management Trainee; Order Clerk; Payroll Clerk; Property and Real Estate Manager; Receptionist; Services Sales Representative; Systems Analyst; Typist/Word Processor. **Educational backgrounds include:** Accounting; Business Administration; Communications; Finance; Marketing. **Benefits:** Daycare Assistance; Dental Insurance; Disability Coverage; Employee Discounts; Life Insurance; Medical Insurance; Pension Plan; Savings Plan;

Tuition Assistance. **Corporate headquarters location:** This Location. **Parent company:** Old Republic International Corporation. **Operations at this facility include:** Administration; Regional Headquarters; Sales. **Listed on:** New York Stock Exchange. **Number of employees at this location:** 350. **Number of employees nationwide:** 1,220.

RELIASTAR FINANCIAL CORPORATION
20 Washington Avenue South, Minneapolis MN 55401. 612/372-1178. **Fax:** 612/342-3066. **Contact:** Human Resources. **World Wide Web address:** http://www.reliastar.com. **Description:** An insurance and financial services company specializing in both group and individual lines of insurance. Founded in 1884. **NOTE:** Second and third shifts are offered. **Common positions include:** Accountant; Administrative Assistant; Auditor; Computer Operator; Computer Programmer; MIS Specialist; Sales Representative; Software Engineer; Systems Analyst; Underwriter/Assistant Underwriter. **Educational backgrounds include:** Accounting; Business Administration; Communications; Computer Science; Economics; Finance; Marketing; Software Development; Software Tech. Support. **Benefits:** 401(k); Daycare Assistance; Dental Insurance; Disability Coverage; Employee Discounts; Financial Planning Assistance; Flexible Schedule; Life Insurance; Medical Insurance; Pension Plan; Profit Sharing; Public Transit Available; Tuition Assistance. **Special programs:** Internships. **Corporate headquarters location:** This Location. **Other U.S. locations:** Nationwide. **Operations at this facility include:** Administration; Divisional Headquarters; Regional Headquarters; Sales; Service. **Listed on:** New York Stock Exchange. **Stock exchange symbol:** RLR. **Number of employees at this location:** 2,000. **Number of employees nationwide:** 4,000.

SENTRY INSURANCE
12400 Portland Avenue South, Suite 165, Burnsville MN 55337. 612/895-6600. **Contact:** Personnel. **Description:** An insurance company offering all types of insurance.

TITAN INDEMNITY COMPANY
P.O. Box 241029, Apple Valley MN 55124. 612/997-4900. **Contact:** Human Resources Department. **Description:** A property and casualty insurance company covering 45 states and the District of Columbia. **Parent company:** TITAN Holdings is a growing property and casualty insurance company that, through its subsidiaries, underwrites property and casualty insurance for small- and medium-sized cities, towns, counties, school districts, and other public entities. The company also underwrites private passenger, non-standard automobile insurance for individuals in Michigan. In addition to these operations, TITAN Holdings underwrites other specialty insurance programs including miscellaneous and contract surety. The company also has a premium financing subsidiary.

UNITEDHEALTH GROUP
P.O. Box 1459, Mail Routing 008-T150, Minneapolis MN 55440-1459. 612/936-1300. **Contact:** Human Resources. **World Wide Web address:** http://www.unitedhealthgroup.com. **Description:** A managed health care company with a nationwide network of owned/managed health plans and integrated specialty companies (pharmaceutical, mental health/substance abuse, and workers' compensation). **Benefits:** Dental Insurance; Disability Coverage; Life Insurance; Tuition Assistance. **Corporate headquarters location:** This Location.

Note: Because addresses and telephone numbers of smaller companies can change rapidly, we recommend you call each company to verify the information below before inquiring about job opportunities. Mass mailings are not recommended.

Additional small employers:

INSURANCE AGENTS, BROKERS, AND SERVICES

ABI Administrative Services Corp.
7701 York Ave S, Ste 200, Minneapolis MN 55435-5831. 612/830-3000.

ABI Administrative Services Corp.
10159 Wayzata Blvd, Hopkins MN 55305-1504. 612/541-0444.

American Family Insurance Co.
PO Box 1246, Minneapolis MN 55440-1246. 612/933-4884.

Chubb & Son Inc.
200 S 6th St, Ste 1000, Minneapolis MN 55402-1411. 612/373-7300.

Cigna
5500 Cenex Dr, Ste 100, South St. Paul MN 55077-1733. 651/455-1036.

Core Source
PO Box 1195, Minneapolis MN 55440-1195. 612/569-6400.

Fireman's Fund Insurance Company
PO Box 9431, Minneapolis MN 55440-9431. 612/546-8421.

J&H Marsh & McLennan Inc.
333 S 7th St, Ste 1600, Minneapolis MN 55402-2427. 612/692-7400.

Kemper Insurance Co.
PO Box 45, Minneapolis MN
55440-0045. 612/820-6100.

MII Life Inc.
PO Box 64193, St. Paul MN
55164-0193. 612/456-5065.

**Mutual Service Casualty
Insurance Co.**
2 Pine Tree Dr, St. Paul MN
55112-3715. 651/631-4891.

National Benefit Resources
5402 Parkdale Dr, Ste 300,
Minneapolis MN 55416-1604.
612/542-1144.

**Prudential Insurance Co. of
America Inc.**
PO Box 1143, Minneapolis MN
55440-1143. 612/557-4023.

**Prudential Preferred Financial
Services**
600 Hwy 169 S, Ste 1000, St.
Paul Park MN 55071. 612/544-
9533.

Prudential Select Brokerage
3033 Campus Dr, Plymouth MN
55441-2651. 612/553-6641.

**Rural Community Insurance
Services**
3501 Thurston Ave, Anoka MN
55303-1062. 612/427-0290.

**State Farm Mutual Auto
Insurance Co.**
8500 State Farm Way, Woodbury
MN 55125-4879. 651/578-4000.

United Healthcare Services Inc.
1902 Valley Pine Cir,
International MN 56649-2179.
218/285-7550.

INSURANCE COMPANIES

Aetna Health Plans
901 Marquette Avenue,
Minneapolis MN 55402-3205.
612/399-2500.

**American Enterprise Life
Insurance Co.**
PO Box 53434, Minneapolis MN
55440. 612/671-7700.

Araz Group Inc.
8500 Normandale Lake Blvd,
Minneapolis MN 55437-3813.
612/896-1200.

Austin Mutual Insurance Co.
10 2nd St NE, Minneapolis MN
55413-2269. 612/378-8600.

Blue Cross & Blue Shield
PO Box 64560, St. Paul MN
55164-0560. 612/456-8000.

Chicago Title Insurance Co.
222 S 9th St, Minneapolis MN
55402-3389. 612/885-2500.

Citizens Fund Insurance Co.
PO Box 3500, Red Wing MN
55066-3500. 651/388-7171.

**Equitable Life Assurance
Society**
8500 Normandale Lake Blvd,
Minneapolis MN 55437-3813.
612/844-0041.

EW Blanch Holdings Inc.
3500 W 80th St, Ste 700,
Bloomington MN 55431-4439.
612/835-3310.

Farmers Home Group
PO Box 9420, Minneapolis MN
55440-9420. 612/861-4511.

**Federated Insurance
Companies**
PO Box 39850, Minneapolis MN
55439-0850. 612/831-4300.

First Health EDP
435 Ford Rd, St. Louis Park MN
55426-1063. 612/546-4353.

Fortis Benefits Insurance Co.
PO Box 64271, St. Paul MN
55164-0271. 651/738-4000.

General Casualty Co.
11000 Prairie Lake Dr, Ste 300,
Eden Prairie MN 55344. 612/941-
0980.

HBO & Company
2700 Snelling Ave N, Roseville
MN 55113-1732. 651/697-5900.

John Alden Life Insurance Co.
PO Box 9398, Minneapolis MN
55440-9398. 612/544-2993.

**Minnesota Fire and Casualty
Co.**
PO Box 1233, Minneapolis MN
55440-1233. 612/939-7000.

**Minnesota Mutual Life
Insurance Co.**
400 Robert St N, St. Paul MN
55101-2015. 651/665-3500.

MSI Companies
PO Box 64035, St. Paul MN
55164-0035. 651/631-7000.

**North Star Mutual Insurance
Co.**
PO Box 48, Cottonwood MN
56229-0048. 507/423-6262.

Northland Insurance Company
PO Box 64816, St. Paul MN
55164-0816. 612/688-4100.

**St. Paul Fire & Marine
Insurance Co.**
3600 W 80th St, Bloomington
MN 55431-1084. 612/893-5602.

**St. Paul Fire & Marine
Insurance Co.**
385 Washington St, St. Paul MN
55102-1309. 651/221-7911.

**State Fund Mutual Insurance
Co.**
7500 Flying Cloud Dr, Eden
Prairie MN 55344-3748. 612/944-
3260.

Tri-State Insurance Co.
PO Box 142, Luverne MN 56156.
507/283-9561.

United Healthcare Services Inc.
325 S Lake Ave, Ste 400, Duluth
MN 55802-2323. 218/727-2001.

**Western National Mutual
Insurance Co.**
PO Box 1463, Minneapolis MN
55440-1463. 612/835-5350.

World Insurance Company
345 Saint Peter St, St. Paul MN
55102-1211. 651/222-2123.

For more information on career opportunities in insurance:

<u>Associations</u>

ALLIANCE OF AMERICAN INSURERS
3025 Highland Parkway, Suite 800, Downers Grove
IL 60515. 630/724-2100. World Wide Web address:
http://www.allianceai.org.

**HEALTH INSURANCE ASSOCIATION OF
AMERICA**
555 13th Street NW, Suite 600E, Washington DC
20004. 202/824-1600. World Wide Web address:
http://www.hiaa.org.

INSURANCE INFORMATION INSTITUTE
110 William Street, New York NY 10038. 212/669-
9200. World Wide Web address: http://www.iii.org.
Provides information on property/casualty insurance
issues.

**NATIONAL ASSOCIATION OF
PROFESSIONAL INSURANCE AGENTS**
400 North Washington Street, Alexandria VA 22314.
703/836-9340. World Wide Web address:
http://www.pianet.com.

SOCIETY OF ACTUARIES
475 North Martingale Road, Suite 800, Schaumburg IL 60173-2226. 847/706-3500. World Wide Web address: http://www.soa.org.

Directories

INSURANCE ALMANAC
Underwriter Printing and Publishing Company, 50 East Palisade Avenue, Englewood NJ 07631. 201/569-8808. Available at libraries.

INSURANCE PHONE BOOK
Reed Elsevier Inc., 121 Chanlon Road, New Providence NJ 07974. Toll-free phone: 800/521-8110. $89.95, new editions available every other year. Also available at libraries.

NATIONAL DIRECTORY OF HEALTH PLANS
American Association of Health Plans, 1129 20th Street NW, Suite 600, Washington DC 20036. 202/778-3200. World Wide Web address: http://www.aahp.org.

Magazines

BEST'S REVIEW
A.M. Best Company, Ambest Road, Oldwick NJ 08858. 908/439-2200. World Wide Web address: http://www.ambest.com. Monthly.

INSURANCE JOURNAL
Wells Publishing, 9191 Towne Centre Drive, Suite 550, San Diego, CA 92122-1231 619/455-7717. World Wide Web address: http://www.insurancejrnl. com. A biweekly magazine covering the insurance industry for the western U.S.

Online Services

FINANCIAL/ACCOUNTING/INSURANCE JOBS PAGE
http://www.nationjob.com/financial. This Website provides a list of financial, accounting, and insurance job openings.

THE INSURANCE CAREER CENTER
http://connectyou.com/talent. Offers job openings, career resources, and a resume database for jobseekers looking to get into the insurance field.

INSURANCE NATIONAL SEARCH
http://www.insurancerecruiters.com/insjobs/jobs.htm. Provides a searchable database of job openings in the insurance industry. The site is run by Insurance National Search, Inc.

LEGAL SERVICES

 *Prospective lawyers will continue to face intense competition through the year 2006, due to the overabundance of law school graduates. Consequently, fewer lawyers are working for major law firms, and are working instead for smaller firms, corporations, and associations, according to the U.S. Department of Commerce. Firms have reduced their support staffs, while large corporations are establishing in-house legal departments to avoid paying for the services of expensive, big-name law offices.*

According to the U.S. Department of Labor, paralegals comprise the fastest-growing profession in legal services, and will be one of the fastest-growing professions overall through 2006. Paralegals are assuming more responsibilities in areas such as real estate and trademark law. Private law firms will hire the most paralegals, but a vast array of other organizations also employ them including insurance companies, real estate firms, and banks. Legal secretaries will see moderate growth through 2006.

ARTHUR, CHAPMAN, KETTERING, SMETAK, PIKALA
500 Young Quinland Building, 81 South Ninth Street, Minneapolis MN 55402. 612/339-3500. **Contact:** Human Resources Manager. **Description:** A law firm specializing in insurance, liability, product liability, and workers' compensation cases. **Common positions include:** Attorney; Paralegal; Secretary. **Benefits:** Disability Coverage; Life Insurance; Medical Insurance; Profit Sharing.

BARNA, GUZY & STEFFEN LTD.
200 Coon Rapids Boulevard, 400 Northtown Financial Plaza, Minneapolis MN 55433. 612/780-8500. **Contact:** Heidi Burmif, Director of Personnel. **Description:** A law firm covering a variety of areas through its 25 attorneys.

BASSFORD, LOCKART, TRUESDALE & BRIGGS
3550 Multifoods Tower, 33 South Sixth Street, Minneapolis MN 55402. 612/333-3000. **Contact:** Shirley John, Human Resources. **Description:** A law firm specializing in litigation.

BRIGGS & MORGAN PROFESSIONAL ASSOCIATION
2200 West First National Bank Building, St. Paul MN 55101. 651/223-6600. **Fax:** 651/223-6450. **Contact:** Ellen Draysin, Director of Human Resources. **World Wide Web address:** http://www.briggs.com. **Description:** A professional legal services firm specializing in corporate law. **Common positions include:** Accountant/Auditor; Administrative Manager; Attorney; Computer Programmer; Human Resources Manager; Librarian; Library Technician; Paralegal; Systems Analyst. **Educational backgrounds include:** Accounting; Business Administration; Computer Science; Law/Pre-Law; Marketing. **Benefits:** 401(k); Dental Insurance; Disability Coverage; Employee Discounts; Life Insurance; Medical Insurance; Profit Sharing; Tuition Assistance. **Corporate headquarters location:** This Location. **Other U.S. locations:** Minneapolis MN. **Listed on:** Privately held. **Number of employees at this location:** 165. **Number of employees nationwide:** 330.

DORSEY WHITNEY
220 South Sixth Street, Pillsbury Center South, Minneapolis MN 55402. 612/340-2600. **Contact:** Joan Oyaff, Director of Human Resources. **World Wide Web address:** http://www.dorseylaw. com. **Description:** A large law firm specializing in a variety of areas.

FAEGRE & BENSON
2200 Norwest Center, 90 South Seventh Street, Minneapolis MN 55402. 612/336-3000. **Contact:** Director of Human Resources. **World Wide Web address:** http://www.faegre.com. **Description:** A corporate law firm.

FREDRIKSON & BYRON, P.A.
900 Second Avenue South, 1100 International Center, Minneapolis MN 55402. 612/347-7000. **Fax:** 612/347-7077. **Contact:** Personnel. **World Wide Web address:** http://www.fredlaw.com. **Description:** A business and trial law firm with 140 attorneys. **Common positions include:** Attorney. **Educational backgrounds include:** Law/Pre-Law. **Benefits:** Dental Insurance; Disability Coverage; Life Insurance; Medical Insurance; Pension Plan; Profit Sharing; Tuition Assistance. **Corporate headquarters location:** This Location. **Number of employees at this location:** 275.

HINSHAW & CULBERTSON
3100 Piper Jaffrey Tower, 222 South Ninth Street, Minneapolis MN 55402. 612/333-3434. **Contact:** Personnel. **Description:** A corporate law firm. **Common positions include:** Attorney. **Benefits:** Disability Coverage; Life Insurance; Medical Insurance; Pension Plan; Profit Sharing. **Other U.S. locations:** Denver CO; Washington DC; Miami FL.

KINNEY & LANGE, P.A.
312 South Third Street, Minneapolis MN 55415. 612/339-1863. **Contact:** Krista Boddie, Recruitment Coordinator. **Description:** A patent law firm. **Common positions include:** Attorney. **Educational backgrounds include:** Engineering; Law/Pre-Law. **Benefits:** 401(k); Dental Insurance; Disability Coverage; Life Insurance; Medical Insurance; Public Transit Available. **Corporate headquarters location:** This Location. **Operations at this facility include:** Legal/Legal Research. **Number of employees at this location:** 55.

LARKIN, HOFFMAN, DALY & LINDGREN
1500 Norwest Financial Center, 7900 Xerxes Avenue South, Bloomington MN 55431. 612/835-3800. **Contact:** Human Resources. **Description:** A law firm specializing in a wide variety of areas. **Common positions include:** Attorney; Paralegal. **Benefits:** 401(k); Daycare Assistance; Disability Coverage; Employee Discounts; Life Insurance; Medical Insurance; Pension Plan; Profit Sharing; Tuition Assistance. **Special programs:** Internships. **Corporate headquarters location:** This Location.

LINDQUIST & VENNUM P.L.L.P.
4200 IDS Center, 80 South Eighth Street, Minneapolis MN 55402. 612/371-3211. **Contact:** Manager of Human Resources. **World Wide Web address:** http://www.lindquist.com. **Description:** A law firm specializing in a variety of areas, including banking, bankruptcy, corporate, employee benefits, family, and real estate.

LOCKRIDGE, GRINDAL, NAUEN & HOLSTEIN P.L.L.P.
100 Washington Avenue South, Suite 2200, Minneapolis MN 55401. 612/339-6900. **Contact:** Managing Partner. **Description:** A law firm.

MOSS & BARNETT, P.A.
4800 Norwest Center, 90 South Seventh Street, Minneapolis MN 55402. 612/347-0300. **Contact:** Julie Donaldson, Hiring Coordinator. **Description:** A law firm specializing in a variety of areas, excluding criminal law.

OPPENHEIMER WOLFF & DONNELLY
45 South Seventh Street, Plaza VII, Suite 3400, Minneapolis MN 55402. 612/344-9300. **Contact:** Jackie Gunstad, Manager of Legal Recruiting. **Description:** A law firm specializing in several different types of law. **Common positions include:** Attorney; Computer Programmer; Human Resources Manager; Legal Secretary; Librarian; Library Technician; Paralegal; Systems Analyst. **Educational backgrounds include:** Law/Pre-Law. **Benefits:** 401(k); Dental Insurance; Disability Coverage; Life Insurance; Medical Insurance; Pension Plan; Savings Plan; Tuition Assistance. **Special programs:** Internships. **Corporate headquarters location:** This Location. **Operations at this facility include:** Administration; Regional Headquarters; Service. **Listed on:** Privately held. **Number of employees at this location:** 400.

ROBINS, KAPLAN, MILLER & CIRESI
2800 LaSalle Plaza, 800 LaSalle Avenue, Minneapolis MN 55402. 612/349-8500. **Fax:** 612/339-4181. **Contact:** Human Resources. **Description:** A law firm specializing in medical malpractice, product liability, and similar areas. **Common positions include:** Legal Nurse Consultant; Paralegal. **Special programs:** Internships. **Corporate headquarters location:** This Location.

ZELLE & LARSON
33 South Sixth Street, Suite 4400, Minneapolis MN 55402-3710. 612/339-2020. **Contact:** Human Resources. **Description:** A law firm which specializes in insurance litigation.

Note: Because addresses and telephone numbers of smaller companies can change rapidly, we recommend you call each company to verify the information below before inquiring about job opportunities. Mass mailings are not recommended.

Additional small employers:

LEGAL SERVICES

Bernard Friel
322 Minnesota St #2200, St. Paul
MN 55101-1201. 651/223-6422.

Bowman and Brooke
150 S 5th St, Ste 2600,
Minneapolis MN 55402-4226.
612/339-8682.

Briggs & Morgan
2400 IDS Ctr, 80 S 8th St,
Minneapolis MN 55402. 612/339-0661.

Darlene M. Cobian
322 Minnesota St #2200, St. Paul
MN 55101-1201. 651/223-6597.

Doherty Rumble Butler PA
30 E 7th St, World Trade Bldg,
St. Paul MN 55101. 651/291-9333.

Fabyanske Westra & Hart PA
920 2nd Ave S, Ste 1100,
Minneapolis MN 55402-4010.
612/338-0115.

Gray Plant Mooty & Mooty
33 South 6th Street,
Minneapolis MN 55402-3601.
612/343-2800.

Jardine Logan & O'Brien
2100 Piper Jaffray Plaza, St. Paul
MN 55101. 651/290-6500.

Leonard Street & Deinard PA
150 S 5th St, Ste 2300,
Minneapolis MN 55402-4223.
612/335-1500.

Mackall Crounse & Moore
1400 AT&T Tower, 901 Market
Ave, Minneapolis MN 55402.
612/305-1400.

Maslon Edelman Borman & Brand
90 S 7th St, Ste 3300,
Minneapolis MN 55402-4104.
612/672-8200.

Meagher & Geer LLP
4200 Multifoods Tower,
Minneapolis MN 55402. 612/338-0661.

Messerli & Kramer PA
150 S 5th St, Ste 1800,
Minneapolis MN 55402-4218.
612/672-3600.

Popham Haik
222 S 9th St, Minneapolis MN
55402-3389. 612/333-4800.

Quorum/Lanier
3105 E 80th St, Ste A2000,
Minneapolis MN 55425-1587.
612/858-6500.

Rider Bennett Egan Arundel LLP
333 S 7th St, Ste 2000,
Minneapolis MN 55402-2431.
612/340-7951.

Winthrop & Weinstine PA
30 7th St E, Ste 3200, St. Paul
MN 55101-4919. 651/290-8400.

For more information on career opportunities in legal services:

Associations

AMERICAN BAR ASSOCIATION
750 North Lake Shore Drive, Chicago IL 60611.
312/988-5000. World Wide Web address: http://www.abanet.org.

FEDERAL BAR ASSOCIATION
1815 H Street NW, Suite 408, Washington DC 20006-3697. 202/638-0252. World Wide Web address:
http://www.fedbar.org.

NATIONAL ASSOCIATION OF LEGAL ASSISTANTS
1516 South Boston Avenue, Suite 200, Tulsa OK
74119-4013. 918/587-6828. World Wide Web
address: http://www.nala.org. An educational
association. Memberships are available.

NATIONAL FEDERATION OF PARALEGAL ASSOCIATIONS
P.O. Box 33108, Kansas City MO 64114-0108.
816/941-4000. World Wide Web address: http://www.paralegals.org. Offers magazines, seminars, and
Internet job listings.

Directories

MARTINDALE-HUBBELL LAW DIRECTORY
121 Chanlon Road, New Providence NJ 07974.
800/526-4902. World Wide Web address:

http://www.martindale.com. A directory consisting of
the names of legal employers. In all, listings for over
900,000 lawyers and law firms are available. In
addition to information regarding firms and practices,
biographies of many individual lawyers are included.

Newsletters

LAWYERS WEEKLY USA
Lawyers Weekly, Inc., 41 West Street, Boston MA
02111. Toll-free phone: 800/444-5297. World Wide
Web address: http://www.lawyersweekly.com. A
newsletter that profiles law firms, provides general
industry information, and provides information on
jobs nationwide.

Online Services

COURT REPORTERS FORUM
Go: CrForum. A CompuServe networking forum that
includes information from the *Journal of Court Reporting*.

LEGAL EXCHANGE
Jump to: Legal Exchange. A debate forum for lawyers
and other legal professionals, offered through Prodigy.

LEGAL INFORMATION NETWORK
Keyword: LIN. An America Online networking
resource for paralegals, family law specialists, social
security specialists, and law students.

MANUFACTURING: MISCELLANEOUS CONSUMER

Greater globalization is the trend in consumer manufacturing as worldwide and regional trade agreements reduce barriers and provide more uniform trade standards. Demand for household goods is cyclical and depends on the state of the economy and the disposable income of consumers. The distribution of these goods is more dependent on large discount retailers, and despite the strong but turbulent economy of 1998, consumer confidence is still relatively high.

A new trend in manufacturing is toward supercontractors, businesses that contract with a major company to do its manufacturing, distributing, and product servicing. According to Business Week, *one such company is the Solectron Corporation, which manufactures printers for Hewlett-Packard. Such arrangements allow the major company, such as Hewlett-Packard, to devote more of its resources to research and development. The relationship is helping the U.S. manufacturing process to become more efficient, and therefore, globally competitive.*

In general, manufacturing jobs will continue to decrease as the economy shifts toward service industries. The Bureau of Labor Statistics estimates a loss of 350,000 manufacturing jobs by 2006. Companies such as Kodak and Gillette have recently laid off thousands of workers, and Kodak expects to cut more than 12,000 more jobs by 2000. Factory automation -- including wireless communications, distributed intelligence, and centralized computer control -- is one major cause for the loss of manufacturing jobs. Growing competition has forced some companies to streamline production by replacing workers with computers in the areas of inventory tracking, shipping, and ordering. Individuals who have a working knowledge of these software applications will have an edge over less technically experienced jobseekers.

ANCHOR HOCKING PLASTICS, INC./PLASTICS INC.
P.O. Box 2830, St. Paul MN 55102-0830. 651/229-5400. **Fax:** 651/229-5470. **Contact:** Vice President of Human Resources. **World Wide Web address:** http://www.organized.com. **Description:** Manufactures plastic disposable servicewear and kitchen storage containers. **Common positions include:** Accountant/Auditor; Blue-Collar Worker Supervisor; Budget Analyst; Financial Analyst; Industrial Engineer; Operations/Production Manager; Systems Analyst. **Educational backgrounds include:** Accounting; Business Administration; Engineering. **Benefits:** 401(k); Dental Insurance; Disability Coverage; Employee Discounts; Life Insurance; Medical Insurance; Pension Plan; Tuition Assistance. **Corporate headquarters location:** Freeport IL. **Parent company:** Newell Company. **Operations at this facility include:** Administration; Divisional Headquarters; Manufacturing; Sales. **Listed on:** New York Stock Exchange. **Number of employees at this location:** 500. **Number of employees nationwide:** 16,000.

ANDERSON FABRICS
P.O. Box 311, Blackduck MN 56630. 218/835-6677. **Contact:** Human Resources. **Description:** Manufactures draperies and vertical blinds.

AVEDA CORPORATION
4000 Pheasant Ridge Drive, Blaine MN 55449. 612/783-4000. **Fax:** 612/783-6850. **Recorded jobline:** 612/783-4282. **E-mail address:** jobs@aveda.com. **World Wide Web address:** http://www.aveda.com. **Contact:** Human Resources. **Description:** Manufactures perfume, makeup,

and beauty products. The company also operated salons and retail stores. **Special programs:** Internships. **Corporate headquarters location:** This Location. **Other U.S. locations:** New York NY.

CANNON EQUIPMENT
324 West Washington Street, Cannon Falls MN 55009-1142. 507/263-4231. **Contact:** Human Resources. **Description:** A manufacturer, merchandiser, and distributor of metal products ranging from steel curtain rods to wire racks.

CRESTLINER INC.
609 13th Avenue NE, Little Falls MN 56345. 320/632-6686. **Contact:** Human Resources. **World Wide Web address:** http://www.crestliner.com. **Description:** Manufactures pleasure boats.

FEDERAL CARTRIDGE COMPANY
900 Ehlen Drive, Anoka MN 55303. 612/323-2300. **Contact:** Human Resources. **World Wide Web address:** http://www.federalcartridge.com. **Description:** Manufactures ammunition for sporting use and law enforcement.

FIRST TEAM SPORTS, INC.
1201 Lund Boulevard, Anoka MN 55303. 612/576-3500. **Contact:** Human Resources. **World Wide Web address:** http://www.ultrawheels.com. **Description:** Manufactures in-line skates, skateboards, wheels, backpacks, ice hockey products, apparel, and accessories. Brand names include B!G, Crossover, Heavy, Hespeler, Skate Attack, Subcon, 3rd World, Ultra-Ice, and UltraWheels. **Corporate headquarters location:** This Location.

FRIGIDAIRE COMPANY
701 33rd Avenue North, St. Cloud MN 56303. 320/253-1212. **Contact:** Human Resources. **Description:** This location manufactures freezers. Overall, Frigidaire manufactures household appliances including laundry machines, ranges, dishwashers, refrigerators, freezers, air conditioners, and disposals. **Corporate headquarters location:** Dublin OH. **Parent company:** AB Electrolux has four business areas: Household Appliances, Commercial Appliances, Outdoor Products, and Industrial Products. The main operation in Household Appliances is white goods. Other operations of Household Appliances include floor care products, absorption refrigerators for caravans and hotel rooms, room air conditioners, and sewing machines, as well as kitchen and bathroom cabinets. The main operations in Commercial Appliances are food-service equipment for restaurants and institutions, and equipment for such applications as apartment-house laundry rooms and commercial laundries. Other operations of Commercial Appliances include refrigeration equipment and freezers for shops and supermarkets, as well as vacuum cleaners and wet/dry cleaners for commercial use. Outdoor Products include garden equipment, chain saws, and other equipment for forestry operations. Garden equipment refers to portable products such as lawn trimmers and leaf blowers, as well as lawn mowers and garden tractors. Industrial Products comprise the group's second-largest business area. Over 40 percent of sales in this business area come from profiles and other half-finished goods in aluminum, manufactured by Granges. Other operations in Industrial Products include car safety belts and related products for personal safety in cars, as well as materials-handling equipment.

THE GILLETTE COMPANY
310 East Fifth Street, St. Paul MN 55101. 651/292-2900. **Contact:** Julie Emmons, Human Resources. **Description:** This location manufactures shampoos, conditioners, and Liquid Paper.

JEWELMONT CORPORATION
800 Boone Avenue North, Golden Valley MN 55427. 612/546-3800. **Toll-free phone:** 800/328-7173. **Fax:** 612/546-2957. **Contact:** Britt Okland, Director of Human Resources. **Description:** Manufactures jewelry. Founded in 1933. **NOTE:** The company offers entry-level positions. **Benefits:** 401(k); Dental Insurance; Employee Discounts; Life Insurance; Medical Insurance. **Special programs:** Apprenticeships. **Listed on:** Privately held. **Annual sales/revenues:** $21 - $50 million. **Number of employees at this location:** 100.

JOSTENS, INC.
5501 Norman Center Drive, Minneapolis MN 55437. 612/830-3300. **Fax:** 612/897-4126. **Contact:** John Abel, Staffing Specialist. **World Wide Web address:** http://www.jostens.com. **Description:** Jostens, Inc.'s primary business segments are School Products, Recognition, and Jostens Learning. The School Products segment is comprised of five businesses: Printing and Publishing, Jewelry, Graduation Products, U.S. Photography, and Jostens Canada. School Products include yearbooks, commercial printing, desktop publishing curriculum kits, class rings, graduation accessories, diplomas, trophies, plaques and other awards, school pictures, group photographs for youth camps

and organizations, and senior graduation portraits. This segment serves schools, colleges, and alumni associations in the United States and Canada through 1,100 independent sales representatives. Jostens also maintains an international sales force in approximately 50 countries for American schools and military installations. The Recognition segment provides products and services that reflect achievements in service, sales, quality, productivity, attendance, safety, and retirements. It also produces awards for championship team accomplishments and affinity products for associations. This segment serves companies, professional and amateur sports teams, and special interest associations through an independent sales force of approximately 100 people. Jostens Learning produces educational software for kids in kindergarten through grade 12, offering software-based curriculum in reading, mathematics, language arts, science programs, and early childhood instruction, as well as programs for at-risk learning and home learning. As one of the nation's largest providers of curriculum software, Jostens Learning serves more than 4 million students in 10,000 schools nationwide. Customers may purchase programs to meet specific instructional needs, add products in a modular approach, or choose to implement a comprehensive schoolwide solution. **Common positions include:** Accountant/Auditor; Administrative Manager; Advertising Clerk; Attorney; Computer Programmer; Customer Service Representative; Editor; Education Administrator; Human Resources Manager; Management Analyst/Consultant; Operations/Production Manager; Paralegal; Property and Real Estate Manager; Public Relations Specialist; Purchasing Agent/Manager; Quality Control Supervisor; Software Engineer; Systems Analyst. **Educational backgrounds include:** Accounting; Art/Design; Business Administration; Communications; Economics; Finance; Marketing. **Benefits:** 401(k); Daycare Assistance; Dental Insurance; Disability Coverage; Life Insurance; Medical Insurance; Pension Plan; Profit Sharing; Savings Plan. **Corporate headquarters location:** This Location. **Other U.S. locations:** Nationwide. **Operations at this facility include:** Administration; Divisional Headquarters; Regional Headquarters; Sales; Service. **Listed on:** American Stock Exchange; NASDAQ; New York Stock Exchange. **Number of employees at this location:** 330. **Number of employees nationwide:** 10,000.

LAMAUR
5601 East River Road, Fridley MN 55432. 612/571-1234. **Contact:** Human Resources. **Description:** A manufacturer of personal grooming products.

NATIONAL SALON RESOURCES
3109 Louisiana Avenue North, New Hope MN 55427. 612/546-9500. **Contact:** Human Resources. **Description:** Produces and distributes beauty products.

NORDIC WARE
5005 Highway 7, St. Louis Park MN 55416. 612/924-8587. **Toll-free phone:** 800/328-4310x587. **Fax:** 612/924-9655. **Contact:** Diane M. Zeller, Human Resources Manager. **E-mail address:** dianezeller@nordicware.com. **World Wide Web address:** http://www.nordicware.com. **Description:** Produces aluminum cookware and related products. Founded in 1946. **NOTE:** Second and third shifts are offered. **Common positions include:** Accountant; Administrative Assistant; Blue-Collar Worker Supervisor; Buyer; Chief Financial Officer; Credit Manager; Customer Service Representative; Electrical/Electronics Engineer; Graphic Designer; Human Resources Manager; Operations Manager; Production Manager; Sales Manager; Secretary; Systems Analyst; Systems Manager. **Educational backgrounds include:** Accounting; Business Administration; Engineering. **Benefits:** 401(k); Dental Insurance; Disability Coverage; Employee Discounts; Life Insurance; Medical Insurance; Public Transit Available; Tuition Assistance. **Office hours:** Monday - Friday, 8:00 a.m. - 4:00 p.m. **Corporate headquarters location:** This Location. **Parent company:** Northland Aluminum Products, Inc. **Operations at this facility include:** Administration; Manufacturing; Research and Development; Sales; Service. **Listed on:** Privately held. **Number of employees at this location:** 150.

POLARIS INDUSTRIES INC.
301 Fifth Avenue SW, Roseau MN 56751. 218/463-2312. **Contact:** Terri Larson, Human Resources Supervisor. **World Wide Web address:** http://www.polarisindustries.com. **Description:** This location manufactures ATVs and snowmobiles. Overall, Polaris Industries manufactures and markets recreational vehicles. Other company products include personal watercraft garments and accessories, such as snowmobile suits and leathers, wet suits, helmets, goggles, activewear, and tennis shoes. The company has a wholly-owned Canadian subsidiary in Winnipeg, Manitoba, and together with Fuji Heavy Industries Ltd. is developing an engine facility in Hudson WI. Polaris products are sold around the world through a network of nearly 2,000 dealers in North America and 55 distributors covering 82 countries worldwide. **Common positions include:** Accountant/Auditor; Blue-Collar Worker Supervisor; Buyer; Computer Programmer; Customer Service Representative; Draftsperson; Electrical/Electronics Engineer; Human Resources Manager; Industrial Engineer; Mechanical Engineer; Operations/Production Manager; Purchasing Agent/Manager; Quality

Control Supervisor. **Educational backgrounds include:** Business Administration; Computer Science; Engineering. **Benefits:** Disability Coverage; Employee Discounts; Life Insurance; Medical Insurance; Profit Sharing; Savings Plan; Tuition Assistance. **Corporate headquarters location:** Minneapolis MN. **Other U.S. locations:** Spirit Lake IA; Osceola WI. **Operations at this facility include:** Manufacturing; Research and Development. **Listed on:** New York Stock Exchange; Pacific Stock Exchange. **Stock exchange symbol:** PII. **Number of employees at this location:** 1,800. **Number of employees nationwide:** 4,000.

POLARIS INDUSTRIES INC.
1225 Highway 169 North, Minneapolis MN 55441. 612/542-0500. **Contact:** Human Resources. **World Wide Web address:** http://www.polarisindustries.com. **Description:** A worldwide manufacturer and marketer of motorized products for recreational and utility use. Products include snowmobiles, all-terrain vehicles, and personal watercraft. Polaris also manufactures garments and accessories, such as snowmobile suits and leathers, wet suits, helmets, goggles, activewear, and tennis shoes. The company has a wholly-owned Canadian subsidiary in Winnipeg, Manitoba, and together with Fuji Heavy Industries Ltd. is developing an engine facility in Hudson WI. Polaris products are sold around the world through a network of nearly 2,000 dealers in North America and 55 distributors covering 82 countries worldwide. **Corporate headquarters location:** This Location. **Other U.S. locations:** Spirit Lake IA; Roseau MN; Osceola WI. **Listed on:** New York Stock Exchange; Pacific Stock Exchange. **Stock exchange symbol:** PII. **Number of employees nationwide:** 4,000.

RIEDELL SHOES
P.O. Box 21, Red Wing MN 55066. 651/388-8251. **Contact:** Personnel. **Description:** Manufactures ice skates and roller blades.

STEARNS MANUFACTURING COMPANY
P.O. Box 1498, St. Cloud MN 56302. 320/252-1642. **Fax:** 320/252-4425. **Contact:** Loretta Trulson, Director of Human Resources. **Description:** Manufactures life jackets and other flotation devices. **Common positions include:** Buyer; Computer Programmer; Credit Manager; Customer Service Representative; Designer; Financial Analyst; Human Resources Manager; Industrial Engineer; Industrial Production Manager; Systems Analyst. **Educational backgrounds include:** Accounting; Art/Design; Business Administration; Engineering; Finance; Liberal Arts; Marketing; Mathematics. **Benefits:** 401(k); Disability Coverage; Employee Discounts; Life Insurance; Pension Plan; Profit Sharing; Tuition Assistance. **Special programs:** Internships. **Corporate headquarters location:** This Location. **Parent company:** Antheny. **Operations at this facility include:** Administration; Divisional Headquarters; Manufacturing; Sales.

SUNRISE PACKAGING
9937 Goodhue Street NE, Blaine MN 55449. 612/785-2505. **Contact:** James Hartley, Controller. **Description:** Manufactures three-ring binders and storage albums for software, audio, and video use.

THE TORO COMPANY
8111 Lyndale Avenue South, Bloomington MN 55420. 612/887-8924. **Contact:** Dave Tourville, Corporate Human Resources Manager. **World Wide Web address:** http://www.toro.com. **Description:** Toro is engaged in the manufacture and marketing of outdoor power products for consumer, irrigation, and commercial industries. Products include lawn mowers, snowblowers, tractors, trimmers, irrigation systems and components, and appliances marketed under the brand names Toro, Wheel Horse, and Lawn-Boy. The company distributes its products through 10,800 independent retailers worldwide. **Common positions include:** Accountant/Auditor; Attorney; Blue-Collar Worker Supervisor; Buyer; Computer Programmer; Credit Manager; Customer Service Representative; Draftsperson; Industrial Engineer; Marketing Specialist; Purchasing Agent/Manager; Quality Control Supervisor; Systems Analyst; Technical Writer/Editor; Transportation/Traffic Specialist. **Educational backgrounds include:** Accounting; Business Administration; Computer Science; Engineering; Finance; Marketing. **Benefits:** Dental Insurance; Disability Coverage; Employee Discounts; Life Insurance; Medical Insurance; Paid Vacation; Pension Plan; Savings Plan; Tuition Assistance. **Corporate headquarters location:** This Location. **Operations at this facility include:** Administration; Research and Development; Sales; Service. **Listed on:** New York Stock Exchange.

TSUMURA INTERNATIONAL INC.
1000 Valley Park Drive, Shakopee MN 55379. 612/496-4700. **Fax:** 612/496-4720. **Contact:** Patti Howe, Human Resources Manager. **World Wide Web address:** http://www.tsumura.com. **Description:** Tsumura is a market leader in manufacturing fragrances, toiletries, and health care products. **Common positions include:** Blue-Collar Worker Supervisor; Buyer; Chemist; Computer

Programmer; Department Manager; Human Resources Manager; Industrial Engineer; Logistics Support Worker; Mechanical Engineer; Operations/Production Manager; Purchasing Agent/Manager; Quality Control Supervisor; Systems Analyst. **Educational backgrounds include:** Business Administration; Chemistry; Computer Science; Engineering; Liberal Arts. **Benefits:** 401(k); Dental Insurance; Disability Coverage; Employee Discounts; Life Insurance; Medical Insurance; Tuition Assistance. **Corporate headquarters location:** Secaucus NJ. **Operations at this facility include:** Manufacturing; Research and Development. **Listed on:** Privately held. **Number of employees at this location:** 200. **Number of employees nationwide:** 700.

Note: Because addresses and telephone numbers of smaller companies can change rapidly, we recommend you call each company to verify the information below before inquiring about job opportunities. Mass mailings are not recommended.

Additional small employers:

HOUSEHOLD AUDIO AND VIDEO EQUIPMENT

Digital Excellence Inc.
875 Montreal Way, St. Paul MN 55102-4245. 651/290-2800.

LAWN AND GARDEN TRACTORS AND RELATED EQUIPMENT

The Toro Company
600 Valley Industrial Blvd, Shakopee MN 55379-1823. 612/937-3300.

The Toro Company
174 16th St, Windom MN 56101-1224. 507/831-3333.

MISC. FURNITURE AND FIXTURES

Steven Fabrics Co.
1400 Van Buren St NE, Minneapolis MN 55413-1535. 612/781-6671.

TOYS AND SPORTING GOODS

Landscape Structures Inc.
PO Box 198, Delano MN 55328-0198. 612/972-3391.

Life Fitness
6043 Highway 10 Northwest, Anoka MN 55303-4559. 612/323-4500.

Nordic Track Inc.
1400 13th Street West, Glencoe MN 55336-1555. 320/864-6173.

RJ Tackle Inc.
PO Box 248, Ranier MN 56668-0248. 218/286-5321.

Rollerblade Inc.
5101 Shady Oak Road, Hopkins MN 55343-4100. 612/930-7000.

Water Gremlin Company
1610 Whitaker St, White Bear Lake MN 55110-3756. 651/429-7761.

For more information on career opportunities in consumer manufacturing:

Associations

ASSOCIATION FOR MANUFACTURING EXCELLENCE
380 West Palatine Road, Wheeling IL 60090. 847/520-3282. World Wide Web address: http://www.ame.org.

ASSOCIATION FOR MANUFACTURING TECHNOLOGY
7901 Westpark Drive, McLean VA 22102. 703/893-2900. World Wide Web address: http://www.mfgtech.org. Offers research services.

ASSOCIATION OF HOME APPLIANCE MANUFACTURERS
20 North Wacker Drive, Suite 1231, Chicago IL 60606. 312/984-5800. World Wide Web address: http://www.aham.org.

NATIONAL ASSOCIATION OF MANUFACTURERS
1331 Pennsylvania Avenue NW, Suite 600, Washington DC 20004. 202/637-3000. World Wide Web address: http://www.nam.org. National Association of Manufacturers is a lobbying association for manufacturers.

NATIONAL HOUSEWARES MANUFACTURERS ASSOCIATION
6400 Schafer Court, Suite 650, Rosemont IL 60018. 847/292-4200. World Wide Web address: http://www.housewares.org. National Housewares Manufacturers

Association offers shipping discounts and other services.

SOCIETY OF MANUFACTURING ENGINEERS
P.O. Box 930, One SME Drive, Dearborn MI 48121. 313/271-1500. World Wide Web address: http://www.sme.org. Society of Manufacturing Engineers offers educational events and educational materials on manufacturing.

Directories

AMERICAN MANUFACTURER'S DIRECTORY
5711 South 86th Circle, P.O. Box 37347, Omaha NE 68127. Toll-free phone: 800/555-5211. World Wide Web address: http://www.infousa.com. Made by the same company that created *American Big Business Directory*, *American Manufacturer's Directory* lists over 531,000 manufacturing companies of all sizes and industries. The directory contains product and sales information, company size, and a key contact name for each company.

APPLIANCE MANUFACTURER ANNUAL DIRECTORY
Appliance Manufacturer, 5900 Harper Road, Suite 105, Solon OH 44139. 440/349-3060. $25.00.

HOUSEHOLD & PERSONAL PRODUCTS INDUSTRY BUYERS GUIDE
Rodman Publishing Group, 17 South Franklin Turnpike, Ramsey NJ 07446. 201/825-2552. World Wide Web address: http://www.happi.com.

Magazines

APPLIANCE
Dana Chase Publications, 1110 Jorie Boulevard, Oak Brook IL 60522-9019. 630/990-3484. World Wide Web address: http://www.appliance.com. Monthly.

COSMETICS INSIDERS REPORT
Advanstar Communications, 131 West First Street, Duluth MN 55802. Toll-free phone: 800/346-0085. World Wide Web address: http://www.advanstar.com. $189.00 for a one year subscription; 24 issues annually. Features timely articles on cosmetics marketing and research.

Online Services

CAREER PARK - MANUFACTURING JOBS
http://www.careerpark.com/jobs/manulist.html. This Website provides a list of current job openings in the manufacturing industry. The site is run by Parker Advertising Service, Inc.

MO'S GATEWAY TO MANUFACTURING-RELATED JOBS LISTINGS
http://www.chesapk.com/mfgjobs.html. Provides links to sites that post job openings in manufacturing.

MANUFACTURING: MISCELLANEOUS INDUSTRIAL

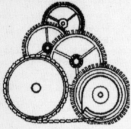

The 1998 General Motors strike proved to be a hard blow for industrial manufacturing, but a strong economy is helping to sustain the industry. In fact, the automobile industry was expecting a record sales year for 1998, despite the GM strike. The Midwest, home to many of the nation's industrial manufacturing companies, continues to do well, recording an unemployment rate of 3.5 percent for August 1998. This was better than the national 4.5 percent rate.

However, the industry is still weak in areas. Deere & Company and Case Corporation both laid off workers in 1998, and due to falling steel prices and increased imports, midwestern steel mills are cutting payrolls and limiting production. Many companies are forging ahead with capital improvements, yet are not increasing their workforce. Companies which specialize in equipment for thriving industries, such as health care and construction, will show the most gains in the future.

ACROMETAL COMPANIES INC.
210 NE 10th Avenue, Brainerd MN 56401. 218/829-4719. **Contact:** Human Resources. **Description:** A manufacturer of metal spools and reels, wire handling and packaging equipment, and other industrial products. **NOTE:** Hiring is done through Acrometal's sister company. Please send resumes to Sue Hilgard, Human Resources Manager, A-Tek, P.O. Box 403, Brainerd MN 56401 and note the location to which you are applying. **Common positions include:** Accountant/Auditor; Administrator; Blue-Collar Worker Supervisor; Buyer; Chemist; Department Manager; Financial Analyst; General Manager; Industrial Engineer; Mechanical Engineer; Operations/Production Manager; Purchasing Agent/Manager; Quality Control Supervisor; Services Sales Representative. **Educational backgrounds include:** Accounting; Business Administration; Economics; Engineering; Finance. **Benefits:** Dental Insurance; Disability Coverage; Life Insurance; Medical Insurance; Pension Plan; Profit Sharing; Savings Plan; Tuition Assistance. **Corporate headquarters location:** Plymouth MN. **Operations at this facility include:** Divisional Headquarters; Manufacturing; Sales.

ADVANTEK
5801 Clearwater Drive, Minnetonka MN 55343-8988. 612/938-6800. **Contact:** Human Resources. **Description:** A manufacturer of carrier tape for the electronics industry.

AG-CHEM EQUIPMENT COMPANY, INC.
5720 Smetana Drive, Minnetonka MN 55343. 612/933-9006. **Contact:** Personnel Department. **World Wide Web address:** http://www.agchem.com. **Description:** Manufactures farm machinery and equipment. **Corporate headquarters location:** This Location. **Number of employees nationwide:** 1,200.

AG-CHEM EQUIPMENT COMPANY, INC.
202 Industrial Park, Jackson MN 56143. 507/847-2690. **Fax:** 507/847-2711. **Contact:** Karen Cross, Human Resources Manager. **World Wide Web address:** http://www.agchem.com. **Description:** A manufacturer of agricultural and industrial application equipment. **Common positions include:** Accountant/Auditor; Agricultural Engineer; Buyer; Draftsperson; Human Resources Manager; Industrial Engineer; Purchasing Agent/Manager; Quality Control Supervisor. **Educational backgrounds include:** Accounting; Business Administration; Engineering. **Benefits:** 401(k); Daycare Assistance; Dental Insurance; Disability Coverage; Employee Discounts; Life Insurance; Medical Insurance; Profit Sharing; Savings Plan; Tuition Assistance. **Corporate headquarters location:** Minnetonka MN. **Operations at this facility include:** Manufacturing. **Number of employees at this location:** 600. **Number of employees nationwide:** 1,200.

ALLIANT TECHSYSTEMS INC.
600 Second Street NE, Hopkins MN 55343. 612/931-6000. **Contact:** Bob Gustafson, Human Resources. **Description:** A developer and manufacturer of munitions and marine systems. The U.S. government is the company's largest client, using products that include the M1A1 tank, tank rounds, infantry weapons, mortar rounds, mines, fuses, and many other munitions and electronic components. Alliant Techsystems also manufactures a variety of products involving sonar and signal processing technologies at its Marine Systems Division. Founded in 1990. **Corporate headquarters location:** This Location. **Listed on:** New York Stock Exchange.

AMCLYDE ENGINEERED PRODUCTS
240 East Plato Boulevard, St. Paul MN 55107. 651/293-4646. **Contact:** Cathy Leritz, Head of Personnel. **Description:** Engaged in the design and construction of custom-engineered lifting and pulling systems. **Parent company:** AMCA.

BEMIS COMPANY INC.
222 South Ninth Street, Suite 2300, Minneapolis MN 55402. 612/376-3000. **Contact:** Lawrence E. Schwanke, Vice President of Human Resources. **World Wide Web address:** http://www.bemis.com. **Description:** Bemis is a diversified producer of consumer and industrial packaging materials, film products, and business products. Packaging products include tapes and paper bags for pharmaceuticals, candy, toilet paper, and detergents. The company also produces sheetprint stock, roll labels, laminates, and adhesive products. **Common positions include:** Accountant/Auditor. **Educational backgrounds include:** Accounting. **Benefits:** 401(k); Dental Insurance; Disability Coverage; Employee Discounts; Life Insurance; Medical Insurance; Pension Plan; Savings Plan; Tuition Assistance. **Corporate headquarters location:** This Location. **Operations at this facility include:** Administration. **Listed on:** New York Stock Exchange.

BLACKBOURN MEDIA PACKAGING
5270 West 84th Street, Suite 200, Bloomington MN 55437. 612/835-9040. **Contact:** Sandy Brooks, Human Resources. **Description:** Manufactures vinyl packaging systems. **NOTE:** All hiring is conducted through the parent company. Jobseekers should direct resumes to Fey Industries, Inc. 200 Fourth Avenue North, Edgertown MN 56128. 507/442-4311. **Common positions include:** Accountant/Auditor; Blue-Collar Worker Supervisor; Industrial Engineer; Manufacturer's/ Wholesaler's Sales Rep.; Operations/Production Manager. **Educational backgrounds include:** Accounting; Business Administration; Communications; Engineering. **Benefits:** Dental Insurance; Disability Coverage; Life Insurance; Medical Insurance; Profit Sharing; Savings Plan; Tuition Assistance. **Corporate headquarters location:** This Location. **Operations at this facility include:** Administration; Manufacturing; Sales.

BUHLER INC.
P.O. Box 9497, Minneapolis MN 55440. 612/545-1401. **Physical address:** 1100 Xenium Lane, Plymouth MN 55441. **Contact:** Frank Lunetta, Director of Personnel. **Description:** Designers and manufacturers of grain milling machinery and other agricultural equipment.

CARTER-DAY INDUSTRIES
500 73rd Avenue NE, Minneapolis MN 55432. 612/571-1000. **Contact:** Tim Ryan, Human Resources. **World Wide Web address:** http://www.carterday.com. **Description:** Engineers, designs, and manufactures to size seed grains and plastic pellets for the agricultural processing and petrochemical industries.

CATERPILLAR PAVING PRODUCTS
P.O. Box 1362, Minneapolis MN 55440. 612/425-4100. **Physical address:** 9401 85th Avenue North, Brooklyn Park MN 55445. **Contact:** Bill Jetson, Manager of Personnel. **World Wide Web address:** http://www.cat.com. **Description:** This location manufactures road construction equipment. Overall, Caterpillar is one of the world's largest manufacturers of construction and mining equipment, natural gas engines, and industrial gas turbines; and a leading global supplier of diesel engines. Products range from track-type tractors to hydraulic excavators, backhoe loaders, motor graders, and off-highway trucks. **Corporate headquarters location:** Peoria IL.

COLEMAN POWERMATE COMPRESSORS
P.O. Box 206, Springfield MN 56087. 507/723-6211. **Physical address:** 118 West Rock Street, Springfield MN. **Contact:** Human Resources. **Description:** A manufacturer of power compressors for use in various industries.

COLORSPAN CORPORATION
7156 Shady Oak Road, Eden Prairie MN 55344. 612/944-9330. **Fax:** 612/944-0377. **Recorded jobline:** 612/943-3457. **Contact:** Corporate Staffing. **E-mail address:** staffing@colorspan.com.

World Wide Web address: http://www.colorspan.com. **Description:** A designer and manufacturer of big color, personal filmsetting, plain-paper typesetting systems for graphic arts, prepress, and desktop publishing applications. Founded in 1985. **Company slogan:** The big color company. **Common positions include:** Account Manager; Accountant; Administrative Assistant; Buyer; Computer Operator; Computer Programmer; Controller; Credit Manager; Customer Service Representative; Database Manager; Design Engineer; Electrical/Electronics Engineer; Graphic Artist; Graphic Designer; Human Resources Manager; Intellectual Property Lawyer; Internet Services Manager; Manufacturing Engineer; Marketing Manager; MIS Specialist; Operations Manager; Paralegal; Production Manager; Purchasing Agent/Manager; Quality Control Supervisor; Sales Executive; Sales Manager; Sales Representative; Software Engineer; Telecommunications Manager; Video Production Coordinator; Webmaster. **Educational backgrounds include:** Engineering; Software Development; Software Tech. Support. **Benefits:** 401(k); Dental Insurance; Disability Coverage; Employee Discounts; Life Insurance; Medical Insurance. **Special programs:** Internships. **Corporate headquarters location:** This Location. **Other U.S. locations:** San Jose CA; Miami FL. **International locations:** Netherlands. **Parent company:** Laser Master Technologies. **Annual sales/revenues:** More than $100 million. **Number of employees nationwide:** 400.

DANA CORPORATION
600 Hoover Street NE, Minneapolis MN 55413. 612/623-1960. **Contact:** Barb Garbey, Human Resources/Personnel Coordinator. **World Wide Web address:** http://www.dana.com. **Description:** This location produces hydraulic pumps, motors, valves, and filters for various industrial uses. Overall, Dana Corporation is a global leader in engineering, manufacturing, and marketing products and systems for the worldwide vehicular, industrial, and mobile off-highway original equipment markets and is a major supplier to the related aftermarkets. Dana is also a leading provider of lease financing services in selected markets. The company's products include drivetrain components, such as axles, driveshafts, clutches, and transmissions; engine parts, such as gaskets, piston rings, seals, pistons, and filters; chassis products, such as vehicular frames and cradles and heavy-duty side rails; fluid power components, such as pumps, motors, and control valves; and industrial products, such as electrical and mechanical brakes and clutches, drives, and motion control devices. Dana's vehicular components and parts are used on automobiles, pickup trucks, vans, minivans, sport-utility vehicles, medium and heavy trucks, and off-highway vehicles. The company's industrial products include mobile off-highway and stationary equipment applications. Dana Corporation has 700 facilities in 27 countries. **Corporate headquarters location:** Toledo OH. **Listed on:** New York Stock Exchange. **Number of employees worldwide:** 55,000.

DATACARD CORPORATION
11111 Bren Road West, Minnetonka MN 55343. 612/933-1223. **Contact:** Human Resources. **World Wide Web address:** http://www.datacard.com. **Description:** A world leader in the development and manufacture of plastic card personalization equipment. Products meet industry needs for conducting transactions, exchanging information, and identification. Customers include financial institutions, health care providers, retailers, oil companies, government, and other industries. **Common positions include:** Accountant/Auditor; Computer Programmer; Draftsperson; Electrical/Electronics Engineer; Manufacturer's/Wholesaler's Sales Rep.; Mechanical Engineer; Software Engineer; Systems Analyst; Technical Writer/Editor. **Educational backgrounds include:** Accounting; Business Administration; Computer Science; Engineering; Marketing. **Benefits:** 401(k); Dental Insurance; Disability Coverage; Life Insurance; Medical Insurance; Pension Plan; Profit Sharing; Tuition Assistance. **Special programs:** Internships. **Corporate headquarters location:** This Location. **Other U.S. locations:** Nationwide. **Operations at this facility include:** Administration; Divisional Headquarters; Manufacturing; Research and Development; Sales; Service. **Listed on:** Privately held. **Number of employees at this location:** 750. **Number of employees nationwide:** 1,400.

DE ZURIK
250 North Riverside Avenue, Sartell MN 56377. 320/259-2000. **Fax:** 320/259-2227. **Contact:** Human Resources. **Description:** An international manufacturer, seller, and servicer of industrial valves and flow control products for process industries such as municipal, HVAC, pulp and paper, chemical, power, and mining. **Common positions include:** Accountant/Auditor; Budget Analyst; Buyer; Chemical Engineer; Computer Programmer; Customer Service Representative; Designer; Draftsperson; Electrician; Environmental Engineer; Financial Analyst; Human Resources Manager; Industrial Engineer; Industrial Production Manager; Materials Engineer; Mechanical Engineer; Metallurgical Engineer; Operations/Production Manager; Public Relations Specialist; Purchasing Agent/Manager; Quality Control Supervisor; Software Engineer; Systems Analyst; Technical Writer/Editor; Transportation/Traffic Specialist. **Educational backgrounds include:** Accounting; Business Administration; Chemistry; Communications; Computer Science; Engineering; Finance; Marketing. **Benefits:** 401(k); Dental Insurance; Disability Coverage; Life Insurance; Medical

Insurance; Pension Plan; Savings Plan; Tuition Assistance. **Special programs:** Internships. **Corporate headquarters location:** This Location. **Other U.S. locations:** Nationwide. **Parent company:** General Signal. **Operations at this facility include:** Administration; Manufacturing; Research and Development; Sales; Service. **Listed on:** New York Stock Exchange. **Number of employees at this location:** 600. **Number of employees nationwide:** 1,000.

DELTAK
P.O. Box 9496, Minneapolis MN 55440. 612/544-3371. **Physical address:** 13330 12th Avenue North, Plymouth MN 55441. **Fax:** 612/541-7253. **Contact:** Human Resources. **World Wide Web address:** http://www.deltak.com. **Description:** Custom designs, manufactures, and constructs heat recovery systems worldwide. **Common positions include:** Account Manager; Accountant/Auditor; Applications Engineer; Buyer; Computer Programmer; Controls Engineer; Designer; Draftsperson; Estimator; Field Engineer; Marketing Manager; Mechanical Engineer; Product Engineer; Project Engineer; Project Manager; Quality Assurance Engineer; Service Engineer; Structural Engineer; Supervisor; Welder. **Benefits:** 401(k); Dental Insurance; Disability Coverage; Life Insurance; Medical Insurance; Profit Sharing; Tuition Assistance. **Corporate headquarters location:** This Location. **Parent company:** Jason Inc. **Listed on:** NASDAQ. **Annual sales/revenues:** $51 - $100 million. **Number of employees nationwide:** 350.

DESPATCH INDUSTRIES
63 St. Anthony Parkway, Minneapolis MN 55418. 612/781-5363. **Fax:** 612/781-5353. **Contact:** Personnel. **World Wide Web address:** http://www.despatch.com. **Description:** A designer and manufacturer of standard and custom industrial heat processing and environmental test equipment including industrial ovens, environmental simulation chambers, and custom-engineered turnkey systems. **Common positions include:** Accountant/Auditor; Buyer; Computer Programmer; Cost Estimator; Customer Service Representative; Designer; Draftsperson; Electrical/Electronics Engineer; Electrician; General Manager; Human Resources Manager; Industrial Engineer; Industrial Production Manager; Manufacturer's/Wholesaler's Sales Rep.; Mechanical Engineer; Purchasing Agent/Manager; Quality Control Supervisor; Software Engineer; Systems Analyst; Technical Writer/Editor. **Educational backgrounds include:** Business Administration; Engineering. **Benefits:** 401(k); Dental Insurance; Disability Coverage; Life Insurance; Medical Insurance; Pension Plan; Profit Sharing; Tuition Assistance. **Corporate headquarters location:** This Location. **Other area locations:** Lakeville MN. **Operations at this facility include:** Administration; Divisional Headquarters; Research and Development; Sales; Service. **Number of employees at this location:** 100.

DONALDSON COMPANY INC.
P.O. Box 1299, Minneapolis MN 55440. 612/887-3131. **Contact:** Human Resources. **World Wide Web address:** http://www.donaldson.com. **Description:** A manufacturer of filtration systems and noise abatement products. **Common positions include:** Accountant/Auditor; Buyer; Chemist; Computer Programmer; Draftsperson; Electrical/Electronics Engineer; Financial Analyst; Industrial Engineer; Manufacturer's/Wholesaler's Sales Rep.; Marketing Specialist; Mechanical Engineer; Systems Analyst. **Educational backgrounds include:** Accounting; Business Administration; Chemistry; Computer Science; Engineering; Marketing. **Benefits:** Dental Insurance; Disability Coverage; Life Insurance; Medical Insurance; Pension Plan; Savings Plan; Tuition Assistance. **Corporate headquarters location:** This Location. **Operations at this facility include:** Administration; Research and Development; Sales. **Listed on:** New York Stock Exchange. **Number of employees at this location:** 700. **Number of employees nationwide:** 4,000.

DOUGLAS MACHINE, LLC
3404 Iowa Street, Alexandria MN 56308. 320/763-6587. **Contact:** Human Resources Director. **World Wide Web address:** http://www.douglas-machine.com. **Description:** A manufacturer of packaging equipment for case packing, palletizing and depalletizing, shrink wrapping, and tray forming.

DRESSER-RAND ELECTRIC MACHINERY
800 Central Avenue NE, Minneapolis MN 55413. 612/378-8000. **Fax:** 612/378-8050. **Contact:** Human Resources. **World Wide Web address:** http://www.electricmachinery.com. **Description:** Custom manufacturers of heavy industrial electric motors and generators and related equipment. **Common positions include:** Accountant; Administrative Assistant; Blue-Collar Worker Supervisor; Buyer; Computer Programmer; Controller; Draftsperson; Electrical/Electronics Engineer; Electrician; Environmental Engineer; Manufacturing Engineer; Marketing Specialist; Mechanical Engineer; Purchasing Agent/Manager; Quality Control Supervisor; Sales Engineer; Secretary. **Educational backgrounds include:** Engineering. **Benefits:** 401(k); Dental Insurance; Disability Coverage; Flexible Schedule; Life Insurance; Medical Insurance; Public Transit Available; Tuition Assistance. **Corporate headquarters location:** Corning NY. **Other U.S.**

locations: Olean NY; Painter Post NY; Wellsville NY; Broken Arrow OK; Houston TX. **Operations at this facility include:** Administration; Manufacturing; Research and Development; Sales; Service. **Number of employees at this location:** 240.

ECO WATER SYSTEMS
P.O. Box 64420, St. Paul MN 55164. 651/739-5330. **Physical address:** 1890 Woodlane Drive, Woodbury MN 55125. **Contact:** David Kell, Human Resources Manager. **World Wide Web address:** http://www.ecowater.com. **Description:** Develops, manufactures, and markets water conditioning equipment, drinking water purifiers, chemical feed pumps, and commercial and industrial water systems. **Common positions include:** Accountant/Auditor; Blue-Collar Worker Supervisor; Buyer; Chemical Engineer; Chemist; Credit Manager; Draftsperson; Electrical/ Electronics Engineer; Financial Analyst; General Manager; Industrial Engineer; Mechanical Engineer; Operations/Production Manager; Purchasing Agent/Manager; Quality Control Supervisor. **Educational backgrounds include:** Accounting; Business Administration; Computer Science; Engineering; Liberal Arts; Marketing. **Benefits:** Dental Insurance; Disability Coverage; Life Insurance; Medical Insurance; Pension Plan; Profit Sharing; Savings Plan; Tuition Assistance. **Corporate headquarters location:** Chicago IL. **Operations at this facility include:** Administration; Manufacturing; Regional Headquarters; Research and Development; Sales; Service.

FARGO ELECTRONICS, INC.
6533 Flying Cloud Drive, Eden Prairie MN 55344. 612/941-9470. **Fax:** 612/941-7836. **Contact:** Human Resources Department. **World Wide Web address:** http://www.fargo.com. **Description:** A manufacturer of plastic card printers. **Corporate headquarters location:** This Location.

FOLDCRAFT COMPANY
615 Centennial Drive, Kenyon MN 55946-1297. 507/789-5111. **Contact:** Human Resources. **E-mail address:** plymold@aol.com. **Description:** A manufacturer of seating and furniture for the restaurant industry.

GRACO INC.
P.O. Box 1441, Minneapolis MN 55440-1441. 612/623-6000. **Physical address:** 4050 Olson Memorial Highway, Golden Valley MN 55422-2322. **Contact:** Human Resources Department. **World Wide Web address:** http://www.graco.com. **Description:** Designs, manufactures, and markets fluid handling systems and equipment for both industrial and commercial applications. Graco's products are used by companies in the manufacturing, processing, construction, and maintenance industries. Founded in 1926. **Corporate headquarters location:** This Location. **Other U.S. locations:** Los Angeles CA; Plymouth MI; Minneapolis MN; Rogers MN; Sioux Falls SD. **International locations:** Argentina; Australia; Belgium; Brazil; Canada; China; France; Germany; Hong Kong; India; Indonesia; Italy; Japan; Korea; Malaysia; Mexico; New Zealand; Philippines; Taiwan; Spain; United Kingdom. **Listed on:** New York Stock Exchange. **Stock exchange symbol:** GGG. **Number of employees nationwide:** 2,080.

HAUENSTEIN & BURMEISTER, INC.
2629 30th Avenue South, Minneapolis MN 55406. 612/721-5031. **Contact:** Marty Deckman, Vice President. **Description:** A diversified manufacturer of elevator entrances and cabs, partitions and ceiling systems, hollow metal and other metal specialties, a complete school equipment line, and telephone and sound systems.

I.M.I. CORNELIUS INC.
One Cornelius Place, Anoka MN 55303. 612/421-6120. **Contact:** Susan Aaker, Human Resources. **Description:** Manufactures food processing machinery.

K&G MANUFACTURING
226 Park Avenue NW, Faribault MN 55021-4804. 507/334-5501. **Contact:** Human Resources. **Description:** A machine shop and precision-parts manufacturer of various components for the automotive, airline, and medical industries.

KURT MANUFACTURING COMPANY
5280 Main Street NE, Minneapolis MN 55421. 612/572-1500. **Contact:** Mr. Kern Walker, Vice President/Human Resources. **World Wide Web address:** http://www.kurt.com. **Description:** A manufacturer of a variety of industrial products including gaging and motion control systems, hydraulic products, precision gears, and workholding devices. Kurt Manufacturing Company also performs die casting, industrial precision machining, and screw machining. **Corporate headquarters location:** This Location.

LIBERTY DIVERSIFIED INDUSTRIES (LDI)

5600 North Highway 169, New Hope MN 55428. 612/536-6600. **Contact:** Dan Petrella, Director of Human Resources. **World Wide Web address:** http://www.libertydiversified.com. **Description:** LDI is a diversified organization comprised of seven companies located throughout the United States. Products include corrugated boxes, metal fabricated products, and plastic extruded products. Other subsidiaries include a paper mill and a manufacturer/wholesaler of office and industrial supplies. **Common positions include:** Accountant/Auditor; Actuary; Administrator; Advertising Clerk; Attorney; Blue-Collar Worker Supervisor; Branch Manager; Buyer; Commercial Artist; Computer Programmer; Credit Manager; Customer Service Representative; Department Manager; Draftsperson; Electrical/Electronics Engineer; General Manager; Human Resources Manager; Industrial Engineer; Marketing Specialist; Operations/Production Manager; Public Relations Specialist; Purchasing Agent/Manager; Quality Control Supervisor; Systems Analyst; Technical Writer/Editor; Transportation/Traffic Specialist. **Educational backgrounds include:** Accounting; Art/Design; Business Administration; Chemistry; Communications; Computer Science; Economics; Engineering; Finance; Marketing; Mathematics. **Benefits:** Disability Coverage; Employee Discounts; Life Insurance; Medical Insurance; Pension Plan; Profit Sharing; Savings Plan; Tuition Assistance. **Corporate headquarters location:** This Location. **Operations at this facility include:** Administration; Research and Development; Service.

LULL INDUSTRIES, INC.

3045 Highway 13, St. Paul MN 55121. 612/454-4300. **Fax:** 612/686-1245. **Contact:** Charlie Weihe, Human Resources Director. **World Wide Web address:** http://www.omniquip.com. **Description:** A manufacturer of rough terrain telescoping boom forklifts. **Common positions include:** Blue-Collar Worker Supervisor; Draftsperson; Inspector/Tester/Grader; Machinist; Mechanical Engineer; Production Manager; Purchasing Agent/Manager; Quality Control Supervisor; Technical Writer/Editor; Welder. **Benefits:** 401(k); Dental Insurance; Disability Coverage; Life Insurance; Medical Insurance. **Parent company:** OmniQuip International. **Operations at this facility include:** Administration; Manufacturing; Sales; Service. **Number of employees at this location:** 200.

MEREEN-JOHNSON MACHINE COMPANY

4401 Lyndale Avenue North, Minneapolis MN 55412. 612/529-7791. **Contact:** Human Resources. **Description:** Manufactures woodworking and plastic cutting machinery.

MINCO PRODUCTS, INC.

7300 Commerce Lane NE, Minneapolis MN 55432. 612/571-3121. **Contact:** Jane Stoner, Human Resources Director. **World Wide Web address:** http://www.minco.com. **Description:** Minco is a manufacturer of temperature sensors, heaters, and flexible interconnecting devices. **Common positions include:** Draftsperson; Electrical/Electronics Engineer; Industrial Engineer; Mechanical Engineer. **Educational backgrounds include:** Engineering. **Benefits:** Dental Insurance; Disability Coverage; Life Insurance; Medical Insurance; Profit Sharing; Tuition Assistance. **Special programs:** Internships. **Corporate headquarters location:** This Location. **Operations at this facility include:** Administration; Divisional Headquarters; Manufacturing; Regional Headquarters; Research and Development; Sales; Service.

MOCON

7500 Boone Avenue North, Suite 111, Minneapolis MN 55428. 612/493-6370. **Contact:** Human Resources. **World Wide Web address:** http://www.mocon.com. **Description:** Develops instruments which test packages and packaging materials for the pharmaceutical market. **Corporate headquarters location:** This Location. **Listed on:** NASDAQ. **Stock exchange symbol:** MOCO.

NILFISK-ADVANCE INC.

14600 21st Avenue North, Plymouth MN 55447-3408. 612/745-3500. **Contact:** Ken Frideres, Director of Human Resources. **World Wide Web address:** http://www.nilfisk-advance.com. **Description:** Manufactures professional floor maintenance equipment. **Common positions include:** Accountant/Auditor; Advertising Clerk; Assistant Manager; Blue-Collar Worker Supervisor; Buyer; Computer Operator; Computer Programmer; Credit Clerk and Authorizer; Credit Manager; Customer Service Representative; Department Manager; Designer; Dispatcher; Draftsperson; Electrical/Electronics Engineer; Electrician; Employment Interviewer; Financial Manager; Graphic Artist; Human Resources Manager; Industrial Engineer; Machinist; Management Trainee; Marketing Manager; Mechanical Engineer; Order Clerk; Payroll Clerk; Photographer/Camera Operator; Precision Assembler; Purchasing Agent/Manager; Quality Control Supervisor; Receptionist; Registered Nurse; Secretary; Services Sales Representative; Sheet-Metal Worker; Stock Clerk; Systems Analyst; Technical Representative; Technical Writer/Editor; Transportation/Traffic Specialist; Truck Driver; Typist/Word Processor; Welder. **Educational**

backgrounds include: Business Administration; Communications; Engineering. **Operations at this facility include:** Administration; Manufacturing; Research and Development; Sales; Service. **Number of employees at this location:** 650.

ONAN CORPORATION
1400 73rd Avenue NE, Minneapolis MN 55432. 612/574-5000. **Contact:** Cathy Klopp, Director of Staffing. **World Wide Web address:** http://www.onan.com. **Description:** Manufactures generators. **Corporate headquarters location:** This Location.

OSMONICS, INC.
5951 Clearwater Drive, Minnetonka MN 55343. 612/933-2277. **Fax:** 612/933-0141. **Contact:** Jeff Joyce, Human Resources Manager. **World Wide Web address:** http://www.osmonics.com. **Description:** Designs, manufactures, and markets fluid processing machines, systems, and components. **Common positions include:** Accountant/Auditor; Agricultural Engineer; Biomedical Engineer; Blue-Collar Worker Supervisor; Buyer; Chemical Engineer; Chemist; Civil Engineer; Clerical Supervisor; Customer Service Representative; Designer; Draftsperson; Electrical/Electronics Engineer; Human Resources Manager; Industrial Engineer; Industrial Production Manager; Mechanical Engineer; Metallurgical Engineer; Operations/Production Manager; Purchasing Agent/Manager; Quality Control Supervisor; Systems Analyst; Technical Writer/Editor. **Benefits:** 401(k); Dental Insurance; Disability Coverage; Employee Discounts; Life Insurance; Medical Insurance; Profit Sharing; Tuition Assistance. **Corporate headquarters location:** This Location. **Other U.S. locations:** AZ; CA; MA; NY; WI. **Operations at this facility include:** Administration; Manufacturing; Research and Development; Sales; Service. **Listed on:** New York Stock Exchange. **Number of employees at this location:** 505. **Number of employees nationwide:** 1,040.

PALM BROTHERS
1031 Madeira Avenue, Minneapolis MN 55405. 612/871-2727. **Contact:** Mike Palm, President. **Description:** A manufacturer and distributor of restaurant equipment.

PARKER HANNIFIN CORPORATION
8145 Lewis Road, Minneapolis MN 55427. 612/544-7781. **Contact:** Human Resources. **World Wide Web address:** http://www.parker.com. **Description:** This location manufactures valves and fittings. Overall, Parker Hannifin Corporation makes motion control products including fluid power systems, electromechanical controls, and related components. Products are sold through direct sales employees and more than 4,900 distributors. The product lines of the industrial sector cover most of the components control systems. The Motion and Control Group makes hydraulic pumps, power units, control valves, accumulators, cylinders, actuators, and automation devices to remove contaminants from air, fuel, oil, water, and other fluids. The Fluid Connectors Group makes connectors, tube and hose fittings, hoses, and couplers which transmit fluid. The Seal Group makes sealing devices, gaskets, and packing which ensure leak-proof connections. The Automotive and Refrigeration Groups make components for use in industrial and automotive air conditioning and refrigeration systems. Principal products of the aerospace segment are hydraulic and pneumatic fuel systems and components. **Corporate headquarters location:** Cleveland OH.

PENTAIR INDUSTRIES
Waters Edge Plaza, 1500 County Road B2 West, St. Paul MN 55113-3105. 651/636-7920. **Contact:** Human Resources. **World Wide Web address:** http://www.pentair.com. **Description:** This location houses the corporate offices. Overall, Pentair Industries is a diverse firm with operations in the manufacturing of portable and stationary woodworking tools, pumps, lubrication systems, jacks, electrical enclosures, and sporting ammunition and accessories. **Common positions include:** Accountant/Auditor; Blue-Collar Worker Supervisor; Branch Manager; Budget Analyst; Computer Operator; Computer Programmer; Customer Service Representative; Department Manager; Designer; Dispatcher; Electrical/Electronics Engineer; Electrician; Employment Interviewer; Financial Manager; General Manager; Human Resources Manager; Industrial Engineer; Industrial Production Manager; Machinist; Management Analyst/Consultant; Management Trainee; Manufacturer's/Wholesaler's Sales Rep.; Marketing Manager; Mechanical Engineer; Metallurgical Engineer; Purchasing Agent/Manager; Quality Control Supervisor; Secretary; Systems Analyst. **Educational backgrounds include:** Accounting; Business Administration; Chemistry; Communications; Computer Science; Economics; Engineering; Finance; Liberal Arts; Marketing. **Corporate headquarters location:** This Location. **Listed on:** NASDAQ. **Number of employees at this location:** 40. **Number of employees nationwide:** 9,300.

RAMSEY TECHNOLOGY, INC.
501 90th Avenue NW, Minneapolis MN 55433. 612/783-2500. **Contact:** Human Resources. **World Wide Web address:** http://www.ramseytsr.com. **Description:** Manufactures industrial

instruments for the measurement, display, and control of process variables. **Common positions include:** Draftsperson; Electrical/Electronics Engineer; Mechanical Engineer. **Educational backgrounds include:** Engineering. **Benefits:** 401(k); Daycare Assistance; Dental Insurance; Disability Coverage; Life Insurance; Medical Insurance; Tuition Assistance. **Corporate headquarters location:** Waltham MA. **Parent company:** Thermo Electron. **Operations at this facility include:** Administration; Divisional Headquarters; Research and Development; Sales; Service. **Listed on:** American Stock Exchange; New York Stock Exchange. **Number of employees at this location:** 255.

REMMELE ENGINEERING
10 Old Highway 8, St. Paul MN 55112. 651/635-4100. **Contact:** Human Resources. **World Wide Web address:** http://www.remmele.com. **Description:** Operates a machine shop for large industrial equipment.

RESEARCH, INC.
P.O. Box 24064, Minneapolis MN 55424. 612/941-3300. **Fax:** 612/941-3628. **Contact:** Karen O'Rourke, Vice President of Human Resources. **World Wide Web address:** http://www.researchinc.com. **Description:** A designer and manufacturer of industrial infrared heating equipment, process control systems, and SMT reflow ovens. **Common positions include:** Accountant/Auditor; Customer Service Representative; Designer; Draftsperson; Electrical/Electronics Engineer; Marketing Specialist; Mechanical Engineer; Sales Representative. **Educational backgrounds include:** Business Administration; Engineering. **Benefits:** 401(k); Dental Insurance; Disability Coverage; Life Insurance; Medical Insurance; Profit Sharing; Tuition Assistance. **Corporate headquarters location:** This Location. **Operations at this facility include:** Administration; Manufacturing; Research and Development; Sales; Service. **Listed on:** NASDAQ. **Number of employees at this location:** 160.

RIMAGE CORPORATION
7725 Washington Avenue South, Minneapolis MN 55439. 612/944-8144. **Fax:** 612/944-7808. **Contact:** Human Resources. **World Wide Web address:** http://www.rimage.com. **Description:** Manufactures the equipment used to duplicate CD-ROMs. Founded in 1978.

ROSEMOUNT INC.
12001 Technology Drive, Mail Stop AL-07, Eden Prairie MN 55344. 612/941-5560. **Contact:** Human Resources. **World Wide Web address:** http://www.rosemount.com. **Description:** Engaged in the design and manufacture of precision measurement and control instrumentation for the aerospace and process control industries. Rosemount's process instrumentation products are used to control flow, level, pressure, and temperature.

RYT-WAY INDUSTRIES
1407 Armstrong Road, Northfield MN 55057. 507/663-1281. **Contact:** Gary Tholkes, Human Resources Director. **Description:** A contract packager of food products.

S-T INDUSTRIES, INC.
301 Armstrong Boulevard North, P.O. Box 517, St. James MN 56081. 507/375-3211. **Toll-free phone:** 800/326-2039. **Fax:** 507/375-4503. **Contact:** Personnel/Employment. **E-mail address:** rjf-st@prairie.lakes.com. **World Wide Web address:** http://www.stindustries.thomasregister.com. **Description:** Manufactures and sells precision measuring instruments, optical comparators, and video inspection systems. **NOTE:** Entry-level positions are offered. **Common positions include:** Accountant/Auditor; Blue-Collar Worker Supervisor; Buyer; Computer Programmer; Design Engineer; Draftsperson; Electrical/Electronics Engineer; Industrial Engineer; Manufacturer's/Wholesaler's Sales Rep.; Mechanical Engineer; Purchasing Agent/Manager; Quality Control Supervisor. **Educational backgrounds include:** Accounting; Business Administration; Engineering; Liberal Arts. **Benefits:** Disability Coverage; Life Insurance; Medical Insurance; Pension Plan; Savings Plan. **Corporate headquarters location:** This Location. **Operations at this facility include:** Administration; Manufacturing; Regional Headquarters; Research and Development; Sales; Service. **Listed on:** Privately held. **President:** Michael J. Smith. **Annual sales/revenues:** $5 - $10 million. **Number of employees at this location:** 125.

SPX CORPORATION
OE TOOL DIVISION
655 Eisenhower Drive, Owatonna MN 55060. 507/455-7046. **Contact:** Human Resources. **Description:** Manufactures specialty hand tools for original equipment and aftermarket automotive and industrial customers. **NOTE:** The company offers entry-level positions and second and third shifts. **Common positions include:** Administrative Assistant; Blue-Collar Worker Supervisor; Buyer; Computer Operator; Computer Programmer; Cost Estimator; Design Engineer;

Draftsperson; Environmental Engineer; Finance Director; Financial Analyst; Human Resources Manager; Manufacturing Engineer; Marketing Specialist; Mechanical Engineer; Operations Manager; Production Manager; Project Manager; Purchasing Agent/Manager; Quality Control Supervisor; Sales Engineer; Secretary; Systems Analyst. **Educational backgrounds include:** Business Administration; Computer Science; Engineering. **Benefits:** 401(k); Dental Insurance; Disability Coverage; Employee Discounts; Financial Planning Assistance; Life Insurance; Medical Insurance; Pension Plan; Savings Plan; Tuition Assistance. **Special programs:** Internships. **Corporate headquarters location:** Muskegon MI. **Listed on:** New York Stock Exchange. **Stock exchange symbol:** SPW. **Annual sales/revenues:** More than $100 million. **Number of employees at this location:** 550.

ST. CLOUD FIRE EQUIPMENT INC.
P.O. Box 1516, St. Cloud MN 56302-1516. 320/252-5562. **Contact:** Owner. **Description:** Manufactures fire protection equipment.

ST. PAUL BAR AND RESTAURANT SUPPLY
655 Payne Avenue, St. Paul MN 55101-4595. 651/774-0361. **Contact:** Human Resources. **Description:** Manufactures and distributes restaurant equipment. **NOTE:** Interested jobseekers should address all inquiries to Mike Palm, President, Palm Brothers, 2727 Nicollet Avenue, Minneapolis MN 55408.

SICO INC.
7525 Cahill Road, Edina MN 55439. 612/941-1700. **Contact:** Human Resources. **World Wide Web address:** http://www.sicoinc.com. **Description:** A manufacturer of a diverse line of products including room-service centers, stages, tables, wall-beds, and other related products. Clients include schools and hotels.

STREATER STORE FIXTURES
411 South First Avenue, Albert Lea MN 56007-1779. 507/373-0611. **Contact:** Human Resources. **Description:** A manufacturer of furniture and shelving fixtures for use in retail stores.

TENNANT
P.O. Box 1452, Minneapolis MN 55440. 612/540-1200. **Physical address:** 701 North Lilac Drive, Minneapolis MN. **Fax:** 612/513-1754. **Contact:** Human Resources. **Description:** Manufactures floor maintenance equipment including industrial sweepers and scrubbers, floor coating machinery, and commercial equipment. **Common positions include:** Automotive Mechanic; Chemist; Customer Service Representative; Services Sales Representative; Systems Engineer. **Educational backgrounds include:** Business Administration; Chemistry; Computer Science; Engineering; Marketing. **Benefits:** 401(k); Dental Insurance; Disability Coverage; Life Insurance; Medical Insurance; Pension Plan; Profit Sharing; Tuition Assistance. **Corporate headquarters location:** This Location. **Operations at this facility include:** Administration; Engineering and Design; Manufacturing; Research and Development; Sales. **Listed on:** NASDAQ. **Number of employees at this location:** 1,000.

TESCOM CORPORATION
19111 Industrial Boulevard, Elk River MN 55330. 612/441-6330. **Contact:** Bruce Tyler, Personnel. **Description:** A manufacturer of industrial control systems.

3M
3M Center, Building 224-1W02, St. Paul MN 55144-1000. 651/733-0687. **Contact:** Human Resources Department. **World Wide Web address:** http://www.3m.com. **Description:** 3M manufactures products in three sectors: Industrial and Consumer; Information, Imaging, and Electronic; and Life Sciences. The Industrial and Consumer Sector includes a variety of products under brand names including 3M, Scotch, Post-it, Scotch-Brite, and Scotchgard. The Information, Imaging, and Electronic Sector is a leader in several high-growth global industries including telecommunications, electronics, electrical, imaging, and memory media. The Life Sciences Sector serves two broad market categories: health care, and traffic and personal safety. In the health care market, 3M is a leading provider of medical and surgical supplies, drug delivery systems, and dental products; in traffic and personal safety, 3M is a leader in products for transportation safety, worker protection, vehicle and sign graphics, and out-of-home advertising. **Corporate headquarters location:** This Location. **International locations:** Worldwide. **Listed on:** Amsterdam Stock Exchange; Chicago Stock Exchange; Frankfurt Stock Exchange; New York Stock Exchange; Pacific Stock Exchange; Paris Stock Exchange; Swiss Stock Exchange; Tokyo Stock Exchange.

TWIN CITY FAN COMPANIES

5959 Trenton Lane, Plymouth MN 55442. 612/551-7600. **Fax:** 612/551-7601. **Contact:** Leslie Barry, Director of Training. **World Wide Web address:** http://www.tcf.com. **Description:** Twin City Fan Companies is a leader in the design and manufacture of air-moving equipment. The company has a complete line of fans and blowers from 1/6 HP to over 1,000 HP for every commercial and industrial air-moving need. Products include airfoil design ventilating fans, packaged ventilating sets, material handling fans, high-pressure and induced draft fans, axial fans, propeller fans, and custom designs and accessories. Each fan and blower produced is manufactured to the customer's specifications. The company operates manufacturing facilities in Mitchell and Brookings SD and maintains a nationwide network of sales representatives. **Corporate headquarters location:** This Location. **Subsidiaries include:** TCF Aerovent, Inc.; Twin City Fan & Blower Company.

U.S. FILTER/JOHNSON SCREENS

P.O. Box 64118, St. Paul MN 55164-0118. 651/636-3900. **Toll-free phone:** 800/VEE-WIRE. **Fax:** 651/636-2916. **Contact:** Ms. Lee Zechmann, Manager of Human Resources. **World Wide Web address:** http://www.johnsonscreens.com. **Description:** Manufactures screens used in industrial, oil and gas, and mining applications. Founded in 1902. **NOTE:** Entry-level positions as well as second and third shifts are offered. **Common positions include:** Advertising Account Executive; Blue-Collar Worker Supervisor; Customer Service Representative; Design Engineer; Draftsperson; Financial Analyst; Human Resources Manager; Manufacturing Engineer; Mechanical Engineer; Operations Manager; Sales Manager; Sales Representative; Systems Analyst. **Educational backgrounds include:** Accounting; Business Administration; Chemistry; Computer Science; Engineering. **Benefits:** 401(k); Dental Insurance; Disability Coverage; Life Insurance; Medical Insurance; Tuition Assistance. **Special programs:** Internships; Apprenticeships. **Corporate headquarters location:** Palm Desert CA. **Other U.S. locations:** Nationwide. **International locations:** Worldwide. **Parent company:** United States Filter Corporation. **Operations at this facility include:** Divisional Headquarters. **Listed on:** New York Stock Exchange. **Stock exchange symbol:** USFILTER. **Number of employees at this location:** 300. **Number of employees worldwide:** 10,000.

UNITED DEFENSE
ARMAMENT SYSTEMS DIVISION

4800 East River Road, Minneapolis MN 55421. 612/571-9201. **Fax:** 612/572-3304. **Contact:** Mark Youngblood, Human Resources Director. **E-mail address:** asd-staffing@udlp.com. **World Wide Web address:** http://www.udlp.com. **Description:** Producers of shipboard missile launching equipment and gun mounts. The company also operates a machine shop and heat-treating, welding, plating, and foundry facilities. **Common positions include:** Accountant; Computer Programmer; Design Engineer; Electrical/Electronics Engineer; Financial Analyst; Industrial Engineer; Mechanical Engineer; Software Engineer; Systems Analyst. **Educational backgrounds include:** Accounting; Computer Science; Engineering; Finance. **Benefits:** 401(k); Dental Insurance; Disability Coverage; Life Insurance; Medical Insurance; Pension Plan; Savings Plan; Tuition Assistance. **Special programs:** Internships. **Corporate headquarters location:** Arlington VA. **Parent company:** The Carlyle Group. **Operations at this facility include:** Divisional Headquarters. **Listed on:** Privately held. **Number of employees at this location:** 1,500. **Number of employees worldwide:** 7,000.

VARITRONIC SYSTEMS, INC.

6835 Winnetka Circle, Brooklyn Park MN 55428. 612/536-6400. **Fax:** 612/536-0769. **Contact:** Human Resources. **World Wide Web address:** http://www.varitronic.com. **Description:** Develops, produces, and sells business graphics products for communication materials. The products are made to satisfy presentation, labeling, and signage in a variety of markets including general office, manufacturing, and education. Varitronic sells lettering and labeling systems that generate print in a variety of styles, in sizes ranging from one-half inch to four inches, using thermal transfer technology. **Corporate headquarters location:** This Location. **Listed on:** NASDAQ. **Number of employees at this location:** 100. **Number of employees nationwide:** 290.

WAGNER SPRAY TECH

1770 Fernbrook Lane, Plymouth MN 55447. 612/553-7000. **Contact:** Human Resources. **World Wide Web address:** http://www.wagnerspraytech.com. **Description:** A manufacturer of all types of paint sprayers.

WATEROUS COMPANY

125 Hardman Avenue South, South St. Paul MN 55075. 651/450-5000. **Fax:** 651/450-5241. **Recorded jobline:** 651/450-5299. **Contact:** Rich Ryan, Personnel Director. **World Wide Web address:** http://www.waterousco.com. **Description:** Manufactures hydrants, pumps, transmissions,

and valves. **NOTE:** Entry-level positions, part-time jobs, and second and third shifts are offered. **Common positions include:** AS400 Programmer Analyst; Accountant; Buyer; Computer Operator; Computer Programmer; Controller; Credit Manager; Customer Service Representative; Desktop Publishing Specialist; Draftsperson; Human Resources Manager; Manufacturing Engineer; Network/Systems Administrator; Operations Manager; Production Manager; Quality Assurance Engineer; Sales Representative; Secretary; Transportation/Traffic Specialist. **Educational backgrounds include:** AS400 Certification; Microsoft Word; Spreadsheets. **Benefits:** 401(k); Casual Dress - Fridays; Dental Insurance; Disability Coverage; Life Insurance; Medical Insurance; Pension Plan; Profit Sharing; Sick Days (6 - 10); Tuition Assistance; Vacation Days (6 - 10). **Corporate headquarters location:** This Location. **Parent company:** American Cast Iron Pipe Company (ACIPCO). **Listed on:** Privately held. **Number of employees at this location:** 360.

WEIGH-TRONIX INC.
1000 Armstrong Drive, Fairmont MN 56031. 507/238-4461. **Contact:** Human Resources. **World Wide Web address:** http://www.weigh-tronix.com. **Description:** Manufactures scales for industrial and agricultural use.

XERXES CORPORATION
7901 Xerxes Avenue South, Suite 201, Bloomington MN 55431. 612/887-1890. **Fax:** 612/887-1870. **Contact:** Barbara J. Meyer, Supervisor of Payroll and Accounting. **World Wide Web address:** http://www.xerxescorp.com. **Description:** Manufactures fiberglass structural products including multi-compartment tanks, oil and water separators, and underground storage tanks. Other tank accessories produced include electronic gauging and leak detection products, hydrostatic monitoring systems, and secondary containment sumps. **Common positions include:** Accountant/Auditor; Attorney; Chemical Engineer; Clerical Supervisor; Computer Programmer; Cost Estimator; Credit Manager; Designer; Draftsperson; Financial Analyst; Human Resources Manager; Industrial Engineer; Manufacturer's/Wholesaler's Sales Rep.; Mechanical Engineer; Purchasing Agent/Manager; Services Sales Representative; Structural Engineer; Systems Analyst. **Educational backgrounds include:** Accounting; Business Administration; Computer Science; Engineering; Finance; Marketing. **Benefits:** 401(k); Dental Insurance; Disability Coverage; Life Insurance; Medical Insurance; Tuition Assistance. **Corporate headquarters location:** This Location. **Other U.S. locations:** Anaheim CA; Lakeland FL; Tipton IA; Hagerstown MD; Avon OH; Seguin TX. **Operations at this facility include:** Divisional Headquarters; Sales. **Listed on:** Privately held. **Number of employees at this location:** 35. **Number of employees nationwide:** 400.

Note: Because addresses and telephone numbers of smaller companies can change rapidly, we recommend you call each company to verify the information below before inquiring about job opportunities. Mass mailings are not recommended.

Additional small employers:

AMMUNITION

Alliant Techsystems Inc.
TCAAP Bldg 103, St. Paul MN 55112. 651/639-3199.

COMMERCIAL FURNITURE AND FIXTURES

Ergotron Inc.
1181 Trapp Rd, St. Paul MN 55121-1248. 612/452-8135.

LSI Corporation of America
2100 Xenium Lane North, Plymouth MN 55441-3629. 612/559-4664.

Safeco Products Company
5600 Highway 169 N, Minneapolis MN 55428-3027. 612/536-6700.

Stylmark Inc.
PO Box 32008, Minneapolis MN 55432-0008. 612/574-7474.

Tuohy Furniture Corporation
42 Saint Albans Pl, Chatfield MN 55923-1457. 507/867-4280.

Wenger Corporation
PO Box 448, Owatonna MN 55060-0448. 507/455-4100.

CONSTRUCTION MACHINERY AND EQUIPMENT

Burro Crane
PO Box 798, Winona MN 55987-0798. 507/454-1563.

Labounty Manufacturing Inc.
100 State Road 2, Two Harbors MN 55616-8010. 218/834-2123.

Mustang Manufacturing Company
PO Box 547, Owatonna MN 55060-0547. 507/451-7112.

Pacal Blades
PO Box 64432, St. Paul MN 55164-0432. 651/631-1111.

Superior Components
PO Box 654, Morris MN 56267-0654. 320/589-3876.

CONVEYORS AND CONVEYING EQUIPMENT

Cannon Conveyor Systems Inc.
1001 Johnson Pkwy, St. Paul MN 55106-3400. 651/776-8501.

FEC
2765 Niagara Ln N, Plymouth MN 55447-4844. 612/559-5200.

Superior Equipment
PO Box 672, Morris MN 56267-0672. 320/589-2819.

Wyard Machinery Group
907 15th St SW, Forest Lake MN 55025-1316. 651/464-4000.

ENGINE PARTS

Cylinder City Inc.
PO Box 49220, Minneapolis MN
55449-0220. 612/780-2550.

Graco Inc.
20500 David Koch Ave, Rogers
MN 55374-8965. 612/379-3750.

Oildyne
4301 Quebec Ave N, Minneapolis
MN 55428-4912. 612/533-1600.

Tol-O-Matic Inc.
3800 County Road 116, Hamel
MN 55340-9342. 612/478-8000.

Victor Fluid Power
1123 Highway 212 W, Granite
Falls MN 56241-1211. 320/564-
2311.

FANS, BLOWERS, AND AIR PURIFICATION EQUIPMENT

King Company Inc.
PO Box 287, Owatonna MN
55060-0287. 507/451-3770.

FARM MACHINERY AND EQUIPMENT

Al Lor Products Inc.
PO Box 289, Benson MN 56215-
0289. 320/843-4161.

Blunt
PO Box 568, Owatonna MN
55060-0568. 507/451-8654.

HD Hudson Manufacturing Co.
2nd St & Eddy St, Hastings MN
55033. 651/437-4121.

HEATING EQUIPMENT

Deltak Corporation
PO Box 55441, Plymouth MN
55441. 612/557-7440.

INDUSTRIAL AND COMMERCIAL MACHINERY AND EQUIPMENT

Audubon Engineering and Manufacturing
PO Box 277, Audubon MN
56511-0277. 218/439-6186.

Classic Manufacturing Inc.
2980 Granada Ln N, St. Paul MN
55128-3607. 651/770-1212.

Com-Tal Machine & Engineering
1239 Willow Lake Blvd, White
Bear Lake MN 55110-5145.
651/483-2611.

Elk River Machine Company
828 4th St, Elk River MN 55330-
1325. 612/441-1581.

Forward Technology Industries
13500 County Road 6, Plymouth
MN 55441-3817. 612/559-1785.

Harmony Engineering Corp.
460 Hoover St NE, Minneapolis
MN 55413-2927. 612/623-0510.

ITW Heartland Parts Division
1601 36th Ave W, Alexandria
MN 56308-3304. 320/762-8138.

Kelco Industries Inc.
6420 Zane Ave N, Minneapolis
MN 55429-4119. 612/535-1174.

Mid-Continent Engineering
405 35th Ave NE, Minneapolis
MN 55418-1126. 612/781-0260.

Motek Engineering and Manufacturing Co.
PO Box 273, Cambridge MN
55008-0273. 612/689-1333.

Straight River Engineering & Manufacturing
PO Box 467, Park Rapids MN
56470-0467. 218/732-4666.

Ver-Sa-Til Associates Inc.
18400 W 77th St, Chanhassen
MN 55317-9308. 612/949-2400.

Washington Scientific Industries
PO Box 340, Long Lake MN
55356-0340. 612/473-1271.

INDUSTRIAL PROCESS FURNACES AND OVENS

Despatch Industries
8860 207th St W, Lakeville MN
55044-9542. 612/469-5424.

Watlow Controls
1241 Bundy Blvd, Winona MN
55987-4873. 507/454-5300.

MEASURING AND CONTROLLING EQUIPMENT

Aetrium Incorporated
2350 Helen Street North,
Maplewood MN 55109-2942.
651/770-2000.

Carl Zeiss IMT Corp.
7008 Northland Dr N,
Minneapolis MN 55428-1524.
612/533-9990.

Circuit Check Inc.
6550 Wedgwood Rd #120, Osseo
MN 55311-3642. 612/550-0050.

Itron Inc.
PO Box 1735, Waseca MN
56093-0745. 507/837-4372.

Micro Control Company
7956 Main St NE, Fridley MN
55432-1842. 612/786-8750.

Nu Aire Inc.
2100 Fernbrook Ln N, Plymouth
MN 55447-4723. 612/553-1270.

Reuter Manufacturing Inc.
410 11th Ave S, Hopkins MN
55343-7844. 612/935-6921.

Rhombus Technology
PO Box 1708, Detroit Lakes MN
56502-1708. 218/847-1317.

Rockwell Automation
14960 Minnetonka Industrial,
Minnetonka MN 55345-2107.
612/935-7704.

Rosemount Measurement Division
PO Box 1126, Chanhassen MN
55317-1126. 612/949-7000.

METAL CUTTING OR FORMING TOOLS

Continental Hydraulics
5505 W 123rd St, Savage MN
55378-1202. 612/890-3300.

Komo Machine Inc.
11 Industrial Blvd, Sauk Rapids
MN 56379-8709. 320/252-0580.

Mate Precision Tooling Inc.
PO Box 728, Anoka MN 55303-
0728. 612/421-0230.

Milltronics Manufacturing Co.
1400 Mill Ln, Waconia MN
55387-1044. 612/442-1410.

Timesavers Inc.
5270 Hanson Ct N, Minneapolis
MN 55429-3111. 612/537-3611.

METALWORKING MACHINERY

PR Systems Inc.
899 Highway 96 W, Shoreview
MN 55126-1912. 651/484-7261.

MISC. INDUSTRIAL MACHINE TOOLS

Viking Drill & Tool Inc.
PO Box 65278, St. Paul MN
55165-0278. 651/227-8911.

MISC. INDUSTRIAL MACHINERY AND EQUIPMENT

Cenco
2930 Anthony Ln, Minneapolis
MN 55418-3239. 612/781-6557.

McQuay International
PO Box 32006, Minneapolis MN
55432-0006. 612/571-5200.

Northern Tool & Equipment
PO Box 1219, Burnsville MN
55337-0219. 612/894-9510.

Ram Center
5140 Moundview Dr, Red Wing
MN 55066-1100. 651/388-1821.

**MISC. PIPE FITTINGS
AND/OR VALVES**

CPC
1001 Westgate Dr, St. Paul MN
55114-1065. 651/645-0091.

**MOTORS AND
GENERATORS**

Katolight Corporation
3201 3rd Ave, Ste B, Mankato
MN 56001-2795. 507/625-7973.

Winco Inc.
225 S Cordova Ave, Le Center
MN 56057-1805. 507/357-6821.

PACKAGING MACHINERY

BPMC Inc.
315 27th Avenue NE,
Minneapolis MN 55418-2715.
612/782-1200.

**POWER TRANSMISSION
EQUIPMENT**

RPM
1259 Wolters Blvd, White Bear
Lake MN 55110-5158. 651/484-
2447.

**PUMPS AND PUMPING
EQUIPMENT**

Hypro Corporation
375 5th Ave NW, St. Paul MN
55112-3239. 651/633-9300.

Oildyne
8811 Science Center Dr,
Minneapolis MN 55428-3619.
612/531-3550.

**SERVICE INDUSTRY
MACHINERY**

Recovery Engineering Inc.
9300 75th Avenue N,
Minneapolis MN 55428-1032.
612/315-5500.

VENDING MACHINES

**Gross Given Manufacturing
Co.**
75 Plato Blvd W, St. Paul MN
55107-2026. 651/224-4391.

For more information on career opportunities in industrial manufacturing:

Associations

**ASSOCIATION FOR MANUFACTURING
EXCELLENCE**
380 West Palatine Road, Wheeling IL 60090.
847/520-3282. World Wide Web address: http://www.
trainingforum.com/ASN/AME.

**ASSOCIATION FOR MANUFACTURING
TECHNOLOGY**
7901 Westpark Drive, McLean VA 22102. 703/893-
2900. A trade association. World Wide Web address:
http://www.mfgtech.org.

INSTITUTE OF INDUSTRIAL ENGINEERS
25 Technology Park, Norcross GA 30092-2988.
770/449-0460. World Wide Web address: http://www.
iienet.org. A nonprofit organization with 27,000
members. Conducts seminars and offers reduced rates
on its books and publications.

**NATIONAL ASSOCIATION OF
MANUFACTURERS**
1331 Pennsylvania Avenue NW, Suite 1500,
Washington DC 20004. 202/637-3000. World Wide
Web address: http://www.nam.org. A lobbying
association.

**NATIONAL TOOLING & MACHINING
ASSOCIATION**
9300 Livingston Road, Fort Washington MD 20744.
Toll-free phone: 800/248-6862. World Wide Web
address: http://www.ntma.org. Reports on wages and
operating expenses, produces monthly newsletters,
and offers legal advice.

**PRECISION MACHINED PRODUCTS
ASSOCIATION**
6700 West Snowville Road, Brecksville OH 44141.
440/526-0300. Provides resource information.

SOCIETY OF MANUFACTURING ENGINEERS
P.O. Box 930, One SME Drive, Dearborn MI 48121.
313/271-1500. World Wide Web address: http://www.
sme.org. Offers educational events and educational
materials on manufacturing.

Directories

AMERICAN MANUFACTURER'S DIRECTORY
5711 South 86th Circle, P.O. Box 37347, Omaha NE
68127. Toll-free phone: 800/555-5211. World Wide
Web address: http://www.infousa.com. Made by the
same company that created *American Big Business
Directory*, *American Manufacturer's Directory* lists
over 531,000 manufacturing companies of all sizes
and industries. The directory contains product and
sales information, company size, and a key contact
name for each company.

Online Services

CAREER PARK - MANUFACTURING JOBS
http://www.careerpark.com/jobs/manulist.html. This
Website provides a list of current job openings in the
manufacturing industry. The site is run by Parker
Advertising Service, Inc.

**MO'S GATEWAY TO MANUFACTURING-
RELATED JOBS LISTINGS**
http://www.chesapk.com/mfgjobs.html. Provides links
to sites that post job openings in manufacturing.

Special Programs

**BUREAU OF APPRENTICESHIP AND
TRAINING**
U.S. Department of Labor, 200 Constitution Avenue
NW, Room N4649, Washington DC 20210. 202/219-
5921.

MINING/GAS/PETROLEUM/ENERGY RELATED

Crude oil prices fell more than 30 percent between November 1997 and November 1998, according to the U.S. Department of Energy. The decline is due to ailing economies in the Far East, mild winters in the U.S. and Europe, and an abundant supply. The trend is likely to continue with Asia in turmoil and a surplus of commodities from heating oil to gasoline. This is good news for consumers who benefited from lower prices.

Metal mining and oil and gas extraction all experienced decreased output during 1998, and the Bureau of Labor Statistics projects that employment opportunities in the mining industry will decrease by 2.5 percent by 2006. Other sectors are expected to remain steady, specifically service companies and drillers. Standard & Poor reported a 22 percent rise in profits for the petroleum services industry through the first half of 1998 versus the same period of 1997.

In other mining sectors, lime production has been reaching higher levels since 1993. The coal mining industry has undergone some changes in order to regain profits, and production is expected to rise 1 percent annually through 2002. Factors that may negatively affect this sector include higher transportation costs, labor disruptions, and government restrictions.

GREAT NORTHERN IRON ORE PROPERTIES
332 Minnesota Street, W-1290 First National Bank Building, St. Paul MN 55101. 651/224-2385. **Contact:** Thomas Janochoski, Vice President. **Description:** A trust company engaged in the leasing of land for use in mining iron ore.

KOCH PETROLEUM GROUP
P.O. Box 64596, St. Paul MN 55164. 651/437-0700. **Contact:** Human Resources. **Description:** An oil refinery.

MARATHON ASHLAND PETROLEUM COMPANY
459 Third Street, P.O. Box 9, St. Paul Park MN 55071. 651/459-9771. **Contact:** Human Resources. **Description:** This location operates a refinery for oil and gasoline to make jet fuels. Overall, Marathon Ashland Petroleum Company is a large, diversified petroleum corporation with a group of non-refining operations. Operations include retail marketing, motor oil marketing, chemicals, engineering and construction, and oil and gas exploration and production.

MINNEGASCO
P.O. Box 59038, Minneapolis MN 55459. 612/372-4664. **Contact:** Human Resources. **Description:** An energy services, products, and communications corporation. **Subsidiaries include:** Minnegasco, Inc., a natural gas distribution company; Dyco Petroleum, an oil and gas exploration and production company; E.F. Johnson Company, providing design, manufacturing, and marketing of radio communications products and systems, electronic components, and specialty products; and EnScan, Inc., which develops and markets energy measurement products and systems.

For more information on career opportunities in the mining, gas, petroleum, and energy industries:

<u>Associations</u>

AMERICAN ASSOCIATION OF PETROLEUM GEOLOGISTS
P.O. Box 979, Tulsa OK 74101. 918/584-2555. World Wide Web address: http://www.aapg.org. International headquarters for petroleum geologists.

AMERICAN GEOLOGICAL INSTITUTE
4220 King Street, Alexandria VA 22302-1502. 703/379-2480. World Wide Web address: http://www. agiweb.org. American Geological Institute publishes *Geotimes* and offers job listings. Scholarships may also be available.

AMERICAN NUCLEAR SOCIETY
555 North Kensington Avenue, La Grange Park IL
60526. 708/352-6611. World Wide Web address:
http://www.ans.org. Offers educational services.

AMERICAN PETROLEUM INSTITUTE
1220 L Street NW, Suite 900, Washington DC 20005.
202/682-8000. World Wide Web address: http://www.
api.org. A trade association.

GEOLOGICAL SOCIETY OF AMERICA
3300 Penrose Place, P.O. Box 9140, Boulder CO
80301. 303/447-2020. World Wide Web address:
http://www.geosociety.org. Membership of over
17,000. Offers sales items and publications. Also
conducts society meetings.

NUCLEAR ENERGY INSTITUTE
1776 I Street NW, Suite 400, Washington DC 20006-
3708. 202/739-8000. World Wide Web address:
http://www.nei.org. Provides a wide variety of
information on nuclear energy issues.

**SOCIETY FOR MINING, METALLURGY, AND
EXPLORATION, INC.**
8307 Shaffer Parkway, Littleton CO 80127. 303/973-
9550. World Wide Web address: http://www.smenet.
org.

**SOCIETY OF EXPLORATION
GEOPHYSICISTS**
P.O. Box 702740, Tulsa OK 74170-2740. 918/497-
5500. World Wide Web address: http://www.seg.org.
A membership association. Offers publications.

SOCIETY OF PETROLEUM ENGINEERS
P.O. Box 833836, Richardson TX 75083. 972/952-
9393. World Wide Web address: http://www.spe.org.

Directories

**BROWN'S DIRECTORY OF NORTH
AMERICAN AND INTERNATIONAL GAS
COMPANIES**
Advanstar Communications, 7500 Old Oak
Boulevard, Cleveland OH 44130. Toll-free phone:
800/225-4569. World Wide Web address: http://www.
advanstar.com.

**DIRECTORY OF MINNESOTA'S ENERGY
EFFICIENT AND RENEWABLE ENERGY
INDUSTRY**
Minnesota Environmental Initiative, 2420 Rand
Tower, 527 Marquette Avenue South, Minneapolis
MN 55402. 612/334-3388.

OIL AND GAS DIRECTORY
Geophysical Directory, Inc., P.O. Box 130508,
Houston TX 77219. 713/529-8789.

Magazines

AMERICAN GAS
1515 Wilson Boulevard, Suite 100, Arlington VA
22209. 703/841-8686.

GAS INDUSTRIES
Gas Industries News, Inc., 6300 North River Road,
Suite 505, Rosemont IL 60018. 847/696-2394.

NATIONAL PETROLEUM NEWS
Adams Business Media, 2101 South Arlington
Heights Road, Suite 150, Arlington Heights IL 60005.
847/427-9512. Fax: 847/427-2006. World Wide Web
address: http://www.petroretail.net.

OIL AND GAS JOURNAL
PennWell Publishing Company, P.O. Box 1260, Tulsa
OK 74101. 918/835-3161. World Wide Web address:
http://www.ogjonline.com.

Online Services

**NATIONAL CENTRE FOR PETROLEUM
GEOLOGY AND GEOPHYSICS**
http://www.ncpgg.adelaide.edu.au/ncpgg.html. This
Website provides links to sites that post job openings
in mining, petroleum, energy, and related fields.

**PETROLEUM & GEOSYSTEMS
ENGINEERING**
http://www.pe.utexas.edu/Dept/Reading/pejb.html.
Offers a vast list of links to sites that are posting
current job openings in petroleum and geosystems
engineering and related fields. The site is run by the
University of Texas at Austin. Links to many relevant
associations are also offered.

PAPER AND WOOD PRODUCTS

Despite an increased demand for U.S. market pulp, the Bureau of Labor Statistics expects a decline in the number of paper industry jobs through 2006. According to the U.S. Department of Commerce, while the pulp sector is expected to enjoy higher sales through 2002, overseas shipment growth should be slower, at 1.8 percent annually.

Profits for the industry as a whole increased 89 percent for the first two quarters of 1998 versus profits for the same period of 1997. Profits rose an amazing 211 percent in the second quarter alone, according to Standard & Poor. *At the same time, industry profit margins more than tripled. Companies such as the Mead Corporation saw varying demand for paper products in 1998.*

Automation is causing a decline in employment opportunities for precision woodworkers and woodworking machine operators, according to the U.S. Department of Labor. Woodworkers who specialize in furniture, cabinets, moldings, and fixtures should find more abundant opportunities. A significant upswing in the demand for wooden household furniture should result in improved employment prospects.

FLOUR CITY PACKAGING
500 Stinson Boulevard, Minneapolis MN 55413. 612/378-2100. **Contact:** Human Resources. **World Wide Web address:** http://www.flourcitypack.com. **Description:** A manufacturer of paperboard boxes.

GEORGIA-PACIFIC CORPORATION
P.O. Box 16267, Duluth MN 55816. 218/720-8200. **Contact:** Human Resources. **World Wide Web address:** http://www.gapac.com. **Description:** Manufactures hardboard. **Corporate headquarters location:** Atlanta GA.

GREAT PLAINS COMPANIES, INC.
P.O. Box 64557, St. Paul MN 55164. 651/639-5751. **Contact:** Human Resources Department. **Description:** Operates 40 lumberyards in the U.S. **Common positions include:** Accountant/ Auditor; Buyer; Construction Contractor; Credit Manager; Customer Service Representative; Draftsperson; Human Resources Manager; Management Trainee; Structural Engineer. **Benefits:** 401(k); Dental Insurance; Disability Coverage; Employee Discounts; ESOP; Life Insurance; Medical Insurance; Tuition Assistance. **Corporate headquarters location:** This Location. **Other U.S. locations:** IA; IL; MT; ND; SD; WI. **Subsidiaries include:** Better Tools; Great Plains Supply, Inc.; Plum Building; Renfrow. **Operations at this facility include:** Administration. **Listed on:** Privately held. **Number of employees at this location:** 35. **Number of employees nationwide:** 700.

GREIF BROTHERS CORPORATION
1821 University Avenue, St. Paul MN 55104-3198. 651/645-5557. **Contact:** Human Resources. **Description:** Produces and sells shipping containers and materials including fibre, steel and plastic drums, multiwall bags, and related items; and produces and sells containerboard and related products including virgin and recycled containerboard, corrugated paper, and corrugated containers. **Other U.S. locations:** Northlake IL; Delaware OH.

INLAND CONTAINER
3900 State Highway 101, Shakopee MN 55379. 612/445-4201. **Contact:** Ms. Pat Holloway, Personnel Director. **Description:** A manufacturer of corrugated shipping containers and boxes.

LAKE SUPERIOR PAPER INDUSTRIES
100 North Central Avenue, Duluth MN 55807. 218/628-5100. **Contact:** Human Resources. **Description:** Manufactures large rolls of paper that are then used in the production of magazines and brochures.

LIBERTY CARTON COMPANY
870 Louisiana Avenue South, Minneapolis MN 55426. 612/540-9600. **Contact:** Mark Tampty, Personnel Director. **Description:** A manufacturer of corrugated and solid fiber boxes.

LYMAN LUMBER COMPANY
P.O. Box 40, Excelsior MN 55331. 612/474-0844. **Contact:** Human Resources. **Description:** A lumber and building materials company with several divisions in the Twin Cities metropolitan area, two in Wisconsin, and one in North Carolina. **Common positions include:** Accountant/Auditor; Architectural Engineer; Blue-Collar Worker Supervisor; Buyer; Credit Manager; Customer Service Representative; Draftsperson; Human Resources Manager; Management Trainee; Manufacturer's/ Wholesaler's Sales Rep.; Operations/Production Manager; Purchasing Agent/Manager; Truck Driver. **Educational backgrounds include:** Accounting; Engineering. **Benefits:** Dental Insurance; Disability Coverage; Employee Discounts; Life Insurance; Medical Insurance; Pension Plan; Profit Sharing; Tuition Assistance. **Corporate headquarters location:** This Location. **Operations at this facility include:** Administration.

MACKAY ENVELOPE CORPORATION
2100 Elm Street SE, Minneapolis MN 55414-2597. 612/331-9311. **Contact:** Human Resources. **World Wide Web address:** http://www.mackayenvelope.com. **Description:** Manufactures envelopes. **Common positions include:** Accountant/Auditor; Customer Service Representative; Manufacturer's/Wholesaler's Sales Rep. **Educational backgrounds include:** Accounting; Business Administration; Liberal Arts. **Benefits:** 401(k); Dental Insurance; Disability Coverage; Life Insurance; Medical Insurance; Profit Sharing; Tuition Assistance. **Corporate headquarters location:** This Location. **Other U.S. locations:** Mount Pleasant IA. **Operations at this facility include:** Manufacturing. **Listed on:** Privately held. **Number of employees at this location:** 250. **Number of employees nationwide:** 350.

QUALITY PARK PRODUCTS
2520 Como Avenue, St. Paul MN 55108-1299. 651/645-0251. **Contact:** Ron Rebeck, Vice President of Human Resources. **World Wide Web address:** http://www.qualitypark.com. **Description:** An envelope manufacturer and wholesaler.

ROCK-TENN
2250 Wabash Avenue, St. Paul MN 55114. 651/641-4938. **Contact:** Human Resources. **Description:** This locations is a paperboard mill. Overall, Rock-Tenn Company is a manufacturer of 100 percent recycled paperboard and paperboard products. Over two-thirds of paperboard production is used by the company's own converting plants to produce folding cartons, book and notebook covers, components for the furniture industry, and solid fiber partitions used in shipping glass and plastic containers.

SMEAD MANUFACTURING COMPANY
600 East Smead Boulevard, Hastings MN 55033. 651/437-4111. **Contact:** Dean Schwanke, Director of Human Resources. **World Wide Web address:** http://www.smead.com. **Description:** A die-cut paper manufacturing firm. **Common positions include:** Accountant/Auditor; Administrator; Blue-Collar Worker Supervisor; Branch Manager; Buyer; Computer Programmer; Credit Manager; Customer Service Representative; Department Manager; Draftsperson; Financial Analyst; General Manager; Human Resources Manager; Industrial Engineer; Industrial Production Manager; Manufacturer's/Wholesaler's Sales Rep.; Marketing Specialist; Mechanical Engineer; Operations/Production Manager; Purchasing Agent/Manager; Quality Control Supervisor; Systems Analyst; Transportation/Traffic Specialist. **Educational backgrounds include:** Accounting; Business Administration; Computer Science; Engineering; Liberal Arts; Marketing. **Benefits:** Disability Coverage; Life Insurance; Medical Insurance; Pension Plan; Savings Plan; Tuition Assistance. **Corporate headquarters location:** This Location. **Operations at this facility include:** Manufacturing.

TENNECO PACKAGING
1821 NE Marshall Street, Minneapolis MN 55418. 612/789-3511. **Contact:** Human Resources. **World Wide Web address:** http://www.tenneco-packaging.com. **Description:** This location houses administrative offices as well as a plant that manufactures boxes and other packaging materials. Overall, Tenneco Packaging is a worldwide manufacturer of paper, corrugated paper, paperboard, aluminum, and plastic packaging material with 60 plant locations. Products are used in the packaging of food, paper and paper products, metal products, rubber and plastics, automotive products, and point-of-purchase displays; the packaging of soap, detergent, and food products; and residential construction. **NOTE:** Please indicate department of interest. **Corporate headquarters location:** Evansville IL. **Parent company:** Tenneco (Greenwich CT).

Note: Because addresses and telephone numbers of smaller companies can change rapidly, we recommend you call each company to verify the information below before inquiring about job opportunities. Mass mailings are not recommended.

Additional small employers:

COATED AND LAMINATED PAPER

3M
PO Box 366, Stillwater MN 55082-0366. 651/737-2000.

3M
710 N State St, Fairmont MN 56031-3851. 507/235-3391.

Lofton Label Inc.
6290 Claude Way, Inver Grove Heights MN 55076-4435. 651/457-8118.

Ritrama Duramark Inc.
800 Kasota Ave SE, Minneapolis MN 55414-2814. 612/378-2277.

CONVERTED PAPER AND PAPERBOARD PRODUCTS

HM Smyth Company
PO Box 64669, St. Paul MN 55164-0669. 651/646-4544.

Modernistic
169 Jenks Ave, St. Paul MN 55117-5068. 651/291-7650.

Weyerhaeuser Company
1699 9th St, White Bear Lake MN 55110-6717. 651/426-0345.

DIE-CUT PAPER AND PAPER PRODUCTS

Fine Impressions
1680 Roe Crest Dr, Mankato MN 56003-2658. 507/625-4355.

INDUSTRIAL PAPER AND RELATED PRODUCTS WHOLESALE

Turnquist Unisource
PO Box 100, Minneapolis MN 55440-0100. 612/536-5600.

LUMBER AND WOOD WHOLESALE

Bayer Built Woodworks Inc.
PO Box 218, Belgrade MN 56312-0218. 320/254-3651.

Truss Joist MacMillan
PO Box 460, Deerwood MN 56444-0460. 218/546-8114.

MILLWORK, PLYWOOD, AND STRUCTURAL MEMBERS

Louisiana Pacific Corporation
PO Box P, Two Harbors MN 55616-0516. 218/834-5652.

Superior Truss & Components
PO Box 366, Minneota MN 56264-0366. 507/872-5195.

PAPER MILLS

Blandin Paper Company
115 SW 1st St, Grand Rapids MN 55744-3662. 218/327-6200.

Boise Cascade
400 2nd St, International MN 56649-2327. 218/285-5011.

Champion International Corporation
PO Box 338, Sartell MN 56377-0338. 320/251-6511.

Hennepin Paper Company
100 5th Ave SW, Little Falls MN 56345-1733. 320/632-3684.

Potlatch Corporation
1801 Mill Ave, Brainerd MN 56401-2158. 218/828-3200.

Potlatch Corporation
Rural Route 3, Box 455, Bemidji MN 56601-9403. 218/751-1708.

Potlatch Corporation
PO Box 503, Cloquet MN 55720-0503. 218/879-2300.

Weyerhaeuser Company
8085 220th St W, Lakeville MN 55044-7245. 612/469-4451.

PAPERBOARD CONTAINERS AND BOXES

Americraft Carton Inc.
403 Fillmore Avenue East, St. Paul MN 55107-1205. 651/227-6655.

International Paper Company
1300 Red Fox Rd, St. Paul MN 55112-6990. 651/636-3300.

Jefferson Smurfit
1050 Kent St, St. Paul MN 55117-4721. 651/488-2551.

Longview Fibre
PO Box 1419, Minneapolis MN 55440. 612/571-4700.

Stone Container Corporation
50 37th Ave NE, Minneapolis MN 55421-3629. 612/789-2485.

Stone Container Corporation
3075 Long Lake Rd, Roseville MN 55113-1025. 651/636-1220.

Stone Container Corporation
PO Box 1287, St. Cloud MN 56302-1287. 320/252-3660.

Tenneco Packaging Inc.
3010 42nd St S, Moorhead MN 56560-6006. 218/233-5000.

Weyerhaeuser Company
7301 Northland Dr N, Minneapolis MN 55428-1005. 612/424-6606.

Weyerhaeuser Company
1900 8th St NE, Austin MN 55912-4932. 507/433-3467.

WOOD MILLS

Woodcraft Industries Inc.
145 Main St, Foreston MN 56330-9631. 320/294-5742.

WOOD PRODUCTS

Diamond Brands Inc.
1800 Cloquet Ave, Cloquet MN 55720-2141. 218/879-6700.

Northwood Panelboard Company
Rural Route 1, Box 2650, Solway MN 56678-9214. 218/751-2023.

Potlatch Corporation
502 County Road 63, Grand Rapids MN 55744-9609. 218/327-3611.

Wincraft Incorporated
PO Box 888, Winona MN 55987-0888. 507/454-5510.

For more information on career opportunities in the paper and wood products industries:

Associations

FOREST PRODUCTS SOCIETY
2801 Marshall Court, Madison WI 53705-2295. 608/231-1361. World Wide Web address: http://www.supranet.com/forestprod. An international, nonprofit, educational association that provides an information network for all segments of the forest products industry, as well as an employment referral service.

NATIONAL PAPER TRADE ASSOCIATION
111 Great Neck Road, Great Neck NY 11021.
516/829-3070. World Wide Web address: http://www.
papertrade.com. Offers management services to paper
wholesalers, as well as books, seminars, and research
services.

PAPERBOARD PACKAGING COUNCIL
201 North Union Street, Suite 220, Alexandria VA
22314. 703/836-3300. Offers statistical and lobbying
services.

**TECHNICAL ASSOCIATION OF THE PULP
AND PAPER INDUSTRY**
P.O. Box 105113, Norcross GA 30092. 770/446-1400.
World Wide Web address: http://www.tappi.org. A
nonprofit organization offering conferences and
continuing education.

Directories

**DIRECTORY OF THE WOOD PRODUCTS
INDUSTRY**
Miller Freeman, Inc., 600 Harrison Street, San
Francisco CA 94107. 415/905-2200. World Wide
Web address: http://www.woodwideweb.com.

**INTERNATIONAL PULP AND PAPER
DIRECTORY**
Miller Freeman, Inc., 600 Harrison Street, San
Francisco CA 94107. 415/905-8166. World Wide
Web address: http://www.pulp-paper.com.

**LOCKWOOD-POST'S DIRECTORY OF THE
PULP, PAPER AND ALLIED TRADES**
Miller Freeman, Inc., 600 Harrison Street, San
Francisco CA 94107. 415/905-2200. World Wide
Web address: http://www.pulp-paper.com/lpdisk.htm.

Magazines

PAPERBOARD PACKAGING
Advanstar Communications, 131 West First Street,
Duluth MN 55802. 218/723-9200. World Wide Web
address: http://www.advanstar.com.

PULP & PAPER
Miller Freeman, Inc., 600 Harrison Street, San
Francisco CA 94107. 415/905-2200. World Wide
Web address: http://www.mfi.com.

WOOD TECHNOLOGY
Miller Freeman, Inc., 600 Harrison Street, San
Francisco CA 94107. 415/905-2200. World Wide
Web address: http://www.woodtechmag.com.

Visit our exciting job and career site at http://www.careercity.com

PRINTING AND PUBLISHING

The publishing industry saw profit gains of 20 percent during the first six months of 1998 as compared to the same period of 1997. New printing production and editorial systems, Web publishing software, and digital color proofs are just a few of the high-tech offerings which continue to revolutionize the book publishing industry. At this point, technology is outpacing the industry and analysts think it will take a few more years before these new technologies are fully integrated into book publishing.

A recent survey by Arthur Andersen reveals that industry mergers may be a continuing trend. Results showed that 79 percent of book publishing executives are considering a merger or acquisition transaction. Bertelsmann AG purchased Random House, Inc. from Advance Publications, Inc. in 1998. Other acquisitions included Pearson Plc.'s purchase of Viacom's educational, professional, and reference publishing divisions, and Barnes and Noble's purchase of the Ingram Book Group, a leading U.S. book distributor. The Arthur Andersen survey also indicates that publishers are motivated to agree to these deals in order to broaden product lines and increase market share in the industry. Overall, book sales have risen only about 5 percent since 1992, according to Veronis Suhler & Associates Inc.

According to the Association of American Publishers, the best book sales in 1997 were in education and professional book publishing. Another area that will be looking to expand is travel publishing. The World Tourism Organization predicts that by 2020 travel will be one of the leading industries in the United States. Look for publishers to expand their selections of travel books in an attempt to capture very specific audiences.

Newspapers lost 5.5 million customers between 1986 and 1996, due in part to higher prices and online news access. However, several newspapers are starting to see incremental sales growth. This growth is the result of new advertising campaigns, changes in production schedules to deliver papers earlier, and utilization of the Internet. Most regional and national newspapers now have their own Websites, allowing for topical research and access to current news and archives.

ABC NEWSPAPERS & SHOPPER
P.O. Box 99, Anoka MN 55303. 612/421-4444. **Contact:** General Manager. **World Wide Web address:** http://www.ecm-inc.com. **Description:** A newspaper and commercial printer. **Common positions include:** Advertising Clerk; Commercial Artist; Editor; Reporter; Sales Executive. **Educational backgrounds include:** Communications; Marketing. **Benefits:** 401(k); Dental Insurance; Disability Coverage; Employee Discounts; Life Insurance; Medical Insurance; Profit Sharing; Tuition Assistance. **Corporate headquarters location:** Princeton MN. **Parent company:** ECM Publishers, Inc. publishes a variety of newspapers including *Anoka County Union, Elk River Star News, Mille Lacs County Times,* and *Princeton Union-Eagle.* **Operations at this facility include:** Administration; Manufacturing; Sales; Service. **Listed on:** Privately held. **Number of employees at this location:** 70.

ABDO PUBLISHING COMPANY
ROCKBOTTOM BOOKS
4940 Viking Drive, Suite 622, Edina MN 55435. 612/831-2120. **Contact:** Jill Hansen, Personnel Director. **World Wide Web address:** http://www.abdopub.com. **Description:** A publisher of children's books.

ACME TAG AND LABEL COMPANY
2838 Fremont Avenue South, Minneapolis MN 55408. 612/872-0333. **Contact:** Ms. Arlene Ludvigson, Human Resources. **Description:** Manufactures tags, printed gum labels, and printed pressure-sensitive labels.

ADVERTISING UNLIMITED
1000 Highway 4 South, Sleepy Eye MN 56085-0008. 507/794-8000. **Contact:** Human Resources. **Description:** Prints calendars.

AUGSBURG FORTRESS PUBLISHERS
P.O. Box 1209, Minneapolis MN 55440-1209. 612/330-3300. **Contact:** Jean Stanley, Human Resources Manager. **World Wide Web address:** http://www.augsburgfortress.org. **Description:** The publishing house of the Evangelical Lutheran Church of America. **Common positions include:** Administrative Manager; Advertising Clerk; Attorney; Blue-Collar Worker Supervisor; Branch Manager; Budget Analyst; Clerical Supervisor; Computer Programmer; Credit Manager; Customer Service Representative; Designer; Editor; Financial Analyst; General Manager; Human Resources Manager; Librarian; Operations/Production Manager; Quality Control Supervisor; Services Sales Representative; Systems Analyst; Wholesale and Retail Buyer. **Educational backgrounds include:** Accounting; Art/Design; Business Administration; Communications; Computer Science; English; Finance; Journalism; Liberal Arts; Marketing. **Benefits:** Dental Insurance; Disability Coverage; Employee Discounts; Life Insurance; Medical Insurance; Pension Plan; Tuition Assistance. **Corporate headquarters location:** This Location. **Other U.S. locations:** Los Angeles CA; Omaha NE; Hicksville NY; Columbus OH; Harrisburg PA; Philadelphia PA; Columbia SC; Austin TX; Mountlake Terrace WA. **Operations at this facility include:** Administration; Manufacturing; Research and Development; Sales; Service. **Number of employees at this location:** 320. **Number of employees nationwide:** 570.

BANTA CATALOG MINNEAPOLIS
7401 Kilmer Lane, Maple Grove MN 55369. 612/424-7446. **Contact:** Human Resources. **World Wide Web address:** http://www.banta.com. **Description:** A large volume printer of catalogs and inserts. The company is part of the Banta Catalog Group, whose products and services include consumer catalogs, primarily full-color specialty catalogs; advertising inserts; electronic prepress services; selective binding; inkjet addressing and messaging; zip code sorting; mail list processing and maintenance services; computerized distribution services; and dealer and franchise personalization programs. **Parent company:** Banta Corporation (Menasha WI) is a technology and market leader in printing and digital imaging. The corporation serves publishers of educational and general interest books, special interest magazines, consumer and business catalogs, and direct marketing materials. In addition to printing and digital imaging, Banta offers multimedia and software packages, interactive media, point-of-purchase materials, and single-use products. Banta operates through the following groups: Banta Book Group; Banta Catalog Group; Banta Digital Group; Banta Direct Marketing Group; Banta Information Services Group; Banta Publications Group; Signs, Displays, Labels & Stamps; and Single-Use Products.

BANTA CATALOG ST. PAUL
655 Fairview Avenue North, St. Paul MN 55104. 651/645-0751. **Contact:** Ross Hooge, Human Resources Director. **World Wide Web address:** http://www.banta.com. **Description:** A commercial letterpress printer. The company operates as part of the Banta Catalog Group, whose products and services include consumer catalogs, primarily full-color specialty catalogs; advertising inserts; electronic prepress services; selective binding; inkjet addressing and messaging; zip code sorting; mail list processing and maintenance services; computerized distribution services; and dealer and franchise personalization programs. **Parent company:** Banta Corporation (Menasha WI) is a technology and market leader in printing and digital imaging. The corporation serves publishers of educational and general interest books, special interest magazines, consumer and business catalogs, and direct marketing materials. In addition to printing and digital imaging, Banta offers multimedia and software packages, interactive media, point-of-purchase materials, and single-use products. Banta operates through the following groups: Banta Book Group; Banta Catalog Group; Banta Digital Group; Banta Direct Marketing Group; Banta Information Services Group; Banta Publications Group; Signs, Displays, Labels & Stamps; and Single-Use Products.

BANTA DIGITAL
18790 West 78th Street, Chanhassen MN 55317. 612/937-5005. **Contact:** Laurie Derickson, Human Resources. **World Wide Web address:** http://www.banta.com. **Description:** Services include data management for the creation of film and printing plates (electronic and conventional prepress services); preparation and storage of customers' digital electronic files containing text and images; high-speed transmission of digitized text and graphics; digital photography; electronic layout and design; one- and four-color digital printing; television identity campaigns; corporate image videos; and interactive and alternative media programming. **Parent company:** Banta Corporation (Menasha WI) is a technology and market leader in printing and digital imaging. The corporation serves publishers of educational and general interest books, special interest magazines, consumer and business catalogs, and direct marketing materials. In addition to printing and digital imaging, Banta offers multimedia and software packages, interactive media, point-of-purchase materials, and single-use products. Banta operates through the following groups: Banta Book Group; Banta Catalog Group; Banta Digital Group; Banta Direct Marketing Group; Banta Information Services Group; Banta Publications Group; Signs, Displays, Labels & Stamps; and Single-Use Products.

BANTA DIRECT MARKETING
18780 West 78th Street, Chanhassen MN 55317. 612/937-9764. **Contact:** Lori Storms, Personnel Manager. **World Wide Web address:** http://www.banta.com. **Description:** A nationwide, four-color printing company. This location is part of the Banta Direct Marketing Group, whose products include direct mail products such as brochures; publication and package inserts, coupons, reply cards, return envelopes, and specialty booklets. The group serves national advertisers, direct marketers, publishers, and ad agencies. **Common positions include:** Accountant/Auditor; Blue-Collar Worker Supervisor; Credit Manager; Customer Service Representative; Department Manager; Dietician/Nutritionist; Financial Analyst; Human Resources Manager; Manufacturer's/Wholesaler's Sales Rep.; Operations/Production Manager; Purchasing Agent/Manager. **Educational backgrounds include:** Accounting; Business Administration; Communications; Marketing. **Benefits:** Credit Union; Dental Insurance; Disability Coverage; Life Insurance; Medical Insurance; Pension Plan; Savings Plan; Tuition Assistance. **Parent company:** Banta Corporation (Menasha WI) is a technology and market leader in printing and digital imaging. The corporation serves publishers of educational and general interest books, special interest magazines, consumer and business catalogs, and direct marketing materials. In addition to printing and digital imaging, Banta offers multimedia and software packages, interactive media, point-of-purchase materials, and single-use products. Banta operates through the following groups: Banta Book Group; Banta Catalog Group; Banta Digital Group; Banta Direct Marketing Group; Banta Information Services Group; Banta Publications Group; Signs, Displays, Labels & Stamps; and Single-Use Products. **Operations at this facility include:** Administration; Manufacturing; Regional Headquarters; Sales; Service.

BANTA INFORMATION SERVICES
7000 Washington Avenue South, Eden Prairie MN 55344. 612/941-8780. **Contact:** Sue Lorentz, Human Resources. **World Wide Web address:** http://www.banta.com. **Description:** Prints books and manuals on demand, and also handles some fulfillment orders. **Parent company:** Banta Corporation (Menasha WI) is a technology and market leader in printing and digital imaging. The corporation serves publishers of educational and general interest books, special interest magazines, consumer and business catalogs, and direct marketing materials. In addition to printing and digital imaging, Banta offers multimedia and software packages, interactive media, point-of-purchase materials, and single-use products. Banta operates through the following groups: Banta Book Group; Banta Catalog Group; Banta Digital Group; Banta Direct Marketing Group; Banta Information Services Group; Banta Publications Group; Signs, Displays, Labels & Stamps; and Single-Use Products.

BANTA PUBLICATIONS
100 Banta Road, Long Prairie MN 56347. 320/732-2121. **Contact:** Duane Byers, Human Resources Representative. **World Wide Web address:** http://www.banta.com. **Description:** A magazine printer. This location is part of the Banta Publications Group, which prints special interest, reader-targeted publications with print runs of between 10,000 and 350,000 copies, and provides electronic prepress services, selective binding, inkjet addressing and messaging, zip code sorting, and mail list management and fulfillment services. **Parent company:** Banta Corporation (Menasha WI) is a technology and market leader in printing and digital imaging. The corporation serves publishers of educational and general interest books, special interest magazines, consumer and business catalogs, and direct marketing materials. In addition to printing and digital imaging, Banta offers multimedia and software packages, interactive media, point-of-purchase materials, and single-use products. Banta operates through the following groups: Banta Book Group; Banta

Catalog Group; Banta Digital Group; Banta Direct Marketing Group; Banta Information Services Group; Banta Publications Group; Signs, Displays, Labels & Stamps; and Single-Use Products.

BROWN AND BIGELOW INC.
345 Plato Boulevard East, St. Paul MN 55107. 651/293-7000. **Contact:** Human Resources Department. **Description:** Brown and Bigelow is a commercial lithographer specializing in playing cards and calendars.

BULLETIN NEWSPAPERS
P.O. Box 99, Cottage Grove MN 55016. 651/459-3434. **Fax:** 651/459-9491. **Contact:** Jeff Patterson, General Manager. **Description:** Publishes two weekly newspapers, *The South Washington County Bulletin* and *The Woodbury Bulletin*. **Common positions include:** Editor; General Manager; Graphic Artist; Writer. **Educational backgrounds include:** Art/Design; Business Administration; Communications; Journalism. **Benefits:** 401(k); Life Insurance; Medical Insurance; Profit Sharing; Savings Plan. **Special programs:** Internships. **Corporate headquarters location:** Red Wing MN. **Parent company:** Red Wing Publishing. **Operations at this facility include:** Administration; Sales. **Listed on:** Privately held. **Number of employees at this location:** 15.

THE BUREAU OF ENGRAVING, INC.
GRAPHICS DIVISION
3400 Technology Drive, Minneapolis MN 55418. 612/788-1000. **Contact:** Gary Minlschmidt, Director of Human Resources. **World Wide Web address:** http://www.boe.com. **Description:** The Bureau of Engraving is a diversified printer and engraver. **Number of employees nationwide:** 1,000.

BURGESS INTERNATIONAL
7110 Ohms Lane, Edina MN 55439. 612/831-1344. **Contact:** Kristen Bartsch, Personnel Director. **Description:** Publishes college textbooks, laboratory manuals, and nonfiction general interest trade books.

CITY PAGES, INC.
401 North Third Street, Suite 550, Minneapolis MN 55401. 612/375-1015. **Fax:** 612/372-3737. **Contact:** Human Resources Department. **World Wide Web address:** http://www.citypages.com. **Description:** City Pages is a weekly alternative newspaper. **Common positions include:** Account Manager; Advertising Account Executive; Controller; Credit Manager; Editor; Graphic Designer; Sales Manager; Systems Manager. **Educational backgrounds include:** Art/Design; Business Administration; Liberal Arts. **Benefits:** 401(k); Employee Discounts; Life Insurance; Medical Insurance. **Special programs:** Internships. **Corporate headquarters location:** This Location. **Operations at this facility include:** Administration; Sales; Service. **Listed on:** Privately held. **Publisher:** Mark Bartel. **Number of employees at this location:** 90.

COLWELL INDUSTRIES INC.
123 North Third Street, Minneapolis MN 55401-1625. 612/340-0365. **Contact:** Human Resources Department. **Description:** This location of the company houses administrative offices. Overall, Colwell Industries is involved in the printing of calling cards. **Corporate headquarters location:** This Location.

DELUXE CORPORATION
P.O. Box 64235, St. Paul MN 55164. 651/787-2759. **Physical address:** 3680 Victoria Street North, Shoreview MN. **Contact:** Susan Pierre-Zilles, Employment Specialist. **World Wide Web address:** http://www.deluxe.com. **Description:** Deluxe Corporation provides check printing, electronic funds transfer processing services, and related services to the financial industry; check authorization and collection services to retailers; and electronic benefit transfer services to state governments. Deluxe also produces forms, specialty papers, and other products for small businesses, professional practices, and medical/dental offices; and provides tax forms and electronic tax filing services to tax preparers. Through the direct mail channel, Deluxe sells greeting cards, gift wrap, and related products to households. Founded in 1915. **Corporate headquarters location:** This Location. **Other U.S. locations:** Nationwide. **International locations:** Canada; United Kingdom. **Subsidiaries include:** Deluxe Check Printers, Inc. is engaged in printing and selling a variety of checks, deposit tickets, and related forms to banks and other financial institutions. The company also manufactures documents imprinted on magnetic ink. Printing operations are carried out at more than 50 plants throughout the United States. **Listed on:** New York Stock Exchange. **Number of employees at this location:** 3,000. **Number of employees nationwide:** 18,000.

HOLDEN GRAPHIC SERVICES

607 Washington Avenue North, Minneapolis MN 55401. **Contact:** Human Resources. **Description:** Produces custom business forms. **Common positions include:** Customer Service Representative; Department Manager; General Manager; Human Resources Manager; Manufacturer's/Wholesaler's Sales Rep.; Operations/Production Manager; Services Sales Representative. **Educational backgrounds include:** Business Administration; Communications; Computer Science; Marketing; Printing. **Benefits:** 401(k); Daycare Assistance; Disability Coverage; Life Insurance; Medical Insurance; Savings Plan; Tuition Assistance. **Corporate headquarters location:** This Location. **Other U.S. locations:** Rockford IL; Arlington TX; Dallas TX. **Operations at this facility include:** Administration; Manufacturing; Regional Headquarters; Sales. **Listed on:** Privately held. **Number of employees at this location:** 60. **Number of employees nationwide:** 280.

JAPS-OLSON COMPANY

7500 Excelsior Boulevard, St. Louis Park MN 55426. 612/932-9393. **Contact:** Michael Beddor, President. **World Wide Web address:** http://www.japsolson.com. **Description:** A large commercial printing and direct mailing company. **Number of employees at this location:** 700.

LE SUEUR PUBLISHING INC.

101 Bridge Street, Le Sueur MN 56058. 507/665-3332. **Contact:** Lois Walker, Office Manager. **E-mail address:** dlbstub@prairie.lakes.com. **Description:** A commercial printer.

LIFETOUCH NATIONAL SCHOOL STUDIOS

11000 Viking Drive, Eden Prairie MN 55344. 612/826-5500. **Contact:** Human Resources. **Description:** Engaged in portrait photography. **Common positions include:** Photographer/Camera Operator; Services Sales Representative. **Educational backgrounds include:** Business Administration. **Benefits:** Dental Insurance; Life Insurance; Medical Insurance; Stock Option. **Operations at this facility include:** Administration; Manufacturing; Regional Headquarters; Research and Development; Sales; Service.

MERRILL CORPORATION

One Merrill Circle, St. Paul MN 55108. 651/646-4501. **Contact:** Kathy Larkin, Vice President of Human Resources. **World Wide Web address:** http://www.merrillcorp.com. **Description:** A typesetting company.

MILLER PUBLISHING COMPANY

P.O. Box 2400, Minnetonka MN 55343. 612/931-0211. **Physical address:** 12400 Whitewater Drive, Minnetonka MN. **Contact:** Human Resources. **Description:** Publishers of agricultural trade magazines.

MINNESOTA SUN PUBLICATIONS

10917 Valley View Road, Eden Prarie MN 55344. 612/829-0797. **Contact:** Human Resources. **World Wide Web address:** http://www.mnsun.com. **Description:** Owns a group of suburban Minneapolis newspapers, including *Sun Current, Sun Post,* and *Sun Sailor.* **Common positions include:** Commercial Artist; Editor; Reporter; Sales Representative. **Educational backgrounds include:** Art/Design; Business Administration; Journalism; Liberal Arts; Marketing. **Benefits:** 401(k); Dental Insurance; Disability Coverage; Life Insurance; Medical Insurance. **Corporate headquarters location:** This Location.

MINUTE MAN PRESS

9850 51st Avenue North, Suite 104, Plymouth MN 55442. 612/553-1561. **Contact:** General Manager. **E-mail address:** mmpmn@aol.com. **Description:** Engaged in magazine publishing, commercial printing, and mailing. **Common positions include:** Customer Service Representative; Department Manager; General Manager; Manufacturer's/Wholesaler's Sales Rep.; Marketing Specialist; Operations/Production Manager. **Educational backgrounds include:** Art/Design; Business Administration; Communications; Marketing. **Benefits:** Dental Insurance; Medical Insurance; Tuition Assistance. **Special programs:** Internships. **Corporate headquarters location:** This Location. **Operations at this facility include:** Manufacturing; Sales. **Number of employees at this location:** 15.

MOORE DATA MANAGEMENT SERVICES
MOORE GRAPHICS SERVICES

2117 West River Road North, Minneapolis MN 55411. 612/588-7200. **Contact:** Human Resources. **Description:** A primary provider of online computer services to the real estate industry. This location also houses Moore Graphics Services, which provides commercial printing and electronic, on-demand, and database publishing to *Fortune* 500 companies. **Corporate**

headquarters location: This Location. **Other U.S. locations:** Nationwide. **Parent company:** Moore Corporation. **Operations at this facility include:** Manufacturing. **Listed on:** New York Stock Exchange. **Number of employees at this location:** 100. **Number of employees nationwide:** 1,200.

OAKSTONE LEGAL & BUSINESS PUBLISHING
4635 Nicols Road, Suite 100, Eagan MN 55122. 612/452-8267. **Contact:** Human Resources Department. **Description:** A newsletter and book publishing company. **Common positions include:** Customer Service Representative.

PUBLISH PDQ
6700 France Avenue South, Suite 200, Edina MN 55435. 612/920-9928. **Contact:** Bob Larranaga, President. **Description:** Publishes financial and health articles for inclusion in newsletters. **Common positions include:** Accountant/Auditor; Advertising Clerk. **Educational backgrounds include:** Art/Design; Business Administration; Communications; Finance. **Benefits:** Disability Coverage; Life Insurance; Medical Insurance; Pension Plan; Profit Sharing; Tuition Assistance. **Corporate headquarters location:** This Location.

QUEBECOR PRINTING INC.
1999 Shepard Road, St. Paul MN 55116. 651/690-7200. **Contact:** Sheila Bergern, Director of Human Resources. **World Wide Web address:** http://www.quebecor.com. **Description:** Quebecor Printing Inc. is one of the world's largest commercial printers with 84 printing and related facilities in Canada, the United States, France, the United Kingdom, Mexico, and India. The company's major product categories include inserts and circulars, magazines, books, catalogs, directories, checks, bonds and bank notes, specialty printing, and newspapers. Quebecor Printing also offers web offset, gravure, and sheetfed printing capacity, plus related services that include advanced electronic prepress and imaging, database and list management, shipping and distribution, and CD-ROM mastering and replicating. Quebecor Printing became one of the largest book manufacturers in North America with the formation of Quebecor Printing Book Group, which serves more than 1,000 publishing firms. **Corporate headquarters location:** Boston MA. **Parent company:** Quebecor Printing (USA) Inc. **Listed on:** American Stock Exchange. **Number of employees nationwide:** 13,000.

ST. MARIE'S GOPHER NEWS COMPANY
9000 10th Avenue North, Minneapolis MN 55427. 612/546-5300. **Contact:** Human Resources Department. **Description:** St. Marie's Gopher News Company is a distributor of periodicals, paperback books, trade books, audiotapes, videotapes, and children's toys. **Number of employees at this location:** 105.

ST. PAUL PIONEER PRESS
345 Cedar Street, St. Paul MN 55101. 651/228-5002. **Contact:** Employee Relations Office. **Description:** An area newspaper publisher. **Common positions include:** Customer Service Representative; Editor; Reporter; Services Sales Representative. **Educational backgrounds include:** Business Administration; Communications; Journalism; Marketing. **Benefits:** Dental Insurance; Life Insurance; Medical Insurance; Pension Plan; Tuition Assistance. **Special programs:** Internships. **Parent company:** Knight-Ridder, Inc. (Miami FL). **Operations at this facility include:** Manufacturing. **Listed on:** New York Stock Exchange.

SHAKOPEE VALLEY PRINTING
5101 Valley Industrial Boulevard South, Shakopee MN 55379. 612/445-8260. **Contact:** Human Resources Department. **Description:** Specializes in the printing of newspapers and various types of magazines.

STAR TRIBUNE
425 Portland Avenue, Minneapolis MN 55488. 612/673-4000. **Contact:** Cathy Veidel, Human Resources. **World Wide Web address:** http://www.startribune.com. **Description:** A daily newspaper with a weekday circulation of 412,400 and a Sunday circulation of 696,100. The paper's employees are divided into four components: one to serve reader customers, one to serve marketer customers (primarily advertisers), a production and distribution function, and support services to serve the other three. **Parent company:** McClatchey Newspapers. **Number of employees at this location:** 1,900 full-time; 1,400 part-time.

TECHNIGRAPH CORPORATION
850 West Third Street, Winona MN 55987. 507/454-3830. **Contact:** Personnel. **Description:** Performs screen printing on plastic containers.

WEST GROUP ~~651~~
610 Opperman Drive, Eagan MN 55123. ~~612~~/687-7000. **Toll-free phone:** 800/328-WEST. **Fax:** ~~612~~/687-5827. **Contact:** Human Resources. **E-mail address:** recruiter@westgroup.com. **World Wide Web address:** http://www.westgroup.com. **Description:** Publishes legal research information in CD-ROM and book formats for law practitioners and the judiciary. **Parent company:** Thomson Corporation.

Note: Because addresses and telephone numbers of smaller companies can change rapidly, we recommend you call each company to verify the information below before inquiring about job opportunities. Mass mailings are not recommended.

Additional small employers:

BLANK BOOKS AND BOOKBINDING

Antioch Company
2815 Clearwater Road, St. Cloud MN 56301-5951. 320/251-3822.

Creative Memories
PO Box 767, St. Cloud MN 56302-0767. 320/251-7524.

Liberty Check Printers
2222 Woodale Dr, St. Paul MN 55112-4900. 612/784-8700.

BOOKS, PERIODICALS, AND NEWSPAPERS WHOLESALE

Bookmen Inc.
525 N 3rd St, Minneapolis MN 55401-1201. 612/341-3333.

Minnesota News Service Inc.
7836 2nd Avenue South, Minneapolis MN 55420-1206. 612/703-0075.

BOOKS: PUBLISHING AND/OR PRINTING

America's Network
131 W 1st St, Duluth MN 55802-2005. 218/723-9200.

Creative Publishing International
5900 Green Oak Drive, Hopkins MN 55343-9607. 612/936-4700.

BUSINESS FORMS

Custom Business Forms
210 Edge Pl, Minneapolis MN 55418-1138. 612/789-0002.

Data Forms Inc.
316 Lake Hazeltine Drive, Chaska MN 55318-1089. 612/448-7503.

Northstar Financial Forms
PO Box 64497, St. Paul MN 55164-0497. 651/483-7700.

Northstar Financial Forms
7130 Northland Cir N, Minneapolis MN 55428-1509. 612/531-7340.

COMMERCIAL PHOTOGRAPHY

Weston Engraving Co.
2626 2nd Street Northeast, Minneapolis MN 55418-2724. 612/789-8514.

COMMERCIAL PRINTING

Aarlson Craft Commercial Division
PO Box 3728, Mankato MN 56002-3728. 507/625-2828.

BCSI
3200 143rd Cir, Burnsville MN 55306-6973. 612/894-4904.

Carlson Craft
PO Box 8700, Mankato MN 56002-8700. 507/625-5011.

Challenge Printing Inc.
7500 Golden Triangle Dr, Eden Prairie MN 55344-3734. 612/942-7086.

Corporate Graphics Commercial Division
PO Box 8800, Mankato MN 56002-8800. 507/388-3300.

Corporate Graphics International
PO Box 8464, Mankato MN 56002-8464. 507/625-4400.

Curtis 1000
PO Box 64109, St. Paul MN 55164-0109. 651/483-6651.

DGI
1700 Broadway St NE, Minneapolis MN 55413-2618. 612/331-1111.

Gaines & Hanson Printing Co.
5197 Winnetka Ave N, Minneapolis MN 55428-4256. 612/533-1000.

GML Inc.
500 Oak Grove Parkway, St. Paul MN 55127-8536. 651/490-0000.

Instant Web Inc.
7951 Powers Blvd, Chanhassen MN 55317-9502. 612/474-0961.

Litho Incorporated
1280 Energy Park Dr, St. Paul MN 55108-5106. 651/644-3000.

Maximum Graphics Inc.
1245 Lakeview Dr, Chaska MN 55318-9506. 612/448-5100.

Medical Arts Press Inc.
8500 Wyoming Ave N, Minneapolis MN 55445-1825. 612/493-7300.

Merrill/May Inc.
PO Box 100, St. Cloud MN 56302-0100. 320/656-5000.

Nahan Printing Inc.
PO Box 697, St. Cloud MN 56302-0697. 320/251-7611.

NCS Forms Division
2125 4th St NW, Owatonna MN 55060-4903. 507/451-5137.

Nordic Press Inc.
5017 Boone Ave N, Minneapolis MN 55428-4023. 612/535-6440.

Northprint International
1321 SE 8th Street, Grand Rapids MN 55744-4000. 218/326-9407.

Olympic Graphics
700 Xenia Ave S, Minneapolis MN 55416-1021. 612/544-3939.

PGI Companies Inc.
11354 K-Tel Dr, Hopkins MN 55343-8868. 612/933-5745.

Phoenix Packaging
10949 91st Avenue N, Maple Grove MN 55369-4070. 612/424-5809.

Printed Media Companies
815 Zane Ave North, Golden Valley MN 55422-4601. 612/542-4400.

Process Displays Co.
7108 31st Ave North,

Minneapolis MN 55427-2848.
612/546-1133.

Quality Assured Label Inc.
11563 K-Tel Dr, Hopkins MN
55343-8845. 612/933-7800.

**Quebecor Printing USA
Holdings**
PO Box 1007, St. Cloud MN
56302-1007. 320/654-2400.

Rainbow Signs Inc.
3500 Thurston Avenue,
Anoka MN 55303-1061.
612/576-6700.

Schmidt Printing Inc.
1101 Frontage Road Northwest,
Byron MN 55920-1386. 507/775-
6400.

Scoville Press Inc.
14505 27th Ave N, Plymouth MN
55447-4802. 612/553-1400.

Source Inc.
2000 Energy Park Drive, St. Paul
MN 55108-1506. 651/646-4422.

UV Color Inc.
2430 Prior Avenue North,
Roseville MN 55113-2716.
651/636-3086.

Watt/Peterson Inc.
15020 27th Ave N, Plymouth MN
55447-4815. 612/553-1617.

Winslow Printing Co.
1225 N 7th St, Minneapolis MN
55411-4060. 612/522-3868.

MISC. PUBLISHING

ADX Distribution Co.
8459 10th Ave N, Minneapolis
MN 55427-4422. 612/595-5400.

AGS
4201 Woodland Road, Circle
Pines MN 55014-1745. 612/786-
4343.

Hal Leonard Corporation
PO Box 227, Winona MN 55987-
0227. 507/454-2920.

**Jostens American Yearbook
Co.**
PO Box 527, Owatonna MN
55060-0527. 507/455-6100.

NCS Assessments
PO Box 1416, Minneapolis MN
55440-1416. 612/939-5000.

**NEWSPAPERS: PUBLISHING
AND/OR PRINTING**

Duluth News-Tribune
424 W 1st St, Duluth MN 55802-
1516. 218/723-5240.

Express Line
PO Box 6118, Rochester MN
55903-6118. 507/285-7600.

House of Print
PO Box 6, Madelia MN 56062-
0006. 507/642-3298.

Lillie Newspapers
2515 7th Ave E, Maplewood MN
55109-3004. 651/777-8800.

Minnesota Daily
2301 University Ave SE,
Minneapolis MN 55414-3030.
612/627-4080.

St. Cloud Times
PO Box 768, St. Cloud MN
56302-0768. 320/255-8700.

The Free Press
PO Box 3287, Mankato MN
56002-3287. 507/625-4451.

**PERIODICALS:
PUBLISHING AND/OR
PRINTING**

Graftek Press
PO Box 1549, Waseca MN
56093-0517. 507/835-2410.

MSP Communications
220 S 6th St, Ste 500,
Minneapolis MN 55402-4501.
612/339-7571.

**PHOTOGRAPHIC
EQUIPMENT AND SUPPLIES**

3M
PO Box 95, New Ulm MN
56073-0095. 507/354-8271.

Photo Control Corporation
4800 Quebec Avenue N,
Minneapolis MN 55428-4520.
612/537-3601.

Photoquip
11201 Hampshire Ave S,
Minneapolis MN 55438-2454.
612/829-5444.

**PRINTING TRADE
SERVICES**

Colorhouse Inc.
13010 County Road 6, Plymouth
MN 55441-3828. 612/553-0100.

Graphics Unlimited Inc.
3000 North 2nd Street,
Minneapolis MN 55411-1608.
612/588-7571.

For more information on career opportunities in printing and publishing:

Associations

AMERICAN BOOKSELLERS ASSOCIATION
828 South Broadway, Tarrytown NY 10591. 914/591-
2665. World Wide Web address: http://www.
bookweb.org. Publishes *American Bookseller*,
Bookselling This Week, and *Bookstore Source Guide*.

AMERICAN INSTITUTE OF GRAPHIC ARTS
164 Fifth Avenue, New York NY 10010. 212/807-
1990. World Wide Web address: http://www.aiga.org.
A nationwide organization sponsoring programs and
events for graphic designers and related professionals.

**AMERICAN SOCIETY OF COMPOSERS,
AUTHORS, AND PUBLISHERS (ASCAP)**
One Lincoln Plaza, New York NY 10023. 212/621-
6000. World Wide Web address: http://www.ascap.
com. A membership association which licenses
members' work and pays members' royalties. Offers
showcases and educational seminars and workshops.
The society also has an events hotline: 212/621-6485.
Many events listed are free.

**AMERICAN SOCIETY OF NEWSPAPER
EDITORS**
11690-B Sunrise Valley Drive, Reston VA 20191.
703/453-1122. World Wide Web address: http://www.
asne.org.

**ASSOCIATION OF AMERICAN PUBLISHERS,
INC.**
71 Fifth Avenue, New York NY 10001. 212/255-
0200. Fax: 212/255-7007. World Wide Web address:
http://www.publishers.org. A national trade
association for the book publishing industry that
provides industry updates and news of upcoming
events.

**ASSOCIATION OF GRAPHIC
COMMUNICATIONS**
330 Seventh Avenue, 9th Floor, New York NY
10001-5010. 212/279-2100. World Wide Web
address: http://www.agcomm.org. Association of
Graphic Communications offers educational classes
and seminars.

BINDING INDUSTRIES OF AMERICA
70 East Lake Street, Suite 300, Chicago IL 60601.
312/372-7606. Binding Industries of America offers
credit collection, government affairs, and educational
services.

THE DOW JONES NEWSPAPER FUND, INC.
P.O. Box 300, Princeton NJ 08543-0300. 609/452-
2820. World Wide Web address: http://www.
dowjones.com.

GRAPHIC ARTISTS GUILD
90 John Street, Suite 403, New York NY 10038.
212/791-3400. World Wide Web address: http://www.
gag.org. A union for artists.

**THE GRAPHIC ARTS TECHNICAL
FOUNDATION**
200 Deer Run Road, Sewickley PA 15143-2600.
412/741-6860. World Wide Web address: http://www.
gatf.org. Provides information, services, and training
to those in graphic arts professions.

MAGAZINE PUBLISHERS OF AMERICA
919 Third Avenue, 22nd Floor, New York NY 10022.
212/752-0055. World Wide Web address: http://www.
magazine.org. A membership association.

**NATIONAL ASSOCIATION OF PRINTERS
AND LITHOGRAPHERS**
75 West Century Road, Paramus NJ 07652. 201/634-
9600. World Wide Web address: http://www.napl.org.
National Association of Printers and Lithographers
offers consulting services and a publication.
Membership required.

THE NATIONAL NEWSPAPER ASSOCIATION
1010 North Glebe Road, Suite 450, Arlington VA
22201. 703/907-7900. World Wide Web address:
http://www.oweb.com/nna.

NATIONAL PRESS CLUB
529 14th Street NW, 13th Floor, Washington DC
20045. 202/662-7500. World Wide Web address:
http://npc.press.org. National Press Club offers
professional seminars, career services, and conference
facilities, as well as members-only restaurants and a
health club.

NEWSPAPER ASSOCIATION OF AMERICA
1921 Gallows Road, Suite 600, Vienna VA 22182.
703/902-1600. World Wide Web address: http://www.
naa.org. The technology department publishes
marketing research.

PRINTING INDUSTRIES OF AMERICA
100 Dangerfield Road, Alexandria VA 22314.
703/519-8100. World Wide Web address: http://www.
printing.org. Members are offered publications and
insurance.

**TECHNICAL ASSOCIATION OF THE
GRAPHIC ARTS**
68 Lomb Memorial Drive, Rochester NY 14623.
716/475-7470. World Wide Web address: http://www.
taga.org. Technical Association of the Graphic Arts
conducts an annual conference and offers newsletters.

WRITERS GUILD OF AMERICA WEST
7000 West Third Street, Los Angeles CA 90048.
310/550-1000. World Wide Web address: http://www.
wga.org. A membership association which registers
scripts.

<u>Directories</u>

**EDITOR & PUBLISHER INTERNATIONAL
YEARBOOK**
Editor & Publisher Co., 11 West 19th Street, New
York NY 10011. 212/675-4380. World Wide Web
address: http://www.mediainfo.com. Offers
newspapers to editors in both the United States and
foreign countries.

GRAPHIC ARTS BLUE BOOK
A.F. Lewis & Company, 245 Fifth Avenue, Suite
2201, New York NY 10016. 212/679-0770. $85.00.
Manufacturers and dealers.

**JOURNALISM CAREER AND SCHOLARSHIP
GUIDE**
The Dow Jones Newspaper Fund, P.O. Box 300,
Princeton NJ 08543-0300. 609/452-2820.

<u>Magazines</u>

AIGA JOURNAL OF GRAPHIC DESIGN
American Institute of Graphic Arts, 164 Fifth Avenue,
New York NY 10010. 212/807-1990. World Wide
Web address: http://www.aiga.org. $22.00. A 56-page
magazine, published three times per year, that deals
with contemporary issues.

THE EDITOR & PUBLISHER
Editor & Publisher Co., 11 West 19th Street, New
York NY 10011. 212/675-4380. World Wide Web
address: http://www.mediainfo.com. *The Editor &
Publisher* is a periodical focusing on the newspaper
publishing industry.

GRAPHIS
141 Lexington Avenue, New York NY 10016.
212/532-9387. $90.00. Magazine covers portfolios,
articles, designers, advertising, and photos.

PRINT
104 Fifth Avenue, 19th Floor, New York NY 10011.
212/463-0600. Offers a graphic design magazine.
$55.00 for subscription.

PUBLISHERS WEEKLY
245 West 17th Street, New York NY 10011. 212/463-
6758. Toll-free phone: 800/278-2991. World Wide
Web address: http://www.publishersweekly.com.
Weekly magazine for book publishers, book sellers,
and jobseekers looking for work in publishing. Each
issue includes a listing of job openings.

<u>Special Book and Magazine Programs</u>

CENTER FOR BOOK ARTS
626 Broadway, 5th Floor, New York NY 10012.
212/460-9768. Offers bookbinding, printing, and
papermaking workshops.

**EMERSON COLLEGE WRITING AND
PUBLISHING PROGRAM**
100 Beacon Street, Boston MA 02116. 617/824-8500.
World Wide Web address: http://www.emerson.edu.

**THE NEW YORK UNIVERSITY SUMMER
PUBLISHING PROGRAM**
11 West 42nd Street, Room 400, New York NY
10036. 212/790-3232.

THE RADCLIFFE PUBLISHING COURSE
6 Ash Street, Cambridge MA 02138. 617/495-8678.

**THE STANFORD PROFESSIONAL
PUBLISHING COURSE**
Stanford Alumni Association, Bowman Alumni
House, Stanford CA 97305-4005. 650/723-2027. Fax:
650/723-8597. E-mail address: publishing.courses@
stanford.edu. World Wide Web address: http://www.
stanfordproed.org.

**UNIVERSITY OF DENVER PUBLISHING
INSTITUTE**
2075 South University Boulevard, #D-114, Denver
CO 80210. 303/871-2570.

Online Services

BOOKS AND WRITING
Jump to: Books and Writing BB. A bulletin board
service, available through Prodigy, that allows writers
to discuss issues in publishing and gain advice on
writing style.

JOURNALISM FORUM
Go: Jforum. A CompuServe discussion group for
journalists in print, radio, or television.

PHOTO PROFESSIONALS
Go: Photopro. A CompuServe forum for imaging
professionals.

PROPUBLISHING FORUM
Go: Propub. CompuServe charges a fee for this forum
which caters to publishing and graphic design
professionals.

REAL ESTATE

 *After rising from 7.96 million in 1993 to 9.14 million in 1997, employment growth in the real estate industry continues to level off. Support for the real estate industry may come from both a strong economy and a strong construction industry. For the period of January through September 1998, housing starts were up approximately 9 percent, according to the U.S. Census Bureau.*

The trend that is sweeping the industry is ownership of real estate investment trusts (REITs). REITs are companies that own, manage, and develop a number of diversified properties. These companies must follow strict guidelines and in the end remain exempt from corporate taxation. The REIT industry saw profits soar from $8 billion in 1990 to $120 billion in 1997.

The best opportunities for investment and sales are in office space. Industry analysts say that suburbs and downtowns, specifically in the Boston, Chicago, New York, San Francisco, and Seattle areas, will be the hot-spots for new construction. Due to the high turnover rate, real estate agents and brokers should continue to see opportunities, though the sector will see slow growth through 2006. With the increase in apartment and rental space, real estate managers are expected to see average growth into the next decade.

Business Week reported that the retail sector may have been the hardest hit in 1998. Overbuilding and changes in shopping habits have produced a glutted market of malls and shopping centers. Another negative is a potential overabundance in apartment space, most notably in the Sunbelt.

BRUTGER EQUITIES, INC.
P.O. Box 399, St. Cloud MN 56302-0399. 320/529-2837. **Contact:** Thomas Etienne, Vice President of Human Resources. **Description:** Engaged in real estate development and management of properties including motels and apartments. **Common positions include:** Accountant/Auditor; Hotel Manager; Property and Real Estate Manager. **Educational backgrounds include:** Accounting; Business Administration; Hotel Administration; Marketing. **Benefits:** 401(k); Disability Coverage; Employee Discounts; Life Insurance; Medical Insurance; Tuition Assistance. **Special programs:** Internships. **Corporate headquarters location:** This Location. **Other U.S. locations:** AZ; CO; ID; MT; ND; SD; WY. **Operations at this facility include:** Administration; Sales. **Listed on:** Privately held. **Number of employees at this location:** 25. **Number of employees nationwide:** 325.

COLDWELL BANKER BURNET
7550 France Avenue South, Suite 300, Edina MN 55435. 612/844-6400. **Fax:** 612/844-6407. **Recorded jobline:** 612/844-6495. **Contact:** Human Resources. **World Wide Web address:** http://www.coldwellbanker.com. **Description:** A real estate agency. Overall, Coldwell Banker is one of the largest residential real estate companies in the United States and Canada in terms of total home sales transactions. Coldwell Banker also provides relocation services to businesses worldwide.

COLDWELL BANKER BURNET
19400 Highway 7, Excelsior MN 55331. 612/474-2525. **Contact:** Human Resources. **World Wide Web address:** http://www.coldwellbanker.com. **Description:** A real estate agency. Overall, Coldwell Banker is one of the largest residential real estate companies in the United States and Canada in terms of total home sales transactions. Coldwell Banker also provides relocation services to businesses worldwide.

GENERAL GROWTH MANAGEMENT, INC.
400 South Highway 169, Suite 800, Minneapolis MN 55426. 612/525-1200. **Contact:** Human Resources Manager. **Description:** General Growth Management is engaged in the third-party

management of malls. **Common positions include:** Accountant/Auditor; Assistant Manager; Department Manager; General Manager; Marketing Specialist; Operations/Production Manager; Paralegal. **Educational backgrounds include:** Accounting; Business Administration; Communications; Economics; Liberal Arts; Marketing. **Benefits:** 401(k); Disability Coverage; Life Insurance; Medical Insurance; Savings Plan; Spending Account; Stock Option; Tuition Assistance. **Corporate headquarters location:** This Location. **Other U.S. locations:** Nationwide. **Operations at this facility include:** Administration; Regional Headquarters; Research and Development. **Listed on:** Privately held. **Number of employees at this location:** 250. **Number of employees nationwide:** 2,700.

Note: Because addresses and telephone numbers of smaller companies can change rapidly, we recommend you call each company to verify the information below before inquiring about job opportunities. Mass mailings are not recommended.

Additional small employers:

LAND SUBDIVIDERS AND DEVELOPERS

Nicco Corp.
12102 Gantry Lane, Apple Valley MN 55124-6204. 612/891-2872.

REAL ESTATE AGENTS AND MANAGERS

AIC
1530 Greenview Dr SW, Rochester MN 55902-1080. 507/280-6663.

LaSalle Management Group Ltd.
2001 Killebrew Dr, Ste 308, Minneapolis MN 55425-1886. 612/854-8800.

Towncrest Management Inc.
4820 Minnetonka Blvd,

Minneapolis MN 55416-2263. 612/922-1002.

United Properties/Encore
3500 W 80th St, Ste 200, Bloomington MN 55431-4432. 612/831-1000.

Welsh Companies Inc.
8200 Normandale Blvd, Minneapolis MN 55437-1053. 612/897-7700.

REAL ESTATE OPERATORS

CB Richard Ellis Services
11455 Viking Dr, Ste 300, Eden Prairie MN 55344-7254. 612/944-7100.

Donatelle Properties
401 County Road E2 West, St. Paul MN 55112-6863. 651/633-4200.

Grace Management Inc.
3701 Winnetka Ave N, Minneapolis MN 55427-1203. 612/544-9934.

Great Lakes Management
5000 Glenwood Ave, Ste 150, Crystal MN 55422-5153. 612/375-0212.

Klodt Inc.
50 Groveland Terrace, Minneapolis MN 55403-1145. 612/374-1770.

Mid Continent Management Corp.
26 Concord Street, St. Paul MN 55107-2224. 651/291-0111.

Sandpiper Bend Inc.
9637 NE West Sandpiper Dr, Minneapolis MN 55434. 612/784-3508.

For more information on career opportunities in real estate:

<u>Associations</u>

INSTITUTE OF REAL ESTATE MANAGEMENT
430 North Michigan Avenue, Chicago IL 60611. 312/661-1930. World Wide Web address: http://www. irem.org. Institute of Real Estate Management is dedicated to educating and identifying real estate managers who are committed to meeting the needs of real estate owners and investors.

INTERNATIONAL ASSOCIATION OF CORPORATE REAL ESTATE EXECUTIVES
440 Columbia Drive, Suite 100, West Palm Beach FL 33409. 561/683-8111. World Wide Web address: http://www.nacore.com. International Association of Corporate Real Estate Executives is an association of real estate brokers.

INTERNATIONAL REAL ESTATE INSTITUTE
1224 North Nokomis, Alexandria MN 56308. 320/763-4648. Offers seminars on issues relating to the real estate industry.

NATIONAL ASSOCIATION OF REAL ESTATE INVESTMENT TRUSTS
1875 Eye Street NW, Suite 600, Washington DC

20006. 202/739-9400. Toll-free phone: 800/3-NAREIT. World Wide Web address: http://www. nareit.com. Contact: Matt Lentz, Membership. Membership required.

NATIONAL ASSOCIATION OF REALTORS
430 North Michigan Avenue, Chicago IL 60611. 312/329-8200. World Wide Web address: http://www. realtor.com. A membership organization compiling statistics, advising the government, and publishing several magazines including *Real Estate Today* and *Today's Realtor*.

<u>Magazines</u>

JOURNAL OF PROPERTY MANAGEMENT
Institute of Real Estate Management, 430 North Michigan Avenue, Chicago IL 60610. 312/329-6000. World Wide Web address: http://www.irem.org.

NATIONAL REAL ESTATE INVESTOR
PRIMEDIA Intertec, 6151 Powers Ferry Road NW, Suite 200, Atlanta GA 30339. 770/955-2500. World Wide Web address: http://www.intertec.com.

Online Services

JOBS IN REAL ESTATE
http://www.cob.ohio-state.edu/dept/fin/jobs/realest.
htm. This Website provides resources for jobseekers
who are looking to work in the real estate field.

REAL JOBS
http://www.real-jobs.com. This Website is designed to
help real estate professionals who are looking for jobs.

RETAIL

Retail trade will likely see annual employment growth of only 1 percent through 2006, according to the Bureau of Labor Statistics. Cashiers will see the largest gains, with the projected creation of 530,000 new positions. Retail salespersons are expected to see more than 400,000 new positions by 2006. Competition will be greatest for supervisory and management positions, which provide higher pay, yet often don't require an advanced degree.

Overall, job growth will depend on the segment of the retail industry, such as computers or home furnishings. The Federal Reserve Board anticipates a continued drop in retail prices due to an increase in lower-priced imports, such as apparel and electronics products.

Frequent fluctuations in the stock market in 1998 helped large discounters, such as Kmart and Wal-Mart, to see an increase in sales. Over the past several years, large discounters have seen their market share increase by 20 percent, whereas major department store chains have seen their market share fall 10 percent. Kmart continues to increase its number of refurbished Big Kmart stores, and planned on converting 528 of its existing stores into modern Big Kmart stores in 1998. Supermarkets are reaping the benefits of lower food prices but facing increased competition. Wal-Mart, the number one discount retailer, is branching into the grocery business, having already opened three test stores.

Online buying totaled more than $4 billion in sales in 1998. Amazon.com, a leading online bookseller, expected sales of approximately $400 million in 1998. Barnes & Noble, a leading retail bookseller which has seen its market share rise more than 100 percent, recently started its own online bookstore, with $14 million in sales for 1997, and expected $100 million in sales for 1998.

In order to see profits continue to rise, retailers will need to consistently offer lower, fair prices. Stores that also provide consumers with added incentives and reward benefits will draw more customers.

BACHMAN'S INC.
6010 Lyndale Avenue South, Minneapolis MN 55419. 612/861-7675. **Fax:** 612/861-7748. **Recorded jobline:** 612/861-9242. **Contact:** Julie Kingsley, Employment Manager. **E-mail address:** hr@bachmans.com. **Description:** A retail florist, landscaper, garden center, nursery, and greenhouse growing range. **Common positions include:** Blue-Collar Worker Supervisor; Designer; Landscape Architect; Management Trainee. **Educational backgrounds include:** Horticulture. **Benefits:** 401(k); Dental Insurance; Disability Coverage; Employee Discounts; Life Insurance; Medical Insurance; Profit Sharing. **Special programs:** Internships. **Corporate headquarters location:** This Location. **Number of employees at this location:** 1,000.

BEST BUY COMPANY, INC.
P.O. Box 9312, Minneapolis MN 55440-9312. 612/947-2000. **Physical address:** 7075 Flying Cloud Drive, Eden Prairie MN 55344. **Recorded jobline:** 612/947-2555. **Contact:** Rick Dear, Region 1 Recruiter. **World Wide Web address:** http://www.bestbuy.com. **Description:** A national retailer of consumer electronics, appliances, and home office products. **Common positions include:** Accountant/Auditor; Advertising Clerk; Buyer; Computer Programmer; Customer Service Representative; General Manager; Human Resources Manager; Management Trainee; MIS Specialist; Systems Analyst. **Educational backgrounds include:** Accounting; Business Administration; Communications; Computer Science; Economics; Finance; Liberal Arts; Marketing. **Benefits:** 401(k); Dental Insurance; Employee Discounts; Life Insurance;

Medical Insurance; Pension Plan; Public Transit Available; Tuition Assistance. **Corporate headquarters location:** This Location. **Other U.S. locations:** Nationwide. **Operations at this facility include:** Administration. **Listed on:** New York Stock Exchange. **Stock exchange symbol:** BBY. **Annual sales/revenues:** More than $100 million. **Number of employees at this location:** 1,500. **Number of employees nationwide:** 40,000.

BUMPER TO BUMPER
2565 Kasota Avenue, St. Paul MN 55108. 651/644-6448. **Contact:** Human Resources. **World Wide Web address:** http://www.midwestbumpertobumper.com. **Description:** This location houses the distribution center and corporate offices. Overall, Bumper to Bumper distributes automotive parts through 150 retail stores in Iowa, Minnesota, North Dakota, South Dakota, Wisconsin, and Wyoming. **Corporate headquarters location:** This Location.

DAMARK INTERNATIONAL, INC.
7101 Winnetka Avenue North, Minneapolis MN 55428. 612/531-0066. **Contact:** Human Resources. **World Wide Web address:** http://www.damark.com. **Description:** Markets general merchandise through catalogs. Products include computers, home office, home decor, consumer electronics, home improvements, and sporting/fitness goods. **Number of employees at this location:** 750.

DAYTON HUDSON CORPORATION
DEPARTMENT STORE DIVISION
700 On the Mall, Minneapolis MN 55402. **Fax:** 612/375-2795. **Contact:** Josh Youman, Human Resources/Recruitment Manager. **World Wide Web address:** http://www.dhc.com. **Description:** Operates 65 upscale fashion department stores in eight midwestern states. **NOTE:** Interested jobseekers should fax a resume and cover letter to Human Resources. Part-time jobs are also offered. **Company slogan:** The best store in town! **Common positions include:** Auditor; Financial Analyst; Industrial Engineer; Management Trainee; Merchant Trainee; Sales Manager; Sales Representative. **Benefits:** 401(k); Casual Dress - Fridays; Daycare Assistance; Dental Insurance; Disability Coverage; Employee Discounts; Life Insurance; Medical Insurance; Pension Plan. **Special programs:** Training. **Corporate headquarters location:** Minneapolis MN. **Other U.S. locations:** Chicago IL; Detroit MI. **Listed on:** New York Stock Exchange. **Number of employees nationwide:** 34,000.

DOWNTOWN PONTIAC JAGUAR
222 Hennepin Avenue, Minneapolis MN 55401. 612/371-1400. **Contact:** Brenda Swanson, Controller. **World Wide Web address:** http://www.downtownpontiac.com. **Description:** A new and used automobile dealership.

FASTENAL COMPANY
P.O. Box 978, Winona MN 55987. 507/454-5374. **Contact:** Human Resources. **World Wide Web address:** http://www.fastenal.com. **Description:** Markets and distributes threaded fasteners such as bolts, nuts, screws, studs, and washers, as well as other related construction supplies such as cutting tools, paints, chains, pins, machinery keys, concrete anchors, masonry drills, flashlights, batteries, sealants, metal framing systems, wire rope, and related accessories through company-operated stores. **Number of employees nationwide:** 870.

FINGERHUT COMPANY INC.
4400 Baker Road, Minnetonka MN 55343. 612/932-3100. **Contact:** Human Resources. **World Wide Web address:** http://www.fingerhut.com. **Description:** Markets general merchandise including electronics, home furnishings, household goods, women's and men's apparel, and jewelry through catalogs and other direct mail solicitations.

FULLERTON COMPANIES
P.O. Box 30, Minneapolis MN 55440-0030. 612/543-2700. **Contact:** Human Resources. **Description:** Owns 16 retail lumber yards. **Corporate headquarters location:** This Location.

GABBERTS INC.
3501 Galleria, Minneapolis MN 55435. 612/828-8500. **Contact:** Human Resources. **Description:** A retail furniture store. **Common positions include:** Accountant/Auditor; Computer Programmer; Credit Manager; Customer Service Representative; Department Manager; General Manager; Human Resources Manager; Operations/Production Manager; Retail Sales Worker. **Benefits:** Dental Insurance; Disability Coverage; Employee Discounts; Life Insurance; Medical Insurance; Profit Sharing; Savings Plan; Stock Option. **Corporate headquarters location:** This Location. **Other U.S. locations:** Dallas TX; Fort Worth TX. **Operations at this facility include:** Administration; Service. **Number of employees nationwide:** 700.

GROW BIZ INTERNATIONAL
4200 Dahlberg Drive, Minneapolis MN 55422-4837. 612/520-8500. **Contact:** Human Resources. **World Wide Web address:** http://www.growbiz.com. **Description:** A retail franchiser which sells a variety of new and used merchandise. **Corporate headquarters location:** This Location. **Subsidiaries include:** It's About Games; Music Go Round; Once Upon A Child; Play It Again Sports; ReTool.

HOIGAARD'S
3550 South Highway 100, St. Louis Park MN 55416. 612/929-1351. **Contact:** Personnel. **World Wide Web address:** http://www.hoigaards.com. **Description:** A retailer of sporting goods.

HOLIDAY STATIONSTORES
4567 West 80th Street, Bloomington MN 55437. 612/832-8530. **Toll-free phone:** 800/745-7411. **Fax:** 612/832-8551. **Recorded jobline:** 612/832-8585. **Contact:** Justin Olsen, Recruiting Manager. **Description:** Operates retail convenience stores/gas stations with 241 locations in 10 states. **NOTE:** Some post-secondary education in business management, accounting, or marketing is helpful for jobseekers, but not required. Entry-level positions are offered. **Common positions include:** Assistant Manager; Cashier; Management Trainee. **Benefits:** Bonus Award/Plan; Dental Insurance; Disability Coverage; Employee Discounts; Life Insurance; Medical Insurance; Profit Sharing; Tuition Assistance. **Special programs:** Internships; Training. **Corporate headquarters location:** This Location. **Other U.S. locations:** IA; ID; MI; MT; ND; NE; WA; WI; WY. **Parent company:** Holiday Companies. **Operations at this facility include:** Administration; Divisional Headquarters. **Listed on:** Privately held. **Annual sales/revenues:** More than $100 million. **Number of employees at this location:** 500. **Number of employees nationwide:** 6,000.

JCPENNEY COMPANY, INC.
1600 Miller Trunk Highway, Duluth MN 55811. 218/727-8111. **Contact:** Human Resources. **World Wide Web address:** http://www.jcpenney.com. **Description:** This location is a department store. Overall, JCPenney sells apparel, home furnishings, and leisure lines in catalogs and 1,900 stores. **Subsidiaries include:** JCPenney Life Insurance Company, which sells life, health, and credit insurance; JCPenney National Bank.

JERRY'S ENTERPRISES
5101 Vernon Avenue South, Edina MN 55436. 612/922-8335. **Contact:** Personnel. **Description:** Operates a chain of grocery stores.

KMART STORES
1734 Mall Drive, Duluth MN 55811. 218/727-0816. **Contact:** Human Resources. **Description:** One location of the discount department store chain. Overall, Kmart is one of the nation's largest owners and operators of general merchandising stores. These stores include 19 super Kmart stores, which offer the same general merchandise plus foodstuffs. Kmart engages in specialty retailing through Borders-Walden, a 1,203-store bookseller; 177 Builders Square home improvement centers; 328 OfficeMax stores; and 80 Sports Authority stores.

KNOWLAN'S SUPER MARKETS
111 East County Road F, Vadnais Heights MN 55127. 651/483-9242. **Contact:** Andrea Wellman, Human Resources Director. **Description:** Operates a chain of retail grocery stores. **Corporate headquarters location:** This Location.

KOHL'S DEPARTMENT STORE
2115 Miller Trunk Highway, Duluth MN 55811. 218/722-9699. **Contact:** Human Resources. **Description:** A location of the department store chain. Overall, Kohl's sells apparel, shoes, accessories, home products, and housewares.

LUND FOOD HOLDINGS
BYERLY'S INC.
4100 West 50th Street, Edina MN 55424. 612/927-3663. **Contact:** Tamra Laska, Personnel Department. **Description:** Lund Food Holdings owns and operates Byerly's, a retail grocery store chain with seven stores in the Minneapolis-St. Paul region. **Corporate headquarters location:** This Location.

McGLYNN BAKERIES, INC.
7350 Commerce Lane NE, Minneapolis MN 55432. 612/574-2222. **Toll-free phone:** 800/624-5966. **Fax:** 612/574-2210. **Contact:** Human Resources. **World Wide Web address:** http://www. mcglynn.com. **Description:** A producer of cookies and other baked goods that operates in three divisions: McGlynn's Retail Bakeries, which operates over 200 locations; Concept 2 Bakers, which

produces and markets frozen bakery foods; and DecoPac, which markets cake decorating sets and supplies in the United States and Canada. **Corporate headquarters location:** This Location. **Parent company:** Pillsbury Company manufactures and markets food products for consumer, industrial, and international markets.

MUSICLAND GROUP, INC.
10400 Yellow Circle Drive, Minnetonka MN 55343. 612/931-8000. **Fax:** 612/931-8300. **Contact:** Kathleen Miller, Manager of Employment. **Description:** This location houses the corporate headquarters for the retail chain of specialty music stores.

NASH FINCH COMPANY
7600 France Avenue South, Edina MN 55435. 612/832-0534. **Contact:** Edgar Timberlake, Personnel Administration. **Description:** Engaged in wholesale distribution, retail distribution, and produce marketing. The wholesale distribution segment supplies products to approximately 5,700 affiliated and independent supermarkets, military bases, convenience stores, and other customers in 31 states. The retail distribution segment consists of approximately 120 company-owned retail stores in 16 states. Nash Finch's corporate stores operate under names such as Econofoods, Sun Mart, Family Thrift Center, Food Folks, and Easter's. Nash DeCamp markets fresh fruits and vegetables to wholesalers and retailers worldwide. **Corporate headquarters location:** This Location. **Listed on:** NASDAQ.

PLANTENBERG MARKET INC.
P.O. Box 399, Richmond MN 56368. 320/597-2385. **Physical address:** 132 West Main Street, Richmond MN 56368. **Contact:** Human Resources. **Description:** A grocery store.

PLAY IT AGAIN SPORTS
1401 First Avenue SW, Austin MN 55912. 507/433-2881. **Contact:** Human Resources. **Description:** One location of a chain of retail stores selling used sporting equipment. **Parent company:** Grow Biz International (Minneapolis MN).

PROEX PHOTO SYSTEMS
7101 Ohms Lane, Edina MN 55439. 612/893-1915. **Contact:** Becky Reinmann, Director of Human Resources. **Description:** A retail, one-hour photo finishing firm. Proex operates 19 retail, one-hour labs in the Minneapolis-St. Paul area, 10 portrait studios, and a specialty lab. **Common positions include:** Assistant Manager; Laboratory Technician; Management Trainee; Photographer/Camera Operator. **Educational backgrounds include:** Business Administration; Communications; Liberal Arts; Management/Planning; Phototechnology. **Benefits:** 401(k); Dental Insurance; Disability Coverage; Employee Discounts; Life Insurance; Medical Insurance; Tuition Assistance. **Corporate headquarters location:** This Location.

RAINBOW FOODS
8000 Excelsior Boulevard, Hopkins MN 55343. 612/931-1100. **Contact:** Mr. Randy Theesfield, Personnel Director. **Description:** Operates a chain of retail grocery stores.

SCHMITT MUSIC
88 South 10th Street, Minneapolis MN 55403. 612/339-4811. **Contact:** Debbie Reinhardt, Director of Personnel. **Description:** Operates a chain of retail music stores.

SNYDER DRUG STORES
14525 Highway 7, Minnetonka MN 55345. 612/935-9441. **Fax:** 612/936-2512. **Contact:** Lisa Kraft, Manager of Human Resources Development. **E-mail address:** snyhr@fishnet.com. **World Wide Web address:** http://www.snyderdrug.com. **Description:** Operates a chain of retail drug stores. **Common positions include:** Accountant/Auditor; Advertising Clerk; Buyer; Human Resources Manager; Management Trainee; Pharmacist; Systems Analyst. **Educational backgrounds include:** Business Administration; Computer Science; Liberal Arts; Marketing. **Benefits:** 401(k); Dental Insurance; Disability Coverage; Employee Discounts; Life Insurance; Medical Insurance. **Corporate headquarters location:** This Location. **Operations at this facility include:** Administration. **Listed on:** Privately held. **Number of employees at this location:** 125. **Number of employees nationwide:** 1,300.

SPEEDWAY SUPERAMERICA
1240 West 98th Street, Bloomington MN 55431. **Toll-free phone:** 800/782-8232. **Contact:** Pam Graupensperger, Recruiter. **Description:** Operates a chain of over 600 convenience store/gas stations in 11 states in the upper Midwest. **NOTE:** Entry-level positions are offered. **Common positions include:** Assistant Manager; Customer Service Representative; General Manager; Management Trainee; Restaurant/Food Service Manager. **Educational backgrounds include:**

Accounting; Business Administration; Finance; Liberal Arts; Marketing. **Benefits:** 401(k); Dental Insurance; Disability Coverage; Employee Discounts; Life Insurance; Medical Insurance; Pension Plan; Profit Sharing; Savings Plan; Tuition Assistance. **Special programs:** Internships. **Corporate headquarters location:** Lexington KY. **Other U.S. locations:** IL; IN; MI; ND; OH; PA; SD; WI; WV. **Parent company:** Ashland, Inc. **Operations at this facility include:** Administration; Regional Headquarters. **Listed on:** New York Stock Exchange. **Number of employees at this location:** 100. **Number of employees nationwide:** 10,000.

SUPERVALU INC.
11840 Valley View Road, Eden Prairie MN 55344. 612/828-4000. **Fax:** 612/828-4803. **Contact:** Michael Overline, General Director of Human Resources. **Description:** One of the nation's largest food retailers and distribution companies, supplying grocery, health and beauty aids, and general merchandise products to over 4,800 customers. In the corporate retail sector, SUPERVALU operates over 300 stores under the following names: bigg's, Cub Foods, Shop 'n Save, Save-A-Lot, Scott's Foods, Laneco, and Hornbachers. **Common positions include:** Buyer; Computer Programmer; Human Resources Manager; Management Trainee; Pharmacist; Transportation/ Traffic Specialist; Wholesale and Retail Buyer. **Corporate headquarters location:** This Location. **Other U.S. locations:** Nationwide. **Subsidiaries include:** Hazelwood Farms Bakeries manufactures frozen bakery products. **Listed on:** New York Stock Exchange. **Stock exchange symbol:** SVU. **Number of employees nationwide:** 48,000.

TARGET STORES
P.O. Box 1392, Minneapolis MN 55440-1392. 612/304-6073. **Physical address:** 33 South Sixth Street, Minneapolis MN 55402. **Contact:** Human Resources. **Description:** Operates a retail chain of discount department stores. **Benefits:** Dental Insurance; Disability Coverage; Employee Discounts; Life Insurance; Medical Insurance; Pension Plan; Profit Sharing; Savings Plan; Tuition Assistance. **Corporate headquarters location:** This Location.

THRIFTY WHITE STORES
55 West Office Center, Suite 300, 10700 Highway 55, Minneapolis MN 55441. 612/513-4300. **Contact:** David Rueter, Personnel Manager. **Description:** Operates a retail drugstore chain with over 50 rural locations in Minnesota, the Dakotas, Iowa, and Montana. **Common positions include:** Accountant/Auditor; Advertising Clerk; Buyer; Clerical Supervisor; Credit Clerk and Authorizer; Department Manager; General Manager; Marketing Manager; Payroll Clerk; Pharmacist; Receptionist; Wholesale and Retail Buyer. **Educational backgrounds include:** Accounting; Business Administration; Liberal Arts. **Benefits:** 401(k); Dental Insurance; Employee Discounts; Life Insurance; Medical Insurance; Pension Plan; Profit Sharing. **Corporate headquarters location:** This Location. **Operations at this facility include:** Administration; Sales. **Number of employees at this location:** 60. **Number of employees nationwide:** 1,150.

TOM THUMB FOOD MARKETS, INC.
POLKA DOT DAIRY, INC.
110 East 17th Street, Hastings MN 55033. 651/437-9023. **Fax:** 651/438-2638. **Contact:** Todd Huffman, Director of Human Resources. **Description:** Tom Thumb Food Markets operates an area grocery and convenience store chain. Polka Dot Dairy (also at this location) is a distributor of bottled milk. **Common positions include:** Management Trainee. **Educational backgrounds include:** Accounting; Business Administration; Economics; Finance; Marketing. **Benefits:** Dental Insurance; Disability Coverage; Life Insurance; Medical Insurance; Profit Sharing. **Corporate headquarters location:** This Location. **Operations at this facility include:** Administration; Regional Headquarters; Sales; Service.

UNITED HARDWARE DISTRIBUTION COMPANY
P.O. Box 410, Minneapolis MN 55440. 612/559-1800. **Contact:** Renee Bourget, Human Resources. **Description:** This location houses the corporate offices. Overall, United Hardware Distribution Company operates the Hardware Hank and Trustworthy Hardware chains of hardware stores, and the Golden Rule Lumber chain of retail lumber stores. **Corporate headquarters location:** This Location.

WAL-MART STORES, INC.
4740 Mall Drive, Duluth MN 55811. 218/727-1310. **Contact:** Human Resources. **Description:** This is a department store location of the retail chain. One of the largest retail merchandise chains in the country, Wal-Mart Stores, Inc. operates a series of full-service discount department stores, and has opened several stores in Mexico through a joint venture with Cifta, one of that country's largest retailers. Wal-Mart Stores, Inc. has also begun an expansion into Canada.

Note: Because addresses and telephone numbers of smaller companies can change rapidly, we recommend you call each company to verify the information below before inquiring about job opportunities. Mass mailings are not recommended.

Additional small employers:

AUTO DEALERS

Barnett Chrysler-Plymouth
3610 Highway 61 N, White Bear Lake MN 55110-4164. 651/429-3391.

Bloomington Chrysler Plymouth
8000 Penn Ave S, Bloomington MN 55431-1317. 612/888-9541.

Buerkle Buick-Honda Co.
3350 Highway 61 N, White Bear Lake MN 55110-5212. 651/484-0231.

Clements Chevrolet Cadillac
1000 12th St SW, Rochester MN 55902-3833. 507/289-0491.

Friendly Chevrolet Geo Inc.
7501 Highway 65 NE, Fridley MN 55432-3544. 612/786-6100.

Grossman Chevrolet-Geo
1200 W 141st St, Burnsville MN 55337-4437. 612/435-8501.

Iten Chevrolet Co.
6701 Brooklyn Blvd, Minneapolis MN 55429-1713. 612/561-9220.

Jeff Belzer's Chevrolet
PO Box 965, Lakeville MN 55044-0965. 612/469-4444.

Jim Lupient Harold Chevrolet
1601 Southtown Dr, Bloomington MN 55431-1431. 612/884-2341.

Jim Lupient Oldsmobile Co.
7100 Wayzata Blvd, St. Louis Park MN 55426-1616. 612/546-2222.

Main Motors Chevrolet/Cadillac
435 W Main St, Anoka MN 55303-2019. 612/421-2700.

Metropolitan Ford
12790 Plaza Dr, Eden Prairie MN 55344-3632. 612/943-9000.

Midway Ford Company Inc.
2777 Snelling Ave N, Roseville MN 55113-1731. 651/636-8200.

Midway Hyundai Suzuki
1389 University Ave W, St. Paul MN 55104-4002. 651/646-2561.

Minar Ford Inc.
1100 Silver Lake Rd NW, St. Paul MN 55112-6325. 651/633-9010.

Polar Chevrolet-Geo-Mazda
1801 County Road F E, White Bear Lake MN 55110-3882. 651/429-7791.

Ron Saxon Ford Inc.
225 University Ave W, St. Paul MN 55103-2045. 651/222-0511.

Southview Chevrolet Jeep
1055 Highway 110, Inver Grove Heights MN 55077-1111. 651/451-2211.

Stephens Buick-Jeep-Eagle
2370 Highway 100 S, Minneapolis MN 55416-1703. 612/929-0081.

Superior Ford Inc.
9700 56th Ave N, Minneapolis MN 55442-1613. 612/559-9111.

Tenvoorde Ford Inc.
PO Box 1045, St. Cloud MN 56302-1045. 320/251-0540.

Town and Country Dodge Inc.
1710 Highway 7, Hopkins MN 55343-6901. 612/935-3371.

Universal Ford-Toyota
4900 Highway 52 N, Rochester MN 55901-0163. 507/288-7564.

White Bear Lake Pontiac-GMC-Hyundai
3880 Highway 61 N, White Bear Lake MN 55110-4645. 651/426-5441.

BOOKSTORES

Minnesota's Book Store
117 University Ave W, St. Paul MN 55155-2202. 651/297-3000.

CATALOG AND MAIL-ORDER HOUSES

Fingerhut Corporation
PO Box 9999A, Waite Park MN 56387. 320/654-4100.

Fingerhut Corporation
847 Howe Ave, Mora MN 55051-1606. 320/679-1600.

Fingerhut Corporation
1910 Aga Dr, Alexandria MN 56308-2772. 320/762-1115.

Sales Guides Inc.
4937 Otter Lake Rd, White Bear Lake MN 55110-6603. 651/426-6006.

Signals Catalog
PO Box 64428, St. Paul MN 55164-0428. 651/659-3700.

Sportsman's Guide Inc.
411 Farwell Ave, South St. Paul MN 55075-2428. 651/451-3030.

CONSUMER ELECTRONICS STORES

Best Buy
1555 Queens Dr, Woodbury MN 55125-1581. 651/731-1090.

Best Buy
1000 West 78th Street, Minneapolis MN 55423-3912. 612/861-3917.

Best Buy
13513 Ridgedale Dr, Hopkins MN 55305-1813. 612/544-0377.

Best Buy
5925 Earle Brown Dr, Brooklyn Center MN 55430-2503. 612/566-1830.

Best Buy
1350 50th St E, Inver Grove Heights MN 55077-1249. 651/457-5817.

Best Buy
304 Northtown Dr NE, Minneapolis MN 55434-1039. 612/780-8668.

Best Buy
1885 County Road D E, Maplewood MN 55109-5307. 651/777-6090.

Best Buy
5105 Burning Tree Rd, Duluth MN 55811-1875. 218/722-8767.

Best Buy
4050 Highway 52 North, Rochester MN 55901-0108. 507/281-5855.

Best Buy
1647 County Road B2 W, Roseville MN 55113-3001. 651/636-6456.

Best Buy
4130 W Division Street, St. Cloud MN 56301-3706. 320/259-5208.

Skyvision Inc.
1010 Frontier Dr, Fergus Falls MN 56537-1023. 218/739-5231.

CONSUMER SUPPLY STORES

Fleet Wholesale Supply Co.
920 E Highway 61, Winona MN
55987-5354. 507/454-5124.

Tires Plus
PO Box 1012, Burnsville MN
55337-0012. 612/894-2700.

DEPARTMENT STORES

Carson Pirie Scott
204 17th Ave NW, Rochester
MN 55901-0329. 507/282-7471.

Dayton Hudson
12411 Wayzata Blvd, Hopkins
MN 55305-1925. 612/591-6600.

Dayton Hudson
1100 Brookdale Ctr, Brooklyn
Center MN 55430-2802. 612/569-
6601.

Dayton Hudson
14251 Fernhaven Dr, Burnsville
MN 55337. 612/435-8811.

Dayton Hudson
900 Fairview Ave S, St. Paul MN
55116-2418. 651/639-6600.

Herbergers
209 12th Ave E, Sartell MN
56377-2327. 320/251-1946.

Herbergers
14781 59th St N, Stillwater MN
55082-6300. 651/430-9229.

Herbergers
1440 S 12th Ave, Virginia MN
55792-3247. 218/741-4747.

Herbergers
1850 Adams St, Mankato MN
56001-4864. 507/388-8884.

Herbergers
PO Box 1386, Willmar MN
56201-1386. 320/231-1300.

JCPenney
12421 Wayzata Blvd, Hopkins
MN 55305-1925. 612/544-6000.

JCPenney
Hwy 100, Brooklyn Center MN
55430. 612/566-2100.

JCPenney
14301 Burnhaven Dr, Savage MN
55306-4927. 612/435-8551.

JCPenney
66 France Ave S, Minneapolis
MN 55435. 612/920-7240.

JCPenney
400 Southdale Ctr, Minneapolis
MN 55435-2405. 612/920-8101.

JCPenney
200 Western Ave NW, Ste A,
Faribault MN 55021-4515.
507/334-1893.

JCPenney
101 Apache Mall, Rochester MN
55902-2104. 507/288-8383.

JCPenney
1700 County Road B2 W,
Roseville MN 55113-3006.
651/631-3330.

JCPenney
4101 W Division St, St. Cloud
MN 56301-6600. 320/252-6020.

Kmart
7575 153rd St W, Apple Valley
MN 55124-7184. 612/432-9100.

Kmart
1201 Hwy 2 W, Bemidji MN
56601. 218/751-5630.

Kmart
7191 10th St N, St. Paul MN
55128-5943. 651/739-3550.

Kmart
4747 Central Ave NE,
Minneapolis MN 55421-1945.
612/571-4801.

Kmart
7282 Point Douglas Dr S, Cottage
Grove MN 55016. 651/459-7030.

Kmart
404 Schilling Dr, Dundas MN
55019. 507/645-8484.

Kmart
1100 W Hwy 10, Anoka MN
55303. 612/427-7507.

Kmart
4300 Xylon Ave North,
Minneapolis MN 55428-4842.
612/535-4830.

Kmart
400 E Travelers Trl, Burnsville
MN 55337-2811. 612/894-1200.

Kmart
3201 White Bear Ave N, White
Bear Lake MN 55110-5402.
651/770-2911.

Kmart
1111 S Pokegama Ave, Grand
Rapids MN 55744-3905.
218/326-0583.

Kmart
4850 228th St N, Forest Lake MN
55025-9301. 651/646-0128.

Kmart
1401 South 12th Avenue,
Virginia MN 55792-3247.
218/749-1131.

Kmart
17501 Highway 7, Minnetonka
MN 55345-3338. 612/934-3800.

Kmart
215 N Central Ave, Duluth MN
55807-2473. 218/624-9335.

Kmart
300 7th St W, Monticello MN
55362-8325. 612/295-0040.

Kmart
201 9th St SE, Rochester MN
55904-6452. 507/288-9567.

Kmart
1400 18th Ave NW, Austin MN
55912-1858. 507/433-1228.

Kmart
1122 W Highway 61, Winona
MN 55987-5349. 507/454-7030.

Kmart
1215 N State St, Fairmont MN
56031-3742. 507/235-8080.

Kmart
2107 North Garden Street, New
Ulm MN 56073-2302. 507/359-
1465.

Kmart
6501 Lyndale Ave S,
Minneapolis MN 55423-1407.
612/861-7251.

Kmart
245 Maryland Avenue East, St.
Paul MN 55117-4617. 651/488-
0555.

Kmart
1640 Robert Street South, St. Paul
MN 55118-3918. 651/451-9000.

Kmart
1605 1st St S, Willmar MN
56201-4234. 320/235-9501.

Kmart
1305 Highway 10 W, Detroit
Lakes MN 56501-2214. 218/847-
9777.

Kmart
1001 N Highway 23 Byp,
Marshall MN 56258-2616.
507/532-2737.

Kmart
10 W Lake St, Minneapolis MN
55408-3116. 612/827-5491.

Kohl's
13900 Aldrich Ave S, Burnsville
MN 55337-6215. 612/890-2450.

Kohl's
450 Prairie Center Dr, Eden
Prairie MN 55344-5382. 612/829-
1314.

Kohl's
1651 County Road B2 W,
Roseville MN 55113-3001.
651/636-8322.

Kohl's
1350 Town Centre Dr, St. Paul
MN 55123-2310. 612/688-8388.

Kohl's
145 2nd St S, Waite Park MN
56387-1364. 320/240-8808.

Kohl's
8080 Wedgewood Ln, Garrison
MN 56450. 612/420-4919.

Kohl's
7100 Valley Creek Pl, Woodbury
MN 55125. 651/731-8456.

Kohl's
8440 Highway 7, St. Louis Park
MN 55426-3900. 612/988-9100.

Kohl's
2501 County Road 10, Brooklyn
Center MN 55430-2501. 612/560-
3665.

Kohl's
7931 Southtown Ctr,
Bloomington MN 55431-1323.
612/881-8861.

Kohl's
3001 Maplewood Dr, Maplewood
MN 55109-1080. 651/779-8110.

Marshall's
2100 Snelling Ave N, Roseville
MN 55113-6000. 651/636-6688.

Mervyn's
Hwy 36 & Snelling NW,
Roseville MN 55113. 651/636-
1120.

Montgomery Ward & Co. Inc.
1400 University Ave W, St. Paul
MN 55104-4001. 651/647-3200.

Montgomery Ward & Co. Inc.
3435 W Broadway Ave, Crystal
MN 55422-2922. 612/520-6400.

Montgomery Ward & Co. Inc.
7831 Southtown Ctr,
Bloomington MN 55431-1324.
612/885-1000.

Montgomery Ward & Co. Inc.
99 Northtown Dr NE,
Minneapolis MN 55434-1034.
612/780-7400.

Montgomery Ward & Co. Inc.
1600 Miller Trunk Hwy, Duluth
MN 55811-5640. 218/727-6677.

Montgomery Ward & Co. Inc.
600 Rosedale Ctr, Roseville MN
55113-3002. 651/631-6800.

Neiman Marcus
505 Nicollet Mall, Minneapolis
MN 55402-1113. 612/339-2600.

Proffitt's
37 Signal Hills Ctr, St. Paul MN
55118-2309. 651/457-9261.

Sears, Roebuck & Co.
2000 Northeast Ct, Minneapolis
MN 55425-5506. 612/853-0500.

Sears, Roebuck & Co.
12431 Wayzata Blvd, Hopkins
MN 55305-1925. 612/542-2101.

Sears, Roebuck & Co.
1297 Brookdale Ctr, Brooklyn
Center MN 55430-2803. 612/572-
3101.

Sears, Roebuck & Co.
14250 Buck Hill Rd, Burnsville
MN 55306-4925. 612/435-2380.

Sears, Roebuck & Co.
3001 White Bear Ave N,
Maplewood MN 55109-1215.
651/770-4301.

Sears, Roebuck & Co.
13050 Riverdale Dr NW,
Minneapolis MN 55448-1057.
612/421-1218.

Sears, Roebuck & Co.
8301 Flying Cloud Dr, Eden
Prairie MN 55344-5381. 612/944-
4912.

Sears, Roebuck & Co.
1001 Apache Mall, Rochester
MN 55902-2178. 507/280-2500.

Sears, Roebuck & Co.
41st & Divison St, St. Cloud MN
56301. 320/251-7760.

Sears, Roebuck & Co.
425 Rice St, St. Paul MN 55103-
2123. 651/291-4397.

Shopko
801 W Central Entrance, Duluth
MN 55811-5468. 218/727-7131.

Shopko
125 Main St N, Hutchinson MN
55350-1807. 320/587-4994.

Shopko
2820 Highway 63, Rochester MN
55904-5571. 507/281-0686.

Shopko
3708 Highway 63 N, Rochester
MN 55906-3902. 507/281-0656.

Shopko
1209 18th Ave NW, Austin MN
55912-1881. 507/437-7785.

Shopko
405 Cottonwood Dr, Winona MN
55987-1914. 507/452-1611.

Shopko
1850 E Madison Ave, Mankato
MN 56001-5448. 507/387-6511.

Shopko
2610 Bridge Ave, Albert Lea MN
56007-2075. 507/373-6600.

Shopko
1001 Highway 15 S, Fairmont
MN 56031-4456. 507/238-9481.

Shopko
1755 N Humiston Ave,
Worthington MN 56187-1757.
507/376-9300.

Shopko
PO Box 547, Marshall MN
56258-0547. 507/532-3266.

Shopko
4161 2nd St S, St. Cloud MN
56301-3761. 320/253-5150.

Shopko
501 Highway 10 SE, St. Cloud
MN 56304-1250. 320/253-0344.

Target
700 Dellwood Dr N, Baxter MN
56425-7929. 218/828-3535.

Target
7200 Valley Creek Rd,
Woodbury MN 55125-2208.
651/735-7083.

Target
3601 Highway 100 S,
Minneapolis MN 55416-2500.
612/926-8855.

Target
3301 Highway 10 E, Moorhead
MN 56560-2516. 218/233-2326.

Target
755 53rd Ave NE, Minneapolis
MN 55421-1240. 612/571-9361.

Target
8655 E Point Douglas Rd S,
Cottage Grove MN 55016-4086.
651/458-8179.

Target
6100 Shingle Creek Pkwy,
Brooklyn Center MN 55430-
2110. 612/566-0739.

Target
2555 W 79th St, Bloomington
MN 55431-1250. 612/888-7701.

Target
11000 Crooked Lake Blvd N,
Coon Rapids MN 55433-3830.
612/421-0260.

Target
2199 Highway 36 E, Maplewood
MN 55109-2215. 651/770-1351.

Target
851 W 78th St, Chanhassen MN
55317-9579. 612/470-0206.

Target
8600 Springbrook Dr NW, Coon
Rapids MN 55433-6033.
612/785-0322.

Target
7000 York Ave S, Minneapolis
MN 55435-4213. 612/925-4610.

Target
19146 Freeport Ave, Elk River
MN 55330-1264. 612/441-5511.

Target
810 County Road 42 W,
Burnsville MN 55337-4426.
612/435-8611.

Target
8225 Flying Cloud Dr, Eden
Prairie MN 55344-5315. 612/944-
0700.

Target
1902 Hwy 53, Duluth MN 55811.
218/727-8851.

Target
3900 Highway 52 N, Rochester
MN 55901-5800. 507/289-0607.

Target
1515 County Road B W,
Roseville MN 55113-6005.
651/631-0330.

Target
1850 Adams St, Mankato MN
56001-4864. 507/625-1011.

Target
777 Nicollet Mall, Minneapolis
MN 55402-2004. 612/370-6948.

Target
1744 Suburban Ave, St. Paul MN
55106-6619. 651/778-1188.

Target
1776 Robert St S, St. Paul MN
55118-3919. 651/455-6671.

Target
2505 1st St S, Willmar MN
56201-4215. 320/235-0916.

Target
2500 East Lake Street,
Minneapolis MN 55406-1909.
612/721-5701.

Target
4201 W Division St, St. Cloud
MN 56301-6601. 320/253-4740.

Target
701 W Broadway Ave,
Minneapolis MN 55411-2611.
612/588-7581.

Target
4404 Highway 29 S, Alexandria
MN 56308-2915. 320/763-6661.

Target
2000 Cliff Lake Rd, Eagan MN
55122-2400. 612/688-8706.

Wal-Mart
1800 1st Ave NE, Little Falls MN
56345-3381. 320/632-9268.

Wal-Mart
1360 Town Centre Dr, St. Paul
MN 55123-2310. 651/686-7428.

Wal-Mart
385 Edgewood Dr N, Baxter MN
56425-9681. 218/829-2220.

Wal-Mart
1711 Highway 10 W, Dilworth
MN 56529-1342. 218/233-8226.

Wal-Mart
3300 Highway 210 W, Fergus
Falls MN 56537-4002. 218/739-
5552.

Wal-Mart
715 W 78th St, Minneapolis MN
55420-1038. 612/854-2262.

Wal-Mart
150 Western Ave NW, Faribault
MN 55021-4504. 507/332-0232.

Wal-Mart
8450 University Ave NE, Fridley
MN 55432-1164. 612/780-9400.

Wal-Mart
1315 Highway 25 N, Buffalo MN
55313-1937. 612/682-2958.

Wal-Mart
5815 Norell Ave N, Stillwater
MN 55082-1766. 651/439-7476.

Wal-Mart
8000 Lakeland Ave N,
Minneapolis MN 55445-2403.
612/424-7077.

Wal-Mart
100 Wal-Mart Ln, Cambridge
MN 55008. 612/689-0606.

Wal-Mart
13020 Riverdale Dr NW,
Minneapolis MN 55448-1057.
612/421-9562.

Wal-Mart
12195 Singletree Ln, Eden Prairie
MN 55344-7921. 612/829-9040.

Wal-Mart
1308 Highway 33 S, Cloquet MN
55720-2653. 218/878-0737.

Wal-Mart
225 33rd St W, Hastings MN
55033-3636. 651/438-2400.

Wal-Mart
1400 S Pokegama Ave, Grand
Rapids MN 55744-4266.
218/326-9682.

Wal-Mart
1300 Trunk Hwy 15 S,
Hutchinson MN 55350. 320/587-
1020.

Wal-Mart
3400 55th St NW, Rochester MN
55901-0123. 507/280-7733.

Wal-Mart
1881 E Madison Ave, Mankato
MN 56001-6200. 507/625-9318.

Wal-Mart
200 12th St SW, Forest Lake MN
55025-1482. 651/464-9740.

Wal-Mart
1010 Hoffman Dr, Owatonna MN
55060-1110. 507/455-0049.

Wal-Mart
1721 W Main St, Albert Lea MN
56007-4385. 507/377-2059.

Wal-Mart
PO Box 416, Blue Earth MN
56013-0416. 507/526-4766.

Wal-Mart
850 County Road E E, St. Paul
MN 55127-7117. 651/486-7001.

Wal-Mart
1300 N State St, Waseca MN
56093-2708. 507/835-2250.

Wal-Mart
3031 1st St S, Willmar MN
56201-4240. 320/231-3454.

Wal-Mart
1101 E Main St, Marshall MN
56258-1133. 507/532-9383.

Wal-Mart
2202 W Hwy 7, Montevideo MN
56265. 320/269-5390.

Wal-Mart
1410 E Bridge St, Redwood Falls
MN 56283-1906. 507/644-6278.

Wal-Mart
380 33rd Avenue South, St.
Cloud MN 56301-3716. 320/259-
1527.

Wal-Mart
515 50th Ave W, Alexandria MN
56308-9588. 320/762-2850.

DRUG STORES

Festival Family Pharmacy
205 Washington Ave E,
Hutchinson MN 55350-2612.
320/587-8233.

Ivanhoe Pharmacy
PO Box G, Ivanhoe MN 56142-0136. 507/694-1414.

**GROCERY AND
CONVENIENCE STORES**

Byerly's
401 W 98th St, Minneapolis MN 55420-4711. 612/881-6294.

Byerly's
13081 Ridgedale Dr, Hopkins MN 55305-1807. 612/541-1414.

Byerly's
401 County Road 42 E, Burnsville MN 55306-5706. 612/892-5600.

Byerly's
800 W 78th St, Chanhassen MN 55317-9578. 612/474-1298.

Byerly's
8090 County Road 50, Rockford MN 55373-9428. 612/477-5803.

Byerly's
1601 W County Rd C, Hugo MN 55038. 651/633-6949.

Byerly's
1959 Suburban Ave, St. Paul MN 55119-7002. 651/735-6340.

Byerly's
2510 W Division St, St. Cloud MN 56301-3815. 320/252-4112.

Byerly's
1299 Promenade Pl, St. Paul MN 55121-2293. 651/686-9669.

Cash Wise Foods
3300 Highway 10 E, Moorhead MN 56560-2512. 218/236-4910.

Cash Wise Foods
495 W North St, Owatonna MN 55060-1107. 507/451-9073.

Cash Wise Foods
1300 3rd St SE, Willmar MN 56201-5302. 320/235-2485.

Coborns
110 1st St S, Sauk Rapids MN 56379-1404. 320/252-2141.

Coborns
1101 2nd Ave NE, Little Falls MN 56345-2943. 320/632-6762.

County Market
305 7th St W, Northfield MN 55057-2421. 507/645-4251.

County Market
PO Box 720, Prior Lake MN 55372-0720. 612/440-7900.

County Market
503 NW 4th St, Grand Rapids MN 55744-2505. 218/326-9695.

County Market
1300 N Frontage Rd, Hastings MN 55033-2377. 651/437-3171.

County Market
310 Brainerd Mall, Brainerd MN 56401. 218/828-1816.

County Market
1100 Shakopee Town Sq, Shakopee MN 55379-1909. 612/445-3866.

County Market
1619 W Main St, Albert Lea MN 56007-1868. 507/373-7357.

County Market
405 Country Club Dr, Marshall MN 56258-1611. 507/532-4338.

Cub Foods
1440 University Ave W, St. Paul MN 55104-4001. 651/646-1003.

Cub Foods
1059 Meadowlands Dr, St. Paul MN 55127-2323. 651/426-6534.

Cub Foods
5937 Nicollet Ave, Minneapolis MN 55419-2421. 612/866-7471.

Cub Foods
3930 Silver Lake Rd NE, Minneapolis MN 55421-4351. 612/789-8689.

Cub Foods
7555 W Broadway Ave, Minneapolis MN 55428-1287. 612/424-2510.

Cub Foods
10520 France Ave S, Bloomington MN 55431-3538. 612/884-8288.

Cub Foods
5633 Memorial Ave N, Stillwater MN 55082-1092. 651/430-2950.

Cub Foods
585 Northtown Dr NE, Minneapolis MN 55434-1044. 612/780-4323.

Cub Foods
6775 York Ave S, Minneapolis MN 55435-2514. 612/929-9330.

Cub Foods
2900 Highway 13 W, Burnsville MN 55337-1742. 612/894-9040.

Cub Foods
3550 Vicksburg Ln N, Plymouth MN 55447-1322. 612/559-2110.

Cub Foods
12900 Riverdale Dr NW, Minneapolis MN 55448-1063. 612/421-4252.

Cub Foods
8015 Den Rd, Eden Prairie MN 55344-8017. 612/941-9050.

Cub Foods
4801 County Road 101, Minnetonka MN 55345-2636. 612/938-1404.

Cub Foods
8150 Wedgewood Ln N, Maple Grove MN 55369-9400. 612/494-8364.

Cub Foods
1800 E Madison Ave, Mankato MN 56001-5448. 507/625-9222.

Cub Foods
8690 E Point Douglas Rd S, Cottage Grove MN 55016-4007. 651/458-1771.

Cub Foods
100 County Road B W, St. Paul MN 55117-1931. 651/489-8217.

Cub Foods
2850 26th Ave S, Minneapolis MN 55406-1529. 612/721-2787.

Cub Foods
250 33rd Ave S, St. Cloud MN 56301-3715. 320/255-9193.

Cub Foods
15350 Cedar Avenue, Apple Valley MN 55124-7021. 612/432-6300.

Cub Foods
1001 4th St SE, St. Cloud MN 56304-1272. 320/253-1322.

Cub Foods
1940 Cliff Lake Rd, Eagan MN 55122-2400. 612/454-4606.

Econo Foods
205 1 St, Buffalo MN 55313. 612/682-2244.

Econo Foods
1858 Service Dr, Winona MN 55987-2125. 507/454-8630.

Econo Foods
1131 Oxford St, Worthington MN 56187-1665. 507/376-3727.

Elden's Inc.
707 3rd Ave E, Alexandria MN 56308-1507. 320/763-3446.

Erdman's Food Center
PO Box 338, Kasson MN 55944-0338. 507/634-2731.

Erickson's
601 Division St S, Northfield MN 55057-2426. 507/645-9514.

Erickson's
2600 Rice Creek Rd, St. Paul MN 55112-5344. 651/636-2277.

Erickson's
621 Main St, Red Wing MN
55066-2249. 651/388-2869.

Food Bonanza
3249 Services, Red Wing MN
55066. 651/388-7189.

Food For Less
1313 Paul Bunyan Dr NW,
Bemidji MN 56601-4153.
218/751-2537.

Food For Less
123 Beltrami Ave NW, Bemidji
MN 56601-4005. 218/751-4977.

Holiday Foods
500 W 84th St, Minneapolis MN
55420-2205. 612/881-4299.

Holiday Foods
250 57th Ave NE, Fridley MN
55432-5420. 612/571-3744.

Hornbachers Food
101 11th St S, Moorhead MN
56560-2837. 218/236-6333.

Hy-Vee
200 Western Ave NW, Faribault
MN 55021-4510. 507/334-2085.

Hy-Vee
1620 S Cedar Ave, Owatonna
MN 55060-3922. 507/451-0138.

Hy-Vee
500 37th St NW, Rochester MN
55901-3404. 507/289-1815.

Hy-Vee
1607 Highway 14 E, Rochester
MN 55904-5192. 507/289-7500.

Hy-Vee
1001 18th Ave NW, Austin MN
55912-1890. 507/437-7626.

Hy-Vee
410 South Riverfront Dr,
Mankato MN 56001-3773.
507/625-1107.

Hy-Vee
PO Box 1126, Albert Lea MN
56007-1126. 507/377-2257.

Hy-Vee
907 S State St, Fairmont MN
56031-4441. 507/238-4323.

Hy-Vee
PO Box 250, New Ulm MN
56073-0250. 507/354-8255.

Hy-Vee
1230 Hwy 13 N, Waseca MN
56093. 507/835-8030.

Hy-Vee
PO Box 489, Worthington MN
56187-0489. 507/372-7354.

Hy-Vee
1000 E Southview Dr, Marshall
MN 56258-2401. 507/532-2247.

Jerry's Foods
5801 Xerxes Ave N, Brooklyn
Center MN 55430-2414. 612/561-
5900.

Kowalski's Market
1261 Grand Ave, St. Paul MN
55105-2603. 651/698-3366.

Kowalski's Market
4391 Lake Ave S, White Bear
Lake MN 55110-3455. 651/429-
5913.

Luekens Village Foods
1171 Paul Bunyan Dr NW,
Bemidji MN 56601-4121.
218/751-1700.

Lund's
6228 Penn Ave S, Minneapolis
MN 55423-1135. 612/861-1881.

Lund's
1151 Wayzata Blvd E, Wayzata
MN 55391-1935. 612/476-2222.

Marketplace Foods
935 Lake St S, Forest Lake MN
55025-2616. 651/464-6111.

Midtown Foods
126 E 5th St, Winona MN 55987.
507/452-4335.

Nelson Foods
430 2nd Ave NW, Faribault MN
55021-5142. 507/334-1661.

Rainbow Foods
1566 University Ave W, St. Paul
MN 55104-3908. 651/644-4321.

Rainbow Foods
4300 Central Ave NE,
Minneapolis MN 55421-2924.
612/781-6916.

Rainbow Foods
3505 W Broadway Avenue,
Crystal MN 55422-2936.
612/522-4445.

Rainbow Foods
140 W 66th St, Minneapolis MN
55423-2371. 612/798-0189.

Rainbow Foods
892 Arcade St, St. Paul MN
55106-3852. 651/776-5808.

Rainbow Foods
2501 White Bear Ave N,
Maplewood MN 55109-5134.
651/777-7849.

Rainbow Foods
10200 6th Avenue North,
Plymouth MN 55441-6367.
612/541-9044.

Rainbow Foods
8020 Brooklyn Blvd, Minneapolis
MN 55445-2407. 612/424-6331.

Rainbow Foods
970 Prairie Center Dr, Eden
Prairie MN 55344-7304. 612/934-
6595.

Rainbow Foods
4800 Highway 191, Minnetonka
MN 55345. 612/474-7993.

Rainbow Foods
1201 Larpenteur Ave W,
Roseville MN 55113-6318.
651/488-1825.

Rainbow Foods
3960 W Frontage Rd N,
Rochester MN 55901-0108.
507/288-0907.

Rainbow Foods
1201 S Broadway, Rochester MN
55904-3862. 507/289-3884.

Rainbow Foods
1643 County Road B2 W,
Roseville MN 55113-3001.
651/639-9956.

Rainbow Foods
2919 26th Ave S, Minneapolis
MN 55406-1555. 612/724-4605.

Randall's International Inc.
PO Box 695, New Ulm MN
56073-0695. 507/354-3195.

Sax Food & Drug
19424 Evans St NW, Elk River
MN 55330-1074. 612/441-1400.

Schaefer's Model Market
15 Smiley Rd, Nisswa MN
56468-9515. 218/963-2265.

Sidco Food Company LLC
1750 County Road 42 W,
Burnsville MN 55337-6200.
612/435-8300.

Summart Foods
824 30th Ave S, Moorhead MN
56560-5006. 218/236-0001.

Super One
1101 E 37th St, Hibbing MN
55746-2971. 218/262-5275.

Super One
5401 Burning Tree Rd, Duluth
MN 55811-1874. 218/722-6019.

Supervalu
219 S Main St, Blue Earth MN
56013-2015. 507/526-2161.

Supervalu
5327 Lyndale Ave S,
Minneapolis MN 55419-1229.
612/822-2935.

Supervalu
1600 Woodland Ave, Duluth MN 55803-2628. 218/728-3665.

Tersteegs Inc.
1111 E Bridge St, Redwood Falls MN 56283-1807. 507/637-8332.

Whole Foods Market Group Inc.
30 Fairview Avenue South, St. Paul MN 55105-1463. 651/690-0197.

MISC. FOOD STORES

Lakewinds Natural Foods
17523 Minnetonka Blvd, Minnetonka MN 55345-1009. 612/473-0292.

MISC. GENERAL MERCHANDISE STORES

Sam's Club
3745 Louisiana Ave S, St. Louis Park MN 55426-4361. 612/924-9452.

Sam's Club
1300 Mendota Rd, Inver Grove Heights MN 55077-1255. 651/451-9801.

Sam's Club
8150 University Ave NE, Fridley MN 55432-1864. 612/784-6153.

Sam's Club
3601 2nd St S, St. Cloud MN 56301-3762. 320/253-8882.

OPTICAL GOODS STORES

Vision World Inc.
2277 Highway 36 W, Roseville MN 55113-3830. 651/633-7736.

RECORD AND PRERECORDED TAPE STORES

Musicland Group Inc.
7500 Excelsior Blvd, St. Louis Park MN 55426-4503. 612/932-7700.

SPORTING GOODS STORES

Cabela's Inc.
3900 E Frontage Rd, Owatonna MN 55060-5646. 507/451-4545.

Galyan's Trading Company Inc.
8292 Tamarack Village, Woodbury MN 55125-3385. 651/731-0200.

Galyan's Trading Company Inc.
11260 Wayzata Blvd, Hopkins MN 55305-2000. 612/525-0200.

Nike Factory Store
400 County Rd, Medford MN 55049. 507/451-9133.

REI
750 W 79th St, Minneapolis MN 55420-1059. 612/884-4315.

Supersports USA
Mall of America, Minneapolis MN 55425. 612/854-9444.

For more information on career opportunities in retail:

Associations

INTERNATIONAL COUNCIL OF SHOPPING CENTERS
665 Fifth Avenue, New York NY 10022-5370. 212/421-8181. World Wide Web address: http://www. icsc.org. Offers conventions, research, education, a variety of publications, and awards programs.

NATIONAL AUTOMOTIVE DEALERS ASSOCIATION
8400 Westpark Drive, McLean VA 22102. 703/821-7000. World Wide Web address: http://www.nadanet. com.

NATIONAL INDEPENDENT AUTOMOTIVE DEALERS ASSOCIATION
2521 Brown Boulevard, Arlington TX 76006. 817/640-3838. World Wide Web address: http://www. niada.com.

NATIONAL RETAIL FEDERATION
325 Seventh Street NW, Suite 1000, Washington DC 20004. 202/783-7971. World Wide Web address: http://www.nrf.com. Provides information services,

industry outlooks, and a variety of educational opportunities and publications.

Directories

AUTOMOTIVE NEWS MARKET DATA BOOK
Crain Communications, 1400 Woodbridge Avenue, Detroit MI 48207-3187. 313/446-6000.

Online Services

THE INTERNET FASHION EXCHANGE
http://www.fashionexch.com. An excellent site for those industry professionals interested in apparel and retail. The extensive search engine allows you to search by job title, location, salary, product line, industry, and whether you want a permanent, temporary, or freelance position. The Internet Fashion Exchange also offers career services such as recruiting, and outplacement firms that place fashion and retail professionals.

RETAIL JOBNET
http://www.retailjobnet.com. This site is geared toward recruiting professionals and jobseekers in the retail industry.

Visit our exciting job and career site at http://www.careercity.com

STONE, CLAY, GLASS, AND CONCRETE PRODUCTS

Largely dependent on the success of the construction market, the stone, clay, glass, and concrete industry experienced steady demand in 1998, as new construction projects began nationwide. Overall population and business growth will require new buildings and the renovation of existing structures. Coupled with a trend in brick and stone decorative structures and a decrease in the number of people entering the trade, bricklayers and stonemasons should see plentiful opportunities. Concrete masons will see less growth, yet will be heavily relied upon in new infrastructure projects. Glaziers will see slow growth, but the strong construction market could increase opportunities for jobseekers in this trade. Technological advances may also increase opportunities for glaziers, as homeowners and businesses upgrade to more efficient windows. Ceramic tile imports will likely increase due to Mexico's duty-free access to the U.S. market and a projected 10 percent cut in tariffs.

ANCHOR GLASS CONTAINER CORPORATION
4108 Valley Industrial Boulevard North, Shakopee MN 55379. 612/445-5000. **Contact:** Human Resources. **Description:** Produces glass containers and bottles.

THE CARDINAL IG COMPANY
7115 West Lake Street, Minneapolis MN 55426. 612/929-0317. **Contact:** Human Resources. **World Wide Web address:** http://www.mhtc.net/~cardinal. **Description:** Manufactures insulated glass for window units. **Corporate headquarters location:** Spring Green WI.

THE CARDINAL IG COMPANY
12301 Whitewater Drive, Minnetonka MN 55343. 612/935-1722. **Contact:** Human Resources. **World Wide Web address:** http://www.mhtc.net/~cardinal. **Description:** Manufactures insulated glass for window units. **Corporate headquarters location:** Spring Green WI.

COLD SPRING GRANITE COMPANY
202 South Third Avenue, Cold Spring MN 56320. 320/685-3621. **Contact:** Chuck Goores, Personnel Manager. **World Wide Web address:** http://www.coldspringgranite.com. **Description:** Mines, quarries, and sells granite.

HARDRIVES INC.
14475 Quiram Drive, Rogers MN 55374-9461. 612/428-8886. **Contact:** Human Resources. **Description:** Engaged in road construction and the manufacture of paving mixes and associated material. **NOTE:** When sending a resume, please indicate to which department you are applying.

HARDRIVES INC.
P.O. Box 579, St. Cloud MN 56302. 320/251-7376. **Physical address:** 1892 74th Avenue South, St. Cloud MN. **Contact:** Human Resources. **Description:** Engaged in road construction and the manufacture of paving mixes and associated material.

VIRACON
800 Park Drive, Owatonna MN 55060. 507/451-9555. **Contact:** Jim Wendorff, Human Resources. **World Wide Web address:** http://www.viracon.com. **Description:** Manufactures high-performance glass products such as insulating, laminated, security, silk-screened, and tempered coatings. **Corporate headquarters location:** This Location. **Parent company:** Apogee Enterprises, Inc. **Number of employees at this location:** 1,200.

WYATT READY MIX
8502 Central Avenue NE, Blaine MN 55434. 612/784-3512. **Contact:** Personnel. **Description:** A national producer of ready-mix concrete.

For more information on career opportunities in stone, clay, glass, and concrete products:

Associations

THE AMERICAN CERAMIC SOCIETY
P.O. Box 6136, Westerville OH 43086-6136.
614/890-4700. World Wide Web address:
http://www.acers.org. Offers a variety of publications,
meetings, information, and educational services. Also
operates Ceramic Futures, an employment service
with a resume database.

NATIONAL GLASS ASSOCIATION
8200 Greensboro Drive, Suite 302, McLean VA
22102. 703/442-4890. World Wide Web address:
http://www.glass.org.

Magazines

GLASS MAGAZINE
National Glass Association, 8200 Greensboro Drive,
McLean VA 22102. 703/442-4890. World Wide Web
address: http://www.glass.org.

ROCK PRODUCTS
PRIMEDIA Intertec, 29 North Wacker Drive,
Chicago IL 60606. 312/726-2805.

TRANSPORTATION/TRAVEL

 *All sectors of the transportation industry appear stable, particularly the domestic airline sector, which boasted record profits for the 12-month period ending in June 1998. Despite an increase in labor costs and high fuel prices, air carriers have maintained high profits due to strong consumer demand coupled with high ticket prices. Budget airlines, such as Southwest Airlines, continue to do well and are attracting competition from industry leaders who want to get into this growing market. An increasing number of public airports, in need of capital to increase their services, are undergoing privatization, which is resulting in improved services for customers, and profits for new owners.*

Rising labor costs and deregulation have forced the trucking industry to lower operating costs, but the U.S. Department of Commerce forecasts that industrial and commercial shipments should increase by about 17 percent annually through 2005. The Bureau of Labor Statistics estimates an increase of 404,000 truck driving jobs through 2006.

The acquisition of Southern Pacific by Union Pacific has caused a great deal of havoc for the railroad industry. The merger is estimated to have cost business customers more than $2 billion. To correct the problem, Union Pacific has ordered hundreds of millions of dollars worth of new locomotives and plans on hiring 2,000 new train operators.

As imports increase, ship travel will increase. Transport ships, the main vehicle for U.S. imports, are increasing in size, some greater than four football fields in length. According to Business Week, *these large ships require deep channels in which to travel, and eastern ports are dredging and redredging to meet the requirements. New York, currently the hub for ships on the East Coast, is dredging its shipping channels, in fear of losing business to deeper ports such as Norfolk and Halifax.*

ALLSTATE LEASING INC.
3575 Highway 13, Eagan MN 55122. 612/681-4900. **Contact:** Controller. **Description:** A truck leasing company.

BERGER TRANSFER
2950 Long Lake Road, St. Paul MN 55113. 612/788-9393. **Contact:** Tom Miller, Director of Administration. **Description:** An interstate trucking company.

BURLINGTON NORTHERN AND SANTA FE RAILWAY
176 East Fifth Street, 11th Floor, St. Paul MN 55101. 651/298-2121. **Contact:** James Dailey, Human Resources. **World Wide Web address:** http://www.bnsf.com. **Description:** Operates a railroad system which transports coal, agricultural commodities, and industrial products. **Common positions include:** Accountant/Auditor; Financial Manager; Management Trainee; Systems Analyst. **Educational backgrounds include:** Accounting; Business Administration; Finance. **Benefits:** Daycare Assistance; Dental Insurance; Disability Coverage; Employee Discounts; Life Insurance; Medical Insurance; Pension Plan; Profit Sharing; Tuition Assistance. **Special programs:** Internships. **Corporate headquarters location:** Fort Worth TX.

C.P. RAIL SYSTEM
P.O. Box 530, Minneapolis MN 55440. 612/347-8390. **Physical address:** 105 South Fifth Street, Minneapolis MN. **Contact:** Personnel Department. **Description:** A railroad transportation company.

CARGO CARRIERS INC.
P.O. Box 5608, Minneapolis MN 55440. 612/742-6763. **Contact:** Personnel. **World Wide Web address:** http://www.cargo.com. **Description:** A water transportation company.

CARLSON COMPANIES, INC.
CARLSON MARKETING GROUP
P.O. Box 59159, Minneapolis MN 55459-8246. 612/540-5000. **Contact:** Vern Lovstad, Human Resources. **World Wide Web address:** http://www.carlson.com. **Description:** A highly diversified corporation doing business through a variety of subsidiaries. Business areas include hotels, restaurant operations, and retail and wholesale travel. Carlson Marketing Group (also at this location) provides a variety of marketing services for sporting events and airlines; incentive programs for employees of other companies; and strategic consulting to help client companies create customer/brand loyalty. **Corporate headquarters location:** This Location. **Number of employees nationwide:** 50,000.

DART TRANSIT COMPANY
P.O. Box 64110, St. Paul MN 55164-0110. 800/366-9000. **Contact:** Human Resources. **World Wide Web address:** http://www.dartadvantage.com. **Description:** A trucking company.

DAYTON'S TRAVEL SERVICE
900 Rosedale Shopping Center, St. Paul MN 55113. 651/639-6777. **Contact:** Human Resources. **Description:** A travel agency.

DULUTH MESABE IRON RANGE RAILWAY COMPANY
227 West First Street, Suite 500, Duluth MN 55802. 218/723-2171. **Contact:** Human Resources. **Description:** A railroad company.

GE CAPITAL FLEET SERVICES
3 Capital Drive, Eden Prairie MN 55344. 612/828-1000. **Contact:** Human Resources. **World Wide Web address:** http://www.ge.com. **Description:** One of the largest vehicle leasing companies in the U.S. and Canada, providing fleet financing and related management services to corporate clients. **Parent company:** General Electric Company (Fairfield CT) operates in the following areas: aircraft engines (jet engines, replacement parts, and repair services for commercial, military, executive, and commuter aircraft); appliances; broadcasting (NBC); industrial (lighting products, electrical distribution and control equipment, transportation systems products, electric motors and related products, a broad range of electrical and electronic industrial automation products, and a network of electrical supply houses); materials (plastics, ABS resins, silicones, superabrasives, and laminates); power systems (products for the generation, transmission, and distribution of electricity); technical products and systems (medical systems and equipment, as well as a full range of computer-based information and data interchange services for both internal use and external commercial and industrial customers); and capital services (consumer services, financing, and specialty insurance). **Number of employees worldwide:** 230,000.

GENMAR INC.
100 South Fifth Street, Suite 2400, Minneapolis MN 55402. 612/339-7900. **Contact:** David Vigdal, Senior Vice President. **World Wide Web address:** http://www.genmar.com. **Description:** A holding company for boat manufacturers.

INTERNATIONAL TRAVEL ARRANGERS
1320 East Lake Street, Minneapolis MN 55407. 612/724-1484. **Contact:** Human Resources. **Description:** A tour wholesaler specializing in charter air travel packages to many destinations.

JEFFERSON PARTNERS L.P.
2100 East 26th Street, Minneapolis MN 55404-4101. 612/332-8745. **Contact:** Human Resources Manager. **Description:** An intercity bus line and travel company. **Common positions include:** Accountant/Auditor; Customer Service Representative; Department Manager; Driver; Human Resources Manager; Operations/Production Manager; Payroll Clerk; Planner; Purchasing Agent/Manager; Services Sales Representative; Transportation/Traffic Specialist. **Educational backgrounds include:** Accounting; Business Administration; Communications; Finance; Liberal Arts; Marketing. **Benefits:** 401(k); Daycare Assistance; Dental Insurance; Disability Coverage; Employee Discounts; Flexible Benefits; Life Insurance; Medical Insurance; Savings Plan; Tuition Assistance. **Corporate headquarters location:** This Location. **Other U.S. locations:** Fort Smith AR; Des Moines IA; Kansas City MO; Oklahoma City OK; Tulsa OK. **Operations at this facility include:** Administration; Divisional Headquarters; Sales; Service. **Listed on:** Privately held. **Number of employees at this location:** 65. **Number of employees nationwide:** 250.

LARSON BOATS
Paul Larson Memorial Drive, Little Falls MN 56345. 320/632-5481. **Contact:** Jean Wolfe, Human Resources. **Description:** Manufactures boats.

M.L.T. INC.
5130 County Road 101, Minnetonka MN 55345. 612/474-2540. **Contact:** Ava Pratte, Human Resources Director. **Description:** A travel and vacation service.

MESABA AIRLINES
7501 26th Avenue South, Minneapolis MN 55450. 612/726-5151. **Recorded jobline:** 612/726-5189x815. **Contact:** Human Resources. **World Wide Web address:** http://www.mesaba.com. **Description:** A scheduled passenger airline carrier located in over 40 cities and Canada. **Common positions include:** Accountant/Auditor; Aircraft Mechanic/Engine Specialist; Buyer; Clerk; Computer Programmer; Customer Service Representative; Flight Attendant; Human Resources Manager; Pilot; Purchasing Agent/Manager. **Educational backgrounds include:** Accounting; Aviation. **Benefits:** 401(k); Dental Insurance; Disability Coverage; Employee Discounts; Life Insurance; Medical Insurance. **Corporate headquarters location:** This Location. **Other U.S. locations:** Detroit MI. **Listed on:** NASDAQ. **Number of employees at this location:** 300. **Number of employees nationwide:** 1,400.

METRO TRANSIT
560 Sixth Avenue North, Minneapolis MN 55411. 612/349-7400. **Contact:** Human Resources. **World Wide Web address:** http://www.metrotransit.org. **Description:** The metropolitan transportation authority.

MINNESOTA COACHES
307 West 59 1/2 Street, Minneapolis MN 55419. 612/866-6628. **Contact:** Human Resources. **Description:** Provides school bus and charter motor coach services. **NOTE:** Interested applicants should apply in person, Monday through Friday.

MONSON TRUCKING INC.
5102 South Cant Road, Duluth MN 55804. 218/525-6681. **Contact:** Human Resources. **Description:** An over-the-road trucking company.

NATIONAL CAR RENTAL SYSTEM, INC.
7700 France Avenue South, Minneapolis MN 55435. 612/893-6060. **Contact:** Sandra Morrison, Director of Human Resources. **World Wide Web address:** http://www.nationalcar.com. **Description:** A car rental agency. **Common positions include:** Accountant/Auditor; Claim Representative; Reservationist; Sales Manager. **Educational backgrounds include:** Accounting; Business Administration; Finance; Marketing. **Benefits:** 401(k); Dental Insurance; Disability Coverage; Employee Discounts; Life Insurance; Medical Insurance; On-Site Exercise Facility; Tuition Assistance. **Corporate headquarters location:** This Location. **Other U.S. locations:** Nationwide. **Operations at this facility include:** Administration; Sales; Service. **Number of employees at this location:** 900. **Number of employees nationwide:** 8,500.

NORTHWEST AIRLINES
5101 Northwest Drive, Mail Stop A-1480, St. Paul MN 55111. 612/726-3600. **Fax:** 612/726-4325. **Recorded jobline:** 612/726-3600. **Contact:** Vivian Tanniehill, Manager of Diversity Sourcing. **World Wide Web address:** http://www.nwa.com. **Description:** One of the world's largest airlines and one of America's oldest carriers. Northwest serves more than 240 cities in 22 countries on four continents: Asia, Europe, North America, and Australia. The U.S. system spans 45 states. Hub cities are Detroit, Minneapolis/St. Paul, Memphis, and Tokyo. Maintenance bases are Atlanta and Minneapolis/St. Paul. Crew bases are Anchorage, Chicago, Detroit, Memphis, San Francisco, Minneapolis/St. Paul, New York, Seattle/Tacoma, Boston, Los Angeles, Honolulu, and several international cities. Founded in 1926. **NOTE:** Jobseekers should call the jobline or view postings on the company's Website before sending a resume. **Common positions include:** Accountant/Auditor; Aerospace Engineer; Aircraft Mechanic/Engine Specialist; Budget Analyst; Computer Programmer; Customer Service Representative; Economist; Electrical/Electronics Engineer; Financial Analyst; Human Resources Manager; Mathematician; Operations/Production Manager; Statistician; Systems Analyst. **Educational backgrounds include:** Accounting; Business Administration; Computer Science; Economics; Finance; Marketing. **Benefits:** 401(k); Dental Insurance; Disability Coverage; Employee Discounts; Life Insurance; Medical Insurance; Pension Plan; Tuition Assistance. **Corporate headquarters location:** This Location. **Other U.S. locations:** Nationwide. **Operations at this facility include:** Administration; Sales. **Listed on:** NASDAQ.

PADELFORD PACKET BOAT COMPANY
Harriet Island, St. Paul MN 55107. 651/227-1100. **Fax:** 651/227-0543. **Recorded jobline:** 800/543-3908. **Contact:** Human Resources. **Description:** Provides Mississippi riverboat cruises in St. Paul and Minneapolis. Operations include sight-seeing cruises, dinner cruises, and private charters from April through October. **Common positions include:** Boat Crew; Caterer; Customer Service Representative; Reservationist; Restaurant/Food Service Manager.

SAFETRAN SYSTEMS CORPORATION
4650 Main Street NE, Minneapolis MN 55421. 612/572-1400. **Contact:** Ms. Robin Hanson, Manager of Human Resources. **World Wide Web address:** http://www.safetran.com. **Description:** Manufactures railroad accessories and safety devices. **Common positions include:** Accountant/Auditor; Blue-Collar Worker Supervisor; Buyer; Computer Programmer; Customer Service Representative; Draftsperson; General Manager; Operations/Production Manager; Purchasing Agent/Manager; Systems Analyst. **Educational backgrounds include:** Accounting; Business Administration; Engineering; Finance. **Benefits:** Dental Insurance; Disability Coverage; Life Insurance; Medical Insurance; Pension Plan; Tuition Assistance. **Parent company:** BTR, plc. **Operations at this facility include:** Administration; Divisional Headquarters; Manufacturing; Research and Development; Sales; Service. **Number of employees at this location:** 250.

THERMO KING CORPORATION
314 West 90th Street, Bloomington MN 55420. 612/887-2200. **Fax:** 612/885-3404. **Contact:** Human Resources Manager. **Description:** Serves the refrigeration and air conditioning needs of buses and tractor-trailer centers. Thermo King is a world leader in temperature-controlled transport. **Common positions include:** Accountant/Auditor; Computer Programmer; Customer Service Representative; Designer; Draftsperson; Electrical/Electronics Engineer; Industrial Engineer; Materials Engineer; Mechanical Engineer; Purchasing Agent/Manager; Software Engineer; Systems Analyst; Test Engineer. **Educational backgrounds include:** Engineering. **Benefits:** 401(k); Dental Insurance; Disability Coverage; Employee Discounts; Life Insurance; Medical Insurance; Pension Plan; Savings Plan; Tuition Assistance. **Corporate headquarters location:** This Location. **Parent company:** Westinghouse. **Operations at this facility include:** Administration; Manufacturing; Research and Development; Sales; Service.

TRANSPORT CORPORATION OF AMERICA, INC.
1769 Yankee Doodle Road, Eagan MN 55121. 651/686-2500. **Fax:** 651/686-2540. **Contact:** Karen Vesovich, Human Resources Manager. **Description:** An irregular route truckload motor carrier, covering 48 states. Founded in 1984. **Common positions include:** Accountant; Computer Operator; Computer Programmer; Customer Service Representative; MIS Specialist; Software Engineer; Systems Analyst; Systems Manager; Transportation/Traffic Specialist. **Educational backgrounds include:** Accounting; Business Administration; Software Development; Software Tech. Support. **Benefits:** 401(k); Dental Insurance; Disability Coverage; Life Insurance; Medical Insurance; Tuition Assistance. **Corporate headquarters location:** This Location. **Operations at this facility include:** Administration; Sales; Service. **Listed on:** NASDAQ. **Annual sales/revenues:** More than $100 million. **Number of employees at this location:** 275. **Number of employees nationwide:** 1,150.

Note: Because addresses and telephone numbers of smaller companies can change rapidly, we recommend you call each company to verify the information below before inquiring about job opportunities. Mass mailings are not recommended.

Additional small employers:

AIR TRANSPORTATION AND SERVICES

American Airlines Inc.
4300 Glumack Drive,
St. Paul MN 55111-3002.
612/726-5833.

Beech Transportation
9960 Flying Cloud Dr, Eden Prairie MN 55347-4011. 612/727-1303.

Carlton County Airport
PO Box 130, Carlton MN 55718-0130. 218/384-4281.

Northwest Airlines Inc.
601 Iron Dr, Chisholm MN
55719. 218/254-7575.

Sun Country Airlines Inc.
2520 Pilot Knob Rd, Ste 250,
Mendota Heights MN 55120-1137. 612/681-3900.

COURIER SERVICES

Federal Express Corporation
4700 Park Glen Rd, Minneapolis
MN 55416-5701. 612/920-1698.

Road Runner Parcel Service
2395 Capp Rd, St. Paul MN
55114-1258. 651/644-8787.

UPS of St. Cloud
3057 Highway 10 SE, St. Cloud
MN 56304-9763. 320/253-4100.

LOCAL AND INTERURBAN PASSENGER TRANSIT

Greyhound Bus Lines
29 N 9th St, Minneapolis MN
55403-1326. 612/371-3332.

Handi-Cabs International Inc.
1154 N 5th St, Minneapolis MN
55411-4304. 612/332-3323.

Kottkes Bus Service Inc.
13625 Jay St NW, Anoka MN
55304-4018. 612/755-3100.

Lakeville Lines
21160 Holyoke Ave, Lakeville
MN 55044-8576. 612/469-2256.

Life Link III
2124 University Ave W, St. Paul
MN 55114-1838. 651/917-5200.

Mayflower/Laidlaw
1717 County Road C W,
Roseville MN 55113-1322.
651/628-0046.

National School Bus Service
1090 Snelling Ave N, St. Paul
MN 55108-2704. 651/645-1959.

Rehbein Transit Inc.
6298 Hodgson Rd, Circle Pines
MN 55014-1430. 651/484-1809.

Reichert Bus Service
1200 Industrial Park Rd S,
Brainerd MN 56425-8084.
218/829-6955.

Ryder Student Transportation
6349 Stillwater Blvd N, St. Paul
MN 55128-3717. 651/777-2319.

Ryder Student Transportation
1530 Brewster St, St. Paul MN
55108-2676. 651/645-5665.

Ryder Student Transportation
1901 Lake Valentine Rd, St. Paul
MN 55112-2835. 651/631-1755.

Sleepy Eye Bus Line
200 2nd Ave NW, Osseo MN
55369-1004. 612/425-2542.

Voyageur Bus Co.
3941 E Calvary Rd, Duluth MN
55803-1318. 218/724-1707.

MAINTENANCE FACILITIES FOR MOTOR FREIGHT TRANSPORTATION

Consolidated Freightways Corp.
3701 85th Ave NE, Shoreview
MN 55126-1125. 612/780-3801.

Yellow Freight System Inc.
12400 DuPont Ave S, Burnsville
MN 55337-1664. 612/890-7550.

MISC. TRANSPORTATION SERVICES

Loram Maintenance Inc.
PO Box 188, Hamel MN 55340-
0188. 612/478-6014.

PASSENGER TRANSPORTATION ARRANGEMENT SERVICES

Northwestern Travel Management
7250 Metro Blvd, Minneapolis
MN 55439-2128. 612/921-3700.

RAILROAD EQUIPMENT

ZTR Control Systems Inc.
901 W 94th St, Minneapolis MN
55420-4236. 612/888-4121.

RAILROAD TRANSPORTATION

Burlington Northern and Santa Fe Railroad
324 Washington Street NE,
Brainerd MN 56401-3155.
218/828-7281.

Burlington Northern and Santa Fe Railroad
80 44th Ave NE, Minneapolis
MN 55421-2599. 612/782-3276.

Burlington Northern and Santa Fe Railroad
PO Box 216, St. Cloud MN
56302-0216. 320/259-3208.

CP Rail System
1000 Shop Rd, St. Paul MN
55106-6706. 651/646-6044.

Soo Line Railroad Company
PO Box 530, Minneapolis MN
55440-0530. 612/337-8608.

SHIP/BOAT BUILDING AND REPAIRING

Alumacraft Boat Co.
315 Saint Julien St, St. Peter MN
56082-1875. 507/931-1050.

Glastron Boats
700 W River Rd, Little Falls MN
56345. 320/632-8395.

Lund Boats
PO Box 248, New York Mills
MN 56567-0248. 218/385-2235.

Premier Marine Inc.
PO Box 509, Wyoming MN
55092-0509. 651/462-2880.

TRANSPORTATION EQUIPMENT

Arctic Cat Inc.
PO Box 810, Thief River Falls
MN 56701-0810. 218/681-8558.

TRUCKING

Allied Systems
PO Box 98, Cottage Grove MN
55016-0098. 651/458-3005.

Allied Systems
PO Box 21428, St. Paul MN
55121-0428. 612/454-9260.

Allstate Delivery Service Co.
PO Box 2061, Minneapolis MN
55402-0061. 612/884-0765.

Anderson Trucking Service
PO Box 1377, St. Cloud MN
56302-1377. 320/255-7400.

Beltmann Group
2480 Long Lake Rd, Roseville
MN 55113-2534. 651/639-2800.

Bud Meyer Truck Lines Inc.
PO Box 453, Lake City MN
55041-0453. 651/345-4591.

Caledonia Haulers Inc.
PO Box 31, Caledonia MN
55921-0031. 507/724-5236.

Daggett Implement Company
PO Box 158, Frazee MN 56544-
0158. 218/334-3711.

Dedicated Logistics Inc.
PO Box 75121, St. Paul MN
55175-0121. 651/631-5918.

Dee Spee Delivery Service Inc.
PO Box 1635, St. Cloud MN
56302-1635. 320/251-6697.

Fil-Mor Express Inc.
PO Box 518, Cannon Falls MN
55009-0521. 507/263-2608.

Floyd Wild Inc.
PO Box 1063, Marshall MN
56258-0863. 507/537-0531.

Freightmasters Inc.
3703 Kennebec Dr, Eagan MN
55122-1055. 612/688-6800.

Gazda Transportation System
9445 East River Rd, Coon Rapids
MN 55433-5597. 612/755-0320.

GW Transportation Services
5871 Cedar Lake Rd S,
Minneapolis MN 55416-1481.
612/593-1300.

J&R Schugel Trucking
PO Box 278, New Ulm MN
56073-0278. 507/359-2037.

Lakeville Motor Express Inc.
PO Box 130280, St. Paul MN
55113-0003. 651/636-8900.

Metcalf AA Moving & Storage Co.
1255 Hwy 36 East, Maplewood
MN 55109-2046. 651/484-0211.

Quast Transfer Inc.
PO Box 7, Winsted MN 55395-
0007. 320/485-2101.

Quicksilver Express Courier
203 Little Canada Road E, St.
Paul MN 55117-1396. 651/484-
1111.

Roadway Express Inc.
2950 Lone Oak Cir, St. Paul MN
55121-1425. 612/452-1710.

Summit Transportation Inc.
PO Box 75338, St. Paul MN
55175-0338. 651/631-5920.

USF Holland Inc.
400 1st St SW, St. Paul MN
55112-7755. 651/631-8400.

Walbon and Company Inc.
4230 Pine Bend Trl, Rosemount
MN 55068-2562. 651/437-2011.

**WAREHOUSING AND
STORAGE**

Bergquist Company
5330 E Bush Lake Rd,

Minneapolis MN 55439. 612/835-
2322.

Holiday Companies
PO Box 1224, Minneapolis MN
55440-1224. 612/921-5200.

**Iron Mountain Records
Management Inc.**
9715 James Avenue S,
Bloomington MN 55431-2513.
612/888-3852.

For more information on career opportunities in transportation and travel industries:

Associations

**AIR TRANSPORT ASSOCIATION OF
AMERICA**
1301 Pennsylvania Avenue NW, Suite 1100,
Washington DC 20004. 202/626-4000. World Wide
Web address: http://www.air-transport.org. A trade
association for the major U.S. airlines.

AMERICAN BUREAU OF SHIPPING
2 World Trade Center, 106th Floor, New York NY
10048. 212/839-5000. World Wide Web address:
http://www.abs-group.com.

AMERICAN SOCIETY OF TRAVEL AGENTS
1101 King Street, Suite 200, Alexandria VA 22314.
703/739-2782. World Wide Web address: http://www.
astanet.com.

AMERICAN TRUCKING ASSOCIATION
2200 Mill Road, Alexandria VA 22314-4677.
703/838-1700. World Wide Web address: http://www.
trucking.org. A national federation of the trucking
industry representing all types of trucking companies.
ATA is affiliated with 51 independent state trucking
associations and 14 national conferences. The
association also publishes *Transport Topics*, a weekly
trade newspaper.

ASSOCIATION OF AMERICAN RAILROADS
50 F Street NW, Washington DC 20001. 202/639-
2100. World Wide Web address: http://www.aar.com.

**INSTITUTE OF TRANSPORTATION
ENGINEERS**
525 School Street SW, Suite 410, Washington DC
20024-2797. 202/554-8050. World Wide Web
address: http://www.ite.org.

MARINE TECHNOLOGY SOCIETY
1828 L Street NW, Suite 906, Washington DC 20036.
202/775-5966. World Wide Web address: http://www.
cms.udel.edu/mts.

**NATIONAL MOTOR FREIGHT TRAFFIC
ASSOCIATION**
2200 Mill Road, Alexandria VA 22314-4654.
703/838-1810. World Wide Web address:
http://www.erols.com/nmfta/index.htm. Works
towards the improvement and advancement of the
interests and welfare of motor common carriers.

NATIONAL TANK TRUCK CARRIERS
2200 Mill Road, Alexandria VA 22314. 703/838-
1700. A trade association representing and promoting
the interests of the highway bulk transportation
community.

Books

**FLIGHT PLAN TO THE FLIGHT DECK:
STRATEGIES FOR A PILOT CAREER**
Cage Consulting, Inc., 13275 East Fremont Place,
Suite 315, Englewood CO 80112-3917. Toll-free
phone: 888/899-CAGE. Fax: 303/799-1998. World
Wide Web address: http://www.cageconsulting.com.

**WELCOME ABOARD! YOUR CAREER AS A
FLIGHT ATTENDANT**
Cage Consulting, Inc., 13275 East Fremont Place,
Suite 315, Englewood CO 80112-3917. Toll-free
phone: 888/899-CAGE. Fax: 303/799-1998. World
Wide Web address: http://www.cageconsulting.com.

Directories

MOODY'S TRANSPORTATION MANUAL
Financial Information Services, 60 Madison Avenue,
6th Floor, New York NY 10010. Toll-free phone:
800/342-5647.

**NATIONAL TANK TRUCK CARRIER
DIRECTORY**
National Tank Truck Carriers, 2200 Mill Road,
Alexandria VA 22314. 703/838-1700.

OFFICIAL MOTOR FREIGHT GUIDE
CNC Publishing, 1700 West Cortland Street, Chicago
IL 60622. 773/278-2454.

Magazines

AMERICAN SHIPPER
Howard Publications, P.O. Box 4728, Jacksonville FL
32201. 904/355-2601. Monthly.

FLEET OWNER
PRIMEDIA Intertec, 11 Riverbend Drive South, P.O.
Box 4211, Stamford CT 06907-0211.

HEAVY DUTY TRUCKING
Newport Communications, P.O. Box W, Newport
Beach CA 92658. 714/261-1636.

ITE JOURNAL
Institute of Transportation Engineers, 525 School
Street SW, Suite 410, Washington DC 20024-2797.
202/554-8050. World Wide Web address: http://www.
ite.org. One year subscription (12 issues): $60.00.

**MARINE DIGEST AND TRANSPORTATION
NEWS**
Marine Publishing, Inc., P.O. Box 3905, Seattle WA
98124. 206/682-3607.

SHIPPING DIGEST
Geyer-McAllister Publications, 51 Madison Avenue, New York NY 10010. 212/689-4411.

TRANSPORT TOPICS
American Trucking Associations, Inc., 2200 Mill Road, Alexandria VA 22314. 703/838-1778. World Wide Web address: http://www.ttnews.com.

<u>Newsletters</u>

AIR JOBS DIGEST
World Air Data, Department 700, P.O. Box 42360, Washington DC 20015. World Wide Web address: http://www.tggh.net/wad. Provides current job openings in aerospace, space, and aviation industries. Subscription rates: $96.00 annually, $69.00 for six months, and $49.00 for three months.

<u>Online Services</u>

THE AIRLINE EMPLOYMENT ASSISTANCE CORPS.
World Wide Web address: http://www.avjobs.com.

Site for aviation jobseekers providing worldwide classified ads, resume assistance, publications, and over 350 links to aviation-related Websites and news groups. Certain resources are members-only access.

COOLWORKS
World Wide Web address: http://www.coolworks. com. This Website provides links to 22,000 job openings on cruise ships, at national parks, summer camps, ski areas, river areas, ranches, fishing areas, and resorts. This site also includes information on volunteer openings.

JOBNET: HOSPITALITY INDUSTRY
World Wide Web address: http://www.westga.edu/ ~coop/joblinks/subject/hospitality.html. Provides links to job openings and information for airlines and cruise ships.

TRAVEL PROFESSIONALS FORUM
Go: Travpro. To join this CompuServe forum, you will need to send an e-mail to the sysop for permission.

UTILITIES: ELECTRIC/GAS/WATER

Deregulation has greatly increased competition throughout all segments of the utilities industry. For example, many states now permit independent power producers to build electric power generating plants. In an effort to lower prices and compete with the new entrants, many existing electric utilities have resorted to layoffs and other cost-cutting measures. Other electric companies, such as Illinova Corporation, are spending millions to increase capacity. Water utilities continue to see growth, and the Bureau of Labor Statistics estimates 51 percent growth for this segment through 2006. Philadelphia Suburban Corporation, a water utility, reported a significant rise in profits due to an increase in customers in 1998. Overall, Standard & Poor reports a drop in both profits and profit margins for the utilities industry, and the U.S. Department of Labor forecasts that job growth will only be 12 percent through 2005, a rate much slower than the average for all industries.

GREAT RIVER ENERGY
P.O. Box 800, Elk River MN 55330. 612/441-3121. **Physical address:** 17845 East Highway 10, Elk River MN 55330. **Contact:** Margaret Zachman, Administrator of Employment Services. **Description:** An electric utility company. **Common positions include:** Accountant/Auditor; Administrative Assistant; Administrator; Attorney; Chief Financial Officer; Computer Programmer; Customer Service Representative; Department Manager; Dietician/Nutritionist; Draftsperson; Electrician; Financial Analyst; Forester/Conservation Scientist; General Manager; Geologist/Geophysicist; Insurance Agent/Broker; Marketing Manager; Marketing Specialist; Mechanical Engineer; Metallurgical Engineer; Mining Engineer; Petroleum Engineer; Public Relations Specialist; Purchasing Agent/Manager; Sales Manager; Statistician; Systems Analyst. **Educational backgrounds include:** Accounting; Chemistry; Communications; Computer Science; Economics; Engineering; Finance; Geology; Liberal Arts; Marketing; Mathematics; Physics; Software Development; Software Tech. Support. **Benefits:** 401(k); Disability Coverage; Life Insurance; Medical Insurance; Pension Plan; Profit Sharing; Savings Plan; Tuition Assistance; Wellness Program. **Corporate headquarters location:** This Location. **Operations at this facility include:** Regional Headquarters. **Number of employees at this location:** 200. **Number of employees nationwide:** 400.

MINNESOTA POWER, INC.
30 West Superior Street, Duluth MN 55802. 218/722-2641. **Contact:** Human Resources. **World Wide Web address:** http://www.mnpower.com. **Description:** An electric utility. **Listed on:** New York Stock Exchange. **Stock exchange symbol:** MPL.

NORTHERN STATES POWER COMPANY (NSP)
414 Nicollet Mall, Minneapolis MN 55401. 612/330-5500. **Contact:** Human Resources. **World Wide Web address:** http://www.nspco.com. **Description:** Northern States Power generates, transmits, and distributes electric energy. The company also transports and distributes natural gas. **Corporate headquarters location:** This Location.

NORTHERN STATES POWER COMPANY (NSP)
MONTICELLO NUCLEAR GENERATING STATION
2807 West County Road 75, Monticello MN 55362. 612/295-5151. **Contact:** Holly Palmer, Human Resources. **Description:** This location houses a nuclear power plant. Overall, Northern States Power generates, transmits, and distributes electric energy. The company also transports and distributes natural gas. **Corporate headquarters location:** Minneapolis MN.

OTTER TAIL POWER COMPANY
215 South Cascade, Fergus Falls MN 56537. 218/739-8200. **Contact:** Human Resources. **World Wide Web address:** http://www.otpco.com. **Description:** Produces, transmits, distributes, and sells electricity in Minnesota, North Dakota, and South Dakota. Founded in 1907. **Corporate**

headquarters location: This Location. **Listed on:** NASDAQ. **Stock exchange symbol:** OTTR. **Number of employees nationwide:** 800.

Note: Because addresses and telephone numbers of smaller companies can change rapidly, we recommend you call each company to verify the information below before inquiring about job opportunities. Mass mailings are not recommended.

Additional small employers:

COMBINATION UTILITY SERVICES

Energy Masters International
1385 Mendota Heights Rd, Mendota Heights MN 55120-1129. 651/686-4000.

NRG Energy Center Inc.
1221 Nicollet Mall, Minneapolis MN 55403-2420. 612/373-5300.

Riverside Steam Plant
3100 Marshall St NE, Minneapolis MN 55418-1821. 612/520-6800.

Rochester Public Utilities
201 4th St SE, Rochester MN 55904-3708. 507/285-8082.

Rochester Public Utilities
4000 E River Rd NE, Rochester MN 55906-3414. 507/280-1540.

ELECTRIC SERVICES

Boswell Steam Electric Station
PO Box 128, Cohasset MN 55721. 218/328-5711.

Connexis Energy
14601 Ramsey Blvd NW, Anoka MN 55303-6024. 612/323-2600.

Cooperative Power Association
14615 Lone Oak Rd, Eden Prairie MN 55344-2200. 612/937-8599.

Dakota Electric Association
4300 220th St W, Farmington MN 55024-9003. 612/463-7134.

Northern States Power
13999 Industrial Blvd, Becker MN 55308-8800. 612/261-4100.

Prairie Island Nuclear Generating Plant
1717 Wakonade Dr E, Welch MN 55089-9642. 651/388-1165.

For more information on career opportunities in the utilities industry:

Associations

AMERICAN PUBLIC GAS ASSOCIATION
11094-D Lee Highway, Suite 102, Fairfax VA 22030. 703/352-3890. World Wide Web address: http://www. apga.org. Publishes a bi-weekly newsletter.

AMERICAN PUBLIC POWER ASSOCIATION (APPA)
2301 M Street NW, Washington DC 20037. 202/467-2903. World Wide Web address: http://www.appanet. org. Represents publicly-owned utilities. Provides many services including government relations, educational programs, and industry-related information publications.

AMERICAN WATER WORKS ASSOCIATION
6666 West Quincy Avenue, Denver CO 80235. 303/794-7711. World Wide Web address: http://www. awwa.org.

NATIONAL RURAL ELECTRIC COOPERATIVE ASSOCIATION
4301 Wilson Boulevard, Arlington VA 22203. 703/907-5500. World Wide Web address: http://www. nreca.org.

Directories

MOODY'S PUBLIC UTILITY MANUAL
Financial Information Services, 60 Madison Avenue, 6th Floor, New York NY 10010. Toll-free phone: 800/342-5647. World Wide Web address: http://www. fisonline.com. Annually available at libraries.

Magazines

PUBLIC POWER
American Public Power Association, 2301 M Street NW, Suite 300, Washington DC 20037-1484. 202/467-2900.

Visit our exciting job and career site at http://www.careercity.com

MISCELLANEOUS WHOLESALING

According to the U.S. Department of Commerce, the need to cut costs is increasing as wholesaling and distributing businesses become more global and competitive, leading to changes in manufacturer-distributor working relationships. The most significant of these is an improved efficiency in inventory management, whereby the distributor manages inventory at the customer's site.

Wholesaling has evolved into an industry driven by customer needs, and while companies now prefer to do business with fewer suppliers, they still expect quality services. Overall, the wholesale industry may see employment growth of 1.1 percent by 2006, according to the Bureau of Labor Statistics.

BELL INDUSTRIES
P.O. Box 538, South St. Paul MN 55075. 651/450-9020. **Contact:** Joyce Wonsmos, Human Resources. **World Wide Web address:** http://www.bellind.com. **Description:** A wholesaler of parts and equipment for recreational vehicles, ATVs, boats, and mobile homes.

CAMERON ASHLEY BUILDING PRODUCTS
5110 Main Street NE, Fridley MN 55421. 612/571-5100. **Contact:** Human Resources. **Description:** A wholesaler of building supplies including ceiling tiles, coatings, gutters, nails, roofing, screws, siding, and ventilation equipment.

CUMMINS NORTH CENTRAL
P.O. Box 64578, St. Paul MN 55113. 651/636-1000. **Contact:** Betty Aschenbrener, Human Resources. **World Wide Web address:** http://www.cummins.com. **Description:** A distributor of diesel engines.

ECOLAB INC.
370 North Wabasha Street, St. Paul MN 55102. 651/293-2233. **Contact:** Vice President of Corporate Human Resources. **World Wide Web address:** http://www.ecolab.com. **Description:** Ecolab provides cleaning, sanitizing, and maintenance products and services for the food service, lodging, health care, laundry, dairy, and food and beverage processing markets in the U.S., Canada, Latin America, Asia, and Europe. Products include dispensers, kitchen supplies, cleaners, sanitizers, janitorial products, textile care products, and commercial pest control items.

HOBART CORPORATION
1610 Broadway Street NE, Minneapolis MN 55413. 612/379-7544. **Contact:** Human Resources. **Description:** Sells and services commercial food preparation equipment used in the food service industry and in the retail food (supermarket) industry. **Common positions include:** Branch Manager; General Manager; Management Trainee; Services Sales Representative; Technician. **Benefits:** Dental Insurance; Life Insurance; Medical Insurance; Pension Plan; Savings Plan. **Corporate headquarters location:** Troy OH. **Parent company:** Premark International. **Operations at this facility include:** Administration; Regional Headquarters; Sales; Service. **Listed on:** New York Stock Exchange.

IKON OFFICE SOLUTIONS
1715 Commerce Drive, North Mankato MN 56003. 507/625-7440. **Contact:** Human Resources. **World Wide Web address:** http://www.ikon.com. **Description:** Resells computers, faxes, and other office equipment.

NAPCO INTERNATIONAL INC.
11111 Excelsior Boulevard, Hopkins MN 55343. 612/931-2460. **Contact:** Judy Winkler, Human Resources Administrator. **World Wide Web address:** http://www.napcointer.com. **Description:** A distributor of defense-related products. **Common positions include:** Accountant/Auditor; Administrative Assistant; Blue-Collar Worker Supervisor; Buyer; Computer Programmer; Credit Manager; Customer Service Representative; Purchasing Agent/Manager; Quality Control Supervisor; Transportation/Traffic Specialist. **Educational backgrounds include:** Accounting; Computer Science; Finance; Marketing. **Benefits:** 401(k); Dental Insurance; Disability Coverage; Life Insurance; Medical Insurance; Profit Sharing; Tuition Assistance. **Corporate headquarters**

location: This Location. **Parent company:** Venturian Corporation. **Operations at this facility include:** Divisional Headquarters; Regional Headquarters; Sales; Service. **Number of employees at this location:** 85.

For more information on career opportunities in the wholesaling industry:

<u>Associations</u>

NATIONAL ASSOCIATION OF WHOLESALERS (NAW)
1725 K Street NW, Suite 300, Washington DC 20006. 202/872-0885. Offers publications on industry trends and how to operate a wholesaling business.

262/The Minneapolis-St. Paul JobBank

Many people turn to temporary agencies, permanent employment agencies, or executive recruiters to assist them in their respective job searches. At their best, these resources can be a valuable friend -- it's comforting to know that someone is putting his or her wealth of experience and contacts to work for you. At their worst, however, they are more of a friend to the employer, or to more experienced recruits, than to you personally, and it is best not to rely on them exclusively.

That said, there are several types of employment services for jobseekers to check out as part of their job search efforts:

TEMPORARY EMPLOYMENT AGENCIES

Temporary or "temp" agencies can be a viable option. Often these agencies specialize in clerical and support work, but it's becoming increasingly common to find temporary assignments in other areas like accounting or computer programming. Working on temporary assignments will provide you with additional income during your job search and will add experience to your resume. It may also provide valuable business contacts or lead to permanent job opportunities.

Temporary agencies are listed in your local telephone directory and in *The JobBank Guide to Employment Services* (Adams Media Corporation), found in your local public library. Send a resume and cover letter to the agency, and call to schedule an interview. Be prepared to take a number of tests at the interview.

PERMANENT EMPLOYMENT AGENCIES

Permanent employment agencies are commissioned by employers to find qualified candidates for job openings. The catch is that their main responsibility is to meet the employer's needs -- not necessarily to find a suitable job for the candidate.

This is not to say that permanent employment agencies should be ruled out altogether. There are permanent employment agencies specializing in specific industries that can be useful for experienced professionals. However, permanent employment agencies are not always a good choice for entry-level jobseekers. Some will try to steer inexperienced candidates in an unwanted direction or offer little more than clerical placements to experienced applicants. Others charge a fee for their services -- a condition that jobseekers should always ask about up front.

Some permanent employment agencies dispute the criticisms mentioned above. As one recruiter puts it, "Our responsibilities are to the applicant and the employer equally, because without one, we'll lose the other." She also maintains that entry-level people are desirable, saying that "as they grow, we grow, too, so we aim to move them up the ranks."

In short, as that recruiter states, "All services are not the same." If you decide to register with an agency, your best bet is to find one that is recommended by a friend or associate. Barring that, names of agencies across the country can be found in *The Adams Executive Recruiters Almanac* (Adams Media Corporation) or *The JobBank Guide to Employment Services* (Adams Media Corporation). Or you can contact:

National Association of Personnel Services (NAPS)
3133 Mount Vernon Avenue
Alexandria VA 22305
703/684-0180

Be aware that there are an increasing number of bogus employment service firms, often advertising in newspapers and magazines. These "services" promise even inexperienced jobseekers top salaries in exciting careers -- all for a sizable fee. Others use expensive 900 numbers that jobseekers are encouraged to call. Unfortunately, most people find out too late that the jobs they have been promised do not exist.

As a general rule, most legitimate permanent employment agencies will never guarantee a job and will not seek payment until after the candidate has been placed. Even so, every agency you are interested in should be checked out with the local chapter of the Better Business Bureau (BBB). Find out if the agency is licensed and has been in business for a reasonable amount of time.

If everything checks out, call the firm to find out if it specializes in your area of expertise and how it will go about marketing your qualifications. After you have selected a few agencies (three to five is best), send each one a resume with a cover letter. Make a follow-up phone call a week or two later, and try to schedule an interview. Once again, be prepared to take a battery of tests at the interview.

Above all, do not expect too much. Only a small portion of all professional, managerial, and executive jobs are listed with these agencies. Use them as an addition to your job search campaign, not a centerpiece.

EXECUTIVE SEARCH FIRMS

Also known as "headhunters," these firms consist of recruiters who are paid by client companies that hire them to fill a specific position. Executive search firms seek out and carefully screen (and weed out) candidates for high-salaried technical, executive, and managerial positions and are paid by the employer. The prospective employee is generally not charged a fee. Unlike permanent employment agencies, they often approach viable candidates directly, rather than waiting for candidates to approach them. Some prefer to deal with already employed candidates. Whether you are employed or not, do not contact an executive search firm if you aren't ready to look for a job. If a recruiter tries to place you right away and finds out you are not really looking yet, it is unlikely they will spend much time with you in the future.

Many search firms specialize in particular industries, while generalist firms typically provide placements in a wide range of industries. Look for firms that specialize in your field of interest or expertise, as well as generalist firms that conduct searches in a variety of fields. While you should concentrate on firms in your geographic area, you do not have to limit yourself to these as many firms operate nationally or internationally.

There are two basic types of executive search firms -- retainer-based and contingency-based. Note, however, that some firms conduct searches of both types. Essentially, retainer firms are hired by a client company for a search and paid a fee by the client company regardless of whether or not a placement is made. Conversely, contingency firms receive payment from the client company only when their candidate is hired. Fees are typically based on the position's first-year salary. The range is usually between 20 and 35 percent, and retainer firm fees tend to be at the higher end of that scale, according to Ivan Samuels, President of Abbott's of Boston, an executive search firm that conducts both types of searches.

Generally, companies use retainer firms to fill senior-level positions, with salaries over $60,000. In most cases, a company will hire only one retainer firm to fill a given position, and part of the process is a thorough, on-site visit by the search firm to the client company so that the recruiter may check out the operation. These search firms are recommended for a highly experienced professional seeking a job in his or her current field. Confidentiality is more secure with these firms, since a recruiter may only use your file in consideration for one job at a time, and most retainer firms will not freely circulate your resume without permission. This is particularly important to a jobseeker who is currently employed and insists on absolute discretion. If that's the case, however, make sure you do not contact a retainer firm used by your current employer.

Contingency firms make placements that cover a broader salary range, so these firms are more ideal for someone seeking a junior or mid-level position. Unlike retainer firms, contingency firms may be competing with other firms to fill a particular opening. As a result, these firms can be quicker and more responsive to your job search. In addition, a contingency firm will distribute your resume more widely. Some firms require your permission before sending your resume to any given company, while others ask that you trust their discretion. You should inquire about this with your recruiter at the outset, and choose according to your needs.

That said, once you've chosen the specific recruiter or recruiters that you will contact, keep in mind that recruiters are working for the companies that hire them, not for you, the jobseeker. Attempting to fill a position -- especially amongst fierce competition with other firms -- means your best interests may not be the recruiter's only priority. For this reason, you should contact as many search firms as possible in order to increase your chances of finding your ideal position.

A phone call is your first step, during which you should speak with a recruiter and exchange all relevant information. Ask lots of questions to determine the firm's credibility, whether they operate on a retainer or contingency basis (or both), and any and all questions you have regarding the firm's procedures. Offer the recruiter information about your employment history, as well as what type of work you are seeking. Make sure you sound enthusiastic, but not pushy. The recruiter will ask that you send a resume and cover letter as soon as possible.

Occasionally, the recruiter will arrange to meet with you, but most often this will not occur until he or she has received your resume and has found a potential match. James E. Slate, President of F-O-R-T-U-N-E Personnel Consultants in Topsfield, Massachusetts, advises that you generally not expect an abundance of personal attention at the beginning of the relationship with your recruiter, particularly with a large firm that works nationally and does most of its work over the phone. You should, however, use your recruiter's inside knowledge to your best advantage. Some recruiters will help coach you before an interview and many are open about giving you all the facts they know about a client company.

Not all executive search firms are licensed, so make sure those you plan to deal with have solid reputations and don't hesitate to check with the Better Business Bureau. Also keep in mind that it is common for recruiters to search for positions in other states. For example, recruiters in Boston sometimes look for candidates to fill positions in New York City, and the reverse is true as well. Names of search firms nationwide can be found in *The Adams Executive Recruiters Almanac* or *The JobBank Guide to Employment Services*, or by contacting:

Association of Executive Search Consultants (AESC)
500 Fifth Avenue, Suite 930, New York NY 10110. 212/398-9556.

Top Echelon, Inc.
World Wide Web address: http://www.topechelon.com.
A cooperative placement networking service of recruiting firms.

CONTRACT SERVICES FIRMS

Firms that place individuals on a contract basis commonly receive job orders from client companies that can last anywhere from a month to over a year. The function of these firms differs from that of a temporary agency in that the candidate has specific, marketable skills they wish to put to work, and the contract recruiter interviews the candidate extensively. Most often, contract services firms specialize in placing technical professionals, though some do specialize in other fields, including clerical and office support. The use of these firms is increasing in popularity, as jobseekers with technical skills recognize the benefit of utilizing and demonstrating their talents at a sampling of different companies, and establishing contacts along the way that could lead to a permanent position, if desired. Most contract services firms do not charge a fee to the candidate.

For more information on contract services, contact:

C.E. Publications, Inc.
Contract Employment Weekly Magazine
P.O. Box 3006, Bothell WA 98041-3006. 425/806-5200.
World Wide Web address: http://www.ceweekly.com.

RESUME/CAREER COUNSELING/OUTPLACEMENT SERVICES

These firms are very diverse in the services they provide. Many nonprofit organizations -- colleges, universities, private associations -- offer free or very inexpensive counseling services. For-profit career/outplacement counseling services, on the other hand, can charge a broad range of fees, depending on what services they provide. Services offered include career counseling, outplacement, resume development/writing, interview preparation, assessment testing, and various workshops. Upon contacting one of these firms, you should ask about the specific services that firm provides. Some firms provide career counseling only, teaching you how to conduct your own job search, while others also provide outplacement services. The difference here is that those which provide outplacement will conduct a job search for you, in addition to the counseling services. Firms like these are sometimes referred to as "marketing firms."

According to a representative at Career Ventures Counseling Services in Salem, Massachusetts, fees for career counseling average about $85 per hour. Counseling firms located in major cities tend to be more expensive. Furthermore, outplacement fees can range from $170 to over $7,000! As results are not guaranteed, you may want to check on a firm's reputation through the local Better Business Bureau.

For more information on resume services, contact:

Professional Association of Resume Writers
3637 Fourth Street, Suite 330, St. Petersburg FL 33704.
Attention: Mr. Frank Fox, Executive Director.

Note: On the following pages, you will find employment services for this JobBank *book's coverage area. Because contact names and addresses can change regularly, we recommend that you call each company to verify the information before inquiring about opportunities.*

TEMPORARY EMPLOYMENT AGENCIES

ABBY BLU INC.
821 Marquette Avenue, Suite 515, Minneapolis MN 55402. 612/338-3200. **Fax:** 612/349-2983.
Contact: Manager. **Description:** A temporary and permanent placement agency that focuses on office support positions. **Specializes in the areas of:** Accounting/Auditing; Advertising; Architecture/Construction; Banking; Computer Science/Software; General Management; Insurance; Legal; Manufacturing; Nonprofit; Personnel/Labor Relations; Secretarial. **Positions commonly filled include:** Accountant/Auditor; Claim Representative; Clerical Supervisor; Credit Manager; Customer Service Representative; Financial Analyst; Human Resources Specialist; Market Research Analyst; Medical Records Technician; Paralegal; Typist/Word Processor. **Benefits available to temporary workers:** 401(k); Paid Holidays; Paid Vacation. **Number of placements per year:** 1000+.

ANSWER PERSONNEL SERVICE, INC.
220 Robert Street South, Suite 208, St. Paul MN 55107-1626. 651/293-1887. **Contact:** Bruce Labelle, Coordinator. **Description:** A temporary agency. **Specializes in the areas of:** Engineering; Food; Industrial; Manufacturing. **Positions commonly filled include:** Clerical Supervisor; Computer Programmer. **Average salary range of placements:** $20,000 - $29,999. **Number of placements per year:** 500 - 999.

AWARD STAFFING
6800 France Avenue South, Suite 173, Edina MN 55435-2004. 612/561-5444. **Contact:** Staffing Manager. **Description:** A temporary agency that also provides some permanent placements. **Specializes in the areas of:** Accounting/Auditing; Clerical; Data Entry; Industrial; Light Industrial; Office Support; Word Processing. **Positions commonly filled include:** Accounting Clerk.

DESIGN PERSONNEL RESOURCES INC.
3585 North Lexington Avenue, Suite 180, St. Paul MN 55126. 651/482-0075. **Contact:** Manager. **Description:** A temporary and temp-to-perm agency. **Specializes in the areas of:** Architecture/Construction; Design.

ENVIROSTAFF, INC.
4500 Park Glen Road, Suite 140, St. Louis Park MN 55416. 612/925-8655. **Contact:** Manager. **Description:** A temporary agency. **NOTE:** Interested jobseekers should call EnviroStaff to speak with a placement specialist before sending a resume. **Specializes in the areas of:** Environmental.

GRAPHIC STAFFING INC.
1710 Douglas Drive, Suite 202, Golden Valley MN 55422. 612/546-1292. **Fax:** 612/546-7822. **Contact:** Dick Haines, Graphics Manager. **E-mail address:** cptgraphic@aol.com. **World Wide Web address:** http://www.graphicstaffing.com. **Description:** A temporary and temp-to-perm agency. **Specializes in the areas of:** Advertising; Art/Design; Publishing. **Positions commonly filled include:** Art Director; Computer Animator; Copy Editor; Desktop Publishing Specialist; Graphic Artist; Graphic Designer; Layout Specialist; Multimedia Designer; Proofreader; Technical Illustrator; Video Production Coordinator; Webmaster. **Other U.S. locations:** Chicago IL. **Average salary range of placements:** $30,000 - $50,000. **Number of placements per year:** 100 - 199.

HEALTH PERSONNEL OPTIONS CORPORATION
2550 University Avenue West, Suite 315 North, St. Paul MN 55114. 651/647-1160. **Fax:** 651/647-1903. **Contact:** Martin Kieffer, President. **Description:** A temporary agency. **Specializes in the areas of:** Health/Medical. **Positions commonly filled include:** Dental Assistant/Dental Hygienist; Dentist; EEG Technologist; EKG Technician; Health Services Manager; Licensed Practical Nurse; Medical Records Technician; Nuclear Medicine Technologist; Occupational Therapist; Physical Therapist; Physician; Radiological Technologist; Registered Nurse; Respiratory Therapist; Social Worker; Speech-Language Pathologist; Surgical Technician. **Other U.S. locations:** Nationwide. **Number of placements per year:** 100 - 199.

INTERIM LEGAL PROFESSIONALS
80 South Eighth Street, Suite 3630, Minneapolis MN 55402. 612/339-7663. **Fax:** 612/339-9274. **Contact:** Holly Bilderback, Branch Manager. **Description:** A temporary agency. **Specializes in the areas of:** Legal. **Positions commonly filled include:** Attorney; Paralegal. **Benefits available to temporary workers:** Dental Insurance; Medical Insurance; Vision Insurance. **Corporate headquarters location:** Fort Lauderdale FL. **Average salary range of placements:** $30,000 - $50,000. **Number of placements per year:** 500 - 999.

JOHNSON ASSOCIATES
1396 White Bear Avenue North, Suite B, St. Paul MN 55106. 651/774-5843. **Contact:** Dana Johnson, Director. **Description:** A temporary agency. **Specializes in the areas of:** Health/Medical. **Positions commonly filled include:** Counselor; Human Service Worker; Psychologist; Recreational Therapist; Registered Nurse; Social Worker. **Average salary range of placements:** $20,000 - $29,999. **Number of placements per year:** 200 - 499.

KELLY SCIENTIFIC RESOURCES
6465 Wayzata Boulevard, Suite 155, St. Louis Park MN 55426. 612/797-0500. **Fax:** 612/797-0611. **Contact:** Branch Manager. **World Wide Web address:** http://www.kellyscientific.com. **Description:** A temporary agency for scientific professionals. **Specializes in the areas of:** Biomedical; Chemicals; Food; Pharmaceuticals.

KELLY SERVICES, INC.
200 South Sixth Street, Suite 145, Minneapolis MN 55402. 612/339-7154. **Contact:** Supervisor. **Description:** A temporary agency. **Specializes in the areas of:** Clerical; Secretarial. **Positions commonly filled include:** Accountant/Auditor; Actuary; Administrative Assistant; Bookkeeper; Claim Representative; Clerk; Commercial Artist; Computer Programmer; Customer Service Representative; Data Entry Clerk; Draftsperson; Factory Worker; General Manager; Legal Secretary; Light Industrial Worker; Marketing Specialist; Medical Secretary; Public Relations Specialist; Sales Representative; Secretary; Stenographer; Typist/Word Processor. **Number of placements per year:** 1000+.

LYNN TEMPORARY
1821 University Avenue West, Suite 106 South, St. Paul MN 55104-2801. 651/645-9233. **Contact:** Carol Glewwe, President. **Description:** A temporary agency. **Specializes in the areas of:** Clerical; Computer Science/Software; Engineering; Nonprofit; Personnel/Labor Relations; Publishing; Secretarial; Technical. **Positions commonly filled include:** Accountant/Auditor; Administrative Manager; Architect; Biomedical Engineer; Buyer; Chemical Engineer; Clerical Supervisor; Computer Programmer; Customer Service Representative; Design Engineer; Designer; Draftsperson; Editor; Electrical/Electronics Engineer; Landscape Architect; Library Technician; Mathematician; Mechanical Engineer; Medical Records Technician; MIS Specialist; Purchasing Agent/Manager; Science Technologist; Services Sales Representative; Software Engineer; Systems Analyst; Technical Writer/Editor; Typist/Word Processor; Video Production Coordinator. **Average salary range of placements:** $20,000 - $29,999. **Number of placements per year:** 200 - 499.

MANPOWER TEMPORARY SERVICES
150 South Fifth Street, Suite 336, Minneapolis MN 55402. 612/375-9200. **Contact:** Branch Manager. **Description:** A temporary agency. **Specializes in the areas of:** Data Processing; Industrial; Secretarial; Technical; Telephone Technical Support; Word Processing. **Positions commonly filled include:** Accountant; Accounting Clerk; Administrative Assistant; Biological Scientist; Bookkeeper; Chemist; Customer Service Manager; Designer; Desktop Publishing Specialist; Electrician; Inspector/Tester/Grader; Inventory Control Specialist; Machine Operator; Packaging/Processing Worker; Painter; Project Engineer; Proofreader; Receptionist; Research Assistant; Secretary; Software Engineer; Stenographer; Systems Analyst; Technical Writer/Editor; Technician; Telemarketer; Transcriptionist; Typist/Word Processor; Welder. **Benefits available to temporary workers:** Life Insurance; Medical Insurance; Paid Holidays; Paid Vacation.

MANPOWER TEMPORARY SERVICES
2564 Bridge Avenue, Albert Lea MN 56007. 507/377-7410. **Toll-free phone:** 800/371-1262. **Fax:** 507/377-7521. **Contact:** Cindy Lunning, Service Representative. **Description:** A temporary agency. **Positions commonly filled include:** Accountant/Auditor; Factory Worker; Receptionist; Support Personnel. **Benefits available to temporary workers:** Life Insurance; Medical Insurance; Paid Holidays; Paid Vacation. **Other U.S. locations:** Milwaukee WI.

MIDWEST FARM WORKERS EMPLOYMENT & TRAINING
P.O. Box 1231, St. Cloud MN 56302. 320/253-7010. **Contact:** Manager. **Description:** An employment agency that provides seasonal placements and training services for farm workers.

MIDWEST STAFFING SERVICES
1145 Canterbury, Shakopee MN 55379. 612/896-2055. **Fax:** 612/896-2059. **Contact:** Director of Operations. **Description:** Midwest Staffing Services is a temporary agency. **Specializes in the areas of:** Accounting/Auditing; Legal; Manufacturing; Personnel/Labor Relations; Secretarial. **Positions commonly filled include:** Blue-Collar Worker Supervisor; Claim Representative; Clerical Supervisor; Credit Manager; Customer Service Representative; General Manager; Human Resources Manager; Librarian; Library Technician; Medical Records Technician; Paralegal; Public Relations Specialist; Typist/Word Processor. **Average salary range of placements:** $20,000 - $29,999.

MINNESOTA WORKFORCE CENTER
P.O. Box 67, St. Cloud MN 56302. 320/255-3266. **Contact:** Manager. **Description:** A state-operated temporary and permanent placement service.

THOMAS MOORE INC.
608 Second Avenue South, Suite 465, Minneapolis MN 55402-1907. 612/338-4884. **Contact:** Recruiter. **Description:** A temporary agency. **Specializes in the areas of:** Accounting/Auditing; Banking; Finance. **Positions commonly filled include:** Accountant/Auditor; Budget Analyst; Credit Manager; Financial Analyst. **Benefits available to temporary workers:** Paid Holidays; Paid Vacation.

OLSTEN FLATLEY TECHNICAL SERVICES, INC.
3600 West 80th Street, Suite 535, Bloomington MN 55431. 612/896-3435. **Contact:** Tami Pulkrabek, General Manager. **Description:** Olsten Flatley Technical Services, Inc. is a temporary agency. **Specializes in the areas of:** Architecture/Construction; Consulting; Engineering; Manufacturing; Materials; Publishing; Technical. **Positions commonly filled include:** Architect; Architectural Engineer; Civil Engineer; Designer; Draftsperson; Electrical/Electronics Engineer; Industrial Engineer; Manufacturing Engineer; Mechanical Engineer; Production Manager; Purchasing Agent/Manager; Quality Control Supervisor; Software Engineer; Structural Engineer; Technical Illustrator; Technical Writer/Editor; Technician. **Number of placements per year:** 500 - 999.

PI ENTERPRISES INC.
900 Second Avenue South, Suite 440, Minneapolis MN 55402-3322. 612/337-5220. **Fax:** 612/371-0865. **Contact:** Shari Bohnhoff, Staffing Director. **Description:** A full-service temporary agency. **Specializes in the areas of:** Office Support.

PRO STAFF
1610 14th Street NW, Suite 102, Rochester MN 55901. 507/288-8878. **Contact:** Manager. **Description:** A temporary agency.

PRO STAFF PERSONNEL SERVICES
500 North Main Street, Suite 108, Le Sueur MN 56058. 507/665-6493. **Contact:** Manager. **Description:** A temporary agency. **Specializes in the areas of:** Light Industrial.

PRO STAFF PERSONNEL SERVICES
101 Seventh Avenue South, Suite 100, St. Cloud MN 56301. 320/656-9777. **Contact:** Manager. **Description:** A temporary agency.

STS TEMPORARY SERVICES
8437 University Avenue NE, Spring Lake Park MN 55432. 612/571-0508. **Contact:** Branch Supervisor. **Description:** A temporary agency. **Corporate headquarters location:** Minneapolis MN. **Average salary range of placements:** $20,000 - $29,999. **Number of placements per year:** 500 - 999.

SUPPORT SERVICES NETWORK
221 Jefferson Street North, Wadena MN 56482-1370. 218/631-4946. **Fax:** 218/631-4946. **Contact:** Ms. Chris Dunrud, Owner. **Description:** A temporary agency. **Specializes in the areas of:** Office Support; Secretarial. **Positions commonly filled include:** Clerical Supervisor; Support Personnel. **Average salary range of placements:** Less than $20,000. **Number of placements per year:** 50 - 99.

TEMP FORCE
6550 York Avenue South, Suite 640, Edina MN 55435. 612/920-9119. **Contact:** Manager. **Description:** A temporary agency. **Specializes in the areas of:** Industrial; Secretarial; Technical.

TEMPORARY ASSETS
7777 Highway 65, Spring Lake Park MN 55432. 612/784-8980. **Contact:** Manager. **Description:** A temporary agency. **Specializes in the areas of:** Clerical; Industrial; Office Support. **Positions commonly filled include:** Electronics Technician; Machine Operator.

JEANE THORNE INC.
336 North Robert Street, Suite 100, St. Paul MN 55101. 651/298-0400. **Toll-free phone:** 800/848-0402. **Fax:** 651/298-0448. **Contact:** Christine Kelleher, Recruitment Manager. **World Wide Web address:** http://www.jeane-thorne.com. **Description:** A temporary agency. Jeane Thorne also provides employee training. **Specializes in the areas of:** Accounting/Auditing; Banking; Office Support; Secretarial. **Positions commonly filled include:** Accountant/Auditor; Administrative Assistant; Customer Service Representative; Data Entry Clerk; Executive Assistant; Legal Assistant; Receptionist. **Benefits available to temporary workers:** Dental Insurance; Life Insurance; Medical Insurance; Referral Bonus Plan. **Other U.S. locations:** Arden Hills MN; Crystal MN; Eagan MN; Eden Prairie MN; Mankato MN; Midway MN; Minneapolis MN; St. Louis Park MN; Woodbury MN; Fargo ND.

WHITNEY PROFESSIONAL STAFFING
619 Kinnard Financial Center, 920 Second Avenue South, Minneapolis MN 55402-4035. 612/337-5100. **Fax:** 612/336-4499. **Contact:** David L. Whitney, President. **E-mail address:** wa625@aol.com. **World Wide Web address:** http://www.whitneyinc.com. **Description:** A temporary and temp-to-perm agency specializing in the placement of accounting professionals with four-year degrees. **Specializes in the areas of:** Accounting; Bookkeeping; Finance; Tax. **Positions commonly filled include:** Accountant; Accounting Clerk; Auditor; Bookkeeper; Budget Analyst; Chief Financial Officer; Controller; CPA; Finance Director; Financial Analyst; Financial Consultant; Tax Specialist; Treasurer. **Average salary range of placements:** $30,000 - $125,000. **Number of placements per year:** 200 - 499.

YOUTH EMPLOYMENT PROJECT, INC.
300 11th Avenue NW, Suite 120, Rochester MN 55901. 507/252-2442. **Fax:** 507/252-2444. **Contact:** Theresa Bigalk, Executive Director. **Description:** A temporary employment agency for youth between the ages of 13 and 19. **Specializes in the areas of:** Agri-Business; Child Care, In-Home; Hotel/Restaurant; Office Support; Retail. **Positions commonly filled include:** Daycare Worker; Retail Sales Worker. **Average salary range of placements:** Less than $20,000. **Number of placements per year:** 500 - 999.

PERMANENT EMPLOYMENT AGENCIES

ADVANTAGE PERSONNEL INC.
408 West 65th Street, Richfield MN 55423-1402. 612/861-9930. **Fax:** 612/861-9543. **Contact:** W. John Knopf II, General Manager. **Description:** A permanent employment agency. **Specializes in the areas of:** Industrial; Light Industrial. **Average salary range of placements:** Less than $20,000. **Number of placements per year:** 50 - 99.

AGRO QUALITY SEARCH INC.
7260 University Avenue NE, Suite 305, Fridley MN 55432-3129. 612/572-3737. **Fax:** 612/572-3738. **Contact:** Jerry L. Olson, President. **Description:** A permanent placement agency. **Specializes in the areas of:** Agriculture; Food; Sales; Technical. **Positions commonly filled include:** Agricultural Engineer; Design Engineer; Food Scientist/Technologist; General Manager; Human Resources Specialist; Industrial Engineer; Manufacturer's/Wholesaler's Sales Rep.; Mechanical Engineer; Purchasing Agent/Manager; Transportation/Traffic Specialist. **Average salary range of placements:** $30,000 - $50,000. **Number of placements per year:** 1 - 49.

ALTERNATIVE STAFFING, INC.
8120 Penn Avenue South, Suite 570, Bloomington MN 55431-1326. 612/888-6077. **Contact:** Kim Howard, President. **Description:** A permanent employment agency. **Specializes in the areas of:** Accounting/Auditing; Clerical; Computer Hardware/Software; Legal; Manufacturing; Publishing; Sales; Secretarial. **Positions commonly filled include:** Accountant/Auditor; Administrative Assistant; Bookkeeper; Claim Representative; Clerk; Computer Programmer; Credit Manager; Customer Service Representative; Data Entry Clerk; Draftsperson; Factory Worker; Financial Analyst; Human Resources Manager; Legal Secretary; Light Industrial Worker; Marketing

Specialist; Medical Secretary; Purchasing Agent/Manager; Receptionist; Sales Representative; Secretary; Stenographer; Typist/Word Processor. **Number of placements per year:** 1000+.

BARTZ ROGERS & PARTNERS
6465 Wayzata Boulevard, Minneapolis MN 55426. 612/936-0657. **Fax:** 612/936-0142. **Contact:** Douglas Bartz, Partner. **Description:** A permanent employment agency. **Specializes in the areas of:** Computer Science/Software. **Positions commonly filled include:** Computer Programmer; Systems Analyst. **Number of placements per year:** 100 - 199.

DIVERSIFIED EMPLOYMENT INC.
1710 Douglas Drive, Suite 200, Golden Valley MN 55422. 612/546-8255. **Fax:** 612/546-4106. **Contact:** Recruiter. **Description:** A permanent employment agency that also provides contract services and career counseling. **Specializes in the areas of:** Accounting/Auditing; Administration; Advertising; Art/Design; Engineering; General Management; Industrial; Manufacturing; Publishing; Sales; Secretarial; Technical. **Positions commonly filled include:** Accountant/Auditor; Administrative Manager; Advertising Clerk; Automotive Mechanic; Blue-Collar Worker Supervisor; Buyer; Clerical Supervisor; Construction and Building Inspector; Counselor; Customer Service Representative; Design Engineer; Designer; Draftsperson; Electrical/Electronics Engineer; Electrician; General Manager; Human Resources Specialist; Industrial Engineer; Industrial Production Manager; Mechanical Engineer; Multimedia Designer; Operations/Production Manager; Purchasing Agent/Manager; Quality Control Supervisor; Restaurant/Food Service Manager; Services Sales Representative; Software Engineer; Structural Engineer; Systems Analyst; Technical Writer/Editor; Typist/Word Processor; Underwriter/Assistant Underwriter. **Average salary range of placements:** $20,000 - $29,999. **Number of placements per year:** 200 - 499.

EMPLOYMENT ADVISORS
6600 France Avenue South, Suite 515, Edina MN 55435. 612/925-3666. **Toll-free phone:** 800/488-8634. **Fax:** 612/924-0111. **Contact:** Manager. **Description:** A permanent employment agency. **Specializes in the areas of:** Banking; Customer Service; General Management; Sales. **Number of placements per year:** 500 - 999.

EMPLOYMENT ADVISORS
STAFF IT PERSONNEL SERVICES
526 Nicollet Mall, Suite 300, Minneapolis MN 55402-1008. 612/339-0521. **Toll-free phone:** 800/959-0521. **Fax:** 612/338-4757. **Contact:** Vicky Sherman, General Manager. **Description:** A permanent employment agency that focuses on the placement of college graduates in entry- and mid-level business positions. Staff It Personnel Services (also at this location) provides temporary and temp-to-perm placements. **Specializes in the areas of:** Customer Service; Finance; General Management; Retail; Sales. **Positions commonly filled include:** Credit Manager; Customer Service Representative; Management Trainee; Public Relations Specialist; Restaurant/Food Service Manager; Sales Representative. **Average salary range of placements:** $20,000 - $29,999. **Number of placements per year:** 200 - 499.

EXPRESS PERSONNEL SERVICES
7101 France Avenue South, Edina MN 55435. 612/915-2000. **Contact:** Jim Johnson, Owner. **Description:** A permanent employment agency that also provides temporary placements. **Specializes in the areas of:** Industrial; Manufacturing; Personnel/Labor Relations; Secretarial. **Positions commonly filled include:** Accountant/Auditor; Administrative Manager; Blue-Collar Worker Supervisor; Branch Manager; Brokerage Clerk; Buyer; Claim Representative; Clerical Supervisor; Credit Manager; Customer Service Representative; General Manager; Human Resources Manager; MIS Specialist; Purchasing Agent/Manager; Quality Control Supervisor; Services Sales Representative; Technical Writer/Editor; Typist/Word Processor. **Benefits available to temporary workers:** Paid Holidays; Paid Vacation. **Corporate headquarters location:** Oklahoma City OK. **Average salary range of placements:** $20,000 - $29,999.

FINANCIAL STAFF RECRUITERS
1600 West 82nd Avenue, Suite 170, Bloomington MN 55431. 612/885-3040. **Contact:** Manager. **Description:** A permanent employment agency. **Specializes in the areas of:** Accounting/Auditing; Finance.

HUMAN RESOURCES PERSONNEL SERVICES
6800 France Avenue South, Suite 173, Edina MN 55435-2007. 612/929-3000. **Fax:** 612/927-4313. **Contact:** Susan Miller, Manager. **E-mail address:** hrps@hrsearch.com. **World Wide Web address:** http://www.hrsearch.com. **Description:** A permanent employment agency that also provides temporary placements. **Specializes in the areas of:** Human Resources; Personnel/Labor Relations. **Positions commonly filled include:** Human Resources Manager.

KAPOSIA, INC.
380 East Lafayette Frontage Road South, St. Paul MN 55107-1216. 651/224-6974. **Fax:** 651/224-7249. **Contact:** Peg Ring, Human Resources/Administrative Assistant. **Description:** A permanent employment agency for individuals with developmental disabilities. **Specializes in the areas of:** Human Services; Nonprofit; Social Services. **Positions commonly filled include:** Accountant/Auditor; Counselor; Human Service Worker; Services Sales Representative. **Benefits available to temporary workers:** Paid Vacation. **Number of placements per year:** 1 - 49.

PALESCH & ASSOCIATES, INC.
530 Kristen Lane, Maple Plain MN 55359. 612/955-3390. **Contact:** Tom Palesch, President. **Description:** A permanent employment agency. **Specializes in the areas of:** Metals. **Positions commonly filled include:** Operations/Production Manager. **Number of placements per year:** 50 - 99.

PROFESSIONAL ALTERNATIVES, INC.
926 Twelve Oaks Center, 15500 Wayzata Boulevard, Wayzata MN 55391. 612/404-2600. **Contact:** Vice President. **Description:** A full-service, permanent employment agency focusing on placing mid- and upper-level professionals. **Specializes in the areas of:** Accounting/Auditing; Advertising; Finance; General Management; Personnel/Labor Relations; Sales. **Positions commonly filled include:** Accountant/Auditor; Administrative Manager; Advertising Clerk; Bank Officer/Manager; Blue-Collar Worker Supervisor; Branch Manager; Buyer; Claim Representative; Clerical Supervisor; Computer Programmer; Credit Manager; Customer Service Representative; Financial Analyst; Financial Services Sales Representative; General Manager; Human Resources Manager; Management Analyst/Consultant; Management Trainee; Manufacturer's/Wholesaler's Sales Rep.; Market Research Analyst; MIS Specialist; Operations/Production Manager; Property and Real Estate Manager; Public Relations Specialist; Purchasing Agent/Manager; Quality Control Supervisor; Securities Sales Representative; Services Sales Representative; Strategic Relations Manager; Systems Analyst; Telecommunications Manager. **Average salary range of placements:** $30,000 - $50,000. **Number of placements per year:** 50 - 99.

SECRETARY & ACCOUNTING SERVICES
50 West Second Street, Winona MN 55987-3440. 507/454-5804. **Fax:** 507/454-5804. **Contact:** Lucia Bartsh, Owner. **Description:** An employment agency that places professionals in both permanent and temporary positions. **Specializes in the areas of:** Accounting/Auditing; Secretarial. **Positions commonly filled include:** Accountant/Auditor; Administrative Manager; Clerical Supervisor; Computer Programmer; Draftsperson; General Manager; Human Resources Manager; Management Trainee; Medical Records Technician; MIS Specialist; Paralegal; Purchasing Agent/Manager; Software Engineer; Systems Analyst; Technical Writer/Editor; Typist/Word Processor. **Average salary range of placements:** $20,000 - $29,999. **Number of placements per year:** 50 - 99.

ULTIMATE SEARCH UNLIMITED
TEMPS UNLIMITED
2233 University Avenue West, St. Paul MN 55114-1629. 651/649-3131. **Fax:** 651/649-3041. **Contact:** Robert H. Draack, Vice President/General Manager. **Description:** A permanent employment agency. Temps Unlimited (also at this location) provides temporary placements. **Specializes in the areas of:** Administration; Banking; Engineering; Finance; Food; General Management; Health/Medical; Legal; MIS/EDP; Sales; Secretarial. **Positions commonly filled include:** Account Manager; Account Rep.; Administrative Manager; Attorney; Bank Officer/Manager; Branch Manager; Certified Nurses Aide; Chief Financial Officer; Claim Rep.; Clerical Supervisor; Computer Operator; Computer Programmer; Credit Manager; Customer Service Rep.; Database Manager; Design Engineer; EEG Technologist; EKG Technician; Electrical/Electronics Engineer; Emergency Medical Technician; Finance Director; Financial Analyst; General Manager; Human Resources Manager; Industrial Engineer; Industrial Production Manager; Insurance Agent/Broker; Licensed Practical Nurse; Management Trainee; Marketing Manager; Medical Records Technician; Occupational Therapist; Operations Manager; Paralegal; Pharmacist; Physical Therapist; Physician; Production Manager; Quality Control Supervisor; Registered Nurse; Respiratory Therapist; Sales Engineer; Sales Executive; Sales Representative; Secretary; Services Sales Representative; Software Engineer; Speech-Language Pathologist; Surgical Technician; Telecommunications Manager; Transportation/Traffic Specialist; Typist/Word Processor. **Benefits available to temporary workers:** Paid Holidays; Paid Vacation. **Average salary range of placements:** $30,000 - $50,000. **Number of placements per year:** 200 - 499.

WEST EMPLOYMENT SOLUTIONS
112 North Third Street, Suite 201, Minneapolis MN 55401-1650. 612/338-8035. **Fax:** 612/338-8057. **Contact:** Don Westrum, President. **Description:** A full-service, permanent employment

agency that focuses on the placement of recent college graduates in entry-level business trainee positions. **Specializes in the areas of:** Banking; Finance; Food; Retail; Sales; Secretarial; Transportation. **Positions commonly filled include:** Bank Officer/Manager; Branch Manager; Credit Manager; Customer Service Representative; Hotel Manager; Management Trainee; Manufacturer's/Wholesaler's Sales Rep.; Restaurant/Food Service Manager; Services Sales Representative. **Average salary range of placements:** $20,000 - $29,999. **Number of placements per year:** 200 - 499.

WORKING RELATIONSHIPS INC.
1405 Lilac Drive, Suite 150, Minneapolis MN 55422. 612/546-2999. **Fax:** 612/546-2898. **Contact:** Recruiter. **World Wide Web address:** http://www.workingrelationships.com. **Description:** A permanent placement agency. **Specializes in the areas of:** Accounting/Auditing; Administration; General Management; Sales; Secretarial. **Positions commonly filled include:** Administrative Assistant; Buyer; Customer Service Representative; Operations/Production Manager; Project Manager; Sales Representative; Secretary; Typist/Word Processor. **Average salary range of placements:** $20,000 - $29,999. **Number of placements per year:** 100 - 199.

EXECUTIVE SEARCH FIRMS

ACCOUNTANTS EXCHANGE, INC.
Roseville Professional Center, 2233 Hamline Avenue North, Suite 509, Roseville MN 55113. 651/636-5490. **Contact:** Chuck McBride, President. **Description:** An executive search firm. **Specializes in the areas of:** Accounting/Auditing; Finance. **Number of placements per year:** 1 - 49.

ACCOUNTANTS EXECUTIVE SEARCH
ACCOUNTANTS ON CALL
45 South Seventh Street, Suite 3004, Minneapolis MN 55402. 612/341-9900. **Contact:** Manager. **Description:** An executive search firm. Accountants on Call (also at this location) is a temporary agency. **Specializes in the areas of:** Accounting/Auditing; Finance.

ACCOUNTANTS PLACEMENT REGISTRY, INC.
1705 Cope Avenue, Suite A, Maplewood MN 55109. 651/773-9018. **Fax:** 651/770-8071. **Recorded jobline:** 651/773-0648. **Contact:** Robert S. Culver, President. **Description:** An executive search firm. **Specializes in the areas of:** Accounting/Auditing; Finance. **Positions commonly filled include:** Accountant/Auditor; Bank Officer/Manager; Budget Analyst; Cost Estimator; Credit Manager; Financial Analyst. **Average salary range of placements:** $30,000 - $50,000. **Number of placements per year:** 50 - 99.

ADD ON STAFFING SOLUTIONS
255 East Roselawn Avenue, Suite 49, St. Paul MN 55117. 651/488-1000. **Toll-free phone:** 800/305-7761. **Fax:** 651/488-9585. **Contact:** Linda Longlet, President. **E-mail address:** addon@onecalltelcom.com. **World Wide Web address:** http://www.interpage.com/addon.htm. **Description:** An executive search firm. **Specializes in the areas of:** Telecommunications. **Positions commonly filled include:** Customer Service Representative; Sales Executive; Sales Manager; Sales Representative; Software Engineer; Telecommunications Manager. **Average salary range of placements:** $30,000 - $50,000. **Number of placements per year:** 1 - 49.

ADVANCE PERSONNEL RESOURCES
715 Florida Avenue South, Suite 301, Golden Valley MN 55426-1729. 612/546-6779. **Fax:** 612/546-2523. **Contact:** Larry Happe, CPC, Owner. **Description:** An executive search firm. **Specializes in the areas of:** Accounting/Auditing; Finance; General Management; Manufacturing; Personnel/Labor Relations; Publishing; Sales; Transportation. **Positions commonly filled include:** Accountant/Auditor; Attorney; Human Resources Specialist; Management Analyst/Consultant; Manufacturer's/Wholesaler's Sales Rep.; Market Research Analyst; Operations/Production Manager; Quality Control Supervisor; Services Sales Representative; Strategic Relations Manager; Telecommunications Manager. **Average salary range of placements:** $30,000 - $80,000. **Number of placements per year:** 1 - 49.

AGRI-BUSINESS SERVICES, INC.
P.O. Box 1237, Lakeville MN 55044. 612/469-6767. **Fax:** 612/469-6768. **Contact:** Michael J. Morrison, President. **Description:** An executive search firm operating on a contingency basis.

Specializes in the areas of: Agri-Business; Biology; Engineering; Food; General Management; Manufacturing; Sales; Technical. Positions commonly filled include: Biochemist; Biological Scientist; Blue-Collar Worker Supervisor; Branch Manager; Chemical Engineer; Chemist; Civil Engineer; Customer Service Representative; Design Engineer; Dietician/Nutritionist; Food Scientist/Technologist; Forester/Conservation Scientist; General Manager; Manufacturer's/Wholesaler's Sales Rep.; Quality Control Supervisor; Services Sales Representative; Veterinarian.

ARCHAMBAULT GROUP
5831 Cedar Lake Road South, St. Louis Park MN 55416. 612/545-6296. Contact: Manager. Description: An executive search firm. Specializes in the areas of: Finance.

BRADLEY & ASSOCIATES
5341 River Bluff Curve, Suite 116, Bloomington MN 55437. 612/884-2607. Fax: 612/884-2019. Contact: John Bradley, President. Description: An executive search firm. Specializes in the areas of: Accounting/Auditing; Engineering; Food; Manufacturing. Positions commonly filled include: Account Manager; Biological Scientist; Chemical Engineer; Controller; Electrical/Electronics Engineer; Mechanical Engineer.

BRIGHT SEARCH/PROFESSIONAL STAFFING
8120 Penn Avenue South, Suite 167, Bloomington MN 55431-1326. 612/884-8111. Fax: 612/881-9197. Contact: Leo Bright, Owner/President. Description: An executive search firm operating on both retainer and contingency bases. Specializes in the areas of: Consulting; Engineering; General Management; Health/Medical; Industrial; Legal; Manufacturing; Personnel/Labor Relations; Sales; Technical. Positions commonly filled include: Attorney; Chemical Engineer; Design Engineer; Electrical/Electronics Engineer; General Manager; Human Resources Specialist; Industrial Engineer; Industrial Production Manager; Management Analyst/Consultant; Mechanical Engineer; Metallurgical Engineer; Purchasing Agent/Manager; Quality Control Supervisor; Services Sales Representative; Software Engineer; Systems Analyst; Technical Writer/Editor; Transportation/Traffic Specialist.

CERTIFIED ACCOUNTING PROS
333 Washington Avenue North, Suite 300, Minneapolis MN 55401. 612/373-9495. Contact: Manager. Description: An executive search firm. Specializes in the areas of: Accounting/Auditing.

COMPUTER EMPLOYMENT
5151 Edina Industrial Boulevard, Suite 299, Edina MN 55439. 612/831-4566. Fax: 612/831-4684. Contact: Marty Koepp, Owner. E-mail address: mkoepp@computeremployment.com. Description: An executive search firm operating on a contingency basis. Specializes in the areas of: Administration; Computer Science/Software. Positions commonly filled include: Computer Programmer; Management Analyst/Consultant; MIS Specialist; Software Engineer; Systems Analyst; Telecommunications Manager. Average salary range of placements: $50,000 - $75,000. Number of placements per year: 50 - 99.

COMPUTER PERSONNEL
5353 Wayzata Boulevard, Suite 604, Minneapolis MN 55416. 612/542-8053. Contact: Manager. Description: An executive search firm. Specializes in the areas of: Computer Science/Software. Other U.S. locations: Seattle WA.

ROBERT CONNELLY AND ASSOCIATES INC.
P.O. Box 24028, Minneapolis MN 55424. 612/925-3039. Contact: Robert F. Olsen, President. Description: An executive search firm. Number of placements per year: 50 - 99.

CUSTOM SEARCH INC.
9800 Shelard Parkway, Suite 104, Plymouth MN 55441. 612/591-6111. Contact: Manager. Description: An executive search firm. Specializes in the areas of: Software Engineering; Technical.

CHARLES DAHL ASSOCIATES
77 13th Avenue NE, Minneapolis MN 55143-1001. 612/331-7777. Contact: Manager. Description: An executive search firm. Specializes in the areas of: Engineering; Finance; Information Technology.

DEVELOPMENT SEARCH SPECIALISTS
W-3072 First National Bank Building, St. Paul MN 55101-1308. 651/224-3750. Contact: Fred J. Lauerman, Principal. Description: An executive search firm. Specializes in the areas of:

Nonprofit. **Positions commonly filled include:** Fundraising Specialist; General Manager; Public Relations Specialist. **Number of placements per year:** 1 - 49.

DIETRICH & ASSOCIATES
5775 Wayzata Boulevard, Suite 700, Minneapolis MN 55416. 612/525-2205. **Fax:** 612/545-0856. **Contact:** Marilyn Dietrich, Owner. **Description:** An executive search firm. **Specializes in the areas of:** Engineering; Manufacturing. **Positions commonly filled include:** Design Engineer; Electrical/Electronics Engineer; Industrial Engineer; Industrial Production Manager; Mechanical Engineer; Operations/Production Manager; Purchasing Agent/Manager; Quality Control Supervisor; Transportation/Traffic Specialist. **Average salary range of placements:** More than $50,000. **Number of placements per year:** 1 - 49.

EHS & ASSOCIATES, INC.
1005 West Franklin, Minneapolis MN 55405. 612/870-1337. **Contact:** Brian Hirt, Vice President. **Description:** An executive search firm. **Specializes in the areas of:** Hotel/Restaurant. **Positions commonly filled include:** Hotel Manager; Restaurant/Food Service Manager. **Number of placements per year:** 200 - 499.

ESP SYSTEMS PROFESSIONALS
701 Fourth Avenue South, Suite 1800, Minneapolis MN 55415-1819. 612/337-3000. **Fax:** 612/337-9199. **Contact:** Robert R. Hildreth, President. **E-mail address:** careers@esp.com. **World Wide Web address:** http://www.esp.com. **Description:** An executive search firm. **Specializes in the areas of:** Information Systems. **Positions commonly filled include:** Computer Programmer; Internet Services Manager; MIS Specialist; Software Engineer; Systems Analyst. **Average salary range of placements:** $35,000 - $60,000. **Number of placements per year:** 500 - 999.

EMERGING TECHNOLOGY SERVICES
1600 Arboretum Boulevard, Suite 209, P.O. Box 215, Victoria MN 55386. 612/443-4141. **Contact:** Manager. **Description:** An executive search firm. **Specializes in the areas of:** Information Systems.

ENTERPRISE SEARCH SERVICES
3639 Admiral Lane, Brooklyn Center MN 55429. 612/537-7310. **Contact:** Manager. **Description:** An executive search firm. **Specializes in the areas of:** Computer Science/Software.

ERSPAMER ASSOCIATES
4010 West 65th Street, Suite 100, Edina MN 55435. 612/925-3747. **Fax:** 612/925-4022. **Contact:** Roy C. Erspamer, Principal. **Description:** An executive search firm. **Specializes in the areas of:** Health/Medical; Medical Technology. **Positions commonly filled include:** Biochemist; Biomedical Engineer; Chemical Engineer; Chemist; Design Engineer; Electrical/Electronics Engineer; Manufacturing Engineer; Mechanical Engineer; Metallurgical Engineer; Project Manager; Quality Control Supervisor; Regulatory Affairs Director; Software Engineer; Statistician. **Number of placements per year:** 1 - 49.

THE ESQUIRE GROUP
105 South Fifth Street, Suite 1800, Minneapolis MN 55402. 612/340-9068. **Fax:** 612/340-1218. **Contact:** Patricia A. Comeford, President. **Description:** An executive search firm. **Specializes in the areas of:** Legal. **Positions commonly filled include:** Attorney.

EXECU-TECH SEARCH INC.
3500 West 80th Street, Suite 20, Bloomington MN 55431. 612/893-6915. **Contact:** Manager. **Description:** An executive search firm specializing in the placement of chemical, electrical, and mechanical engineering professionals. **Specializes in the areas of:** Engineering.

EXECUTIVE SEARCH INC.
5401 Gamble Drive, Suite 275, Minneapolis MN 55416. 612/541-9153. **Contact:** Manager. **Description:** An executive search firm.

FAIRFAX GROUP
9800 Shelard Parkway, Suite 110, Plymouth MN 55441. 612/541-9898. **Fax:** 612/541-9124. **Contact:** Manager. **Description:** An executive search firm. **Specializes in the areas of:** Information Systems; Logistics; Manufacturing.

FALLS MEDICAL SEARCH
34 Forest Dale Road, Minneapolis MN 55410. 612/922-0207. **Contact:** Manager. **Description:** An executive search firm. **Specializes in the areas of:** Physician Executive.

FOCUS EXECUTIVE SEARCH
2852 Anthony Lane South, St. Anthony MN 55418. 612/706-4444. **Contact:** Tim McLafferty, President. **Description:** Focus Executive Search is an executive search firm that places mid- to executive-level professionals. **Specializes in the areas of:** Food; Pharmaceuticals. **Positions commonly filled include:** Agricultural Engineer; Biological Scientist; Chemical Engineer; Dietician/Nutritionist; Food Scientist/Technologist; Human Resources Manager; Pharmacist. **Average salary range of placements:** More than $50,000. **Number of placements per year:** 100 - 199.

FOGARTY & ASSOCIATES
6600 France Avenue, Suite 210, Edina MN 55435. 612/831-2828. **Contact:** Manager. **Description:** Fogarty & Associates is an executive search firm. **Specializes in the areas of:** Health/Medical.

GATEWAY SEARCH INC.
15500 Wayzata Boulevard, Building 604, Suite 221, Wayzata MN 55391-1438. 612/473-3137. **Fax:** 612/473-3276. **Contact:** James Bortolussi, President. **Description:** An executive search firm operating on a contingency basis. **Specializes in the areas of:** Computer Science/Software. **Positions commonly filled include:** Client/Server Specialist; Computer Programmer; Database Manager; Network Administrator; Software Engineer; Systems Analyst; UNIX System Administrator. **Average salary range of placements:** More than $50,000. **Number of placements per year:** 1 - 49.

GERDES SINGER & ASSOCIATES INC.
120 South Sixth Street, Suite 2480, Minneapolis MN 55402. 612/335-3553. **Contact:** Manager. **Description:** An executive search firm that focuses primarily on the creative side of advertising. **Specializes in the areas of:** Advertising.

ROGER G. GILMER AND ASSOCIATES
14581 Grand Avenue South, Burnsville MN 55306. 612/469-3652. **Contact:** Roger Gilmer, Owner. **Description:** An executive search firm. **Specializes in the areas of:** Engineering; Manufacturing. **Positions commonly filled include:** Biomedical Engineer; Electrical/Electronics Engineer; Mechanical Engineer; Quality Control Supervisor. **Number of placements per year:** 1 - 49.

GLEASON DALE KEENE & ASSOCIATES, INC.
7401 Metro Boulevard, Suite 460, Minneapolis MN 55439. 612/844-0121. **Contact:** Manager. **Description:** An executive search firm.

HR SERVICES OF PLYMOUTH
P.O. Box 564, Rockford MN 55373. 612/477-6595. **Fax:** 612/477-6609. **Contact:** Manager. **Description:** An executive search firm. **Specializes in the areas of:** Architecture/Construction; Engineering; Food; Industrial; Manufacturing; Personnel/Labor Relations. **Positions commonly filled include:** Blue-Collar Worker Supervisor; Ceramics Engineer; Chemical Engineer; Chemist; Civil Engineer; Construction Trade Worker; Electrical/Electronics Engineer; Industrial Engineer; Manufacturing Engineer; Mechanical Engineer; Metallurgical Engineer; Operations/Production Manager; Purchasing Agent/Manager; Quality Control Supervisor; Structural Engineer; Technical Illustrator. **Average salary range of placements:** $30,000 - $50,000. **Number of placements per year:** 50 - 99.

ROBERT HALF INTERNATIONAL
ACCOUNTEMPS
80 South Eighth Street, Suite 2850, Minneapolis MN 55402. 612/339-9001. **Contact:** Manager. **World Wide Web address:** http://www.roberthalf.com. **Description:** An executive search firm. Accountemps (also at this location) provides temporary placements. **Specializes in the areas of:** Accounting/Auditing. **Corporate headquarters location:** Menlo Park CA. **Other U.S. locations:** Nationwide.

ROBERT HALF INTERNATIONAL
ACCOUNTEMPS
10405 Sixth Avenue North, Suite 220, Plymouth MN 55441. 612/545-0911. **Contact:** Manager. **World Wide Web address:** http://www.roberthalf.com. **Description:** An executive search firm. Accountemps (also at this location) provides temporary placements. **Specializes in the areas of:** Accounting/Auditing. **Corporate headquarters location:** Menlo Park CA. **Other U.S. locations:** Nationwide.

HAYDEN & ASSOCIATES
7825 Washington Avenue South, Suite 120, Bloomington MN 55439. 612/941-6300. **Contact:** Manager. **Description:** An executive search firm. **Specializes in the areas of:** Advertising; Data Processing; Finance; Medical Sales and Marketing.

HAYDEN SEARCH GROUP
505 North Highway 169, Suite 275, Plymouth MN 55441. 612/593-2400. **Contact:** Todd Hayden, President. **Description:** An executive search firm. **Specializes in the areas of:** Accounting/ Auditing; Finance. **Positions commonly filled include:** Accountant/Auditor; Administrative Manager; Budget Analyst; Cost Estimator; Credit Manager; Financial Analyst; Finance Manager; Public Accountant. **Number of placements per year:** 50 - 99.

HEALTHCARE RECRUITERS OF MINNESOTA
6442 City West Parkway, Suite 303, Eden Prairie MN 55344. 612/942-5424. **Fax:** 612/942-5452. **Contact:** Steven J. Yungner, President. **World Wide Web address:** http://www.hcrintl.com/ minnesot.html. **Description:** An executive search firm that places sales, sales management, marketing, and executive professionals in the health care industry. **Specializes in the areas of:** Health/Medical; Medical Sales and Marketing. **Positions commonly filled include:** Branch Manager; General Manager; Health Services Manager; Marketing Manager; Medical Sales; Pharmacist; Physical Therapist; Physician; Product Manager; Regulatory Affairs Director; Sales Manager; Sales Representative. **Corporate headquarters location:** Minneapolis MN. **Other U.S. locations:** Nationwide. **Average salary range of placements:** $30,000 - $50,000. **Number of placements per year:** 50 - 99.

HEINZE & ASSOCIATES
6125 Blue Circle Drive, Suite 218, Minnetonka MN 55343. 612/938-2828. **Contact:** Manager. **Description:** An executive search firm. **Specializes in the areas of:** General Management. **Average salary range of placements:** $100,000+.

HILLEREN & ASSOCIATES
3800 West 80th Street, Suite 880, Bloomington MN 55431. 612/956-9090. **Fax:** 612/956-9009. **Contact:** Jerry Hilleren, Owner. **Description:** An executive search firm. **Specializes in the areas of:** Health/Medical; Medical Sales and Marketing. **Positions commonly filled include:** Health Services Manager; Radiological Technologist; Services Sales Representative. **Average salary range of placements:** More than $50,000. **Number of placements per year:** 50 - 99.

T.H. HUNTER, INC.
526 Nicollet Mall, Suite 310, Minneapolis MN 55402. 612/339-0530. **Fax:** 612/338-4757. **Contact:** Martin Conroy, Executive Recruiter. **Description:** An executive search firm. **Specializes in the areas of:** Accounting/Auditing; Administration; Advertising; Banking; Biology; Computer Science/Software; Economics; Engineering; Finance; Food; Health/Medical; Insurance; Legal; Manufacturing; Nonprofit; Personnel/Labor Relations; Publishing; Retail; Sales; Technical. **Positions commonly filled include:** Accountant/Auditor; Actuary; Attorney; Bank Officer/Manager; Biomedical Engineer; Branch Manager; Budget Analyst; Buyer; Computer Programmer; Credit Manager; Economist; Electrical/Electronics Engineer; Financial Analyst; General Manager; Health Services Manager; Human Resources Manager; Internet Services Manager; Licensed Practical Nurse; Management Analyst/Consultant; Manufacturer's/Wholesaler's Sales Rep.; Mechanical Engineer; Mortgage Banker; Occupational Therapist; Physical Therapist; Physician; Quality Control Supervisor; Registered Nurse; Science Technologist; Software Engineer; Speech-Language Pathologist; Systems Analyst; Technical Writer/Editor; Telecommunications Manager; Urban/Regional Planner. **Average salary range of placements:** More than $50,000. **Number of placements per year:** 50 - 99.

JFK SEARCH
10 South Fifth Street, 600 Lumber Exchange Building, Minneapolis MN 55402. 612/332-8082. **Contact:** Manager. **Description:** An executive search firm. **Specializes in the areas of:** Advertising.

JACKLEY SEARCH CONSULTANTS
14581 Grand Avenue South, Burnsville MN 55306. 612/831-2344. **Contact:** Manager. **Description:** An executive search firm. **Specializes in the areas of:** Engineering; High-Tech.

ERIC KERCHEVAL & ASSOCIATES, EXECUTIVE RECRUITERS
15 South First Street, Suite A4, Minneapolis MN 55401. 612/338-7944. **Contact:** Manager. **Description:** An executive search firm. **Specializes in the areas of:** Advertising; Hotel/Restaurant.

GEORGE KONIK ASSOCIATES INC.
7242 Metro Boulevard, Minneapolis MN 55439. 612/835-5550. **Contact:** Manager. **Description:** An executive search firm. **Specializes in the areas of:** Human Resources; Technical.

KORN/FERRY INTERNATIONAL
4816 IDS Center, Minneapolis MN 55402. 612/333-1834. **Contact:** Manager. **Description:** An executive search firm that places upper-level managers in a variety of industries. **Corporate headquarters location:** Los Angeles CA. **International locations:** Worldwide. **Average salary range of placements:** More than $50,000.

LaBREE & ASSOCIATES
5201 Winnetka Avenue North MN 55428. 612/535-5191. **Contact:** Manager. **Description:** LaBree & Associates is an executive search firm. **Specializes in the areas of:** Construction; Finance; Insurance.

SUSAN LEE & ASSOCIATES
6100 Green Valley Drive, Suite 150, Bloomington MN 55438. 612/897-1170. **Contact:** Manager. **Description:** An executive search firm. **Specializes in the areas of:** Printing; Publishing.

HOWARD LIEBERMAN & ASSOCIATES INC.
311 First Avenue North, Suite 503, Minneapolis MN 55401. 612/338-2432. **Fax:** 612/332-8860. **Contact:** Howard Lieberman, President. **E-mail address:** hla503@aol.com. **World Wide Web address:** http://member.aol.com/HLA503/index.html. **Description:** An executive search firm. **Specializes in the areas of:** Legal. **Positions commonly filled include:** Attorney. **Number of placements per year:** 1 - 49.

MANAGEMENT RECRUITERS OF MINNEAPOLIS
SALES CONSULTANTS OF MINNEAPOLIS
7550 France Avenue South, Suite 180, Edina MN 55435. 612/830-1420. **Contact:** Manager. **Description:** An executive search firm operating on a contingency basis. **Specializes in the areas of:** Accounting/Auditing; Administration; Advertising; Architecture/Construction; Banking; Chemicals; Communications; Computer Hardware/Software; Construction; Design; Electrical; Engineering; Finance; Food; General Management; Health/Medical; Industrial; Insurance; Legal; Manufacturing; Operations Management; Personnel/Labor Relations; Pharmaceuticals; Procurement; Publishing; Real Estate; Retail; Sales; Technical; Textiles; Transportation.

MANAGEMENT RECRUITERS OF ROCHESTER
1652 Greenview Drive SW, Suite 600, Rochester MN 55902. 507/282-2400. **Contact:** Nona Vierkant, Chief Financial Officer. **Description:** An executive search firm operating on a contingency basis. **Specializes in the areas of:** Computer Science/Software. **Positions commonly filled include:** Computer Programmer; Systems Analyst. **Average salary range of placements:** $30,000 - $50,000. **Number of placements per year:** 1 - 49.

LEE MARSH & ASSOCIATES
1469 Highview Avenue, Eagan MN 55121. 612/452-5412. **Fax:** 612/452-9051. **Contact:** Lee Marsh, Owner. **E-mail address:** marsh042@gold.tc.umn.edu. **Description:** Lee Marsh & Associates is an executive search firm. **Specializes in the areas of:** Software Engineering; Technical. **Positions commonly filled include:** Computer Programmer; Design Engineer; Electrical/Electronics Engineer; Sales Representative; Software Engineer; Systems Analyst. **Number of placements per year:** 50 - 99.

BRAD MARTIN & ASSOCIATES
5353 Wayzata Boulevard, Suite 403, Minneapolis MN 55416. 612/544-4130. **Contact:** Manager. **Description:** Brad Martin & Associates is an executive search firm. **Specializes in the areas of:** Manufacturing.

MARY L. MAYER, LTD.
P.O. Box 250, Medina MN 55340-0250. 612/473-7700. **Fax:** 612/449-0772. **Contact:** Mary Mayer, President. **Description:** An executive search firm focusing on the property/casualty insurance industry. **Specializes in the areas of:** Insurance; Sales. **Positions commonly filled include:** Actuary; Adjuster; Administrative Manager; Branch Manager; Claim Representative; Clerical Supervisor; Customer Service Representative; General Manager; Human Resources Specialist; Insurance Agent/Broker; MIS Specialist; Systems Analyst; Underwriter/Assistant Underwriter. **Average salary range of placements:** More than $50,000. **Number of placements per year:** 1 - 49.

MEDSEARCH CORPORATION
6545 France Avenue South, Edina MN 55435. 612/926-6584. **Contact:** Manager. **Description:** An executive search firm. **Specializes in the areas of:** Health/Medical. **Positions commonly filled include:** Physician.

METRO HOSPITALITY CONSULTANTS
9448 Lyndale Avenue South, Suite 223, Bloomington MN 55420. 612/884-4299. **Contact:** Debra Kiefat, President. **Description:** An executive search firm. **Specializes in the areas of:** Food; Hotel/Restaurant. **Positions commonly filled include:** Restaurant/Food Service Manager. **Corporate headquarters location:** Minneapolis MN. **Number of placements per year:** 1 - 49.

C.A. MOORE & ASSOCIATES, INC.
15500 Wayzata Boulevard, Suite 803C, Wayzata MN 55391. 612/473-0990. **Contact:** Connie Moore, President. **E-mail address:** camoore@mcg.net. **Description:** An executive search firm operating on both retainer and contingency bases. **Specializes in the areas of:** Accounting/Auditing; Direct Marketing; Finance; Insurance; Legal; Risk Management. **Positions commonly filled include:** Accountant/Auditor; Adjuster; Administrative Worker/Clerk; Attorney; Controller; Finance Director; Financial Analyst; General Manager; Human Resources Manager; Insurance Agent/Broker; Operations/Production Manager; Sales Executive; Sales Manager; Sales Representative; Underwriter/Assistant Underwriter. **Number of placements per year:** 1 - 49.

NER, INC. (NATIONAL ENGINEERING RESOURCES)
6200 Shingle Creek Parkway, Suite 160, Brooklyn Center MN 55430. 612/561-7610. **Toll-free phone:** 800/665-7610. **Fax:** 612/561-7675. **Contact:** Technical Recruiter. **E-mail address:** nerinc@sprynet.com. **World Wide Web address:** http://www.occ.com/ner. **Description:** An executive search firm focusing on the placement of engineering, technical, and scientific personnel. **Specializes in the areas of:** Administration; Clerical; Computer Hardware/Software; Engineering; Industrial; Medical Technology; Oil and Gas; Petrochemical; Publishing; Technical. **Positions commonly filled include:** Administrative Manager; Agricultural Engineer; Aircraft Mechanic/Engine Specialist; Ceramics Engineer; Computer Programmer; Materials Engineer; Medical Assistant; Metallurgical Engineer; Nuclear Engineer; Quality Control Supervisor; Software Engineer; Structural Engineer; Systems Analyst. **Number of placements per year:** 1 - 49.

NESS GROUP INC.
52 East Pleasant Lake Road, St. Paul MN 55127-2117. 651/482-8004. **Fax:** 651/482-0993. **Contact:** Manager. **E-mail address:** recruitur@aol.com. **Description:** An executive search firm.

G.J. NIENHAUS & ASSOCIATES
2800 East Cliff Road, Suite 260, Burnsville MN 55337. 612/890-5702. **Contact:** Manager. **Description:** An executive search firm. **Specializes in the areas of:** Packaging.

NORTH AMERICAN RECRUITERS
4725 Olson Memorial Highway, Suite 100, Golden Valley MN 55422. 612/591-1951. **Toll-free phone:** 800/886-7598. **Fax:** 612/591-5850. **Contact:** David Knutson, President. **Description:** An executive search firm operating on a retainer basis. **Specializes in the areas of:** Accounting/Auditing; Administration; Computer Science/Software; Engineering; Finance; General Management; Health/Medical; Industrial; Manufacturing; Sales; Technical. **Positions commonly filled include:** Accountant/Auditor; Computer Programmer; Customer Service Representative; Electrical/Electronics Engineer; Financial Analyst; General Manager; Industrial Engineer; Industrial Production Manager; Mechanical Engineer; Operations/Production Manager; Purchasing Agent/Manager; Services Sales Representative; Software Engineer; Systems Analyst; Telecommunications Manager. **Average salary range of placements:** More than $50,000. **Number of placements per year:** 100 - 199.

NORTHLAND EMPLOYMENT SERVICES INC.
10801 Wayzata Boulevard, Suite 325, Minnetonka MN 55305. 612/541-1060. **Fax:** 612/595-9878. **Contact:** David Gavin, President. **World Wide Web address:** http://www.jobsmn.com. **Description:** An executive search firm operating on both retainer and contingency bases. **Specializes in the areas of:** Architecture/Construction; Biology; Computer Science/Software; Engineering; Technical. **Positions commonly filled include:** Biochemist; Biological Scientist; Biomedical Engineer; Chemical Engineer; Chemist; Civil Engineer; Computer Animator; Computer Operator; Construction Contractor; Database Manager; Design Engineer; Electrical/Electronics Engineer; Environmental Engineer; Geologist/Geophysicist; Industrial Engineer; Manufacturing Engineer; Mechanical Engineer; MIS Specialist; Project Manager;

Quality Control Supervisor; Software Engineer; Systems Analyst; Systems Manager; Webmaster. **Average salary range of placements:** More than $50,000. **Number of placements per year:** 200 - 499.

NYCOR SEARCH INC.
4930 West 77th Street, Suite 300, Minneapolis MN 55435-4809. 612/831-6444. **Fax:** 612/835-2883. **Contact:** Manager. **E-mail address:** jobs@nycor.com. **World Wide Web address:** http://www.nycor.com. **Description:** An executive search firm that focuses on the placement of experienced professionals in engineering and other technical disciplines. **Specializes in the areas of:** Architecture/Construction; Computer Science/Software; Engineering; General Management; Industrial; Manufacturing; Technical. **Positions commonly filled include:** Biomedical Engineer; Chemical Engineer; Chemist; Civil Engineer; Clinical Lab Technician; Computer Programmer; Design Engineer; Designer; Draftsperson; Electrical/Electronics Engineer; Food Scientist/Technologist; General Manager; Industrial Engineer; Internet Services Manager; Materials Engineer; Mathematician; Mechanical Engineer; Metallurgical Engineer; MIS Specialist; Multimedia Designer; Operations/Production Manager; Petroleum Engineer; Purchasing Agent/Manager; Quality Control Supervisor; Science Technologist; Software Engineer; Systems Analyst; Technical Writer/Editor; Telecommunications Manager. **Benefits available to temporary workers:** Medical Insurance; Paid Holidays; Paid Vacation. **Average salary range of placements:** More than $50,000. **Number of placements per year:** 200 - 499.

PERSONNEL ASSISTANCE CORPORATION
1242 Homestead Trail, Long Lake MN 55356. 612/476-0674. **Contact:** Donald E. Pearson, President. **Description:** An executive search firm operating on a contingency basis. **Specializes in the areas of:** Engineering; Industrial; Manufacturing; Technical. **Positions commonly filled include:** Agricultural Engineer; Design Engineer; Designer; General Manager; Industrial Production Manager; Mechanical Engineer; Operations/Production Manager. **Average salary range of placements:** $30,000 - $100,000. **Number of placements per year:** 1 - 49.

PIONEER SEARCH, INC.
P.O. Box 277, Center City MN 55012. 651/257-3957. **Contact:** Manager. **Description:** An executive search firm. **Specializes in the areas of:** Computer Hardware/Software; Engineering.

PROFESSIONAL RECRUITERS, INC.
17641 Kettering Trail, Lakeville MN 55044-9344. 612/892-3700. **Fax:** 612/892-3711. **Contact:** Robert Reinitz, Principal. **E-mail address:** headhunt@primenet.com. **World Wide Web address:** http://professionalrecruiters.com. **Description:** An executive search firm operating on both retainer and contingency bases. **Specializes in the areas of:** Electrical; Electronics; High-Tech; Industrial; Management; Marketing; Sales. **Positions commonly filled include:** Account Representative; Applications Engineer; Marketing Manager; Product Manager; Sales Engineer; Sales Manager; Vice President of Marketing; Vice President of Sales. **Average salary range of placements:** More than $50,000. **Number of placements per year:** 1 - 49.

PROGRAMMING ALTERNATIVES OF MINNESOTA, INC.
7701 France Avenue South, Suite 100, Edina MN 55435. 612/841-1188. **Contact:** Kenneth Rosaro, Divisional Manager. **Description:** An executive search firm that focuses on information technology staffing and consulting. **Specializes in the areas of:** Biotechnology; Computer Science/Software; Data Processing; Engineering; Industrial; Information Technology; Manufacturing; Technical. **Positions commonly filled include:** Aerospace Engineer; Biological Scientist; Biomedical Engineer; Chemical Engineer; Computer Programmer; Design Engineer; Electrical/Electronics Engineer; Industrial Designer; Mechanical Engineer; Metallurgical Engineer; MIS Specialist; Operations/Production Manager; Physicist; Purchasing Agent/Manager; Quality Control Supervisor; Software Engineer; Systems Analyst; Technical Writer/Editor; Telecommunications Manager. **Corporate headquarters location:** Minneapolis MN. **Average salary range of placements:** More than $50,000. **Number of placements per year:** 50 - 99.

QUANTUM CONSULTING & PLACEMENT
6600 City West Parkway, Suite 310, Eden Prairie MN 55344. 612/829-5950. **Fax:** 612/829-5988. **Contact:** Doug Berg, President/Recruiter. **World Wide Web address:** http://www.qconsult.com. **Description:** An executive search firm. **Specializes in the areas of:** Computer Science/Software. **Positions commonly filled include:** Computer Programmer; Systems Analyst. **Number of placements per year:** 1 - 49.

RAUENHORST RECRUITING COMPANY
7600 Parklawn Avenue, Suite 215, Edina MN 55435. 612/897-1420. **Contact:** Manager. **Description:** A generalist executive search firm.

REGENCY RECRUITERS, INC.
7101 York Avenue South, Suite 248, Edina MN 55435-4450. 612/921-3377. **Contact:** David Tetzloff, President. **Description:** An executive search firm focusing on engineering positions, including electrical and mechanical design, software, and manufacturing. **Specializes in the areas of:** Computer Science/Software; Electrical; Engineering; Industrial; Manufacturing; Mechanical; Technical. **Positions commonly filled include:** Aerospace Engineer; Biomedical Engineer; Chemical Engineer; Computer Programmer; Draftsperson; Electrical/Electronics Engineer; Mechanical Engineer; Metallurgical Engineer; Quality Control Supervisor; Software Engineer. **Average salary range of placements:** More than $50,000.

RESOURCE SEARCH
8301 Golden Valley Road, Suite 240, Golden Valley MN 55427. 612/546-0099. **Fax:** 612/546-4102. **Contact:** John Breczinski, President. **Description:** An executive search firm. **Specializes in the areas of:** Advertising; Art/Design; Engineering; Food; General Management; Health/Medical; Industrial; Manufacturing; Sales. **Positions commonly filled include:** Design Engineer; Designer; Electrical/Electronics Engineer; General Manager; Manufacturer's/Wholesaler's Sales Rep.; Market Research Analyst; Mechanical Engineer; Operations/Production Manager; Public Relations Specialist; Services Sales Representative. **Average salary range of placements:** More than $50,000. **Number of placements per year:** 1 - 49.

ROTH YOUNG EXECUTIVE RECRUITERS
4620 West 77th Street, Suite 290, Edina MN 55435-4924. 612/831-6655. **Fax:** 612/831-7413. **Contact:** Donald Spahr, President. **Description:** An executive search firm. **Specializes in the areas of:** Fashion; Food; Health/Medical; Hotel/Restaurant; Personnel/Labor Relations; Retail; Sales. **Positions commonly filled include:** Buyer; Food Scientist/Technologist; Hotel Manager; Human Resources Manager; Manufacturer's/Wholesaler's Sales Rep.; Occupational Therapist; Physical Therapist; Quality Control Supervisor; Recreational Therapist; Restaurant/Food Service Manager; Retail Manager; Sales Representative; Speech-Language Pathologist. **Number of placements per year:** 50 - 99.

RUSSELL REYNOLDS ASSOCIATES, INC.
90 South Seventh Street, Suite 3050, Minneapolis MN 55402. 612/332-6966. **Contact:** Manager. **Description:** A generalist executive search firm.

SATHE & ASSOCIATES EXECUTIVE SEARCH
5821 Cedar Lake Road, St. Louis Park MN 55416. 612/546-2100. **Fax:** 612/546-6930. **Contact:** Mark Sathe, President. **Description:** An executive search firm. **Specializes in the areas of:** Accounting/Auditing; Administration; Architecture/Construction; Banking; Engineering; Finance; Food; General Management; Industrial; Manufacturing; Nonprofit; Personnel/Labor Relations; Sales. **Positions commonly filled include:** Accountant/Auditor; Bank Officer/Manager; Buyer; Electrical/Electronics Engineer; Hotel Manager; Industrial Engineer; Mechanical Engineer; Purchasing Agent/Manager; Quality Control Supervisor. **Number of placements per year:** 1 - 49.

SCHALEKAMP & ASSOCIATES, INC.
2608 West 102nd Street, Minneapolis MN 55431-3346. 612/948-1948. **Fax:** 612/948-9677. **Contact:** Paul D. Schalekamp, President. **E-mail address:** schalekamp@aol.com. **Description:** An executive search firm that focuses on placing property and casualty insurance professionals. **Specializes in the areas of:** Insurance. **Positions commonly filled include:** Adjuster; Claim Representative; Insurance Agent/Broker; Loss Prevention Specialist; MIS Specialist; Risk Manager. **Average salary range of placements:** More than $50,000. **Number of placements per year:** 1 - 49.

SEARCH SPECIALISTS
2655 North Shore Drive, Wayzata MN 55391. 612/449-8990. **Fax:** 612/449-0369. **Contact:** Tim Lindell, Vice President of Administration. **E-mail address:** clindell@sprynet.com. **World Wide Web address:** http://www.cities-online.com/search. **Description:** An executive search firm. Employer pays fee. **Specializes in the areas of:** Architecture/Construction; Computer Science/Software; Data Processing; Engineering; Marketing; Sales; Software Development. **Positions commonly filled include:** Architect; Civil Engineer; Design Engineer; Draftsperson; Electrical/Electronics Engineer; Landscape Architect; Mechanical Engineer; MIS Specialist; Software Engineer; Structural Engineer. **Average salary range of placements:** $50,000 - $100,000. **Number of placements per year:** 1 - 49.

SEARCHTEK
4900 North Highway 169, Suite 309, New Hope MN 55428. 612/531-0766. **Fax:** 612/531-0667. **Contact:** Gerald Otten, President. **World Wide Web address:** http://www.usinterpage.com/

searchtek.htm. **Description:** A high-tech recruiting firm that operates on both retainer and contingency bases. **Specializes in the areas of:** Engineering; High-Tech. **Positions commonly filled include:** Biomedical Engineer; Computer Programmer; Electrical/Electronics Engineer; Industrial Engineer; Industrial Production Manager; Manufacturing Engineer; Mechanical Engineer; Metallurgical Engineer; Production Manager; Quality Control Supervisor; Software Engineer. **Corporate headquarters location:** This Location. **Other U.S. locations:** Nationwide. **International locations:** Worldwide. **Average salary range of placements:** More than $50,000. **Number of placements per year:** 1 - 49.

SOURCE SERVICES CORPORATION
Pillsbury Center South, 220 South Sixth Street, Suite 810, Minneapolis MN 55402. 612/332-6460. **Contact:** Manager. **Description:** An executive search firm. Other divisions at this location include Source EDP and Accountant Source Temps. **Specializes in the areas of:** Accounting/Auditing; Computer Hardware/Software; Information Technology.

STAFF CONNECTION, INC.
15500 Wayzata Boulevard, Wayzata MN 55391. 612/475-1554. **Contact:** Craig Lyon, Secretary/Treasurer. **E-mail address:** sci@mm.com. **Description:** An executive search firm operating on a contingency basis. **Specializes in the areas of:** Computer Science/Software; Engineering; Technical. **Positions commonly filled include:** Computer Programmer; Internet Services Manager; MIS Specialist; Software Engineer; Systems Analyst. **Corporate headquarters location:** Minneapolis MN. **Other U.S. locations:** Phoenix AZ; Las Vegas NV. **Average salary range of placements:** $30,000 - $90,000.

SYSTEMS SEARCH, INC.
P.O. Box 600, Anoka MN 55303. 612/323-9690. **Contact:** Mike Fitzpatrick, President. **E-mail address:** 74352.3305@compuserve.com. **Description:** An executive search firm that recruits and places computer professionals including systems analysts, consultants, engineers, administrators, and programmers. **Specializes in the areas of:** Administration; Computer Science/Software. **Positions commonly filled include:** Computer Programmer; Internet Services Manager; Management Analyst/Consultant; MIS Specialist; Multimedia Designer; Software Engineer; Systems Analyst; Telecommunications Manager. **Average salary range of placements:** $30,000 - $50,000. **Number of placements per year:** 1 - 49.

RICHARD THOMPSON ASSOCIATES
701 Fourth Avenue South, Suite 500, Minneapolis MN 55415. 612/339-6060. **Contact:** Manager. **Description:** An executive search firm.

TOTAL SEARCH
1541 Berne Road, Fridley MN 55421. 612/571-0247. **Contact:** Tom Harrington, President. **Description:** An executive search firm operating on a contingency basis. **Specializes in the areas of:** Computer Science/Software; Food; Retail. **Positions commonly filled include:** Computer Programmer; Restaurant/Food Service Manager; Retail Manager; Systems Analyst. **Number of placements per year:** 50 - 99.

TWIN CITY SEARCH
3989 Central Avenue North, Suite 215, Minneapolis MN 55421. 612/789-4537. **Contact:** Manager. **Description:** An executive search firm. **Specializes in the areas of:** Computer Hardware/Software; Technical.

WILLIAMS EXECUTIVE SEARCH
4200 Norwest Center, 90 South Seventh Street, Minneapolis MN 55402. 612/339-2900. **Contact:** Manager. **Description:** An executive search firm.

CONTRACT SERVICES FIRMS

CDI CORPORATION
510 First Avenue North, Suite 600, Minneapolis MN 55403. 612/541-9967. **Fax:** 612/541-9605. **Contact:** Manager. **World Wide Web address:** http://www.cdicorp.com. **Description:** A contract services firm. **Specializes in the areas of:** Technical. **Corporate headquarters location:** Philadelphia PA. **Other U.S. locations:** Nationwide. **International locations:** Worldwide.

CDI CORPORATION
1915 Highway 52 North, Suite 222-B, Rochester MN 55901. **Toll-free phone:** 888/686-8979. **Contact:** Manager. **World Wide Web address:** http://www.cdicorp.com. **Description:** A contract services firm. **Specializes in the areas of:** Engineering; Technical. **Corporate headquarters location:** Philadelphia PA. **Other U.S. locations:** Nationwide. **International locations:** Worldwide.

CONSULTIS
8500 Normandale Lake Boulevard, Suite 1670, Bloomington MN 55437. 612/921-8866. **Contact:** Manager. **Description:** A contract services firm. **Specializes in the areas of:** Information Technology.

HUMAN RESOURCE STAFFING, INC.
7242 Metro Boulevard, Minneapolis MN 55439. 612/835-5550. **Fax:** 612/835-7294. **Contact:** Cindy Ridley, Recruiter. **Description:** A contract services firm. **Specializes in the areas of:** Human Resources; Personnel/Labor Relations. **Positions commonly filled include:** Human Resources Manager; Recruiter. **Benefits available to temporary workers:** 401(k); Dental Insurance; Medical Insurance; Paid Holidays; Paid Vacation. **Average salary range of placements:** $30,000 - $50,000. **Number of placements per year:** 1 - 49.

MANPOWER TECHNICAL
3800 West 80th Street, Suite 260, Bloomington MN 55431. 612/820-0365. **Fax:** 612/820-0350. **Contact:** Manager. **Description:** A contract services firm. **Specializes in the areas of:** Administration; Computer Science/Software; Engineering; Finance; Industrial; Manufacturing; Personnel/Labor Relations; Publishing; Technical. **Positions commonly filled include:** Accountant/Auditor; Administrative Manager; Aerospace Engineer; Aircraft Mechanic/Engine Specialist; Bank Officer/Manager; Biochemist; Biological Scientist; Biomedical Engineer; Blue-Collar Worker Supervisor; Branch Manager; Broadcast Technician; Chemical Engineer; Computer Programmer; Credit Manager; Customer Service Representative; Design Engineer; Designer; Draftsperson; Editor; Electrical/Electronics Engineer; Environmental Engineer; Financial Analyst; Food Scientist/Technologist; General Manager; Geologist/Geophysicist; Human Resources Specialist; Industrial Engineer; Industrial Production Manager; Insurance Agent/Broker; Internet Services Manager; Library Technician; Management Analyst/Consultant; Management Trainee; Manufacturer's/Wholesaler's Sales Rep.; Market Research Analyst; Materials Engineer; Mathematician; Mechanical Engineer; Metallurgical Engineer; MIS Specialist; Multimedia Designer; Nuclear Engineer; Operations/Production Manager; Paralegal; Physicist; Purchasing Agent/Manager; Quality Control Supervisor; Science Technologist; Securities Sales Representative; Services Sales Representative; Software Engineer; Structural Engineer; Systems Analyst; Technical Writer/Editor; Telecommunications Manager; Typist/Word Processor; Underwriter/Assistant Underwriter; Video Production Coordinator. **Benefits available to temporary workers:** 401(k); Medical Insurance. **Corporate headquarters location:** Milwaukee WI. **Other U.S. locations:** Nationwide. **Average salary range of placements:** More than $50,000. **Number of placements per year:** 500 - 999.

PRECISION DESIGN, INC.
15 10th Avenue South, Suite 102, Hopkins MN 55343-7561. 612/933-6550. **Fax:** 612/933-0344. **Contact:** Larry Helgerson, President. **World Wide Web address:** http://www.mn-jobs.com/precisiondesign/index.html. **Description:** A contract services firm. **Specializes in the areas of:** Engineering. **Positions commonly filled include:** Design Engineer; Draftsperson; Electrical/Electronics Engineer; Industrial Engineer; Manufacturing Engineer; Mechanical Engineer; Software Engineer; Technical Writer/Editor. **Benefits available to temporary workers:** 401(k); Medical Insurance; Paid Holidays; Paid Vacation. **Average salary range of placements:** More than $50,000. **Number of placements per year:** 100 - 199.

THE RESOURCE GROUP
LABORATORY RESOURCES INC.
7700 Equitable Drive, Suite 101, Eden Prairie MN 55344. 612/974-9225. **Toll-free phone:** 800/298-5627. **Contact:** Account Manager. **E-mail address:** lri@rsgi.com. **Description:** A contract services firm. **Specializes in the areas of:** Biology; Technical. **Positions commonly filled include:** Biological Scientist; Biomedical Engineer; Chemical Engineer; Chemist; Clinical Lab Technician; Food Scientist/Technologist; Forester/Conservation Scientist; Geologist/Geophysicist; Quality Control Supervisor; Science Technologist. **Benefits available to temporary workers:** 401(k); Dental Insurance; Medical Insurance; Paid Holidays; Paid Vacation. **Average salary range of placements:** $30,000 - $50,000. **Number of placements per year:** 50 - 99.

SOURCE SERVICES CORPORATION
8500 Normandale Lake Boulevard, Suite 2160, Bloomington MN 55437-3833. 612/835-5100. **Fax:** 612/835-1548. **Contact:** Recruiter. **E-mail address:** weibyek@sourcesvc.com. **World Wide Web address:** http://www.sourceminnesota.com. **Description:** A contract services firm that also offers temporary placements. **Specializes in the areas of:** Accounting/Auditing; Computer Science/Software; Secretarial. **Positions commonly filled include:** Accountant/Auditor; Budget Analyst; Computer Programmer; Financial Analyst; MIS Specialist; Software Engineer; Systems Analyst; Telecommunications Manager; Typist/Word Processor. **Benefits available to temporary workers:** Medical Insurance; Paid Vacation; Profit Sharing. **Corporate headquarters location:** Dallas TX. **Other U.S. locations:** Nationwide. **Average salary range of placements:** $30,000 - $50,000. **Number of placements per year:** 200 - 499.

STROM AVIATION
10501 Wayzata Boulevard, Minnetonka MN 55305. 612/544-3611. **Toll-free phone:** 800/743-8988. **Fax:** 612/544-3948. **Contact:** Lead Recruiter. **Description:** A contract services firm that provides experienced aircraft maintenance personnel to heavy maintenance overhaul repair stations for all types of aircraft. **Positions commonly filled include:** Aircraft Mechanic/Engine Specialist. **Benefits available to temporary workers:** Paid Holidays; Paid Vacation. **Corporate headquarters location:** Minneapolis MN. **Other U.S. locations:** Tempe AZ; Dallas TX. **Average salary range of placements:** $20,000 - $29,999.

SYSDYNE CORPORATION
1660 South Highway 100, Suite 424, Minneapolis MN 55416-1533. 612/541-9889. **Toll-free phone:** 888/797-3963. **Fax:** 612/541-9887. **Contact:** Jannie Crabtree Higgins, Recruiter. **E-mail address:** techjobs@sysdyne.com. **World Wide Web address:** http://www.sysdyne.com. **Description:** A contract services firm that provides professional technical staffing. **Specializes in the areas of:** Computer Science/Software; Engineering; Technical. **Positions commonly filled include:** Biomedical Engineer; Computer Programmer; Design Engineer; Draftsperson; Electrical/Electronics Engineer; Mechanical Engineer; MIS Specialist; Sales Engineer; Software Engineer; Technical Writer/Editor. **Benefits available to temporary workers:** 401(k); Cafeteria; Savings Plan. **Average salary range of placements:** $30,000 - $50,000. **Number of placements per year:** 50 - 99.

H.L. YOH COMPANY
2626 East 82nd Street, Suite 355, Bloomington MN 55425. 612/854-2400. **Toll-free phone:** 888/243-3557. **Fax:** 612/854-0512. **Contact:** Linda Eisenzimmer, Technical Recruiter. **E-mail address:** lindayoh@skypoint.com. **Description:** A contract services firm. **Specializes in the areas of:** Computer Science/Software; Engineering; Industrial; Technical. **Positions commonly filled include:** Administrative Assistant; Buyer; Chemical Engineer; Chemist; Computer Operator; Computer Programmer; Database Manager; Design Engineer; Draftsperson; Electrical/Electronics Engineer; Environmental Engineer; Graphic Artist; Graphic Designer; Industrial Engineer; Industrial Production Manager; Manufacturing Engineer; Mechanical Engineer; Metallurgical Engineer; Operations Manager; Project Manager; Purchasing Agent/Manager; Quality Control Supervisor; Secretary; Software Engineer; Systems Analyst; Systems Manager; Technical Writer/Editor; Typist/Word Processor. **Benefits available to temporary workers:** 401(k); Credit Union; Disability Coverage; Medical Insurance. **Corporate headquarters location:** Philadelphia PA. **Other U.S. locations:** Nationwide. **International locations:** China. **Average salary range of placements:** $30,000 - $50,000. **Number of placements per year:** 200 - 499.

RESUME/CAREER COUNSELING SERVICES

ALLEN & ASSOCIATES
6600 France Avenue South, Suite 615, Minneapolis MN 55435. 612/925-9646. **Toll-free phone:** 800/562-7925. **Fax:** 612/925-9662. **Contact:** Manager. **World Wide Web address:** http://www.allenandassociates.com. **Description:** A career/outplacement counseling firm. **Corporate headquarters location:** Maitland FL. **Other U.S. locations:** Nationwide.

QUALITY OFFICE SERVICES
12710 Falcon Court North, White Bear Lake MN 55110. 651/426-2516. **Contact:** Mrs. Lois M. Rather, Owner. **Description:** A professional resume writing service.

WORKING OPPORTUNITIES FOR WOMEN
1295 Bandana Boulevard North, Suite 110, St. Paul MN 55108. 651/647-9961. **Contact:** Yvette Oldendorf, President. **Description:** A career/outplacement counseling firm that provides career development and planning services for women.

INDEX OF PRIMARY EMPLOYERS

NOTE: *Below is an alphabetical index of primary employer listings included in this book. Those employers in each industry that fall under the headings "Additional employers" are not indexed here.*

C

D

E

F

Your Job Hunt
Your Feedback

Comments, questions, or suggestions? We want to hear from you! Please complete this questionnaire and mail it to:

The JobBank Staff
Adams Media Corporation
260 Center Street
Holbrook, MA 02343

or send us an e-mail at **jobbank@adamsonline.com**

Did this book provide helpful advice and valuable information which you used in your job search? What did you like about it?

How could we improve this book to help you in your job search? Is there a specific company we left out or an industry you'd like to see more of in a future edition? No suggestion is too small or too large.

Would you recommend this book to a friend beginning a job hunt?

Name: _____

Occupation: _____

Which JobBank did you use? _____

Mailing address: _____

E-mail address: _____

Daytime phone: _____

JobBank List Service
Custom-Designed For Your Job Search

Generated by the same editors who bring you the nationally renowned *JobBank* series, the electronic *JobBank List Service* is a compilation of company information that is important to you. Our huge database is updated year-round to ensure that our data is as accurate as possible. Our company information is available to you by e-mail or on disk in ASCII delimited text format.

Whether you're looking for a small company to work for, or a large corporation to do business with, *JobBank List Service* can help! *JobBank List Service* is not mass-produced for the general public; it is built for *you* through a personal consultation with a member of the *JobBank* staff.

While other services offer their company information on pre-generated disk or CD-ROM, we construct the data explicitly to match your criteria. Your *JobBank* consultant will work with you to find the company information that applies to your specific job search needs. Criteria for companies or employment agencies can be specified geographically, by industry, by occupation, or any variation or combination you can imagine... you decide.

With the most current information on companies in more than thirty industries, job-seekers, recruiters, and businesses alike will find the *JobBank List Service* the perfect solution to their personal and professional needs. Industries covered include:

- *Accounting and Management Consulting*
- *Advertising, Marketing, and Public Relations*
- *Aerospace*
- *Apparel, Fashion & Textiles*
- *Architecture, Construction, and Engineering*
- *Arts, Entertainment, Sports, & Recreation*
- *Automotive*
- *Banking/Savings and Loans*
- *Biotechnology, Pharmaceuticals & Scientific R&D*
- *Charities and Social Services*
- *Chemicals/Rubber & Plastics*

- *Communications: Telecommunications & Broadcasting*
- *Computer Hardware, Software, and Services*
- *Educational Services*
- *Electronic/Industrial Electrical Equipment*
- *Environmental & Waste Management Services*
- *Fabricated/Primary Metals & Products*
- *Financial Services*
- *Food & Beverages/Agriculture*
- *Government*
- *Health Care: Services, Equipment & Products*

- *Hotels & Restaurants*
- *Insurance*
- *Manufacturing*
- *Mining/Gas/Petroleum/Energy Related*
- *Paper & Wood Products*
- *Printing and Publishing*
- *Real Estate*
- *Retail*
- *Stone, Glass, Clay, and Concrete Products*
- *Transportation*
- *Utilities*
- *Miscellaneous Wholesaling and many others*

- NO MINIMUM ORDER — NO ORDER IS TOO SMALL!
- THOUSANDS OF PRIVATE & PUBLIC COMPANIES IN <u>ALL</u> 50 STATES & DC
- THOUSANDS OF EMPLOYMENT SERVICES
- EACH LISTING INCLUDES THE SAME TYPE OF DETAILED CONTACT & BUSINESS INFORMATION OFFERED IN THE *JOBBANK* BOOK SERIES
- STANDING ORDER DISCOUNTS ARE AVAILABLE

Contact a *JobBank* staff member now for your individual consultation and pricing information.
E-mail: jobbank@adamsonline.com
Phone: 800/872-5627 x5304 (in MA: 781/767-8100 x5304)
Fax: 781/767-2055

Other Adams Media Books

The Adams Jobs Almanac

Updated annually, *The Adams Jobs Almanac* includes names and addresses of over 7,000 U.S. employers; information on which positions each company commonly fills; industry forecasts; geographical cross-references; employment prospects in all 50 states; and advice on preparing resumes and cover letters and standing out at interviews. $5\frac{1}{2}$" x $8\frac{1}{2}$", 952 pages, paperback, $16.95.

The JobBank Series

There are 35 *JobBank* books, each providing extensive, up-to-date employment information on hundreds of the largest employers in each job market. The #1 best-selling series of employment directories, the *JobBank* series has been recommended as an excellent place to begin your job search by the *New York Times*, the *Los Angeles Times*, the *Boston Globe*, and the *Chicago Tribune*. *JobBank* books have been used by millions of people to find jobs. Titles available:

The Atlanta JobBank • The Austin/San Antonio JobBank • The Boston JobBank • The Carolina JobBank • The Chicago JobBank • The Connecticut JobBank • The Dallas-Fort Worth JobBank • The Denver JobBank • The Detroit JobBank • The Florida JobBank • The Houston JobBank • The Indiana JobBank • The Las Vegas JobBank • The Los Angeles JobBank • The Minneapolis-St. Paul JobBank • The Missouri JobBank • The Northern New England JobBank • The New Jersey JobBank • The New Mexico JobBank • The Metropolitan New York JobBank • The Upstate New York JobBank • The Ohio JobBank • The Greater Philadelphia JobBank • The Phoenix JobBank • The Pittsburgh JobBank • The Portland JobBank • The Salt Lake City JobBank • The San Francisco Bay Area JobBank • The Seattle JobBank • The Tennessee JobBank • The Virginia JobBank • The Metropolitan Washington DC JobBank • The Wisconsin JobBank • The JobBank Guide to Computer & High-Tech Companies • The JobBank Guide to Health Care Companies

EACH JOBBANK BOOK IS 6" X $9\frac{1}{4}$", OVER 300 PAGES, PAPERBACK, $16.95.

 JobBank List Service: If you are interested in variations of this information in electronic format for sales or job search mailings, please call 800-872-5627 x5304, or e-mail us at jobbank@adamsonline.com.

Available Wherever Books Are Sold

If you cannot find these titles at your favorite retail outlet, you may order them directly from the publisher. BY PHONE: Call 1-800-872-5627. We accept Visa, Mastercard, and American Express. $4.95 will be added to your total order for shipping and handling. BY MAIL: Write out the full titles of the books you'd like to order and send payment, including $4.95 for shipping and handling, to: Adams Media Corporation, 260 Center Street, Holbrook, MA 02343. 30-day money-back guarantee. BY FAX: 800-872-5628. BY E-MAIL: jobbank@adamsonline.com. *Discounts available for standing orders.*

Visit our exciting job and career site at http://www.careercity.com

Other Adams Media Books

The Adams Electronic Job Search Almanac 1999

Uncover thousands of jobs in minutes using your own computer! This comprehensive guide features hundreds of online resources available through commercial online services, the World Wide Web, newsgroups, and more. *The Adams Electronic Job Search Almanac 1999* also includes a selection of company joblines, advice on posting an electronic resume, and strategies for researching companies on the Internet. The book also features information on a variety of job-hunting software. $5\frac{1}{2}$" x $8\frac{1}{2}$", 312 pages, paperback, $10.95.

The Adams Executive Recruiters Almanac

The Adams Executive Recruiters Almanac contains comprehensive, up-to-date information on 7,000 executive search firms, permanent employment agencies, contract services firms, temporary agencies, and career/outplacement counseling firms nationwide. Recruiter profiles include names, addresses, phone and fax numbers, agency descriptions, information on each recruiter's areas of specialization, positions commonly filled, and benefits provided. Indexed by specialization and alphabetically. $5\frac{1}{2}$" x $8\frac{1}{2}$", 762 pages, paperback, $16.95.

The Adams Job Interview Almanac

The Adams Job Interview Almanac includes answers and discussions for over 1,800 interview questions. There are 100 complete job interviews for all fields, industries, and career levels. Also included is valuable information on handling stress interviews, strategies for second and third interviews, and negotiating job offers to get what you want. $5\frac{1}{2}$" x $8\frac{1}{2}$", 840 pages, paperback, $12.95.

Available Wherever Books Are Sold

If you cannot find these titles at your favorite retail outlet, you may order them directly from the publisher. BY PHONE: Call 1-800-872-5627. We accept Visa, Mastercard, and American Express. $4.95 will be added to your total order for shipping and handling. BY MAIL: Write out the full titles of the books you'd like to order and send payment, including $4.95 for shipping and handling, to: Adams Media Corporation, 260 Center Street, Holbrook, MA 02343. 30-day money-back guarantee.

Visit our exciting job and career site at http://www.careercity.com

Other Adams Media Books

The Adams Cover Letter Almanac

The Adams Cover Letter Almanac is the most detailed cover letter resource in print, containing 600 cover letters used by real people to win real jobs. It features complete information on all types of letters, including networking, "cold," broadcast, and follow-up. In addition to advice on how to avoid fatal cover letter mistakes, the book includes strategies for people changing careers, relocating, recovering from layoff, and more. 5½" x 8½", 736 pages, paperback, $12.95.

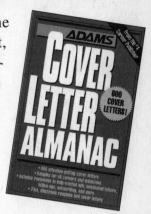

The Adams Resume Almanac

This almanac features detailed information on resume development and layout, a review of the pros and cons of various formats, an exhaustive look at the strategies that will definitely get a resume noticed, and 600 sample resumes in dozens of career categories. *The Adams Resume Almanac* is the most comprehensive, thoroughly researched resume guide ever published. 5½" x 8½", 768 pages, paperback, $10.95.

Available Wherever Books Are Sold

If you cannot find these titles at your favorite retail outlet, you may order them directly from the publisher. BY PHONE: Call 1-800-872-5627. We accept Visa, Mastercard, and American Express. $4.95 will be added to your total order for shipping and handling. BY MAIL: Write out the full titles of the books you'd like to order and send payment, including $4.95 for shipping and handling, to: Adams Media Corporation, 260 Center Street, Holbrook, MA 02343. 30-day money-back guarantee.

Visit our exciting job and career site at http://www.careercity.com

From the publishers of the *JobBank* and *Knock'em Dead* books

Visit our Web Site: www.careercity.com

...free access to tens of thousands of current job openings plus the most
comprehensive career info on the web today!

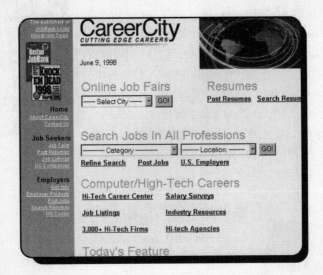

- Current job listings at top employers in all professions

- Descriptions and hot links to 27,000 major US employers

- Free resume posting gets noticed by top hiring companies

- Access to thousands of executive search firms and agencies

- Comprehensive salary surveys cover all fields

- Directories of associations and other industry resources

- Hundreds of articles on getting started, changing careers,
  job interviews, resumes, cover letters and more

Post your resume at CareerCity and have the job offers come to you!

It's fast, free and easy to post your resume at CareerCity—and you'll get noticed
by hundreds of leading employers in all fields.